Schriftenreihe der Österreichischen Gesellschaft
für Europaforschung (ECSA Austria)

Band 5

European Community Studies Association of Austria
(ECSA Austria) Publication Series

Volume 5

SpringerWienNewYork

Stefan Griller (ed.)

International Economic Governance and Non-Economic Concerns

New Challenges for the International Legal Order

SpringerWienNewYork

Prof. Dr. Stefan Griller

Research Institute for European Affairs, Wirtschaftsuniversität Wien,
Vienna, Austria

Financial support was given by the *Bundesministerium für Bildung,
Wissenschaft und Kultur,* Vienna

© 2003 Springer-Verlag Wien
Printed in Austria

Typesetting: Camera ready by editor
Printing: Ferdinand Berger & Söhne Gesellschaft m.b.H., A-3580 Horn
Printed on acid-free and chlorine-free bleached paper
CIP data applied for
SPIN: 10875839

ISBN 3-211-83823-6 Springer-Verlag Wien New York

Preface

In December 1999, shortly after the WTO Ministerial meeting in Seattle, ECSA Austria organised a conference in Vienna on "The WTO after the Seattle Ministerial Conference: Recent Developments and Future Perspectives". As it happened, Seattle drew attention to new, though sometimes unwarranted, "Future Perspectives" of the WTO and also of global economic relations and the so-called globalisation.

As a result, not only some of the actors but also many of the items on the agenda appeared to be provocative. Legitimacy, democracy, human rights, environmental protection, labour standards, and sustainable economic development suddenly became as important as "world trade classics" like the reduction of barriers to trade, even if already extended to services and intellectual property rights. In addition, the style of the discussion changed considerably: Seattle itself, and later Prague and Genoa became synonyms for the new, and partly very controversial, public interest in trade issues. One might feel tempted to conclude that globalisation entails the end of "pure" economic governance (if that ever existed), and a pressure towards a more thorough balancing of diverging interests, closer as ever to what is supposed to happen primarily at state level.

Against the background of these developments as well as the WTO Ministerial meeting in Doha, ECSA Austria, in co-operation with the Research Institute for European Affairs – IEF, and the Federal Economic Chamber of Austria, convened another meeting two years after the above-mentioned conference. Thus, on December 10 and 11, 2001, European and American scientists met in Vienna to discuss "International Economic Governance and Non-Economic Concerns: Transparency, Legitimacy, and International Economic Law". As all the "new" issues were at stake, the debate proved to be a *tour d'horizon*, covering the *status quo* of international economic governance at the beginning of the 21st century and also the future perspectives at least in some instances.

This volume not only documents the proceedings of this conference, but also includes attempts to develop further concepts such as democracy and legitimacy, the crucial importance of which is in general only acknowledged with regard to states or supranational entities like the European Communities. Hence, fundamental concepts are discussed side by side with more practical aspects of the "new" agenda. Furthermore, both theory and practice are analysed in their relation to an international public law framework, which itself is now composed of traditional and new elements and institutions.

May this volume contribute to a better understanding of the present change in international economic governance and help to discover firm ground for a promising path forward.

The realisation of the conference "International Economic Governance and Non-Economic Concerns: Transparency, Legitimacy, and International Economic Law" as well as this book was only possible with the financial support provided by the European Commission, DG Education and Culture, the Federal Economic Chamber of Austria and the Austrian Ministry for Science, Education and Culture. On behalf of ECSA Austria, I would like to thank these institutions for their help.

Special thanks go to *Roman Puff*, who not only mastered the technical difficulties to produce the text of this book camera-ready. He was the motivating force of the whole project, not the least in encouraging the authors to finish their contributions.

Vienna, November 2002

Stefan Griller

Table of Contents

Meinhard Hilf / Goetz J. Goettsche

The Relation of Economic and Non-Economic Principles in International Law

I.   No better Case than the *Shrimp* Case

More than three years ago the Appellate Body ruled in its land-mark decision of 12 October 1998 that the US Shrimp embargo was legitimate under Article XX (g) GATT 1994, because it related to the conservation of exhaustible natural resources (sea turtles)[1] and was made effective in conjunction with restrictions on domestic production.[2]

This marked the first time that a trade embargo was found to be WTO-compatible under Article XX (g) GATT 1994 despite of its violation of the obligation not to institute import restrictions other than taxes, duties or other charges (Article XI GATT 1994).[3] However, the Appellate Body did blame the United States for the discriminatory way in which the import ban was carried out and concluded *'that the United States measure, while qualifying for provisional justification under Article XX (g), fails to meet the requirements of the chapeau of Article XX, and, therefore, is not justified under Article XX of the GATT 1994.'*

A wealth of scholarly attention has since been devoted to this Appellate Body report[4] and it has divided both the environmental and the trade community. Environmental community divisions were manifest on 30 October 1998 when the WTO Director General was hit by a pie after leaving a London meeting where he had been fa-

---

[1]   Appellate Body Report, United States – Import Prohibition of Certain Shrimp and Shrimp Products (AB Report *US – Shrimp*), WT/DS58/AB/R, adopted 6 November 1998, paras 127-134.

[2]   AB Report *US – Shrimp*, paras 143-145.

[3]   Before the *US – Shrimp* ruling there has been a number of Article XX GATT related disputes in the GATT/WTO: e.g. Panel Report, United States – Prohibition of Imports of Tuna and Tuna Products from Canada, adopted on 22 February 1982, BISD 29S/91; Panel Report, Canada – Measures affecting Exports of unprocessed Herring and Salmon, adopted on 22 March 1988, BISD 35S/98; Panel Report, Thailand – Restrictions on Importation of and Internal Taxes on Cigarettes, adopted on 7 November 1990, BISD 37S/200; Panel Report, United States – Restriction on Imports Of Tuna, not adopted, circulated on 3 September 1991, BISD 39S/155; Panel Report, United States – Restrictions on Imports of Tuna, not adopted, circulated on 16 June 1994, DS29/R; Panel Report, United States – Taxes on Automobiles, not adopted, circulated on 11 October 1994, DS31/R; Appellate Body Report, United States – Standards for Reformulated and Conventional Gasoline (AB Report *US – Gasoline*), WT/DS2/AB/R, adopted on 20 May 1996; cf. *Hilf* (2000) 319 et seqq..

[4]   *Appleton* (1999) 477 et seqq.; *Beyerlin* (2000) 323 et seqq.; *Dailey* (2000) 331-383; *Cone* (1999) 51 et seqq.; *Pyatt* (1999) 815 et seqq.; *Mavroidis* (2000) 73 et seqq.; *Ahn* (1999) 819 et seqq.; *Ginzky* (1999) 216 et seqq.; *Hilf* (2000) 481 et seqq.; *Sampson* (2001) 1122 et seqq..

vourably received by members of this same community. With respect to the trade community, the same split was evident a week
later when the Dispute Settlement Body (DSB) debated and adopted
the Shrimp decision. In an unusual reversal of form the appellees,
who prevailed, were critical of this decision, whereas the losing
party, the appellant, welcomed the decision and urged its adoption.[5]

The latest WTO compliance Panel on the shrimp-turtle dispute
found in favour of the United States on all essential points. It ended
its report with an exhortation to Malaysia and the United States to
*'cooperate fully in order to conclude as soon as possible an agree-
ment which will permit the protection and conservation of sea turtles to the satisfaction of all interests involved and taking into account the principle that States have common but differentiated responsibilities to conserve and protect the environment'.*[6] The
concluding remark reflected the 'leitmotiv' of the Panel report,
released on 15 June 2001.[7] It repeatedly emphasised the preference
for multilateral solutions to environmental problems, but upheld the
US import embargo[8] on marine shrimp caught without turtle excluder devices.[9]

Malaysia appealed against the report of the compliance Panel on
23 July 2001. However, in its latest report on the shrimp-turtle dispute, the Appellate Body confirmed that the United States' import
embargo on marine shrimp did not, as currently applied, violate its
WTO obligations. In the report of 22 October 2001 the Appellate
Body *'finds that the Panel correctly fulfilled its mandate under 21.5
of the [Dispute Settlement Understanding] DSU (...); and upholds
the findings of the Panel, (...), that 'Section 609 of Public Law 101-
162, as implemented by the Revised Guidelines of 6 July 1999 and
as applied so far by the United States authorities, is justified under*

---

[5]   Cf. *Appleton* (1999) 477 et seq..

[6]   Panel Report, United States – Import Prohibition of certain Shrimp and
Shrimp Products, Recourse to Article 21.5 by Malaysia, WT/DS58/-
RW, adopted 21 November 2001, para 7.2.

[7]   The background of the dispute is set out in detail in the Panel Report,
Recourse to Article 21.5 by Malaysia, paras 1.1-1.5 and 2.12-2.21.

[8]   The US-embargo was established pursuant to Section 609 of Public
Law 101-162, adopted in 1989 as complementary legislation to the
Endangered Species Act, which protects all species of sea turtles that
occur in the United States; cf. AB Report *US – Shrimp*, paras 1-6.

[9]   Turtle excluder devices (TEDs) allow highly endangered sea turtles to
escape from shrimp trawl nets where they often drown.

Article XX of the GATT 1994 as long as the conditions stated in the findings of this Report, in particular the ongoing serious good faith efforts to reach a multilateral agreement, remain satisfied'.[10]

The shrimp-turtle dispute has now been through all stages of the WTO dispute settlement process: Panel and Appellate Body reports, a compliance review and, finally, its appeal.

But even after the second Appellate Body decision in the Shrimp/Turtle litigation, the remaining difficulty in the trade and environment debate is evident: How to balance the two important goals of free trade and environmental protection? Or, in a broader context, how to best strike a balance between the pursuit of economic and non-economic principles in general?

II.   Drawing the Lines ...

In trying to uncover the relationship between economic and non-economic principles in international law, some limitations of scope have to be made at the outset. The focus of attention will be just one section of the wider scope of international law, namely 'international economic law'.[11] This term itself can cover a wide range of subjects. Defined broadly, almost all international law could be called international economic law, because almost every aspect of international relations touches in one way or another on economic matters. A more restrained definition would encompass only economic relations between nations, a kind of public international law of economic relations. Since other scholars and practitioners have given their differing ideas about the meaning of this term, no attempt at a precise definition will be volunteered here.[12]

Today, in fact, international economic law is most visible in the European Union (EU) and in the GATT/WTO system, although it is growing in other regional organisations and in multilateral or pluri-

---

[10]   Appellate Body Report, United States – Import Prohibition of Certain Shrimp and Shrimp Products, Recourse to Article 21.5 of the DSU by Malaysia (AB Report *US – Shrimp*, 21.5), WT/DS58/AB/RW, adopted 21 November 2001, para 152.
[11]   This relates to the theme of the 2001 Vienna Conference on "International Economic Governance and Non-Economic Concerns – Transparency, Legitimacy, and International *Economic* Law", Vienna 10./11. Dec. 2001.
[12]   See e.g.: *Jackson* (1995) 596 et seqq.; *Jackson* (1999) 25 et seq.; *Schwarzenberger* (1966) 7; *Verloren van Themaat* (1981) 9 et seqq..

lateral organisations with sectoral responsibilities, too.[13] For this reason a second limitation has to be made here, namely apart from some brief comparative references to the legal system of the European Community (EC) the focus will be on the WTO legal system and its usage of economic and non-economic principles.

III.   What are Principles?

The term 'principle' is not always used with great precision in international law. Overlaps with other terms, as for example, objectives, values, interests, rights or maxims are common.[14] *Petersmann*, for example, defines 'principle' as a legal term of art implying various categories of legally binding norms having their origin in national law or in international law or as applied to all kinds of legal relations regardless of the legal order to which they belong.[15] *Oppermann/Conlan* prefer a definition of principles as regulative concepts expressed at a greater level of generality than rules, allowing a goal to be identified, without necessarily identifying the detailed instruments to achieve that goal.[16] For the given purpose *principles* formulate general and flexible imperatives. They exist in contrast to *rules*, which lay down specific rights and obligations and assert a specific form of behaviour.[17] This distinction between rules and principles as two types of legal norms was first developed in English texts[18] in order to attack positivism. It has since been used to describe and analyse positive law phenomena[19] and can therefore legitimately be employed.

No legal order incorporates only written provisions and in no legal system it is possible for the written law to supply a response to each arising question. Therefore, principles have to complement the written rules.[20] They help to guide the applicant and interpreter of legal texts in cases of conflicting legal opinions regarding the content of the rules under dispute and the ambiguities and lacunae in

---

[13]   *Trachtmann* (1996) 46 et seq..
[14]   See e.g. *Röhl* (2001) 253 et seq..
[15]   *Petersmann* (1987) 209.
[16]   *Oppermann/Conlan* (1990) 81; see also: *Roessler* (1978) 56.
[17]   *Hilf* (2001) 112; see also: *Röhl* (2001) 255; *Larenz* (1991) 421; *Benedek* (1990) 50; *Tietje* (1998) 175 et seqq..
[18]   *Dworkin* (1977) 14, 22 et seqq.; *Hart* (1994) 259 et seqq..
[19]   *Alexy* (1985) 71 et seqq.; *Esser* (1974) 39 et seqq.; *Roessler* (1978) 56 et seqq..
[20]   *Fastenrath* (1991) 125.

such texts.[21] These often unwritten principles represent the fundamental legal concepts and essential values of any legal system.[22] They are founded in the moral purpose of the law and are essential to a just legal order no matter how technical the rules applicable to a specific dispute are.[23]

According to *Pescatore* only legal principles transform the law into a coherent system.[24] In contrast to rules principles as such are not directly applicable in a specific dispute. They always need to be balanced with competing principles and additional objectives. In any legal order written rules should reflect this finely tuned balance between the principles and objectives underlying the system as a whole.[25]

IV.   A Principle-oriented Approach to WTO Law

International economic law is predominantly treaty-based.[26] Having said this, the WTO treaty law forms both the basis as well as the limits of the search for principles underlying the WTO system. There are, of course, some who suggest that during the drafting of the WTO agreement[27] the drafters did not consider and therefore did not agree to any 'principles'. A quick reference to the Preamble of the Agreement Establishing the World Trade Organization (WTO Agreement)[28] may be sufficient to rebut this argument. In

---

[21]   *Hart* and *Dworkin* both agree that judges must necessarily fill gaps in legal systems, though they disagree on whether law is being made or merely applied in these cases. *Hart* (1994) 124 et seqq.; *Dworkin* (1977) 22; see also: *Larenz* (1991) 421.

[22]   *Esser* (1974) 39; *Benedek* (1990) 49.

[23]   *Cameron/Gray* (2001) 298; see also *Larenz* (1991) 474.

[24]   *Pescatore* (1960) 120; see also: *Tietje* (1998) 179.

[25]   *Hilf* (2001) 112; *Benedek* (1990) 50.

[26]   *Oppermann* (1987) 194.

[27]   „WTO agreement" is used here to denominate the Final Act Embodying the Results of the Uruguay Round of Multilateral Trade Negotiations (15. April 1994), printed in: The Results Of The Uruguay Round Of Multilateral Trade Negotiations: The Legal Texts (1995) 2 (which includes not only the WTO Agreement with its four annexes, but also a series of ministerial declarations and decisions); reprinted in: 33 ILM (1994) 1125.

[28]   Marrakesh Agreement Establishing the World Trade Organization (15. April 1994), printed in: The Results Of The Uruguay Round Of Multilateral Trade Negotiations: The Legal Texts (1995) 6; reprinted in: 33 ILM (1994) 1144.

the last paragraph of the preamble, the Parties to the agreement declared their determination *'to preserve the basic principles and to further the objectives underlying this multilateral trading system'*. Thus, the WTO Agreement confirms the existence of 'basic principles' in the WTO context.[29]

But what are those principles? And are they of an economic or even non-economic nature? The WTO Agreement itself gives no list of such principles to be applied. It is therefore unclear if these 'basic principles' mentioned in the preamble, encompass only the economic rationale of the GATT, including e.g. characteristics such as non-discrimination and open markets. In a wider context, the notion might also refer to basic legal principles such as due process, good faith or natural justice.[30] It seems that in a number of its decisions, the Appellate Body has followed the second alternative.

In their early years the WTO dispute settlement bodies, i.e. Panels and Appellate Body, made considerable efforts to avoid judicial activism when interpreting the WTO agreements. In its very first report, the Appellate Body made clear that the new adjudicators in world trade law should interpret the text of the agreements primarily in accordance with the ordinary meaning of the words of the treaty.[31] In subsequent case law, the Appellate Body regularly reversed creative departures from the text and instructed Panels to stick to their dictionaries.[32]

This approach of the Appellate Body finds strong support in the Dispute Settlement Understanding, since Art. 3.2 and Art. 19.2 DSU clearly state that *'recommendations and rulings of the DSB [Dispute Settlement Body] cannot add to or diminish rights and obligations provided in the covered agreements'*. However, in the WTO system, as in any other legal system, rules have to be inter-

---

[29] See in this context also the Doha Ministerial Declaration of 14 November 2001, WT/MIN(01)/DEC/W/1, para 1.

[30] *Hilf* (2001) 112.

[31] AB Report *US – Gasoline*, sec. III B.

[32] See e.g.: Canada – Measures Affecting the Importation of Milk and the Exportation of Dairy Products, WT/DS103,113/AB/R, adopted 27 October 1999, para 97 (citing: Black's Law Dictionary, West Publishing 1990; The New Shorter Oxford English Dictionary, Clarendon Press 1993, Merriam Webster's Collegiate Dictionary, 1993); Japan – Taxes on Alcoholic Beverages (AB Report *Japan – Alcoholic Beverages*), WT/DS8, 10, 11/AB/R, adopted 1 November 1996, sec. D; AB Report *US – Shrimp*, para 114.; cf. *Desmedt* (2001) 442.

preted and interpretation often requires the judiciary bodies to go beyond the given text of the rules. This applies even more, when legal clarity is not the prime characteristic of the rule in question. In fact, there are situations, in which rules are deliberately left vague, since they reflect a lack of consensus amongst the negotiators. And in a world becoming increasingly complex, new rules need to contain open concepts that require further implementation and interpretation.[33] Given these circumstances, it is difficult for a judge to avoid establishing case law with additional sources of law – such as legal principles. They represent a vast reservoir of legal concepts and values that helps to add colour and shading, or even to fill in the gaps left in the text of the treaty.[34] Despite the often explicit hostility of the WTO Members to any kind of judicial activism of the DSB, the legal system of the WTO is no different in this respect.

The case law of the European Court of Justice (ECJ) has prompted EC Member States to recognize an increasing number of general principles of European Community Law.[35] Similarly, the legally binding dispute settlement reports of Panels and the Appellate Body are likely to prompt WTO Members to increasingly accept the application of 'external principles' derived from public international law.

V.   Sources of WTO Law

A search for economic and non-economic principles, which are relevant for the legal system of the WTO, must take into account the sources of WTO law. *Palmeter* and *Mavroidis* suggested in an early paper, that the texts of the 'covered agreements'[36] are only a 'first of all' and do not exhaust the sources of potentially relevant law.[37] Conversely, Article 3.2, along with Article 7 DSU, has the

---

[33] *Bronckers* (1999) 554.

[34] *Bogdan* (1977) 51.

[35] For more details see: *de Búrca/Scott* (2001) 22.

[36] In its report Brazil – Measures Affecting Desiccated Coconut (AB Report *Brazil – Coconut*), WT/DS22/AB/R, adopted 20 March 1997, in sec. IV B the AB stated: „The 'covered agreements' include the WTO Agreement, the Agreements in Annexes 1 and 2, as well as any Plurilateral Trade Agreement in Annex 4 where its Committee of signatories has taken a decision to apply the DSU"; see also: *Palmeter/ Mavroidis* (1998) 399.

[37] *Palmeter/Mavroidis* (1998) 399.

effect of bringing into the WTO system all sources of law stated in Article 38 (1) of the Statute of the International Court of Justice (ICJ). These include not only WTO Panel and Appellate Body reports, GATT Panel reports,[38] custom, the teachings of highly qualified publicists, but also other international instruments, such those referred to in the WTO agreements and those between the parties concerned and, last but not least, general principles of law.[39] This view has occasionally been contested by authors who take the view that Panels and the Appellate Body may only apply the rules expressly set out in the covered agreements as interpreted in accordance with the rules of customary international law on the interpretation of treaties.[40] But it is argued here that this view is too restrictive and does not reflect the actual practice of Panels and the Appellate Body.[41]

In its very first report *US – Gasoline* the Appellate Body enunciated that the WTO system, like any other sub-system, cannot be construed in 'clinical isolation' from the widespread sources of

---

[38] With reference to its Report *Japan – Alcoholic Beverages*, sec. E, the AB distinguishes between adopted and unadopted GATT Panel Reports: "*adopted* panel reports are an important part of the GATT acquis. They are often considered by subsequent panels. They create legitimate expectations among WTO Members, and, therefore, should be taken into account where they are relevant to any dispute. However, they are not binding, except with respect to resolving the particular dispute between the parties to that dispute. In short, their character and their legal status have not been changed by the coming into force of the WTO Agreement. *Unadopted* panel reports "have no legal status in the GATT or WTO system since they have not been endorsed through decisions by the CONTRACTING PARTIES to GATT or WTO Members". Likewise, we agree that "a panel could nevertheless find useful guidance in the reasoning of an unadopted panel report that it considered to be relevant"; compare also: Argentina – Measures affecting Imports of Footwear, Apparel and Other Items (*Argentina – Footwear*), WT/DS56/AB/R, adopted 22 April 1998, para 43; see also: *Chua* (1998a) 171 et seqq..

[39] *Palmeter/Mavroidis* (1998) 399; see also: *Trebilcock/Howse* (1999) 72 et seqq..

[40] See e.g.: *Marceau* (1999) 109-115; *Trachtman* (1999) 342; *Guruswamy* (1998) 311.

[41] *McRae* (2000) 37.

public international law.[42] And in a recent report a Panel rejected
the *argumentum e contrario* that reference in Article 3.2 DSU only
to rules of treaty interpretation of customary international law has
the effect of excluding all other international law.[43]

It is true that the DSU limits the *jurisdiction* of Panels and the
Appellate Body to claims under WTO covered agreements (Articles
1.1, 3.2 and 11 DSU).[44] This, however, does not mean that the applicable law is also limited in the same way. Much has been said
about the creation and continuing existence of the WTO agreements
in the wider context of general international law and other non-
WTO treaties.[45] Like international environmental law or human
rights law, WTO law is just a branch of public international law.[46]
And therefore the WTO dispute settlement system, which was set
up by the WTO agreement, does not exist in a legal vacuum and is
not a self-contained regime.[47] Although the DSU does not explicitly
include a provision on 'applicable law',[48] nowhere else does a
WTO rule preclude Panels or the Appellate Body from addressing
and applying other rules of international law in order to decide disputes before them. Therefore, apart from the limited jurisdiction of
both Panels and the Appellate Body and apart from special conflict
rules either in the WTO agreement, general international law or

---

[42] AB Report *US – Gasoline*, WT/DS2/AB/R, adopted 20 May 1996, sec. III B.

[43] Panel Report Korea – Measures Affecting Government Procurement, WT/DS163/R, adopted 19 June 2000, para 7.96, footnote 753: „We should also note that we can see no basis here for an *a contrario* impli-cation that rules of international law other than rules of interpretation do not apply. The language of 3.2 in this regard applies to a specific problem that had arisen under the GATT to the effect that, among other things, reliance on negotiating history was being utilized in a manner arguably inconsistent with the requirements of the rules of treaty interpretation of customary international law.“

[44] *Bartels* (2001) 502 et seq..

[45] With one exception, no academic author or any WTO decision or document denies that WTO rules are part of the wider corpus of public international law: *Jackson* (1998) 89; *Pauwelyn* (2001) 538; *McRae* (2000) 28; *Bartels* (2001) 499 et seqq.; the exception is: *Hippler Bello* (1996) 417.

[46] *Pauwelyn* (2001) 538.

[47] See for this discussion: *Mavroidis* (1991) 497 et seqq.; *Kujper* (1994) 227 et seqq.; *Simma* (1985) 111 et seqq..

[48] *Pauwelyn* (2001) 561.

other non-WTO agreements,[49] international law from all sources is potentially applicable as WTO law, unless the DSU or any other WTO rule has expressly contracted out of them.[50]

The following elaboration will demonstrate, that the Appellate Body has so far been quite prepared to invoke economic as well as non-economic principles in order to resolve those cases for which the covered agreements, properly interpreted, give no sufficient answer ('hard cases'[51]).[52]

VI.   Principles Expressed in WTO Agreements: 'Internal Principles'

A. 'Classical' GATT/WTO Principles

A rather short overview shall be given of those principles already contained in the classical GATT 1947 and now embodied in the legal system of the WTO. International trade has always been largely influenced by economic principles. Their origin dates back to the interregional commerce of ancient and medieval times and is much older than the theoretical explanations of the mutual benefits of trade.[53] With the conclusion of GATT in 1947, these principles were put on a multilateral legal basis for the first time. During the history of GATT a complex legal system has evolved, the principles of which have often been enumerated[54] and continue to apply with the text of the GATT 1994. Several more fundamental principles were added to the list for the WTO, namely by the General Agree-

---

[49]   See for more details: *Pauwelyn* (2001) 550 et seqq. and 560; and also: *Bartels* (2001) 506 et seqq..

[50]   *Pauwelyn* (2001) 562; see also the recent AB Report: United States – Transitional Safeguard Measure on Combed Cotton Yarn from Pakistan (AB Report *US – Cotton Yarn*), WT/DS192/AB/R, adopted 5 November 2001, para 120.

[51]   The problem of hard cases is dealt with extensively in: *Dworkin* (1977) 81 – 130; see also: *Röhl* (2001) 259.

[52]   For an overview see e.g.: *Waincymer* (2001) 1262 et seqq.; *Cameron/ Gray* (2001) 248 et seqq.; *Hilf* (2001) 117 et seqq..

[53]   *Petersmann* (1985) 1542 with reference to the theories of *Adam Smith* and *David Ricardo*.

[54]   *Petersmann* (1987) 211 et seqq.; *Benedek* (1990) 51 et seqq.; *Oppermann/Conlan* (1990) 83; *Dolzer* (2001) 479 et seqq.; *Hohmann* (2001) 650.

ment on Trade in Services (GATS) and the Trade-Related Intellectual Property Agreement (TRIPS).[55]

The Preamble of the WTO Agreement suggests that 'basic principles' are 'underlying' the WTO system. They might not always be visible at first glance or expressed in positive rules. Indeed, there might even be a reference to those principles overarching the numerous rules laid down in the WTO agreements.[56] Furthermore, basic 'objectives' of a more substantive nature are also mentioned in the Preamble, including e.g. sustainable development and the raising of the standard of living. Finally, the Preamble refers to the multilateral trading 'system', which is a rather vague notion. But from a legal perspective, a 'system' would refer to a specific legal order which links the various principles and objectives to form a coherent unit.[57] A list of those core principles, which are laid down in the WTO agreements and have also been acknowledged by several Appellate Body reports, certainly entails the following for sure: *trade liberalization*[58] and *least distortion* respectively,[59] *non-discrimination*,[60] which includes the two sub-principles of *most favoured nation treatment* (MFN)[61] and *national treatment*,[62] co-

---

[55]   *Jackson* (1998) 23; with respect to TRIPS see also: *Stegemann* (2000) 1243 et seqq..

[56]   *Hilf* (2001) 112.

[57]   *Esser* (1974) 44.

[58]   Cf. Preamble of the WTO Agreement 'liberalization efforts'; Preamble of GATT 1994 'substantial reduction of tariffs and other barriers to trade'; or e.g. Preamble Agreement on Technical Trade Barriers (TBT Agreement) 'facilitating the conduct of international trade'.

[59]   See e.g. Articles II, XXVIII and XXVIIIbis GATT 1994 or Art. 2.2 TBT Agreement.

[60]   Appellate Body Report, European Communities – Regime for the Importation, Sale and Distribution of Bananas (AB Report *EC – Bananas*), WT/DS27/AB/R, adopted 25 September 1997, paras 160, 161, 241; Appellate Body Report, European Communities – Measures Affecting the Importation of Certain Poultry Products (AB Report *EC – Poultry*), WT/DS69/AB/R, adopted 23 July 1998, para 100.

[61]   Art. I and XIII GATT 1994; see also: AB Report *EC – Bananas*, para 232; Appellate Body Report, Canada – Certain Measures Affecting the Automotive Industry (AB Report *Canada – Automotive Industry*), WT/DS139, 142/AB/R, adopted 19 June 2000, paras 69, 82 et seq..

[62]   Art. III GATT 1994 AB Report *EC – Bananas*, para 231; AB Report *Japan – Alcoholic Beverages*, sec. F; Appellate Body Report, Canada – Certain Measures Concerning Periodicals (AB Report *Canada – Peri-*

operation and *multilateralism*[63] including *reciprocity*[64] but also the *preferential treatment of developing countries,*[65] *(economic) sovereignty*[66] and *national deference,*[67] *sustainable development*[68], *transparency,*[69] the *rule of law*[70] and the *peaceful settlement of disputes.*[71]

---

odicals), WT/DS31/AB/R, adopted 30 July 1997, sec. VI A; AB Report *US – Gasoline*, sec. IV; Appellate Body Report, Canada – Term of Patent Protection, (AB Report *Canada – Patent Protection*), WT/DS170/AB/R, 12 October 2000, para 56.

[63] AB Report *US – Shrimp*, paras 166-172; see also now: AB Report *US – Shrimp, 21.5*, para 152.

[64] Cf. third recital of the Preamble of the WTO Agreement, which urges states to enter into 'reciprocal and mutually advantageous arrangements' in order to achieve further liberalization; see also e.g.: Appellate Body Report, European Communities – Customs Classifications of Certain Computer Equipment (AB Report *EC – Computer Equipment*), WT/DS62, 67, 68/AB/R, adopted 22 June 1998, para 82.

[65] Some regard this as the 'principle of solidarity': *Benedek* (1990) 54; see also: *Ipsen/Haltern* (1991) 27.

[66] See e.g. Articles 3.2 and 19.2 DSU; various 'escape clauses' can also be seen as a means to protect national interests in case of need; Articles XX and XXI GATT 1994.

[67] Article 17.6 of the Agreement on the Implementation of Art. IV GATT (Anti-Dumping Agreement) can for example be seen as a specific reference to national deference in the field of fact-finding; with respect to a certain level of deference in environmental protection under national law see: AB Report *US – Shrimp*, paras 160, 184.

[68] AB Report *US - Shrimp*, paras 129-131, 153; *Marceau* (1999) 138.

[69] Article X GATT 1994, Article 10 TBT Agreement, Article 7 and Annex B of the Agreement on the Application of Sanitary and Phytosanitary Measures (SPS Agreement); see also: Appellate Body Report, United States – Restrictions on Import of Cotton and Man-Made Fibre Underwear (AB Report *US – Underwear*), WT/DS24/AB/R, adopted 25 February 1997, sec. IV; AB Report *Canada – Periodicals*, sec. VII.

[70] An essential expression of this principle is the DSU. As the AB pointed out in a recent report, the 'procedural rules of the WTO dispute settlement are designed to promote (...) the fair, prompt and effective resolution of trade disputes'; see: Appellate Body Report, United States – Tax Treatment for „Foreign Sales Corporations" (AB Report *US – FSCs*), WT/DS108/AB/R, adopted 20 March 2000, para 166.

[71] See e.g.: *Petersmann* (1985) 1549; *Hilf* (2001) 117 et seqq.; *Senti* (2000) 154; *Beise* (2001) 47 et seqq.; *Oppermann/Conlan* (1990) (83).

B. The Principle of Proportionality

Another principle, that implicitly underlies the WTO system as a whole, which shall be discussed in greater detail, is the principle of proportionality.[72] In many legal systems the principle of proportionality is an important tool for judges to check the regulatory freedom of governments.[73] In EC Law, for example, it is one of the most important unwritten principles commonly invoked before the ECJ in challenging European legislation.[74] And with the entry into force of the Maastricht Treaty 1992, an explicit reference can be found in Article 5 (3) EC Treaty, which provides that 'any action by the Community shall not go beyond what is necessary to achieve the objectives of this Treaty'.[75] The principle of proportionality holds that the individual should not have his or her freedom of action limited beyond the degree necessary for the protection of public interest.[76] It therefore imposes a general limitation on the exercise by both Community and national authorities of the powers conferred upon them by Community law by requiring the measures they adopt to be in proportion to their ultimate objectives.[77] Its application generally consists of a number of stages: first, identifying what legally protected right or interest is at stake; secondly, identifying the extent to which this right or interest has been interfered with or restricted; thirdly, identifying the reason (the purported justification) for its restriction, whether for the protection of another right or public interest, etc., and if so what weight is to be given to

---

[72] *Hilf/Puth* (2002); and also: *Hilf* (2001) 117 et seqq.; *Hilf* (2000) 488; *Epiney* (2000) 83 et seq.; *Tietje* (1998) 313 et seqq..

[73] For the German principle of '*Verhältnismäßigkeit*' see e.g.: BVerfGE 3, 383 (399); 17, 108 (117 et seqq.); 23, 127 (133); see also: *Maurer* (1999) 233 et seqq.; *Grabitz* (1973) 568-616; for an overview in the law of the European Convention on Human Rights (ECHR) see: *McBride* (1999) 23 et seq.; for an overview with respect to public international law: *Delbrück* (1997) 1141 et seqq..

[74] See generally: *Ellis* (1999); *Emiliou* (1996) 115 et seqq.; and also: *Neumayer* (2001) 151 et seq..

[75] Although the term 'proportionality' is not mentioned, most commentators regard this provision as an act of recognition of the existing case law, even though a partial and unsuccessful one.

[76] ECJ, Internationale Handelsgesellschaft v Einfuhr- und Vorratsstelle Getreide, Case 11/70 ECR [1970], 1125 at 1127.

[77] For a detailed analysis see: *Emiliou* (1996); *de Búrca* (1993) 105 et seqq..

that other interest. Ultimately, the question is, whether in the light of this balancing of interests, the interference with the protected legal interest is excessive or not.[78]

With respect to the WTO legal system it is questionable whether the principle of proportionality also plays a significant role when judging the regulations of WTO Members. In a recent paper *Desmedt* gives a detailed analysis on the topic concluding that 'there is not one single overarching (unwritten) principle of proportionality in WTO law' and 'that at this stage of the WTO's development it would not be appropriate for the WTO dispute settlement organs to assert such a principle'.[79] Other scholars seem to have intermittently supported this view.[80]

It has to be admitted that the texts of the agreements contain no explicit reference to a 'principle of proportionality'.[81] And, until recently,[82] both Panels and the Appellate Body have never expressly used the term 'proportionality' in any of their decisions. However, the basic idea of the proportionality, i.e. the due balancing of competing rights or values,[83] is not only reflected in several provisions of the WTO agreements, but has also found its way into the jurisdiction of the Appellate Body.

Almost no WTO provision mentions the word 'proportionality' as such.[84] What can be found as common language of the GATT 1994 and other multilateral trade agreements are e.g. textual requirements to employ 'necessary',[85] 'appropriate'[86] or 'reason-

---

[78] *de Búrca* (2000) 97.
[79] *Desmedt* (2001) 441 and 478 et seqq..
[80] See e.g. *Marceau* (1999) 138; and also: *Neumayer* (2001) 153.
[81] *Hilf* (2001) 120; *Desmedt* (2001) 443.
[82] Cf. the recent AB Report *US – Cotton Yarn*, paras 119, 120 and 122.
[83] *Delbrück* (1997) 1140.
[84] See, for example, Article 46 TRIPS with a reference to 'the need for proportionality' in the context of enforcement provisions; see also: footnote 9 Article 4.10 SCM Agreement, where the word 'disproportionate' is used in connection with countermeasures; for both examples cf. *Desmedt* (2001) 443, Fn. 6.
[85] Articles VIII:3, XI:2(b) and (c), XII:2(a), XII:3(c)(i), XVIII:9, XIX:1(a) and (b), XX(a), (b) and (d) GATT 1994; Articles 2.2, 3.2, 9.1 SPS Agreement; Article 5.2.7 TBT Agreement; Articles 7.1(iii), 11.1 Anti-Dumping Agreement.
[86] Article 2.8 TBT Agreement.

able'[87] measures dealing with international trade problems and to take measures 'imposed for',[88] 'essential to',[89] or 'relating to'[90] the aim sought to be realised.[91] Another example is Article 2.2 of the Agreement on Technical Barriers to Trade (TBT Agreement) providing that '(...) technical regulations shall not be more trade-restrictive than necessary to fulfil a legitimate objective (...)'. And according to Article 5.6 of the Agreement on the Application of Sanitary and Phytosanitary Measures (SPS Agreement) 'Members shall ensure that [sanitary and phytosanitary] measures are not more trade-restrictive than required to achieve their appropriate level of sanitary or phytosanitary protection (...)'. Finally, the Agreement on Implementation of Article VI of the GATT 1994 (Anti-Dumping Agreement) states in Article 9.1 that '[i]t is desirable that [...] the duty be less than the margin [of dumping] if such lesser duty would be adequate to remove the injury to the domestic industry'. This treaty language, which appears longwinded and unconventional, illustrates the presence of a principle of proportionality in WTO law. All of the given examples are to be seen as special forms and expressions of the basic philosophy behind the principle of proportionality, namely: sensitive measures must be strongly and genuinely related to a legitimate objective and must take into account the legitimate interests possibly affected, all that with the intention to establish a due balance between the competing rights, interests and objectives.[92]

This view finds support in the position of the Appellate Body. As an analysis of the following three AB Reports demonstrates, the Appellate Body at least with respect to Article XX GATT 1994 already employs an approach similar, if not identical, to a proportionality test.[93] [94]

---

[87] Articles XII:3(c)(ii), XVIII:10 GATT 1994; Article 2.9.4 TBT Agreement.

[88] Article XX(f) GATT 1994.

[89] Article XX(j) GATT 1994.

[90] Article XX (c), (e) and (g) GATT 1994.

[91] *Hilf/Puth* (2002).

[92] *Hilf/Puth* (2002).

[93] In the same context compare also: Panel Report, European Communities – Measures affecting Asbestos and Asbestos-Containing Products (AB Report *EC – Asbestos*), WT/DS135/R, adopted 5 April 2001, para 8.207 with reference to 'proportionate' administrative resources.

[94] *Hilf* (2001) 121; see also: *Cass* (2001) 66 et seqq..

1. AB Report *US – Gasoline*

The Appellate Body laid the ground for its systematic and well-founded approach to Article XX GATT 1994 in its very first and long expected report *US – Gasoline*. Both Venezuela and Brazil brought a complaint concerning the effects of rules prescribed under the US Clean Air Act to foreign exported gasoline, while the United States attempted to justify its measure under Article XX of the GATT 1994.

With regard to the structure of the Article, the Appellate Body pointed out that the analysis is comprised of two elements: first, provisional justification under one of the paragraphs (a) to (j); and second, further appraisal of the same measure under the standards of the introductory clauses of Article XX GATT 1994, the so-called chapeau clause.[95] In contrast to the provisional justification under one of the paragraphs of Article XX GATT 1994 that directs the attention to the abstract rules maintained by the Member, the chapeau clause addresses mainly the manner in which these rules are applied.[96]

In the first step of its analysis of Article XX 1994, the Appellate Body stressed:

'In enumerating the various categories of governmental acts, laws or regulations which WTO Members may carry out or promulgate in pursuit of differing legitimate state policies or interests outside the realm of trade liberalisation, Article XX [GATT 1994] uses different terms in respect of different categories:

"necessary" – in paragraphs (a), (b) and (d);
"essential" – in paragraph (j);
"relating to" – in paragraphs (c), (e) and (g);
"for the protection of" – in paragraph (f);
"in pursuance of" – in paragraph (h); and
"involving" – in paragraph (i).

It does not seem reasonable to suppose that the WTO Members intended to require, in respect of each and every category, the same kind or degree of connection or relationship between the measure under appraisal and the state interest or policy sought to be promoted or realised.'[97]

---

[95] AB Report *US – Gasoline*, sec. IV; and also: *Correa* (2000) 94 et seq..
[96] See AB Report *US – Gasoline*, sec. III B and IV.
[97] AB Report *US – Gasoline*, sec. III B.

Clearly, this passage deals with the relationship of ends and means that differs from one exception to the other. In other words, the measure under consideration must be connected to the legitimate aim pursued in the special kind and degree required. Another section of the report might be understood as an indication that the legal rights of the other Members have to be taken into account and, accordingly, be balanced with the legitimate objectives acknowledged in the exceptions of Article XX GATT 1994:

'the phrase "relating to the conservation of exhaustible natural resources" may not be read so expansively as seriously to subvert the purpose and object of Article III:4 [GATT 1994]. Nor may Article III:4 [GATT 1994] be given so broad a reach as effectively to emasculate Article XX(g) [GATT 1994] and the policies and interests it embodies. The relationship between the affirmative commitments set out in, e.g., Articles I, III and XI [GATT 1994], and the policies and interests embodied in the "General Exceptions" listed in Article XX [GATT 1994], can be given meaning within the framework of the General Agreement and its object and purpose by a treaty interpreter only on a case-to-case basis, by careful scrutiny of the factual and legal context in a given dispute, without disregarding the words actually used by the WTO Members themselves to express their intent and purpose. [98]

This passage is anything but clear. It puts more emphasis on the general approach taken, rather than the balancing of competing rights. It is in the second step of the analysis in the examination of the concrete application of the measure under the chapeau clause that the Appellate Body takes care of the legitimate trade interests of the other Members. The report reads as follows:

'The chapeau is animated by the principle that while the exceptions of Article XX [GATT 1994] may be invoked as a matter of legal right, they should not be so applied as to frustrate or defeat the legal obligations of the holder of the right under the substantive rules of the General Agreement. If those exceptions are not to be abused or misused, in other words, the measures falling within the particular exceptions must be applied reasonably, with due regard both to the legal duties of the party claiming the exception and the legal rights of the other parties concerned. [99]

---

[98] AB Report *US – Gasoline*, sec. III B.
[99] AB Report *US – Gasoline*, sec. IV.

Here, the Appellate Body examines the effects of the measure under appraisal of the legal rights of the other Members concerned. Above all, the trade restrictive measure must be reasonable. As this is the fundamental theme of the chapeau clause, the single standards 'arbitrary discrimination', 'unjustifiable discrimination' and 'disguised restriction on international trade' take second place and 'may [...] be read side-by-side'.[100] In practice, the evaluation of reasonableness implies a due balancing of competing rights. And that is, as pointed out earlier, the basic idea of proportionality.

2. AB Report *US – Shrimp*

In the Shrimp-Turtle dispute, the Appellate Body followed the two-tiered analysis elaborated in *US – Gasoline* and added some more specifications to the understanding of Article XX GATT 1994. Most importantly, the Appellate Body stressed that '[t]he general design of a measure, as distinguished from its application is [...] to be examined in the course of determining whether that measure falls within one or another paragraph of Article XX [GATT 1994] following the chapeau'.[101] That means, the paragraphs (a) to (j) address the abstract measure, whereas the chapeau clause addresses the application of the abstract measure in the single case.

With regard to the provisional justification of the abstract measure under Article XX (g) GATT 1994,[102] the Appellate Body stated:

'The means are, in principle, reasonably related to the ends. The means and ends relationship between Section 609 and the legitimate policy of conserving an exhaustible, and, in fact, endangered species, is observably a close and real one [...].'[103]

The cited passage can be read as including almost all constitutive elements of proportionality. Not only that the connection between the trade restrictive measure and the 'legitimate policy' must be 'a close and real one', a language very similar to 'effective' and 'suitable', the relationship must also be 'reasonably'.

---

[100] AB Report *US – Gasoline*, sec. IV.
[101] AB Report *US – Shrimp*, para 116.
[102] Article XX (g) GATT 1994 uses the term 'relating to' to specify the required degree of connection between the measure under appraisal and the 'conservation of exhaustible natural resources'.
[103] AB Report, *US – Shrimp*, para 141.

In respect of the chapeau clause of Article XX GATT 1994 the Appellate Body considered first of all the fundamental logic of the clause:

'*The chapeau of Article XX [GATT 1994] is, in fact, but one expression of the principle of good faith. This principle, at once a general principle of law and a general principle of international law, controls the exercise of rights by states. One application of this general principle, the application widely known as the doctrine of abus de droit, prohibits the abusive exercise of a state's rights and enjoins that whenever the assertion of a right "impinges on the field covered by [a] treaty obligation, it must be exercised bona fide, that is to say, reasonably.* "'[104]

According to the Appellate Body, the chapeau clause of Article XX GATT 1994 is an expression of the principle of good faith and, consequently requires the Members acting under one of the exceptions to exercise their rights *reasonably*. In greater detail, the Appellate Body proceeds with the statement:

'*the task of interpreting and applying the chapeau is [...] one of locating and marking out a line of equilibrium between the right of a Member to invoke an exception under Article XX [GATT 1994] and the rights of the other Members under varying substantive provisions [...] of the GATT 1994, so that neither of the competing rights will cancel out the other and thereby distort and nullify or impair the balance of rights and obligations constructed by the Members themselves in that Agreement. The location of the line of equilibrium, as expressed in the chapeau, is not fixed and unchanging; the line moves as the kind and the shape of the measures at stake vary and as the facts making up specific cases differ.* '[105]

3. AB Report *Korea – Beef*

In *Korea – Beef*, a case which involved two separate measures, each tending to protect the Korean beef industry from import competition, the Appellate Body discussed *in extenso* the meaning of the term 'necessary' in Article XX (d) GATT 1994. The report summarises the results of the interpretation with the following words:

'*In sum, determination of whether a measure, which is not "indispensable", may nevertheless be "necessary" within the contemplation of Article XX(d) [GATT 1994], involves in every case a*

---

[104] AB Report, *US – Shrimp*, para 158.
[105] AB Report *US – Shrimp*, para 159.

process of weighing and balancing a series of factors which prominently include the contribution made by the compliance measure to the enforcement of the law or regulation at issue, the importance of the common interests or values protected by that law or regulation, and the accompanying impact of the law or regulation on imports or exports'.[106] [emphasis added]

Again, the Appellate Body employs a 'process of weighing and balancing' in order to determine the necessity of a trade restrictive measure. According to the passage cited, the decisive elements are: (1) the suitability of the measure to achieve the legitimate objective, i.e. to secure compliance with another law or regulation; (2) the legitimacy of the values protected by that law or regulation; and (3) the trade effects of that law or regulation. This balancing process is also described elsewhere in the report laying more weight on the reasonableness of the measure:

'In our view, the weighing and balancing process we have outlined is comprehended in the determination of whether a WTO-consistent alternative measure which the Member concerned could "reasonably be expected to employ" is available, or whether a less WTO-inconsistent measure is "reasonably available".'[107]

All of these excerpts of Appellate Body reports present a clear picture. They either give effect to certain aspects of the proportionality principle, or have at least a direct connection to the components and single elements of this principle.[108] In the interpretation and application of Article XX GATT 1994, elements of the principle of proportionality are relevant both in the examination of the design of a measure in order to assign it to one of the paragraphs and in the appraisal of the application of the measure under the chapeau clause. The only difference between the proportionality concepts applied at the two stages of justification under Article XX GATT 1994 might be seen in the differing degrees of complexity and flexibility. The design of the measure, on the one hand, is measured under one of the exceptions of Article XX GATT 1994 with respect to both its close and genuine relationship to a legitimate objective and the competing legal rights and objectives. The required relationship of ends and means, along with other requirements are specified in the text of each of the paragraphs of Article

---

[106] AB Report *Korea – Beef*, para 164.
[107] AB Report *Korea – Beef*, para 166.
[108] *Epiney* (2000) 84; *Tietje* (1998) 313 et seqq..

XX GATT 1994. These differences must be given meaning in the interpretation and application of the exceptions. As a consequence, the 'process of weighing and balancing' is bound by these specific requirements. On the other hand, the chapeau clause, addressing the application of the measure in the given case, consists of three broad limitation clauses that are open to a variety of interpretations and value-decisions. The fundamental task under the chapeau clause is to maintain a due balance between the rights and obligations of the Members concerned. Keeping the differences in the texts of the agreements in mind, there exists no apparent reason why the recognition of the principle of proportionality should be denied in WTO law.

4. AB Report *US – Cotton Yarn*

This characterisation of the principle of proportionality as one of the more basic principles underlying the multilateral trading system is now supported by the most recent decision of the Appellate Body. In the AB Report *US – Cotton Yarn*,[109] adopted on 5 November 2001, the Appellate Body for the first time explicitly referred to the 'principle of proportionality'. In its ruling, issued on 8 October 2001, the Appellate Body upheld an earlier Panel decision,[110] which found that a US safeguard-investigation leading to restrictions in imports of combed cotton yarn from Pakistan[111] was not carried out in accordance with WTO rules (Agreement on Textiles and Clothing, ATC).[112]

---

[109] United States – Transitional Safeguard Measure on Combed Cotton Yarn from Pakistan (AB Report *US – Cotton Yarn*), WT/DS192/AB/R, adopted 5 November 2001.

[110] Panel Report, United States – Transitional Safeguard Measure on Combed Cotton Yarn from Pakistan, WT/DS192/R, adopted 5 November 2001.

[111] The US decision adopted by the *Clinton* administration in 1999 imposes an annual import restraint of 5.26 million kilograms on Pakistani combed cotton yarn. The decision was based on a US investigation covering the period 1996-1998 which concluded that significant increases in imports of cotton yarn had caused serious damage, or threat of damage to domestic manufacturers producing similar or competitive products.

[112] For Pakistan and other developing countries, the decision was considered important, as it marked a victory in their struggle with the US's 40-year old textile trade policy.

The relevant part of the report that refers to the principle of proportionality deals with Pakistan's previous claim before the Panel that the United States acted inconsistently with the requirements of Article 6.4 ATC thus attributing serious damage to imports from Pakistan without making a comparative assessment of the imports of other Member countries. In its report, the Panel held for Pakistan on this issue stating that the United States acted inconsistently with its obligations under Article 6.4 ATC, not having examined the effect of imports from other (appropriate) Members individually.

This conclusion was then appealed against by the United States arguing, among other things, that Article 6.4 ATC, second sentence, permits a comparative analysis of the effect of imports from a particular Member, without conducting a similar kind of analysis for the other Members from whom imports have also increased sharply and substantially. Noting the unclear wording of the relevant provision the Appellate Body in its report held contrary to the view of the United States *'that Article 6.4 [ATC], second sentence does not permit the attribution of the totality of serious damage to one Member, unless the imports from that Member alone have caused all the serious damage.'* The position of the United States would *'amount to a 'mis-attribution' of damage and would be inconsistent with the interpretation in good faith of the terms of Article 6.4 [ATC]. Therefore, the part of the total serious damage attributed to an exporting Member must be proportionate to the damage caused by the imports from that Member.'*

In the following paragraph the Appellate Body supports this view of the principle of proportionality as a limiting device by referring not just to the rules of general international law on state responsibility (Article 51 of the International Law Commission's Draft on Responsibility of States is quoted in the footnote) but also to Article 22.4 DSU. And within the ensuing two paragraphs, the principle of proportionality is explicitly referred to by the Appellate Body when stating:

'In our view, such an exorbitant derogation from the principle of proportionality in respect of the attribution of serious damage could be justified only if the drafters of the ATC had expressly provided for it, which is not the case.'

And further on:

'We now turn to the question of how to conduct the comparative analysis required by Article 6.4. This analysis is to be seen in the light of the principle of proportionality as the means of

determining the scope or assessing the part of the total serious damage that can be attributed to an exporting Member' [emphasis added].

This recent decision clearly indicates that the Appellate Body has now overcome its reluctance to explicitly recognizing proportionality as an unwritten and overarching principle in the current body of WTO law. This tendency to apply legal principles as additional sources of law once again testifies to the growing maturity of the WTO legal system.

VII. Principles Originated in Public International Law or the Internal Legal Regimes of WTO Members: 'External Principles'

As already mentioned above, the Appellate Body acknowledged in its very first report *US – Gasoline*, *"[t]hat direction [in Article 3.2 of the DSU] reflects a measure of recognition that the General Agreement [GATT 1994] is not to be read in clinical isolation from public international law."*[113] This statement of the Appellate Body amounted to a death blow to those maintaining that WTO rules were not rule of public international law and brought to an end the ill-founded concept of the GATT as being a 'self-contained' system.[114] In *US – Shrimp*, the Appellate Body then presented Article 31 (3) (c) of the Vienna Convention on the Law of the Treaties (VCLT)[115] as the key to finding 'additional interpretative guidance' from public international law.[116] This article directs that in interpreting a treaty, account must be taken not only of the treaty itself, but also of *"any relevant rules of international law applicable in the relations between the parties"*. Those rules referred to in Article 31 (3) (c) VCLT may derive from any source of international law, i.e. treaty provisions, customary international law, or general principles of law.[117] In terms of customary international law, this approach was confirmed in the Panel Report *Korea – Government*

---

[113] AB Report *US – Gasoline*, sec. III B.
[114] *Marceau* (1999) 107 et seqq.; *Pauwelyn* (2001) 542.
[115] Reprinted in: 8 ILM (1969) 679.
[116] AB Report *US – Shrimp*, para 158, footnote 157; detailed: *Marceau* (1999) 123 et seqq.; also: *Waincymer* (2001) 1261 et seq..
[117] Cf. *Pauwelyn* (2001) 575 with reference to the *Golder* Case, 57 ILR 201, 217 (European Court of Human Rights 1975), in which it was held that the reference to "relevant rules of international law" includes general principles of international law.

Procurement. In this report, which had not been appealed, the Panel even went a step further and employed the rules and principles of customary international law to fill unintended gaps in the WTO agreements.[118] It also held that *"such [customary] international law applies to the extent that the WTO treaty agreements do not "contract out" from it"*. This point of view, which finds even more support in the recent Appellate Body decision *US – Cotton Yarn*,[119] shows the increasingly prominent position, which the legal environment has gained in the process of the application and interpretation of WTO agreements.

In the jurisprudence of the Appellate Body, references have been made to various principles originating from different legal spheres, e.g. other international treaties, statutes of WTO-related international organisations,[120] custom, general principles of law, or principles common to the internal legal regimes of WTO Members. A non-comprehensive enumeration of applied principles encompasses, amongst other things, the following: the principle of good faith,[121] the principle of fundamental fairness,[122] the principle of

---

[118] Panel Report Korea – Measures Affecting Government Procurement, WT/DS163/R, adopted 19 June 2000, para 7.101; and also with comments: *Pauwelyn* (2001) 543 and 570 et seq..

[119] AB Report *US – Cotton Yarn*, para 120.

[120] Although the WTO is not a formal Member of the UN family, various WTO Agreements refer to the rules governing other international organisations, such as the IMF, WIPO, WHO, FAO or ISO.

[121] AB Report *US – Shrimp*, para 158; AB Report *US – Cotton Yarn*, para 81; AB Report *US – Shrimp, 21.5*, para 134, footnote 97; AB Report *US – FSCs*, para 166; AB Report *EC – Computer Equipment*, para 83; Appellate Body Report, Canada – Measures Affecting the Export of Civilian Aircraft (AB Report *Canada – Aircraft*), WT/DS70/AB/R, adopted 20 August 1999, para 190; Appellate Body Report, United States – Anti-Dumping Measures on Certain Hot-Rolled Steel Products from Japan (AB Report *US – Japan Hot-Rolled Steel*), WT/DS184/AB/R, adopted 23 August 2001, para 101: "(...) the principle of good faith, which is, at once, a general principle of law and a principle of general international law (...)"; on good faith in WTO jurisprudence see generally: *Petersmann* (1998) 189 et seqq..

[122] AB Report *US – Japan Hot-Rolled Steel*, para 193; Appellate Body Report, Mexico – Anti-Dumping Investigation of High-Fructose Corn Syrup (HFCS) from the United States, Recourse to Article 21.5 of the DSU by the United States (AB Report *Mexico – HFCS, 21.5*), para 107.

estoppel,[123] the principle of the abuse of rights,[124] the principle of due process,[125] the principle of effectiveness in treaty interpretation,[126] the principle of judicial economy,[127] the principle of non-

---

[123] AB Report *US – FSCs*, para 165; AB Report *EC – Asbestos*, para 180; Appellate Body Report, Thailand – Anti-Dumping Duties Angles, Shapes and Sections of Iron or Non-Alloy Steel and H-Beams from Poland (AB Report *Thailand – Steel*), WT/DS122/AB/R, adopted 5 April 2001, para 95; see also: *Cameron/Gray* (2001) 293 et seq..

[124] AB Report *US – Shrimp*, para 158; AB Report *US – Cotton Yarn*, para 81, footnote 53; see also: *Waincymer* (2001) 1264.

[125] AB Report *Brazil – Coconut*, sec. VI (with respect to Art. 7.3 DSU); AB Report *EC – Computer Equipment*, para 70 (interpreting Art. 6.2 DSU); Appellate Body Report, European Communities – Measures Concerning Meat and Meat Products (Hormones) (AB Report *EC – Hormones*), WT/DS26, 48/AB/R, adopted 13 February 1998, paras 133 (referring to "fundamental fairness", "due process" and "natural justice" in the context of Art. 11 DSU), 152, footnote 138, 154; Appellate Body Report, Australia – Measures Affecting Importation of Salmon (AB Report *Australia – Salmon*), WT/DS18/AB/R, adopted 6 November 1998, paras 271, 272, 278; on due process in WTO law see generally: *Gaffney* (1999) 1173 et seqq..

[126] AB Report *US – Gasoline*, sec. IV; AB Report *Japan – Alcoholic Beverages*, sec. G (interpreting Art. III GATT 1994); AB Report *US – Shrimp*, para 131 (interpreting Art. XX (g) GATT 1994); AB Report *US – Underwear*, sec. IV (with reference to *US – Gasoline* and *Japan – Alcoholic Beverages*).

[127] Appellate Body Report, United States – Measures Affecting Imports of Woven Wool Shirts and Blouses from India (AB Report *US – Shirts and Blouses*), WT/DS33/AB/R, adopted 23 May 1997, pages 18 et seq.; in AB Report *Australia – Salmon*, paras 219 et seqq.; in para 223 this principle was further refined as meaning in the WTO context: "A panel has to address those claims on which a finding is necessary in order to enable the DSB to make sufficiently precise recommendations and rulings so as to allow for prompt compliance by a Member with those recommendations and rulings "in order to ensure effective resolution of disputes to the benefit of all Members"; AB Report *Canada – Automotive Industry*, paras 115 et seqq.; AB Report *EC – Hormones*, paras 250 et seq.; AB Report *EC – Poultry*, para 135; see also: *Waincymer* (2001) 1260 et seqq..

retroactivity,[128] the principle of state responsibility[129] and the principle of *effet utile*.[130]

One striking example in which the Appellate Body applied a principle common to the internal legal regimes of WTO Members, can be found in the Report *US – Shirts and Blouses*. Here, with respect to the burden of proof, the Appellate Body applied the *'generally-accepted canon of evidence in civil law, common law and, in fact, most jurisdictions that the burden of proof rests upon the party, whether complainant or defending, who asserts the affirmative of a particular claim or defence'*.[131] Principles, however, which might be common to the internal legal systems of WTO Members are generally difficult to verify, given the number of Members representing a wide range of legal systems. In contrast to the European Community, for example, where principles common to the legal systems of all Member States have become one of the major sources of law,[132] there is far less homogeneity in the WTO system and, therefore, any such reference should be used with caution.

Within the jurisdiction of the Appellate Body, there are also rulings in which the Appellate Body Members rejected to apply or refer to certain legal principles. In *EC – Hormones*, for example, the Appellate Body was faced with an EC claim that the so-called 'precautionary principle' constitutes customary international law, or at least a general principle of law.[133] It was found in the report that it was *"unnecessary, and probably imprudent, for the Appellate Body in this appeal to take a position on this important, but abstract, question"*.[134] It noted, though, that *"the precautionary prin-*

---

[128] AB Report *Canada – Patent Protection*, paras 71 et seqq..

[129] AB Report *US – Shrimp*, para 173.

[130] AB Report *Canada – Milk*, para 133 (with reference in footnote 116 to AB Report *US – Gasoline*, page 23; AB Report *Japan – Alcoholic Beverages*, page 12).

[131] AB Report *US – Shirts and Blouses*, page 14; see also: India Quantitative Restrictions on Imports of Agricultural, Textile and Industrial Products (AB Report *India – Quantitative Restrictions*), WT/DS90/AB/R, adopted 22 September 1999, paras 135 et seqq. (citing *US – Shirts and Blouses*).

[132] See *Arnull* (1999) 190.

[133] Cf. AB Report *EC – Hormones*, para 121; see also: *Neumayer* (2001) 157 et seq..

[134] AB Report *EC – Hormones*, para 123, referring to a detailed list of academic literature on the debate (fn. 92).

ciple, at least outside the field of international environmental law, still awaits authoritative formulation."[135] It further stated that *"the principle has not been written into the SPS Agreement as a ground for justifying SPS measures that are otherwise inconsistent with the obligations of Members set out in particular provisions of that Agreement."*[136] But nevertheless, the Appellate Body recognized that the principle *"finds reflection"* in various SPS provisions.[137] Noting that *"the precautionary principle does not, by itself, and without a clear textual directive to that effect, relieve a Panel from the duty of applying the normal [...] principles of treaty interpretation",*[138] the Appellate Body finally agreed with the Panel that *"the precautionary principle does not override the provisions of Articles 5.1 and 5.2 of the SPS Agreement".*[139]

In the decision *India – Quantitative Restrictions*, the Appellate Body had to answer the arguments of India which supported the existence of a 'principle of institutional balance' in WTO law.[140] However, the Appellate Body rejected India's line of argumentation and held *'that India failed to advance any convincing arguments in support of the existence of a principle of institutional balance'.*[141]

In addition to the above, numerous other principles could be mentioned, which occur either in the texts of the WTO agreements, or have been referred to by the Appellate Body, without mentioning whether they are inherent to the WTO system or whether they have their explicit source in the law outside the WTO system. Reference in this sense could be made for example to the principle of judicial economy.[142] Many, if not all of the principles listed above have also found their expression in legal systems 'outside' the WTO system, i.e. in public international law, or in the internal legal regimes of WTO Members. Thus, it is often difficult to see whether the Ap-

---

[135] AB Report *EC – Hormones*, para 123 with reference to case law of the ICJ.
[136] AB Report *EC – Hormones*, para 124.
[137] AB Report *EC – Hormones*, para 124.
[138] AB Report *EC – Hormones*, para 124.
[139] AB Report *EC – Hormones*, para 125.
[140] AB Report *India – Quantitative Restrictions*, paras 8 et seqq. and 98 et seqq..
[141] AB Report *India – Quantitative Restrictions*, para 105; for the principle of separation of powers in the WTO context see: *Cass* (2001) 55 et seqq..
[142] AB Report *US – Shirts and Blouses*, page 14.

pellate Body by applying a given principle not explicitly expressed in the texts of the WTO agreements wants to confirm that such a principle is underlying the WTO system, or is part of the 'external' sources of law.[143]

VIII.   Balancing Rules and Principles in WTO Law

Coming back to the initial question of the relationship of economic and non-economic principles in international law, one must examine how to relate conflicting rules and/or principles in WTO law. This is a difficult task because of the lack of any inherent hierarchy between general international law and treaties – as well as, more generally, between any two rules of international law. This lack of hierarchy, to which rules of *ius cogens* are the prominent exception, is explained on the grounds that both derive, in one way or another, from the will or acquiescence of states as the same source and must therefore be equal in value.[144]

In the legal system of the WTO, a number of rules on hierarchy exist, which have to be applied first. According to Article XVI (3) WTO Agreement rules and principles expressed in the WTO Agreement shall prevail over those in the GATT 1994 and all other multilateral agreements. In the event of conflict between the GATT 1994 and another agreement on trade in goods in Annex 1A to the WTO Agreement, the latter shall prevail.[145] Various other conflict rules to solve 'intra WTO-conflicts'[146] can be found within the texts of the different Agreements.[147]

If no conflict rule can be found for either intra-WTO conflicts in the WTO agreement itself, or for conflicts between WTO rules or principles and other rules or principles of international law, further guidance on how to solve normative conflicts must be sought in general international law, as reflected, for example, in the provisions of the Vienna Convention. This encompasses not only the rules of logic of general international law, i.e. the general principle

---

[143] *Hilf* (2001) 121.
[144] *Pauwelyn* (2001) 536.
[145] Interpretative Note at Annex 1A to the WTO Agreement.
[146] *Pauwelyn* (2001) 560.
[147] Art. 21 Agreement on Agriculture; Art. 1.5 TBT Agreement; Art. 1 (2) DSU; for more details see: *Pauwelyn* (2001) 560; and also: *Montaguti/ Lugard* (2000) 473 et seqq.; AB Report *Canada – Automotive Industry*, para 159 et seqq..

of *lex posterior*,[148] the customary rule of *lex specialis*,[149] but also the *pacta tertiis* principle[150] or the *presumption against conflict*.[151] However, the principles dealing with treaty conflicts do not always lead to a satisfactory solution.

The *lex posterior* rule, expressed in Article 30 (3) VCLT, refers to the constellation of successive treaties between exactly the same states expressing their contractual freedom to change their minds. But, as already noted by *Sinclair*, with regards to the interplay between multilateral treaties the *lex posterior* rule is *'in many respects not entirely satisfactory'*.[152] Most modern multilateral conventions exist as a regulatory framework or legal system created at one point in time, but they continue to exist and evolve over a mostly indefinite period. If a norm of such an 'evolving treaty' conflicts with norms of other treaties, in particular of the same evolving nature, the *lex posterior* principle would only focus on the time of conclusion of the later treaty. Such a 'guillotine-approach'[153] does not make any sense and mostly leads to arbitrary results.

The same holds true for the idea of *lex specialis*. WTO rules regulate the trade relations between Members. However, in today's highly interdependent world WTO rules cut across almost all other areas of international law (e.g. environment, human rights).[154] Given this complex situation, the difficult question has to be answered which of the conflicting legal systems provides the more focused or detailed solution to the problem at stake, since advocates of both regimes would tend to invoke the principle in their own favour.[155] Furthermore, the notion of *lex specialis* leads to the as-

---

[148] Cf. Articles 30 (3), 59 VCLT; see also: *Marceau* (2001) 1091 et seq.; *Waincymer* (2001) 1263.

[149] See for further references: *Marceau* (2001) 1092 et seq.; *Waincymer* (2001) 1263.

[150] Pacta tertiis nec nocent nec prosunt.

[151] See e.g.: *Marceau* (2001) 1089; *Waincymer* (2001) 1263.

[152] *Sinclair* (1984) 96 et seqq..

[153] *Pauwelyn* (2001) 546.

[154] See on these topics e.g. *Petersmann* (2001) 3 et seqq. (Human Rights); *Rollo /Winter* (2000) 561 et seqq. (Environmental and Labour Standards); *Correa* (2000) 89 et seqq. (National Public Health Policies).

[155] *Hilf* (2000) 481; See for the difficult issue of the legal relationship between the WTO and Multilateral Environmental Agreements (MEAs) for example: *Marceau* (2001) 1081 et seqq.; *Runge* (2001) 399 et seqq.; *Schoenbaum* (1997) 281 et seqq.; *Motaal* (2001) 1215 et seqq..

sumption that rules generally take precedence over principles. The ruling of the Appellate Body in *EC – Hormones* seems to support this view, since it was held that a principle of customary international law could not override a specific obligation under treaty law.[156]

If the principles of *lex specialis* and *lex posterior* cannot solve every dispute that arises in a satisfactory manner, other solutions have to be found. Assuming that no rule of priority gives higher rank to written rules and principles in relation to unwritten ones, every interpreter of law has to evaluate, on a case-by-case basis, how to weigh each conflicting principle. Unwritten principles, in particular, normally have a fundamental importance based on their wide acceptance. Additionally, it may be unreasonable to presume that rules and principles from the WTO system carry more weight in the balancing process than general principles being developed on the basis of either public international law, or the national laws of WTO Members.[157]

With respect to Article XX GATT 1947, Panels have, at times, applied the principle of interpretation that exceptions should be construed narrowly.[158] This indicates a ranking of interests that favours free trade. Although the Appellate Body referred to the exceptions under Article XX GATT 1994 as being 'limited exceptions from obligations under certain other provisions of the GATT 1994'[159] it did not confirm the approach of the GATT Panels.[160] In fact, the Appellate Body in its report *US – Shrimp* searched for a balance of the right of a Member to invoke a general exception under Article XX GATT 1994, on the one hand, and the substantive rights of the other Members under GATT 1994, on the other hand, with due regard to the interests at stake.[161] In such a situation it is for the principle of proportionality to balance the conflicting interests in light of the further legal requirements as listed in the chapeau of Article XX GATT 1994. However, a narrow interpretation

---

[156] AB Report *EC – Hormones*, para 124.

[157] *Hilf* (2001) 128.

[158] Panel Report, Canada – Administration of the Foreign Investment Review Act, adopted 7 February 1984, BISD 30S/140, para 5.20; Panel Report, United States – Section 337 of the Tariff Act of 1930, adopted 7 November 1989, BISD 36S/345, para 5.27.

[159] AB Report *US – Shirts and Blouses*, page 16.

[160] AB Report *EC – Hormones*, para 104.

[161] AB Report *US – Shrimp*, para 156,

should be applied in cases where an exception refers to the same or similar interests. Thus safeguard clauses invoked for economic reasons should be interpreted narrowly in the light of the general principles of the GATT 1994, including the exclusion of quantitative trade restrictions under Article XI. On the contrary, when non-economic interests and principles are invoked, for example, under Articles XX and XXI GATT 1994, there seems to be no reason why, from the outset, a narrow interpretation of non-economic interests of imperative public importance should be warranted.[162]

IX.   Prospects and Conclusions

The search for principles underlying WTO law seems to be typical of a civil law approach, since it tends to construe law from top to bottom, whereas in common law a case would be decided first and the principles determined afterwards.[163] In addition, the foregoing reflections on the relevance of principles in WTO law have probably been influenced by the efforts of interpretation within the EC legal system, although the functional differences between the WTO and the EC should not be overlooked.[164] Of course, the EU represents a unique construct, i.e. a supra-national institution, the existence and development of which is heavily influenced by historical circumstances and the political will for European integration. In contrast to European Union law, the WTO regime has not been built by teleologically-driven judges,[165] but has rather grown from the GATT through a much more laborious bottom-up process. But the fact that the EU and the WTO represent substantially different levels of integration, and will most likely continue to do so, does not imply that lessons cannot be drawn from the former for a reform of the latter.[166]

As this paper has tried to illustrate, there has been a remarkable development towards the use of economic as well as non-economic principles in WTO law. In particular, the Appellate Body employs those principles not just in order to enhance legal security and con-

---

[162] *Hilf* (2001) 129; also: *Manzini* (1999) 825 et seqq..

[163] *Holmes* (1870) 1.

[164] The legal system of the former shall provide a stable and reliable framework for international trade and not the integration of the legal and economic systems of its Member States, which is the function of the latter; see for example: *Rollo/Winters* (2000) 566 et seq..

[165] *Weiler* (1991) 2416.

[166] *Neumayer* (2001) 146.

sistency within the WTO legal system and to meet the requirements of a coherent 'multilateral trading system' as referred to in the Preamble of the WTO Agreement, but also to contribute to a further sophistication of international economic law in general.

It was the Appellate Body in its report *US – Shrimp* that indicated its obligation to interpret the often fragmentary rules of WTO law.[167] The openness of the Appellate Body to the use of economic as well as non-economic principles, in its jurisprudence, is of considerable importance in bringing the relevant diverse values and interests into the process of dispute settlement, especially in disputes relating to the interface between the liberal trade regime and other policy regimes, both national and international.[168] Its rulings develop international legal jurisprudence, and at the institutional level, the global community becomes more secure with the knowledge that an international dispute resolution regime can function in a mutually satisfactory, principled and efficient way.[169]

It has already been mentioned that Appellate Body reports may only lead to binding settlements of specific disputes. To some extent, the use of (unwritten) economic and non-economic principles might appear to contravene the rule in Articles 3.2. and 19.2 DSU against adding to or diminishing the rights and obligations provided in the covered agreements. But even though the reports of the Appellate Body do not have the effect of creating a precedent[170] and do not have any law-making powers,[171] they certainly serve to verify the existence of underlying principles – just as court decisions in any other legal system. And it seems that the actions of the Appellate Body have been approved by WTO Members in its basing decisions, at least in part, on basic principles which find their expres-

---

[167] AB Report *US – Shrimp*, para 155.

[168] *Trebilcock/Howse* (1999) 74.

[169] *Cameron/Gray* (2001) 297.

[170] The findings and recommendations of the panels and the Appellate Body do not create precedents. Each panel process and each appeal is independent of any other such process. However, in actual practice the panels and the Appellate Body go over the previous decisions and are guided by them. For a discussion on *stare decisis* in WTO Law see: *Lester* (2001) 522 (524 et seqq.); *Chua* (1998b) 45 et seqq..

[171] The competence to give binding interpretations of the various agreements is exclusively conferred to the Ministerial Conference or the General Council, see Article IX (2) WTO Agreement.

sion in the legal underpinnings of the WTO system.[172] This method of consistent, coherent and authoritative interpretation not only strengthens the development of the trade regime, connecting adjudication with the constitutional function of the WTO, but also provides the interested parties with grounds for trust.

In the case of a conflict between different principles, especially between those of economic and non-economic nature, all relevant principles shall be taken into account on an equal basis and have to be balanced according to their respective relevance for the given case (*'process of optimisation'*).[173] With a view to obtaining a due relation between the different interests at stake, this sensitive balancing process shall be guided by the principle of proportionality. It may be seen as the more sophisticated sister of the queen of all principles, namely the principle of good faith.

Such an approach is a prerequisite for any satisfactory settlement of trade disputes and the maintenance of a stable, reliable and coherent multilateral trading system.

Summary

The Relation of Economic and Non-Economic Principles in International Law

1. What are principles?
   In view of the confusion about principles one should look for fundamental and high ranking concepts of general acceptance which are underlying the specific legal rules. Principles can hardly be isolated and are in permanent collision with other principles.
2. Economic and non-economic principles can be discussed in the broader context of the WTO. It seems difficult to distinguish principles from other basic concepts including e.g. objectives, values and interests.
3. The Preamble of the Agreement Establishing the WTO refers to "basic principles and (...) objectives underlying this multilateral trading system". This has been strongly affirmed in the Ministe-

---

[172] *Waincymer* (2001) 1270.
[173] See e.g. *Larenz* (1991) 475.

rial Declaration of Doha (WT/MIN(01)/DEC/W/1, 14 November 2001, para. 1).

4. The recognition of (often unwritten) principles does not "add or diminish the rights and obligations provided in the covered agreements" (Art. 3.2 DSU).

5. The obligatory nature of the dispute settlement system requires the continuing recognition of general principles coming from various sources inside, as well as outside the legal framework of the WTO.

6. Both a number of economic and non-economic principles are referred to in the different agreements covered under the WTO (internal sources).

7. The Appellate Body (AB) has construed the law of the WTO as being part of general public international law (no "clinical isolation", no "legal vacuum", no "self-contained regime"). Likewise, reference has been made to treaties covering "non-economic" fields such as those relating to the environment, human rights etc.. In addition, principles common to the legal systems of its Members have been taken into account (external sources).

8. In case of conflict, formal rules or principles of treaty interpretation such as the rules "*lex posterior*" or "*lex specialis*" or "exceptions to be interpreted narrowly" may be helpful, but often do not lead to convincing results.

9. In case of conflicting principles especially between economic and non-economic principles all relevant principles have to be taken into account on an equal basis. They have to be balanced according to their respective relevance for the given case ("process of optimisation").

10. The principle of proportionality is helpful in this process of balancing conflicting principles as well as in defining the "end and means relationship". Its final recognition by the AB (*US – cotton Yarn*) testifies to the growing maturity of the WTO legal system.

11. The essential elements of the principle of proportionality are mentioned in various provisions of the WTO ("effective", "necessary" as well as "reasonable").

12. The principle of good faith may be qualified as being the "queen of all principles". The principle of proportionality then may be seen as her more sophisticated sister.

Bibliography:

D. Ahn (1999), Environmental Disputes in the GATT/WTO: Before and after US-Shrimp Case, Michigan Journal of International Law 19 (1999), 819-870.

R. Alexy (1985), Theorie der Grundrechte, Baden-Baden 1985.

A. E. Appleton (1999), *Shrimp / Turtle*: Untangling the Nets, Journal of International Economic Law 2 (1999) No. 3, 477-496.

A. Arnull (1999), The European Union and its Court of Justice, Oxford 1999.

L. Bartels (2001), Applicable Law in WTO Dispute Settlement Proceedings, Journal of World Trade 35 (2001) No. 3, 499-519.

M. Beise (2001), Die Welthandelsorganisation (WTO), Funktion, Status, Organisation, Baden-Baden 2001.

W. Benedek (1990), Die Rechtsordnung des GATT aus völkerrechtlicher Sicht, Berlin 1990.

U. Beyerlin (2000), Umweltvölkerrecht, München 2000.

M. Bogdan (1977), General Principles of Law and the Problem of Lacunae in the Law of Nations, Nordic Journal of International Law 46 (1977), 37-53.

M. C. E. J. Bronckers (1999), Better Rules for a New Millennium: A Warning against Undemocratic Developments in the WTO, Journal of International Economic Law 2 (1999) No. 4, 547-566.

G. de Búrca (1993), The principle of proportionality and its application in EC law, Yearbook of European Law 13 (1993), 105-150.

G. de Búrca (2000), Proportionality and Subsidiarity as General Principles of Law, in *U. Bernitz / J. Nergelius* (eds.), General Principles of European Community Law, Den Haag / London / Boston 2000, 95-112.

G. de Búrca /J. Scott (2001), The Impact of the WTO on EU Decision-making, in *G. de Búrca /J. Scott* (eds.), The EU and the WTO, Oxford 2001, 1-30.

J. Cameron /K. R. Gray (2001), Principles of International Law in the WTO Dispute Settlement Body, International and Comparative Law Quarterly 50 (2001) April, 248-298.

D. Z. Cass (2001), The 'Constitutionalization' of International Trade Law: Judicial Norm-Generation as the Engine of Constitutional Development in International Trade, European Journal of International Law 12 (2001), 39-75.

A. T. L. Chua (1998a), Precedent and Principles of WTO Panel Jurisprudence, Berkeley Journal of International Law 1998, 171-196.

A. T. L. Chua (1998b), The Precedential Effect of WTO Panel and Appellate Body Reports, Leiden Journal of International Law 11 (1998), 45-61.

S. M. Cone, III (1999),The Appellate Body, the Protection of Sea Turtles and the Technique of "Completing the Analysis", Journal of World Trade 33 (1999) No. 2, 51-61.

C. M. Correa (2000), Implementing National Public Health Policies in the Framework of WTO Agreements, Journal of World Trade 34 (2000) No. 5, 89-121.

V. Dailey (2000), Sustainable Development: Reevaluating the Trade vs. Turtles Conflict at the WTO, Journal of Transnational Law and Policy, Spring 2000, 331-383.

J. Delbrück (1984), "Proportionality", in *R. Bernhard* et al. (eds.), Encyclopedia of Public International Law III (1997), 1140-1144.

A. Desmedt (2001), Proportionality in WTO Law, Journal of International Economic Law 4 (2001) No. 3, 441-480.

R. Dolzer (2001), Wirtschaft und Kultur im Völkerrecht, in: *W. Graf Vitzthum*, Völkerrecht, Berlin [2]2001, 469-544.

R. Dworkin (1977), Taking Rights Seriously, London 1977.

E. Ellis (1999), The Principle of Proportionality in the Laws of Europe, Oxford 1999.

N. Emiliou (1996), The Principle of Proportionality in European Law, London 1996.

A. Epiney (2000), Welthandel und Umwelt, Deutsches Verwaltungsblatt 2000, 77-86.

J. Esser (1974), Grundsatz und Norm in der richterlichen Fortbildung des Privatrechts, Tübingen [3]1974.

U. Fastenrath (1991), Lücken im Völkerrecht, Berlin 1991.

J. P. Gaffney (1999), Due Process in the World Trade Organization: The Need for Procedural Justice in the Dispute Settlement System, American University International Law Review 14 (1999) No. 4, 1173-1221.

H. Ginzky (1999), Garnelen und Schildkröten – zu den umweltpolitischen Handlungsspielräumen der WTO-Mitgliedstaaten, Zeitschrift für Umweltrecht 11 (1999), 216-222.

E. Grabitz (1973), Der Grundsatz der Verhältnismäßigkeit in der Rechtsprechung des Bundesverfassungsgerichts, Archiv des öffentlichen Rechts 98 (1973), 568-616.

L. D. Guruswamy (1998), Should UNCLOS or GATT/WTO Decide Trade and Environment Disputes?, Minnesota Journal of Global Trade Summer 1998, 287-328.

H. L. A. Hart (1994), The Concept of Law, Oxford [2]1994.

M. Hilf (2000), Freiheit des Welthandels contra Umweltschutz?, Neue Zeitschrift für Verwaltungsrecht 2000, 481-490.

M. Hilf (2001), Power, Rules and Principles in WTO /GATT Law, Journal of International Economic Law 4 (2001) No. 1, 111-130.

M. Hilf/S. Puth (2002), The Principle of Proportionality on its Way into WTO/GATT Law, in *A. von Bogdandy* et. al. (ed.), European Integration and International Coordination, Festschrift für C. D. Ehlermann (2002), forthcoming.

J. Hippler Bello (1996), The WTO Dispute Settlement Understanding: Less is more, American Journal of International Law 90 (1996), 416-418.

H. Hohmann (2001), Die WTO-Streitbeilegung im Jahr 2000, Recht der internationalen Wirtschaft 2001, 649-658.

O. W. Holmes (1870), Codes and the Arrangement of the Law, American Law Review 5 (1870) No. 1.

K. Ipsen / U. R. Haltern (1991), Reform des Welthandelssystems?: Perspektiven zum GATT und zur Uruguay-Runde, Frankfurt am Main 1991.

J. H. Jackson (1995), International Economic Law: Reflections on the „Boilerroom" of International Relations, American University Journal of International Law and Policy, Winter 1995, 595-606.

J. H. Jackson (1998), The World Trade Organization, Constitution and Jurisprudence, London 1998.

J. H. Jackson (1999), The World Trading System, London ²1999.

P. J. Kuijper (1994), The Law of GATT as a Special Field of International Law, Netherlands Yearbook of International Law 1994, 227-257.

K. Larenz (1991), Methodenlehre der Rechtswissenschaft, Berlin ⁶1991.

S. N. Lester (2001), WTO Panel and the Appellate Body Interpretations of the WTO Agreement in US Law, Journal of World Trade 35 (2001) No. 3, 521-543.

P. Manzini (1999), Environmental Exceptions of Art. XX GATT 1994 Revisited in the Light of the Rules of Interpretation of General International Law, in *P. Mengozzi* (ed.), International Trade Law on the 50th Anniversary of the Multilateral Trade System, Milano 1999, 811-848.

G. Marceau (1999), A Call for Coherence in International Law: Praises for the Prohibition Against „Clinical Isolation" in WTO Dispute Settlement, Journal of World Trade 33 (1999) No. 5, 87-152.

G. Marceau (2001), Conflicts of Norms and Conflicts of Jurisdictions, The Relationship between the WTO Agreement and MEAs and other Treaties, Journal of World Trade 35 (2001) No. 6, 1081-1131.

H. Maurer (1999), Staatsrecht, München 1999.

P. C. Mavroidis (1991), Das GATT als „self-contained" Regime, Recht der interantionalen Wirtschaft 1991, 497-501.

P. C. Mavroidis (2000), Trade and Environment after the *Shrimps-Turtles* Litigation, Journal of World Trade 34 (2000) No. 1, 73-88.

J. McBride (1999), Proportionality and the European Convention on Human Rights, in *E. Ellis*, The Principle of Proportionality in the Laws of Europe, Oxford 1999, 23-35.

D. M. McRae (2000), The WTO in International Law: Tradition Continued or New Frontier, Journal of International Economic Law 3 (2000) No. 1, 27-41.

E. Montaguti/M. Lugard (2000), The GATT 1994 and Other Annex 1A Agreements: Four Different Relationships?, Journal of International Economic Law 3 (2000) No. 3, 473-484.

D. A. Motaal (2001), Multilateral Environmental Agreements (MEAs) and WTO Rules, Journal of World Trade 35 (2001) No. 6, 1215-1233.

E. Neumayer (2001), Greening the WTO Agreements, Can the Treaty Establishing the European Community be of Guidance? Journal of World Trade 35 (2001) No. 1, 145-166.

T. Oppermann (1987), On the Present International Economic Order, in *T. Oppermann/E.-U. Petersmann* (eds.), Reforming the International Economic Order (1987), 187-199.

T. Oppermann/P. Conlan (1990), „Principles" – Legal Basis of Today's International Economic Order?, Jahrbuch für die Ordnung von Wirtschaft und Gesellschaft, ORDO 41 (1990), 75-91.

D. Palmeter/P. C. Mavroidis (1998), The WTO Legal System: Sources of Law, American Journal International Law 92 (1998), 398-413.

J. Pauwelyn (2001), The Role of Public International Law in the WTO: How far can we go?, American Journal International Law 95 (2001), 535-578.

P. Pescatore (1960), Introduction à la Science du Droit, Luxembourg 1960.

E.-U. Petersmann (1985), World Trade, Principles, in *R. Bernhard* et al. (eds.), Encyclopedia of Public International Law IV (1985), 1542-1552.

E.-U. Petersmann (1987), International Trade Order and International Trade Law, in *T. Oppermann /E.-U. Petersmann* (eds.), Reforming the International Economic Order, Berlin 1987, 201-241.

E.-U. Petersmann (1998), From the Hobbesian International Law of Coexistence to Modern Integration Law: The WTO Dispute Settlement System, Journal of International Economic Law 1 (1998) No. 1, 175-198.

E.-U. Petersmann (2001), Human Rights and International Economic Law in the 21st Century. The need to clarify their interrelationships, Journal of International Economic Law 4 (2001) No. 1, 3-39.

S. Pyatt (1999), The WTO Sea Turtle Decision, Ecology Law Quaterly 1999, 815-839.

F. Roessler (1978), Law, De Facto Agreements and Declarations of Principle in International Economic Relations, German Yearbook of International Law 21 (1978), 27-59.

K. F. Röhl (2001), Allgemeine Rechtslehre, Köln [2]2001.

J. Rollo /L. A. Winters (2000), Subsidiarity and Governance Challenges for the WTO: Environmental and Labour Standards, The World Economy 23 (2000), 561-576.

C. F. Runge (2001), A Global Environment Organization (GEO) and the World Trading System, Journal of World Trade 35 (2001) No. 4, 399-426.

G. P. Sampson (2001), Effective Multilateral Environment Agreements and Why the WTO Needs Them, The World Economy 24 (2001), 1109-1134.

T. J. Schoenbaum (1997), International Trade and Protection of the Environment: The Continuing Search for Reconciliation, American Journal of International Law 91 (1997), 268-313.

G. Schwarzenberger (1966), The Principles of International Economic Law, Recueil de Cour 1966 I, 5-96.

R. *Senti* (2000), WTO, System und Funktionsweise der Welthandelsordnung, Zürich 2000.

B. *Simma* (1985), Self-Contained Regimes, Netherlands Yearbook of International Law 1985, 111-136.

I. *Sinclair* (1984), The Vienna Convention on the Law of Treaties, Manchester 1984.

K. *Stegemann* (2000), The Integration of Intellectual Property Rights into the WTO System, The World Economy 23 (2000), 1244-1267.

C. *Tietje* (1998), Normative Grundstrukturen der Behandlung nichttarifärer Handelshemmnisse in der WTO /GATT Rechtsordnung, Berlin 1998.

J. P. *Trachtmann* (1996), The International Economic Law Revolution, University of Pennsylvania Journal of International Economic Law, Spring 1996, 33-61.

J. P. *Trachtmann* (1999), The Domain of WTO Dispute Resolution, Harvard International Law Journal 40 (1999) No. 2, 333-377.

M. J. *Trebilcock*/R. *Howse* (1999), The Regulation of International Trade, London ²1999.

P. *Verloren van Themaat* (1981), The Changing Structure of International Economic Law, Den Haag 1981.

J. *Waincymer* (2001), Settlement of Disputes Within the World Trade Organisation: A Guide to the Jurisprudence, The World Economy 24 (2001), 1247-1278.

J. H. H. *Weiler* (1991), The Transformation of Europe, Yale Law Journal 100 (1991), 2403-2483.

J. H. H. Weiler / Iulia Motoc

Taking Democracy Seriously: The Normative Challenges to the International Legal System*

---

*   © 1999-2002 *J. H. H .Weiler*. Over the last three years unpublished
     earlier versions were presented at workshops or conferences at Michi-
     gan Law School; Duke Law School; the Legal Theory Section of the
     ILA London 2000 meeting; the *Gulbenkian* Foundation Conference on
     Globalism, Lisbon; The Globalization and its Discontents Colloquium,
     New York University Law School. The many comments and criticisms
     received are gratefully acknowledged.

I.   International Law and Democracy: A Classical Approach

Our point of departure is rooted in three trite, even banal affirmations about classical international law and democracy.

A. *The Rule of Law and Democracy*

Despite widespread use, the concepts of both Democracy and the Rule of Law are under-specified terms in the vocabulary of political theory and social science. Different theories give different meanings in different contexts to both. But however defined, it seems to us banal to recognize that in *domestic* settings democracy and the rule of law have become at least since the second half of the 20th Century inextricably linked, indeed interdependent. In our modern practices, the Rule of Law encapsulates, among other things, the claim to, and justification of, obedience to the law.[1] Such obedience can neither be claimed, nor justified, if the laws in question did not emanate from a legal system embedded in some form of democracy. Democracy, on this reading, is one (though not the only one) of the indispensable normative components for the legitimacy of a legal order. In a departure from previous understandings, if obedience, as a matter of fact, is secured without the legitimacy emanating from the practices of democracy, we are no longer willing to qualify such as the Rule of Law. A dictatorship that followed strictly its internal legal system, would be just that: A dictatorship following legal rules. It would not qualify as a system upholding the Rule of Law. The reverse is also true: It is to rules of law that we turn to define whether the practices of democracy have indeed been followed and, more generally, the Rule of Law, with its constraint on the arbitrary use of power, is considered an indispensable material element of modern democracy.[2] An attempt to vindicate even verifiable expressions of popular will outside legally defined procedures is regarded by us as the rule of the mob, rather than democracy.

---

[1]   Cf. *Raz* (1979)

[2]   Thus, typically in considering the requirements of "good government", judicial supremacy (as a manifestation of the Rule of Law) is considered an essential element for democracy like free and fair elections and the like. Cf. *Franck* (2001).

B. The Rule of International Law:
A Chronicle of Indifference and Hostility

This interdependence and symbiosis is not the case when describing the "Rule of International Law". In discussing the relationship between International Law and democracy, it is useful to examine two different facets: First, doctrinally, the extent to which democracy forms, part of the primary, material rules of international law and / or is part of its various doctrines; and, second, in a more self-referential process-oriented notion utilizing again the *Hart*ian distinction, the extent to which democracy is integrated into the process of international *law making* and forms part of International Law's own set of secondary rules of recognition.

Our second trite or banal observation is that traditionally, as regards both facets, for most of the 20th Century, generally speaking International Law has displayed indifference, even hostility, to the concept of democracy.[3] Certainly, its claims to, and justification of, obedience were not rooted in notions of democratic legitimation.[4] We do not propose here fully to demonstrate this claim but simply to illustrate it as regards both its doctrinal and its self-referential aspects.

As regards the former even a cursory survey of some of the fundamental doctrines of classical international law will illustrate the point.

- *Pacta Sunt Servanda*, the primordial norm of international law, has never depended for its validity on the internal democratic arrangements of its subjects – States.[5] Democracy or lack of it is

---

[3]   We feel a close affinity and acknowledge an intellectual debt to *Crawford* (1994). There has been a resurgence of writing on international law and democracy often with a somewhat less skeptical approach to our own. We have profited from and are indebted to *Franck* (1992) and the vast literature it has spawned. For the most recent thinking of these issues see the contributions in *Fox / Roth* (2000).

[4]   See, e.g. *Watts* (1993).

[5]   The general rule of international law does not allow, except in the narrowest of circumstances, for a state to use its own domestic law, including its own domestic constitutional law, as an excuse for non-performance of a treaty. That is part of the a, b, c of international law and is reflected in the Vienna Convention Article 27. "A party may not invoke the provisions of its internal law as justification for its failure to perform a treaty. This rule is without prejudice to article 46". See too the more recent Article 32 of the Draft Articles on the Responsibility

not among the vitiating or exculpating factors from an international legal obligation.[6]

---

of States for International Wrongful Acts, ILC 2001: "The Responsible State May not rely on the provisions of its internal law as justification for failure to comply with the obligations under this Part" (Official Records of the General Assembly, Suppl. No.10 (A/56/10) ch. IV, E1, nov.2001). Doctrine demonstrates an equal constancy in this respect. Compare for example *Verdross* (1927) with *Quadri* (1952). The most authoritative of texts in the "Anglo-Saxon" world, *Oppenheim's International Law*, is clear: "It is firmly established that a state when charged with a breach of its international obligations cannot in international law validly plead as a defense that it was unable to fulfill them because its internal law ... contained rules in conflict with international law; this applies equally to a state's assertion of its inability to secure the necessary changes in its law by virtue of some legal or constitutional requirement ..." *Jennings / Watts* (1992) 84-85. What is true for formal constitutional requirements would, *a fortiori* apply to softer notions such as the general requirements of democracy.

[6] The "hardness" of the "*pacta*" has remained intact even in the post '89-'90 epoch despite the widespread turn to democracy, formal or otherwise, in many countries previously hostile to such notions. Whether the turn to democracy could qualify under the doctrine of *rebus sic stantibus* was discussed recently by the ICJ in the *Gabcikovo / Nagymaros Project (Hungary-Slovakia)* case. "Hungary further argued that it was entitled to invoke a number of events which, cumulatively, would have constituted a fundamental change of circumstances. In this respect it specified profound changes of a political nature, the Project's diminishing economic viability, the progress of environmental knowledge and the development of new norms and prescriptions of international environmental law. ... The prevailing political situation was certainly relevant for the conclusion of the 1977 Treaty. But the Court will recall that the Treaty provided for a joint investment program for the production of energy, the control of floods and the improvement of navigation on the Danube. In the Court's view, the prevalent political conditions were thus not so closely linked to the object and purpose of the Treaty that they constituted an essential basis of the consent of the parties and, in changing, radically altered the extent of the obligations still to be performed" (ICJ, Rep. 1997 par. 104). Two points are of interest: First the fact that Hungary itself did not expressly refer to the dictatorial nature of the previous regime as a reason, *per se,* to escape responsibility. More interestingly, though the Court's language suggests the possibility in principle that the nature of the "political conditions" could be relevant to the essential basis of consent (the classical condi-

- In defining subjecthood, for most of the past century, it was the efficiency of government, and its effective control over national territory that were critical to acceptance of both new States and new regimes – almost penalizing the more messy emergence of democracy.[7]
- The complex norms of State succession are not about vindicating democracy but about vindicating identity. The new State, which invokes the *Tabula Rasa* components of the laws of State Succession, did not do this on the grounds that they were non-democratically approved by, say, a previous colonial regime. Indeed, the rule of the newly independent state could be, and often was, as undemocratic as the displaced Metropolitan power. Prior obligations were rejected because approval, democratic or otherwise, did not emanate from the right "Self".[8]
- In the law of State Responsibility, unlike traditional concepts such as attribution, *dolus, cupla,* necessity – democracy has classically had no status as such as affecting the responsibility of states vis-à-vis other international actors.[9]
- In the central area of Use of Force, until recently,[10] intervention to vindicate democracy and / or to combat its overthrow was

---

tion for the doctrine of *rebus sic stantibus* to apply), it is hard to imagine where that would be the case in relation to most treaties.

[7] For classical treatment see *Crawford* (1994). Practice has in this respect changed, notably in the post '89 epoch. Cf. *Roth* (1999).

[8] *Craven* (1998) repays careful study. See generally *O'Connell* (1968).

[9] There is movement in this domain. Article 22 of the Draft Articles of Responsibility of States for International Wrongful Acts, ILC 2001 envisages legal counter measures to be taken where "the obligation breached is owned to the international community as a whole" (cf. Article 48.2.b). The ICJ has considered respect for Self-Determination as an *erga omnes* norm (*East Timor / Portugal* v. *Australia*, ICJ, Rep. 1995, par. 29). To the extent that, say, toppling a democratic regime constitutes a violation of Self Determination under modern law, one can see the concept creeping into to the general law of State Responsibility.

[10] Haiti is considered the turning point. A careful reading of the relevant decision of the Security Council will however reveal that it was careful not to link the right to intervention directly with a lack of democratic legitimacy but rather with [un] "climat de peur, de persécution et de désorganisation économique, lequel pourrait accroître le nombre des Haïtiens cherchant refuge dans les Etats membres voisins". The Coun-

condemned not only as an interference with the internal affairs of a state, but also as a violation of Self-Determination.[11] Nowhere is the tension between International Law and democracy more noted than in the different understanding of self-determination. In democratic theory, democracy is almost ontological to the notion of Self Determination: It is the only means for determination of (and by) the collective self. In International Law, democracy was considered an ideology,[12] one among others, the acceptance or rejection of which were part of the determination

---

cil also qualified the Haiti circumstances as "uniques et exceptionnelles" and as part of a *humanitarian* crisis because of massive dislocation of persons (see Security Council Resolution 940). Compare, however, with the 1997 Sierra-Leone situation where the Council declared to be "Gravely concerned at the continued violence and loss of life in Sierra Leone following the military coup of 25 May 1997, the deteriorating humanitarian conditions in that country, and the consequences for neighbouring countries" and added that it "Demands that the military junta take immediate steps to relinquish power in Sierra Leone and make way for the *restoration of the democratically-elected Government and a return to constitutional order* (Security Council Resolution 1132, emphasis added). But here, too, one may ask whether the essential was the loss of democracy or the deteriorating humanitarian conditions? And had the constitutional order been one of, say, an Islamic *Sharia* State (which is non-democratic) or the a Communist State (which is equally non-democratic) would the Security Council Resolution have been any different? Would it not have equally demanded a return to "constitutional order" (democratic or otherwise) in the face of a deteriorating humanitarian condition? In other words was the operative part a return to constitutional order (whatever its nature?) or a restoration of democracy? Was democracy simply the contingent condition of the constitutional order?

[11] Earlier in USA interventions in Granada in 1983 and Panama in 1989 were sought to be justified on many grounds of which restoration of democracy was only one (see UN Doc, S/PV 2487 and UN Doc S/PV 2902). The US avoided condemnation because of its veto. In the *Nicaragua* Case the ICJ was even careful in allowing intervention in case of violation of human rights (ICJ Rep. 1986, par. 202-204).

[12] And not simply an ideology, but a Western, First World, ideology in competition with, and no superior to, Second and Third World competing ideologies. Détente was based on this premise and there was a tacit acceptance of the *Brezhnev* and *Reagan* Doctrines. Cf. *Tunkin* (1965) 232; *Fischer* (1968); and the spirited discussion of *Schachter* (1984).

of the Self. Indeed, if we were to apply to this field the same methods which are applied in making claims about the existence of this or that human right protected under international law (e.g. the right to development; the right to a clean environment) it would be easy enough to demonstrate a right in international law *not* to be a democracy, the right to be an "undemocracy"[13]

- Recent developments in the practice of Recognition of new States and in some form of a right to democracy and even an alleged right to intervene to protect democracy, only underscore the ambivalence of the system and provides a useful transition point from which to reflect on the second, self-referential, relationship between International Law and democracy.[14] There is a double irony in a system which has begun to insist that newcomers to the club pass some democratic entrance exam, however crude, and transitory, but which, first, turns out to be like tenure for professors: Once you have proven that you can write, you can stop writing for the rest of your life. And where, second, the club in question contains dozens of vile dictatorships. It is equally ironic that the new so-called right to democracy (whatever its parameters) has emerged in a manner, which is difficult to reconcile with even the crudest understanding of what democracy means.[15] Put differently, if there is under the international legal doctrine of sources a sustainable claim to the emergence of a "right to democracy", it is doubtful whether the rules which

---

[13] For the difficulty of classical International Law to come to terms with a consonance between democracy and a valid determination of the identity of the collective self, see *Salmon* (1993) and *Koskenniemi* (1994) 241.

[14] See, e.g., Declaration on the "Guidelines on the Recognition of New States in Eastern Europe and in the Soviet Union" adopted by the EU on 16 December 1991. See *Charpentier* (1992) where one can also find a text of the declaration. And one should always recall that even in the new epoch, recognition is still political and States which seem to correspond to the new conditions might still be denied recognition. Particularly embarrassing to the EU in this context was the case of Macedonia – cf. Conference on Yugoslavia, Arbitration Commission Opinion no. 3-6, in ILM (1992), 1499-1507.

[15] In the literatures which have emerged and claim the right to democracy as part of international law, there is not even an attempt to claim that this right emerged in a manner which may be called democratic.

govern these sources, whether international law making itself, represent a credible structure of democratic law making.

What, then, of international law making? It would be tempting to conflate the principle of Consent, so deeply rooted in the normative discourse of international law and its principal legitimating artifact, with democracy: A phrase such as: A customary law cannot emerge without the consent, active or tacit, of [all states bound by it]; [the principal legal families]; [those most affected by the norm] etc. sounds very much like democracy at the international level. But, in fact and in law, in theory and in practice, this is part of a very different vocabulary, namely that of sovereignty and sovereign equality.[16] It is, in some ways, the opposite of democracy, since it is based on the legal premise, even if at times a fiction, that the collectivity has neither the power nor, certainly, the authority to impose its will on individual subjects other than through their specific or systemic consent, express or implied. Put differently, it is based on the premise, an extreme form of which claims that there is no collectivity with normative power, and, in less extreme form claims that even if there is such a collectivity, there is an inherent power of opting out – through non-signature; reservations, persistent objector etc. This, of course, is the opposite of any functioning notion of democracy which is based on the opposite premise, however justified in political theory, that a majority within a collectivity, a *demos*, has the authority to bind its individual members, even against their will.

There are of course exceptions to these observations; we will return to these exceptions as part of a narrative of change.

Against this indifference or hostility, the concern for democracy of International Law has typically found expression outside international law – in the domestic foreign relations law of states through the so called democratic control of foreign policy. From this perspective, even if international law making itself does not follow any recognizable sensibility to democracy, its democratic legitimation could perhaps be sought at the internal level of the subjects which make it.

This, at best, would be a very problematic proposition.

First, as a matter of empirical observation, democratic control of foreign policy does not only remain an exception among States, but

---

[16]   *Kingsbury* (1998) repays careful study as a fundamental text on these issues.

is often derided from an international legal perspective: Democratic control of foreign policy is good when it approves and ratifies new treaties (which are typically considered progressive and normatively positive).[17] It is bad when it consigns such treaties to some graveyard.

Second, even when democratic control exists, it is never accompanied by an enquiry whether the Treaty that is democratically debated and approved in country A, was also democratically debated and approved in country B. The assumption of the democratic discourse in, say, the German Bundestag or the US Congress or the European Parliament is that if consent is given, the Treaty will be binding independently of the democratic quality of consent given in another State. In other words, democratic control of foreign policy at the level of the State, is not only formally but substantively part of the foreign relations law of the consenting state and not part of the validating matrix of international law itself.[18] There is simply no norm, not even an alleged norm, that the "bindingness" of an international treaty or customary law, or general principle, or "new source" should depend on internal democratic validation by the subjects and objects of such norms. Indeed, the great enthusiasm in the 60s and 70s for "Soft Law" and "New Sources" was result, rather than process, oriented. These were mechanisms which, *inter alia,* enabled international legal authority to be given to a variety of progressive norms which the traditional methods with their greater insistence on express consent were unable to do. But the oft-justified celebration of human rights, ecological norms and other such

---

[17] In the classical tradition of political theory, foreign policy is often excluded as a domain which would be subjected to normal democratic controls. Cf. *Tocqueville* (1981); *Mill* (1981) 211-212. Also great contemporary democrats are cautious. Thus *Aron* explains: "Les relations entre les Etats ont un caractère singulier, pour ainsi dire paradoxal: d'une part, il s'agit des relations globales, macroscopiques, puisqu'en cas de guerre les Etats sont aux prises les unes avec les autres comme des entités de dimensions considérables, mais, d'une autre part, les décisions d'où résultent les événements sont souvent prises par des personnes. Il y a donc une espèce de contradiction interne dans ce monde des relations interétatiques, dans la mesure où il existe souvent en apparence une disproportion entre le rôle qui jouent les individus et les conséquences de leurs actions". *Aron* (1989) 334.

[18] For a characteristically down to earth, realistic approach to foreign affairs and democratic control see *Dahl* (1999).

truly noble causes which the "Soft Law" and "New Sources" occasioned, was accompanied by a willful blindness to, even contempt of, any notion of democratic legitimation of these norms either at the international level or within the States that became subject to these norms. Equally, the typical critiques of "Soft Law" and "New Sources" were either result oriented, based an hostility to the content of the proclaimed norm, or systemic, usually challenging, as a matter of legal doctrine, the *consent* basis of the alleged new norm and hence its legal validity. We have already argued that to root international legal validity or legitimacy in consent has little to do with a democratic sensibility and might, indeed, be the opposite of such as sensibility. In the critique of New Sources there has been, with few exceptions, little concern for democratic legitimation. And, indeed, why should there have been? "New Sources" are not less democratic or more democratic than "Old Sources".

What makes them worthy of observation is the ironic dissonance between their progressive content and their regressive method of adoption.

C. International Law Vindicated:
Evaluating the Indifference and Hostility

In describing the relationship of International law to a democracy we have deliberately used an affective, anthropomorphic terminology – indifference, hostility, contempt – in order to provoke a normative reaction of censure or even outrage. Isn't that how one is meant to feel in the face of a legally binding norms adopted with little concern to the very vocabulary of democracy, let alone its habits and practices? Yes it is. And is one not justified in using an anthropomorphic terminology in order to counter the typical reification of law thereby ascribing responsibility to those behind the law – the real human beings, flesh and blood, who ultimately make international law? Yes it is.

And yet the outrage or censure would be out of place and one should not be overly scandalized by the indifference and hostility.[19]

---

[19] Indeed, there is a growing critical literature skeptical of the very use of democracy in international discourse – both dogma and praxis. See, e.g., *Carothers* (1992); *Koskienniemi* (1996) 231; *Marks* (1997) which is in part a response to the optimistic "progress" vision seen in the writings of, say, *Franck* and *Slaughter*, which *Marks* qualifies as "liberal millennialism". There are two strands to this literature. Part of it belongs to the more general reaction against classical liberal pluralism

For here is our third banal affirmation: Democracy is premised on the co-existence of *demos*, polity and government, and the relationships among them.

The *indifference* of International Law to democracy emanates from the absence of those elements in international life: There is International Law but traditionally there has been no "international *demos*", no international polity and no international government. You cannot be concerned with tonality or rhythm if there is no music. If traditional international law understands itself as a series of autonomous sovereigns, all equal, contracting legal obligations on a more or less enlightened *Adam-Smith*ian notion of liberalism, so as to maximize the interests of each with minimum friction to the interests of others, democracy is, indeed, no more relevant to international law as it is to the law of contract in domestic law. We may be concerned, both in a domestic or international contractarian universe, with inequalities of bargaining power, but that concern goes to notions of consent, coercion and, perhaps, fairness to which democracy or its absence are neither part of the problem nor part of the remedy. International law is maybe a response to a *Hobbes*ian brute world, but it is not a democratic *Locke*ian response.

---

of the *J. S. Mill* or *Isaiah Berlin* variety. *J. Gray* articulates this strand well: "Liberalism was the political theory of the modernity. As we enter the closing phase of the modern age, we confront the spectre of renascent atavistic barbarisms, which threaten to ruin the modern inheritance of civil society. Our task, as post-moderns no longer sustained by the modernist fictions of progress, rights and the universal civilization or by classical conceptions of natural law as embodied in Greco-roman and judeo-christian traditions, is to preserve the practice of liberty that is transmitted to us by inherited institutions of civil society" (*Gray* (1993) 328). A second strand of the literature is more pragmatic in nature and is rooted in a critique of the use democracy has been put to in international law. In this essay we premise democracy as a positive "good". It is not our intention fully to work out this position – but it is rooted in our belief that democracy with all its imperfections and with the need always to attend to these imperfections, is the best chance of political organization of the social which will honor the dignity of man created in the image of God, and equally the best chance of a political organization of the social to vindicate liberty consistent with that dignity. "Progress" not least in the world of ideas may well be a fiction, but we find nothing fictive in the conceptions of human dignity embodied in the Judeo-Christian tradition with their attendant consequences to political organization.

The classical *hostility* of International Law to democracy emanates from the fact that the absence of those three elements was (and in many cases still is) normatively desired. The essential language of modern democracy, its grammar, syntax and vocabulary, revolves not only around people, nation and State, but also about a shared self-understanding of authority, legitimacy and the relationship of people to each other and to their government institutions. Thus, even to accept that democracy is merely relevant to international law, would not be an organic extension of an evolving normative sensibility from a domestic setting to the international system. It would seem to imply a contested new self-understanding of that very international system. The breathtaking radicalism of the French Revolution was surely not simply in changing the structure and process of government, but in changing the very way society was to understand itself. A turn to democracy by and in International Law would be every bit as revolutionary.

Given the rootedness of democratic discourse in a Statal setting, if a turn to democracy would imply a corresponding turn to a Statal self-understanding of the international legal system, within the classical premises of international law, it could appear to many, and rightly so, as a very undesirable revolution.

II.   A Methodological Excursus: The Geology of International Law – A Differentiated Response to a Non-Monolithic Legal Universe

International law and the international legal system are not static and have changed over time. No less importantly, the understanding of legitimacy and democracy has not been static and has changed – both as an empirical social phenomenon and as a normative concept. How, does one relate these two moving targets to each other? As noticed from our title, we employ the metaphor of geology. This is not just a cutesy affect but represents a serious methodological commitment. It signals our particular approach for dealing with time, with history.

First, our approach to the past is instrumental. We are interested in the past not *per se* but primarily in the sense that it can illuminate the present.

Second, and more importantly, whereas the classical historical method tends to periodize, geology stratifies. Typically, a geological snapshot is taken and then the accumulated strata of the past are identified, analyzed, conceptualized. By stratifying geology folds the whole of the past into any given moment in time – that moment in which one examines a geological section. This method turned out to be crucial for our understanding of the international legal system.[20] For the proverbial reasons of time and space we are unable to provide here the full empirical apparatus on which our analysis is based. But we can provide an illustration.

We took, to give but one example, a snapshot of international treaty making and more generally international law making in 1900-10 in 1950s and 60s and in 1990-2000.

In the first decade of the 20th century we discovered a predominance of bilateral, contractual treaties and a very limited number of multilateral law making treaties. We also discovered, in that earlier part of the century a very sedate, almost "magisterial", and backward looking practice of customary law typified by a domestic case such as *The Paquette Habana* which leisurely takes in four hundred years of state practice in order to affirm the existence of a binding rule. A case such as *The Lotus* is also typical as an illustration of the typical use of the methodology of custom to privilege the status quo and chill change.

In mid-century we discovered a huge enterprise of actual and in-the-making multilateral law making treaties ranging from the Law of the Sea to Human Rights and even what may be called "constitutional" treaties. Customary law reincarnated itself into the so-called New Sources. The New Sources, though often using (indeed, piggy-backing on) notions of classical custom to justify the emergence of a binding norm, were the opposite of custom in that the sedate, backward looking and magisterial were replaced by an aggressive, cheeky and forward looking sensibility, privileging change and transformation and in which both treaty and "custom" often prized the communal and universal over the particularistic.[21]

Towards the end of the century, in addition to the bilateral, multilateral and constitutional layers of law making, we detected the emergence, or thickening, of a fourth layer, which has perhaps been less discussed. This is a regulatory layer. It is notable in the fields

---

[20] We acknowledge, of course, that even this "geology" is a form of history though one less interested in both a chronicle of events or in a sophisticated historiography.

[21] The literature is immense. We particularly profited from *Jiménez de Aréchega* (1988); *Lillich* (1995/96); *Meron* (1989); *Reisman* (1987); *Roberts* (2001); *Van Hoof* (1984).

of trade with the explosion of Regional Economic Agreements (whose numbers are in the hundred) as well as the new WTO and associated agreements, and in other similar fields: Environment, Asylum, Finance. In terms of content the regulatory layer addresses issues associated with the risk society in which we live.

The regulatory layer is distinct from its predecessors in a variety of ways: Its subject matters tend to be away from what traditionally was considered high politics and more towards what was traditionally considered low politics. (They are typically neither about Security nor even about Human Rights?) The obligations created are often positive in nature, not simply negative interdictions. Certain things have to be accomplished – note for example Article 16 of the WTO or the "conditions" imposed by the IMF and World Bank. The regulatory regime is often associated with an international bureaucratic apparatus, with international civil servants, and, critically, with mid-level State officials as interlocutors. Regulatory regimes have a far greater "direct" and "indirect" effect on individuals, markets, and more directly if not always as visibly as human rights, come into conflict with national social values.

We noted, too, in that period a much higher index than before of a new kind of "Practice" – not the old style State practice but "International Practice" of a variety of bodies ranging from well established international organizations to allusive entities such as the Group of Seven – a practice covering even classical fields such as security and human rights which can best be described as international management. Couple the regulatory layer of treaties with the international practice of management and a new form of international legal command may justifiably be conceptualized as governance.

Analogies to domestic law are impermissible, though most of us are habitual sinners in this respect. We can present the geology of international law as replicating to some extent the geology of domestic law – the turn from the 19th Century very contractarian emphasis, to the interventionist State of the Mixed Economy, to the Constitutional State (which is mostly a post World War II phenomenon) to the Administrative State of the 70s , 80s and beyond.

Similar results emerged from our soundings in the area of dispute settlement. We can afford to be even more synoptic here, for this story is even better known than the law making story: Here too we saw an initial strata of horizontal, dyadic, self-help through mechanisms of counter-measures, reprisals and the like. This is still an important feature of enforcement of international legal obligation. Then, through the century we saw a consistent thickening of a triadic stratum – through the mechanisms with which we are all familiar – arbitration, courts and panels and the like. The thickening consisted not only in the emergence of new areas subject to third party dispute settlement but in the removal of optionality, in the addition of sanctions and in a general process of "juridification". Dispute Settlement, the hall mark of diplomacy, has been replaced, increasingly, by legal process especially in the legislative and regulatory dimensions of international law making.[22] And there is, here too, a third stratum of dispute settlement which may be called constitutional, and consists in the increasing willingness, within certain areas of domestic courts to apply and uphold rights and duties emanating from international obligations. The appellation constitutional may be justified because of the "higher law" status conferred on the international legal obligation.[23]

Based on these finding, our initial temptation was to characterize the turn of the last century as a period of transactional legal relations, to look at the mid-century, especially the decades following World War II as one characterized by emergence of Community and the fin-de-siècle as the period of international governance. (We will, in short order, give more thickness to these labels – transaction, community and governance). But on closer look at the data we stumbled on the obvious. Even in the early part of the 20th century there were, alongside the thick stratum of bilateral, transactional treaty making, already thin strata of the multilateral and even of governance style of international command. Equally, we noted that mid-century, and fin-de-siècle, along side the constitutional and law making treaties there continued a very rich practice of the bilateral and transactional, that for every assertion of the New Sources and Communal values there was an old style *Texaco* a dignified late century heir to *The Lotus*. Change, thus, would not be adequately described as a shift from, say, bilateralism to multilateralism. What had changed was the stratification. Bilateralism persists and even

---

[22] See, e.g. *Slaughter / Helfer* (1997); *Stone Sweet* (1999); *Kupfer Schneider* (1999); *Reich* (1996/97); *Weiler* (2000). Generally see the special issue of International Organization: Legalization and World Politics, International Organization 54 (2000) No. 3.

[23] Cf. *Cass* (2001); *Petersmann* (1996/97). For a different approach, see *Trachtman / Weiler* (1996/97).

thrives as an important stratum of international law throughout the century till this day. Thus, geology allows us to speak not so much about transformations but of layering, of change which is part of continuity, of new strata which do not replace earlier ones, but simply layer themselves alongside. Geology recognizes eruptions, but it also allows a focus on the regular and the quotidian. It enables us to concentrate on physiognomy rather than pathology. As is always the case, the vantage point, the prism through which the subject is examined determines in no small measure the picture which emerges. The geology of international law is, thus, both the window and the bars on the window, which frame and shape our vision.

Against this background we develop our current theses. The ideas behind these theses are conventional enough and we hope, of course, that they will appear persuasive to the reader. They do, however, involve multiple strands and require keeping several balls in the air simultaneously. Here then is a little nutshell.

Firstly, and put bluntly, we believe that classical approaches, such as the one we ourselves developed in the introductory passages of this essay, which examine democracy in relation to "international law" or the "international legal system", are less than optimal because of the monolithic assumption on which they are typically based. The ways and means of international norm setting and law making, the modes in which international law "commands", are so varied, sometimes even radically so, that any attempt to bring them into the laboratory of democracy as if belonging to a monolithic species called "international law" will result in a reductionist and impoverished understanding of international law, of democracy and of the actual and potential relationship between the two.

We suggest that much can be gained, in this context, by conceptually unpacking international law or the international legal system into different "command" modes which the "geological" survey reveals: International law as Transaction, international law as Community, and International law as Governance. Each one of these modes presents different normative challenges, entails a different discourse of democracy and legitimacy, and, eventually, will require a different set of remedies.

Second, and put simply, we believe that democracy, too, cannot be treated monolithically. In this case it does not require unpacking but the opposite – repacking as part of a broader discourse of legitimacy. In municipal settings the absence of "democracy" (at least in the narrow sense of the word) in all aspects of domestic governance, is not always a lacuna, nor even a "necessary evil" and does not in all situations *per se* delegitimate such domestic systems. Legitimacy encompasses other elements too.

What complicates the matter is, as mentioned above, that notions of, and sensibilities towards, the legitimacy of international law have changed too.[24] Transactionalism was a prominent layer of early 20th Century international law. It was legitimated by reference to that old world and its prevailing norms. Transactionalism persists to early 21st Century international law and is a prominent layer also today. But to the extent that its old world legitimating features still accompany it, we have the makings of the legitimacy crisis in this respect. Communitarianism is most prominent as in Mid 20th Century international law and finds its original legitimating features in that epoch. It is still an important layer in the universe of 21st Century international law, but its legitimacy raises new Questions. And finally, Governance, though present in earlier epochs emerges as a thick and critical layer towards the end of 20th Century international law. It requires an altogether new discourse of legitimacy.

III.   Transaction, Community, Governance and the Emerging Legitimacy Crisis of International Law

A. Coordinating the National Interest – International Law as Transaction

Historically transactional international law was the predominant command mode. It is still a large and important part of the overall universe of international law. In its purest form it is dyadic and represented best by the bilateral transactional treaty. It is premised on an understanding of a world order composed of equally sovereign states pursuing their respective national interest through an enlightened use of law to guarantee bargains struck. There can be multipartite expressions and even international organizations which are an expression of dyadic transactional international law. The Universal Postal Union to give an ancient but still extant and relevant organization and the GATT in its 1947 incarnation of examples. Although multipartite in form (and suggesting, thus, a more multilateral communitarian self-understanding of the international legal order), they are in substance just more efficient structures

---

[24]   See *Franck* (1988); *Georgiev* (1993); *Weiler / Paulus* (1997) and the literature cited therein.

enabling their parties to transact bilateral agreements. Many other examples abound.

It is interesting to explore the legitimacy, both internal and external, of the dyadic, transactional international legal obligation. The key interlinking concepts underlying this mode of command were Sovereign Equality, Consent and *Pacta Sunt Servanda*. Sovereign Equality is critical for the transactional world view since in it is encapsulated the rejection of a community which can impose its will on its members. Consent is, in similar vein, not just a technical condition for obligation, but a reference to status and a signifier of the self-understanding of the (non)system. And *Pacta Sunt Servanda* is not just the indispensable and tautological axiom of obligation, but a signifier of the world of honor in which the equally sovereign understood themselves to be in. Indeed, in our view, the transactional mode of international law in its early historical context owed its deepest roots and claim to legitimacy to the pre-state chivalrous world of feudalism. Although transformed to the State, the vocabulary, rhetoric and values of sovereign equality, consent and *Pacta Sunt Servanda* were picked up almost intact.

There were huge pay-offs for this rootedness of international legal obligations in that pre-modern world of chilvary. There was, first, a confluence of internal and external authority of the State the legitimacy of each feeding on the other. It was also, paradoxically, a way of actually legitimating war against and subjugation of other states. As in chivalry where only other knights – peers – were legitimate targets for force (subject to ritualistic challenges etc.) the elevation of all states to the formal category of Sovereign and Equal is what allowed the playing out of the real life inequality among states.[25]

The principal legitimacy concern of this "slice" of the international legal system concerns on the one hand the continued centrality of dyadic transactional international law which is situated, on the other hand, within a "normative environment" to which the old formal legitimacy has little traction.

We will only hint at some of the normative problems. One major problem is the confluence between external and internal sovereignty exhibited in the very notion of national interest. There maybe some continued currency to national interest in matters of, say, war

---

[25] We do not expect that all will agree with this interpretation. We find some support in *Skinner* (1978); *Skinner* (1998)

and peace and consequently in their reflection in things like mutual defense pacts and the like. But no one can today credibly argue that bilateral treaties of the "Friendship, Navigation and Commerce" type of which, say, the United States continues to have a plethora, or the bilateral "free trade areas" which the European Union has with more than half the countries of the world are a non-contested manifestation of the "national interest". They are agreements rooted in a certain worldview, which vindicate certain internal socio-economic interests. This, in turn, presents two delicate issues: One is the measure of democratic scrutiny, which treaties such as these receive, in developed democracies such as the USA or the EU. We contend that often they receive far less democratic scrutiny than domestic legislation with the same socio-economic redistributive impact. This is certainly quite commonly the case in Europe and not at all infrequent in the USA. The second problem is that Economic giants such as the USA and the EU can impose such Treaties on lesser states not only leaving them with little or no margin of negotiation, but with even less concern to *their* (the would be partner's) internal democratic scrutiny.

B. The Constitutional and Legislative:
International Law as Community[26]

An interpretation of the legislative and constitutional strata of geological map yields the much noted, and positively commented upon phenomenon of the emergence, in certain areas, of some form of international community. There are both structural and material hall marks to the emergence of such community. Structurally we detect the emergence of new types of international organization. Some international organization, say, the International Postal Union, is mostly a mechanism to serve more efficiently the contractarian goals of States. At the other extreme, you take the UN or the EU and you find organizations whose objectives articulate goals a part of which is independent of, or distinct to, the specific goals of its Member States. They are conceived, of course, as goals which are in the interest of the Member States, but they very often transcend any specific transactional interest and are of a "meta" type – i.e. the overall interest in having an orderly or just international community.

---

[26] See generally the comprehensive study of *Simma* (1994).

Materially, the hallmark of Community may be found in the appropriation or definition of common assets. The common assets could be material such as the deep bed of the high sea, or territorial such as certain areas of space. They can be functional such as certain aspects of collective security and they can even be spiritual: Internationally defined Human Rights or ecological norms represent common spiritual assets where States can no more assert their exclusive sovereignty, even within their territory, then they could over areas of space which extend above their air-space.

Explaining these common assets in contractarian regimes is, at best, unconvincing and at worst silly. One has to stipulate a community which is composed of, but whose objectives and values may be distinct from the specific objectives of, any one of its Members.

Here, too, there are a myriad of legitimacy problems. We will list briefly only four: the fictions of consent, the closure of exit, the unpacking of the State and, finally, the existence of "Community" without Polity.

The growth in the number of States and the complexity of international legal obligations makes the forms of consent as a means of justifying norms increasingly fictitious, requiring the invocation of presumptions, silence, meta consent and the like. Many of those very norms which were the hallmark of community are often the very ones for which meaningful consent is little more than a fiction. This is particularly true for norms, the validity of which depends on some employment of "custom" or "general principles".[27]

But this is also the case in relation to many multilateral treaties. Increasingly international regimes, such as, say, the Law of the Sea, the WTO are negotiated on a Take-it-or-leave-it basis. WTO officials are always ready with the "what do you want: sovereign governments signed and ratified this" pleas. But for most States both the Take it is fictitious and the Leave it is even more. The consent given by these "sovereign" states is not much different to the "consent" that each of us gives, when we upgrade the operating system of our computer and blithely click the I Agree button on the Microsoft Terms and Conditions. One cannot afford to be out, and one cannot afford to leave. The legitimation that comes from sovereignty is increasingly untenable. The ability to chose one's obligations has gone: The Single Undertaking; the No Reservations Treaty are today increasingly the norm, rather than the exception. It

---

[27]   Cf. *Tomuschat* (1993).

is either all, or nothing, and nothing is not an option, so it has to be all. So even those States where there is a meaningful internal democratic control of foreign policy are obliged, democratically, to click the I Agree button of, say, the WTO or the Law of the Sea.

Further, classical consent was based on a conflation of government with State. That conflation is no longer tenable. As noted, the breakdown in terms of subject matter between what is "internal" and what is "international" means that most international normativity is as contested socially as domestic normativity. The result of international law continuing to conflate government with State is troubling: You take the obedience claim of International Law and couple it with the conflation of government and State which International Law posits and you get nothing more than a monstrous empowerment of the executive branch at the expense of other political estates or an empowerment of those internal special interest who have a better capture of the executive branch.

Finally, despite the "progressive" values with which the turn to Community is normally associated – notably human rights and the environment – the absence of true polity is highly problematic.

Few areas of contemporary international law have been presented as challenging the past and have excited as much rhetoric about transformation as human rights. The "turn" to the individual, the "valorizing" of the individual, the "piercing of the statal veil" et cetera. That international law has taken an interest in human rights as it has in the environment is of course an important material development. That it has defined them as common assets is an important structural development. Situating human rights along side the environment is helpful. For, seen through the prism of political theory, international law deals with humans the way it deals with whales and trees. Precious objects which require very special regimes for their protection. The surface language of international legal rights discourse may be neo-*Kant*ian. Its deep structure is utterly pre-modern. It is a rights notion that resembles the Roman Empire which regards individuals as an object on which to bestow or recognize rights, not as agents from whom emanates the power to do such bestowing. It is a vision of the individual as an object or, at best, as a consumer of outcomes, but not as an agent of process. In one respect the international legal system is even worse than the Roman Empire: International law generates norms. But there are no, and cannot be, a polity and citizens by whom these norms are generated. The individual in International law is seen, structurally, only as an object of rights but not as the source of authority, is no different from women in the pre-emancipation societies, or indeed of slaves in Roman times whose rights were recognized – at the grace of others.

And, of course, what gives a sharper edge to these issues is the frequent situation of all forms of international obligation in a far more effective and binding enforcement mechanism.

C. The Regulatory: International Law as Governance

Finally, interpreting primarily the regulatory dimension of international law, points at the end of the century not to the emergence of World Government (a horrible thought in itself) but something no less otiose: Governance without Government.[28]

What are the hallmarks of international governance?

- The increasing importance of the administrative or regulatory strata of Treaties. There is now increasingly international regulation of subject matter which hitherto was not only within the domain of States but within the domain of the administration within the State.
- There are increasingly new forms of obligation:
  - Direct regulatory obligation where international norm replaces the domestic one. What is interesting here is also to note new forms whereby increasing the obligation of international law is positive in nature, rather than a negative interdiction. Also, increasingly it requires not only obtaining cer-

---

[28] Cf. *Rosenau / Czempiel* (1992) " ... [T]he concept of governance without government is especially conducive to the study of world politics inasmuch as centralized authority is conspicuously absent from this domain of human affairs even though it is equally obvious that a modicum of order, of routinized arrangements, is normally present in the conduct of global life. Given an order that lacks a centralized authority with the capacity to enforce decisions on a global scale, it follows that a prime task of inquiry is that of probing the extent to which the functions normally associated with governance are performed in world politics without the institutions of government" (7). The Governance without Government is associated with the literature, at times overstated, about the "disappearance" or weakening of the classical Nation-State or in the most minimalist version, its loss of total domination of international legal process. We have profited from and acknowledge a debt to *Spruyt* (1995); *Spruyt* (1997); *Schachter* (1997); *Ruiz-Fabri* (1992).

tain results but insists on a specific process in working towards that result.

- Indirect regulatory norms where the international norm does
  not replace the government regulatory regime but seriously
  limits it. The most common example is the discipline of non-
  discrimination in trade regimes.
- Governance incentives, transforming to the international regime the US Federal invention of Grants-in-Aid. These can
  be financial – as is often the case with World Bank or IMF
  conditions are regulatory – as in the case of the *Codex Alimentarius* which promises material and procedural advantages to those who follow its norms. The State is free to follow, but it stands to lose a lot if it does not. All but the very
  rich and powerful can ill afford to say No.

- The emergence of International Civil Service and International
  Management.
- International Proceduralization and international insistence on
  domestic proceduralization.
- An invasion or subtle reversal of internal order of values – especially in the law of justification, burdens of proof and legal presumptions.

Here, too, what gives a sharper edge to governance, and to the
normative problems that we will shortly explore, is the situation of
these obligations and regimes and a much more effective enforcement regime.[29]

There is, thus, governance, but critically there is no government
and no governed. It is Governance without government and without
the governed – i.e. polity. At the international level, we do not have
the branches of government or the institutions of government we
are accustomed to from Statal settings. This is trite but crucial.
When there is governance it should be legitimated democratically.
But democracy presumes *demos* and presumes the existence of
government. Whatever democratic model one may adopt it will
always have the elements of accountability, representation and

---

[29] The "Regulatory" does not fully overlap with International Organizations as such. Nonetheless, some of the burgeoning literature on the legitimacy and democracy of international organizations is most helpful
in understanding the democratic and legitimacy challenges to which
the regulatory stratum gives rise. See *Stein*, (2001); *Esty* (2002);
Howse (2000).

some deliberation. There is always a presumption that all notions of representation, accountability, deliberation can be grafted on to the classical institutions of government. Likewise, whatever justification one gives to the democratic discipline of majority rule, it always presumes that majority and minority are situated within a polity the definition of which is shared by most of its subjects. The International system form of governance with government and without *demos* means there is no purchase, no handle whereby we can graft democracy as we understand it from Statal settings on to the international arena.

Moreover, the usual fall back position that this legitimacy may to be acquired through democratic control of foreign policy at the State level loses its persuasive power here even more than in relation to international community values. Meso- and micro- international regulation is hardly the stuff of effective democratic control by state Institutions. The fox we were chasing in the traditional model was the executive branch – our state government. In the universe of transnational regulation, even governments are no longer in control.

Democratic theories also creak badly, be they liberal or neo-liberal, consociational or even *Schumpeter*ian elite models when attempting to apply them to these forms of governance. Who is Principal, who is Agent? Who are the stake holders? We may define *demos* and *demoi* in different ways. But there is no convincing account of democracy without *demos*. *Demos* is an ontological requirement of democracy. There is no *demos* underlying international governance, but it is not even easy to conceptualize what that *demos* would be like? Network theory and constructivism are helpful in describing the form of international governance and explain how they work. But if anything they aggravate the normative and legitimacy dilemmas rather than solve them.

The "democracy" issue for International Law is no longer whether there is a right to democracy – which would, for example justify denial of recognition, or even intervention to restore a denial of democracy through a coup. Instead the issue is how in the face of International community which "appropriates" and defines common material and spiritual assets and in the face of international governance which increasingly appropriates administrative functions of the state, we can establish mechanisms which, in the vocabulary of normative political theory, would legitimate such governance. If an answer is not found to this, the huge gains attained in the systemic evolution of law making and law enforcement may be normatively and even politically nullified.

IV.   Conclusion: The Tragedy of Democracy and the Rule of Law in the International Legal Order

We end by returning to our point of departure: The nexus between the Rule of (International) Law and Democracy.

Over much of the 20th Century there has been a considerable widening and deepening in the scope of the international legal order. We tried to capture such widening and deepening by our reference to the transactional, the communitarian and the regulatory dimensions of international command modes buttressed by a similar widening and deepening of compliance mechanisms. We argued that the concept of international governance in important, if discrete, areas of international life is fully justified, albeit governance without government. We further argued that both a change in sensibility towards the legitimation of power generally and the turn to governance of international law create a considerable normative challenge to the international legal order in its classical (transactional) and more modern forms (communitarian and regulatory). And yet, we also argued that in all these spheres the challenge has been neither fully appreciated nor fully met. What's more, given that the vocabulary of democracy is rooted in notions of *demos*, nation and state, there is no easy conceptual template from the traditional array of democratic theories one can employ to meet the challenge. A simplistic application of the majoritarian principle in world arenas would be normatively ludicrous. It is not a question of a adapting national institutions and processes to international contexts. That could work in only limited circumstances. What is required is both a rethinking of the very building blocks of democracy to see how these may or may not be employed in an international system which is neither State nor Nation and to search for alternative legitimating devices which would make up for the non applicability of some of the classical institutions of democracy where that is not possible.

We speak about the tragedy of the international legal order in an altogether non-sentimental way. On the one hand, as a matter of our own values, we believe that much of the widening and deepening of international law over the last century, especially in the accelerated fashion of the last few decades, has been beneficial to mankind and has made the world a better place in which to live for a large number of persons.[30] We also believe, as indicated in the premises of this essay, that as in domestic situations where the rule of law is a necessary element and a condition for a functioning democracy, the same, *mutatis mutandis*, would be true for the international system. From this perspective we would regard as regressive a call for a wholesale dismantling of the international legal regime.

On the other hand, we believe too that in the international sphere as elsewhere the end can justify the means only so far. That a legitimacy powerfully skewed to results and away from process, based mostly on outputs and only to a limited degree on inputs, is a weak legitimacy and sometimes none at all.

The first sentiment would be a call for States, their internal organs (notably courts) and other actors and to embrace international normativity. The second sentiment would be a call to the same agents to treat international normativity with considerable reserve. The traditional opposition to "internationalism" came from nationalism and was conceptualized as a tension between national sovereignty and international law. The opposition we are alluding to is, instead, not a concern with sovereignty – at least not with the classical sovereignty of the State. It takes the international legal order as an *acquis* – but it is unwilling to the benefits of that *acquis* gained by a disenfranchisement of people and peoples. There is, thus, in our view a deep paradox in the spread of liberal democracies to an increasing number of States and populations around the world. This spread does not automatically go hand-in-hand with a normative call for a respect of international norms and for various degrees of constitutionalization of international regimes at least among and within the group of liberal States. It also means calling into question of those very norms by those very States in the name of that very same value, liberal democracy.

---

[30] There is, of course, much to qualify this statement. There are many international regimes, notably in the economic area, which overlook, compromise or even damage the interests and claims for justice of many people and groups. Universal justice, however it may be defined, is still far from being achieved.

Bibliography:

R. Aron (1989), Leçons sur l'histoire, Paris 1989.

Th. Carothers (1992), Empirical Perspectives on the Emerging Norm of Democracy in International Law, American Society of International Law, Proceedings 84 (1992), 261-267.

D. Z. Cass (2001), The Constitutionalization of International Trade Law: Judicial Non-Generation as the Engine of Constitutionalization, European Journal of International Law, 13 (2001), 39-77.

J. Charpentier (1992), Les déclarations des douze sur la reconnaissance des nouveau Etats, Revue Générale de Droit International Public, 1992, 343-355.

M. C. R. Craven (1998), The Problem of State Succession and the Identity of States under International Law, European Journal of International Law, 9 (1998), 142-162.

J. Crawford (1994), Democracy in International Law, Cambridge / New York 1994.

R. A. Dahl (1999), Can International Organizations be Democratic? A Skeptical View, in *I. Shapiro / C. Hacker-Cordon* (eds.), Democracy's Edges, Cambridge / New York 1999, 23-28.

D. Esty (2002), The World Trade Organization's Legitimacy Crisis, World Trade Review 1 (2002), 7-22.

G. Fischer (1968), Quelques problèmes juridiques découlant de l'affaire tchécoslovaque, Annuaire Français de Droit International 1968, 15-42.

G. Fox / B. Roth (2000) (eds.), Democratic Governance and International Law, Cambridge / New York 2000.

Th. M. Franck (1992), The Emerging Right to Democratic Governance, American Journal of International Law, 86 (1992), 46-91.

Th. M. Franck (1998), Legitimacy in the Legal System, American Journal of International Law, 82 (1988), 705-759

Th. M. Franck (2001), Democracy, Legitimacy and the Rule of Law'', in *N. Dorsen / P. Gifford* (eds.), Democracy and the Rule of Law, Washington, DC 2001, 169-177.

D. Georgiev (1993), Politics of Rule of Law: deconstruction and legitimacy in International Law, European Journal of International Law 4 (1993) No. 1, 1-14.

J. Gray (1993), Postliberalism. Studies in Political Thought, London/New York 1993.

R. Howse (2000), Adjudicative Legitimacy and Treaty Interpretation in International Trade Law: The Early Years of WTO Jurisprudence, in *Joseph H. H. Weiler* (ed.), The EU, the WTO and the NAFTA: Towards a Common Law of International Trade, Oxford/New York 2000, 35-69.

R. Jennings / A. Watts (1992) (eds.), Oppenheim's International Law, Vol. I: Peace, Harlow ⁹1992.

E. Jiménez de Aréchega (1998), Custom, in *A. Cassese / J. H. H. Weiler* (eds.), Change and stability in international law-making, Berlin/New York 1988, 1-4.

B. Kingsbury (1998), Sovereignty and Inequality, European Journal of International Law 9 (1998) No. 4, 599-626.

M. Koskenniemi (1994), National Self-determination Today: Problems of Legal Theory and Practice, International and Comparative law Quarterly 43 (1994), 241-269.

M. Koskienniemi (1996), Intolerant Democracies: A Reaction, Harvard International Law Journal 37 (1996), 231-235.

A. Kupfer Schneider (1999), Getting Along: The Evolution of Dispute Resolution Regimes in International Trade Organizations, Michigan Journal of International Law 20 (1999) No. 4, 697-773.

R. B. Lillich (1995/96), The Growing Importance of Customary International Law, Georgia Journal of International and Comparative Law, 25 (1995/96) No. 1.

S. Marks (1997), The End of History? Reflections on Some International Legal Theses, European Journal of International Law 8 (1997) No. 3, 449-477.

T. Meron (1989), Human Rights and Humanitarian norms as Customary Law, Oxford 1989.

J. S. Mill (1981), Considerations on Representative Government, in Three Essays, Oxford 1981.

D. P. O'Connell (1968), State Succession in Municipal and International Law, vols. I and II, Cambridge 1968.

E.-U. Petersmann (1996/97), Constitutionalism and International Organizations, Northwestern Journal of International Law and Business 17 (1996/97), 398-469.

R. Quadri (1952), Le fondement du caractère obligatoire du droit international public, in Recueil de cours 80 (1952), Tome I., 579-633.

J. Raz (1979), The Authority of Law - Essays on Law and Morality, Oxford/New York 1979.

A. Reich (1996/97), From Diplomacy to Law: The Juridicization of International Trade Relations, Northwestern Journal of International Law and Business 17 (1996/97), 775 et seqq.

W. R. Reisman (1987), The Cult of Custom in the late 20th Century, California Western International Law Journal 17 (1987) 133-145.

A. E. Roberts (2001), Traditional and Modern Approaches to Customary International Law: A Reconciliation, American Journal of International Law 95 (2001) No. 4, 757-791.

J. Rosenau / E. O. Czempiel (1992) (eds.), Governance without Government: Order and Change in World Politics, Cambridge 1992.

B. Roth (1999), Governmental Illegitimacy in International Law, Oxford/New York 1999.

H. Ruiz-Fabri (1992), Genèse et disparition de l'Etat à l'époque contemporaine, Annuaire Français de Droit International 1992, 153-178.

J. Salmon (1993), Internal Aspects of the Right to self-determination: Towards a Democratic legitimacy principle? in *C. Tomuschat* (ed.), Modern Law of Self Determination, Dordrecht 1993, 253-282.

O. Schachter (1984), The legality of pro-democratic invasion, American Journal of International Law 78 (1984), 645-650.

O. Schachter (1997), The Decline of the Nation State and Its Implications for International Law, Columbia Journal of Transnational Law, 7 (1997),pp.7-23

B. Simma (1994), From Bilateralism to Community Interest in International Law, Recueil de cours 250 (1994), tome IV, 217-384.

Q. Skinner (1978), The foundations of modern political thought, 2 vols., Cambridge 1978.

Q. Skinner (1998), Liberty before Liberalism, Cambridge 1998.

A.-M. Slaughter / L. Helfer (1997), Toward a Theory of Effective Supranational Adjudication, Yale Law Journal 107 (1997), 273-391.

H. Spruyt (1995), The Sovereign State and its Competitors, Princeton/NJ 1995.

H. Spruyt (1997), The Changing Structure of International Law Revisited, European Journal of International Law 8 (1997) No. 3, 399-448.

E. Stein (2001), International Integration and Democracy: No Love at First Sight, American Journal of International Law 95 (2001) No. 3, 489-534.

A. Stone Sweet (1999), Judicialization and the Construction of Governance, Comparative Policy Studies 31 (1999), 147-184.

A. de Tocqueville (1981), De la démocratie en Amérique, Paris 1981.

C. Tomuschat (1993), Obligations Arising for States Without or Against their Will, Recueil de cours 241 (1993), tome IV, 195-374.

J. P. Trachtman / J. H. H. Weiler, European Constitutionalism and its Discontents, Northwestern Journal of International Law and Business 17 (1996/97), 354- 397.

G. Tunkin (1965), Droit international public, Paris 1965.

G. H. F. Van Hoof (1984), Rethinking the Sources of International Law, Dordrecht 1984.

A. Verdross (1927), Le fondement du droit international, Recueil de cours 16 (1927) tome I, 251-321.

A. Watts (1993), The International Rule of Law, German Yearbook of International Law 36 (1993), 15-45.

J. H. H. Weiler (2000), The Rule of Lawyers and the Ethos of Diplomats, Reflections on the Internal and External Legitimacy of WTO, http://www Jeanmonnetprogram.org/papers/2000/001901.

J. H. H. Weiler / A. L. Paulus (1997), The Structure of Change in International Law or Is There a Hierarchy of Norms in International Law?, European Journal of International Law 8 (1997) No. 4, 545-565.

Robert Howse

How to Begin to Think About the 'Democratic Deficit' at the WTO[1]

I.   Introduction: Disaggregating the Democratic Deficit

There is an increasingly widespread intuition that the World Trade Organization lacks adequate democratic legitimacy, or has a 'democratic deficit' to use an expression derived from debates about the European Union. Views on the issue of the WTO and democracy range from the dismissal of the 'democratic deficit' based on the notion that since the WTO rules are approved by national governments they must be democratic or adequately so, to claims that the WTO along with other institutions and actors of globalization as essentially destroyed democracy as we have known it.[2]

Despite the intensity with which the issue of democracy and the WTO is contested there is essentially no literature aimed at bringing analytical clarity to the problem. As *Susan Marks* notes, democracy

---

[1]   Many thanks to *Sylvia Ostry, Andrew Moravcsik, Armin von Bogdandy, Kalypso Nicolaidis, Claude Barfied, Marco Bronckers, Debra Steger, Joseph Weiler* and *Claus Ehlermann* for stimulating conversations on some of the issues discussed in this paper. All of the many shortcomings are entirely my responsibility, of course.

[2]   *Hertz* (2002).

itself "is a hugely contested concept".[3] In other work, I have identified a range of conceptions of 'democracy' that is at play in debates
about democracy and governance beyond the nation state, including
representative democracy, deliberative democracy, corporatist or
consociational democracy, republican or communitarian
democracy, and democracy as decentralization.[4] All of these views
of democracy have salience in determining democratic legitimacy,
and they are in important ways inter-related. For example, while
representative democracy is identified with formal representative
institutions, such as elected parliaments, the legitimacy that flows
from such processes surely presumes elements of deliberative democracy, such as the possibility – and reality – of debate and confrontation of different points of view on public policy. Not only
dreamy academics but politicians and activists for secession and
regional autonomy movements, among others, invoke republican
conceptions of democracy to justify their cause, despite the reality
that representative institutions in modern democracies appear to
offer on a daily basis little of the collective self-determination of
which *Rousseau* waxed eloquent in his more poetic moments.

A further complication, often forgotten, is that democracy is not
the *only* source of legitimacy for policy outcomes.[5] Decisions of a
constitutional court to constrain majority will, for example, may be
legitimated in significant measure by deontological conceptions of
human autonomy or equality.[6] Decisions of autocratic or authoritarian regimes may have a certain legitimacy, even in the absence
of 'democracy', if they are respectful of social diversity, and reflect
a process of *consultation* with the people.[7]

As if the complexity, interrelationship, and contestability of sali-
ent alternative conceptions of democracy didn't make the task of
analytical clarity hard enough, the perception of a democratic deficit in institutions of globalization such as the WTO occurs at a time
when there is significant disillusionment with *domestic* democratic
institutions and practices, indeed with domestic governance.[8] Thus,

---

[3]   *Marks* (2000) 2.
[4]   *Howse* (2000).
[5]   I have discussed the multiple sources or claims of legitimacy in the
      WTO context in *Howse* (2001).
[6]   See an excellent paper on the 'Democratic Deficit' in the EU by *An-
      drew Moravcsik*, from which I have learnt much (*Moravcsik* (2002)).
[7]   See *Rawls* (1999).
[8]   See *Ostry* (2002).

it is not sufficient to address the 'democratic deficit' from a static perspective, merely asking to what extent outcomes in the WTO are *less* democratically legitimate than policy outcomes within domestic polities. Many of the most outspoken critics of the WTO are also outspoken critics of the real world of democracy within the nation state – of course, it isn't the fault of the WTO that the goal posts, as it were, are being moved, but to some extent they are, and if the claims for a higher standard of legitimation domestically are well-founded, then it is besides the point, or at least somewhat inadequate, to point out that the WTO doesn't fare that badly measured against the arguably low *domestic* 'status quo'.

Within the confines of this essay, it is possible only to begin to suggest what sort of analytical framework could clarify issues of this complexity. Thus, I have proceeded by looking at one model of democracy, representative democracy, as it has been actually practiced in the 'West' in the post-war period, as well as how its practice has been conceived ideally by scholars of democracy. In order to attempt to refine the inquiry into the existence of a democratic deficit, I have identified four separate issues or questions that are of relevance, which often get elided or confused with one another, in debates about the WTO and the democratic deficit.

The first, which is the most obvious, relates to whether WTO rules are sufficiently underpinned by democratic consent. A second concern is whether the substance of the rules themselves is democracy-enhancing or undermining. A third kind of concern relates the nature of WTO rules as pre-commitments – assuming *arguendo* that there is an adequate initial act of consent to the rules, today's majority is purporting to bind tomorrow's. WTO rules are not reversible without cost, should there be a change in popular will in a given Member country – nor would such rules have much value, if they could be abandoned freely. There is nothing inherently undemocratic about democratic pre-commitment – most liberal democratic constitutions purport to bind and constrain the majority will in the future. Yet such pre-commitments usually require special or extraordinary procedural justifications – super-majority votes in the legislature, referenda and plebiscites – or extraordinary substantive ones (such a deontological account of the primacy of certain rights over any expression of popular will). The question is whether such justifications exist with respect to WTO rules, and whether they are strong enough, given what appear to be the costs of reversibility in response to a change in the direction of the popular will in a Mem-

ber State. A forth concern arises from the character of democracy as
not merely a set of legitimating institutional mechanisms, but also
as a set of values or behaviors. Among the values often plausibly
associated with democracy are openness, accountability, equality,
value pluralism and inclusiveness. One dimension of the issue of
democracy at the WTO is whether the behaviors and attitudes of the
actors in the system, or closely associated with it, are appropriately
reflective of such values.

II.   Democratic 'Consent' and the Legitimacy of WTO Rules

Under the model of representative democracy, consent for particular policies and actions of the government is almost always indirect (however, the occasional use of referenda or plebiscites is not
inconsistent with the representative model, and indeed reflects often
the special situation involved where today's majority seeks to bind
tomorrow's, i.e. constitution-making). Consent of the people's representatives normally substitutes for a direct expression of popular
will. Thus representative democracy is fundamentally constituted
by a principal-agent relationship, that of the people to their representatives. In the case of multilateral trade negotiations, as in other
areas, these representatives themselves then delegate to others –
officials, experts, etc. – the task of bargaining with other 'states'.

As *Coglianese* and *Nicolaidis* suggest, given that representative
democracy operates through principal-agent relationships, there is
no reason why agency theory, although developed in the context of
explaining economic institutions, should not be applicable to political institutions as well. They usefully summarize the key propositions of agency theory as follows: "The challenges in the principal
agent relationship arises from two sources: (1) differences in interests between agents and principals which lead them to prefer different goals and strategies; and (2) information asymmetries" which
come from the fact that agents "typically know more about their
task than their principals do, though principals know more about
what they want accomplished". As a result, the agent may be able
to perform tasks in ways which do not conform the goals of the
principal while the latter might not be able to do much about it".[9]

---

[9]   *Coglianese / Nicolaidis* (2001) 281. On agency theory generally see
       Pratt / Zeckhauser (1985).

Under a representative democracy model, the problem of 'democratic deficit' is essentially a problem of agency costs. To the extent to which their attitudes and behavior has been studied, the experts involved in the negotiation of WTO rules can be said to have some interests and goals not necessarily shared, at least not to the same extent, by their principals: agents, for instance, may well have a personal commitment, for example, to free trade or to the good of international cooperation as such, which is not shared, or fully shared, with principals.[10] As members of what *Anne-Marie Slaughter* calls a "government network",[11] the agents of different governments also have an interest in maintaining good working relationships with each other over time – they tend to be repeat players in these negotiations. We know from studies in the risk regulation area that experts perceive risk very different than do lay people, and in trade negotiations that relate to rules on domestic health and safety policies, for example, these differences in perceptions and perhaps also preferences about risk as between agents and principals may lead to agency costs, of a kind that are not often fully recognized by standard agency theory, which focuses on divergence of interests between agents and principals; there may be also differences of perception and value that can lead agents to act differently in making delegated decisions than would principals if they had full or as full information in the circumstances.

GATT/WTO law is also an area where information asymmetries have traditionally been very severe – there is very little understanding about trade rules and how they function, even among other agents of the people, such as legislators and senior bureaucrats concerned with domestic matters directly affected by trade rules. Negotiations have taken place in secret, making the account by negotiating agents of what went on in the room very difficult to verify independently. Further, governments (and ultimately citizens) have been highly dependent in most cases on the expert community to which the negotiating agents belong in making judgments about what the rules being negotiated 'mean', or, more precisely, the future consequences of those rules for various relevant interests.

It is thus not difficult to make an intuitively plausible case that there will be significant agency costs entailed in delegation of negotiating authority for multilateral trade rules. The real issue is

---

[10] See *Weiler* (2001); *Drake/Nicolaidis* (1992). See also *Perez* (1996).
[11] *Slaughter* (2000).

whether the existing institutional mechanisms for managing these agency costs are adequate or not.

Those who believe that the WTO is adequately 'democratic' usually point to the process of *ex post* legislative approval of negotiated WTO rules as an appropriate and effective democratic safeguard.[12] However, those who have examined the role of *ex post* legislative control in the case of the Uruguay Round Agreements tend to the conclusion that in all jurisdictions aside from the United States, *ex post* legislative scrutiny of negotiated rules was largely perfunctory.[13]

The mere fact, however, that such scrutiny was perfunctory in this case does not itself show that it was not optimized in the Uruguay Round, nor that it is *in principle* ineffective to control agency costs. For instance, one reason why such scrutiny might have been perfunctory and yet optimal is that legislators might have perceived agency costs to be small – that is to say they might have trusted negotiators to have closely reflected the interests of citizens in bargaining to an agreement. Legislators have scarce resources – it could well be that the opportunity cost of using legislative time and money to closely scrutinizing the Uruguay Round bargain was simply too high. There are *many* international negotiations where legislative oversight is minimal, just as legislative oversight of domestic agency rule-making varies greatly from agency to agency and regulatory context to regulatory context.

Here, it makes a great deal of difference how one perceives the choices of trade negotiators as they make WTO rules. Is this a matter largely of applying some kind of expertise – technical economics, for instance – to further a relatively uncontested conception of the public interest? Or do the rules in question, or the choices about the content of the rules, engage directly competing public values and constituencies? Especially after the Uruguay Round WTO rules have been increasingly perceived, and rightly so, as more conforming to the latter description. Because this essay is aimed not at taking sides in the debate over the 'democratic deficit' as in clarifying what is at stake, and alternative remedies, I cannot prove this

---

[12] See for example statement of three former DGs of the GATT/WTO at Davos.

[13] See *Petersmann* (2001) 98, citing the various country studies in *J. Jackson / A. Sykes* (eds.), Implementing the Uruguay Round, Oxford 1997; *Bellman / Gerster* (1996).

point here. I have attempted to do so elsewhere, however.[14] Agency theory must be considered here along with a conception of politics or the political. Legislatures are not just one link in the chain between principals, the people, and subordinate agents, such as expert trade negotiators. The legislative process, at least ideally, is *political* in a manner that makes it appropriate to the determination, or at least scrutiny, of policy choices that involve contested values and warring constituencies.[15]

One explanation for the absence of meaningful legislative oversight and control in the case of the Uruguay Round outcomes, is that the public and the legislators were not yet adequately sensitized to the extent to which the rules engaged competing or contested public values. In other words, the implications were not well-understood, and obviously the 'experts' were not well-positioned to explain them – given that the 'experts' still believed that in many respects what they were doing was applying a rational economic policy model.

At the same time, a disincentive to legislative activism may be the limited effectiveness of *ex post* legislative scrutiny of outcomes negotiated by agents. First of all, there is the fact that legislators face a stark choice of either approving an entire package as is,

---

[14] *Howse* (2002). See also *Stein* (2001).

[15] The conception of 'politics' I am attempting to articulate here is admittedly underdeveloped and partly intuitive – it is really a notion of the sorts of processes and institutions appropriate to making decisions that cannot be derived from a universally recognized higher authority, whether divine or natural law, scientific or technical expertise. I do not think this reduces to democracy as majority rule or the aggregation of preferences, but that something of a conception of deliberative politics has been built into the ideal of the legislature in the theory of representative government. These concerns have often come to be expressed today in terms of another model of *democracy*, the deliberative. Perhaps this is in part a reflection of the gap between the ideal of the legislative process and its reality. Perhaps also in the tendency to reduce *political* legitimacy to democratic legitimacy. But the emphasis on rationality in deliberation in the deliberative model suggests that decision by politics is not reduced simply to reflection of mass or popular will. *But* at the same time, it differs greatly from the manner of decision based on the *Wissenschaft* or *techne* claimed by experts. On the distinctiveness of politics as a mode of collective choice among competing values or ideals, see *Weber* (1965). On the 'political' deficit of the WTO, see *Bogdandy* (2001).

without amendment, or rejecting it. They have no possibility, at least taking the law-making structure operated in recent multilateral trade rounds as paradigmatic, to reshape the package in a manner that makes it better reflect voter preferences. This kind of structure gives agents considerable capacity to increase the costs of an ultimate rejection of their package, since agents have considerable agenda-setting ability, including the linkage of issues, and (as the Uruguay Round demonstrates) even the ability to establish negotiating parameters that tie the continued enjoyment of benefits from existing rules to agreement to new rules. Agents know that a legislature will be hard put to reject a rule that poorly reflects the preferences of citizens, if in so doing they have to reject many other rules, or even entire agreements, that are popular with citizens. Moreover, if they are able to load enough matters of importance into a single 'package', agents may be able to create a sense that catastrophic consequences would ensue from legislative rejection of the 'package'. If agents know that principals can only reverse their choices *ex post* at catastrophic cost, they will consider themselves relatively free to act autonomously from principals' preferences.

A further reason why *ex post* legislative scrutiny of outcomes negotiated by agents may be ineffective to control agency costs, is that there are significant information asymmetries between legislators and negotiating agents. Legislators whose only real involvement in WTO matters is a periodic examination of the results of negotiating rounds, will come to this task with few analytical tools and a very limited knowledge base, with which to assess critically the claims of agents as to the costs, benefits, and more generally the consequences, of accepting or rejecting the negotiated outcome. In the case of the Uruguay Round Agreements, the texts themselves were in many cases not available to legislators in native languages.

Since negotiating agents tend to be invested in the outcomes that they have negotiated, they face strong incentives to exaggerate the benefits, and minimize the costs, or negative consequences of the deal. Moreover, since negotiating agents tend to be in most jurisdictions career civil servants with a strong presumption of lifetime job tenure, it is very difficult to discipline agents, when their statements about the implications of legal rules turn out to be erroneous. And even if they could be disciplined, there would be the very difficult task of distinguishing good faith interpretations or predictions about the effects of legal rules, from self-interested misrepresentations. It is likely therefore that agents face few disincentives not to self-interestedly put the best face on the outcomes they negotiate.

These observations suggest that other mechanisms may be necessary to control the agency costs that arise from multilateral trade negotiations. One such mechanism, which addresses the ability of negotiating agents to set agendas and tie issues in a manner that makes *ex post* legislative control ineffective, is *ex ante* hands tying of negotiating agents. Indeed, the current practice of 'fast track' in the United States appears to reflect a recognition that, if it is put in a position where the only effective *ex post* control over a negotiated outcome involves the power to vote it up or down as a package, the legislature should attach *ex ante* constraints on the exercise of discretion by negotiating agents.

Formulating *ex ante* constraints that are effective is not an easy task. The US 1988 Omnibus Trade and Competitiveness Act, for instance, set out certain parameters for US negotiators in terms of US negotiating priorities, among which was labour standards, also stated as a priority in the 1974 trade bill. However, in the Uruguay Round, US negotiators came up empty handed on labour.[16] It seems that, unless expressed in terms of legal directives that mandate or prohibit certain outcomes in precise terms, agents can relatively easily avoid such constraints, perhaps stating claims (largely unverifiable in secret negotiations), that they made best efforts to make the negotiated outcome conform to the instructions in a legislative mandate, but failed due to the intransigence of other parties. Negotiating agents may also resort to window-dressing – the inclusion of relatively meaningless legal provisions that nevertheless give the appearance of fulfilling the mandate. The adequacy of such provisions could be hard to question, unless one has a very fine understanding of the operation of international law in general and trade law in particular.

On the other hand, *ex ante* constraints in the form of precise legal directives have the obvious disadvantage that they substantially limit the capacity of negotiating agents to achieve compromise with the positions of other member states. It may be possible to meet the underlying concerns of the legislature using a different formula of words, or a different structure of disciplines that give other member states less difficulty. In such a situation, too specific *ex ante* constraints would impede a negotiated outcome that might closely re-

---

[16]   *Aronson* (2001).

flect the preferences of principals. Moreover, very specific mandates or instructions may create a problem for negotiating agents of other Member states – they may appear like ultimatums, the acceptance of which could well carry the optics of having 'caved'. Here, one need only think of the recent example of the 'rider' placed on 'fast track' (Trade Promotion Authority) for the US President in the Senate that essentially makes it a condition of the smooth functioning of 'fast track' that the executive not agree to any treaty provisions that would require changes to US trade remedy law.

A third approach to controlling agency costs is monitoring of agents' on-going activities. As *Odell* suggests, writing in the context of multilateral trade negotiations, "tighter institutional requirements to hear changing constituent demands and interim reactions will calibrate the agent more exactly as the negotiation evolves".[17] According to *Odell*, beginning with the Trade Act of 1974, the US Congress has required extensive consultation of legislators, and directly with interest groups, *throughout* the negotiating process.[18] Indeed, consistent with the concern about information asymmetries that exist due to a secret negotiating process, negotiators have been required to share confidential information with legislators and interest group representatives. *Odell* claims that the result of such requirements has been a much better alignment of principals' interests and agents' behavior in the Uruguay Round. The United States appears to be an exceptional case, however, in the involvement of legislators extensively in the negotiating process.[19]

Monitoring may be facilitated by a greater role for NGOs in the negotiating process; open access to negotiating offers or proposals; and regular public reports by WTO officials and by governments to the public on the future of negotiations. Current attitudes of secrecy and the continuing 'Club' approach to negotiations, to use the expression of *Keohane* and *Nye*,[20] frustrate the use of monitoring as a means of reducing agency costs. WTO Members cannot even agree concerning the presence of other *intergovernmental* organization representatives as mere observers in for a such as the WTO Committee on Trade and Environment. This stands in sharp contrast to,

---

[17]   *Odell* (1997) 159.
[18]   Ibid. 176-178.
[19]   *Bellman / Gerster* (1996) 41-45.
[20]   *Keohane / Nye* (2001).

for example, the recent negotiations on the Biosafety Protocol.[21] There has been some marginal progress with respect to transparency of negotiating proposals. For example, proposals concerning the structure of negotiations on services were posted to the WTO web site. However, the actual offers that Members are making with respect to commitments on market access are not a matter of public record. Despite these limitations, NGOs with considerable competence in trade law and policy have been playing an important role in monitoring what negotiating agents have been doing and saying in Geneva, and informing domestic constituencies of the possible impact on their values and interests. Critics of NGO involvement in the WTO such as *Claude Barfield*,[22] who argue that NGOs run interference as it were with the formal mechanisms of accountability in representative democracy, which entail the brokerage of interests at the *domestic* level, simply ignore the problem of agency costs and therefore are unable to see that, in their monitoring function, NGOs that are present at the level of the negotiations themselves, can help to reduce agency costs, and therefore make classic *representative* democracy function *better*.

III.   Are WTO Rules Democracy-Facilitating or -Undermining?

It is trivial that WTO rules constrain governments from acting in the future. We know that not all legal constraints on government action are democracy-undermining, however. Constitutional rules guaranteeing freedom of association and expression and periodic free elections are, for instance, widely regarded as democracy-enhancing.

In the case of the WTO, the kind of rules characteristic of the GATT could plausibly be presented as largely democracy-enhancing, on the theory that these rules largely constrain trade *protectionism*. Since protectionism is often considered by trade economists and policy analysts to be almost always an inefficient instrument for achieving legitimate public aims, it is often assumed that protectionism is a result of distortions or imperfections in the democratic process that allow concentrated interest groups to capture government policymaking and win rents. To the extent that

---

[21]   See the discussion in depth of the role of NGOs in this negotiation process, in *Bail/Falkner/Marquard* (2002) chs. 27-30.

[22]   *Barfield* (2001), especially ch. 6.

GATT-type rules either constrain protectionism, or require a justification of trade protection as a necessary or legitimate public policy in the circumstances, they could be argued to prevent the corruption of the democratic process of special interests.

Elsewhere I have been critical of the notion that one should assume that whenever a government resorts to trade protection as a policy instrument it is captive to special interests.[23] This debate cannot be resolved in this brief essay. However, it is clear that many of the newer WTO rules cannot be understood this way, for example the rules on intellectual property protection. Indeed, in the case of patents, these rules could themselves be understood as a product of special interest group capture at the WTO itself, namely in that case the pharmaceutical industry.

A complex example is that of the rules embodied in the Agreement on Sanitary and Phytosanitary Measures, which were at issue in the infamous *Beef Hormones* case. These rules impose scrutiny on non-discriminatory domestic health and safety regulations where these affect trade. As such they threaten the ability to make such choices on the basis of democratic will. However, when read properly, the rules can be understood mostly as requiring a procedure of public justification for such regulations, including the gathering of scientific evidence, which may enhance democracy, by allowing fuller public debate of the issues, and better public information.

In the *Hormones* case itself, the European Community of course was found to be in violation of the WTO rules, suggesting the capacity of those rules to frustrate the democratic expression of citizen concerns through regulation. It should be noted however that the Appellate Body of the WTO was faced with a situation where the EC had not tabled even a single relevant scientific study as a basis for its regulations, while the EC lawyers themselves refused to rely on a clause in the SPS Agreement that would allow provisional measures pending further scientific investigation. The Appellate Body went to great lengths to emphasize that it would not second-guess a WTO Member's regulatory choices, provided there was some scientific evidence on the record concerning the risks in question, and even stated that a Member could act on the basis of 'non-mainstream' science, thereby ensuring that 'science' does not become an orthodoxy precluding democratic contestability in the area of risk regulation.

[23] *Howse* (2002).

One could similarly view the Agreement on Technical Barriers to Trade as primarily aimed not at constraining democratic regulatory choices, but disciplining the *process* by which those choices are arrived at, including requiring policymakers to have at least turned their minds to alternatives less restrictive of trade. Understood in this way, again as with SPS rules that appear democracy-threatening when they are understood as inviting WTO tribunals to second guess democratic regulatory *outcomes*, may be understood as democracy-enhancing with respect to regulatory *processes*.[24]

Rules on services and particularly the binding of market access commitments have the potential to be especially democracy-threatening. Such commitments are often tantamount to the 'lock in' at the international level of domestic experiments with regulatory reform and / or privatization in services industries with 'public goods' or network aspects. Moreover, many of the policies in question could be at the regional or local level, where the implications of a WTO market access commitment are even less likely to be fully understood and democratically debated. One needs only to think of examples like electricity reform in California to realize that even if justified at some level of generality in terms of economic theory the precise design of regulatory reform may well need to be fine tuned as the effects of the original experiments on the public interest become known. The freezing of early approaches to the design of regulatory reform an demonopolization and / or privatization in WTO market access commitments obviously frustrates the possibilities for such fine-tuning.

Finally there are provisions in the WTO Agreements that require transparency of domestic laws and regulations, such as Article X of the GATT. These could be potentially democracy-enhancing. Relatively little attention has been paid to such provisions, however. In

---

[24] However, in its first decision on the substantive obligations in the TBT Agreement, the WTO Appellate Body appears to have endorsed a view of certain provisions of the TBT that is more demanding of harmonization, and thusmore threatening of regulatory diversity than is warranted by the text of the Agreement. This stands in contrast to the more deferential and sensitive approach in *Hormones*. See *EC-Sardines*, Report of the Appellate Body, 2002. However, the *Sardines* case did not involve fundamental questions of human health and life, or environmental protection. In cases that implicate such values, the AB may well find itself rethinking its support of the panel's intrusive approach in *Sardines*.

the case of the Trade Policy Review mechanism, where trade and related policies are put under review at the WTO on a periodic basis, the democratic potential of such review has not been realized, due to the narrowness of the policy perspective adopted in examining Members' policies and a failure to realize the potential of broad civil society input. Appropriately reformed, the TPRM could enhance domestic democratic accountability for trade and related policies and their affects on citizens.

IV.   Pre-Commitment and Reversability

Adhesion to international agreements is a mechanism by which today's government, or today's majority, can bind tomorrow's. This is a straightforward result of the basic public international law rule of state responsibility that treaty obligations are not extinguished – nor is there a right to modify or re-negotiate them when a government changes. Pre-commitment of this nature is, of course, a common feature of domestic constitutionalism in liberal democracies. What is pre-committed is usually basic structural rules for the processes of government, or division of competences, as well as individual rights (and in some instances minority and collective rights). Pre-commitment exists inasmuch as a new government, or even a shift in majoritarian opinion under the existing government cannot easily result in the rules being suspended or abandoned. This requires some kind of extraordinary democratic process, such as a supramajority vote of both houses of the legislature, in a federal state approval of all or most of the federal sub-units and so forth.

Pre-commitment outside the constitutional context can be dangerous for democracy. A government waning in popular appeal could sign a trade agreement that locks in an ideological agenda that is already becoming illegitimate or not broadly supported by citizens.

When such pre-commitment occurs at the international level, what are the options when the polity changes its mind, a new government comes to power, and so forth? The rule that a government is bound by the international obligations undertaken by previous governments must be understood in light of the traditional, decentralized approach to interpretation and enforcement in international law. Getting a state to abide by its international legal commitments has generally required the cooperation of that state itself, both in terms of an acceptance that it has in fact acted in contravention of its obligations, and the appropriate remedy. In this respect, from the point of view of democracy, there is a sense in which international law involves in *Renan*'s sense "une plébiscite de tous les jours". Many contemporary international lawyers lament this fact about traditional international law, and are keenly interested in mechanisms for creating more centralized interpretation and enforcement, with a view to 'compliance'. Many social scientists have been skeptical as to whether international law is really law at all, given the absence of automatic or relatively automatic identification and sanctioning of non-compliance.

The WTO operates, or purports to operate, in stark contrast to this traditional picture of international law. Judicial dispute settlement is both compulsory and binding. Whether the measures a Member found to be in violation has taken to remedy the violation are adequate is also a matter of binding judicial arbitration. And failure to comply triggers a right of the aggrieved Member to take retaliatory action in the form of withdrawal of trade concessions of 'equivalent commercial effect' to the violation.

Where a WTO rule, or its interpretation, has come to be seen as democratically illegitimate, or unduly constraining of the democratic will, non-compliance remains of course an option of sorts. Some WTO scholars, most notably *Alan Sykes*, even suggest that the provisions of the WTO Dispute Settlement Understanding that provide for, and limit, retaliation, constitute a kind of 'efficient breach' mechanism. They fix a price at which a Member is within its rights in walking away from WTO legal commitments. As a matter of interpretation of the WTO rules, as well as the general international law rules of state responsibility, I do not agree with *Sykes*.[25] However, from the perspective of democracy, it is significant that the cost of reversing or suspending pre-commitment, albeit through what I would described as 'civil disobedience' has been fixed. In some instances, such as the case of Europe's hormone ban, the price has been obviously not prohibitive.

When a WTO ruling lacks legitimacy or the rules lose legitimacy the options for that Member within what I understand to be the law, are to apply for a waiver or an authoritative interpretation by the Membership that supports a democratically legitimate meaning for the rule, to negotiate an amendment of the WTO treaty,

---

[25] *John Jackson* and *Marco Bronckers* have explained persuasively, I believe, why the interpretation is flawed (*Bronckers* (2001); *Jackson* (1997)).

or finally to withdraw from the WTO. All but the last option require consent of a supra-majority, and in practical terms, probably consensus of the entire WTO Membership. The last option would probably have very serious, if not catastrophic consequences for many Members, given the dependence of private economic actors on the rules in question and their binding character.

Thus, the fact is that WTO rules, or even interpretations of those rules, are not reversible within the law in any kind of way that is analogous to the ability of domestic polities to change all but a small number of constitutional rules through a routine expression of democratic will within that country.

To my mind, these costs of and constraints on reversibility, combined with the impact of new era trade rules in freezing or limiting regulatory choices in many policy areas depending on how they are interpreted, constitute the most troubling aspect of the WTO's 'democratic deficit'. One answer to the problem is to simply argue that WTO rules are like many domestic constitutional rules, a kind of 'higher law', the substantive normative content of which justifies a mechanism that creates high costs for reversibility. This is, in substance, the argument of *Ernst-Ulrich Petersmann*. *Petersmann*'s view of the WTO law as constitutional 'human rights' is however subject to certain powerful difficulties. *Petersmann* himself admits that such rights are nevertheless subject to limits, and that some rights need to be balanced against others. The question then becomes whether it makes sense for a domestic polity to confer upon the dispute settlement organs of the WTO, which in any case don't seem to have particular credentials to deal with 'human rights', the ultimate authority in deciding such balances or limits, at a very high cost of reversibility.[26]

Petersmann accepts that one implication of the constitutional status that he claims for WTO rules, is a need for greater democratic legitimacy. But his proposals in this regard – greater involvement of domestic parliamentarians in the WTO and NGO advisory committees – are weak and seem highly manipulable by those, whether in the executive branch of government in many cases, or in the WTO, who will be selecting the parliamentarians and the NGOs who have these participatory rights.

---

[26] See *Petersmann*'s latest articulation of his point of view and my response to it (*Petersmann* (2002); *Howse* (2002a)). See also *Howse / Nicolaidis* (2001).

In my view, one can address the problem of the high costs of re-versibility either by returning to a system that is more flexible, diplomatic[27] and less legally compelling (building more room for reversibility into services commitments, i.e. opt outs and safeguards or considering alternatives to legally binding judicial dispute set-tlement in new areas of considerable policy sensitivity such as envi-ronment or competition). Instead, one could move forward as it were, in recognition of the implications of pre-commitment, and start employing extraordinary mechanisms of democratic consent that are used domestically in constitutional contexts where today's majority is purporting to bind tomorrows. Thus, serious considera-tion should be given to a referendum or plebiscite at the national, or even at local and regional levels, on the outcome of the Doha Round of negotiations. To be meaningful, this would require a campaign governed by appropriate rules and procedures, including access to national media – especially electronic media – for oppos-ing groups or parties. The proposals would need to be translated into local languages and widely distributed to the public.

But the problem even here is that the decision is of a take it or leave it nature. The public can ultimately veto a pre-commitment, but that is a blunt instrument, applied to a large package of rules. Perhaps then a further implication is to no longer negotiate new WTO rules in such 'packages', a point of view that had some favor among *Clinton* Administration officials, while it was and is quite antithetical to the EU approach to new negotiations. However, a referendum or plebiscite requirement would, theoretically at least, provide an incentive for governments to make increased efforts to engage public opinion in the negotiating process itself, to create 'ownership' of the result, and thereby reduce the likelihood of an eventual rejection.

V.   Do the Actors in the WTO System Exemplify or Prac-tice Democratic Political Ethics?

Among the most original and important contributions of *Alexis de Tocqueville* to democratic theory was to locate democracy and its legitimating force not only in a set of institutions, procedures or rules for decision-making, but also in the habits of soul or ethics that form and are formed by such institutions, procedures or rules. *Joseph Weiler* has offered a compelling description of the range of

---

[27]   See *Barfield* (2001).

actors that has traditionally dominated the evolution and operation
of the post-war multilateral trading regime: "A dominant feature of
the GATT was its self-referential and even communitarian ethos
explicable in constructivist terms. The GATT successfully managed
a relative insulation from the 'outside' world of international relations and established among its practitioners a closely knit environment revolving round a certain set of shared normative values
(of free trade) and shared institutional (and personal) ambitions
situated in a matrix of long term first name contacts and friendly
personal relationships. GATT operatives became a classical 'network' ... Within this ethos there was an institutional goal to prevent
trade disputes from spilling over or, indeed, spilling out into the
wider circles of international relations: ...".[28] These observations
are broadly consistent with what *Keohane* and *Nye* have identified
as a 'club' atmosphere in multilateral trade negotiations and regime
management.[29]

Many of the values that can be identified as at the core of democratic political ethics are antithetical to this kind of closed club or
network approach. The problem here is not that networks can't be
held accountable through normal representative processes: subject
to agency costs, observers such as *Anne-Marie Slaughter* are generally speaking right that they can. The problem is that being subject
to accountability mechanisms of representative democracy does not
excuse them from the expectation that their own conduct will reflect democratic values and attitudes.

Some of the key values and attitudes are inclusiveness, transparency, and value pluralism. On all three scores the trade policy network fails miserably. It clings to traditions of cloak-and-dagger
diplomacy, has had to be led kicking and screaming to the modest
de-restriction of documents that was insisted upon by the United
States, particular the *Clinton* Administration. It is reluctant to let
other intergovernmental organizations, including environmental
health and human rights organisms of the United Nations participate even as observers in WTO processes that directly concern or
affect the interests and constituencies that those organisms are pre-
occupied with. It even defends secrecy in dispute settlement proceedings, whereas secret trials have long been discredited as inconsistent with liberal democratic values essentially everywhere.

---

[28] *Weiler* (2001).
[29] *Keohane / Nye* (2001).

There is however one agent within the WTO system that is an exception to this characterization – the Appellate Body. Particularly in its manner of interpreting open-ended or general provisions of the WTO Agreements in cases where there are contested values, the Appellate Body has been sensitive to value pluralism, in a manner appropriate to a public law adjudicator in a pluralistic liberal democratic society.[30] The approach of the Appellate Body is well-expressed by its remark in the *Hormones* case that WTO treaty provisions may represent a "delicate and carefully negotiated balance ... between ... shared but sometimes, competing interests ...".[31] In interpreting the text, the political ethics of democracy – as appropriate to the judicial branch[32] – demand a sensitivity to and acceptance of the pluralism of legitimate values and constituencies at stake.

Along similar lines, the Appellate Body has also displayed the value of inclusiveness in its decision to interpret its broad discretion over its own operations as a judicial body to accept *amicus curiae* briefs from Non-Governmental Organizations.[33]

It should be said that generational change within the WTO Secretariat, for instance, is yielding some incremental advance towards the embrace of the political ethics of democracy. These changes are hard to notice, since these younger people operate within a formal structure that still reflects the old 'club' ethics. But, at a personal level, and consistent with the instructions of their superiors, they do

---

[30] See *Sunstein* (1996).

[31] Para 177.

[32] Thus my observation of this sensitivity should not be confused with the irresponsible and indeed defamatory allegation, for instance by *Jagdish Bhagwati* that in some cases the Appellate Body has actually corrupted the law under political pressure from particular constituencies. On the sensitivity of the Appellate Body to value pluralism, see *Howse* (2000a). For an examination of a single case in this light, see *Howse / Tuerk* (2001).

[33] *Shrimp-Turtle* and *Carbon Steel* cases. Despite the very negative reaction from the 'club' of diplomatic representatives at the WTO, the Appellate Body has once again, in the recent the *EC-Sardines* case, affirmed that it has the discretion to accept such briefs and indeed did find one amicus brief, by the author of this essay, to be 'admissible'. However, the AB also stated it did not have to rely on the brief to decide the appeal.

prove open to and sensitive to groups and values previously excluded for consideration or dialogue by the trade 'club'.

Lord *Dahrendorf* has suggested – and this an insight of *Eric Stein*, too – that formal institutional change or development is not easy to imagine, at least in the foreseeable future as a response to the democratic challenge posed by institutions of globalization. But as Lord *Dahrendorf* argues, one can have 'Democrats without Democracy' to the extent to which those who decide within or influence the system have the political ethics of democrats. It is thus worth shifting some of the immense attention from mechanisms and institutions that might 'democratize' the WTO (parliamentary assemblies etc.) to the challenge of establishing or widening a political ethics that reflects democratic values in existing institutions of global economic governance.[34] At the same time, the kind of practices of transparency and inclusiveness that would result from the entrenchment of such a political ethics would help reduce agency costs, and therefore also strengthen the role of existing domestic institutions of representative democracy in ensuring the democratic legitimacy of the WTO.

Bibliography:

S. A. Aronson (2001), Taking to the Streets: The Lost History of Public Efforts to Shape Globalization, Ann Arbor 2001.

C. Bail / R. Falkner / H. Marquard (2002) (eds.), The Cartagena Protocol on Biosafety: Reconciling Trade in Biotechnology with Environment & Development?, London 2002.

C. Barfield (2001), Free Trade, Sovereignty, Democracy: The Future of the World Trade Organization, Washington D.C. 2001.

C. Bellman / R. Gerster (1996), Accountability in the World Trade Organization, Journal of World Trade 30 (1996), No. 6, 31-74.

A. von Bogdandy (2001), Law and Politics in the WTO – Strategies to Cope with a Deficient Relationship, in *J. A. Frowein / R. Wol-*

---

[34] See *Dahrendorf* (2001). On the idea of a political ethics of supranational governance, see also *Howse / Nicolaidis* (2002).

frum (eds.), Max Planck Yearbook of United Nations Law 5/2001, Heidelberg 2001.

M. C. E. J. Bronckers (2001), More Power to the WTO?, Journal of International Economic Law 4 (2001) No. 1, 41-65.

C. Coglianese / K. Nicolaidis (2001), Securing Subsidiarity: The Institutional Design of Federalism in the United States and Europe, in *K. Nicolaidis / R. Howse* (eds.), The Federal Vision: Legitimacy and Levels of Governance in the United States and the European Union, Oxford 2001), 277-299.

R. Dahrendorf (2001), Can Democracy Survive Globalization?, National Interest Fall 2001

W. J. Drake / K. Nicolaidis (1992), 'Trade in Services' and the Uruguay Round, International Organization 46 (1992) No. 4, 37-100.

N. Hertz (2002), The silent takeover: global capitalism and the death of democracy, New York 2002.

R. Howse (2000), Transatlantic regulatory cooperation and the problem of democracy, in *G. Bermann* et al. (eds.), Transatlantic Regulatory Cooperation: Legal Problems and Political Prospects, Oxford 2000.

R. Howse (2000a), Adjudicative Legitimacy and Treaty Interpretation in International Trade Law: The Early Years of WTO Jurisprudence, in *J. H. H. Weiler* (ed.), The EU, the WTO and the NAFTA: Towards a Common Law of International Trade, Oxford 2000, 35-70.

R. Howse (2001), The Legitimacy of the WTO, in *J.-M. Coicaud / V. Heiskanen* (eds.), The Legitimacy of International Organizations, New York / Tokyo 2001, 355-407.

R. Howse (2002), From Politics to Technocracy – and Back Again: The Fate of the Multilateral Trading Regime, American Journal of International Law 96 (2002) No. 1, 94-117.

Robert Howse (2002a), Human Rights in the WTO: Whose Rights, What Humanity? Comment on Petersmann, European Journal of International Law 13 (2002) No. 3, 651-660.

R. Howse / K. Nicolaidis (2001), Legitimacy and Global Governance: Why Constitutionalizing the WTO is a Step Too Far, in *R.*

Porter et al. (eds.), Efficiency, Equity and Legitimacy: The Multilateral Trading System at the Millenium, Washington D.C. 2001, 227-263.

R. Howse/K. Nicolaidis (2002), 'This is my EUtopia ...': Narrative as Power, Journal of Common Market Studies 40 (2002) No. 4, 767-792.

R. Howse / E. Tuerk (2001), The WTO Impact on Intenal Regulations-A Case Study of the Canada-EC Asbestos Dispute, in *G. de Búrca /J. Scott* (eds.), The EU and the WTO: Legal and Constitutional Issues, Oxford 2001, 283-328.

J. H. Jackson (1997), The WTO Dispute Settlement Understanding – Misunderstandings on the Nature of Legal Obligation, American Journal of International Law 91 (1997) No. 1.

R. O. Keohane /J. S. Nye (2001), The Club Model of Multilateral Cooperation and the World Trade Organization: Problems of Democratic Legitimacy, in *R. Porter* et al. (eds.), Efficiency, Equity and Legitimacy: The Multilateral Trading System at the Millenium, Washington, D.C. 2001, 264-307.

S. Marks (2000), The Riddle of all Constitutions: International Law, Democracy, and the Critique of Ideology, Oxford 2000.

A. Moravcsik (2002), In Defence of the 'Democratic Deficit': Reassessing Legitimacy in the European Union, Journal of Common Market Studies 40 (2002) No. 4, 603-624.

J. S. Odell (1997), Negotiating the World Economy, Ithaca / NY 1997.

S. Ostry (2002), External Transparency: The Policy Process at the National Level of the Two Level Game, WTO Advisory Group, Geneva, April 2002.

A. F. Perez (1996), Who Killed Sovereignty? Or: Changing Norms Concerning Sovereignty in International Law, Wisconsin International Law Journal 14 (1996), 463 et seqq.

E.-U. Petersmann (2001), European and International Constitutional Law: Time for Promoting 'Cosmopolitan Democracy' in the WTO in *G. de Burca /J. Scott* (eds.), The EU and the WTO: Legal and Constitutional Issues, Oxford 2001, 81-110.

E.-U. Petersmann (2002), Time for a United Nations 'Global Compact' for Integrating Human Rights into the Law of Worldwide

Organizations: Lessons from European Integration, European Journal of International Law 13 (2002) No. 3, 621-650.

J. Pratt / R. Zeckhauser (1985) (eds.), Principals and Agents: the Structure of Business, Boston 1985.

J. Rawls (1999), The Law of Peoples, Cambridge/MA 1999.

A.-M. Slaughter (2000), Governing the Global Economy through Government Networks, in *M. Byers* (ed.), The Role of Law in International Politics, Oxford 2000, 177-206.

E. Stein (2001), International Integration and Democracy: No Love at First Sight, American Journal of International Law 95 (2001) No. 3, 489-534.

C. Sunstein (1996), Legal Reasoning and Political Conflict, New York 1996.

M. Weber (1965), The profession and vocation of politics, in *ibidem*, Political Writings, Cambridge 1965.

J. Weiler (2001), The Rule of Lawyers and the Ethos of Diplomats: Reflections on the Internal and External Legitimacy of Dispute Settlement, in *R. Porter* et al. (eds.), Efficiency, Equity and Legitimacy: The Multilateral Trading System at the Millenium, Washington D.C. 2001, 334-350.

Armin von Bogdandy

Legitimacy of International Economic Governance: Interpretative Approaches to WTO law and the Prospects of its Proceduralization*

The organizer of this conference asked me to present a paper on legitimacy in today's evolving models of national, supranational and international governance. This is a most challenging topic, first of all, because legitimacy has become the dominant external reference point of law after the victory of positivism and legal sociology. As *Immanuel Kant* observed, lawyers are often uncomfortable with such grand reference points, and – even worse – the concept of legitimacy can be founded on the most diverse criteria, from anything between opinion polls to complex philosophical or economic considerations.[1] But for other reasons as well the organizer of the conference asked me to speak on a topic that is – as I eventually found out – hardly within my province. The term "governance" is vague and hardly allows the application of the instruments of legal scholarship.[2] The nearest object of legal investigation is "international economic law". In order to avoid becoming an amateurish political scientist or essayist, I will therefore dedicate myself to some hermeneutical issues concerning international economic law. From this more legal perspective, however, some light might be shed on the grand issues.

The challenge of legitimacy with respect to WTO law has been raised mainly because of its impact on domestic law. Therefore the first part of this paper investigates this impact in the tradition of continental constitutional theory. Conventionally the main source of legitimacy is considered to be the operation of the legislative process in a constitutionally organized political community responding to the values, needs and convictions of that community. WTO law deeply affects the operation of this process and therefore what is conventionally considered to be one of the main sources of legiti-

---

*   This article develops some ideas first laid down in a much longer article titled "Law and Politics in the WTO. Strategies to cope with a deficient relationship", *Max Planck Yearbook of United Nations Law* 5 (2001), 609 – 674. Many thanks to *Eric Pickett* for most valuable assistance.

[1]   *Hofmann* (1997) 11 et seq., 47 et seq.

[2]   *Zumbansen* (2001) 13, 35 et seq.; *Möllers* (2001) 41 et seq.; *Archibugi/ Beetham* (1998) 86 et seq.; *Kohler-Koch* (1998); see also references in note 77. Given the developed institutional structure of the Union, the relevant discussion can hardly be applied to the international sphere; on the latter *European Commission* (2001) 428.

macy.[3] Scholars of WTO law should take this aspect into consideration when interpreting WTO law.

The second part will present three hermeneutic models which respond differently to this phenomenon. Drawing on similar discussions regarding the European economic constitution, three *ideal types* of understandings[4] of transnational trade law can be distinguished: the model of *economic liberalism*, the *federal* or *governance* model, and the *coordinated interdependence model.*[5] The last one is, as shall be seen, the most convincing for responding to the legitimacy problem described in part I.

The third part will investigate the perhaps most intriguing approach to securing WTO law's legitimacy through a certain *proceduralization.* Succinctly stated, it develops WTO law into a body of law that attempts to remedy some undemocratic features of lawmaking even within the political communities that respect the democratic principle as it is conventionally understood. WTO law thus extends certain features of the democratic system so that domestic legal and political systems live up to their responsibility to take account of the legitimate interests of foreign economic actors when their measures impact them.[6] This does not mean *overturning* the democratic principle; on the contrary, it means *extending* its reach and thereby, perhaps, better realizing it.

I.   The Impact of International Institutions on National Legitimacy

A. International Treaties and Democratic Sovereignty

Many seem to assume that the main relationship between international economic law and legitimacy is that the former undermines the latter.[7] International economic law is treaty law. This law nega-

---

[3]   BVerfGE 89, 155, 186.

[4]   *Weber* (1988) 146 et seq., 190 et seq.

[5]   This part has been inspired by *Poiares Maduro* (1998) 103 et seq.

[6]   As will be seen below, this is often indirect because the Appellate Body's proceduralization usually gives a voice to WTO Members in internal regulatory systems, though not necessarily to individual corporations as such.

[7]   *Brand /Brunnengräber /Schrader /Stock /Wahl* (2000) 104; see also the critique of public citizen *Wallach / Sforza* (1999) 3, 217 et seq. This latter, quite influential critique is interesting as an astonishingly incorrect presentation of many legal issues.

tively impacts on national legitimacy, if that legitimacy is understood in the terms of effective democratic sovereignty.[8] From the
static perspective, the drawback can be found in the fact that, although national (and consequently democratic[9]) sovereignty is formally respected, the content of the rules is determined in intergovernmental negotiations according to traditional diplomatic procedures. An open public discourse that can influence the rules, an
essential element for democratic legitimacy according to most theories, is severely limited.[10] The autonomy of the bureaucratic-gov-
ernmental élites is far greater than in the national political process.[11]
If this is a general feature of international relations, it is particularly
so in international trade relations: the GATT 1947 and WTO have
so far been one of the most secretive organizations in the world, and
this secrecy is considered an instrument to strengthen national negotiators who are in favor of trade liberalization.[12] Furthermore,
with the possible exception of the US-Congress,[13] national parliaments show a far greater deference to governmental proposals if
they concern international treaties rather than autonomous domestic
legislation. As the discussion on the role of national parliaments in
the EU legislative process has clearly revealed, there is also little
hope of improving the input of national parliaments into transnational rule-making during negotiations.[14]

The democratic problem grows even worse from a dynamic perspective. In modern times, *law* means *positive law*.[15] The main
feature of the positivity of law is the legislature's grasp of and responsibility for the law:[16] the law is posited by a legislature or is at

---

[8] For the respective US-American debate cf. *Jackson* (1998a); for the
     EU *de Búrca/Scott* (2001) 1.

[9] My entire argument only applies to WTO Members whose internal
     structures can be considered democratic. The problem with respect to
     citizens living under autocratic rule needs a separate investigation.

[10] For attempts to further the participation of NGOs in the work of the
     WTO *Marceau/Pedersen* (1999) 5.

[11] For a detailed account which calms some preoccupations see *Shaffer*
     (2001), 1.

[12] *Goldstein/Martin* (2000) 603, 612.

[13] *Jackson* (2000) 44-45, 377-378.

[14] *Norton* (1998) 209; *Judge* (1995) 79.

[15] *Hegel* (1821/1970), § 3.

[16] *Böckenförde* (1991) 289, 322.

least – in case of the common law or other judge made law – under its responsibility due to the legislature's competence to intervene at any given moment, amending or derogating a rule which an autonomous adjudicative process has developed.[17] This positivity of the law is an important aspect of the democratic sovereignty of a polity: in democratic societies, the majority, usually conceived as a unitary subject organized through the elected government, can at any moment intervene in the body of law and change it.[18] Under all constitutional systems, the economic process is subject to rules that can be enacted by a simple majority or through delegated legislation: the possibility of fast intervention is a leading principle in framing the respective rule-making competence.[19]

WTO law undermines the positivity of law in this sense. Once a treaty is set up, the political grasp on its rules is severely restricted – not normatively, but in all practical terms. Although international legislation respects the democratic principle insofar as treaties are negotiated and concluded by democratically elected governments, mostly even with parliamentary assent, it totally modifies the relationship between law and politics. By ratifying WTO law the current majority in a polity puts its decision largely outside the reach of any new majority.[20] This restriction is particularly important in the case of the WTO since "corrective" political influence, i. e. noncompliance, becomes difficult because of the obligatory WTO adjudication. Certainly, the democratic autonomy of the new majority is preserved to some extent through the right of withdrawal, Art. XV WTO. However, this right supports the democratic legitimacy of the WTO as much as the individual's right to emigrate does the democratic legitimacy of a State.[21] It can hardly be considered as sufficient as it is not a realistic option.

---

[17] For the specific situation in Common Law countries *Atiyah /Summers* (1991) 141 et seq.

[18] *von Bogdandy* (2000) 35 et seq. The guarantee of an efficient legislature is a *leitmotiv* of many constitutional developments in the last fifty years.

[19] In detail *Hilf/Reuß* (1997) 289, 290 et seq.; *Schmidt* (1988) § 83; on the economic constitution in Germany and the European Union see *Gerber* (1998) 232 et seq.

[20] *Abbott /Snidal* (2000), 421 et seq., (439); *Goldstein /Kahler /Keohane / Slaughter* (2000) 385 et seq., consider this a common political strategy.

[21] See Art. 13.2 Universal Declaration of Human Rights (1948), Art. 12.2 of the International Covenant on Civil and Political Rights (1966), Art.

One might say that this limitation on democratic self-governance inevitably comes with the need for treaty-based international cooperation. This argument can also take the form that this kind of limitation has been generally accepted as intrinsic to international law. Yet necessity and inevitability are bad normative grounds since they collide with the principle of freedom. Moreover, it has to be borne in mind that WTO law has an impact on democratic self-government far beyond most international rules: very few other international rules constrain domestic legislation on the economic process beyond the principle of non-discrimination.[22] Even most international environmental law instruments – which in many respects can be considered as providing cutting-edge mechanisms for international governance – do not prescribe specific regulative instruments or prohibit others, but mostly operate with objectives that must be attained.[23]

WTO law must be regarded as an unprecedented step in the development of international economic law which goes far beyond the GATT 1947.[24] One need only recall the importance of the TRIPs Agreement, the Agreement on the Application of Sanitary and Phytosanitary Measures, the Agreement on Technical Barriers to Trade, the Agreement on Subsidies and Countervailing Measures and the new dispute settlement procedures. One could challenge this thesis by pointing to the treaties aiming at international harmonization of private law, in particular international private law and intellectual property law.[25] The difference between these fields and many parts of WTO law, however, is that these areas of law do not call for frequent political intervention. Moreover, given the lack of a centralized adjudication in these treaties, the domestic legal

---

2.2 Protocol No. 4 of the European Convention on Human Rights; see *Weis/Zimmermann* (1995) 74.

[22] See in particular the friendship, trade and shipment treaties or on the protection of investment, *Blumenwitz* (1984) 318, 321.

[23] In detail *Bothe* (2001).

[24] On the main innovations see *Benedek* (1995) 532; on the development see *Senti* (1994) 301; *Stoll* (1994) 241; *Meng* (1998) 19.

[25] For an overview *Kegel/Schurig* (2000) 69 et seq.

[26] Ibid., 5, 8 et seq.

orders keep some autonomy in the evolution of these instruments.[26] Also in this respect, WTO law leads to a diminution of domestic autonomy because it incorporates other instruments outside the WTO. For example, TRIPs incorporates many intellectual property treaties into the WTO adjudicative mechanism (Art. 1 – 39 TRIPs). Similarly, the TBT and SPS Agreements refer in various provisions (e.g. Annex A no. 3 (a) SPS) to rules of other bodies, such as the Codex Alimentarius Commission (CAC), International Office of Epizootics (IOE), International Plant Protection Convention (IPPC). The respective provisions are among the most problematic and most discussed of the whole of WTO law.[27]

While these organizations may be more flexible and able to respond more quickly to changing market needs and scientific insights, thereby functioning as a substitute legislator for the WTO, they are also problematic for the WTO's legitimacy for several reasons. First, it must be pointed out that not all WTO Members are members of these organizations. This may mean that, at crucial points in WTO law, they have not been adequately represented.[28] Second, these organizations may not always function in the most democratic of fashions, thus prejudicing the WTO's legitimacy insofar as it relies on such rules. Third, these organizations may cater to or even be captured by special interests, thus undermining the democratic legitimacy of their rules. The hormones standardization case in the CAC provides a case in point.[29]

---

[27] *Eggers* (1998) 148; *Hilf/Eggers* (1997) 559; *Quick/Blüthner* (1999) 637; *Ritter* (1997) 133, 133 et seq., 136 et seq.; *Sander* (2000) 335; *Pauwelyn* (1999) 641.

[28] A similar issue was discussed in Appellate Body Report of 2 August 1999, WT/DS46/AB/R *Brazil – Export Financing Programme for Aircraft*. The Appellate Body held that the Brazilian export finance regime for Brazilian aircraft violated Art. 3.1. lit a) Agreement on Subsidies and Countervailing Measures (SCMA) because it was "used to secure a material advantage in the field of export credit terms" which, according to the definition under lit k) of the illustrative list in Annex I SCMA, is a prohibited export subsidy. As a possible benchmark for the definition of a material advantage the Appellate Body referred to the "Commercial Interest Reference Rate" developed by a sub-body of the OECD, even though this standard appears nowhere in the SCMA and even though the defendant, Brazil, was not member of the OECD and had therefore not participated in the development of this standard (para. 181).

[29] In detail *von Bogdandy* (2001) 609 – 674.

The legitimacy problem can also be considered from another angle. Legislative efficiency is a constitutional value in most constitutional systems.[30] Treaty-making procedures are slow and cumbersome, a feature that becomes particularly problematic if the social sector in question is in rapid evolution as is the case with the national and international economy. This entails the danger that rules become inadequate or anachronistic, a danger the authors of the WTO were aware of, as proven by clauses which require periodic revision of a number of provisions.[31] Given the acknowledged probability of the need to amend legislation, the procedures of Art. X WTO are deeply inadequate.

B. International Adjudication and Democratic Sovereignty

The necessity of an efficient democratic legislator has been argued so far with respect to the need to adopt rules to changing social and economic conditions, fears and convictions. A further aspect must be considered: the need of an adjudicative body to have a political counterpart when developing a body of law through reasoned dispute settlement decisions. At a first glance, the DSU appears to minimize this need through provisions such as Art. 3.2 DSU, which curtail the adjudicative bodies' opportunities to "creatively develop" the law. Such a clause might effectively exclude decisions that introduce "revolutionary" principles such as the direct effect of WTO law or its supremacy over domestic law.[32] It

---

[30] *von Bogdandy* (2000), see also note 18.

[31] E.g., Art. 15.4 TBT Agreement stipulates that the TBT Committee must review the implementation and operation of the agreement every three years. The first report has just been published, http://www.wto.org/english/tratop_e/tbt_e/tbt5.htm. For further evidence cf. Art. 20 Agreement on Agriculture; Art. 12.7 Agreement on the Application of Sanitary and Phytosanitary Measures; Art. 15.3, 15.4 Agreement on Technical Barriers to Trade; Art. 9 Agreement on Trade-Related Investment Measures; Art. 7.1 Agreement on Import Licensing Procedures; Art. 31 Agreement on Subsidies and Countervailing Measures; Art. 71.1 TRIPs.

[32] On the lack of direct effect explicitly WT/DS152/R *United States – Sections 301-310 of the Trade Act of 1974*, Report of the Panel, para. 7.72. For an earlier attempt to introduce direct effect and supremacy cf. DS 23/R *United States-Measures Affecting Alcoholic and Malt Beverages*, Report by the Panel adopted on June 19, 1992, BISD 39 (1991-1992), 206, 297.

cannot, however, exclude the creation of a body of law through reasoned reports. Rather, such a development is inevitable if the adjudicative organs faithfully follow the DSU. Art. 11 DSU requires an "objective assessment of the matter". An "objective assessment" requires giving reasons.[33] Any reasoned decision will, however, inevitably lead to the creation of a body of law.[34] The building of such case law is normatively supported by Art. 3.2 DSU, which sets out the objective of "providing security and predictability to the multilateral trading system." From here flows – as the Appellate Body pointed out – the obligation to take previously adopted reports and interpretations into consideration.[35] Even though reports do not have a binding force in and of themselves, they create legitimate expectations and must therefore be taken in account.[36] In a system with compulsory adjudication, this objective can only be attained through consistent adjudicative practice.

The adjudicative mechanism in itself is a law generating procedure, and some even consider it the engine driving neo-liberal globalization.[37] The WTO sets up not only a substantive body of law, but moreover one which is autonomously developing through the dispute settlement procedure. In fully developed legal systems, the creative function of the judges is democratically embedded since the legislator can intervene at any given moment. This possibility of intervention entails political responsibility and, consequently, democratic legitimacy for those developments. As pointed out, such a legislator does not exist for WTO law.[38]

---

[33]   In detail *Ross* (1929) 283 et seq.; *Kriele* (1976) 167 et seq.

[34]   *Shapiro* (1999) 321, 340.

[35]   Appellate Body Report of 4 October 1996, WT/DS8/AB/R, WT/DS10/AB/R, WT/DS11/AB/R, *Japan – Taxes on Alcoholic Beverages*, 15.

[36]   Ibid. For the common ground between civil law systems and common law systems on this point cf. *Esser* (1990). As *Behboodi* (2000) 578-579, points out, security and predictability in the sense of coherent judicial interpretation is fundamental to the WTO's legitimacy. While the WTO tribunals do at times reverse previous jurisprudence, they are reluctant to do so and careful to try to make coherent case law. For example, the panel was careful to explain the effects of its ruling on mandatory and discretionary legislation on previous decisions in WT/DS152/R (see note 32), footnote 675.

[37]   *Brand/Brunnengräber/Schrader/Stock/Wahl* (2000) 104, 105.

[38]   On the question whether the WTO should be considered a constitu-

A comparison between WTO law and other international treaties which set up compulsory adjudicative organs gives further account of the specificity of the WTO with respect to the issue of legitimacy.[39] In most cases, such organs adjudicate either on the basis of specific and limited obligations with little impact on the domestic legislative and regulatory process or on the basis of international human rights obligations, which have a special standing.[40] WTO law is similar to other international instruments insofar as it is a body of law that is difficult to change. This general feature of international law is, however, especially problematic with respect to WTO law because it addresses a dynamic, rapidly changing field. The WTO does not set up politico-legislative mechanisms to tackle this dynamism, for sound reasons. For example, there are still no international procedures which guarantee sufficient democratic legitimacy at the global level.[41] Since the Member States remain the crucial actors, far more than at the EU level, it is only logical that the proper form of law-making for the WTO remains the treaty amendment procedure.

As a consequence we have a body of law which is linked to the political process only through extremely cumbersome procedures. Once this body of rules has been ratified, corrections by the political process are very difficult.[42] Changes in the will of the majority of citizens within a State (or the European Union) will hardly ever

---

tional order and would therefore lead to a different conclusion see below, part III, 1.

[39] This is also the evidence from *Goldstein /Kahler /Keohane /Slaughter* (2000), 385, 389, 398, analyzing a number of international agreements under the categories of "obligation, precision, and delegation".

[40] The international law of human rights appears to have taken a separate development since the total submission of politics to essential human rights standards has become an established feature, *A. Cassese* (1999) 5 et seq., 85 et seq.; *Tomuschat* (1998) 1 et seq.; *Zimmermann* (1998) 47 et seq.

[41] On the relationship to civil society see *Scholte /O'Brien /Williams* (1999) 107; in more general terms *Bodansky* (1999) 596.

[42] Some scholars assume that for that reason the most important processes of forming new law have moved from the traditional institutions to societal actors, *Teubner* (2000) 437; see also *Ipsen* (1999) § 3, para. 29, 30.

lead to changes in the relevant WTO law. The possibility of with-drawal pursuant to Art. XV WTO will generally be prohibitively expensive.[43] In traditional international law, a possible inroad of national politics was non-compliance to international law. This inroad has become severely restricted owing to the WTO's compul-sory jurisdiction.[44]

Given all these elements, WTO law has severe consequences on the ability of domestic legislative procedures to generate legiti-macy. This entails that the legitimacy of WTO law itself comes under question.[45] How can legal scholarship respond to this chal-lenge?[46]

II.   Models of Construction of WTO Law with a View to its Legitimacy

There is a possibility of various and even contradictory inter-pretations of important WTO provisions, as proven by regular di-vergences between the panels and the Appellate Body. Given this scope, general understandings of the nature and objective of WTO law influence the meaning attributed to disputed provisions in many instances. They might be used as inroads for legitimacy enhancing interpretations of WTO law.

---

[43]   It is telling that only the US – the most influential member of the WTO – has considered withdrawal, *Abbott/Snidal* (2000), 438 et seq.

[44]   The substantive debate today is whether a WTO Member is free to choose between fulfilling the recommendations of a dispute settlement report – and thus being obliged to adapt its internal order – or mere compensation, Art. 22 DSU. The opinion that a Member must adapt appears more convincing, *Jackson* (1998b) 41 et seq., 85 et seq.; *Rosas* (2001) 131, 135; for the opposite view *Sack* (1997) 650, 688. Also the debate on direct applicability of WTO law can be understood in this light.

[45]   This article does not develop to what extent particular provisions of WTO law might display forms of one-sidedness in favor of particular interests, thereby casting further doubt on their legitimacy; on this as an unsuspicious source, *Petersmann* (2000a) 1363, 1368, 1371, 1374.

[46]   One crucial strategy is to deny direct applicability of WTO law within the domestic legal orders. This is probably the most controversial point in legal scholarship, for the point made cf. *von Bogdandy* (2002).

A. The Liberal Model

1. The Model's Main Features and Currents

The first conception, historically, in number of proponents and in level of sophistication, is the *liberal model*. It interprets WTO law as an instrument to substantially restrain the grasp of domestic politics on the economy and – in different variants – to increase international competition and to some extent deregulation. What this article has so far considered to be a substantial problem for the WTO – limiting the (domestic) political interference in the economic process – is, from this perspective, a crucial asset and perhaps a main source of this law's legitimacy. The *liberal model* represents the most elaborate position in international trade law, and corresponds to the dominant positions in international trade theory.[47] It comes in various alternatives.

John Jackson is the best known, although cautious representative of the traditional variant. Albeit sometimes ambiguous, he usually presents WTO law in the liberal light: "The basic purpose of GATT is to constrain governments from imposing or continuing a variety of measures that restrain or distort international trade".[48] The basic rational comes from economic theory on which he relies when he cites *Coase*'s thesis that "[e]conomic policy consists of choosing those legal rules, procedures and administrative structures which will maximize the value of production".[49] WTO law is seen as an instrument to limit intervention in the markets. Settled insights from mainstream economic theory provide the main interpretative horizon with few intermediate steps.

A theoretically more developed variant of the *liberal model* is presented by private law scholars who consider WTO law as instrumental to rolling back regulatory public law interfering in the

---

[47] *The Economist* (1990) 5 et seq.; *The Economist* (1998) 4 et seq.; *Frey* (1985) 12 et seq.; *Glismann/Horn/Nehring/Vaubel* (1992) 72 et seq.

[48] *Jackson* (2000), 22-3, similarly, ibid., p. 102: "... to prevent member nation states from abusing their national powers when those would damage the operation of world markets". Sometimes, however, he presents the objective of GATT as far more limited, being simply "to prevent arbitrary and unfair decisions or policies from undermining the other rules of GATT"; ibid., 23; *Jackson* (1991) 305; this latter position corresponds to the understanding proposed in this article.

[49] *Jackson* (1991) 102, quoting *R. Coase* in his authority as a Nobel Prize winner.

private law domain of shaping economic relations. Also from this point of view States are an "interference factor" (*Störfaktor*) in international trade.[50] The private law approach sees WTO law as instrumental to fostering the "global private law society" (*globale Privatgesellschaft*). According to this model, social integration largely occurs through the triad of contractual freedom, competition and property.[51] The global private law society is formed through transnational private law relationships, and is conceptually distinguished from the discrete political communities with their different regulatory schemes which interfere with the private law relations. According to this understanding, which reads WTO law as the basis of a global economic constitution, substantive WTO law obliges Members to follow an liberal economic policy.[52] Securing this private law society endows transnational law with a purpose, form and legitimacy. On this reading, WTO law is to allow only those public interventions which maintain the framework of an efficient market and of the global private law society.[53] This does not completely exclude regulatory intervention for social or environmental protection, but it requires doing so by the means least detrimental to the operation of markets.

From a public law perspective, the most important contribution is that of *Ernst-Ulrich Petersmann*'s constitutional reading of the WTO. His contribution has been particularly important since it is largely due to his courageous, well-founded and far-reaching constructions that a rich theoretical debate on international economic law has developed. Since his thought is prolific and continuously developing, the following presentation might not do justice to his current position. Nevertheless, it will be presented as an ideal type.

On this reading, WTO law respects the principle of the separation of powers (as a crucial tenet of constitutional legitimacy) and is based on an adequate relationship between law and politics. According to this reading, the critique developed in the first part of this article is therefore misguided.

---

[50] *Fikentscher* (1983) 255. *Fikentscher*'s great monograph interprets the whole of international economic law as parts of an emerging world competition order, ibid., 204 et seq.

[51] *Mestmäcker* (1989) 273; *Mestmäcker* (1991) 177; for a criticism *Günther* (1992) 473.

[52] For a thorough theoretical review cf. *Gerber* (1998), 232 et seq.

[53] *Drexl* (1998), 841, 846; for the theoretical underpinning cf. *Goodhart* (1997) 1, 17 et seq..

His conception has some strong foundations. It is beyond dispute that there is a specific relationship between politics and *constitutional* law. There is also agreement that constitutional law should stand beyond the "normal" political process. In fact, there is a difference between the legislator's ability to change "normal" law and its much more limited ability to alter constitutional law. Constitutional law guides and channels the "normal" political process and provides the core mechanism to convincingly stabilize the separation *and* interaction of law and politics in contemporary societies.[54] Even though constitutional rules are also subject to constitutional politics, it is the essence of the separation of powers doctrine that the constitutional political process be much more burdensome, requiring specific majorities and/or procedures.[55] If WTO law had a constitutional function, its remoteness from the normal political process would be in accordance with established constitutional principles, political thinking and legitimacy generating.[56]

In order to attribute a constitutional function to WTO law, *Petersmann* considers – in a *Kant*ian tradition[57] – substantive WTO law as functional to realizing the basic individual freedom of choice of entrepreneurs and consumers.[58] The main thrust of this argument so far has been to interpret WTO provisions as giving rights to individuals against domestic legislation and other acts of public authorities.[59] Yet *Petersmann* also assumes that the WTO is an *integration* agreement with the internal European economic constitution – understood as a deregulatory constitution – as a model.[60]

The basic argument of the liberal model in all its different variants is economic rationality, which asserts that there are optimal

---

[54] For a theoretical account *Luhmann* (1995) 407 et seq.

[55] *Vergottini* (1999) 206 et seq., 234 et seq.

[56] For further uses of this category on the international level cf. *Fassbender* (1998) 25 et seq.

[57] *Petersmann* (2000) 19, 24.

[58] The leading work is *Petersmann* (1991) in particular 210 et seq.; furthermore *Hauser* (1986), 171; *Roessler* (1986), 467; *Tumlir* (1983), 71 et seq.

[59] The question of the direct effect of WTO law is the subject of the richest and most controversial discussion in international trade law; its adequate presentation is not the object of this contribution; see Advocate General *A. Saggio,* conclusions of 25. 2. 1999 in case C-149/96, *Portugal* v. *Council,* para. 14 et seq., para. 24; *Meng* (1995) 1064.

[60] *Petersmann* (1995) 189.

and sub-optimal instruments to correct market failures.[61] The protection of the operation of the economic process in its wealth-creating function against interfering political majorities using sub-optimal instruments is an old demand of liberal economic theory.[62] This school of thought gives a broad scope to most obligations under the WTO, while granting only a narrow scope to the exceptions. They thus limit regulatory and legislative intervention by the domestic political systems. On a radical reading, WTO law shall help to bring to an end a historic interplay whose main feature has been the close grip of politics on the economy through law. The restriction of public interference and even de-regulation at the domestic level would be the consequence, in particular since WTO duties require not only avoiding a concrete collision (the standard requirement under international law), but also adapting the domestic legal order, Art. XVI.4 WTO. In contrast to the EU, a re-regulation at the global level would not take place in view of the cumbersome WTO political process.[63] The law's function as a political instrument to forward political aims in the sphere of economics would therefore atrophy. At the same time, it would re-establish its more traditional functions of providing a stabilization of expectations and a forum for conflict resolution. Regulatory competition is, in this light, a WTO objective.[64]

2. A Critique

This is an impressive model. Yet, ultimately, I do not find it convincing.[65] To the extent that it draws on economic theory one might question to what extent that science's models are capable of grasping the real world where "people live and work and die".[66] Also the assertion that protectionist lobbies are usually stronger

---

[61] In detail *Meng* (1995), 1080 et seq.; *Petersmann* (1997).

[62] *Friedman* (1962) 11; see also *Mestmäcker* (1989), 273; this vision is shared by powerful economic actors, see the chairman of Deutsche Bank, *Breuer* (1999) 9.

[63] In detail *Beise* (2001) 197 et seq.

[64] For a discussion of costs and benefits cf. *Petersmann* (1996), 5, 12, 15 et seq.

[65] In detail *Langer* (1995) 18 et seq.; *Howse / Nicolaidis* (internet); *Krajewski* (2001), 167.

[66] Report of the Panel on *EC Measures Concerning Meat and Meat Products (Hormones)* of 18 August 1997, WT/DS26/R/USA, EC and report of the Appellate Body of 16 January 1998, WT/DS26/AB/R, WT/DS48/AB/R, para. 187.

than free trade lobbies[67] is not beyond doubt.[68] The normative quality appears equally questionable. It is not convincing to fasten the
interpretation of a body of law which is hard to change to an economic theory which is – in contrast to human rights – fiercely disputed.[69] At this point, legal research should be careful: neither constitutional theory nor legal theory possess the tools to decide the
controversies involved. They should, however, for the sake of the
legitimacy of the body of rules they investigate, fend off attempts to
seize the field in the name of a particular theory.[70]

It is also useful to conceive of this issue in terms of jurisdiction.
Under domestic constitutional law, it is quite legitimate for a political community to opt for less wealth and less integration in the
global market and give preference to other values to be realized
through economically sub-optimal instruments. These decisions go
to the core of social structures and solidarity: they concern the equitable distribution of wealth, the relative positions of civic organizations such as unions and business associations, the distribution of
risks between individuals and the society collectively and so on.[71]
Such fundamental and sensitive decisions should be democratically
decided within the polity.[72] It is unconvincing to interpret an international treaty in a way that severely hampers the ratifying parties
to do what their constitutions consider perfectly legitimate. Even if
a Member should deliberately and democratically decide to be a
"competition state" rather than a "welfare state",[73] there is no con-

---

[67] *Petersmann* (1991) 96 et seq.

[68] *Goldstein/Martin* (2000), 609 et seq.; *Shaffer* (2001).

[69] In detail *Irwin* (1996) 180 et seq.; *Hobsbawm* (1995) 703; *Lofdahl*
      (1998), 339, 351; *Perkins* (1998) 46, 51; see also *Drexl* (1998); *Esser*
      (1999) 117 et seq.

[70] As the economist *Goodhart* (1997) 2, puts it: "Economics has become
      an increasingly and unashamedly imperialist social science in recent
      decades. And you in the law provide one of our finest colonies."

[71] *Charny* (2000) 281, 297.

[72] This is not to say that a polity may not be bound by human rights. For
      example, if certain labour rights – such as the right not to work in
      sweatshop conditions – are also human rights, then no polity may deny
      these rights, even if a decision to deny this right were taken democrati-
      cally. Cf. *Charny* (2000) 295-296. The discussion here, however, does
      not concern such core rights. It should be noted that, while there may
      be few such core rights, there is broad international consensus on them.

[73] On this distinction *Altvater/Mahnkopf* (1999) 45, 63 et seq., 133 et seq.,
      219 et seq.

stitutional ground to assume that this choice should be "written in stone", out of the reach of later majorities. Such decisions are generally not at the constitutional level in domestic law nor are conceived of in terms of constitutional rights precisely because it is considered necessary for a variety of reasons to keep such decisions within the reach of the current majority. It is also telling that WTO law does not provide any hint that its provisions, even the most central ones, should be considered as international human rights. In fact, human rights is simply a non-issue in WTO law. Thus, for the WTO to bind the Members to a particular economic theory would undermine the organization's legitimacy at a fundamental level.

Beyond this more ideological confrontation, there are also important arguments which are more focussed on specific problems of adjudication. There are inherent limits to any adjudicative process convincingly drawing the line between political intervention and economic freedom:[74] regulatory problems can only exceptionally be settled through litigation. In general, adjudicative organs lack the expertise for such policies; their information is dependent on those who participate in the adjudicative process and issues may be decided without hearing affected interests which do not participate. The total costs of adjudicative procedures are usually far higher than those of administrative procedures.[75] All these considerations are confirmed by the ECJ's approach. An analysis of the ECJ's jurisprudence on the basic freedoms discourages an interpretation of WTO law that aims at negative integration and deregulation. The ECJ's jurisprudence is based on the premise that legislative correction is possible at the supranational level.[76] That possibility does not obtain within the WTO.

B. The Federal or Governance Model

The second model, here called the *federal* or *governance model*, aims to equip the international legal regimes with more policy functions. This model comes in different variants: one variant calls for federal elements, another variant proposes still vaguely defined forms of international *governance*.[77] The supranational understanding aims to reproduce the relationship between law and poli-

---

[74] In detail *Poiares Maduro* (1998) 59 et seq.

[75] For further arguments cf. *Poiares Maduro* (1998) 145 et seq.

[76] In detail *Poiares Maduro* (1998) 76 et seq., 78.

[77] *Commission on Global Governance* (1995) 9 et seq.; *Zürn* (1998) 329 et seq.; *Altvater/Mahnkopf* (1999) 397.

tics of more developed political communities at the transnational
level. There are those who argue in favor of a global federation.[78]
Those who – more realistically – propose that the WTO develop
similar to the European Union are more numerous in trade law.[79]
This position is not necessarily in opposition to the first reading;
new forms of international policy-making can be integrated into the
liberal model's understanding.[80] The very idea is that the political
process within the WTO should be organized in such a way that
necessary legislation can be enacted on a global level. *Roessler*'s
proposed interpretation of Art. XXV GATT 1947 provides an example.[81]

However, given the restricted possibilities of the WTO's
autonomous political procedures, the *federal* or *governance* model
cannot inform the interpretation of the current law: the simple possibility that sometime in the future adequate policy mechanisms
might develop does not permit an interpretation of current WTO
law as if such mechanisms actually existed. Moreover, the difficulties of the European Union in developing into a constitutional
community which satisfies the tenets of democratic government
justifies a deep scepticism as to whether such a development is
feasible for an organization with a global reach. From the experience of the European Union one might rather conclude that the
necessary conditions are not given and that attempts in this direction would likely shatter the WTO.

C. Coordinated Interdependence

1. The Idea

The third understanding – termed the *coordinated interdependence model* – tries to find another balance between the increasingly
transnational nature of the economy and the WTO Members' re-

---

[78] *Höffe* (1999) 310 et seq.; convincing the critique by *Günther* (2000)
      232 et seq.; similarly the ideas of a cosmopolitan democracy, *Held*
      (1998) 59.
[79] *Nettesheim* (2001) 381, 382, 407; *Messner/Nuscheler* (1997) 337, 351;
      Shell (1995) 829 et seq.
[80] *E.-U. Petersmann* has made important proposals, see *Petersmann*
      (1995) 161, 189 ("Global Integration Agreement") 221; *Petersmann*
      (2001) 81; as a possible model for future development *Langer* (1995),
      330; *Howse/Nicolaidis* (internet) 13 et seq.
[81] See *Roessler* (1987) 73.

sponsibilities under their respective constitutions.[82] It considers those parts of WTO law affecting the domestic regulatory processes as merely an instrument to prevent (intentional) protectionism *and* to force Members to take the economic interests of other Members into account.[83] When it comes to internal regulation,[84] WTO law is an instrument to politically coordinate different regulatory systems, not an instrument to curtail such regulatory systems for the sake of wealth-creation or in the name of economic freedom. The *coordinated interdependence model* is predicated on the widespread conviction that non-discrimination is the central principle of WTO law.[85] Members remain free to regulate their national economy, and neither deregulation nor regulatory competition are among the objectives of the WTO. Unlike the liberal model, in this conception WTO law has neither a domestic policy function nor constitutional function. This model corresponds best to the problem of legitimacy which this article has analyzed. The following section will flesh out this proposal with respect to the objectives of WTO law.

2. An Application of the Objectives of WTO Law

The proposed reading of WTO law is based on understanding its objectives as being rather limited. It collides with other conceptions which assume that the WTO aims at free trade[86] or even market integration.[87] "Free trade" and "market integration" do not appear anywhere as a WTO objective. In the first recital of the preamble to the WTO Agreement, the objective is "expanding the production of

---

[82] To my knowledge, those fundamentally critical of the WTO have not yet proposed a scholarly model for interpretation.

[83] In a similar vein *Langer* (1995) 65 et. seq.; *Robert Howse*, with his concept of "embedded liberalism" (see also *Ruggie* (1983) 195) proposes what is, perhaps, the most elaborate position within this school of thought, cf. *Howse /Nicolaidis* (internet); *Howse* (2000); *Howse* (2002).

[84] On the broad understanding of laws and government action see WT/DS152/R (note 32), para. 7.26-7.27 and WT/DS103/AB/RW, WT/DS113/AB/RW *Canada – Measures Affecting the Importation of Milk and the Exportation of Dairy Products*, Report of the Appellate Body adopted on 03 December 2001, para. 112, respectively.

[85] *Howse* (2002).

[86] This is often assumed by critics, *Altvater/Mahnkopf* (1999) 396.

[87] *Petersmann* (1995).

and trade in goods and services".[88] This does not determine to what extent impediments to trade should be removed. More precise information about the aims is laid down in the third recital of the WTO preamble, according to which the WTO agreements are "directed to the substantial reduction of tariffs and other barriers to trade and the elimination of discriminatory treatment in international trade relations".[89] Accordingly, not even with respect to specific trade restrictive measures does WTO law aim at their elimination, but rather aims only at their "substantial reduction". Judging by its own standards laid down in Art. XXIV.8 GATT, WTO law does not aim at market integration and "is [...] not a free trade instrument".[90]

Free trade could nevertheless be the objective, if the words "substantial reduction of [...] other barriers to trade" meant that international trade flows should not be hampered. Yet the recital continues: "and to the elimination of discriminatory treatment in international trade relations". Obviously, the Contracting Parties had a narrow understanding of the term "trade barriers", as a broad understanding would include discriminatory measures. Consequently, to interpret the preamble as including free trade as an objective would render the second part of the recital meaningless, thus violating a basic rule of interpretation.[91] Accordingly, such an interpretation is unconvincing.

The understanding proposed here finds further support in a comparative analysis which takes Art. 2 EU and Art. 2 EC into account. These two treaties aim at economic and political integration. Art. 2 EC supports far-reaching interpretations of treaty provisions which force Member States to grant market access to products originating

---

[88]   It should be noted that the tribunals also make legal arguments from the preambles to the agreements. See for example, WT/DS202/R *US – Definitive Safeguard Measures on Imports of Circular Welded Carbon Quality Pipeline from Korea*, report of the panel adopted on 29 October 2001, para. 7.49; WT/DS152/R (note 32), para. 7.74 – 7.75; WT/DS108/R *US – Tax Treatment for "Foreign Sales Corporations"*, Report of the Panel adopted on 08 October 1999, para. 7.173 et seq; WT/DS108/RW *US – Tax Treatment for "Foreign Sales Corporations"*, Report of the Panel adopted on 20 August 2001, para. 8.144.

[89]   Similarly the 2nd recital of GATT; see also the 2nd and 4th recitals of GATS, 1st recital of TRIPs.

[90]   *Tumlir* (1986) 1, 7, with respect to GATT, of course.

[91]   *Bydlinski* (1991) 444.

in other Member States irrespective of questions of discrimination. However, Art. 2 EC aims at the establishment of a "Common Market", whereas WTO law only aims at "substantial reduction of barriers to trade" and the "elimination of discrimination". The difference is even more striking when considering the relevant normative context. Art. 2 EC has been continuously enriched through complementary objectives, such as cohesion, solidarity and numerous regulatory policies; WTO law lacks this entirely. As already set out above, cohesion, solidarity and regulatory policies complement the creation of new spheres of economic freedom, at least according to current constitutional thought.

The gulf separating EU law from WTO law grows even greater when looking at the preambles of the EC- and EU-Treaties, which aim at an "ever closer union of the European peoples" in order to further peace, democracy and human rights. None of this is contained in the WTO Agreement. One can assume that this omission was deliberate, because European integration – so far the most successful attempt to liberalize international trade – must have been in the minds of the negotiating parties. Moreover, the WTO lacks the political mechanisms to accompany liberalization and deregulation brought about by adjudication.[92]

This vision of limited ambitions and objectives of the WTO finds further support in a telling omission in the Appellate Body's reasoning: it never assumes a "WTO interest"; rather, it appears that only the Members have an interest to be considered.[93] Hereby the Appellate Body distances itself from understandings which aim at the creation of a new polity.[94] According to the Appellate Body,

---

[92] For further differences see *Ehlermann/Campogrande* (1988) 481, 482 et seq.; in detail *Holmes* (2001) 59, 64 et seq.

[93] See e.g., WT/DS2/AB/R *US – Standards for Reformulated and Conventional Gasoline*, Report of the Appellate Body adopted on 29 April 1996, 22; WT/DS58/AB/R *United States – Import Prohibition of certain Shrimp and Shrimp Products, Recourse to Article 21.5 DSU*, para. 164, 167. This does not mean that private persons (i.e., importers and exporters) do not have interests which are irrelevant to the WTO. Instructive in this regard US – Sections 301 – 310 (note 32) para. 7.81 et seq. See also e.g., WT/DS2/AB/R *US – Standards for Reformulated and Conventional Gasoline*, Report of the Appellate Body adopted on 29 April 1996. However, this question is at a different level than the one being discussed here.

[94] The assumption of a *global common good* or *interest* is crucial for

WTO law only serves its Members and no further interest. The assumption of a "Community interest" and a "Community common good" is, in contrast, a core concept of European Union law (e.g. Art. 43.1 lit. a EU, Art. 86.2 EC) and is among the most important argumentative tools in the ECJ's jurisprudence.[95] This is confirmed by the fact that – different to the EU-Commission – no WTO organ, including none of the surveillance bodies, has the competence to bring a case before a panel. This also speaks for the *coordinated interdependence model.*

A similar result comes to the fore with respect to the question of whether harmonization of domestic rules is a WTO objective. Certainly, some parts of WTO law leave Members little discretion in shaping legal instruments. For example, any WTO conform anti-dumping instrument or countervailing duties instrument will have to closely follow the detailed rules in the respective WTO agreements. The same might happen with national subsidies under the relevant WTO provisions.[96] TRIPs is even more stringent. Legally TRIPs does not impose an obligation on the Members to harmonize their legislation.[97] Yet any implementation limited to foreigners may result in reverse discrimination against the Member's own citizens: a result which is obviously politically untenable. Moreover, in several important areas of intellectual property, some developing countries did not even have any legislation on intellectual property rights when TRIPs was introduced. It can therefore be expected that TRIPs will result in a substantial restructuring of the domestic legal systems: they will have to bow to some form of *de facto* harmonization.

Given this article's analysis, the rush towards harmonization should be contained, and it is important to emphasize that harmonization does not appear as an overall objective in the WTO pream-

---

those who argue in favor of the development of global governance *Messner/Nuscheler* (1996) 12, 21.

[95] Case 26/62, *van Gend & Loos*, ECR 1963, 1, 24; *Heintzen* (2000) 377, 381 et seq.

[96] For an interpretation in the sense of "coordinated interdependence" *Langer* (1995) 264 et seq.

[97] TRIPs only sets up certain minimum standards for the treatment of foreigners and does not address the treatment of nationals. According to Art. 1.3 TRIPs "Members shall accord the treatment provided for in this Agreement to the nationals of other Members". See also *Schäfers* (1996) 763, 770 et seq.

ble. This cautious analysis also finds support in Appellate Body's reports on the SPS Agreement. This may appear surprising, as the SPS Agreement aims – according to its preamble – "to further the use of harmonized sanitary and phytosanitary measures between Members". The Appellate Body, however, interprets even this agreement in such a manner that the Members retain the autonomy to regulate their national economy. The Appellate Body reversed the panel report in the Hormones case, in which the panel held that Members were obliged to adopt harmonized international standards on phytosanitary measures.[98] Instead, the Appellate Body reasoned that the harmonization mentioned in the preamble of the SPS is "a *goal, yet to be realized in the future.*"[99] The Appellate Body understands the relevant SPS-provision as simply preventing "the use of such measures for arbitrary and unjustified discrimination between Members"[100] without hindering them to regulate their national economies according to their legitimate needs.[101] This confirms the position proposed in this article: that most substantive and procedural WTO law is limited to upholding the principle of non-discrimination.

The principle of national treatment should not be underestimated. In addition to its economic dimension it also has an important political function.[102] The perception that products are being discriminated against on the basis of nationality is offensive to political and moral sensibilities. The principle of non-discrimination thus helps to maintain at least the appearance of impartiality. Consequently it facilitates not only trade but also political stability between the trading partners. This principle thus contributes to the WTO's legitimacy in multiple ways.

Summing up, the preamble of the WTO confirms the proposed reading that WTO law – beyond the reduction of tariffs and of trade measures of a similar nature and, of course, the elimination of discrimination – does *not* aim at the general elimination of barriers as envisaged in the ECJ's *Cassis de Dijon* doctrine *or* at market inte-

---

[98] WT/DS26/AB/R (see note 66), para. 8.75 et seq.
[99] WT/DS26/AB/R, WT/DS48/AB/R, (see note 66), para. 165, emph. in original.
[100] Ibid., para. 177.
[101] Similarly WT/DS58/AB/R (see note 93), para. 193; WT/DS2/9 (see note 93), 30.
[102] *Culbertson* (1925), 185 et seq.; *Gardner* (1956), 16, 17.

gration *or* at regulatory competition *or* at free trade. They are not even envisaged in the recitals which set out the overall aims the Contracting Parties want to achieve through further negotiations (Art. III.2 WTO). They cannot *a fortiori* guide the interpretation of current WTO law. All this supports the *coordinated interdependence model*. This understanding can also be applied to the understanding of exceptions and the procedural law of the DSU.[103]

D. WTO Legitimacy Through the Imposition of a New Model of Democratic Legitimacy in an Interdependent World?

1. The Appellate Body's Approach

A most intriguing attempt to deal with the WTO's crisis of legitimacy might be the Appellate Body's attempt to counter a current legitimacy deficit in domestic constitutional systems. It is the nature of the domestic political process that the interests of the polity's citizens enjoy a priority over those of foreigners.[104] Even when the process does not aim at protectionism, home interests tend to be favored and foreign interests neglected. Information, participation and regulatory traditions are control-elements of the regulatory process that reflect domestic interests.[105] Foreign interests, sometimes deeply affected through domestic decisions, do not generally have a standing in domestic procedures. This situation is one of the undemocratic features of globalization: more and more purely "domestic" decisions are having a transnational impact with ever greater significance. This contribution suggests that the Appellate Body's interpretation of WTO law can be understood as aiming to rectify this feature of globalization with multilateralism: when a sovereign decision affects the economic interests of people in other States, their interests must be taken into account, either through a negotiated solution between the affected States, or, if impossible, through "simulated multilateralism" in the domestic process of legislation.

Dependence on external factors, including decisions made in foreign jurisdictions, has become greater. External relations have therefore become more important to the democratic principle, and a self-respecting democracy can no longer afford to keep foreign relations outside the mechanisms of democratic accountability. The

---

[103] On this in more detail *von Bogdandy* (2001) 609, 663 et seq.

[104] *McRae* (2000) 29.

[105] *Poiares Maduro* (1996), 146 et seq.

Appellate Body's decisions can be understood as an attempt to respond to this situation.

In several reports, panels and the Appellate Body have interpreted WTO law as requiring Members who are in non-compliance with basic obligations to seek multilateral solutions with the negatively affected Members, without, however, giving concrete guidance as to the substantive prerequisites.[106] More recently, in *US – Shrimps Recourse to Art. 21.5 of the DSU by Malaysia*, the Appellate Body elaborated to a certain extent as what the requirements regarding the obligation to seek multilateral solutions are.

In this instance the US had successfully conducted multilateral negotiations concerning shrimp harvesting methods that were "turtle friendly" with some of the WTO Members. In the original case, the Appellate Body had found that the US measure as applied to other WTO Members was not consistent with the chapeau to Art. XX GATT in part because the US had failed to conduct similar negotiations with the other trading partners.[107] In the latest case, the Appellate Body specified that the previous negotiations (in this case the Inter-American Convention) should operate as a basis for comparison for negotiations with other Members.[108] The later negotiations "must be comparable in the sense that comparable efforts are made, comparable resources are invested, and comparable energies are devoted to securing an international agreement."[109] Thus, the initial negotiations do not operate as a legal standard, but rather as a factual reference point for the comparison.[110] The negotiations do not need to be successful; there is no requirement that a multilateral agreement actually be concluded.[111] Rather, what is required are "serious, good faith efforts", comparable to the other negotiations,

---

[106] WT/DS2/9 (see note 93), 27; WT/DS58/AB/R (see note 93), para. 174 et seq.

[107] WT/DS58/AB/R (see note 93) para. 172.

[108] WT/DS58/AB/RW *United States – Import Prohibition of Certain Shrimp and Shrimp Products. Recourse to Article 21.5 DSU*, Report of the Appellate Body, para. 130.

[109] Ibid, para. 122.

[110] Ibid, para. 130.

[111] Ibid, para. 123, 124. With respect to taking foreign interests into account, the Appellate Body reiterates that the obligation only amounts to "serious, good faith efforts" to arrive at an international agreement with an affected country, but not to the conclusion of such an agreement since that would amount to a veto of that other country.

aimed at the conclusion of a multilateral agreement. Thus, when it comes to negotiations with WTO Members not included in the original negotiations, the Members now have concrete guidance as to the substantive requirements that must be met in order to comply with the chapeau to Art. XX GATT. Moreover, the Members themselves can, to a significant extent, shape what those substantive requirements are through the extent of their contributions in the original negotiations. What is left unclear, however, is what the substantive requirements are for the initial negotiations, though it has been clear since the *US – Reformulated Gasoline* case that such obligations exist.[112]

This approach is particularly decisive for the analysis of domestic rules primarily aimed at the protection of non-economic interests, e.g. the environment or consumer protection. The importance of the new Shrimps decision can hardly be overemphasized: on the one hand, the legitimacy of trade-limiting environmental measures with an extra-territorial reach has been confirmed.[113] On the other, the obligation to seek multilateral solutions not only serves to guard against protectionist trade barriers,[114] but also to ensure that the needs of the other trade partners are taken into account. In critical situations the Appellate Body proceduralizes the substantive WTO obligations and compels the Members to try to achieve a multilateral consensus. The Members are thus spared from being forced to harmonize their domestic legal orders according to substantive WTO rules.[115]

---

[112] The obligation of cooperation is *also* regarded as the overriding principle in international environmental law, see International Tribunal for the Law of the Sea, Order of 03 December 2001, *The Mox Plant* Case, Separate Opinion of Judge *Wolfrum*, 7 (internet: www.itlos.org). While in the Shrimps case the Appellate Body also argued from international environmental conventions such as the Rio Declaration to establish its claim for international cooperation, it is apparent from *US – Reformulated Gasoline* that this obligation is independent from such conventions. *C. Tietje* correctly claims that international cooperation is one of the most important criteria for the legality of a measure under Art. XX GATT, *Tietje* (2000) 285, 294.

[113] On the importance *Jackson* (2000a) 303, 304; *Shaffer* (1999) 507, 511; *Berger* (1999) 355, 358.

[114] *Neumann* (2001) 529, 538.

[115] This is not to say that the disciplines will not create strong pressure to have similar or substantially the same regimes in many respects. As

This is not to suggest that a general transformation of substantive obligations into procedural requirements should occur: such an understanding is not supported by the reports thus far issued and would contradict the system of many WTO treaties. Procedural requirements have the function of serving the accomplishment of substantive obligations and cannot function as a general substitute for them. This general rule does not, however, exclude interpreting a substantive provision in such a way that it lays down certain procedural and organizational requirements which further the aim of the provision in question.[116]

The procedural requirements, which aim at a multilateral solution to conflicts, have two steps, though the relationship between them remains vague. First, the Appellate Body forces the Members to pursue multilateral cooperation as a means to keeping the effects of trade restrictive measures arising from domestic rules to a minimum.[117] The negotiations should not only be conducted with the other Member States, but also directly with the affected exporters.[118] By requiring negotiations to be conducted with the trading partners as well as with affected private interests, the Appellate Body introduced a procedural prerequisite which extends an important element of the democratic principle to foreign interests. The WTO thus induces an international political process that occurs outside of its institutional framework to come to an international agreement coordinating domestic rules, something which could hardly be convincingly achieved by WTO law on its own.

If the efforts to achieve a multilateral solution to the conflict fail, then the Member may proceed to the second step. In this case, WTO law requires that the Member, in its domestic proceedings, take the interests of the affected Members and their citizens into account, even if there is no special international obligation to do

---

pointed out above, some may consider systematic pressures towards policy convergence to amount to a *de facto* harmonization. Such a harmonization is, however, far less intrusive and far more respectful of legislative autonomy than a *de jure* harmonization.

[116] Some details in WT/DS58/AB/RW (note 108), para. 115 et seq. Most important in this respect is the discussion which derives organizational and procedural standards from fundamental rights, *Vesting* (1997) 94 et seq.

[117] WT/DS2/9 (see note 93), 27; WT/DS58/AB/R (see note 93), para. 174 et seq.

[118] WT/DS2/9 (see note 93), 27.

so.[119] This is especially evident in the Appellate Body's report in the *Reformulated Gasoline* case. There the Appellate Body found that "while the United States counted the cost for its domestic refiners [...], there is nothing [...] to indicate that it did other than disregard that kind of consideration when it came to foreign refiners."[120] It concluded that this "goes well beyond what was necessary for the Panel to determine that a violation of Article III:4 [GATT] had occurred"[121] and that there had been arbitrary discrimination. In other words, the costs and appropriateness of the measures for the trading partners must be included in the policy. This was confirmed in the *United States – Shrimps* case, when the Appellate Body, in finding that there had been arbitrary discrimination, gave weight to the fact that there was no inquiry into the appropriateness of the program for the conditions prevailing in the exporting countries.[122] The application of this regulatory program imposed "a single, rigid and unbending requirement" with "little or no flexibility" and consequently also constituted arbitrary discrimination within the meaning of the chapeau to Art. XX GATT.[123] The implication is that such measures must be designed and applied flexibly, i.e., so that they acknowledge comparable policies adopted by other Members. Although taking foreign interests into account when creating domestic regulations does not achieve "real" multilateralism, it does achieve a "simulated" form of multilateralism. This "simulated multilateralism" preserves the democratic principle by insuring that affected foreign interests are adequately recognized and taken into account in policy formulation. Only after the domestic legislative process has taken these interests into account is it permissible to restrict imports to protect a recognized public good.[124]

---

[119] WT/DS2/9 (see note 93), 28; WT/DS58/AB/R (see note 93), para. 169, 172 et seq.
[120] WT/DS2/9 (see note 93), 26.
[121] Ibid.
[122] WT/DS58/AB/R (see note 93), para. 177.
[123] Ibid.
[124] On such goods see WT/DS135/R *EC – Measures Affecting Asbestos and Asbestos – Containing Products*, Report of the Panel adopted on 18 September 2000, para. 8.180. In the *Canada – Periodicals* case, Canada's argument that its measure was necessary to protect its culture was unsuccessful because this is not a recognized exception under GATT. This creates significant problems for those interested in protecting human or labour rights.

The Appellate Body has not only created prerequisites for the legislative process but also for the application of the norms. The main criteria are the principles of due process and basic fairness, which the Appellate Body developed on the basis of Art. X.3 GATT.[125] In an *a forteriori* conclusion, the Appellate Body applied these principles to measures based on the provisions providing exceptions to GATT.[126] Thus the protection of other Members is to be ensured by procedural means, as is highlighted in the *United States – Shrimps* case. Here the United States relied on an origin-based method to exclude the import of shrimp from its market that were caught with nets not certified as being "turtle friendly" by the US.[127] In concluding that arbitrary discrimination had occurred, the Appellate Body attached great significance to the "singularly informal and casual" nature of the certification process, concluding that it resulted in a denial of both basic fairness and due process.[128] This led the Appellate Body to conclude that the minimum standards for transparency and procedural justice established by Art. X.3 GATT had not been met.[129]

The Appellate Body also found that the measure's lack of flexibility constituted arbitrary or unjustified discrimination:[130] exporting Members were required to adopt essentially the same policies and practices as the US. This constituted unjustifiable discrimination "because the application of the measure at issue did not allow for any inquiry into the appropriateness of the regulatory program for the conditions prevailing in the exporting countries."[131] The revised guidelines condition market access on the adoption of a program of comparable effectiveness. The Appellate Body found that the revised guidelines are sufficiently flexible to take into ac-

---

[125] Due process first used in WT/DS24/AB/R, *US – Restrictions on Cotton and Man-Made Fibre Underwear*, Report of the Appellate Body adopted on 10 February 1997, para. 16.

[126] WT/DS58/AB/R (see note 93), para. 190.

[127] The importing countries had to comply with the guidelines under Section 609(b)(2)(A) and (B). In practice this meant that they were required to use turtle extractor devices. See e.g. ibid., para. 177 et seq.

[128] Ibid., para. 181.

[129] Ibid., para. 183.

[130] Ibid, para. 177 et seq.

[131] WT/DS58/RW *United States – Import Prohibition of certain Shrimp and Shrimp Products,* Report of the panel adopted on 15 June 2001, para. 5.92.

count the specific conditions prevailing in the exporting Member.[132] Moreover, the Appellate Body appeared to be satisfied that its previous concerns about basic fairness and due process had been met by the introduction of new procedures in the certification process.[133] These new procedures include the provision of reasons if the preliminary assessment appears to be negative, the ability of the applicant to supply new information and the correspondent obligation of the US authority to consider this information. Thus, the exporting Members were given a voice so that their individual circumstances can be taken into account. This implies that treatment no less favorable will require different treatment, depending on the circumstances of the exporting Member.

From the foregoing it can be concluded that, in terms of the application of domestic regulatory programs, foreign interests must enjoy a right to be heard. Furthermore, Members are obliged to give reasons in proceedings for the permission to import and sufficient legal protection against the denial of such permission. The far-reaching scope of the publication requirement also serves to protect other Members.[134] The Appellate Body thus extended basic elements of the democratic principle and the rule of law to aliens. Only if these requirements have been met, does the importing Member remain free to pursue its domestic preferences and interests.[135]

The Appellate Body thereby avoids the extremely problematic situation of establishing substantive requirements through concre-

---

[132] WT/DS58/AB/RW (note 108), para. 148, see also para. 142 et seq. It is important to note that this finding concerned the measure on its face, and not its application. Clearly, the application of the measure must also be applied with this flexibility.

[133] Ibid, para. 147.

[134] An important provision of this type is Art. 7 SPS in conjunction with Annex B SPS Agreement. It contains a publication requirement, obliges the Members to create a national information office and provides for a special notification procedure. The Appellate Body gives significant weight to these provisions. In WT/DS76/AB/R *Japan – Measures Affecting Agricultural Products* it decided that the publication requirement for measures regulated by the SPS Agreement was not only applicable to legally enforceable instruments but also to other instruments which are applicable generally and similar in character to those explicitly mentioned, para. 102 – 108. This publication requirement goes well beyond what is constitutionally required in most Member States, *von Bogdandy* (2000) 484 et seq.

[135] WT/DS58/AB/R (see note 93), para. 169 et seq.

tizing WTO provisions; however, it remains to be seen whether and in how far these procedural prerequisites can be implemented effectively in domestic legislative and administrative procedures.

2. Some Remarks

This development might not surprise political scientists insofar as they assume that there is an established principle in international relations that – at least between democratic States – those States negatively affected by a regulation have "full rights of participation".[136] However, from a legal perspective it is most spectacular and a general legal duty can certainly not be assumed.[137] Moreover, this most remarkable interpretation raises a number of constitutional questions. On this reading, WTO law might call on domestic legislatures to introduce major reforms in domestic law. Important changes might have to be introduced into domestic procedures if the requirements of "multilateralism" and of "more objective and rational rule-making" should become a reality.[138] Democratic politics do not always lead to what from a legal or scientific perspective appears as objective and rational rule-making.

Procedural requirements might present even greater challenges for the WTO Members than substantive requirements.[139] Considerable resistance is to be expected, since preferential treatment of the State's own citizens is a basic feature of most current constitutions. WTO law could have a revolutionary impact, because it may require a re-thinking and re-framing of the principle of democracy, the most basic of the principles of the constitutional system of government.

From another perspective such requirements might, however, be more easily squared with established constitutional thinking. It is well acknowledged that sovereignty entails responsibility.[140] For the

---

[136] *Zürn* (1998), 348.
[137] *Wolfrum* (1995) 1242; this is even true in the much developed context of international environmental law; *Stoll* (1996) 39, 44 et seq.
[138] With respect to the European Union, it probably entails that the Directorate General for Agriculture loses its competence to develop policies on health issues and consumer protection, given its protectionist bias.
[139] For the challenges see *S. Cassese* (1999) 321, 326 et. seq.
[140] This is an organizing principle for example for the Charter of Fundamental Rights of the European Union, see Art. 1, 51 I.

domestic dimension of sovereignty, constitutional sovereignty entails constitutional responsibility for those affected. So far this dimension has been based mainly on national fundamental rights which impose duties on the State to protect core interests of the individuals on its territory.[141] The basic idea, applied to the external side of sovereignty in an interdependent world, entails some constitutional responsibility for people living outside the polity as well.[142] Hence, the requirements of WTO law could be construed as concretizing what might be implicit in an adequate constitutional understanding of a State in an interdependent world. To put it another way, a WTO Member is forced to adequately protect the legitimate core interests of its trading partners' subjects when they are affected by the Member's measures. Particularly in an increasingly interdependent world, it is difficult to see why this should be objectionable.[143] Understood this way, WTO law might be seen to complement rather than conflict with the principle of sovereignty.[144] The fundamental changes brought about by this paradigm shift might represent the true constitutional dimension of the WTO, though its implications need much further research.

Beyond these theoretical aspects, a host of more practical institutional questions need to be answered. Procedures have to be devised to identify relevant foreign interests in the course of the domestic legislative or administrative process and to ensure that they can be properly represented. To my knowledge, the relevant reforms have yet to be introduced, and even worse: the relevant provisions are still to be invented.[145] The main reports which led to this interpretation were directed against the United States of America. For a number of reasons rooted in the unique features of its constitutional system, the US has a system of open rule-making which can rather easily accommodate these requirements. For continental European systems a similar development is far more difficult. One might be tempted to observe that the American solution is the most democratic one, with the implication that all other nations should conform to its regulatory mode.[146] Such a premise would need,

---

[141] *Pieroth/Schlink* (1998) 23 et seq., 47 et seq.

[142] Pathbreaking *Langer* (1995) 23 et seq., 51.

[143] Cf. *Petersmann* (2000) 19 et seq.

[144] On this aspect of sovereignty *Dahm/Delbrück/Wolfrum* (1989) § 23 IV 1.

[145] More details in WT/DS58/AB/RW (see note 93), para. 115 et seq.

[146] In this sense *Rose-Ackermann* (1995).

however, further justification. As the importance attributed to institutional and procedural autonomy of the Member States within the framework of the European Union proves,[147] such steps within the far more heterogeneous WTO should be carefully considered.

Also the example of international environmental law, probably the leader with respect to the issue of foreign interest representation, provides only limited help. It is certainly one of environmental law's (soft, customary, treaty) greatest achievements that domestic decision-makers have to adequately take foreign interests affected by the decision into account.[148] However, the idea of representation of foreign interests is mainly based on the good neighbor principle and is directed at administrative decisions.[149] The Aarhus-Convention[150] which leads to harmonized minimum standards with respect to interest representation is telling in this respect: the controversies regarding its elaboration and ratification as well as its limited scope in comparison with the respective obligations that might flow from WTO law clearly show what is at stake.[151]

The Appellate Body is probably aware of these implications of proceduralization. It carefully proves in great detail that in the concrete cases an alternative course has been practically available to and even partly applied by the trade restricting Member.[152] Most important in this respect is its report issued on October 22, 2001.[153] As seen above, in the most recent Shrimps report the Appellate

---

[147] See in particular the Protocol on subsidiarity and proportionality.

[148] In detail *Bothe* (1983) 1; *Bothe* (1988) 186; *Haedrich* (2000) 547, 554 et seq.

[149] *Beyerlin* (2000) 222 et seq.; *OECD* (1976) and *OECD* (1978) 7 et seq., 13 et seq.

[150] Convention on Access to Information, Public Participation in Decision-Making and Access to Justice in Environmental Matters of June 25, 1998, 38 I.L.M. 517 (1999), in particular Art. 6 to 9.

[151] Similarly *Ruffert* (2001) 304, 320.

[152] WT/DS58/AB/R (see note 93), para. 169 et seq., 171.

[153] Another most important feature of the report, namely the final acceptance of the legality of unilateral trade barriers enforcing extraterritorial PPMs (processes and production methods), will not be discussed. It should, however, be noted that any such measures will need to be justified under Art. XX GATT and are not to influence the concept of "like products" under Art. III.4 GATT. For the view that such measures are to be handled under Art. III.4 GATT see *Howse/Regan* (2000) 249.

Body avoids establishing concrete procedural rules regarding the obligation to conduct "serious, good faith negotiations". This is certainly a minimalist reading of the obligations developed in the reports on *Reformulated Gasoline* and *Shrimps*, which appear to leave the domestic constitutional procedures largely unaffected. Similarly cautious is the answer of what is required with respect to "simulated multilateralism". The "simulated multilateralism" requires taking foreign interests autonomously into account in the internal law making procedures. That entails that regulatory progams comparable in effectiveness must be admitted.[154] However, this requirement of flexibility does not imply that specific provisions must address all specific situations in the world; it is enough if the provisions are sufficiently flexible to take the particular situation of any Member adequately into account.[155]

The panel and the Appellate Body appear cautious in advancing the proceduralization of WTO law in order to further global democracy by forcing States to allow affected interests of citizens from other countries access to the domestic procedures. Given the difficult situation of the WTO in general and of the dispute settlement procedure in particular as well as the far-reaching theoretical and practical effects, this strategy appears reasonable. It rather underscores the far-sightedness of these bodies: they have indicated a possible new avenue for global democracy, but leave enough room for the political and scientific arenas to test and develop this avenue.

III. Conclusions

The crisis of legitimacy of WTO law has surprised international lawyers. Most international lawyers assume an inherent legitimacy in multilateral treaty law given its ordering effect on the otherwise *Hobbes*ian relationship between States.[156] Moreover, given the number of studies proving the wealth creating effect of international trade, a substantial "out put legitimacy" of this body of law appears assured because it provides the multilateral rules necessary for a viable trading system. Similarly, the WTO system in principle should enhance the relative position of weaker States against the

---

[154] WT/DS58/AB/RW (see note 108), para. 141.
[155] Ibid, para. 146 et seq.
[156] *Zürn* (1998) 230.

more powerful actors in international trade.[157] Yet, there is no measure by which trade-offs between different forms and bases of legitimacy can be scientifically argued,[158] and it is – as pointed out in this article – undeniable that WTO law presents serious challenges to the established forms of legitimacy-creation through the domestic democratic process. What legal science can do is to investigate the different aspects involved and elaborate the cost and benefits of possible institutional and legal responses, thereby helping to further a more rational debate on a most challenging political and social topic.

Bibliography:

K. Abbott /D. Snidal (2000), Hard and Soft Law in International Governance, International Organization 54 (2000), 421.

E. Altvater /B. Mahnkopf (1999), Grenzen der Gobalisierung. Ökonomie, Ökologie und Politik in der Weltgesellschaft, Münster ⁴1999.

---

[157] This statement reflects the transition from a power-based to a rule-based forum. Furthermore, the jurisprudence of the Appellate Body examined in this article has obviously helped to improve the position of the developing countries. It is not the aim of this article to assess the relative position of the developing countries in the WTO. Nevertheless, a few remarks need to be made because it must be borne in mind that developing countries face many difficulties. First, the WTO still has power oriented elements, see *Salazar-Xirinachs* (2000) 381. Second, the developing countries may face greater problems in either bringing a complaint or defending against a complaint within the WTO because they lack the human and financial resources. Third, and in particular in the context of the TRIPs Agreement, many developing countries face problems implementing the various regimes. Fourth, there are certain asymmetries in the WTO instruments themselves. For example, the GATS does not include rights of mobility for unskilled workers. Fifth, they face difficulties in fully participating, especially in critical sub-WTO bodies such as the CAC. Thus, in assessing the relative position of the developing countries in the WTO a nuanced and differentiated view is required.

[158] *Klein* (1981) 661.

D. Archibugi /D. Beetham (1998), Diritti umani e democrazia cosmopolita, Milano 1998.

P. S. Atiyah /R. S. Summers (1991), Form and Substance in Anglo-American Law, Oxford 1991.

R. Behboodi (2000), 'Should' Means 'Shall': A Critical Analysis of the Obligation to Submit Information under Article 13.1 of the DSU in the *Canada – Aircraft Case*, Journal of International Economic Law 3 (2000) No. 4, 563-592.

M. Beise (2001), Die Welthandelsorganisation (WTO). Funktion, Status, Organisation, Baden-Baden 2001.

W. Benedek (1995), GATT - The Uruguay Round to WTO, in *R. Wolfrum /C. Philipp* (eds.), United Nations: law, policies, and practice, Dordrecht/Boston 1995, 532.

J. Berger (1999), Unilateral Trade Measures to Conserve the World's Living Resources: An Environmental Breakthrough for the GATT in the WTO Sea Turtle Case, Columbia Journal of Environmental Law 24 (1999), 355.

U. Beyerlin (2000), Umweltvölkerrecht, München 2000.

D. Blumenwitz (1984) , Treaties of Friendship, Commerce and Navigation, in *R. Bernhardt* (ed.), Encyclopedia of Public International Law Vol. 7, Amsterdam/London/New York 1984, 318.

E. W. Böckenförde (1991), Demokratie als Verfassungsprinzip, in *idem* (ed.) Staat, Verfassung, Demokratie, Frankfurt am Main 1991, 289.

D. Bodansky (1999), The Legitimacy of International Governance: A Coming Challenge for International Environmental Law?, American Journal of International Law 93 (1999), 596-624.

A. von Bogdandy (2000), Gubernative Rechtsetzung, Tübingen, 2000.

A. von Bogdandy (2001), Law and Politics in the WTO. Strategies to cope with a deficient relationship, Max Planck Yearbook of United Nations Law Vol. 5 (2001), 609-674.

A. von Bogdandy (2002), Legal Equality, Legal Certainty, and Subsidiarity in Transnational Economic Law, in *Y. Mény /P. C.*

Mavroidis / A. von Bogdandy (eds.), Liber amicorum Claus-Dieter Ehlermann, 2002, forthcoming.

M. Bothe (1983), Grenzüberschreitender Verwaltungsrechtsschutz gegen umweltbelastende Anlagen, Umwelt- und Planungsrecht 3 (1983), 1-8.

M. Bothe (1988), Le Tribunal administratif fédéral allemand reconnaît le principe de l'égalité d'accès, Revue juridique de l'environnement 1988, 186-188.

M. Bothe (2001), Environment, Development, Resources, Hague Academy of International Law, Den Haag 2001, forthcoming.

U. Brand / A. Brunnengräber / L. Schrader / C. Stock / P. Wahl (2000), Global Governance. Alternativen zur neoliberalen Globalisierung?, Münster 2000.

R. Breuer (1999), Offene Bürgergesellschaft in der globalisierten Weltwirtschaft, Frankfurter Allgemeine Zeitung, Jan. 4, 1999, 9.

G. de Búrca / J. Scott (2001), The Impact of WTO on EU Decision-Making, in *idem* (eds.), The EU and the WTO. Legal and Constitutional Issues, Oxford 2001, 1-30.

F. Bydlinski (1991), Juristische Methodenlehre, Wien [2]1991.

A. Cassese (1999), I diritti umani nel mondo contemporaneo, Roma [4]1999.

S. Cassese (1999), Gli studi nella rete internazionale di poteri pubblici, Rivista Trimestrale di Diritto pubblico 1999 No. 2, 321-330.

D. Charny (2000), Regulatory Competition and the Global Coordination of Labor Standards, Journal of International Economic Law 3 (2000) No. 2, 281-302.

Commission on Global Governance (1995), Our Global Neighbourhood, Bonn 1995.

W. Culbertson (1925), International Economic Policies, New York 1925.

G. Dahm / J. Delbrück / R. Wolfrum (1989), Völkerrecht I/1, Stuttgart [2]1989.

J. Drexl (1998), Unmittelbare Anwendbarkeit des WTO-Rechts in der globalen Privatrechtsordnung, in *B. Grossfeld* (ed.), Festschrift W. Fikentscher, Tübingen 1998, 841.

The Economist (1990), "World Trade Survey", 22 Sept. 1990, 5.

The Economist (1998), "A Survey of World Trade", 3 Oct. 1998, 4.

B. Eggers (1998), Die Entscheidung des WTO Appelate Body im Hormonfall, Europäische Zeitschrift für Wirtschaftsrecht 5-6/1998, 147-151.

C.-D. Ehlermann/G. Campogrande (1988), Rules on Services in the EEC: A Model for Negotiating World-Wide Rules?, in *E.-U. Petersmann/M. Hilf* (eds.), The New GATT Round of Multilateral Trade Negotiations. Legal and economic problems (= Studies in transnational economic law, Vol. 5), Den Haag 1988, 481.

J. Esser (1990), Grundsatz und Norm, Tübingen ⁴1990.

J. Esser (1999), Der kooperative Nationalstaat im Zeitalter der Globalisierung, in *D. Döring* (ed.), Sozialstaat in der Globalisierung, Frankfurt am Main 1999, 117-144.

European Commission (2001), European Governance: A White Paper, Brussels 2001.

B. Fassbender (1998), UN Security Council Reform and the Right of Veto. A Constitutional Perspective, Den Haag 1998.

W. Fikentscher (1983), Wirtschaftsrecht, Vol. I, München 1983.

B. S. Frey (1985), Internationale Politische Ökonomie, München 1985.

M. Friedman (1962), Kapitalismus und Freiheit, Frankfurt am Main 1962.

R. N. Gardner (1956), Sterling-Dollar Diplomacy, Oxford 1956.

D. J. Gerber (1998), Law and Competition in Twentieth Century Europe, Oxford 1998.

H. H. Glismann /E.-J. Horn /S. Nehring /R. Vaubel (1992), Weltwirtschaftslehre, Vol. I, Göttingen ⁴1992.

J. Goldstein/M. Kahler/R. Keohane/A. Slaughter (2000), Introduction: Legalization and World Politics, International Organization 54 (2000) Special Issue 3, 385-399.

J. Goldstein /L. Martin (2000), Legalization, Trade Liberalization, and Domestic Politics: A Cautionary Note, International Organization 54 (2000), 603-632.

C. A. E. Goodhart (1997), Economics and the Law: Too Much One-Way Traffic?, The Modern Law Review 60 (1997) No. 1, 1-22.

K. Günther (1992), „Ohne weiteres und ganz automatisch?" Zur Wiederentdeckung der „Privatrechtsgesellschaft", Rechtshistorisches Journal 11 (1992), 473-499.

K. Günther (2000), Alles Richtig, Rechtshistorisches Journal, 19 (2000), 232.

M. Haedrich (2000), Internationaler Umweltschutz und Souveränitätsverzicht, Der Staat 39 (2000), 547-569.

H. Hauser (1986), Domestic Policy Foundation and Domestic Policy Function on International Trade Rules, Außenwirtschaft 41 (1986), 171.

G. W. F. Hegel (1821/1970), Grundlinien der Philosophie des Rechts, 1821 (reprint 1970), § 3.

M. Heintzen (2000), Die Legitimation des Europäischen Parlaments, Zeitschrift für Europarechtliche Studien 3 (2000), 377-389.

D. Held (1998), Rethinking Democracy: Globalization and Democratic Theory, in *W. Streek* (ed.), Internationale Wirtschaft, nationale Demokratie, Frankfurt am Main 1998, 59.

M. Hilf /B. Eggers (1997), Der WTO-Panelbericht im EG /USA-Hormonstreit, Europäische Zeitschrift für Wirtschaftsrecht 18/1997, 559-566.

M. Hilf/M. Reuß (1997), Verfassungsfragen lebensmittelrechtlicher Normierung, Zeitschrift für das gesamte Lebensmittelrecht 24 (1997), 289.

E. Hobsbawm (1995), Das Zeitalter der Extreme, München 1995.

O. Höffe (1999), Demokratie im Zeitalter der Globalisierung, München 1999.

H. Hofmann (1997), Legitimität und Rechtsgeltung. Verfassungstheoretische Bemerkungen zu einem Problem der Staatslehre und der Rechtsphilosophie, Berlin 1997.

P. Holmes (2001), The WTO and the EU: Some Constitutional Comparisons, in *G. de Búrca /J. Scott*, The EU and the WTO. Legal and Constitutional Issues, Oxford 2001, 59-80.

R. Howse (2000), Democracy, Science, and Free Trade: Risk Regulation on Trial at the World Trade Organization, Michigan Law Review 98 (2000) No. 7, 2329-2357.

R. Howse (2002), Eyes Wide Shut in Seattle: The Legitimacy of the World Trade Organization, in *V. Heiskanen /J.-M. Coicaud* (eds.), The Legitimacy of International Institutions, Tokyo/New York 2002.

R. Howse /D. Regan (2000), The Product/Process Distinction – An Illusory Basis for Disciplining 'Unilateralism' in Trade Policy, European Journal of International Law 11 (2000) No. 2, 249-290.

R. Howse /K. Nicolaidis (internet), Legitimacy and Global Governance: Why Constitutionalizing the WTO is a Step Too Far, available in the internet at http://www.ksg.harvard.edu/cbg/Conferences/trade/howse.htm.

K. Ipsen (1999), Völkerrecht, München [4]1999.

D. A. Irwin (1996), Against the Tide: An Intellectual History of Free Trade, Princeton 1996.

J. H. Jackson (1991), The world trading system, Cambridge [3]1991.

J. H. Jackson (1998a), The Great 1994 Sovereignty Debate: United States Acceptance and Implementation of the Uruguay Round Results, Columbia Journal of Transnational Law 36 (1998), 157-188.

J. H. Jackson (1998b), The World Trade Organization. Constitution and Jurisprudence, London 1998.

J. H. Jackson (2000), The Jurisprudence of the GATT and the WTO: Insights on Treaty Law and Economic Relations, Cambridge 2000.

J. H. Jackson (2000a), Comments on *Shrimp/Turtle* and the Process /Product Distinction, European Journal of International Law 11 (2000) No. 2, 303-308.

D. Judge (1995), The Failure of National Parliaments?, West European Politics 18 (1995) No. 2, 79-100.

G. Kegel /K. Schurig (2000), Internationales Privatrecht, München [8]2000.

E. Klein (1981), Die Kompetenz- und Rechtskompensation, Deutsches Verwaltungsblatt 1981, 661-667.

B. Kohler-Koch (1998), Regieren in entgrenzten Räumen, Politische Vierteljahresschrift, Sonderheft 29, Opladen 1998.

M. Krajewski (2001), Democratic Legitimacy and Constitutional Perspectives of WTO Law, Journal of World Trade 35 (2001) No. 1, 167-186.

M. Kriele (1976), Theorie der Rechtsgewinnung, Berlin [2]1976.

S. Langer (1995), Grundlagen einer internationalen Wirtschaftsverfassung, München 1995.

C. L. Lofdahl (1998), On the Environmental Externalities of Global Trade, International Political Science Review 19 (1998) No. 4, 339-356.

N. Luhmann (1995), Das Recht der Gesellschaft, Frankfurt am Main 1995.

G. Marceau /P. N. Pedersen (1999), Is the WTO Open and Transparent? A Discussion of the Relationship of the WTO with Nongovernmental Organisations and Civil Society's Claims for more Transparency and Public Participation, Journal of World Trade 33 (1999) No. 1, 5-49.

D. McRae (2000), The WTO in International Law: Tradition Continued or New Frontier?, Journal of International Economic Law 3 (2000) No. 1, 27-41.

W. Meng (1995), Gedanken zur Frage unmittelbarer Anwendung von WTO-Recht in der EG, in *U. Beyerlin/M. Bothe/R. Hofmann /E.-U. Petersmann* (eds.), Recht zwischen Umbruch und Bewahrung, Festschrift für Rudolf Bernhardt, Berlin 1995, 1061-1086.

W. Meng (1998), WTO-Recht als Steuerungsmechanismus der neuen Welthandelsordnung, in *M. Klein/W. Meng/F. Rode* (eds.), Die neue Welthandelsordnung der WTO, Amsterdam 1998, 19-74.

D. Messner /F. Nuscheler (1996), Global Governance. Organisationselemente und Säulen einer Weltordnungspolitik, in *idem* (eds.), Weltkonferenzen und Weltberichte. Ein Wegweiser durch die internationale Diskussion, Bonn 1996, 12-36.

D. Messner /F. Nuscheler (1997), Global Governance. Herausforderungen an der Schwelle zum 21. Jahrhundert, in *D. Senghaas* (ed.), Frieden machen, Frankfurt am Main 1997, 337-361.

E.-J. Mestmäcker (1989), Der Kampf ums Recht in der offenen Gesellschaft, Rechtstheorie 20 (1989), 273-288.

E.-J. Mestmäcker (1991), Die Wiederkehr der bürgerlichen Gesellschaft und ihres Rechts, Rechtshistorisches Journal 10 (1991), 177-192.

C. Möllers (2001), Globalisierte Jurisprudenz, in *M. Anderheiden et al.* (eds.), Globalisierung als Problem von Gerechtigkeit und Steuerungsfähigkeit des Rechts, Stuttgart 2001.

M. Nettesheim (2001), Von der Verhandlungsdiplomatie zur internationalen Verfassungsordnung, in *C. D. Classen* (ed.), In einem vereinten Europa dem Frieden der Welt zu dienen, Liber amicorum Thomas Oppermann, Berlin 2001, 381-409.

J. Neumann (2001), Die materielle und prozessuale Koordination völkerrechtlicher Ordnungen. Die Problematik paralleler Streitbeilegungsverfahren am Beispiel des *Schwertfisch*-Falls, Zeitschrift für ausländisches öffentliches Recht und Völkerrecht 61 (2001), 529-572.

P. Norton (1998), National Parliaments and the European Union: where to from here, in *P. Craig/C. Harlow* (eds.), Lawmaking in the European Union, London 1998, 209-222.

OECD (1976), Recommendation of the Council on Equal Right of Access in Relation to Transfrontier Pollution, Res. C(76) (Final), in *OECD*, Non-Discrimination in Relation to Transfrontier Pollution, Paris 1978.

OECD (1978), Report on the Implementation of a Regime of Equal Right of Access and Non-Discrimination in Relation to Transfrontier Pollution, Report by the OECD Secretary General, in *OECD*, Non-Discrimination in Relation to Transfrontier Pollution, Paris 1978.

J. Pauwelyn (1999), The WTO agreement on sanitary and phyto-sanitary (SPS) measures as applied in the first three SPS disputes. *EC – Hormones, Australia – salmon and Japan – varietals*, Journal of International Economic Law 2 (1999) No. 4, 641-664.

P. Perkins (1998), Sustainable Trade: theoretical approaches, in *R. Keil/L. Fawcett* (eds.), Political Ecology, London 1998, 46-67.

E.-U. Petersmann (1991), Constitutional Functions and Constitutional Problems of International Economic Law, Fribourg 1991.

E.-U. Petersmann (1995), The Transformation of the World Trading System through the 1994 Agreement Establishing the World Trade Organization, European Journal of International Law 6 (1995) No. 2, 161-221.

E.-U. Petersmann (1996), International Competition for Governments and for Private Business, Journal of World Trade 30 (1996) No. 3, 5-35.

E.-U. Petersmann (1997), International Trade Order and International Trade Law, in *T. Oppermann /E.-U. Petersmann* (eds.), Reforming the International Economic Order, Berlin 1997.

E.-U. Petersmann (2000), The WTO Constitution and Human Rights, Journal of International Economic Law 3 (2000) No. 1, 19-25.

E.-U. Petersmann (2000a), From "negative" to "positive" integration in the WTO, Common Market Law Review 37 (2000) No. 6, 1363-1382.

E.-U. Petersmann (2001), European and International Constitutional Law: Time for Promoting "Cosmopolitan Democracy" in the WTO, in *G. de Búrca/J. Scott*, The EU and the WTO. Legal and Constitutional Issues, Oxford 2001, 81-110.

B. Pieroth/B. Schlink (1998), Grundrechte Staatsrecht II, Heidelberg [14]1998.

M. Poiares Maduro (1998), We, the court. The European Court of Justice and the European Economic Constitution, Oxford 1998.

A. Quick/R. Blüthner (1999), Has the Appellate Body Erred?, Journal of International Economic Law 2 (1999) No. 4, 603-639.

M. Ritter (1997), Das WTO-Übereinkommen und seine Auswirkungen auf das Deutsche und Europäische Lebensmittelrecht, Europäische Zeitschrift für Wirtschaftsrecht 5/1997, 133-138.

F. Roessler (1986), Competition and Trade Politics, Außenwirtschaft 41 (1986), 467.

F. Roessler (1987), The Competence of GATT, Journal of World Trade Law 21 (1987) No. 3, 73-83.

A. Rosas (2001), Implementation and Enforcement of WTO Dispute Settlement Findings: An EU Perspective, Journal of International Economic Law 4 (2001) No. 4, 131-144.

S. Rose-Ackermann (1995), Umweltrecht, Baden-Baden 1995.

A. Ross (1929), Theorie der Rechtsquellen, Leipzig/Wien 1929.

M. Ruffert (2001), Der Entscheidungsmaßstab im WTO-Streitbeilegungsverfahren – Prozessuale Relativierung materieller Verpflichtungen?, Zeitschrift für Vergleichende Rechtswissenschaft 100 (2001), 304-321.

J. G. Ruggie (1983), International Regimes, Transactions, and Change. Embedded Liberalism in the Postwar Economic Order, in *S. Krasner* (ed.), International Regimes, Ithaca 1983, 195-231.

J. Sack (1997), Von der Geschlossenheit und den Spannungsfeldern in einer Weltordnung des Rechts, Europäische Zeitschrift für Wirtschaftsrecht 21/1997, 650-651.

J. Salazar-Xirinachs (2000), The Trade-Labour Nexus: Developing Countries' Perspectives, Journal of International Economic Law 3 (2000) No. 2, 377-385.

G. Sandner (2000), Gesundheitsschutz in der WTO – eine neue Bedeutung des Codex Alimentarius im Lebensmittelrecht?, Zeitschrift für europäische Studien 3 (2000), 335-375.

A. Schäfers (1996), Normsetzung zum geistigen Eigentum in internationalen Organisationen, WIPO und WTO – ein Vergleich, Zeitschrift für gewerblichen Rechtsschutz und Urheberrecht – internationaler Teil 1996, 763-778.

R. Schmidt (1988), Staatliche Verantwortung für die Wirtschaft, in *J. Isensee /P. Kirchhof* (eds.), Handbuch des Staatsrechts des Bundesrepublik Deutschland, Vol. III, Heidelberg 1988, § 83.

J. Scholte/R. O'Brien/M. Williams (1999), The WTO and Civil Society, Journal of World Trade 33 (1999) No. 1, 107-123.

R. Senti (1994), Die neue Welthandelsordnung. Ergebnisse der Uruguay-Runde, Chancen und Risiken, ORDO 45 (1994), 301-314.

G. C. Shaffer (1999), International decisions, US-Shrimp, American Journal of International Law 93 (1999), 507.

G. C. Shaffer (2001), The World Trade Organization Under Challenge: Democracy and the Law and Politics of the WTO's Treatment of Trade and Environment Matters, Harvard Environmental Law Review 25 (2001) No. 1, 1-50.

M. Shapiro (1999), The European Court of Justice, in *P. Craig/G. de Búrca* (eds.), The Evolution of EU Law, Oxford 1999, 321-348.

G. Shell (1995), Trade Legalism and International Relation Theory, Duke Law Journal 44 (1995), 829.

P.-T. Stoll (1994), Die WTO: Neue Welthandelsorganisation, neue Welthandelsordnung, Zeitschrift für ausländisches öffentliches Recht und Völkerrecht 54 (1994), 241-338.

P.-T. Stoll (1996), The International Environmental Law of Cooperation, in *R. Wolfrum* (ed.), Enforcing Environmental Standards: Economic Mechanisms as Viable Means, Berlin 1996, 39-93.

G. Teubner (2000), Privatregimes: Neo-Spontanes Recht und duale Sozialverfassung in der Weltgesellschaft, in *D. Simon/M. Weiss* (eds.), Zur Autonomie des Individuums, liber amicorum Spiros Simitis, Baden-Baden 2000, 437-453.

C. Tietje (2000), Die völkerrechtliche Kooperationspflicht im Spannungsverhältnis Welthandel /Umweltschutz und ihre Bedeutung für die europäische Umweltblume, Europarecht 35 (2000) No. 2, 285-296.

C. Tomuschat (1998), Das Strafgesetzbuch der Verbrechen gegen den Frieden und die Sicherheit der Menschheit, Europäische Grundrechte-Zeitschrift 25 (1998) No. 1-4, 1-7.

J. Tumlir (1983), International Economic Order and Democratic Constitutionalism, ORDO 34 (1983), 71-83.

J. Tumlir (1986), GATT Rules and Community Law, in *M. Hilf/F. Jacobs/E.-U. Petersmann* (eds.), The European Community and GATT, Baden-Baden 1986, 1.

G. de Vergottini (1999), Diritto costituzionale comparato, Padova ⁵1999.

T. Vesting (1997), Prozedurales Rundfunkrecht, Baden-Baden 1997.

L. Wallach/M. Sforza (1999), Whose Trade Organization?, Washington D. C. 1999.

M. Weber (1988), Die ‚Objektivität' sozialwissenschaftlicher Erkenntnis, in *idem* (ed.), Gesammelte Aufsätze zur Wissenschaftslehre, Tübingen ⁷1988.

P. Weis/A. Zimmermann (1995), Emigration, in *R. Bernhardt* (ed.), Encyclopedia of Public International Law, Vol. II, Amsterdam 1995.

R. Wolfrum (1995), International Law of Cooperation, in *R. Bernhardt* (ed.), Encyclopedia of Public International Law, Consolidated Edition Vol. 2, Amsterdam 1995.

A. Zimmermann (1998), Die Schaffung eines ständigen Internationalen Strafgerichtshofes, Zeitschrift für ausländisches öffentliches Recht und Völkerrecht 58 (1998), 47-107.

P. Zumbansen (2001), Spiegelungen von "Staat und Recht". Governance-Erfahrungen in der Globalisierungsdebatte, in *M. Anderheiden et al.* (eds.), Globalisierung als Problem von Gerechtigkeit und Steuerungsfähigkeit des Rechts, Stuttgart 2001.

M. Zürn (1998), Regieren jenseits des Nationalstaates, Frankfurt am Main 1998.

Gerhard Hafner

The Effect of Soft Law on International Economic Relations

I. Introduction

In modern times, the question of the possible impact of soft law on international economic relations has become an issue of major importance as this problem affects the whole field of international relations. Soft law is increasingly considered as an appropriate instrument to shape international relations in general and hardly any issue of international relations can be deemed to be free of economic aspects. Therefore to the extent that general conclusions on soft law will necessarily apply to economic matters, the economic aspect of the soft law problematic will be addressed as far as necessary.

In order to reach certain conclusions it is necessary first to identify and define soft law, second, to discuss the differences and similarities of soft and hard law and ponder on the possible disadvantages of soft law; third, to discuss the effects such instruments could have on international relations; fourth, to assess the means to increase its effectiveness, and fifth, to identify the reasons why States increasingly resort to it.

II.   Soft Law

Since the middle of the XXth century, a long discussion on the definition of soft law in contrast to hard law or black letter law has emerged. One could very quickly end the discussion on this issue by denying the existence of any soft law at all: Either it is law or not; soft law is a *contradictio in adiecto* so that it would be impossible to speak about it.

Although this sounds quite logical, international practice did, however, not follow this logic but uses this term of soft law with increasing intensity so that it can no longer be ignored when dealing with international matters.

As used in international practice, this term covers an extremely broad range of international instruments; they may be

- resolutions of international organisations,
- resolutions or declarations of international conferences,
- declarations of summit meetings of high political personalities,
- conclusions in the framework of the OSCE,
- even, conclusions of the presidency of the EU,
- results of meetings of bilateral nature such as the meeting of Melk,[1] or the Memorandum of Moscow,[2]

---

[1]   The Meeting of Melk was a meeting of the Federal Chancellor of Austria and the Prime Minister of the Czech Republic on 12 December 2000 concerning the issue of the nuclear power station Temelín situated in Czech Republic near the common border. This agreement resulted in an "Agreement" which was not considered as amounting to a treaty in the formal sense.

[2]   The Memorandum of Moscow of 13 March 1955 which was agreed upon by the delegations of Austria and the Soviet Union opened the way to the Austrian State Treaty 1955. It is seen as constituting not a

- even unilateral statements,
- or recommendations in the framework of the WTO Dispute Settlement procedure.[3]

Hence, dealing with soft law, one faces the broadest spectrum of international instruments so that it would be extremely difficult to identify the features common to them. But in any case, two distinctive elements can be singled out which separate these instruments on the one side from acts which fall neither under soft law nor under hard law and on the other from acts qualifying as hard law:

- These acts are performed by officials of State in their capacity as such so that they are attributable to the States and
- they do not constitute hard law in the sense that they have not that legally binding effect which is accorded to hard law.

A. Attributability

Although the distinction according to whom the act is attributable, to the individual person or to the State, seems to be a relatively easy issue, it nevertheless could pose problems since a certain confusion exists concerning the so-called gentlemen's agreements: In the Anglo-Saxon doctrine they are conceived as acts which are attributable only to the persons involved and not to the State they normally represent[4] whereas in French doctrine this term includes also acts which are attributable to the States.[5] For the sake of clarity, it seems more useful to proceed from the conception that gentlemen's agreements produce effects only in relations of the persons involved in their personal capacity.

---

treaty, but a commitment of the both delegations (*Neuhold/Hummer/ Schreuer* (1997) 55).

[3]   Cf. Article 19 Dispute Settlement Understanding: "Panel and Appellate Body Recommendations".
"1.Where a panel or the Appellate Body concludes that a measure is inconsistent with a covered agreement, it shall recommend that the Member concerned bring the measure into conformity with that agreement. In addition to its recommendations, the panel or Appellate Body may suggest ways in which the Member concerned could implement the recommendations. 2. In accordance with paragraph 2 of Article 3, in their findings and recommendations, the panel and Appellate Body cannot add to or diminish the rights and obligations provided in the covered agreements".

[4]   *Sinclair/Dickson* (1995) 225; *Fiedler* (1984) 105.
[5]   *Eisemann* (1979).

But even the resort to the criterion of attributability does not entirely rule out problems in the distinction between soft law instruments and acts which do not possess even this quality. To give an example: The Memorandum of Moscow has been qualified as a "Verwendungszusage", i.e. a commitment of endeavour of the delegations. Should this mean that this instrument did not at all concern the State itself? This conclusion is to be doubted; one could rather conclude that this instrument was attributable to States since it was the result of official State-to-State negotiations, but imposed duties only on the delegations. And despite this restriction of the effect of the obligations, it was attributable to the State insofar as the delegations accepted the obligations as State organs and not in their private capacity. Contrary to this, the qualification of the results of meetings like the World Economic Forum in St Moritz or, more recently in New York,[6] where high State officials participate are attributable only to the persons involved. However, the question whether the declarations of the G-7 (G-8) Summit are attributable only to the persons in their private capacity or to States is to be answered in favour of the attributability to the States. This conclusion is warranted by the terminology used in the results of the G-8 meetings since the text clearly establishes a direct link between the declaration and the persons articulating it:

"We, the Heads of State and Government of eight major industrialised democracies and the Representatives of the European Union, met in Genoa for the first Summit of the new millennium. In a spirit of co-operation, we discussed the most pressing issues on the international agenda".[7]

The first result to be deduced from these examples is that a precise categorization can only be based on the text of these instruments and on the context in which these instruments are drawn up. The second conclusion is that acts which are not attributable to States should be excluded from the further discussion of soft law since otherwise this latter term would lose any significance. To include also instruments such as texts elaborated by NGOs would – irrespective of the authority they could develop – certainly totally obfuscate and render meaningless the term of soft law.

---

[6]   The most recent Forum was held in New York, 3-5 February 2002.
[7]   Final Communiqué of the Genoa Meeting, July 22, 2001.

B. The Particular Legal Effect of Hard Law

As to the other side of the spectrum of international instruments, those of hard law nature, some more complex discussions on the particular effects of hard law which distinguishes it from soft law are needed.

Any enunciation has an effect either on the actor himself or on others to whom it is communicated. This effect can be of different nature: moral, political, or legal. In this context, it is the legal effect which is decisive to separate acts which are called hard law from others. In international law, this legal effect means that the non-compliance has a certain negative effect which materializes in the law of State responsibility.[8] Non-compliance triggers off consequences such as the duty of restoration, compensation, satisfaction, etc.[9] At the same time the injured State can take countermeasures and invoke the violation before an international dispute settlement instrument entailing binding decisions.[10] In economic terms, these consequences of non-compliance can be regarded as some sort of costs[11] which a State has to take into account when it evaluates the consequences of its decisions. The State must include into its foreign policy analysis these consequences which present themselves as external effects or costs. In this respect, an analogy could be drawn to the "polluter-pays-principle" according to which a State would have to internalize the external effects of its activities. And this internalization must be done already in the course of the first stages of the decision making process. These costs also include the possibility that the other State will resort to an international dispute settlement procedure in case of alleged non-compliance, what undoubtedly also entails substantial costs.

These facts exercise a certain preventive effect since States because of these consequences will rather abstain from breaching such rules and the other States could rely on this position. Hence, these costs are an important factor which contributes to a greater efficiency and effect of instruments of such kind. In more legal terms,

---

[8] See the Articles on Responsibility of States for internationally wrongful acts, elaborated by the International Law Commission 2001, Official records of the GA, 56th session, Supplement No 10 (A/56/10), (chp. IV.E.1).

[9] Article 28, article 34 ILC Draft Articles *supra* note 7

[10] Article 49, article 52 ILC Draft Articles *supra* note 7

[11] *Neuhold* (1999) 91 et seq.

it must also be borne in mind that these instruments have a certain legal effect also within the domestic legal order insofar as – speaking *grosso modo* – they are able to amend national laws.

A further effect consists in the reduction of the complexities of international relations.[12] If a State deviates from the established patterns of behaviour, other States would also be free to do the same so that any predictability and certainty of future behaviour would be lost. Applying the concept developed by *Luhmann*,[13] one could come to the conclusion that because of costly consequences of non-compliance with legal regulations a State could expect that the other State would rather comply with the regulation than deviate therefrom. It can be expected that the conduct of this other State will remain within the boundaries of the relevant regulation unless extremely important reasons compel the State to deviate therefrom. Legal instruments are therefore the most effective means (in legal terms) to ensure a certain predictability of the conduct of States, a predictability which is required for any stable and smooth development of international, in particular economic, relations.

Instruments which do not entail such consequences lack a certain mechanism which ensures their compliance. In such a situation, a State cannot be sure to the same extent as in the case of legal regulation that the other States will abide by the provisions of the instrument. The question might therefore arise as to how far such instruments are in effect able to ensure a certain predictability of behaviour of States. In any case these instruments are less able to produce such an effect than legal texts.

III.   Distinction Between Hard and Soft Law

A. The Form of the Act

The different legal effect of hard law and soft law, however, is only a consequence of the distinction between them so that the question remains how to distinguish between them on the basis of their outer appearance.

As far as bi- or multilateral instruments are concerned, the distinction seems to be rather clear insofar as the hard law instruments must materialize in the form of treaties which are very formal instruments. They require formal expressions of consent in order to

---

[12]   According to *Luhmann* (1973) *passim*.
[13]   *Luhmann* (1973) *passim*.

be effective on a State. Although the Vienna Convention on the Law of Treaties of 1969 (VCLT) defines the various means by which the consent to be bound can be expressed such as signature, exchange of instruments constituting a treaty, ratification, acceptance, approval or accession,[14] the distinction between these two categories of instruments is not always easy to achieve: The most recent example is the legal nature of the Brussels Agreement regarding Temelín[15] since it was argued that this instrument did not amount to a treaty. Another example is the 1997 Founding Act on Mutual Relations, Cooperation and Security between NATO and the Russian Federation which was subject of controversies concerning its legal nature. The categorization certainly depends on the intention of the parties which is reflected in certain objective elements of the treaty text.[16]

A much more difficult issue is the distinction between unilateral acts or joint unilateral acts which entail a legal effect and therefore belong to the category of hard law and other unilateral enunciations. The ILC is presently discussing the issue of unilateral acts; but already the definition seems rather doubtful.[17] What can be acknowledged at the moment is that the intention of the author of the declaration to produce a legal effect is decisive. To give an example: The

---

[14] Article 11 of the VCLT reads as follows:
"Means of expressing consent to be bound by a treaty
The consent of a State to be bound by a treaty may be expressed by signature, exchange of instruments constituting a treaty, ratification, acceptance, approval or accession, or by any other means if so agreed."

[15] In December 2001, the heads of the Governments of Austria and Czech Republic, accompanied by a Member of the Commission of the European Union, signed a text relating to the Nuclear Power Station Temelín, which was neither submitted to the respective Parliaments for approval nor ratified by the Heads of states. The question was raised whether this text amounted to a treaty in the technical sense, but met with a negative answer.

[16] Cf the view of the ILC reflected in the commentary on draft article 2, reproduced in *Rauschning* (1978) 83; *Rotter* (1971) 432.

[17] The most recent definition runs as follows: "For the purpose of the present articles, 'unilateral act of a State' means an unequivocal expression of will which is formulated by a State with the intention of producing legal effects in relation to one or more other States or international organizations, and which is known to that State or international organization", ILC 52nd session 2000, Third report on unilateral acts of States, A/CN.4/505, 13.

CSCE Final Act 1975 belongs undoubtedly to soft law: however, it was also argued that it consists of unilateral promises entered into by the participating States.[18] Certainly this document contains such unilateral commitments; however, they could hardly be deemed as promises with full legal effect since the context was not such which did generate such effect.

B. The Process of Formation

One particular distinction has also to be stated without any indication as to whether it has negative or positive implications: Foreign policy is usually target of criticism since it is mostly performed by the executive power of a State and therefore subject to a democratic deficit. However, as far as binding rules are concerned they are to a certain extent subject to the principle of democracy insofar as the parliaments are mostly implied in the process of the decision-making on the binding effect. In Austria this is achieved through articles 50 and 65 of the Austrian Constitution (B-VG) which ensure parliamentary participation in this procedure so that the executive power cannot act without co-operation of the legislative power.[19] The only exceptions are agreements according to article 66

---

[18] So the Austrian Federal Chancellor Dr. *Bruno Kreisky* in the answer to a parliamentary question where he stated that the provisions of the Helsinki Act included "a broad range of declarations of intent, concessions and norms of conduct" (*Hafner* (1980) 320).

[19] Article 50 reads: "(1) Political treaties, and others in so far as their contents modify or complement existent laws and do not fall under Art. 16 para. 1, may only be concluded with sanction of the National Council. In so far as such treaties settle matters within the autonomous sphere of competence of the Laender, they require in addition the approval of the Federal Council. (2) At the time of giving its sanction to a treaty which falls under para. 1 above, the National Council can vote that the treaty in question shall be implemented by the issue of laws. (3) Art. 42 paras. 1 to 4 inclusive and, should constitutional law be modified or complemented by treaty, Art. 44 paras. 1 and 2 shall be analogously applied to resolutions of the National Council in accordance with paras. 1 and 2 above. In a vote of sanction adopted pursuant to para. 1 above, such treaties or such provisions as are contained in treaties shall be explicitly specified as "modifying the constitution"; article 65 (1) reads: "(1) The Federal President represents the Republic internationally, receives and accredits envoys, sanctions the appointment of foreign consuls, appoints the consular representatives of the Republic abroad and concludes treaties. At the

(2) B-VG which empowers the Federal President to delegate the treaty-making competence to the government or individual ministers.[20] Non-legal instruments, however, remain exclusively within the competencies of the executive power. Whereas treaties which even do not need parliamentary approval must remain within the parameters of the legislation, the non-legal instruments are not restricted in this way, they could and do exceed such limits.[21] There is only one exception to this rule insofar as, in Austria, even in the field of soft law the parliament is involved, but this involvement is restricted to the area of the EU: Article 23 e B-VG ensures the possible participation of the parliament, represented by its main committee, in the decision-making process within the EU.[22] It is only to

---

time of conclusion of a treaty not falling under Art. 50 or a treaty pursuant to Art. 16 para. 1 which neither modifies nor complements existent laws, he can direct that the treaty in question shall be implemented by the issue of ordinances", English version edited by Bundeskanzleramt, Bundespressedienst Wien 2000, http://www. bka.gv.at/bka/service/publikationen/verfassung.pdf.

[20] Article 66 (2) reads: "(2) The Federal President can authorize the Federal Government to conclude certain categories of treaties which do not fall under Art. 16 para. 1 nor under Art. 50; such an authorization extends also to the powers to order that these treaties shall be implemented by the issue of ordinances", see *supra* note 15.
The declaration of the Federal President of 31 December 1920 established the treaty-making power of the Federal Government, individual Federal Ministries either in conjunction with the Foreign Ministry or alone.

[21] See, *Hillgenberg* (1999) 503 et seq. considering the German Basic Law.

[22] Article 23 e reads: "(1) The competent member of the Federal Government shall without delay inform the National Council and the Federal Council about all projects within the framework of the European Union and afford them opportunity to vent their opinion. (2) Is the competent member of the Federal Government in possession of an opinion by the National Council about a project within the framework of the European Union which shall be passed into Federal law or which bears upon the issue of a directly applicable juridical act concerning matters which would need to be settled by Federal legislation, then the member is bound by this opinion during European Union negotiations and voting. Deviation is only admissible for imperative foreign and integrative policy reasons. (3) If the competent member of the Federal Government wishes to deviate from an opinion by the National Council pursuant to para. 2 above, then the National

be questioned whether the parliament is in a position to make use of this competence in order to develop a foreign policy on its own.

C. Certainty of Compliance

Furthermore, non-legal instruments certainly cannot develop such a certainty of compliance as treaties. So for instance, the investigations on how far the G-7/8 summit declarations were com-

---

Council shall again be approached. In so far as the juridical act under preparation by the European Union would signify an amendment to existing Federal constitutional law, a deviation is at all events only admissible if the National Council does not controvert it within an appropriate time. (4) If the National Council has pursuant to para. 2 above delivered an opinion, then the competent member of the Federal Government shall report to the National Council after the vote in the European Union. In particular the competent member of the Federal Government shall, if deviation from an opinion by the National Council has occurred, without delay inform the National Council of the reasons therefore. (5) The maintenance of the National Council's competencies pursuant to paras. 1 to 4 above is in principle incumbent on its Main Committee. The more detailed provisions relating to this will be settled by the Federal law on the National Council's Standing Orders. On this occasion there can be settled in particular the extent to which a separate standing sub-committee of the Main Committee shall for the treatment of projects within the framework of the European Union be competent and the maintenance of the National Council's competencies pursuant to paras. 1 to 4 above is reserved to the National Council itself. Art. 55 para. 2 holds good for the standing sub-committee. (6) Is the competent member of the Federal Government in possession of an opinion by the Federal Council about a project within the framework of the European Union which needs imperatively be implemented by a Federal constitutional law that would be in accordance with Art. 44 para. 2 require the agreement of the Federal Council, then the member is bound by its opinion during European Union negotiations and voting. Deviation is only admissible for imperative foreign and integrative policy reasons. The maintenance of the Federal Council's competencies pursuant to para. 1 above and this paragraph will be settled in more detail by the Standing Order of the Federal Council. On this occasion there can be settled in particular the extent to which a specifically designated committee shall for the treatment of projects within the framework of the European Union be competent instead of the Federal Council and the extent to which the maintenance of the Federal Council's competencies pursuant to the first paragraph and this paragraph is reserved to the Federal Council itself", see *supra* note 15.

plied with led to the following result: The question was asked as to what extent has the summit process in fact influenced and shaped the course of economic and political events. How effective has it actually been in building co-operative relations between states? Generally speaking, the compliance score was extremely dispersed, the record showed compliance from even 0% to 100%, depending on the state investigated, the particular obligation and the circumstances of compliance. American compliance scores for debt relief have increased progressively from 0% concerning the results of the summit in Lyon to 80% with relation to that in Cologne while its record on trade was more variable: 0% in 1996, 40% in 1997, 0% in 1998, and 80% in 1999. In contrast to the United States, the pattern of Canada's results were not consistent for the issue of debt relief, in that Canada scored 80% compliance in 1996 and 1999 and 0% in 1997 and 1998. On the trade front, Canada observed more stable compliance levels, scoring in the 70% to 80% compliance level range for all the summits except Denver 1997, where it scored a low of 40%. Hence, it is difficult to expect a certain compliance record for such instruments, because too many factors are involved. However, it can quite safely be stated that 0% is extremely exceptional so that a record of between 55 and 75% can easily be expected.[23]

D. Acceptance Procedure

Treaties require a formal commitment in order to be binding upon a State. No State can be forced to accept a treaty as binding. For this reason, in order to assess the binding effect of a treaty in a given case, it has always to be established which States are bound by it. It occurs rather frequently that treaties are not applicable at all because of the lack of the necessary ratification or other consent to be bound.[24] Likewise, very often a double standard cannot be avoided where only some States are bound by a certain treaty aiming at a general regulation and the other apply customary international law. Non-legal instruments are different: They do not depend on such formal procedures in order to produce their effect on States

---

[23] *Juricevic* (1999).

[24] In this respect the question about the legal effect of treaties which have not entered into force arises; some authors ascribe such treaties a certain effect insofar as States tend to comply with them in view of the vagueness of customary international law. It could even be assumed that such treaties are comparable to soft law instruments.

and – totally contrary to the treaties – could even produce such an effect for States which were overruled, i.e. which did not consent to the regulation in the case of majority decision-making. In such a situation a double standard could be avoided, albeit at the expense of less stringency.

E. Reservations

Treaties produce a stringent effect and are strictly to be complied with.[25] States have the possibility in case of multilateral treaties to deviate from the treaty only by making reservations (unless there are other means provided in the treaty itself).[26] These reservations again are subject to a relatively strict procedure and to certain limitations.[27] Non-legal instruments are normally not accompanied by reservations. Of course, States frequently declare by explanation of vote that they would have problems to abide by one or the other part of the instrument, but genuine reservations are rather the exception. This is to be explained by the less stringent effect of such instrument so that States see no need to make formal declarations to this effect.

Hence, although in doctrine very often doubts have been raised as to the usefulness of a distinction between hard and soft law,[28] the distinction nevertheless must not be neglected since otherwise the interplay between the different instruments and international relations could not be correctly assessed.

IV.   The Advantages of Soft Law

Despite these weaknesses of soft law, it nevertheless produces a certain steering effect on the attitude of States. It is possible to distinguish the following different aspects of this steering effect:
- Soft law instruments have been used in order to draw the attention of the States to a certain new problems of general importance which have been likely to become significant for the international relations. A striking example is the Declaration on

---

[25] Article 25 VCLT.
[26] See Draft Guideline 1.7.1 (Alternatives to reservations and interpretative declarations) of the Guide to Practice concerning Reservation to Treaties, as adopted by the ILC, see: Report of the ILC, *supra*, fn 8, 455.
[27] Article 19-23 VCLT.
[28] Cf. *Zemanek* (1997) 141.

Human Environment of 1972[29] which, for the first time, raised the issue of the protection of the environment on a global level.

- Soft law has been used in order to make attempts of changing certain basic rules of international relations: So, for instance, through the Charter of Economic Rights and Duties of States[30] developing countries attempted to change the fundamental rules of the North-South relations.

- Soft law instruments can exercise a pre-normative effect insofar as they may become the germ for the creation of binding rules through international customary law or treaty law: The best examples are the General Assembly Resolutions on the Peaceful Uses of Outer Space,[31] on the Peaceful Uses of the International Seabed and Ocean Floor,[32] on the Protection of Human Rights[33] which was referred to in Principle 7 of the CSCE Final Act of Helsinki.[34] But contrary to some conclusions contained in the report of the International Law Association on Customary Law adopted 2001,[35] it can hardly be stated that e.g. unanimously or almost unanimously adopted resolutions of the General Assembly already constitute customary international law. Of course, this particular issue which was discussed in the International Law Association accentuates the political problem involved in

---

[29] UN Doc. A/CONF.48/14.

[30] UN Doc. GA RES 3281 (XXIX).

[31] UN Doc. GA RES 1348 (XIII).

[32] GA RES 2749 (XXV).

[33] The Universal Declaration on Human Rights, GA RES 217 (III).

[34] Principle 7 of the Principles explicitly obliges Participant States to act in conformity with the purposes and principles of the Charter of the United Nations and with the Universal Declaration of Human Rights.

[35] Principle 35 of "Statement of Principles Applicable to the Formation of General Customary International Law" reads:
"32. Resolutions accepted unanimously or almost unanimously, and which evince a clear intention on the part of their supporters to lay down a rule of international law, are capable, very exceptionally, of creating general customary law by the mere fact of their adoption. In the event of a lack of unanimity, (i) a failure to include all representative groups of States will prevent the creation of a general rule of customary international law (see Section 14); and (ii) even if all representative groups are included, individual dissenting States enjoy the benefit of the persistent objector rule (see Section 15)", ILA London Conference 2002, Final Report of the Committee on Formation of Costumary (general) International Law.

it: Developing countries which want to change existing law would certainly be inclined towards furnishing resolutions of the General Assembly with a law creating effect since it would facilitate the change of existing international law in the interest of the majority.

- Sometimes such instruments are used in order to test how far States are prepared to accept the rules contained in them as existing law.
- Soft law may be used to formulate (or even to concretise) existing norms which due to their unwritten form are difficult to ascertain. The best example is certainly the Resolution on the Principles Governing the Friendly Relations among States[36] which formulates the basic principles of international law.
- Soft law could be seen as demonstrating the *opinio iuris* which is required for the proof of international customary law: In the *Nicaragua* case the ICJ referred to such instruments for this purpose.[37]
- Soft law is frequently being used in order to indicate a possible conduct of States with respect to certain problems.
- Soft law has also the effect to legalise conduct which is in compliance with it; such conduct has the *fumus iuris* or the presumption of legality on its side.[38] Anybody who contests the legality would have the onus to prove the wrongfulness.
- Finally, soft law can even be used in order to concretise certain general prescriptions of behaviour: Sometimes black letter rules refer to general terms like "good order" or "safe conditions" which even judicial decisions interpret in a sense given by some soft law instruments such as certain resolutions of international organisations. This situation exists in the framework of the law of navigation, of air traffic or even of customs regulations where the "recommended practices" are sometimes already interpreted in the sense of hard law.

Hence, on the one hand, it cannot be stated that soft law as such has no effect on international relations, it undoubtedly can steer these relations to a certain extent. But, on the other, it is impossible to ascertain one and the same effect to the various instruments. The real effect exercised by a given soft law instrument can be derived

---

[36] GA RES 2625 (XXV).
[37] ICJ Reports 1986, Judgment, Merits, para. 188 et seq.
[38] *Schreuer* (1997).

only from its content, wording and context as they indicate the willingness of the parties addressed by them to abide by them.

V.   Means to Increase the Effectiveness of Soft Law Instruments

Although the effect of such instruments and their capacity to influence international relations *prima facie* seem rather modest, there nevertheless exist certain means to increase their effect. Where legally binding instruments receive their force mainly from the sanction mechanism which is provided by the secondary rules of international law, in particular the law of State responsibility, this mechanism is not applicable to soft law instruments.

However, States are induced to comply with these rules due to the principle of reciprocity or – in legal terms – to the principle *inadimplenti non est adimplendum*. Hence a State will rather comply with the prescription of such an instrument in order not to give the other side reason to depart from this prescription. In the terms of the prisoner's dilemma, States apply in such situation a cooperative rather than a non-cooperative strategy.[39] The principle of reciprocity is certainly the strongest incentive to abide by such rules. However, this mechanism can only work in situations where the rules embodied in the instrument are called to govern synallagmatic relations. Where a standard-setting type of regulations is at stake, i.e. States are obliged to observe a certain conduct in relation to private persons such as rules spelled out in Human Rights instruments, this mechanism would necessarily fail.

Another possibility consists in a substitute for the enforcement mechanisms created by secondary rules, which would make them some sort of a self-contained regime[40] or a subsystem. So for instance some resolutions of the General Assembly contain a mechanism of this kind when e.g. the States are asked to indicate whether or not they would comply with this resolution. The most developed

---

[39]   *Hillgenberg* (1999) 502.

[40]   Self-contained regime is called a regime which includes not only the rules for the conduct of States, but also rules on the consequences of non-compliance with such rules. The International Court of Justice called the law of diplomatic relations a self-contained regime (in the *Hostages* case, ICJ Reports 1980) because of the right of the receiving State to declare a diplomat "*persona non grata*" as a consequence of the breach of a rule of diplomatic law.

system exists in the OSCE: The follow-up conference are clearly such instruments when the implementation of the OSCE commitments are discussed and Participating States have to justify themselves for certain acts which have not been in conformity with the commitments. The most developed mechanism of this kind is formed by the Convention on the Conciliation and Arbitration within the OSCE[41] since the mandatory conciliation procedure has to base its recommendation also on the OSCE commitments despite the absence of a legally stringent effect of the latter.

Hence, the effect of such instruments can be increased by the mechanisms available to ensure them. It can be expected that resolutions adopted within the framework of international organisations therefore have a better chance of being supplemented by such mechanisms than soft law instruments taken outside such institutional framework. This distinction substantially contributes to the varied effects of these acts.

VI.   The Similarities of Hard Law and Soft Law Instruments

Despite all the attempts to draw a clear delimitation line between hard law and soft law instruments, it cannot be ignored that the distinction between hard and soft law becomes increasingly blurred.

Without mandatory dispute settlement procedure which could be resorted to, even hard law can be enforced only to a limited extent, in particular in a system of unequal distribution of power.

And even hard law regulations can be of a different stringency as they can provide for instance only a duty of endeavour or contain even less concrete formulations. If States only "should" instead of "shall" perform certain activities the effect of such a rule of hard law comes very close to soft law despite its original nature. It has therefore already been proposed to abandon the clear distinction between these two categories or to include also soft law regulations within the catalogue of sources of international law.[42] Although there might be a gradual increase of effectiveness of regulations from the softest soft law to the hardest hard law, it is nevertheless still necessary to distinguish between both since otherwise the traditional system of international law which still governs international relations would lose its fundamental structure to the benefit of those who possess the power.

---

[41]   *Hafner* (1994).
[42]   *Klabbers* (1996).

VII.   Reasons for the Resort to Soft Law Instruments

Some of the reasons which induce the States to resort rather to soft law than hard law instruments have already been mentioned; but, there are also additional considerations having such effect in particular in the field of economic relations.

- *Reduced costs*: Soft law instruments certainly reduce the transactions costs as compared to black letter law; their elaboration and adoption do not require costly formal procedures and the non-compliance with them entails also less costs than in the case of hard law.
- *Confidence building*: Irrespective of their lack of legal force these instrument nevertheless produce a certain confidence among the participants and through this confidence narrow the spectrum of actions and reduce the complexities of international relations.[43]
- *Flexibility*: Such instruments are characterised by a high degree of flexibility. Their formulation is very often full of constructive ambiguities in order to leave a certain discretion to States in the concrete implementation of these instruments.
- *Adaptability*: Due to their rather informal nature, it is easier to adjust such instruments to changed circumstances than e.g. treaties. Hence, it is sometimes better to resort to soft law instruments where the need of rapid alteration is foreseeable or cannot be excluded.
- *Abstention from direct regulation*: As far as economic relations are concerned, a further reason seems to surface: According to the neo-liberal approach States presently make efforts to abstain from direct regulation of economic matters by hard law. It could be stated that international law would be reduced to that what can be called a limited regularity.[44] Nevertheless, within the free room left by this limited regularity co-ordination is needed in order to guarantee a safe development of world economy for specific actions. In this case, States resort to soft law such as the G-7/8 summit declarations.

---

[43]   *Luhmann* (1973).
[44]   *Hayek* (1960) 161.

VIII. Conclusions

These considerations permit the following conclusions:

- A judgement regarding soft law instruments can never be generalised: These instruments differ too much among themselves, are of too different structures, and are adopted under too different circumstances to allow general conclusions.
- Their effect on international relations primarily depends on their contents and the context of their elaboration and adoption.
- The distinction of these instruments from those of hard law has still a certain significance, in particular concerning the applicable mechanisms of enforcement.
- Nevertheless, the impact of soft law instruments on international relations must not be ignored.
- Soft law instruments enjoy certain advantages over hard law regulations.

Such instruments are therefore a useful option in particular in circumstances where treaties are not within the reach of the States.

Bibliography:

P. M. Eisemann (1979), Le gentlemen's agreement comme source du droit international, Journal du Droit Internationale, 106 (1979), 326-348.

W. Fiedler (1984), Gentlemen's agreements, in *R. Bernhardt* (ed.), Encyclopedia of Public International Law Vol. 7, Amsterdam / London/New York 1984, 105-107.

G. Hafner (1980), Die österreichische diplomatische Praxis zum Völkerrecht 1979/80, in Österreichische Zeitschrift für Öffentliches Recht und Völkerrecht NF 31 (1980), 319-350.

G. Hafner (1994), Das Streitbeilegungsübereinkommen der KSZE: Cui bono?, in *K. Ginther* (ed.), Völkerrecht zwischen normativem Anspruch und politischer Realität. Festschrift für Karl Zemanek zum 65. Geburtstag, Berlin 1994, 115-154.

F. A. Hayek (1960), The Constitution of Liberty, Chicago 1960.

H. Hillgenberg (1999), A Fresh Look at Soft Law, European Journal of International Law 10 (1999) No. 3, 499-516.

D. Juricevic (1999), Compliance with G8 Commitments: Ascertaining the degree of compliance With Summit debt and international trade commitments. For Canada and the United States 1996-1999, Toronto 1999, available at http://www.g7.utoronto.ca/g7/scholar/juricevic2000/index.html.

J. Klabbers (1996), The Redundancy of Soft Law, Nordic Journal of International Law 65 (1996) No. 2, 167-182.

N. Luhmann (1973), Vertrauen. Ein Mechanismus zur Reduktion sozialer Komplexität, Stuttgart 1973.

H.-P. Neuhold (1999), The Foreign-Policy "Cost-Benefit-Analysis" Revisited, German Yearbook of International Law 42 (1999), 84-124.

H.-P. Neuhold/W. Hummer/C. Schreuer (1997) (eds.), Österreichisches Handbuch des Völkerrechts, Wien [3]1997.

D. Rauschning (1978), The Vienna Convention on the Law of Treaties. Travaux Préparatoires, Frankfurt 1978.

M. Rotter (1971), Die Abmachung zwischen völkerrechtlichem Vertrag und außerrechtlicher zwischenstaatlicher Abmachung, in *R. Marci et al.* (eds.), Internationale Festschrift für Alfred Verdroß zum 80. Geburtstag, München / Salzburg 1971, 426 et seqq.

C. Schreuer (1997), Recommendations and the traditional sources of international law, German Yearbook of International Law 40 (1997), 103-118.

I. Sinclair/S. J. Dickson (1995), United Kingdom, in *M. Leigh/M. R. Blakeslee* (eds.), National Treaty Law and Practice (France, Germany, India, Switzerland, Thailand, United Kingdom), American Society of International Law, Studies in Transnational Legal Policy No. 27, Washington, DC 1995, 223-257.

K. Zemanek (1997), The legal foundation of the international system: General course on Public International Law, in Recueil de cours 266 (1997), 9-336.

Elisabeth Tuerk

The Role of NGOs in International Governance NGOs and Developing Country WTO Members: Is there Potential for Alliance?[*]

[*]   This essay reflects the personal views of the author and does not repre-
      sent those of any of her affiliations. The author would like to thank
      Malini Goel, Markus Krajewski, Mireille Perrin, Alexandra Ruppen
      and *Sabrina Svarma* for the valuable comments on and contributions to
      an earlier draft of this paper. All errors remain the author's only.

"In my view [the TRIPS and Health Declaration] is perhaps the most concrete result of this campaign of NGOs, of public demonstrations that have been seeking to rebalance the system of globalization rules..."[1]

Rubens Ricupero, Secretary General of the United Nations Conference on Trade and Development (UNCTAD) on the TRIPS and Health Declaration adopted at the WTO's Fourth Ministerial Conference in Doha, Qatar, November 2001.

I.   Introduction

This article addresses the role of non-governmental organizations (NGOs)[2] in international governance. In particular, it focuses on the role of NGOs in the work of the World Trade Organization (WTO), one of the central elements of an emerging structure of international economic governance.

Much has been said and written about civil society participation in the WTO. Scholars and activists have elaborated on the potential benefits and pitfalls of increasing NGO participation in different areas of WTO work.[3] While non-governmental participation in the WTO's dispute settlement process has attracted much scholarly interest, civil society participation in WTO rule-making has been given little attention. Nonetheless, civil society participation in the formulation of new WTO disciplines and in the so-called "day-to-

---

[1]   *Rubens Ricupero* interviewed by *Someshwas Singh* in "Doha Set The Stage For Future Negotiations", South Bulletin, 24 / 25, 30 November 2000; A South Centre Publication.

[2]   It is not the purpose of this essay to elaborate on different definitional questions relating to the notions "civil society groups" and "non-governmental organizations" (NGOs). Rather, this essay uses the term "NGOs" and "civil society groups" inter-exchangeably for organizations serving the public interest rather than pursuing commercial goals. Because of their profit orientation, business associations and corporations are therefore not covered by the terms as they are used in this essay. This is in line with the approach taken by the UN, which characterizes civil society groups as "... any non-profit, voluntary citizens' group which is organized on a local, national or international level ...". See, United Nations (1997) "Introduction". On the contrary, the WTO's guidelines for consultation and cooperation with NGOs do not contain any definition of NGOs. See WTO guidelines for relations with NGOs, WT/L/162. For a discussion of the diversity of NGOs see also *Foreign Policy Centre* (2000) 7 and *Kohona* (2001).

[3]   *Esty* (1998) 144 et seqq. classifies areas of NGO involvement into dispute resolution, WTO legislative functions, and trade negotiations.

day work" of the WTO Secretariat and Members merits similar attention. The following essay therefore focuses on these latter areas of WTO work and also to move the debate forward on external transparency in the law-making-function of the WTO.[4]

Proponents of improving NGO access to the multilateral trading system assert that international economic governance, in particular the WTO, is facing a legitimacy crisis. It is argued by some that improved responsiveness to civil society concerns will enhance the organization's legitimacy. Opponents of improving NGO access to the multilateral trading system raise a series of counter-arguments, namely that NGOs themselves lack legitimacy and accountability and that their increased participation will be detrimental to the objectives of developing country Members. While concerns surrounding NGO legitimacy and accountability have been reflected in academic and other literature, this literature rarely discusses other arguments relating to power imbalances within the WTO system. This second set of arguments, however, has figured prominently in the political debate in Geneva, where it is the prevalent view among some groups of trade policy-makers that increasing NGO participation will prove disadvantageous for developing countries. Increasing external transparency, it is argued, will pose an additional burden on developing countries. This burden, it is argued, will be par-

---

[4]   From a democracy/legitimacy point of view, the case for NGO participation appears strongest with respect to WTO negotiations and WTO dispute settlement proceedings. Trade negotiations effectively create new international law, which in turn poses constraints on domestic law making. Dispute settlement proceedings, though they cannot add to or diminish existing obligations (Article 3.2 DSU), nevertheless establish crucial and sometimes far-reaching interpretations of existing obligations. In addition, law making in the day-to-day work of WTO Committees merits closer attention. Whilst formally outside of any negotiating context, many WTO Committees are working to "close the gaps" in existing WTO Agreements (i.e. GATS technical review and classification discussions or the work of the TBT and SPS Committees). Given the breath of some of the gaps and ambiguities in WTO treaty language, much of this work amounts to de-facto law making. Therefore, it could be argued that increasing civil society participation is also required in these areas. This essay builds upon this argument and addresses the contribution of NGOs in all areas of WTO work apart from dispute settlement proceedings. In addition, see *Esty* (1998) 144 et seqq., who classifies areas of NGO involvement into dispute resolution, WTO legislative functions, and trade negotiations.

ticularly problematic for those WTO Members who already face problems when aiming to effectively participate in WTO decision-making processes. Surprisingly, this argument has found little reflection outside of the political debate amongst WTO Members. Again, this article aims to highlight this rather neglected issue and move it to the center stage of discussion.

The premise of this article may be stated very simply: that NGOs and their involvement in the multilateral trading system can provide positive contributions to improving developing countries' participation in that system. In other words, external transparency can be an effective means of addressing problems related to internal transparency. In developing this argument, this article attempts to adopt the perspective of developing country WTO Members and to focus on the challenges that these Members face when aiming to effectively participate in the multilateral trading system. By focusing on developing countries, the debate can evolve in a broader context of global economic governance. This is essential to the discussion, since developing countries' inability to effectively participate in WTO decision-making processes is amongst the main sources of the WTO's legitimacy problems. Second, only a thorough understanding of developing countries' needs, challenges and fears relating to NGOs and their access to the trading system will allow for new solutions which hopefully will be more easily accepted by all who are involved and affected.

The following discussion first highlights the most recent manifestations of WTO legitimacy problems, and thus sets the scene for discussing NGO involvement in WTO processes (section II.). Section III. then briefly re-capitulates the main arguments for and against increasing NGO participation in the multilateral trading system (external transparency). Section IV. lays the groundwork for the main treatise of this essay. Specifically, it argues that developing countries' reluctance towards increasing civil society participation in WTO proceedings can be traced back to the problems developing countries experience when striving to effectively participate in WTO proceedings (internal transparency). Section V. then shows that NGOs can effectively assist developing countries to overcome some of these problems. In particular, section V. discusses the role of NGOs as "resource enhancers", as support in informal and intransparent decision-making processes and as mobilizers of public opinion to remedy developing countries' lack of political clout in the international system. Finally, section VI. concludes with a brief outlook towards the future, taking the Doha Declaration's paragraph on transparency as a starting point.

II.   The WTO's Legitimacy Problems – A Reason for More NGO Involvement?

As the world moved into the 21st century, we saw that the WTO was facing a legitimacy crisis.[5] This crisis was most obvious at the WTO's 3rd Ministerial Conference in Seattle. At the 1999 meeting, public protests surrounding the conference center effectively disrupted the conduct of the meeting.[6] Inside the conference venue, WTO Members failed to overcome fundamental differences as to the organization's future agenda. Many of the differences occurred between developed and developing country WTO Members. For example, developing countries claimed that the WTO and the Members driving its agenda were unwilling to accommodate developing countries' views and thus refused to agree upon any common declaration.

Unlike Seattle, the Doha Ministerial in November 2001 approved a far-reaching agenda for new trade negotiations.[7] At first glance, post-Doha, the WTO appears to have overcome its legitimacy problems. However, the process leading up to the meeting, the conduct of the conference and the events surrounding it reveal the organization's inertia. This inertia in turn is an expression of the

---

[5]   *Wilkinson* (2001); *Krajewski* (2001a) 176; *Krajewski* (2001b); Action Aid / CIEL *et al.* (2001).

[6]   The last years have seen increasing public protests at international economic or political meetings. Apart from the WTO's Seattle Ministerial in December 1999, massive public protests have been taking place at the World Bank / IMF annual meeting in Prague, Czech Republic, October 2000; the G7 Summit in Genoa, Italy, August 2001; or the World Economic Forum's Global Affairs Meetings in Davos, Switzerland, January 2001 and 2000. These street protests, targeted towards international economic institutions and their meetings, are indications for the increasing public suspicion and mistrust towards these organizations and towards international economic governance more broadly. Thus these public protests are also manifestations of these organizations' legitimacy crises.

[7]   Ministerial Declaration, Ministerial Conference, Fourth Session, Doha 9-14 November 2001, WT/MIN(01)/DEC/W/1.

organization's crisis, which is caused and exposed by problems related to internal and external transparency of the WTO.[8]

External transparency problems were evident in the process leading up to the Doha conference, thereby exposing the organization's crisis. Members moved the meeting to the capital of the Emirat Qatar[9] and limited the number of conference accreditations and the number of available entry visas to one representative per NGO. This not only reduced the possibility for on-site public protests, but also reinforced the widespread perception that the WTO is closed to public scrutiny and participation.[10]

While the particularities of the Doha process were widely discussed amongst civil society groups and the interested public, they also are indicative of the fundamental lack of external transparency in WTO processes overall. This more fundamental problem relates to the fact that WTO working meetings are closed to the interested public, both to active participants as well as passive observers. Thereby, lack of external transparency causes the organization's legitimacy problems and current crisis.

Also internal transparency-related problems characterized the process leading up to the Doha conference. Amongst the internal transparency-related procedural flaws were the Secretariat's intense lobbying efforts in favor of a "New Round"[11] and the General Council chairman's issuing of an "un-bracketed" Draft Ministerial

---

[8]   In the following, the notion "internal transparency" will be used to describe issues surrounding the participation of developing countries in WTO processes. Similarly, "external transparency" is the term, which will refer to issues addressing the participation of non-governmental actors in the workings of the multilateral trading system.

[9]   In addition, the location of the conference posed constraints on many NGOs and developing country delegations, amongst others because of purely practical issues such as the high costs for sending a delegate to Qatar.

[10] Action Aid/CIEL *et al.* (2001).

[11] Note that in principle, the WTO Secretariat's role would be to act as a neutral broker in a "member driven" organization. However, it is questionable whether the Director General's shuttle diplomacy to promote a new round of trade negotiations would fall within the scope of such "neutral activities". The Director General's activities were particularly problematic, as he effectively promoted and pushed an issue, which had not overall approval of all of the organization's membership. See *Sharma* (2001).

Declaration.[12] Issuing a draft declaration without any "bracketed" words departed from traditional practice to discuss draft texts, where brackets clearly indicate the points of disagreement amongst Members. Some argued that the "un-bracketed" text was designed to create the impression of broad consensus amongst Members, while in reality views were still widely diverging – mostly between developed and developing country Members. In that context, problems relating to internal transparency played out to the detriment of developing countries, who claim that their views, which often opposed a broad "New Round" negotiating mandate, were not adequately taken into consideration.

Internal transparency problems were also prevalent during the conduct of the Ministerial Conference itself. "Traditional" use of "greenroom"[13] practices to hammer out decisions, along with heavy pressure exerted upon individual delegations were common practices during these November days in 2001. Once again, developing countries were the victims of internal transparency problems.

The above examples, relating to the preparation and conduct of the Ministerial Conference show how lack of internal transparency cause legitimacy problems.

Finally, lack of external transparency as well as the public's discontent with WTO policies found expression in a series of public events surrounding the Doha Conference. During the days of the conference concerted public protests took place all over the world and exposed broad legitimacy concerns amongst WTO Members' citizens.

In sum, problems related to external and internal transparency cause legitimacy problems. Problems related to lacking external and internal transparency are also evidence of a larger WTO crisis and reflect the new challenges the organization needs to face in order to not lose further legitimacy. However, while some Members confidently approach a new set of negotiations after Doha, the organiza-

---

[12] JOB(01)/140, General Council, Preparation for the Fourth Session of the Ministerial Conference, Draft Ministerial Declaration, 26 September 2001.

[13] Green room meetings are a form of informal decision-making, in which only 15-25 chosen WTO Members take part and the composition of which is unknown. In Doha the "green room meetings" were partly replaced by a "green man process", where – rather than convening a meeting – the chairman went round the crucial delegations with the aim to "create consensus".

tion has not yet taken any visible step to face these challenges and to address the underlying causes of its legitimacy problems. Fortunately, questions surrounding the WTO's legitimacy, and more broadly, questions surrounding international economic governance, are increasingly being discussed in academic circles, newspaper editorials and mainstream political and critical civil-society debates.

The growing body of literature, research and discussion on global economic governance seems to constitute the prevalent response to the increasing perception that those who are affected by decisions taken in the WTO are not necessarily those who have a clear say in the decision-making process. This perception applies to the two main subjects of this essay: developing country WTO Members and WTO Members' citizens, who to some extent feel represented by civil society groups. Currently, the WTO lacks internal transparency as developing countries face serious problems to effectively participate in and use WTO decision-making processes. The WTO also falls short of an expected level of external transparency. This is demonstrated by the fact that individual citizens and citizen groups in WTO Member countries (while feeling directly affected by the ramifications of international trade, the WTO and its far-reaching agreements) do not have a direct link or access to WTO decision-making processes.

As traditional trade negotiating processes have lacked both, external and internal transparency, they have led to the conclusion of international agreements, which are inherently imbalanced against the interests of both developing countries and citizens in WTO Members' societies. For example, the Agreement on Trade-Related Aspects of Intellectual Property Rights (TRIPS Agreement)[14] has proven to have vast implications for access to basic medicines. Intellectual property rights and their enhanced protection result in higher prices for medicines, which in turn affect the sick and disadvantaged, particularly in the poorer parts of the world. Similarly, there are concerns that the General Agreement on Trade in Services (GATS)[15] may have negative implications for the provision of basic services, such as education, health or water. Again, those most likely to loose out from increasing liberalization and market based

---

[14] Agreement on Trade Related Aspects of Intellectual Property Rights, Annex 1 C to the Marrakech Agreement Establishing the WTO.

[15] General Agreement on Trade in Services, Annex 1 B to the Marrakech Agreement Establishing the WTO.

provision of such services are the poor and disadvantaged in our societies. It is therefore crucial to remedy existing deficiencies and to ensure that any new negotiations will not add further imbalances to the growing body of international economic rules. Appropriate design of rule-making processes is key to achieve this goal. In turn, external and internal transparency are central elements of any rule making processes.

To date however, rule making processes for international economic law, in particular WTO disciplines, contain serious deficiencies with respect to these two central elements. On the internal transparency front, developing countries fail to effectively participate in WTO processes. On the external transparency front, trade negotiations are still conducted by trade, economic or foreign ministries, frequently without adequate input from and feedback to citizens and other non-trade and non-economic constituencies and their representatives.[16] Continuing with this traditional way of conducting trade negotiations has the potential to bring about serious deficiencies in policy outcomes. Such outcomes may prove particularly harmful because of the vast negotiating agenda contained in the Doha work program. Allowing for increased NGO involvement in policy formation processes at the WTO has been suggested as a means to remedy existing and prevent future deficiencies. The following sub-section will briefly re-capitulate the debate on this issue.

III.   WTO and External Transparency – Status Quo of the Debate

Much has been said both in favor and against increasing NGO participation in WTO proceedings.[17] Some have suggested that

---

[16] Usually, trade or economic ministries hold so-called inter-ministerial co-ordination sessions to consult with other governmental agencies affected by WTO related issues. Increasingly, the entities responsible for trade policy making at the national level, or in the case of Europe at the regional level, also hold consultations with civil society groups or request comments on their negotiating positions. Whilst these are initial positive steps such consultations and comment procedures still suffer from serious deficiencies. For a comprehensive discussion of consultation processes during the Uruguay Round see *Bellmann / Gerster* (1996).

[17] For example see *Benedek* (1999); *Scholte / O'Brien / Williams* (1999); *W. Benedek* (1998); *Dunoff* (1998) 435; *Esty* (1997); *Charnovitz*

formalized relationships between NGOs and the WTO could be
used as a remedy to address concerns about the legitimacy of the
WTO, the multilateral trading system and global economic governance.[18] In this context, proponents argue that increasing NGO participation in WTO proceedings will improve the formation of WTO
law and polices, will ensure that the WTO's actions are perceived
as responsive, and fair and will thus improve the authoritativeness
of policy choices and judgments emanating from the WTO.

Proponents increasing NGO access to WTO processes maintain
that establishing formal procedures for NGO participation in the
international trading system would allow NGOs to serve as "con-
nective tissue", bridging the gap between WTO decision-makers
and the distant constituencies affected by trade policies.[19] It has also
been suggested that NGOs could serve as intellectual competitors to
governments, especially with respect to trade and economic ministries. Indeed, NGOs possess a vast body of knowledge and technical expertise on issue areas affected by trade policies, ranging from
environmental and human rights issues to health, education and
cultural policies.[20] Similarly, NGOs do not view problems through
the so-called "trade-lens", a synonym for the rather narrow view-
point that trade and economic ministries adopt because of their narrow and specialized mandates.[21] NGOs also serve as defenders of
viewpoints that governments do not adequately represent, because
governments in their nature are constrained by political processes or
by their geographically limited mandate.[22] Finally, it is also argued,

---

(1996); *Charnovitz / Wickham* (1995); *Cameron / Ramsay* (1995);
Charnovitz (1997). In addition to these academic and scholary essays
there exist numerous civil society policy statements on that issue.

[18] Action Aid/CIEL *et al.* (2001); see also ICTSD (1999). On page 5 this
document suggests that "[m]ost NGOs consider that formalized relations with the WTO are needed as a way of ensuring transparency,
participation and accountability of the multilateral trading system".

[19] *Esty* (1998) 125.

[20] *Esty* (1998) 135. See also *Dunoff* who touches upon the role private
industry, which with its specific expertise - can contribute as "resource
enhancers" in the case of WTO dispute settlement proceedings; *Dunoff*
(1998) 436.

[21] *Esty* (1998) 136.

[22] See *Esty* who makes these arguments in the context of global environmental problems and discusses the diversity of civil society organizations. *Esty* (1998) 124, 131 and 132. There is also the different view-

that NGOs could prove more directly useful for trade policy-makers or WTO officials because NGOs serve as agents of civil education and as disseminators of information on the WTO. Likewise, NGOs could assist trade officials to better gauge the political viability of proposed measures of programs.[23]

On the other hand, there are counter-arguments to this positive approach towards civil society involvement in the WTO. Opponents of NGO participation claim that allowing non-governmental actors to participate in WTO proceedings would undermine the status of the WTO as an intergovernmental body.[24] Some argue that trade policy-making works best in absence of a "cacophony of voices".[25] Related to this is the fear that opening up the process to private parties will lead to special interest capture at the WTO and thus distort rather than improve the decision-making process.[26] In that context it is also claimed that many NGOs pursue traditionally Northern topics such as the protection of the environment or the promotion of human rights and that granting them greater participatory rights would therefore further tip the balance towards Northern interests vis-à-vis the South. Finally, there is the claim that NGOs are neither representative nor electorally accountable[27] and thus, because of their own lack of legitimacy, cannot serve to remedy the WTO's legitimacy problems.[28]

---

point that there is nothing such as a common set of civil interests that cross national borders or a global civil society with uniform goals and values. For an explanation of this viewpoint see: *Foreign Policy Centre* (2000) 9.

[23] *Esty* (1998) 131

[24] *Dunoff* (1998) 438, and *Esty* (1998) 140. For a discussion of this aspect of trade policy making see other essays in this volume and for a discussion of the role of NGOs in the making of international rules more generally, see *Kohona* (2001).

[25] For example, *Dunoff* (1998) 438. However this "traditional" understanding of trade policy-making is increasingly being criticized, amongst others by theories, which emphasize the importance of different and diverging viewpoints to improve democratic deliberations and thus the results of democratic decision-making processes.

[26] *Dunoff* (1998) 437, see also *Esty* (1998) 138.

[27] *Dunoff* (1998) 438, and *Esty* (1998) 141.

[28] *The Foreign Policy Centre* discusses problems related to transparency, accountability of NGOs and the accuracy of their statements and concludes that the "thorny issue of legitimacy" is frequently used as an ar-

Overall, the issue of NGO participation has given rise to much controversy and discussion. Most interesting however is that outside the WTO most of the debate no longer discusses *whether* to involve NGOs, but *how* to best involve NGOs.[29] Thus, ways and modalities of NGO involvement have moved to the center stage of the current discussions, which aim to provide policy recommendations to maximize benefits and minimize potential pitfalls of NGO involvement.[30] In that context, research has provided extensive information on different options used for formal civil society participation in international fora. Furthermore, individual organizations have made specific policy recommendations for accreditation procedures.[31] Similar efforts to provide practical suggestions have been undertaken with respect to *amicus briefs* in the WTO dispute settlement.[32]

It should be noted that his debate has not been supported by political agreement amongst WTO Members to constructively move forward on the NGO participation issue. Not only have WTO Members carefully avoided any clear commitment to external transparency in the Doha Ministerial Declaration, but they have also, in some instances, reacted extremely sensitive to any actions which could be perceived as granting the WTO Secretariat greater leeway to define its relationships with civil society groups without appropriate consultation with Members.[33] Interestingly, much of this reluctance and opposition originates from developing country WTO Members. Thus, there is some evident need to strengthen the case for NGO participation and in particular, to address the specific sets of concerns and counter arguments, which are raised by devel-

---

gument against increasing the external transparency of the WTO. *Foreign Policy Centre* (2000) 17 et seqq., in particular 19.

[29] *Marceau/Pedersen* (1999) 45.

[30] See *Esty* (1998), discussing practicalities for NGO involvement (141); see also *Chaytor* (1999) 10 et seqq.; and see, *Foreign Policy Centre*, which on a more broader basis suggests three principles for a "New Deal" between governments and civil society actors in global governance: 1) a voice not a vote, 2) minimum standards for NGO integrity and performance, 3) a level playing field for NGO involvement. *Foreign Policy Centre* (2000) 4, 5.

[31] ICTSD (1999) and Action Aid/CIEL *et al.*2001).

[32] *Marceau/Stilwell* (2001).

[33] See below for WTO Members' reactions to the Appellate Body's request for leave procedure in the *Asbestos* case

oping country Members. Given that developing country concerns with greater NGO participation have proven to be one of the main stumbling blocks impeding the move forward, this essay aims to recast the scene for the debate on external transparency from a developing country perspective. Hopefully it will also mean that more detailed proposals on the specifics of civil society participation will be regarded with greater openness and enthusiasm.

IV.   Developing Countries in the WTO: Their Reluctance to Greater NGO Involvement and Their Problems to Effectively Participate in WTO Processes

Amongst all WTO membership, developing countries have proven to be most reluctant to greater NGO involvement in WTO proceedings. Recently, this reluctance has been most evident with respect to *amicus briefs* in the WTO dispute settlement.[34] In that context, the controversy exacerbated in the *Asbestos* case,[35] where upon appeal, a significant number of unsolicited non-governmental submissions were expected. The Appellate Body thus established a so-called "request for leave procedure"[36] which was designed to govern the admission of *amicus briefs*. Though the "request for leave" procedure was created for this individual case only, it gave rise to significant "disquiet and anxiety"[37] amongst developing country Members. Amongst others, developing countries argued that the Appellate Body's move "will have the implication of putting the developing countries at an even greater disadvantage" and these Members then stressed "the relative unpreparedness of their

---

[34]   For discussions of issues related to *amicus briefs* in WTO dispute settlement procedures see: *Appleton* (2000); *Marecau / Stilwell* (2001); *Mavroidis* (2001); and *Zonnekeyn* (2001).

[35]   WTO, Appellate Body Report, *European Communities – Measures Affecting Asbestos and Asbestos – Containing Products*, WT/DS135/ AB/R, 12 March 2001.

[36]   WTO, Communication from the Appellate Body, *European Communities – Measures Affecting Asbestos and Asbestos-Containing Products*, WT/DS135/9, 8 November 2000.

[37]   Statement by India in the General Council Special Session, Wednesday 22 November 2000, subject: Appellate Body's Communication to the Chairman of the DSB [WT/DS135/9], on file with the author, hereinafter: Indian statement (2000) 1.

[38]   Indian statement (2000) 8.

[Southern] NGOs who have much less resources ... to send briefs ...".[39]

However, many of the developing country arguments against *amicus briefs* also apply to other areas of NGO involvement, including NGO participation in the formulation of WTO laws and policies. While developing countries' arguments against increasing NGO participation in the WTO are multi-fold and diverse, the following are those most relevant for the purpose of this essay. First, developing countries point out that many NGOs stand for inherently Northern concerns, such as the protection of the environment or the promotion of labour rights and social issues in the context of the WTO. From a traditional developing country viewpoint, both labour and environment – though possibly to a different extent – are considered to pose threats to increasing developing countries' exports and improving their economic performance.[40] Opening up WTO processes to NGOs, it was argued, would further favor such Northern interests at the expense of Southern national interests.

Secondly, developing countries highlight that Northern NGOs have access to financial resources, which go beyond those available to many developing countries, their delegations or their trade ministries. Similarly, Northern NGOs' budgets go far beyond what would ever be available to similar Southern organizations.[41] The financial aspect is particularly relevant since allowing greater access to NGOs would most likely also provide business and multinational corporations with better avenues to pursue their policies in

---

[39] ibid.

[40] Several other contributions in this volume analyze issues and challenges surrounding the inter-linkages between economic and non-economic concerns, such as the protection of the environment or social issues. *Joanne Scott* discusses how environmental considerations can be integrated into international economic law, amongst which WTO dispute settlement. *Gerhard Loibl* examines the relationship between one specific multilateral environmental agreement, the Biosafety Protocol, and WTO rules and obligations. For a developing country approach to the inclusion of labour issues into international economic law see the contribution of *José Manuel Salazar – Xirinachs* and *Jorge Mario Martínez Piva*. Finally, *Michael J. Trebilcock* outlines objectives, instruments and institutions in the context of international trade and international labour standards.

[41] Indian statement (2000) 8.

the WTO.[42] Developing countries are thus reluctant to grant such business or multinational "non-governmental" interests this additional avenue, since many perceive corporate interests to be the main driving force behind the trade policy position of the Quad.[43] Arguably, such corporate interests should not have "two bites at the same apple", domestically and at the international level.[44]

A third argument against increasing NGO participation relates to developing countries' general reluctance and suspicion towards the issues, which are mainly pushed by industrialized WTO Members. It has been argued that external transparency is a "public relations strategy" of the Quad, which aims to deflect from addressing internal imbalances and to rally public support for the WTO. Thus it would diminish possibilities for a fundamental re-balancing of the system to better accommodate Southern considerations.

Finally, some WTO Members might be reluctant to grant NGOs a greater voice in the WTO because of their respective domestic policies. For example, some countries have not organized their do-

---

[42] For official statistics about the number of business and "public interest / non-profit" NGOs accredited to the different WTO Ministerial Conferences see http://www.wto.org/english/forums_e/ngo_e/meet_e.htm. The numbers varied between 48 business out of 108 participating organizations at the 1996 Singapore Ministerial and 46 business out of 128 participating entities at the 1998 Geneva Ministerial (the non-business entities encompassing developmental, environmental, environment / development, consumer, trade unions and others). There are no official statistics available for the 1999 Seattle and 2001 Doha Ministerials, because it proved difficult to draw distinctions between the different types oforganizations. Unofficial calculations for the Doha Ministerial count 114 business out of 365 others (on file with the author). Note that the financial contribution of "business" interest groups is widely acknowledged in the WTO dispute settlement proceedings, where private business parties can play an important role, particularly in resource intensive cases. See also *Dunoff* (1998) 441 et seqq.

[43] The Quad is an informal grouping of the four main driving forces of WTO processes, namely the US, Canada, the EC and Japan.

[44] Similar, Action Aid / CIEL *et al.* (2001). At the same time, some trade policy circles positively acknowledge the financial contribution of "business" interest groups. Apart from negotiations this is also the case for dispute settlement proceedings where private business parties can play an important role, particularly in resource intensive cases. See *Dunoff* (1998) 441 et seqq.

mestic decision-making processes according to democratic principles or have even pursued an active policy against civil society
involvement. Approving a role for non-governmental views and
entities at the international level would certainly strengthen similar
calls for more open and more democratic decision-making processes at the national level.

Given that the argument relating to domestic democratic processes in itself raises legitimacy concerns, and that the argument
suggesting a Quad "strategy" remains unsubstantiated, most of the
remaining arguments reflect developing countries' fears that more
external transparency will further exacerbate structural imbalances
between North and South in WTO processes. It is further feared
that this will worsen developing countries' inability to effectively
participate in WTO processes.

Thus, in order to genuinely address developing countries' disquiet with external transparency, it is crucial to analyze the causes
and problems of these structural imbalances and of developing
countries' inability to effectively participate in the WTO system.[45]
These problems can be traced back to a series of different factors,
namely that there is a lack of financial resources and technical expertise, that WTO informal decision-making processes are slanted
towards the North, and that developing countries lack political clout
in general.[46]

First, we address lack of financial resources – the probably most
evident of the above factors. Lack of finances impedes more than

---

[45] While this paper mainly addresses imbalances with respect to the
WTO's law-making function in trade negotiations, similar issues also
arise with respect to WTO dispute settlement proceedings. In the context of dispute settlement, the recently established Advisory Center on
WTO Law aims to address such imbalances. In the second recital of
the Agreement establishing the Advisory Center on WTO Law, the
Parties to the Agreement note "... that developing countries...have
limited expertise in WTO law and the management of complex trade
disputes and their ability to acquire such expertise is subject to severe
financial and institutional constraints"; see http://www.acwl.ch/
MainFrameset.htm.

[46] For a thorough analysis of developing countries problems to effectively participate in WTO proceedings see South Centre (2001); Krajewski (2000).

29 countries[47] from having a permanent representation in Geneva. Nevertheless, decisions made in the Geneva based WTO are binding even for "non-resident" WTO Members. Lack of financial resources impedes developing countries from maintaining and adequately staffing their Geneva missions, both in terms of number of staff members and technical and legal expertise.

Inequality is clear when looking at the number of staff members in developing country and developed country missions. While delegations such as the EC or US have between 12 (EC) and 16 (US) permanent Geneva staff members[48] to work substantively on WTO issues, most developing country missions vary between 3 and 6 staff members dedicated to trade,[49] with countries such as Brazil (9) and India (7) being valuable exceptions.[50] As the increasing proliferation of the WTO agenda results in more and also more overlapping meetings, continuous representation in all the meetings is becoming increasingly difficult, if not impossible, for small and understaffed delegations.[51]

Inequality is also obvious when looking at the technical and legal expertise available in WTO delegations. Though the need for trade-related education, teaching and training activities has been

---

[47] 20 of these countries are WTO Members, all of them least-developed countries, while the remaining nine are observers to the WTO. Note that in January 2002 the European Commission assisted in setting up an office for ACP Countries, to improve their participation in WTO processes. See 16 January 2002 press release; EU backs launch of Geneva-based office to help African, Caribbean and Pacific countries boost World Trade Organization presence.

[48] Such imbalances not only exist with respect to Geneva based missions but also in national capitals or with respect to delegations for WTO Ministerials. In Doha, for example the EC was represented with about 500 staff members, while Malawi only managed to send three individuals.

[49] Bangladesh for example, only has two persons working on trade in Geneva. Note that these staff members usually not only cover WTO trade issues, but also meetings in the United Nations Conference on Trade and Development (UNCTAD) or the International Trade Center (ITC) and frequently also cover non-trade bodies, such as the UN human rights bodies.

[50] Similar imbalances also exist with respect to the staffing of the WTO Secretariat; see *Krajewski* (2000) 11 and 12 and South Centre (2001) 11.

[51] See above, *Krajewski* (2000) and South Centre (2001).

widely acknowledged[52] developing countries still lag far behind, unable to provide necessary in-house expertise or hire out-side consultants. Continuing access to high quality expertise becomes even more relevant as the expanding WTO agenda proves to be increasingly technical.[53]

As a result of insufficient financial resources and technical expertise, many developing countries are unable to effectively participate in WTO decision-making processes. Consequently, developing countries frequently are not among the agenda setters, and are left to defend their positions rather than taking an assertive role. Often their issues simply get stuck. These negative consequences of insufficient resources and expertise are aggravated by the specific way in which WTO decision-making works.

This is related to the second main problem, namely that the WTO's informal decision-making processes are slanted towards the North. While on paper, WTO decision-making processes work along the pattern of one country-one vote and most decisions require "consensus",[54] in practice, the informal and in-transparent handling of such decision-making disadvantage developing country Members. For the most part, the WTO follows old GATT practice to move "real" decision-making to informal gatherings[55] instead of

---

[52] The Doha Declaration dedicates four entire paragraphs to technical cooperation and capacity building (paras 38 et seqq.). In spring 2002 Members pledged CHF 30 million to a global trust fund, to "boost technical assistance and help developing countries to build capacity and participate fully in the Doha Development Agenda". See WTO press release, Press/279, 11 March 2002. Subsequently, he WTO Secretariat set up a special process, hiring additional staff to meet capacity building targets. There are concerns, however, that some of these efforts are Northern driven and may prove detrimental to Southern interests.

[53] South Centre (2001) 8.

[54] For a discussion of the consensus requirement from a developing country perspective, see South Centre (2001) 6. Note that even where there is no consensus requirement from a strictly speaking legal point, WTO Members attach great importance to such consensus. This political importance of "consensus" was most evident in the 1999 selection of the Director General, where failure of WTO Members to agree upon one candidate led to the practical solution of splitting an extended term amongst the two candidates.

[55] The ill-famous "Greenroom" is one of these decision-making practices. For a discussion from an NGO perspective see, *Krajewski* (2000) 8 et

deciding according to formalized procedures. Informal and non-transparent decision-making processes require even more detailed technical and political understanding, together with a good overall "big picture view" of the scene. Information is crucial in such processes and lack of, incomplete or late information can significantly alter the bargaining position of individual negotiators. Time is another crucial factor in informal decision-making processes. The ability to quickly and accurately analyze positions and shifts in positions, together with a sound understanding of the legal and political implications of certain drafts or proposals within and outside the particular negotiating context in question, is vital. As explained above, most developing countries lack these resources and therefore do not enter such informal bargaining processes in a well-equipped way.

Finally there is the problem that developing countries in general lack political clout. Again, this plays out negatively in the WTO's informal decision-making processes, which allow countries to selectively exert pressure on others and to and which do not hold anyone accountable. As it is not clear how a decision has been made nor how much support there was for it, these informal decision-making processes are prone to be dominated by Members with significant political clout, which many developing countries lack.

Lack of political clout can be due to the overall low economic performance of a country and the lack of interest by other WTO Members in accessing these low performing markets. Lack of political clout can also be traced back to a country's specific economic or political situation, which effectively allows other WTO trading partners to pressure the troubled country into agreeing to certain decisions. Prominent examples of such situations are the lending policies of international financial institutions, when developing countries' dependence on financial assistance is used as a tool to weaken the country's bargaining situation in the WTO or as was done previously, in the Uruguay Round trade negotiations.[56] Thus, informal decision-making processes and lack of political clout call for increased collaboration and co-ordination amongst developing countries to avoid negative outcomes. While such coordination is

---

seqq., for a discussion from a developing country view, see South Centre (2001) 9 et seqq.

[56] Again the TRIPS Agreement serves as an example for such practices during the Uruguay Round.

increasingly commonplace and is resulting in increased assertive-
ness of developing country WTO Members, these positive developments need to be strengthened and complemented with efforts in
other areas.

In sum, many of the problems which developing countries face
in WTO decision-making processes originate from a combination
of several factors, namely: lack of financial resources and technical
expertise, informal and in-transparent decision-making processes,
and insufficient political clout. It could be argued that NGOs can
provide remedies to improve developing country positions with
respect to all of these aspects and thereby strengthen and complement existing efforts to improve developing countries participation
in the WTO. Whilst the next sub-section of this essay will develop
this argument in more detail, the concluding section then expresses
the hope that developing countries, as they realize the positive contribution that NGOs can make towards furthering their interests,
will react more positively to calls for making WTO processes more
transparent and inclusive.

V.   NGOs as a Means to Assist Developing Countries to More Effectively Participate in WTO Processes

The following section first illustrates that NGOs can act as resource enhancer for developing countries, in particular by providing
much needed technical expertise in trade and trade related areas. It
then explains how NGOs, through their information services, can
prove valuable in addressing problems related to the informal and
in-transparent decision-making processes in the WTO. Finally, this
section argues that NGOs by mobilizing public opinion can assist
developing countries to reduce problems due to lack of political
clout.

A. NGOs as Resource Enhancers –
Providing Technical Expertise First and foremost, NGOs can act as
resource enhancers by providing technical expertise to developing
countries. Many NGOs possess valuable expertise in trade and
trade-related policies or at least possess the ability to hire outside
experts to develop trade-related policy papers and recommendations. For example, civil society expertise exists in the traditional
area of legal and economic issues related to international trade.
International Lawyers and Economists Against Poverty (ILEAP), a
recently founded non-governmental organization states in its Statement of Mission and Principle that it "stems from the conviction

that fresh and low-cost non-governmental inputs from the legal, economics and related professions in the sphere of international trade and trade-related issues can significantly assist development processes and poverty reduction in the materially poorer parts of the world".[57] In a survey on technical assistance providers, ILEAP identified more than ten international and regional non-governmental organizations, inter-university and private practice initiatives providing technical assistance services related to trade-law and economics.[58]

However, technical assistance and resource-related synergies between NGOs and developing countries also exist in other areas, which have only recently been affected by international trade rules. Health policies or policies relating to genetic resources are two prominent examples. With respect to health policies, synergies between NGOs and developing countries have materialized in issues surrounding the TRIPS Agreement. This agreement's excessive standards of intellectual property protection affect governments' health policies and – predominantly in developing countries – caused concern that governments will not be able to maintain or put in place much needed policies to combat AIDS or other diseases. Thus, expertise and knowledge about domestic health policies and in particular about developing countries' health policies is crucial for policy decisions in the context of international trade. *Médecins sans Frontières* has widely acknowledged in-house expertise on issues related to developing countries' health policies and provided useful input to international policy discussions in the trade field. Another organization providing expertise on trade, IPR and health policy issues is the Consumer Project for Technology (CPT).

Similar situations arise also in relation to the other "hot" TRIPS issue, access to genetic resources. Again, non-governmental organizations such as the Quakers[59] or WWF[60] have substantively contributed to and refined the debate. In their work many NGOs analyze linkages between international rules on IPR protection and

---

[57] Statement of Mission and Principles http://www.ileapinitiative.com.

[58] While this survey combines NGOs, inter-university and private practice initiatives in one category, it also reviews existing technical assistance efforts in another category of actors, such as international and regional development/funding organizations.

[59] For a description of the process undertaken by the Quakers United Nations Office see *Tansey* (2001).

[60] See WWF/CIEL (2001).

domestic laws and policies regulating access to genetic resources. Frequently these organizations offer a developing country perspective. GRAIN[61] for example, provides value added by comparing negotiating activities in different fora or between different governments and their implications for developing countries. Some NGOs also formally collaborate with intergovernmental organizations (IGOs), which have a clear development focus. In August 2001 for example, the International Center for Trade and Sustainable Development (ICTSD) together with the United Nations Conference on Trade and Development (UNCTAD) launched a joint project on intellectual property rights and development with the goal to "build capacity among negotiators and other decision-makers from developing countries to effectively participate in rule-making through research, information exchange and stakeholder consultations".[62]

The above issues, health and genetic resources are policy areas which only recently have been affected by international trade rules and many developing country trade ministries have not yet developed necessary expertise in these areas. Long established NGO expertise may therefore be a useful resource. In addition, NGOs can also be useful even if they do not directly possess the relevant in-house expertise. In that case they can provide financial assistance to complement lacking legal or technical skills. In the process leading to the Doha Ministerial Declaration on TRIPS and Health, the Quakers played this valuable role.

TRIPS issues offer good opportunities to create synergies among NGOs and developing country WTO delegations because there is a certain extent of overlap in the policy objectives of NGOs and developing countries.[63] However, it could prove more difficult to re-

---

[61] GRAIN (Genetic Resources Action International) also provides detailed information about how industrialized countries through a range of bilateral and regional agreements pressure developing to go much further than the WTO TRIPS requirements and adopt more hardline standards for intellectual property rights on life forms. http://www. grain.org/front/index.cfm. For a compilation of legal texts see the biodiversity rights section of the webpage http://www.grain.org/brl/trips-plus-brl-en.cfm.

[62] For a comprehensive website see http://www.ictsd.org/unctad-ictsd/deve.

[63] Note that another area for potential synergies is the WTO's Agreement on Agriculture, where many NGOs aim to defend the livelihoods of

alize such synergies in other areas of WTO policies. In particular, technical assistance and skill synergies might be difficult to realize if the receiving end must watch out for a hidden agenda in these exercises. There is the fear that many NGOs stand for "inherently Northern" concerns, such as labour or environment protection and will provide technical expertise only to advance their own agendas. To respond to such concerns, ILEAP for example, explicitly included into its principles that it aims to "respond[ing] to expressed needs, without any other agendas to promote ...".[64]

Regarding NGOs pushing an inherently Northern agenda, this issue is becoming less significant if we look closely at recent developments among civil society groups. While it is outside the scope of this paper to discuss the potential benefits and disadvantages of Northern policy choices such as promoting human rights or protecting the environment, it is important to note that during the last decade, the concept of "sustainable development" has become increasingly popular in both, Northern and Southern civil society groups. The concept of "sustainable development", which encompasses three pillars, namely: the protection of the environment, social advancement and the promotion of economic development[65] has increasingly moved to the center stage of traditionally "green" NGOs' and their trade-policy activities.

Among environmental NGOs, even big Northern players are now actively incorporating the developmental perspective of trade-related issues into their policy formation processes. While having the protection of the environment as their central objective, Northern organizations increasingly work on so-called "developing country friendly" trade related issues, for example questions relating to genetically modified organisms or the relationship between the TRIPS Agreement and the Convention on Biological Diversity

---

Southern small-scale farmers versus the interests of big agribusiness in the North. For example, see http://www.iatp.org.

[64] ILEAP Statement of Mission and Principles, http://www. ileapinitiative.com. Yet, any danger of a hidden agenda in technical assistance must be even more obvious in those cases where technical assistance is provided or financed by developing countries' Northern WTO negotiating partners.

[65] For a discussion of the principle of sustainable development and its evolution from The Stockholm Conference on the Human Environment to The Rio Earth Summit and beyond, see chapter four of *Hunter / Salzman / Zaelke* (2002).

(CBD).[66] Also, they are beginning to push for "sustainable development" rather than "green protectionism". For example, the World Wide Fund for Nature (WWF), a well-known "green" organization recognizes sustainable development as its main policy objective. WWF names as the main objective of its trade and investment program "... to redirect trade and investment policies and flows, including international trade and investment agreements, towards the objective of sustainable development".[67] Similarly, Friends of the Earth, another major player amongst so-called "environmental NGOs" clearly identifies in its mission statement that it is amongst its main objectives to "promote environmentally sustainable development on the local, national, regional and global levels".[68]

Maybe such changes make developing country governments more open to technical expertise offered by civil society organizations also in other "non TRIPS" areas. WWF's expertise on sustainability assessments is an example where NGO technical expertise on what traditionally has been regarded as a Northern policy tool, can assist developing countries and broaden their understanding of an issue. During the last year, services trade assessment has been a standing agenda item in WTO services negotiations.[69] While

---

[66] For Greenpeace's coverage of such developing country friendly "environmental issues", see "Safe Trade in the 21st Century", Greenpeace's campaigning document for the Doha Ministerial Conference. For another indication that traditional environmentally focused groups increasingly work on and incorporate development topics see the Statement to the Monterrey, UN International Conference on Financing for Development, which makes specific suggestion on issues related to Overseas Development Aid (ODA), foreign debt, or trade distorting subsidies. Also Greenpeace signed onto this statement. See www.weedbonn.org/ffd?WSSD_FFD_ 190102_version.doc.

[67] See http://www.panda.org/resources/programmes/trade/about.htm.

[68] See http://www.foei.org/about/mission_statement.html.

[69] Note that services trade assessment is amongst one of the topics of utmost importance for developing country WTO Members. In addition to this more technical advice, many NGOs incorporated the call for a thorough and comprehensive assessment of services trade liberalization into their GATS campaigning messages, see http://focusweb.org/our-world-is-not-for-sale/statements/Stop-gats-attack.html, http://www. wdm.org.uk/campaign/GATS.htm, or http://www.forumue.de/ forumaktuell/positionspapiere/0000001d.html. For a more detailed de-

Members originally focused on assessing purely quantitative and economic aspects of service trade liberalization, recent discussions are broader: WTO Members move towards qualitative assessments and civil society groups point to the value of sustainability impact assessments as a tool to ensure that liberalization brings about the expected benefits. Through a series of public statements,[70] background document[71] and meetings,[72] WWF provided Geneva based trade policy-makers with much needed technical expertise on how to conduct sustainability assessment. Knowledge about the practical challenges and benefits arising in the assessment of trade policies is of crucial importance for trade negotiators covering the current GATS negotiations. Thus, while the road ahead may be long, Northern NGOs increasingly address Southern considerations in their trade-policy formation. Simultaneously, developing countries realize that they benefit by drawing upon NGOs resources and research activities on a wide range of issues.

Perhaps a more peripheral WTO-related area, but nonetheless an important one where civil society expertise can be helpful, is the issue of corporate lobbying and corporate influence in the WTO. While developing countries are reluctant to more external transparency, fearing that this will grant additional influence to multinational corporations, corporate lobbying has been considered a normal part of trade-policy formation. For example, it is widely acknowledged that Northern pharmaceutical companies constituted the main driving force behind the TRIPS Agreements. Similarly, in current GATS negotiations Northern corporations play a major role

---

scription of how NGOs create political space for developing countries to assert their position, see below, section V.C. of this essay

[70] See the four WWF / CIEL Joint Public Statements on Services Trade Assessment, each of them launched for one specific WTO Services negotiating session (July 2001, September 2001, December 2001, May 2001) and giving precise suggestions on how to move forward GATS assessment discussion in the WTO. Available under: www.panda.org/resources/programmes/trade.

[71] See WWF's comprehensive study on how to conduct services trade assessments in the tourism sector (WWF (2001)).

[72] For example, the seminar on GATS assessment which WWF, CIEL, PSI (Public Services International) and WDM (World Development Movement) organized for WTO delegates and civil society groups on 12 March 2002 to complement the WTO's Symposium on GATS Assessment.

in determining industrialized countries' market access requests. This may again result to be to the detriment of developing countries.

At the same time, there are NGOs who consider "corporate lobbying" as their main focus area. They identify, track and analyze the relationships between Northern trade policy-makers and their business constituency. They point to the fact that compared to groups representing non-business interests, industry often has much better avenues to make its views known to the relevant trade policy-makers. In addition, NGOs collect information on the substantive content of such corporate influence. An increasing flow of information between civil society organizations and developing countries could therefore be potentially beneficial for the latter, for example by assisting developing countries to anticipate the moves of industrialized WTO Members or to identify the motives behind certain positions. Thus, rather than providing additional avenues for Northern corporate interests, increasing collaboration with civil society can also provide tools to expose and address imbalances between Northern business and developing country delegations.

Regarding the claim that increasing external transparency will tip the balance towards inherently Northern interests there is yet another argument that dismisses that fear. The last years have seen a proliferation of Northern NGOs, which have "development" policies as their central objectives. These organizations range from research to campaigning organizations amongst which Oxfam, World Development Movement, Christian Aid or Actionaid. These organizations have effectively provided research and analysis or – through their lobbying efforts – influenced international economic policy-making to promote development objectives.

Still, the above analysis might give rise to the impression that NGOs are an inherently Northern phenomenon and that Northern NGOs, due to their financial and technical capacities, play the dominant role.[73] This raises serious concerns relating to the ownership of policy-making and technical expertise in the civil society field. Policy-making should be balanced, not only in terms of content or result, but also in terms of participation. In other words, there are legitimate reasons to call for increasing Southern ownership of NGO policy-making. Fortunately fundamental changes are

---

[73] For example, the concerns expressed by India with respect to *amicus briefs*, see above Indian statement.

taking place. Again, the last decade has seen considerable changes in the structure and composition of the global civil society movement.

Today, many NGOs are organized as international networks, which give adequate consideration to both Southern and Northern views. Friends of the Earth, for example is structured as an international network, a decentralist federation of groups, which are autonomous organizations and many of which are located in the South and were established before joining the federation.[74] Policy positions are to be decided by all Members of the network, and capacity building among Northern and Southern members of the network is a crucial element. Second, the last decade has seen an increasing proliferation of "truly" Southern NGOs. For example, amongst UN accredited NGOs, there is an increasing Southern participation. As many of these organizations are smaller groups, they have the benefit of being closely rooted in local domestic constituencies. Thus, through liaison offices or other loose networks, the interests of domestic grassroot organizations can be directly represented at the international level in Geneva. In addition, there are many well-established players in the Southern NGO world. Third World Network[75] and Focus on the Global South,[76] both have significant capacity in policy analysis, possess long experience in trade related questions, have established an effective presence in Geneva, and have developed strong links and direct access to the relevant Southern delegations and domestic ministries.

In sum, a closer look at the last decade of developments in the NGO field reveals that we indeed witnessed changes that weaken the argument that NGOs push an inherently Northern agenda and that there is an inherent bias in the civil society field towards Northern organizations. While the road ahead remains a long one, there is much evidence that NGOs are and will be useful resource enhancers as they supply technical expertise to developing country delegations and relevant intergovernmental organizations.[77]

---

[74] For a list of Foe groups see all over the world see http://www.foei.org/groups/members/index.html.

[75] http://www.twnside.org.sg/index.htm.

[76] http://www.focusweb.org/.

[77] Another example, where an IGO with a development focus resorts to civil society input in its work is the United Nations Development Programme (UNDP). In December 2001, UNDP commissioned a background paper, entitled "The Multilateral Trading System: A De-

B. NGOs to Balance North / South Power In-balances in Informal
WTO Decision-making Processes –
Supplying Information Services

NGOs can prove valuable to remedy imbalances, which arise from informal WTO decision-making processes. Previously, this paper argued that informal decision-making processes pose challenges for developing country WTO Members. One source of such challenges is the fact that informal decision-making processes require even more detailed technical and political understanding, together with a good overall "big picture view" and complete, reliable and timely information. While sub-section A. has explained how NGOs can be useful in terms of providing much needed technical expertise, this sub-section focuses on the role that NGOs play in addressing specific ex-post and ex-ante information needs arising in informal, power based decision-making processes.

Several private companies have established information services, generally covering recent developments in WTO processes. Whilst these services prove useful by reporting details of the day-to-day processes, including a "behind the scenes" look at developments in the WTO, access entails significant cost.[78] Again, NGOs have stepped into that niche, providing weekly updates on WTO law and policy developments free of charge. For example, ICTSD's "Bridges Weekly"[79] is highly recommended and appreciated by both civil society as well as traditional trade law experts. In effect, ICTSD states that it "plays a unique systemic role as a provider of original, non-partisan reporting … services at the intersection of international trade and sustainable development."[80] Similar services are also provided by Southern NGOs, SUNS, the South-North Development Monitor is a daily bulletin on trade and development issues, again, from a non-governmental source.

Apart from precise, timely and accurate reports on past developments in WTO processes, NGOs can also be a source of not yet

---

velopment Perspective", to Third World Network, one of the most prominent Southern NGOs. Again, this shows that civil society groups and their specific expertise can provide significant value-added and directly improve developing countries' participation in WTO processes.

[78] Examples of such information dissemination services are Inside US Trade or the World Trade Law Reporter.

[79] Bridges Weekly Trade News Digest, to be obtained through bridges@iatp.org.

[80] http://www.ictsd.org/about/index.htm.

readily available information for developing country negotiators. Such ex-ante information can help to avoid that informal, highly complex trade negotiation processes are misused for power politics and splitting of coalitions. Information is particularly crucial in bilateral bargaining processes, in which the potential for power politics frequently originates in the fact that there is only limited information available. In addition, ex-ante information in crucial because informal negotiating processes often imply short time frames for responding to negotiating offers, which in turn requires additional resources and renders the process even more burdensome. Again, NGOs can prove useful by providing relevant, accurate and timely information.

The WTO's services negotiations have seen a recent example for NGOs' information dissemination function. In April 2002 civil society groups obtained part of the EC's draft requests for services trade liberalization[81] and, besides publicizing the event in the media, also transmitted these documents to developing country negotiators. By going to the media, civil society organizations made use of then available details about the content of EC's forthcoming market access request to generate a public discussion criticizing the breath of the EC's negotiating proposals, in particular those EC proposals directed towards developing country Members. NGOs thereby acted as mobilizers of public opinion, a function which will be further discussed in the next sub-section of this essay.[82]

---

[81] In the so-called market access phase of the services negotiations, WTO Members aim to increase the level of services trade liberalization by deepening commitments under the GATS market access (XVI) and national treatment (XVII) obligations. The essentially bilateral negotiating process builds on "requests" and "offers", negotiating documents which one WTO Member directs to another WTO Member. In a "request", a Member indicates the changes in domestic laws and regulations it expects its particular trading partner to undertake to increase this other Member's level of market openness. The responding trading partner then replies to this request with an "offer", indicating which changes it is willing to undertake. The Doha Declaration mandates that initial requests be submitted by 30 June 2002 and initial offers by 30 March 2003. These documents are generally not public, not even to the affected stakeholders within the individual countries. This secrecy has spurred considerable controversy amongst civil society groups.

[82] For example, "A Privatiser's Hit List", The Guardian, 18 April 2002; "EU Plays Down Leaked Trade Plan, Green Angry", Reuters, 18 April 2002; "The Bananas For the Banking Agenda", The Guardian 17 April

At the same time developing country delegations acknowledged the strategic value which prior and broad based access to otherwise unavailable information had for their bargaining position in general, for the time pressure they were under and for the development of their response to the EC requests. With respect to improving their bargaining power, they considered the broad availability of information useful, as it gave each of them the chance to compare its own EC request with the requests addressed to other WTO Members. This, it was said, would provide a good argument to reject a very ambitious demand in a certain area where the EC's requests to another Member was overly far reaching. With respect to the time factor, they acknowledged the value of timely, in-advance information, both for the development of their own request and for increasing the available time for developing their offers. In this context, they acknowledged the value of the information available in the leaked documents for developing their own requests, since the available drafts provided good guidance as to how a request shall be formulated and designed and thus the EC document would serve as an example.

In addition to the strategic value of the leaked documents in the negotiating processes, the leak also provided the basis for broader discussions about the pros and cons of services trade liberalization amongst the interested public. By providing specific information on the potential effects of the liberalization of health, education or water services, NGOs may also serve their role as intellectual competitors to the mainstream economic or trade ministries or simply provide expertise and skills in domestic consultation processes. However, the leak generated heavy reactions within the European Commission, which stated that it "strongly regret[s] this leak" and subsequently was going to great length to prevent any further leaks of their negotiating position.[83] Maybe the Commission is reluctant to share services negotiating proposals – many of which directed against developing country WTO Members – because it would not

---

2002. For additional examples of how NGOs as mobilizers of public opinion can serve developing countries see the next sub-section of this essay.

[83] Apparently, each EU member state only receives a few paper copies and is not allowed to make copies of these documents to distribute within ministries and other involved government agencies. This lack of consultation with concerned parties and affected stakeholders again gives rise to serious legitimacy concerns.

want to offer NGOs another possibility to mobilize public opinion in support of developing countries. This leads us to the third example, how NGOs can effectively assist developing countries to more effectively participate in WTO processes.

C. NGOs to Alleviate Lack of Political Clout– Mobilizing Public Opinion

By disseminating information to the public and by mobilizing public opinion, NGOs can serve to remedy some of the negative effects developing countries experience because of their lack of political clout vis-à-vis their industrialized country WTO counterparts. Traditionally, a WTO Member's political clout depended upon a country's trade volume and share in world trade.[84] For obvious reasons, this places many developing countries at a disadvantage. However, outside the narrow WTO context, political clout can also be generated through the particular issue, content or topic in question. For example, a specific issue can give rise to high public interest and initiate public discussions about the political correctness of a certain position. One could thus argue, that the issue-specific opinion of a broad public movement can effectively support a country's position in the WTO. Again, NGOs, as they disseminate information about WTO negotiating processes and as they act as mobilizers of public opinion, play a valuable role in this context. This sub-section reviews relevant experiences relating to the WTO's Doha Ministerial. It first describes how NGOs created the political space for the TRIPS and Health Declaration to happen and then reviews how NGOs more generally mobilized public opinion in support of developing countries in the Doha process.

While Uruguay Round negotiations on trade related intellectual property rights had not created much controversy outside the specific negotiating context, the last years have seen increasing public debate focusing mostly on questions related to human health and genetic resources. NGOs such as CPT,[85] MSF[86] and Oxfam concerted their efforts in a broad-based "Access to Medicine Campaign", skillfully using their technical expertise, media relations

---

[84] South Centre (2001) which states on page 10 that "for developed countries, shares in international markets where sufficiently high to allow them a voice as agenda-setters and hard bargain drivers in GATT negotiators".

[85] Consumer Project for Technology.

[86] Médecins sans Frontières.

and campaigning practices.[87] The debate on TRIPS and human health culminated in the run-up to the Doha Ministerial in autumn 2001 and the proposal to adopt a Declaration on TRIPS and Health was among the main agenda issues at the WTO Ministerial Conference.

During the months preceding the Doha Conference, NGOs, both Northern and Southern intensified their efforts and mounted campaigns against the constraints that the TRIPS Agreement poses on a country's health policies.[88] Campaigning organizations created a broad public discussion about South Africa's struggle to provide anti-viral drugs to its AIDS victims and about the way, the TRIPS Agreement was used by pharmaceutical companies and their representatives to pressure the South-African government into refraining from issuing compulsory licenses.[89] In addition, the fact that the US lodged a TRIPS-based WTO complaint against Brazil, challenging Brazilian anti-aids policies, also became the subject of public debate. In that context, the question of TRIPS and human health turned into a moral issue of fundamental equity.[90] NGOs had effectively created the political space for the TRIPS and Health Declaration to happen, overcoming previous power-imbalances between promoters and opponents of the WTO intellectual property regime.

---

[87] For an excellent review of the political strategies of the architects of the TRIPS, the effects of TRIPS, and the activities of the Access to Medicine Campaign during the last years until Doha, see *Sell* (2002).

[88] This "campaign" did not only consist of traditional activist-style campaigning activities but also used more technical campaigning tools. For example, the campaign produced detailed rebuttals of industry commissioned papers which had suggested that patents would not pose problems for Southern countries health policies. See *Sell* (2002) describing the October comment which CPT, Essential Action, Oxfam, Treatment Access Campaign, and Health Gap issued as a response to *Attaran / Gillespie-White* and PhRMA Surveys of Patents on Antiretroviral Drugs in Africa and how this significantly diluted the propaganda effect of the industry studies.

[89] Such compulsory licensing processes provide the legal basis for the wide provision of anti AIDS drugs.

[90] The Brazilian and South African examples were mainly North-South issues, pitching the interests of Northern intellectual property holders against those of Southern AIDS victims. Subsequently, the events of September 11 and the fact that both, the US and Canada considered issuing compulsory licenses to increase availability and access to Cipro added another dimension to the debate.

Apart from creating public pressure, NGOs also provided their own technical expertise. When not available in-house, they made finances available to have the world's leading intellectual property experts engage in the drafting, design and negotiating of the TRIPS and Health declaration.[91] By combining both political pressure to overcome lack of political clout and technical expertise to develop well-researched and targeted negotiating positions, NGOs effectively assisted developing countries to better participate in WTO processes.

The Doha Declaration on TRIPS and Health is probably the most prominent and successful example of developing country and NGO collaboration. There are however also other examples that demonstrate how NGOs, by disseminating information to a broad public and by creating awareness of power imbalances in WTO processes, have or will most likely affect pre-Doha and post-Doha decisions-making processes. Several NGOs have also identified the inequalities and power politics of WTO processes as their areas of work and research. Such organizations may prove valuable by establishing a record of individual events, where developing countries have been put under pressure by their industrialized counter parts. Communicating this information to the interested public, both in developing and developed countries, may prove useful to influence future processes.

For example, prior to the Doha Ministerial Conference, several organizations continuously reported on inside developments in Geneva[92] and followed and criticized Commissioner *Lamy*'s, USTR *Zoellick*'s and WTO Director General *Moore*'s "shuttle diplomacy" that aimed to convince developing countries of the benefits of signing onto a new round of trade negotiation. Complementing mainstream media reports on the "positive" concerted efforts of the US, the EC and the WTO to launch a new round of trade negotiations, civil society reports placed a different spin on the issue. They focused on the fact that these concerted efforts of Northern WTO Members and the Secretariat effectively pressured developing

---

[91] For NGOs as resource enhancers, see above sub-section V.A. of this essay.

[92] See *Sharma* (2001). See also the activities of the Trade Information Project (TIP) that monitors WTO activity in Geneva in an effort to facilitate advocacy by civil society actors to redress imbalances in the world trading system. http://www.iatp.org/tradeobservatory/library/index.cfm?c_id=43.

countries, both in Geneva and in their respective capitals, and that such lobbying efforts fell outside the agreed scope of activities to be taken by a Director General. The mandate of the Director General would have been that he or she is supposed to act as a neutral broker amongst WTO Members. NGOs have served to bring about neutrality and have also added value by clarifying misrepresentations of individual country positions in the mainstream press. In the aftermath of the Doha Ministerial, NGOs put together detailed documentation of the events before, during and after the WTO Conference and made this broadly available to the media and interested public, including at the WTO Symposium in spring 2002.[93]

In the aforementioned cases, the infusion of additional data and information, combined with the strategic dissemination of such information to target groups, individuals and the press, created the political space and impetus that allowed developing countries to assert themselves and effectively present and advance their positions. Thus, by mobilizing public opinion in support of developing country issues in the WTO, NGOs can assist developing countries to overcome deficiencies that these countries often experience due to their lack of political clout.

VI.   Building a New Alliance and the Pitfalls of the Doha Declaration - The Road Ahead Remains a Long One

Section V. of this essay has given examples of how NGOs can assist developing country WTO Members to more effectively participate in WTO decision-making processes. By providing much needed technical expertise in trade and trade related areas, NGOs can act as resource enhancers for developing countries. Through their information dissemination services to delegates, NGOs can help to address problems related to the informal and in-transparent decision-making processes in the WTO. Finally, by disseminating information to the public and by mobilizing public opinion, NGOs can create the necessary political space to allow developing countries to overcome problems due to lack of political clout.

---

[93] *Kwa* (2002). The aim of this report is to show with evidence the skewed process of decision-making and rule making in the WTO. For information about the work session on internal transparency and decision-making processes of May 2002 "WTO Symposium on the Doha Development Agenda and Beyond", see http://www.wto.org/english/tratop_e/dda_e/symp_devagenda_prog_02_e.htm.

Hopefully, these most recent developments constitute the beginning of a potentially powerful alliance between civil society groups and the developing world. The extent to which this alliance will truly materialize will depend on a series of factors, including the ability of NGOs to provide political pressure as well as highly qualified advise and expertise on trade-related issues. Arguably, the development of this alliance will also depend on the extent to which NGOs are prepared to constructively work within the ramifications of a system such as the WTO, rather than simply oppose it. Yet, whether this alliance will ultimately come to life or not and whether the WTO will move forward on external transparency depends upon all WTO Membership.

This essay attempts to present arguments which should discourage developing countries from "view[ing] NGOs in simplistic terms of one (i.e. the marginalized member states of the WTO) vs. them / the others (NGOs which tow the line of the developed countries)".[94] Thereby it aims to encourage WTO Members, in particular developing country Members to analyze potentials and pitfalls of increasing NGO access to WTO processes. However, judging upon Members' collective at the Doha Ministerial, prospects for realizing the benefits of increasing NGO participation look bleak.

Ministers in Doha devoted a whole paragraph of the Declaration to transparency-related issues. [95] By addressing both internal and external transparency in one paragraph, Members recognized the systemic link between both aspects of transparency. However, the adoption of new text does not necessarily ensure positive results. First, with respect to internal transparency paragraph 10 of the Doha Declaration mistakenly creates the impression that internal transparency problems are related to expanding WTO membership,

---

[94]   South Centre (2001) 24 et seqq.

[95]   See para 10 of the Doha Ministerial Declaration, which reads as follows: "Recognizing the challenges posed by an expanding WTO membership, we confirm our collective responsibility to ensure internal transparency and the effective participation of all Members. While emphasizing the intergovernmental character of the organization, we are committed to making the WTO's operations more transparent, including through more effective and prompt dissemination of information, and to improve dialogue with the public. We shall therefore at the national and multilateral levels continue to promote a better public understanding of the WTO and to communicate the benefits of a liberal, rules-based multilateral trading system".

rather than originating in systemic structural flaws of both, GATT
and WTO decision-making process and resource allocation amongst
Members. In addition, Members simply aimed to improve internal
transparency by rectifying imbalances in resource allocation and
technical expertise through capacity building and technology transfer.[96] While it is positive that subsequently Members made concerted efforts to move forward on capacity building, it remains to
be seen whether these efforts will prove positive for developing
country WTO Members. There are concerns that ultimately these
capacity building activities will be used to pressure countries into
accepting pertinent commitments at the next Ministerial Conference
in Mexico.

The Declaration's shortcomings with respect to external transparency are equally disappointing. While Members state that they
"are committed to making the WTO's operations more transparent
... and to improve dialogue with the public", the Declaration's only
clear commitment refers to Members assurance to "continue to
promote a better understanding of the WTO and to communicate
the benefits of a liberal, rules-based multilateral trading system".
This direction of action not only fails to promote increased NGO
access to WTO processes, it seems to actually move the WTO's
efforts in the wrong direction. Instead of allowing for a broad set of
views to be heard in international trade policy-making, Members
decided to focus their efforts to "communicate the benefits of a
liberal, rules-based multilateral trading system".

This language clearly fails to recognize that civil society fur-
nishes valuable elements to any trade policy-making processes by
acting as intellectual competitors and resource enhancers. In addi-

---

[96] See paras 38 et seqq. of the Doha Ministerial Declaration.

[97] See above.

[98] See para 10 of the Doha Ministerial Declaration, which reads as follows: "Recognizing the challenges posed by an expanding WTO membership, we confirm our collective responsibility to ensure internal
transparency and the effective participation of all Members. While emphasizing the intergovernmental character of the organization, we are
committed to making the WTO's operations more transparent, including through more effective and prompt dissemination of information,
and to improve dialogue with the public. We shall therefore at the national and multilateral levels continue to promote a better public understanding of the WTO and to communicate the benefits of a liberal,
rules-based multilateral trading system".

tion this explicit commitment to "communicate the benefits" is likely to further the perception that the WTO is unwilling to listen to diverging arguments and remains closed to public scrutiny. By disallowing the integration of non-trade views, which could forseeably improve the quality and authority of the WTO's policy choices and enhance its accountability, the Organization has neglected the opportunity to overcome its increasing legitimacy problems. It seems that both, NGOs and the WTO still have a long way to go to make real progress.

It is hoped that this essay provides a step towards making real progress and thereby towards reducing existing and avoiding further WTO legitimacy problems. In particular, this essay aims to identify new ways to look at external and internal transparency problems, both of which are amongst the main sources of the those legitimacy problems.

With respect to internal transparency, this essay argues that NGOs can assist to address imbalances between developed and developing country WTO Members. In particular, NGOs can provide technical expertise, crucial information and mobilize the public in support of disadvantaged WTO Members. Whilst NGOs cannot fully remedy any internal legitimacy problems they can provide innovative ways and assistance to address them. It is hoped that this essay's focus on internal transparency problems, and innovative ways of addressing them, will provide new input into discussions surrounding fundamental structural problems relating to WTO decision-making processes. Only by truly addressing internal decision-making deficiencies, will the organization overcome this central source of its legitimacy problems.

With respect to external transparency, this essay attempts to overcome the stalemate the issue currently faces in the WTO context. This essay aims to dismiss one of the most prevalent reasons, developing country WTO Members bring to argue against increasing NGO access to the multilateral trading system. By showing that increasing collaboration with NGOs can improve rather than exacerbate problems related to internal transparency and by showing that NGOs can be beneficial for developing county WTO Members this essay aims to encourage developing countries to constructively engage in discussions about issues related to external transparency. Addressing legitimacy problems arising from external transparency related deficiencies is far from simple and much analysis and discussion about the extent and the best way to engage NGOs remains ahead. It is thus crucial that Members have the political will to truly develop, consider and analyze different options.

Hopefully, by focusing on both, external and internal transparency, this essay induces WTO Members - in particular developing country Members - to truly engage in such discussions.

By highlighting the intrinsic link between internal and external transparency this essay also sets certain standards for the process through which the issue of external transparency should move forward. It suggests that any process to move forward on external transparency must fulfill standards related to internal transparency. Any such processes must fully and effectively engage developing country Members, rather than being a process dominated and driven by Northern WTO Members or the WTO Secretariat. This essay aims to assist and induce developing countries to actively engage in such a debate and thereby allow such an inclusive process to happen.

Bibliography:

Action Aid / CIEL / Friends of the Earth International / IATP / WWF International (2001), Open Letter on WTO and Institutional Reform for the Fourth WTO Ministerial and Beyond, http://www. panda.org/resources/programmes/trade/latest.htm.

A. E. Appleton (2000), *Amicus Curiae* Submissions in the *Carbon Steel* Case: Another Rabbit from the Appellate Body's Hat?, Journal of International Economic Law 3 (2000), No. 4, 691-699.

C. Bellmann / R. Gerster (1996), Accountability in the World Trade Organization, Journal of World Trade 30 (1996), No. 6, 31-74.

W. Benedek (1998), Relations of the WTO with other International Organizations and NGOs, in *F. Weiss / E. Denters / P. de Waart* (eds.), International Economic Law with a Human Face, Den Haag / Cambridge, MA 1998, 479-493.

W. Benedek (1999), Developing the Constitutional Order of the WTO – The Role of NGOs, in *W. Benedek / H. Isak / R. Kicker* (eds.), Development and Developing International and European

Law. Essays in Honor of Konrad Ginther on the Occasion of his 65th Birthday, Frankfurt 1999, 228-250.

J. Cameron / R. Ramsay (1995), Participation by NGOs in the WTO, Global Environment and Trade Study (GETS) Working Paper, Minneapolis, MN 1995.

B. Chaytor (1999), Improving transparency and civil society involvement in the World Trade Organization, Foundation for International Environmental Law and Development / FIELD, London, September 1999.

S. Charnovitz (1997), Two Centuries of Participation: NGOs and International Governance, Michigan Journal of International Trade 18 (1997), No. 2, 183-286.

S. Charnovitz (1999), Participation of Nongovernmental Organizations in the World Trade Organization, University of Pennsylvania Journal of International Economic Law 17 (1996), No.1, 331-357.

S. Charnovitz / J. Wickham (1995), Non-Governmental Organizations and the Original International Trade Regime, Journal of World Trade 29 (1995), No. 5, 111-121.

J. L. Dunoff (1998), The Misguided Debate Over NGO Participation at the WTO, Journal of International Economic Law 1 (1998), No. 3, 433-456.

D. Esty (1997), Why the World Trade Organization Needs Environmental NGOs, International Center for Trade and Sustainable Development, Public Participation in the International Trading System Vol. 1, No.3, 1997.

D. Esty (1998), Non-Governmental Organizations at the World Trade Organization: Cooperation, Competition or Exclusion, Journal of International Economic Law 1 (1998), No. 1, 122-147.

Foreign Policy Centre (2000), NGO Rights and Responsibilities - A New Deal for Global Governance, London 2000.

D. Hunter / J. Salzman / D. Zaelke (2002) (eds.), International Environmental Law and Policy, New York, 2002.

ICTSD / International Center for Trade and Sustainable Development (1999), Accreditation Schemes and Other Arrangement for

Public Participation in International Fora, Genève, November 1999.

P. Kohona (2001), The Role of Non-State Entities in the Making and Implementation of International Norms, Journal of World Investment 2 (2001), No. 3, 537-578.

M. Krajewski (2000), From Green Room to Glass Room, Participation of Developing Countries and Internal Transparency in the WTO Decision Making Process, Germanwatch, 2000.

M. Krajewski (2001a), Democratic Legitimacy and Constitutional Perspectives of WTO Law, Journal of World Trade 35 (2001), No. 1, 176-186.

M. Krajewski (2001b), Verfassungsperspektiven und Legitimation des Rechts der Welthandelsorganisation (WTO) (= Hamburger Studien zum Europäischen und Internationalen Recht, Vol. 31), Berlin 2001.

A. Kwa (2002), Power Politics in the WTO – Developing Countries' Perspectives in Decision-making Processes in Trade Negotiations, available at http://www.focusweb.org/publications/2002/power%20politics_final.pdf.

G. Marceau, / P. Pedersen (1999), Is the WTO Open and Transparent? A Discussion of the Relationship of the WTO with Nongovernmental Organizations and Civil Society's Claims for more Transparency and Public Participation, Journal of World Trade 33 (1999), No. 1, 5-51.

G. Marceau / M. Stilwell (2001), Practical Suggestions for *Amicus Curiae* Briefs Before WTO Adjudicating Bodies, Journal of International Economic Law 4 (2001), No. 1, 155-187.

P. Mavroidis (2001), *Amicus Curiae* Briefs Before the WTO: Much Ado About Nothing, Harvard Jean Monnet Working Paper 02/01, Cambridge, MA 2001.

J. A. Scholte / R. O'Brien / M. Williams (1999), The WTO and Civil Society, Journal of World Trade 33 (1999), No. 1, 107-123.

S. Sell (2002), TRIPS and the Access to Medicine Campaign, paper prepared for the Conference "Access to Medicines for the Developing World: International Facilitation or Hindrance?", Madison, Wisconsin, March 9-10, 2002 (forthcoming).

S. Sharma (2001), A Mockery of a Multilateral Trading System: Who Is Accountable? October 2001, available at http://www. wtowatch.org/library/admin/uploadedfiles/Mockery_of_a_Multil ateral_Trading_System_Who_I.htm.

South Centre (2001), WTO Decision-Making and Developing Countries, Trade-Related Agenda, Development and Equity, T.R.A.D.E. Working Paper, Genève November 2001.

G. Tansey (2001), IPRs, food and biodiversity, paper presented at World Bank NGO Agricultural Science and Technology Roundtable Discussion, Washington, DC, 16 April 2001.

United Nations (1997) (ed.), Directory of Non-Governmental Organizations, Associated with the Department of Public Information 1997 – 1998, New York 1997, DPI/ 1696/Rev.1-13569-June 1997-8M.

R. Wilkinson (2001), The WTO in Crisis, Exploring the Dimensions of Institutional Inertia, Journal of World Trade 35 (2001), No. 3, 397-419.

WWF / World Wildlife Fund for Nature (2001) (ed.), Preliminary Assessment of the Environmental and Social Effects of Trade in Tourism, WWF Internal Discussion Paper, May 2001.

WWF / CIEL (2001) (eds.), Biodiversity and Intellectual Property Rights: Reviewing Intellectual Property Rights in Light of the Objectives of the Convention on Biological Diversity, Joint Discussion Paper, March 2001.

G. A. Zonnekeyn (2001), The Appellate Body's Communication on *amicus curiae* briefs in the *Asbestos* case – an Echternach Procession? Journal of World Trade 35 (2001), No. 3, 553-563.

Ernst-Ulrich Petersmann

Constitutional Primacy and 'Indivisibility' of Human Rights in International Law? The Unfinished Human Rights Revolution and the Emerging Global Integration Law

Introduction: How to Overcome the 'Democracy Deficit' of International Law?

From the peace treaties of Westphalia (1648) up to the UN Charter (1945), the *international law of coexistence* evolved as a system of rights and duties of states focusing on the protection of "sovereign equality" of states (Article 2:1 UN Charter) and on effectiveness of government control over a territory and a population. *Inside democracies*, validity of law depends on respect for human rights and for democratic rule-making procedures. The validity of classical international law rules, however, and the recognition of states as subjects of international law into whose "domestic jurisdiction" other states must not intervene, does not depend on the democratic legitimacy of the governments concerned. Due to its power-oriented character, the lack of legitimacy of classical international law has been criticized long since (e.g. by colonial and other suppressed people) and has rendered a worldwide rule-of-law system impossible.

Since the fall of the Berlin wall (1989), human rights have become universally recognized by all 189 UN member states not only as part of international treaty law (e.g. in the UN Charter and the 1989 UN Convention on the Rights of the Child, ratified by 191 states), but also of international customary law and of the "general principles of law recognized by civilized nations" (Article 38, Statute of the International Court of Justice). The UN's *international law of cooperation* includes also intergovernmental rights and obligations to mutually beneficial cooperation across frontiers and obligations to respect human rights. Yet, UN law secures neither democratic governance nor democratic legislation implementing and protecting human rights, nor judicial protection of human rights.[1] Can the necessary "international governance" for the supply of "public international goods" (such as democratic peace, protection of the "global commons", promotion of human rights and of welfare-increasing division of labour across frontiers) be realized through power-oriented worldwide organizations without democratic governance at the international level and without effective protection of individual liberty rights, property rights and other human rights necessary for a mutually beneficial division of labour among free citizens?

The exercise and protection of human rights (e.g. through democratic institutions, parliamentary legislation and judicial remedies) require economic resources. For instance, the human right to health requires production of medicines, formation of medical doctors, access to medical services at affordable prices, construction, equipment and maintenance of hospitals; and the human right to education depends on access to teachers and teaching materials including schools and universities. Since economic resources are scarce and rational individuals tend to compete as "utility maximizers", national and international relations continue to be dominated by economic and trade issues, such as the need for division of labour, for monetary and legal stability as preconditions for savings and investments, production, trade and other international economic transactions necessary for satisfying the unlimited consumer demand for private and public goods and services. Why has it been

---

[1]   See *Petersmann* (2002a).

possible only in the area of regional and worldwide economic law to protect freedom, non-discrimination and mutually beneficial co-operation among citizens across frontiers through legal and judicial remedies which go far beyond those in other areas of international law (e.g. compulsory adjudication in the EC and WTO)?[2]

Regional and worldwide economic integration law, such as the Agreement establishing the World Trade Organization (WTO) and the more than hundred free trade area and customs union agreements pursuant to GATT Article XXIV and GATS Article V, derive legitimacy not only from the ratification of these agreements by national parliaments and from "embedding" the domestic implementation of these agreements into domestic constitutional systems. No less important is that their legal and judicial guarantees protect individual freedom, non-discrimination, rule of law and welfare-increasing cooperation among producers, investors, traders and consumers far beyond the corresponding legal guarantees in national laws and constitutions.[3] Economists have long since recognized that international guarantees of "market freedoms", non-discrimination and rule of law, such as those in the 1944 Bretton Woods Agreements and in GATT 1947, can serve "constitutional functions" for enabling citizens to increase their individual and social welfare through mutually beneficial division of labour – guided by the information functions, coordination functions, allocation and distribution functions of market prices and competition across frontiers – without prejudice to the sovereign rights of governments to correct "market failures" and supply "public goods" through national legislation and other government interventions.[4] The liberal trade order before World War I illustrated that international market mechanisms – provided they are legally protected and restrained by national and international rules – enable the collective supply of international public goods without multilateral governance.

The move from "negative integration" (e.g. reciprocal liberalization of discriminatory border restrictions in GATT) toward worldwide harmonization of non-discriminatory internal regulations (e.g. for trade-related services, investments, property rights, competition and environmental rules) raises new concerns about how worldwide rule-making can be legitimized if it is no longer effec-

---

[2] See e.g. *Petersmann* (1998).
[3] See e.g. *Hilf/Petersmann* (1993).
[4] Cf. *Petersmann* (1991), notably chapter VII.

tively controlled by civil society, parliaments and "deliberative democracy". Can the divergent national traditions of democratic self-governance legitimize intergovernmental rule-making at the international level even though the preconditions of democratic legitimacy – such as a "government of the people, by the people and for the people" (*A. Lincoln*) – do not exist in worldwide organizations where governments often continue to behave like monarchs treating their citizens as mere objects and negotiating rules behind closed doors without transparent democratic discussion?

Since the 1990s, the universal recognition of human rights offers a new source of democratic legitimization of international law. The Universal Declaration of Human Rights (UDHR) recognizes that "everyone is entitled to a social and international order in which the rights and freedoms set forth in this Declaration can be fully realized" (Article 28). Yet, national and international law have so far focused on protection of human rights vis-à-vis *domestic* governments; outside Europe, human rights have not yet been effectively defined and protected vis-à-vis the *collective exercise of government powers in international organizations*.

What are the corresponding human rights obligations of international organizations, for instance as regards the transparency, openness and representative nature of their decision-making practices, their respect for individual freedom of access to information and access to courts, and their standards for the increasingly frequent review by intergovernmental bodies of national regulatory measures? Can the human rights ideal of individual self-government and self-development, and judicial protection of human rights across frontiers, compensate for the ever weaker parliamentary control over international law and international organizations?[5] How can the human rights of those people who are not effectively represented in intergovernmental organizations, be protected more effectively at the international level? Are there other forms of "functional legitimization" of international organizations, different from human rights and parliamentary democracy, for instance similar to the recourse to independent, and thus less politicized organizations

---

[5] For a comparative study of foreign affairs and foreign trade under the liberal 18th century US Constitution, the liberal 19th century Swiss Constitution of 1874, the liberal 20th century German Constitution of 1949, and under the EC Treaty Constitution see *Petersmann* (1991), chapter VIII.

inside democracies (e.g. central banks, competition authorities, regulatory authorities)? Or do functional intergovernmental organizations risk to evolve into a new despotism that is no longer effectively controlled by citizens and parliaments? How can worldwide organizations be more effectively "constitutionalized" either at the international level (e.g. through stronger institutional "checks and balances") or – since a world government, a world parliament and a worldwide *demos* remain undesirable because they are unlikely to protect human rights and individual diversity effectively – through "embedding" and "anchoring" international organizations as a "fourth branch of government" in domestic constitutional systems (e.g. through more effective control of international rule-making by national parliaments, national courts and individuals recognized as legal subjects of the law of international organizations)?

I.   Constitutional Primacy and 'Indivisibility' of Human Rights in International Law? The Unfinished 'Human Rights Revolution'

The focus of classical international law on freedom of governments rested on power-oriented value premises which differ from the modern recognition, in national and international human rights instruments, of "the inherent dignity and of the equal and inalienable rights of all members of the human family (as) the foundation of freedom, justice and peace in the world" (Preamble, UDHR 1948).[6] Human dignity (e.g. in the sense of moral, rational and personal autonomy of individuals), and the universal legal recognition of "inalienable" liberties and other human rights, proceed from the assumption that values must be derived from individuals and from their consent, and that all government powers are constitutionally limited by human rights. As inside constitutional democracies, the legal recognition of an inalienable core of human rights as international *ius cogens* – *acknowledged* but not granted by governments – can be interpreted as constitutional restraint on all government powers, including those of international organizations. Such a *human rights approach* can lead to treaty interpretations (e.g. on the consistency of humanitarian NATO interventions in Kosovo with

---

[6]   On the need for reconciling the international law concepts of "state sovereignty" and "popular sovereignty" with the universal recognition of inalienable human rights ("individual sovereignty") see *Petersmann* (2002b).

UN law) clashing with state-centered interpretations focusing on state sovereignty and government consent rather than on protection of inalienable human rights. Yet, human rights are not absolute and need to be defined, balanced, implemented and protected through democratic legislation and judicial remedies which may legitimately differ from country to country. In contrast to one-sided claims by human rights organizations that the difficult balancing between trade rules and human rights should be solved by reliance on "hierarchy of norms" and by subordination of trade rules to "the principle of pre-eminence of human rights over WTO trade agreements",[7] recognition of the constitutional primacy of human rights does not dispense from the need to balance the "human rights values" underlying many WTO rules with other human rights.

Human rights do not enforce themselves. Historically, recognition, protection and promotion of human rights have usually resulted from "bottom-up pressures" and "glorious revolutions" empowering individuals, parliaments and courts to defend and enforce human rights against abuses of power. The constitutional protection of civil and political ("first generation") human rights preceded economic, social and cultural ("second generation") human rights. Today, however, all governments recognize that "all human rights are universal, indivisible and interdependent and interrelated".[8] This modern legal insight reflects a fundamental fact of life: Most people spend most of their time on their economic activities of producing goods and services and on exchanging the fruits of their labour for other goods and services that are necessary for survival and personal development. Protection, promotion and enjoyment of human rights depend on scarce economic resources and on enabling individuals, through division of labour based on liberty rights and property rights, to acquire, save, invest, produce and exchange resources necessary for their self-development and self-governance.

The 'indivisibility' of civil, political, economic and social human rights entails the need to protect private autonomy in the economy no less than in the polity by basic rights vis-à-vis abuses not only of *political power* but also of *economic power*. The inherent tendency of liberty to destroy itself ("paradox of freedom") exists in

---

[7] See *Habbard/Guiraud* (2001) 3. On the "human rights functions" of WTO rules see e.g. *Petersmann* (2000a).

[8] Vienna Declaration of the UN World Conference on Human Rights (1993), section I.5, cf.: United Nations (1995) 450.

economic markets (e.g. leading to monopolies and cartels) no less
than in political markets (e.g. leading to concentration and abuses
of political power). Most states have therefore adopted not only national constitutions protecting equal human rights in political decision-making processes. More than 100 states have also adopted national competition laws, or international commitments (e.g. in UN
resolutions and Article 45 of the Cotonou Agreement of 2000) to
introduce such laws, so as to protect economic markets against concentration and abuses of economic power (e.g. by monopolization
and other abuses of market power).

In European integration, citizens, parliaments and courts have
forced the EC institutions to recognize that, as stated by the EC
Court of Justice, "fundamental human rights (are) enshrined in the
general principles of Community law and protected by the Court",[9]
and "respect for human rights is a condition of the lawfulness of
Community acts".[10] The European Court of Human Rights has
likewise emphasized that the human rights obligations of the more
than 40 member states of the European Convention on Human
Rights (ECHR) apply not only to national measures but also to *collective* rule-making in international organizations and to the domestic implementation of international rules:

"Where States establish international organizations, or *mutatis
mutandis* international agreements, to pursue cooperation in certain
fields of activities, there may be implications for the protection of
fundamental rights. It would be incompatible with the purpose and
object of the Convention if Contracting States were thereby ab-
solved from their responsibility under the Convention in relation to
the field of activity covered by such attribution".[11]

---

[9]   Case 29/69, *Stauder*, ECR 1969, 419, para. 7.
[10] Opinion 2/94, ECR 1996 I-1759, para. 34.
[11] European Court of Human Rights, Third Section Decision as to the
      Admissibility of Application No. 43844/98 by T.I. against the United
      Kingdom, 7 March 2000, at page 16 (nyr). In *Matthews* v. *UK*, the
      European Court of Human Rights found the United Kingdom in viola-
      tion of the human right to participate in free elections of the legislature
      even though the law which denied voting rights in Gibraltar imple-
      mented a treaty concluded among EC member states on the election of
      the European Parliament: "there is no difference between European
      and domestic legislation, and no reason why the United Kingdom
      should not be required to 'secure' the rights (under the ECHR) in re-
      spect of European legislation in the same way as those rights are re-

In most worldwide organizations, however, human rights have not been effectively integrated into multilateral rule-making and policies and are not effectively protected through worldwide adjudication. In contrast to the *"Matthews* principle" recognized in European law,[12] citizens outside Europe seem to lack effective judicial remedies to ensure that all international obligations undertaken by states must remain consistent with their human rights obligations. The UN Covenant on Economic, Social and Cultural Rights (UNCESCR) offers much looser legal and institutional safeguards for compliance with economic and social human rights compared with the UN Covenant on Civil and Political Rights (UNCCPR).[13] By not mentioning property rights, and by "safeguarding fundamental political and economic freedoms to the individual" only in an indirect and inadequate manner (cf. Article 6:2), the UNCESCR does not protect the legal preconditions for creating the economic resources necessary for the enjoyment of human rights. The now regular civil society protests against non-transparent rule-making in worldwide organizations, and the often one-sided industry-pressures determining multilateral negotiations (e.g. in the GATT and WTO), illustrate a continuing "clash of civilizations" between a citizen-oriented *human rights culture* and power-oriented pressures in intergovernmental negotiations and state-centered organizations.

II.   Time for Replacing the 'Washington Consensus' by a *New Integration Paradigm* Based on Strengthening Universal Human Rights in Global Integration Law

The human rights obligations in the UN Charter and in the UDHR of 1948 were negotiated at the same time as the 1944 Bretton Woods Agreements, the General Agreement on Tariffs and Trade (GATT) of 1947 and the 1948 Havana Charter for an International Trade Organization. All these agreements aimed at protecting liberty, non-discrimination, rule of law, social welfare and other human rights values through a rules-based international order

---

quired to be 'secured' in respect of purely domestic legislation". Cf. European Court of Human Rights, judgment of 18 February 1999 on complaint No. 24833/94, see Europäische Grundrechtszeitschrift (EUGRZ) 1999, 200.

[12] See the judgment by the European Court of Human Rights mentioned above in note 11.

[13] Cf. e.g. *Arambulo* (1999).

and "specialized agencies" (Article 57 UN Charter) committed to the economic principle of "separation of policy instruments":

- *foreign policies* were to be coordinated in the UN so as to promote "sovereign equality of all its Members" (Article 2:1 UN Charter) and collective security;
- *liberalization of payments* and *monetary stability* were collectively pursued through the rules and assistance of the International Monetary Fund (IMF);
- GATT 1947 and the Havana Charter aimed at mutually beneficial *liberalization of international trade and investments*;
- *development aid and policies* were coordinated in the World Bank Group;
- and *social laws and policies* were promoted in the International Labour Organization (ILO) and other specialized agencies (like UNESCO and WHO).

Apart from a few exceptions (such as the references to human rights in the UN Charter and in the statutes of the ILO, UNESCO and WHO), human rights were not effectively integrated into the law of most worldwide organizations so as to facilitate *functional intergovernmental integration* (such as liberalization of trade and payments restrictions) notwithstanding different views on human rights and domestic policies (such as *communism*). In accordance with the "principles of justice" elaborated by modern legal philosophers[14] and reflected in the constitutional law of the leading postwar power,[15] the postwar institutions gave priority to reciprocal interna-

---

[14] See e.g. *Rawls* (1999a), Chapter II, whose conception of "justice as fairness" for defining the basic rights and liberties of free and equal citizens in a constitutional democracy gives priority to maximum equal liberty as "first principle of justice". *Rawls'* "principle of fair equality of opportunity" and his "difference principle" are recognized only as secondary principles necessary for socially just conditions essential for moral and rational self-development of every person. *Kant*ian legal theory also gives priority to a legal duty of states to ensure conditions of maximum law-governed freedom over moral "duties of benevolence" to provide for the needs of the citizens (cf. *Rosen* (1993) 217; *Guyer* (2000) 264 et seq.).

[15] For instance, the Bill of Rights, which had to be appended to the US Constitution in order to secure its ratification, focuses more on "inalienable rights" to life and liberty than on social rights to secure "the general Welfare" (recognized as an objective of the US Constitution in its Preamble).

tional *liberalization* (e.g. in the context of the IMF, GATT, WTO, WIPO and ILO) and to *wealth creation*. *Economic* and *social rights* and *redistribution of wealth* were perceived as primarily the responsibility of *national* governments, depending on national resources and value preferences, to be supplemented by "international benevolence".[16] Article 28 of the UDHR recognized: "Everyone is entitled to a social and international order in which the rights and freedoms set forth in the Declaration can be fully realized". Yet, UN human rights law lacks a coherent theory on transnational economic and social human rights vis-à-vis not only domestic governments but also foreign governments and international organizations.

Regional integration law, by contrast, has moved toward a different "integration paradigm" linking economic integration to constitutional guarantees of human rights, democracy and undistorted competition. For instance, the "human rights clauses" in the European Union (EU) Treaty, in the association and cooperation agreements between the EU and more than twenty countries in Eastern Europe and the Mediterranean, and in the EU's Cotonou Agreement with 77 African, Caribbean and Pacific states make "respect for human rights, democratic principles and the rule of law … essential elements" of these agreements.[17] The Quebec Summit Declaration of April 2001 and the "Inter-American Charter of Democracy" of September 2001, adopted by more than 30 member states of the Organization of American States, likewise link the plans for a Free Trade Area of the Americas (FTAA) to the strengthening of human rights and democracy. Even though "realists" continue to dominate foreign policy-making, human rights are becoming ever more important parts of the national identity and of the foreign and security policies of states, as illustrated by the humanitarian intervention by 19 NATO countries in the Kosovo crisis and their invocation of

---

[16] On legal philosophies concerning moral and legal duties of assistance vis-à-vis "burdened societies", the "principle of just savings", a "property-owning democracy" promoting widespread ownership of economic and human capital, and on "distributive justice among peoples" see e.g. *Rawls* (1999b), chapters 15 and 16. On human rights and "global justice" see *Falk* (2000).

[17] The quotation is from Article 9 of the Cotonou Agreement signed in June 2000 by the EU, the 15 EU member states and 77 ACP countries. On human rights in the external relations law of the EU see e.g. the contributions by *Clapham*, *Simma*, *Aschenbrenner* and *Schulte* to *Alston et alii* (1999).

NATO's mutual defense principle (Article 5) in response to the terrorist attacks in New York and Washington on 11 September 2001.[18] The proposals in the WTO Ministerial Declaration of 14 November 2001,[19] for negotiating competition, investment, environmental and health protection rules in the WTO, are further illustrations of the need to examine whether the European and American "integration paradigm" should not also become accepted at the worldwide level in order to promote consensus on a new kind of global integration law based on human rights and solidary sharing of the social adjustment costs of global integration.

The proposed change from *international functionalism* to *constitutionalism* does not put into question the economic efficiency arguments for "optimizing" and separating policy instruments.[20] However, European integration confirms that the collective supply of public goods (such as global division of labour) may not be politically feasible without comprehensive "package deals" including solidary responses to "market failures" and redistributive "principles of justice".[21] Less-developed countries, for instance, often perceive market competition as a "license to kill" for multinational corporations from developed countries as long as liberal trade rules are not supplemented by competition and social rules (as in the EC) promoting fair opportunities and equitable distribution of the gains from trade.

In order to remain politically acceptable, global integration law (e.g. in the WTO) must pursue not only "economic efficiency" but also "democratic legitimacy" and "social justice" as defined by hu-

---

[18] See International Herald Tribune of 13 September 2001 3. See more generally e.g. *Forsythe* (2000b).

[19] WTO doc. WT/MIN(01)/DEC/W/1 of 14 November 2001.

[20] See e.g. *Corden* (1974); *Viscusi/Vernon/Harrington* (1997).

[21] On the need for international organizations and international aid for the provision of "global public goods" see *Kaul/Grunberg/Stern* (1999). The recent World Bank report on "Globalization, Growth and Poverty: Building an Inclusive World Economy" (2001) emphasizes that open market economies and increased trade offer the best hope for the more than 1 billion people living on less than one dollar a day. Over the past two decades of globalization, the successful integration of more than 24 big developing countries into the global industrial economy has increased their income per head (about 5% p.a.) and reduced the number of people in absolute poverty. Countries not participating in the global division of labour have tended to aggravate their poverty problems.

man rights. Citizens will continue to challenge the democratic and social legitimacy of integration law if it pursues economic welfare without regard to social human rights, for example the *human right to education* of the 130 million children (aged from 6 to 12) who do not attend primary school; the *human right to basic health care* of the 25 million Africans living with AIDS, or of the about 35,000 children dying each day from curable diseases; and the *human right to food and an adequate standard of living* for the 1.2 billion people living on less than a dollar a day. The new opportunities for the worldwide enjoyment of human rights created by global division of labour (such as additional economic resources, job opportunities, worldwide communication systems, access to new medicines and technologies) must be accompanied by stronger legal protection of social human rights so as to limit abuses of deregulation (e.g. by international cartels, trade in drugs and arms, trafficking in women and children), help vulnerable groups to adjust to change without violation of their human rights, and put pressure on authoritarian governments to protect not only the self-interests of the rulers and of big business but the human rights of all their citizens.

III.   **Legal, Economic and Political Arguments for Integrating Human Rights into the Law of Worldwide Organizations**

Most of the 144 WTO member states have ratified or signed the 1966 UN Covenants on civil, political, economic, social and cultural human rights, other UN human rights covenants as well as regional and bilateral treaties on the protection of human rights. In contrast to the judicial remedies provided for in the European and Inter-American Human Rights conventions,[22] however, the worldwide human rights obligations and supervisory bodies under the six "core" UN human rights treaties (on civil, political, economic, social and cultural human rights, rights of the child, prohibition of torture, racial discrimination and discrimination against women) do

---

[22]   The African Charter on Human and Peoples' Rights, in force since October 1986 and now ratified by all 53 member states of the Organization of African Unity, does not provide for access to an African Court of human rights. The *African Commission on Human and Peoples Rights* has, however, received one inter-state and several non-state complaints. In some African countries like South Africa, constitutional protection and justiciability of economic, social and cultural human rights are well established.

not ensure effective protection of human rights by national and international courts.[23] The 183 multilateral treaties on labour and social standards adopted in the ILO suffer likewise from inadequate enforcement mechanisms.[24] In many countries, widespread and unnecessary poverty, health and food problems reflect a lack of effective protection of human rights through legislation, administrative procedures (e.g. in agricultural, health and labour ministries), judicial remedies and assistance by national and international organizations for the protection of human rights (e.g. to health, food and work). The more globalization renders "foreign" and "domestic" affairs" inseparable, the more "realist" claims for separation of policy instruments and for "primacy of foreign policy" (including monetary policy in the IMF and trade policy in the WTO) risk undermining human rights and policy-coherence at home and abroad.

From a human rights perspective, the universal recognition of human rights as part of *general international law* requires a human rights framework for *all areas* of international law and international organizations so as to render human rights more effective and promote better coherence of national and international law and policies. The state-centered tradition of treating individuals as mere objects of international law, and the contradictory behavior of governments paying lip-service to human rights in UN bodies but advocating "realpolitik" without regard to human rights in "specialized" international organizations, are inconsistent with the legal primacy and constitutional functions of human rights. The universal recognition of the *indivisibility of civil, political, economic, social and cultural human rights* has contributed to increasing jurisprudence by national courts (including those of developing countries

---

[23] For critical assessments of the effectiveness of worldwide human rights treaties see e.g. *Alston/Crawford* (2000). For a recent collection of international human rights treaties see e.g. Council of Europe (2000). For the political obstacles to implementing human rights in a world of "realist" power politics see e.g. *Forsythe* (2000a).

[24] For a recent critical assessment of the ILO supervisory and promotional systems and of other mechanisms to promote core labour standards worldwide see e.g.: OECD (2000) 43 et seq. In November 2000, the ILO's Governing Body concluded that the 1998 report and recommendations of the ILO's Commission of Inquiry on forced labour in Myanmar had not been implemented and therefore "sanctions" should take effect. The ILO lacks, however, powers to ensure that economic sanctions are effectively implemented.

like India and South Africa) and by international courts that economic and social rights (such as the EC Treaty guarantees of freedom of trade and non-discrimination of women) may be no less
justiciable than civil and political rights.[25] Also economists, politicians and civil society groups increasingly recognize the relevance
of human rights for economic welfare and define *development* no
longer in purely quantitative terms (e.g. as increase in real income
and national production of goods and services) but also in terms of
substantive freedom and real capability of citizens to have access to
the resources necessary for exercising human rights. European integration offers *three important lessons* why, and how, human rights
can and should be integrated into the law of international organizations so as to better enable citizens to pursue their self-development, peace and prosperity across frontiers.

*A. The Law of International Organizations Must be Construed in
Conformity with the Human Rights Recognized by Member States*

Just as the ratification of the ECHR by all EC member states
prompted the EC Court of Justice to construe EC law in conformity
with the human rights guarantees of the ECHR, the law of worldwide organizations must be interpreted in conformity with universally recognized human rights.[26] The necessary balancing of civil,

---

[25] European jurisprudence (e.g. by the EC Court of Justice and the European Court on Human Rights) has long since recognized that obligations to respect, protect and fulfil economic and social human rights
may be "justiciable" even if they entail not only "negative" but also
"positive" obligations (e.g. to promote non-discriminatory access to
education). On the particular problems of "welfare rights" (such as in-
determinacy of redistributive rights, their dependence on personal responsibility), the distinction between social rights in welfare states and
social human rights, and the need for constitutional safeguards against
abuses of welfare institutions, see e.g. *Arambulo* (1999). Many civil
and political human rights (like the right to vote) also imply not only
"negative" but also "positive obligations" (e.g. to render the right effective through legislation and administrative procedures that involve
economic costs).

[26] As shown below, this follows both from UN human rights law as well
as from the general international law rules on treaty interpretation (cf.
Article 31 of the Vienna Convention on the Law of Treaties), notwithstanding the fact that the statutes of most UN Specialized Agencies
(with the exception of the ILO, WHO and UNESCO) do not explicitly
refer to human rights.

political, economic, social and cultural human rights may legitimately differ from country to country in response to their different
laws and procedures, resources and preferences. In worldwide organizations, governments remain reluctant to limit their foreign
policy discretion by incorporating "human rights clauses" into the
law of specialized organizations that may entail conflicts between
international and domestic legal constraints and policy pressures.
As in the EC, international courts (e.g. the WTO Appellate Body)
and human rights organizations (e.g. the UN Committee on Economic, Social and Cultural Rights) should therefore take the lead –
with due deference to the "margin of discretion" of democratic legislatures, and in cooperation with the growing civil society requests
for more effective protection of human rights in worldwide organizations – in interpreting and progressively developing the law of
specialized organizations in conformity with universally recognized
human rights. The needed human rights framework for coherent
national and international "multi-level governance" requires a "UN
global compact" for promoting respect for human rights not only in
private business practices of international corporations, but – much
more important – also in the *public law* of intergovernmental organizations.[27] The UN should call upon all international organizations to submit annual "human rights impact statements" examining
and explaining the contribution of their respective laws and practices to the promotion of human rights.

B. Human Rights Promote Market Competition and the Effectiveness of International Organizations

The focus of human-rights on personal autonomy and on democratic diversity corresponds with, and reinforces, the decentralized
legal structures of consumer-driven markets and of citizen-driven
democracies. Human rights make not only "better democratic citizens" but, as advocated by the UN Development Program, also
"better economic actors".[28] Legal doctrine has long since neglected
that human rights constitute not only moral and legal rights (e.g. of
a defensive, procedural, participatory or redistributive nature), corresponding obligations of governments at national and international
levels, and objective principles of justice necessary for protecting
"democratic peace" and for limiting abuses of power also by non-
state actors (e.g. freedom of association in labour markets). They

---

[27] See above note 1.
[28] See United Nations Development Program (2000) iii.

also offer decentralized information-, incentive-, coordination-, en-
forcement- and legitimacy-mechanisms for solving social problems
confronting all societies.[29] For instance:

(1) Human rights (e.g. to freedom of information and freedom of the
press) entitle individuals to act on the basis of their own personal
knowledge and to acquire and take into account the personal
knowledge of others. They also protect spontaneous information
mechanisms (such as market prices) which enable individuals to
take into account knowledge dispersed among billions of human
beings even if individuals remain "rationally ignorant" of most
of this dispersed knowledge.

(2) Human rights (e.g. property rights, freedom of contract) set incentives for savings, investments and mutually beneficial division of labour and protect individual rights to acquire, buy and
sell goods and services necessary for their personal self-development but whose supply remains scarce in relation to consumer
demand.

(3) Human rights help to transform the *Hobbes*ian "war of everybody against everybody else" into peaceful cooperation based on
equal legal rights. In the economy no less than in the polity, the
inevitable conflicts of interests (e.g. between producer interests
in high sales prices and consumer interests in low prices) can be
reconciled best on the basis of equal liberty rights (e.g. freedom
of contract) and other human rights. By protecting (e.g. through
freedom of religion, freedom of opinion and freedom of the
press) diversity of individual values and preventing majorities
from imposing their value preferences on minorities, human
rights and markets (as organized dialogues about values) promote peaceful coexistence, tolerance and scientific progress.

(4) The history of "human rights revolutions" demonstrates that
human rights offer "countervailing powers" enabling citizens to
defend their human rights against abuses of government powers
and to limit the constitutional task of governments to the "common public interest" defined in terms of equal human rights.

(5) Human rights (e.g. of access to courts) and corresponding obligations (e.g. for compensation for violations of human rights) set

---

[29] On the instrumental function of human rights for dealing with the
problems of limited knowledge, conflicting interests and abuses of
power see e.g. *Barnett* (2000).

incentives for decentralized enforcement of rules by self-interested, vigilant citizens.

(6) The human rights to "periodic and genuine elections ... by universal and equal suffrage" (Article 21 UDHR), and to democratic participation in the exercise of government powers (Article 25 UNCCPR), promote transparent governance based on "the will of the people" (Article 21 UDHR) and on "deliberative democracy"[30] legitimating the exercise of political power at national and international levels.

As long as unnecessary poverty continues to prevent billions of human beings from enjoying human rights, the empirical evidence on the contribution of human rights to economic welfare is of particular importance for promoting the effectiveness of human rights.[31] For instance, property rights and liberty rights set incentives for efficient use of resources and enable citizens to coordinate their individual investments, production, trade and consumption in a decentralized and welfare-increasing manner. By assigning liberty rights (e.g. to self-development, freedom of contract and freedom of exchange) and property rights (e.g. to acquire, possess, use and dispose of scarce resources), and by defining individual responsibility and liability rules, human rights create incentives for savings, investments, efficient use of dispersed knowledge, mutually beneficial cooperation (e.g. through agreed exchanges of property rights) and decentralized markets (e.g. for labour, capital, goods and services) aimed at satisfying consumer demand and consumer preferences. Such "economic markets" inducing investors, producers and traders to supply private goods and services demanded by consumers involve democratic "dialogues about values"[32] which are no less important for effective enjoyment of human rights than the "political markets" for the supply of "public goods" by governments.

The centuries-old English and American common law tradition of protecting equal freedoms of traders, competitors and consumers

---

[30]   See e.g. *Koh/Slye* (1999).

[31]   See UNDP 2000 as well as *Olson* (2000), explaining why "almost all of the countries that have enjoyed good economic performance across generations are countries that have stable democratic governments" (43), and why "individual rights are a cause of prosperity" (187); *Pipes* (1999), who explains prosperity as resulting from "successful struggle for rights of which the right to property is the most fundamental" (291); World Bank (2000); *North* (1990).

[32]   Cf. *Fikentscher* (1983) 10.

against "unreasonable restraint of trade" and "coercion" reflect an early recognition of the historical experience that markets risk to destroy themselves (e.g. as a result of monopolization and cartel agreements) unless freedom and abuses of power are constitutionally restrained.[33] The history of competition law and constitutional law in Europe and North America confirms the economic insight that the efficiency of market mechanisms (e.g. for allocating resources in a manner coordinating supply and demand) depends, *inter alia*, on effective protection of individual freedoms (e.g. of information, production, trade, competition and freedom of association) and protection of property rights in both material and intellectual resources. If market failures adversely affect human rights, economic theory teaches that governments should correct such market imperfections through "optimal" interventions directly at the source of the problem (e.g. through labour, social and health legislation, prohibitions of cartels and environmental pollution) without preventing citizens to engage in mutually beneficial trade.

The economic and human resources needed for the full enjoyment of human rights thus depend on making human rights an integral part of a social and sustainable market economy.[34] The successful integration of human rights into EC law and policies confirms that the economy and "specialized organizations" must not be regarded as autonomous fields unrelated to the human rights of producers, workers, investors, traders and consumers. In order to strengthen the mutual synergies between human rights and integration law also at the worldwide level, UN human rights law must overcome its longstanding neglect of economic liberty rights, property rights and competition safeguards as indispensable means of promoting widespread ownership of economic and human capital (such as health and education) and of preventing small minorities from controlling the economy and polity. WTO members must likewise interpret their declared treaty objectives of "raising stan-

---

[33] On this common dilemma of market economies and democracy, and on the replacement of the rights-based common law criteria by efficiency-based economic criteria (such as absence of out-put and price restrictions) in modern US antitrust law, see *Amato* (1997); *Gerber* (1998). More generally on the paradoxical dependence of liberty on constitutional restraints see *Elster* (2000).

[34] See e.g. *Robinson* (1999) 187: "if we hope to see human rights flourishing, it will only be in the context of an equitable and sustainable economic order".

dards of living, ensuring full employment and a large and steadily
growing volume of real income ..., while allowing for the optimal
use of the world's resources in accordance with the objective of
sustainable development" (Preamble of the WTO Agreement), in
conformity with their human rights obligations.

C. Human Rights Promote Democratic Legitimacy and Self-Governance in International Organizations

At the *national level*, most of the 189 UN member states now
recognize human rights and the need for constitutional rules protecting, implementing and balancing human rights. In Europe and
North America, almost all countries have introduced also complementary constitutional safeguards of market economies and competition laws based on the insight that equal freedoms of citizens need
to be protected through institutions, procedures, substantive legal
safeguards and individual rights in the *economy* no less than in the
polity so as to prevent abuses of private and public power that were
not consented by citizens and reduce their welfare. At the level of
worldwide organizations, however, protection of universally recognized human rights often remains ineffective because the complementary constitutional principles needed for effectuating human
rights – such as democratic participation, parliamentary rule-making, transparent "deliberative democracy" and judicial protection of
rule of law – have not yet become part of the law and practices of
most worldwide organizations.

The history of European integration suggests that the emergence
of a human rights culture promoting democratic peace and social
welfare depends on empowering individuals to defend not only
their civil and political human rights, but also their economic and
social rights through individual and democratic self-government
and access to courts. Inside the EC, the judicial protection of "market freedoms" and of non-discrimination principles as fundamental
individual rights[35] became an important driving force for the pro-

---

[35] See e.g. Case 240/83, *ADBHU*, ECR 1985 531, para. 9: "the principles
of free movement of goods and freedom of competition, together with
freedom of trade as a fundamental right, are general principles of
Community law of which the Court ensures observance". Especially
the freedom of movements of workers and other persons, access to
employment and the right of establishment have been described by the
EC Court as "fundamental freedoms" (Case C-55/94, *Gebhard*, ECR
1995, I-4165, para. 37) or "a fundamental right which the Treaty con-

gressive realization of the common market and of "an area of freedom, security and justice" (Article 61 EC Treaty). The EC Court
emphasized that economic freedoms "are not absolute but must be
viewed in relation to their social function"[36] and with due regard to
human rights.[37] The EC jurisprudence on social rights (e.g. "the
principle of equal pay for male and female workers for equal work"
in Article 141 EC Treaty) contributed to the emergence of a European "social market economy" in which EC member states are required to extend social rights (e.g. to education and vocational
training) to nationals of other EC member states.[38] The new treaty
objective of "appropriate action to combat discrimination based on
sex, racial or ethnic origin, religion or belief, disability, age or sex-
ual orientation" (Article 13) confirms the functional interrelationships between economic and political order and human rights. The
progressive evolution of European integration from a coal and steel
community to a customs union, common market, monetary and political union would have never been politically feasible without recognition of EC citizens as legal subjects and "citizens of the Union"
(Articles 17-22) with ever more comprehensive individual rights
across frontiers.

Similar "democratic challenges" exist in global integration law
and worldwide organizations like the Bretton Woods institutions
and the WTO.[39] The WTO Ministerial Declaration of November
2001 on "The TRIPS Agreement and Public Health", for example,
was a "deal breaker" for the successful launching of a new "round"

---

fers individually on each worker in the Community" (Case 22/86,
Heylens, ECR 1987, 4097, para. 14). The EC Court avoids "human
rights language" for the "market freedoms", the right to property and
the freedom to pursue a trade or business in EC law.

[36] Case C-44/94, *The Queen* v. *Minister of Agriculture*, ECR 1995 I-
3115, para. 28.

[37] Cf. *Betten / Grief* (1998); *Alston et alii* (1999).

[38] Due to the constitutional limits of EC law, social rights were initially
developed in EC law as a function of market integration rather than of
the more recent EC Treaty guarantees of "citizenship of the Union"
(Article 17) and of "fundamental social rights" (e.g. Article 136). On
the need for integrating social rights into market integration law as a
means for limiting social market failures (e.g. resulting from an unjust
distribution of resources and purchasing power, inadequate opportunities of all market participants to express their "voice" and "exit") see
e.g. *Poiares Maduro* (1999) 459.

[39] See *Stein* (2001) 489.

of worldwide negotiations in the WTO; it affirms "that the Agreement can and should be interpreted and implemented in a manner supportive of WTO Member's right to protect public health and, in particular, to promote access to medicines for all".[40] The withdrawal, in April 2001, of the complaints in the South African Supreme Court by 39 pharmaceutical companies against government regulations facilitating access to AIDS medicaments likewise demonstrated the importance of *civil society* support and of judicial remedies for reconciling national and international economic law (e.g. on trade-related intellectual property rights) with social human rights.

In UN human rights law and global integration law, the *indivisibility of human rights* and *justiciability of economic and social rights* remain inadequately protected and do not empower citizens, economic operators and judges to enforce and progressively develop economic and social rights in domestic and international courts (as inside the EC). UN law, unlike European integration law, does not take into account that effective protection of human rights entails and requires market competition and its legal protection by liberty rights, property rights, other human rights and competition safeguards limiting abuses of power. An anti-market bias of UN human rights law will further reduce its operational potential as a benchmark for the law of worldwide economic organizations and for a rights-based market economy and jurisprudence e.g. in WTO dispute settlement practice. Reconciling civil, economic and social human rights also requires to admit that, in a world of constant change, human rights cannot be rights to be immune from adjustment pressures. Promoting individual responsibility and human capacity to adjust to inevitable change in a manner respecting human dignity remains one of the most difficult tasks of a human rights policy protecting individual liberty and global integration across frontiers.

IV.   **Obstacles on the Way Towards a 'Human Rights Culture' in Global Integration Law: Learning from European Integration**

State-centered international lawyers often ignore that markets are a necessary consequence of, and an indispensable means for,

---

[40] WTO document WT/MIN(01)/DEC/W/2 of 14 November 2001, para. 4.

effective protection of human rights. European integration confirms the insight of "functional theories" that citizen-driven market integration can set strong incentives for transforming "market freedoms" into "fundamental rights" which – if directly enforceable by producers, investors, workers, traders and consumers through courts (as in the EC) – can reinforce and extend the protection of basic human rights (e.g. to liberty, property, food and health). Functionally limited and citizen-driven "low policy integration" may also contribute more effectively to "democratic peace" than it may be possible in government-centered "high policy organizations" (like the UN) whose bureaucracies may pursue strong self-interests (e.g. in preserving foreign policy discretion without judicial control) and often resist democratic power-sharing on grounds of "primacy of foreign policy".

A. Market Integration Law Can Promote Human Rights

Wherever freedom and property rights are protected, individuals start producing and exchanging goods and services so as to increase their income and satisfy consumer demand. Enjoyment of human rights requires use of dispersed information and economic resources that can be supplied most efficiently, and most democratically, through division of labour among free citizens and liberal trade promoting economic welfare, freedom of choice, and the free flow of scarce goods, services and information across frontiers.[41] The fact that most people spend most of their time on their "economic freedoms" (e.g. to produce and exchange goods and services including one's labour and ideas) illustrates that, for ordinary people, economic liberties are no less important than civil and political freedoms (e.g. to participate in the democratic supply of "public goods"). Human rights and consumer-driven markets are both designed to protect individual preferences, voluntarily agreed transactions, and decentralized information-, allocation-, coordination- and enforcement mechanisms. The moral "categorical imperative" of maximizing equal liberties across frontiers[42] justifies both the

---

[41] On the contribution of liberal trade to economic welfare and to protection of human rights (which, like any legal system, involve economic costs), and, *vice versa*, on the reciprocal contribution of human rights to economic welfare, see *Sykes* (2002); and *Petersmann* (2002c).

[42] On *Kant's* moral "categorical imperatives" for acting in accordance with universal laws ("Act only in accordance with that maxim through which you can at the same time will that it become a universal law"),

Ernst-Ulrich Petersmann

idea of inalienable, equal human rights and the economic objective of maximizing consumer welfare through open markets and non-discriminatory competition.

Hence, there is no reason for human rights lawyers to neglect the interrelationships between human rights and market competition, and the economic dimensions of human rights problems – such as the dependence of human rights (e.g. to work, food, education, housing and health-care) on supply of scarce goods, services and job opportunities. Likewise, "economic lawyers" must not disregard the human rights dimensions of economic law, for instance that savings, investments and economic transactions depend on property rights and liberty rights (such as freedom of contract and transfers of property rights).[43] Also foreign policy-makers and economists need to reconsider their often one-sided views that economic development should be defined in purely quantitative terms (e.g. without regard to real human capability to enjoy human rights), or that the economic tasks of "specialized agencies" (like the IMF, the World Bank, and the WTO) should not be "overloaded" with human rights considerations because they may be abused as pretexts for protectionist restrictions.[44]

There is increasing recognition among economists that human rights require to define the goal of economic policy as enabling

---

for respecting human dignity by treating individuals and humanity as ends in themselves ("So act that you use humanity, whether in your own person or that of another, always at the same time as an end, never merely as a means"), and for respecting individual autonomy ("the idea of the will of every rational being as a will giving universal law") and individual right ("Any action is right if it can coexist with everyone's freedom according to a universal law"), and on *Kant*'s theory of the antagonistic human nature promoting market competition and national and international constitutional guarantees of equal freedoms, see e.g. *Wood* (1999); *Petersmann* (1999a).

[43] On the recognition of the importance of human rights for rendering environmental law and environmental protection more effective see *Boyle/Anderson* (1998).

[44] See e.g. *Gianviti* (2001), who emphasizes "the principle of specialization that has governed the establishment of the specialized agencies and their relationships with the United Nations" (44), and concludes that the UN human rights covenants "apply only to States, not to international organizations" (10). These arguments, however, do not preclude the legal relevance of general international human rights law for the IMF.

every citizen to acquire and own the economic resources necessary for exercising his human rights.[45] From a human rights perspective, "market failures" should be defined more broadly as including violations of human rights (e.g. in case of child labour, forced labour and discrimination of women distorting labour markets; discriminatory takings of property rights without adequate compensation distorting capital markets). "Rules of reason" in competition law and the "public interest clauses" in regional and global integration law (e.g. Article XX GATT) should be construed as justifying government interventions necessary for the protection of human rights and for the correction of market failures (e.g. if private markets do not supply necessary medicines at socially affordable prices). Yet, interpreting "market failures" and "public interest clauses" in conformity with human rights does not necessarily imply that import restrictions are an appropriate policy instrument for dealing with human rights violations in an exporting country, or that competition authorities should have regulatory powers and protect competitors rather than competition as a process.[46] The EC Directives and also the worldwide GATS Protocol on Liberalization of Basic Telecommunications, for instance, require the setting-up of independent regulatory bodies in all member states and prescribe other pro-competitive rules for access to "essential facilities", non-discriminatory "interconnection" with major network suppliers, as well as other

---

[45] See e.g. *Sen* (1999), who argues that freedom (in the sense of "capabilities" of persons to lead the kind of lives they have reason to value) is at once the ultimate goal of economic life and the most efficient means of realizing general welfare.

[46] Whereas modern US competition policy emphasizes the competition policy objective of protecting competition as a welfare-maximizing process (rather than protecting competitors), EC competition policy continues to admit the legitimacy of protecting the "economic freedom" of competitors in the marketplace even if e.g. vertical restraints do not limit output and harm consumers. US competition lawyers criticize this European notion of "restriction of economic freedom" on several grounds such as: "(1) its failure to generate precise operable legal rules (i.e. its failure to provide an analytical framework); (2) its distance from and tension with (micro)economics, which does provide an analytical framework; (3) its tendency to favour traders / competitors over consumers and consumer welfare (efficiency); and (4) its capture of totally innocuous contract provisions having no anti-competitive effects in an economic sense" (*Hawk* (1995) 977-978). For an explanation of the EC position see e.g. *Marsden* (2000).

competition safeguards against abuses of market power in oligopo-listic markets.[47] The underlying "separation of policy instruments" (i.e. trade liberalization rules, competition safeguards, pro-competi-tive industrial regulation, access to courts) combines economic effi-ciency arguments with constitutional insights (e.g. need for "checks and balances" between separate trade bureaucracies, competition authorities, independent industrial regulators and independent courts) and illustrates the need for broader constitutional principles ensuring overall policy coherence at national and international lev-els.

The moral and legal recognition of the 'indivisibility of human rights' is thus supported by empirical and economic evidence that economic, political and legal freedoms complement and support each other (e.g. economic liberties contributing to political liberty, democracy forcing governments to prevent famines and other hu-man rights violations). European integration law suggests that linking market integration with human rights offers the most effec-tive political strategy for promoting open markets, economic wel-fare, human rights and democratic peace across frontiers. Inter-preting the global integration law of the WTO in conformity with universally recognized human rights could likewise contribute to the economic WTO objectives of "raising standards of living ..., real income ... and sustainable development" (see the preamble of the WTO agreement).

B. Market Integration Promotes Legal and Political Integration

Contrary to the "logic of 1945" of "specialized agencies", the universal recognition of human rights, of *constitutionalism* and market-based integration offers a coherent framework for a new *global integration paradigm* based on human rights, democracy, open markets and social justice. In both economic and political markets, abuses of private and public power risk to destroy freedom and competition and call for national and international competition law and constitutional law limiting abuses of power. Economic the-ory (e.g. on property rights as decentralized incentives for "inter-nalizing external costs") supports the human rights objective of em-powering citizens to invoke their individual rights before domestic courts so as to counteract and limit "government failures" and other

---

[47] See e.g. the contributions of *W. Baer* in OECD (1997); *Ehlermann/Gosling* (2000). On the GATS Protocols on Trade in Services see WTO Secretariat (2001).

abuses of power. Economic theory (e.g. on "countervailing powers") and human rights law also offer arguments for recognizing
"market citizens" (e.g. investors, producers, traders, consumers) as
legal subjects entitled to judicial protection of their "market rights".
The logic of market economies and the logic of human rights are
mutually consistent and support each other. The successful decentralized enforcement of individual market freedoms, property rights,
non-discrimination rights and social rights in EC law illustrates the
constitutional importance of creating "legal and judicial markets"
for the progressive legal clarification and judicial enforcement by
self-interested citizens, lawyers and judges of equal liberties and
other human rights.

Free trade area agreements, customs unions and common markets were important stages in the historical formation of many federal states. The progressive evolution of the EC Treaty – from a
customs union treaty focusing on economic freedoms to a modern
"treaty constitution" protecting human rights and "democratic
peace" far beyond the economic area – illustrates the functional
interrelationships between economic, political and legal integration.
Just as competition in economic markets aims at maximizing consumer welfare and freedom of choice, human rights and democratic
competition in political markets aim at protecting individual preferences of citizens and respect for e.g. minority values vis-à-vis
democratic majority legislation. Even though human rights require
legislative, administrative and judicial implementing measures, they
protect individual as well as democratic *diversity*. Like economic
markets, human rights and democracy run counter to the idea of
uniformity and worldwide harmonization of national legislation and
of administrative and judicial implementing measures.

The negotiators of the 1957 Treaty establishing the European
Economic Community thought that the human rights guarantees in
the national constitutions of EC member states and in the ECHR
(1950) were sufficient for protecting human rights in the common
market. Hence, similar to GATT 1947 and the WTO Agreement,
the EC Treaty of 1957 did not refer to human rights law based on
the belief that mutually beneficial economic liberalization would
promote, rather than endanger, the national and international human
rights guarantees. Today, however, EU law has evolved into a comprehensive constitutional system for the protection of civil, political, economic and social rights of EU citizens across national frontiers. Also the objective of the EU's common foreign and security

policy is defined by the EU Treaty as "to develop and consolidate democracy and the rule of law, and respect for human rights and fundamental freedoms" (Article 11). The EU has consequently insisted on including "human rights clauses" and "democracy clauses" into international agreements concluded by the EC with more than hundred third countries. The adoption of the Charter of Fundamental Rights of the European Union in December 2000,[48] and the proposals for incorporating this Charter into a European Constitution at the intergovernmental conference scheduled for 2004, confirm the "functional theory" underlying European integration, i.e. the view that *economic market integration* can progressively promote peaceful cooperation and rule of law beyond economic areas, thereby enabling more comprehensive and more effective protection of human rights than has been possible in traditional state-centered international law.[49] In a similar perspective, the worldwide WTO guarantees of freedom, non-discrimination and rule of law, protected by the compulsory WTO dispute settlement system, constitute non-economic legal achievements and "human rights values" that are no less important than the economic welfare gains resulting from liberalization of international trade.

C. Recognition of Citizens as Legal Subjects of Integration Law Promotes Market Integration and International Constitutionalism

Inside the EC and in the European Economic Area between the EC and third European countries, the treaty prohibitions of restrictions of the free movement of goods, services, persons, capital and related payments, as well as the treaty guarantees of non-discrimination (e.g. in Article 141), were construed by the EC Court and national courts as *individual economic freedoms* to be protected by the courts.[50] The national constitutional guarantees of "the princi-

---

[48] See the text published in the Official Journal of the EC, C 364/1-22 of 18 December 2000, and the commentary by *Lenaerts / De Smijter* (2001).

[49] The number of "human rights cases" before the European Court of Human Rights far outnumbers those before the EC Court of Justice. Yet, the guarantees in the ECHR focus on civil and political rights which often do not go beyond those in national constitutions. The EC's common market freedoms and constitutional law, by contrast, go far beyond national and ECHR guarantees and have contributed to unprecedented levels of economic and social welfare, individual freedom and democratic peace of European citizens.

[50] See above note 35.

ples of liberty, democracy, respect for human rights and fundamental freedoms, and the rule of law" were progressively recognized as "principles which are common to the Member States" and
legally binding also on all EU institutions, as later acknowledged in
Article 6 of the EU Treaty. In conformity with the EC Treaty requirements to comply with international law (cf. Articles 300, 307)
and cooperate with other international organizations (cf. Articles
302-306), the EU Treaty now requires explicitly respect for the
European Convention on Human Rights (cf. Article 6:2 EU Treaty),
the 1961 European Social Charter and 1989 Community Charter of
the Fundamental Social Rights of Workers (cf. Article 136 EC
Treaty), and for the 1951 Geneva Convention and 1967 Protocol on
the protection of refugees (cf. Article 63 EC Treaty).

The constitutional guarantees of the EU for economic liberties
and complementary constitutional, competition, environmental and
social safeguards have also induced numerous EU initiatives to
strengthen competition, environmental and social law in *worldwide*
international agreements. The strong competition law of the EC
reflects the constitutional insight that – in the economy no less than
in the polity – equal freedoms of citizens and open markets need to
be legally protected against abuses of *public powers* as well as of
private powers.[51] The EC Treaty prohibitions of cartel agreements
(Article 81) and of abuses of market power (Article 82) are not only
protected by the EC Court as *individual rights* of "market citizens".
They also prompted all EC member states to enact *national* competition laws enforced by independent *national* competition authorities. Likewise, under the influence of EC competition law and of
the incorporation of competition safeguards into the EC's "Europe
agreements" and association agreements, also most third states in
Europe have progressively introduced, since the 1980s, national
competition laws protecting citizens and economic competition

---

[51] Also the US Supreme Court rightly emphasized that "antitrust laws ...
are the Magna Carta of free enterprise. They are as important to the
preservation of economic freedom and our free enterprise system as the
Bill of Rights is to the protection of our fundamental freedoms"
(*United States* v. *Topco Assoc. Inc.*, 405 U.S. 596, 610, 1972). Yet,
unlike the EC, US law does not protect economic liberties and social
rights as fundamental constitutional rights of citizens, and US politicians favor a power-oriented, extraterritorial application of US antitrust
laws vis-à-vis third countries rather than worldwide competition rules
as suggested by the EC.

against abuses of private and public power. By recognizing transnational individual rights and protecting the exercise of equal freedoms and property rights through independent institutions (like national and EC competition, monetary and judicial "guardians" protecting individual rights), European integration enabled a
progessive transformation of a customs union treaty into a *treaty
constitution* protecting *democratic peace* more effectively than ever
before in European history.

D. Lessons for Global Integration Law?

The paradoxical fact that many developing countries remain
poor notwithstanding their wealth of natural resources (e.g. more
than 90% of biogenetical resources in the world), is attributed by an
increasing number of economists to their lack of effective human
rights guarantees and of liberal trade and competition laws. The
absence of effective legal and judicial protection of liberty rights
and property rights inhibits investments and acts as an incentive for
welfare-reducing private and governmental restrictions of trade and
competition and collaboration between cartelized industries and
authoritarian governments.[52] The widespread abuses of private
power in Africa, Asia and Latin America are no less dangerous for
human rights and social welfare than abuses of public government
powers. The EC proposals for complementing the liberal trade rules
of the WTO by worldwide competition rules have met with increasing support notably by less-developed countries who have suf-
fered from discriminatory cartel practices (e.g. of shipping and air
transport cartels) and find it politically difficult to overcome anti-
competitive practices of powerful domestic industries through unilateral national legislation.[53] In the WTO Ministerial Declaration of
November 2001, all WTO member states recognized "the case for a
multilateral framework to enhance the contribution of competition
policy to international trade and development", and agreed to negotiate additional WTO rules on the interaction between trade and
competition policies.[54]

Investments, production, trade and also protection of the environment depend on legal incentives (e.g. freedom and legal secu-

---

[52] See e.g. *de Soto* (2000), who describes why many natural resources in
developing countries remain "dead capital" due to the lack of secure
property titles and legal insecurity.
[53] Cf. *Petersmann* (1999b).
[54] See above note 19, at paragraph 23.

rity) and legal rights for investors, producers, traders, polluters and consumers. The EC's integration approach – notably the recognition and empowerment of citizens as legal subjects not only of human rights but also of competition law and integration law – should serve as a model also for *worldwide integration law*. The modern universal recognition of human rights as part of general international law implies that human rights have become part of the "context" for interpreting the law of worldwide organizations and must be taken into account in all rule-making and policy-making processes at national and international levels.[55] Just as the human rights guarantees and competition safeguards of the EC Treaty have reinforced the legitimacy and effectiveness of European integration and of protection of human rights throughout Europe, human rights law and WTO rules offer mutually beneficial synergies also at the worldwide level for rendering human rights and the social functions and democratic legitimacy of the emerging global integration law more effective. The modern universal recognition of the need for respecting human dignity (e.g. in the sense of moral, rational and personal autonomy), inalienable equal human rights, open markets, non-discriminatory and undistorted competition, and democratic decision-making offers a coherent moral, legal, economic and political framework for a new *global integration paradigm* focusing no longer one-sidedly on liberalization and wealth-creation, but also on protection of human rights, democratic legitimacy, social justice and solidary sharing of the adjustment costs in countries committed to human rights and global integration.

European integration offers important lessons for global integration, notwithstanding the need for diversity of national and international legal and political systems. Functional market integration can promote human rights, economic welfare and democratic peace far beyond what may be possible in political intergovernmental organizations (like the Council of Europe and the UN). The increasing recourse to *constitutional rules* (e.g. on freedom, non-discrimination, rule of law and protection of human health) and *constitutional methods* in the WTO, such as the compulsory WTO dispute settle-

---

[55] See Resolution 1998/12 on "Human rights as the primary objective of international trade, investment and finance policy and practice", adopted by the UN Sub-Commission on Prevention of Discrimination and Protection of Minorities in August 1998 and subsequently endorsed by numerous NGOs, cf. *Mehra* (1999) 123 et seq.

ment system and the GATS requirements of independent national regulatory bodies (e.g. for telecommunications) and access to national courts, confirm the national and international experience of the "paradox of liberty" and of *constitutionalism*, i.e. the need for constitutional limitations on the inherent tendencies of economic markets as well as political markets to endanger individual freedom and non-discriminatory competition through abuses of power.

Neither UN human rights law nor global integration law (e.g. in the IMF, World Bank and WTO) have so far developed a coherent *constitutional strategy* for protecting human rights and other individual rights across frontiers not only vis-à-vis abuses of *domestic* government powers, but also vis-à-vis *foreign* government powers, intergovernmental organizations and abuses of economic power (e.g. by dominant firms). In contrast to the anti-market bias of earlier UN recommendations for a "New International Economic Order",[56] the recent UN Secretary-General's report on "Globalization and its impact on the full enjoyment of all human rights"[57] is characterized by a balanced attempt at reconciling human rights, market competition and globalization. It emphasizes, *inter alia*,

- the worldwide opportunities of increasing the resources available for the realization of human rights through global division of labour provided market competition is accompanied by appropriate domestic policies;[58]
- the complementary functions of international guarantees of freedom and non-discrimination e.g. in IMF and WTO law and in human rights law;
- the need to correct "market failures" so as to ensure that economic growth leads to greater promotion and protection of human rights;
- the importance of human rights (such as the rights to health, food and a clean environment) for the interpretation of "public interest clauses" in the law of worldwide organizations and for

---

[56] See e.g. *Petersmann* (1992).

[57] UN documents A/55/342 of 31 August 2000 and A/56/254 of 31 July 2001.

[58] The recent WTO report on *Trade, Income Disparity and Poverty* (*Ben-David et alii* (1999)) offers empirical evidence that trade contributes to economic growth and promotes alleviation of poverty provided trade liberalization is complemented by appropriate domestic policies (e.g. for education, health and consumer protection) that have much larger effects on poverty alleviation than trade policy.

the structural adjustment programs of international financial institutions;

- the positive effects of new technologies (e.g. for education and
the successful organization of civil society initiatives), but also
their unequal distribution and certain negative effects (e.g. in
terms of increased vulnerability of capital markets, abuses of the
Internet for spread of hate speech, etc);
- the positive contribution of human rights to a geographically
more even distribution of investments and financial flows, and
the adverse effects of trade protectionism on development and
human rights;
- frequent links between lack of democracy and certain negative
aspects of international trade (such as illegal trafficking of
drugs, diamonds and human beings).

Yet, citizens, NGOs, national parliaments and domestic courts
will rightly continue to be suspicious vis-à-vis non-transparent,
multilateral rule-making and policy-making in worldwide organizations like the Bretton Woods institutions and the WTO as long as
these organizations do not follow the example of other regional and
worldwide organizations (such as the EU and the ILO) and commit
themselves to the protection of human rights and to recognition of
citizens as legal subjects also in the law of international organizations.

V.   Human Rights and the 'Constitutional Functions' of
Worldwide Guarantees of Freedoms, Non-Discrimi-
nation, Rule-of-Law and 'Sustainable Development':
Need for Legal Integration

Protection of human rights and democratic participation in the
exercise of government powers rarely come about "top-down"
without prior "bottom-up pressures" and "glorious revolutions" by
citizens, parliaments and courageous judges defending human
rights vis-à-vis abuses of government powers and fighting for
democratic reforms of authoritarian government structures. Like the
"Constitution of the ILO" following World War I, the Bretton-
Woods Agreements and the UN Charter of 1944/45 presented such
"revolutions" in international law designed to extend freedom, non-
discrimination, rule of law and mutually beneficial cooperation
across frontiers. Also the legal and quasi-judicial WTO guarantees
of freedom, non-discrimination and rule of law – in contrast to most

human rights treaties – go far beyond national constitutional guarantees in most democracies which tend to limit economic freedom to domestic citizens and, for centuries, permit welfare-reducing discrimination against foreign goods, foreign services, foreign investors and foreign consumers (e.g. by means of export cartels). Yet, in contrast to European integration law, the increasingly global economic integration has not yet led to a corresponding legal integration of national and worldwide legal and political systems.

By extending equal freedoms across frontiers and subjecting discretionary foreign policy powers to additional legal and judicial restraints ratified by domestic parliaments, reciprocal international guarantees of freedom, non-discrimination, rule of law, transparent policy-making, social safeguard measures and wealth-creation through a mutually beneficial division of labour – such as those in the 1944 Bretton-Woods Agreements, the ILO Constitution, GATT 1947 and the 1994 WTO Agreement – can be understood as serving "constitutional functions" for the legal protection of human rights values across frontiers, similar to national democratic legislation for the protection of human rights inside national borders.[59] Of course, "not all international rules serve constitutional functions", and the lack of adequate constitutional safeguards in the law of international organizations facilitates "intergovernmental collusion" endangering democratic governance and human rights.[60] For example, the general exceptions and safeguard clauses in the WTO Agree-

---

[59] For a detailed explanation see *Petersmann* (1991), as well as *Petersmann* (1993a) 47 et seq. The theory of the "constitutional" and "domestic policy functions" of international guarantees of freedom, non-discrimination and rule of law was developed by economists (e.g. *J. Tumlir*) and lawyers in the 1980s (see *Petersmann* (1986)). The theory focused on the *substantive constitutional values* of the GATT 1947 guarantees of freedom, non-discrimination and rule of law, rather than on the formal primacy of "higher" international law over domestic law, or on the procedural advantages of *reciprocal pre-commitments ("hands-tying")* at the international law level designed to limit mutually harmful "beggar-they-neighbor policies" at domestic policy levels. In view of the "separation of policy instruments" underlying the Bretton Woods Agreements and the cold war dissent on human rights, the theory did not challenge the "logic of 1945" and did not address the impact of the more recent universal recognition of human rights on the law, policies and "integration paradigm" of worldwide organizations.

[60] The quotations are from the titles of various chapters in *Petersmann* (1991), e.g. chapters VI and VII.5.

ment leave each government broad discretion as to how economic freedoms should be reconciled with other human rights subject to "necessity" and non-discrimination requirements (e.g. in GATT Article XX, GATS Article XIV, Article 8 of the TRIPS Agreement) that are similar to those in human rights law. Yet, the move from "negative integration" in GATT 1947 to "positive integration" in the WTO may endanger protection of human rights and democratic governance in areas such as health protection and intellectual property law.[61]

The focus of GATT/WTO law is neither on de-regulation nor on distributive justice, but on *optimal trade regulation* through welfare-increasing *non-discriminatory internal regulation* (rather than welfare-reducing *discriminatory* border restrictions or export subsidies). GATT and WTO jurisprudence has so far hardly ever challenged the sovereign right of GATT and WTO member states to protect the human rights of their citizens through *non-discriminatory* internal or international social rules (e.g. ILO-conventions, human rights treaties, environmental agreements) if procedural due-process requirements had been met (e.g. for risk-assessment procedures prior to the application of sanitary measures, consultations with exporting countries that were adversely affected by environmental regulations unilaterally adopted in importing countries).[62] Is interpretation of WTO law in conformity with human rights, as required by general international law, sufficient for ensuring coherence between human rights and trade law? How should human rights be construed in the particular context of worldwide organizations which offer much less effective constitutional, parliamentary and judicial "checks and balances" than constitutional democracies? Should WTO law follow the example of EU law and integrate human rights and social rules more explicitly into WTO law and jurisprudence? Or should the implementation and protection of human rights in international economic relations be left to other "specialized agencies" like the various UN human rights bodies and the ILO? How to enable citizens to invoke and enforce WTO rules in domestic courts so as to render the "constitutional functions" of

---

[61] These dangers are emphasized e.g. in *Petersmann* (2000a); *idem* (2000b).

[62] In contrast to GATT/WTO law, European Community law has gone much further in challenging and replacing national by EC social, environmental and human rights rules, cf. *Poiares Maduro* (1999).

WTO rules more effective in domestic legal systems and extend corresponding human rights guarantees across frontiers?

A. How to Protect Freedom Across Frontiers? Liberty Rights as 'Negative', 'Positive' and 'Institutional Guarantees'?

The political struggle for "basic individual rights" goes back to the beginnings of written history and is characterized by the progressive extension of equal liberty rights and other human rights to all domestic citizens and across frontiers. Precursors include the rights to asylum granted by Greek city-states; Roman citizenship rights; rights of the nobility in the Middle Ages (e.g. in the *Magna Carta* 1215); religious freedom protected in the constitutional charter adopted by the Dutch provincial assembly at Dordrecht in 1572; the English *Habeas Corpus Act* of 1679 and *Bill of Rights* of 1689; the French Declaration of the Rights of Man and the Citizen of 1789; and the *Bill of Rights* appended to the US Constitution in 1791. The particular focus of liberty rights (e.g. freedom of religion, freedom of association, freedom to demonstrate) was often shaped by historical events (such as the schism of the Christian church from the 16th century onwards) and by political struggles against the rulers. Liberalization of discriminatory border barriers and transnational protection of "global freedom" and other "globalization rights"[63] are human rights challenges of the 21st century.

In the history of federal states (such as the US, Switzerland and Germany) and of customs unions (such as the German Customs Union 1834-1866 and the EC), freedom of trade was first extended across frontiers inside the federation and inside the customs union by means of *objective constitutional guarantees* (such as the *commerce clause* in Article I sect. 8 of the US Constitution and the customs union rules in the EC Treaty) which were only later protected by domestic courts as conferring also individual rights. Federal *human rights catalogues* (e.g. in US, Swiss, German and EC constitutional law) were agreed only at later stages of market integration.[64] The judicial interpretation of liberty rights, and of the constitutional guarantee that no person shall be deprived of "liberty without due process of law" (Fifth and Fourteenth Amendments of the US Constitution), has changed over time both in Europe and

---

[63] See *Pendleton* (1999).

[64] For a comparative legal analysis with numerous references to the relevant legal texts see *Petersmann* (1991), chapter VIII.

North America.[65] In modern welfare states like Germany, for example, human rights are no longer interpreted only as "negative
freedoms" but also as "positive rights" and "institutional guarantees" which require legislation (such as competition and social rules
for a "social market economy") enabling citizens to actively use
their freedom across frontiers and protect themselves against abuses
of power also in transnational relations with third countries.[66] Article 28 of the UDHR likewise recognizes rights of everyone "to a
social and international order in which the rights and freedoms set
forth in this Declaration can be fully realized".

1. Human Liberty Rights Should Be Construed as
Protecting Maximum Equal Freedom Across
Frontiers Subject to Lawful Democratic
Legislation

National and international human rights instruments – from the
US Declaration of Independence of 1776 up to the Universal Declaration of Human Rights of 1948 and the Charter of Fundamental
Rights of the EU adopted in December 2000[67] – recognize not only
specific liberty rights (cf. Article 16 EU Charter: "freedom to conduct a business in accordance with Community law and national
laws"), but also inalienable *general* human rights to liberty (e.g.
Article 2:1 German Basic Law, Article 6 EU Charter, Article 3
UDHR). Most human rights instruments further recognize that
"human dignity is inviolable" and "must be respected and protected" (Article 1 Charter of the EU). If human dignity is interpreted in accordance with the moral "categorical imperative" as
requiring maximum equal liberty for individual self-development
consistent with equal human rights of all others, it is only logical to
construe the general human right to liberty as applying to *all areas
of personal development* which are not protected through specific
human rights. Some constitutional texts explicitly provide for such
general rights to maximum equal liberty subject to other constitutional restraints and democratic legislation (e.g. Article 2:1 of the
German Basic Law).[68] Other constitutional systems (e.g. in the
USA) achieve similar results by the constitutional requirement that
governmental restrictions of individual freedom need a legal basis

---

[65] See e.g. *Garvey/Aleinikoff* (1994) 618 et seq.
[66] Cf. e.g. *Grabitz* (1976).
[67] See above note 48.
[68] See *Petersmann* (1991), chapter VIII.4.

in constitutional law and democratic legislation.[69] Comparative studies of constitutional democracies confirm that in "most of the English-speaking world and most of Western Europe ... there is general acceptance of a principle of maximum individual freedom consistent with equal freedoms for others" subject to democratic legislation.[70]

The Preamble to the US Constitution describes its objectives as, *inter alia*, to "promote the general welfare and secure the blessings of liberty to ourselves and our posterity". In view of the logical impossibility of enumerating all areas of individual liberty protected by the Constitution, and in order to reduce the danger of interpreting human rights catalogues as excluding liberty rights not explicitly listed, the founding fathers of the US Constitution made it explicit in the Ninth Amendment of the Constitution that "the enumeration of certain rights in the Constitution shall not be construed to deny or disparage others retained by the people". In the constitutional deliberations, other law-makers considered the Ninth Amendment as unnecessary because the constitutional principle of limited government prohibited governmental restraints of freedom that were not necessary for the protection of human rights.[71] How justified the concerns of the US founding fathers had been, is illustrated by the denial by US courts of any "vested right to trade with foreign nations".[72] In Europe, it has likewise been claimed that "freedom of trade as a fundamental right" inside the EC, as recognized by the EC Court,[73] should not be protected in trade relations with third countries.[74] One major advantage of interpreting liberty rights as protecting maximum equal freedom across frontiers (i.e.

---

[69]   Cf. *Morrison/Hudec* (1993) 92 et seq.

[70]   *Macpherson* (1977) 7.

[71]   See e.g. *Sherry* (1987), 1127 et seq.

[72]   For a discussion of this jurisprudence see: *Petersmann* (1993a) 14-15.

[73]   On the protection of "freedom of trade as a fundamental right" by the EC Court of Justice see above note 35. The Court has, however, not specified whether this freedom protects – in conformity with the customs union principle of EC and GATT law and the primacy of international obligations (e.g. under GATT Articles II, XI and XXIV) over secondary EC law (cf. Articles 300:7, 307 ECT) – also trade transactions with third countries subject to lawful restrictions by the EC or EC member states.

[74]   E.g. by *Peers* (2001) 129 ("no right to trade deserves to be recognized").

including also trade transactions with third countries) is to enable individuals and courts to review whether legislative or other government restrictions are consistent with substantive and procedural constitutional guarantees (e.g. the customs union principle in EC and GATT law which prohibits non-tariff trade barriers, or the EC Treaty requirement of compliance with international law such as the WTO obligations of the EC).[75]

Modern national constitutions (such as Articles 23 and 24 of the German Basic Law), European Community law and also UN human rights law (e.g. Article 28 of the UDHR) confirm that "inalienable" human rights limit all government powers, regardless of whether they are exercised unilaterally by national government institutions or collectively by international organizations. The German Law on Foreign Economic Relations of 1961, for example, explicitly recognizes that the constitutional guarantees of liberty (e.g. in Articles 2, 12 and 14 of the Basic Law) protect also freedom to import and export subject to legislative restrictions which "are to be limited as to character and extent to the minimum necessary to achieve the purpose stipulated in the empowering legislation" and "are to be formulated in such a way as to interfere as little as possible with the liberty of economic activities" (Article 1 of the German Law on Foreign Economic Relations).[76] Should the same principle

---

[75] This is so in countries like Germany where "basic rights shall bind the legislature, the executive and the judiciary as directly enforceable law" (Article 1:3 Basic Law), and "in no case may the essential content of a basic right be encroached upon" (Article 19:2 Basic Law). Article 19:4 of the Basic Law guarantees recourse to a court against violations by public authority of any person's right, and the possibility of direct constitutional complaints to the Federal Constitutional Court (cf. Article 93 of the Basic Law) is frequently used by individuals requesting the Court to review whether their individual liberty protected by Article 2:1 has been unnecessarily restricted by legislative or administrative measures.

[76] For a detailed discussion of the constitutional and legislative protection of "freedom of trade" in Germany see *Petersmann* (1993a) 22 et seq. In a judgment of 1904, the US Supreme Court likewise recognized: "No one has a vested right to trade with foreign nations, which is so broad in character as to limit and restrict the power of Congress to determine what articles ... may be imported into this country and the terms upon which a right to import may be exercised" (*Buttfield v. Stranahan* (1904), 192 U.S. 470, 493). More recent lower court decisions in the US have, however, denied "any vested right to import"

not also be applied to the discretionary trade policy powers of international organizations like the EC which offer much less effective constitutional safeguards than inside national constitutional democracies?

2. Interpretation of Freedoms of Trade in International Integration Law

The very idea of protecting personal self-development ("human dignity") and maximum equal liberties through human rights requires to protect also mutually beneficial *transnational* cooperation among citizens, as it has been done in the jurisprudence of the EC Court of Justice protecting free movement of goods, services, persons, capital and payments as "fundamental rights" of citizens in the EU. This legal and judicial limitation of the centuries-old tradition in nation states to discriminate against foreigners, foreign goods, foreign services and foreign investments has not only extended the fundamental rights of EC citizens across frontiers. It has also enhanced their social welfare and their potential for personal self-government and self-development. Since the "freedom to conduct a business in accordance with Community law", protected by Article 16 of the EU Charter of Fundamental Rights in accordance with the jurisprudence of the EC Court, must be construed in conformity with the EC Treaty guarantees for free movement of goods, services, persons, capital and payments, it was also logical for the EC Court to recognize "freedom of trade as a fundamental right", as it had been done before by some Constitutional Courts in EC member countries.[77]

The EC Treaty's customs union principle prohibits not only discriminatory tariff and non-tariff trade barriers among EC member states (cf. Articles 28-30, 90) but also vis-à-vis third countries, as specified in the customs union rules of GATT (e.g. GATT Articles II, XI, XXIV) ratified by the EC and by all EC member states.[78] International agreements ratified by the EC, like the GATT and other WTO Agreements, are legally binding on the EC and all its

---

without the qualifications in the Supreme Court judgment, cf. *Petersmann* (1993a) 14-17.

[77] See above note 35 and *Petersmann* (1993a) 17-25.

[78] On the WTO membership of the EC and EC member states see *Van den Bossche* (1997) 23 et seq. On GATT's customs union principle as a constitutional principle explicitly incorporated into the EC Treaty see *Petersmann* (1993b).

member states (cf. Article 300:7) with a legal status inside the EC that is, according to the EC Court, higher than autonomous "secondary law".[79] EC law must be construed consistently with international law binding on the EC, and "the Court of Justice shall ensure that in the interpretation and application of this Treaty the law is observed" (Article 220). The EC Court should therefore guard the rule of law not only with regard to the *internal dimension* of the customs union principle (Articles 28-30, 90 EC Treaty) but also vis-à-vis its precise and unconditional *external prohibitions* of tariffs and non-tariff trade barriers since these GATT and WTO obligations (e.g. in GATT Articles II, III:2, XI:1) are recognized as an "integral part of the Community legal system" with a legal rank superior to EC regulations and other "secondary law". Yet, the EC Court has persistently refused to apply GATT and WTO rules and dispute settlement rulings unless EC regulations were intended to implement particular WTO obligations or made reference to specific WTO provisions.[80]

The EC Court's judicial self-restraint in ensuring the GATT- and WTO-consistency of EC regulations undermines the rule of law and democratic legitimacy of EC law. Since the 1970s, more than 30 GATT and WTO dispute settlement reports have found the EC institutions to violate GATT and WTO guarantees of freedom of trade ratified by the EC and by all national parliaments in EC member states for the benefit of EC citizens. EC citizens and their national parliaments have never granted, neither in EC law nor in WTO law, a mandate to EC institutions to violate precise and unconditional WTO guarantees of freedom of trade, non-discrimination and rule of law.[81] By undermining the rule of EC law and of international law, the EC institutions undermine also their own legal and democratic legitimacy as well as the liberty rights of EC

---

[79] See e.g. Case C-61/94, *Commission* v. *Germany*, ECR 1996 I-3989.

[80] For recent surveys and criticism of the contradictory ECJ jurisprudence concerning the EC's GATT and WTO obligations see *Peers* (2001), and *Zonnekeyn* (2001).

[81] The invocation by the EC Court (in case C-149/96, *Portugal v. Council*, ECR 1999 I-8395) of Article 22 of the WTO's DSU (i.e. the possibility of offering compensation by the EC so as to prevent countermeasures by third countries) can not legally justify the refusal by the EC Court to protect the rule of law inside the EC against manifest violations of EC law and WTO law that were not democratically authorized by national parliaments.

citizens to exercise their human rights across frontiers in conformity with EC law and international law binding on the EC.

The success of the EC's common market law was largely due to decentralized private and judicial enforcement of the pertinent EC rules through self-interested citizens and national and European courts. The EC's proposals for more decentralized enforcement of EC competition law by citizens and national courts are presented as a new paradigm for more democratic governance in the EU.[82] Since liberal trade and competition rules serve complementary functions for promoting individual and social welfare through "a system ensuring that competition in the internal market is not distorted" (Article 3 g EC Treaty), citizens and courts should also be more actively enlisted in the decentralized enforcement of the external customs union rules of the EC. Having recognized that the EC Treaty grants individual rights to freedom of competition and freedom of trade inside the EC, national and EC courts should protect these freedoms also in the external relations of the EC against manifestly illegal restraints of trade and competition by the EC institutions. Legal and judicial protection of such freedoms has nothing to do with "*laissez faire* liberalism" and one-sided protection of "negative liberties". Freedom of competition and freedom of trade protect also "positive liberties" of participating in a mutually beneficial division of labour. Lawyers should no longer ignore the basic insight of modern economic theory that governments should correct "market failures" through domestic interventions directly at the source of the market distortion without restricting the gains from trade. EC lawyers defending illegal and welfare-reducing trade protectionism as "realpolitik" so as not to "disarm politicians and civil servants"[83] undermine the human rights of EC citizens to protection of maximum equal liberties, rule of law and social welfare in the EC.

B. Social Human Rights and the WTO's Public Interest Clauses: *the Human Right to Health and Access to Medicines*

In contrast to the integration of social and labour standards into regional free trade area agreements (such as NAFTA) and customs unions (such as the EC), proposals for integrating ILO social and labour standards into WTO law (e.g. following the precedent of the 1948 Havana Charter) remain controversial on political, economic

---

[82] Cf. *Ehlermann/Atanasiu* (2001) xviii.

[83] *Peers* (2001) 123.

as well as legal grounds (e.g. because trade sanctions are viewed as an inefficient remedy that can hardly ever be "necessary" for addressing e.g. child labour and discrimination of women in exporting countries). The interrelationships between trade rules and the human right to health, however, are increasingly recognized. In the WTO Ministerial Declaration on "The TRIPS Agreement and Public Health" of November 2001, all WTO members "affirm that the Agreement can and should be interpreted and implemented in a manner supportive of WTO Members' right to protect public health and, in particular, to promote access to medicines for all"; WTO members also "reaffirm the right of WTO Members to use, to the full, the provisions in the TRIPS Agreement, which provide flexibility for this purpose".[84] Rather than granting a general waiver from WTO law in favor of the human right to health, WTO members preferred to specify those TRIPS provisions which they understand to grant sufficient flexibility for promoting public health and access to medicines for all. This approach seems consistent with the general principle that human rights are not "absolute" but must be legally implemented through legislative measures taking into account all other human rights.

The universal recognition of human rights requires to construe the numerous public interest clauses in WTO law in conformity with the human rights requirement that individual freedom and non-discrimination may be restricted only to the extent necessary for protecting other equal human rights. The non-discrimination and "necessity" requirements in the "general exceptions" of WTO law (e.g. in GATT Article XX and GATS Article XIV) reflect these human rights principles. WTO law gives clear priority to the sovereign right to restrict trade if this is necessary for the protection of human rights (e.g. to life, health, food, education, a clean and sustainable environment, and social security). The recent WTO panel and Appellate Body reports on US import restrictions of shrimps (aimed at protecting endangered species of sea turtles) confirmed that import restrictions may be justifiable under WTO law for protecting human rights values not only inside the importing country but also in other countries and in the High Seas.[85]

---

[84] See above note 40, para 4.

[85] See the Appellate Body report of 22 October 2001 on *US Import Prohibition of Certain Shrimp and Shrimp Products*, DS58/AB/RW, with references to the earlier WTO panel and Appellate Body reports.

By prohibiting discriminatory and protectionist abuses, the "general exceptions" in WTO law aim at reconciling freedom of trade with the "human rights functions" of safeguard measures restricting liberal trade. In such legal and judicial balancing processes, human rights must guide the interpretation not only of the WTO's "exceptions" and safeguard clauses, but also the interpretation of the basic WTO guarantees of freedom, non-discrimination, property rights and rule of law which protect the corresponding human rights guarantees of individual liberty, non-discrimination, private property and access to courts. Moreover, the right of the importing country to protect the human rights of its citizens needs to be balanced with the corresponding right of the exporting country and also with the economic insight that trade restrictions are only rarely an efficient instrument for correcting "market failures" and supplying "public goods". [86]

In past GATT and WTO practice, governments have only rarely referred to human rights e.g. in their invocations of the "general exceptions" (e.g. in GATT Article XX) and other safeguard clauses in GATT and WTO law so as to justify measures "necessary to protect human, animal or plant life or health". [87] There appears to be no evidence, however, that past GATT practice under Article XX

---

[86] In its Resolution 1999/30 of 26 August 1999 on "Trade Liberalization and its Impact on Human Rights", the Sub-Commission (of the UN Commission on Human Rights) on the Promotion and Protection of Human Rights declared "that sanctions and negative conditionalities which directly or indirectly affect trade are not appropriate ways of promoting the integration of human rights in international economic policy and practice". See also Resolution 1998/12 on "Human rights as the primary objective of trade, investment and financial policy" adopted by the UN Sub-Commission on the Promotion and Protection of Human Rights, and Resolution 1999/30 on "Trade liberalization and its impact on human rights" adopted by the same UN Sub-Commission in 1999.

[87] For an exception, see the submission from Mauritius in WTO document G/AG/NG/W/36/Rev.1 of 9 November 2000, which claims that Article 20 of the Agreement on Agriculture (regarding the taking into account of "non-trade concerns") should be read in conjunction with Article 11 of the ICESCR recognizing the right of everyone to adequate food. A computer search of references to human rights in WTO panel and Appellate Body reports indicates 10 reports since 1996 where parties, third parties, experts, panelists or the Appellate Body refer to human rights.

has been inconsistent with human rights. GATT dispute settlement jurisprudence, for instance, has never challenged the legality of non-discriminatory, "necessary" safeguard measures under GATT Article XX. Also WTO practice seems to be consistent so far with interpreting the "general exceptions" in WTO law (e.g. Article XIV GATS, Article 8 TRIPS Agreement) in conformity with human rights (such as the rights to health, food, adequate housing and education, or the right to protection of moral and material interests resulting from scientific, literary or artistic production of which one is the author).[88] The numerous "human rights clauses" in international economic agreements concluded by the EC with third countries have likewise been used only rarely for trade restrictions as a remedy for human rights violations.[89]

General Comment No. 14 (2000) on the human right to the highest attainable standard of health (Article 12 ICESCR), adopted by the UN Committee on Economic, Social and Cultural Rights in

---

[88] In the negotiations for the WTO Ministerial Declaration of November 2001 on access to medicines and review of Article 27:3(b) of the TRIPS Agreement, the "Africa Group", for instance, referred explicitly to human rights as criteria for interpreting the TRIPS Agreement. The WTO Secretariat also actively contributed to the discussions leading to the report of the UN High Commissioner for Human Rights on the impact of the TRIPS Agreement on human rights (E/CN.4/Sub.2/2001/ 13) and to Resolution 2001/21 by the UN Sub-Commission on Human Rights on "Intellectual Property and Human Rights" (E/CN.4/Sub.2/ RES/2001/21 of 16 August 2001).

[89] The EC's suspension of trade preferences for Yugoslavia in November 1991, for instance, was motivated by the military hostilities in the former Yugoslavia rather than by human rights violations. In the context of the Lomé-Convention, the EC reacted to human rights violations (e.g. in Rwanda) by suspension of financial and technical assistance rather than trade restrictions. The EC's Generalized System of Tariff Preferences (GSP) offers additional preferences to developing countries which respect basic ILO guarantees (such as freedom of association and minimum age for admission to employment); temporary withdrawal of GSP benefits by the EC in response to violations of human rights have been rare (e.g. in the case of Myanmar).There is thus hardly any empirical basis for the criticism (e.g. by *Prove* (1999) 32) of an alleged "bias of the WTO" because "the primary entry point for human rights concerns would be as justifications for sanctions and trade conditionalities".

May 2000,[90] defines the right to health as an inclusive right extending not only to timely and appropriate health care but also to the underlying determinants of health, such as availability, accessibility and affordability of health facilities, goods and services. The legal obligations of states to respect, protect, promote and fulfil this human right requires legislative implementation, judicial protection and health policy measures which, "depending on the availability of resources, ... should facilitate access to essential health facilities, goods and services in other countries, wherever possible and provide the necessary aid when required".[91] The General Comment recognizes that trade restrictions e.g. on individual access to essential food, drugs and health services can be inconsistent with the human right to health, and that cooperation might be required also in the WTO for the implementation of the right to health.[92]

The universalization and expanding subject matters of both human rights and intellectual property law have prompted negotiations in various UN bodies and also in the WTO on the clarification of the complex interrelationships between the TRIPS Agreement and human rights. While the need for intellectual property as reward and incentive for research and development (e.g. of new pharmaceuticals) is no longer contested, the proper balancing between the social objectives of the TRIPS Agreement (see Articles 7 and 8), its "regulatory exceptions" (e.g. in Article 6 for "parallel imports", Article 31 for "compulsory licencing", Article 40 concerning abuses of intellectual property rights), and the appropriate scope of intellectual property protection (e.g. for genetic and other living materials, rights of indigenous peoples) raises numerous controversial questions.[93] Yet, there seems to be broad agreement so far that the TRIPS provisions are flexible enough to permit necessary health protection measures so as to ensure access to affordable medicines to treat AIDS and other pandemics.[94]

---

[90] See UN document E/C.12/2000/4, CESCR of 4 July 2000 and, on the preparatory work *Toebes* (1999).
[91] General Comment No. 14 (note 90), paragraph 39.
[92] See e.g. paragraphs 41, 43 and 64 of the General Comment No. 14 (note 90).
[93] See e.g. *Dutfield* (2000).
[94] See the above-mentioned WTO Ministerial Declaration of November 2001 and e.g. the report of the joint WHO/WTO Workshop on Differential Pricing and Financing of Essential Drugs of 8-11 April 2001 (which notes that about 95% of the WHO list of "essential drugs" are

C. Democratic Balancing of Human Rights:
Are WTO Rules Adequate?

In their continuing evolution, human rights and global integration law require constant mutual balancing and concretization aimed at maximizing human rights. This human rights objective can be realized only if – similar to the bargaining inside national parliaments on the balance of private and public interests in national economic and human rights legislation – international rule-making is constitutionally restrained so as to avoid human rights being "traded away".[95] Just as views on the appropriate balancing of human rights in national legislation tend to differ depending on the interests involved, there continue to be serious doubts whether the trade-oriented TRIPS provisions appropriately balance e.g. the human rights "to benefit from the protection of the moral and material interests resulting from any scientific, literary or artistic production of which he is the author" with the right of everybody "to enjoy the benefits of scientific progress and its applications" (cf. Article 15:1 ICESCR). While national and international judges tend to exercise deference vis-à-vis legislative discretion, human rights require judges to protect the essential core of human rights against unnecessary interference by national and international rule-makers.

The high minimum standards of the TRIPS Agreement for the protection of intellectual property rights are beneficial for industries in developed countries where more than 90% of patented inventions are registered. It remains to be clarified whether the relatively vague TRIPS provisions on prevention of abuses of intellectual property rights (e.g. Articles 8, 40), on the transfer and dissemination of technology (e.g. Article 7), and on the protection of traditional knowledge, genetic resources and "farmers' rights" (e.g. in Article 27) are adequate for less-developed countries which own 90% of the world's biogenetic resources and depend on importation of technology and on more effective property rights protection of their own resources. While intellectual property protection of e.g. biotechnology may be necessary for protecting human rights (in-

---

not or no longer patented, and differential pricing and international financing of essential drugs are consistent with the TRIPS Agreement).

[95] For instance, the inalienable "moral rights" of authors recognized in Article 6*bis* of the Berne Convention for the Protection of Literary and Artistic Works (1896) were not mentioned in the TRIPS Agreement. See also *Garcia* (1999) 51.

cluding the right to food), such protection needs to be balanced with
legitimate protection of e.g. traditional knowledge owned by indigenous people, "farmers' rights" and the human right to health
and access to medicines at affordable prices.[96]

The report by the UN High Commissioner on the impact of the
TRIPS Agreement on human rights confirms that human rights are
important "context" for the interpretation of TRIPS provisions, for
instance as regards "parallel imports" of low-priced medicines,
"exhaustion" of intellectual property rights, compulsory licensing
and "local working" requirements for patented inventions.[97] The
need for balancing human rights arises also in many other areas of
WTO law and practice. The right to work, for instance, may need to
be protected through social adjustment assistance (as permitted under GATT Articles XVI and XIX) if the private adjustment costs
impose unjust sacrifices on workers in import-competing sectors.
Human and labour rights may require governments to promote
labour mobility so that unemployment caused by import
competition can be compensated by new employment opportunities
in the export sector. The WTO rules on non-discriminatory market
access may necessitate complementary competition and social rules
protecting small enterprises and vulnerable groups from abuses of
market power. The WTO's safeguard clauses leave broad discretion

---

[96] See for critical new evaluations e.g. *Elliot* (2001); *Posner* (2001).

[97] See the report mentioned above (note 88). Cf. also e.g. Resolution
No.2/2000 on 'International Trade Law' (notably Annex I on "Ex-
haustion of Intellectual Property Rights and Parallel Trade") adopted
by the worldwide International Law Association on 29 July 2000 (cf.
International Law Association (2000), 18-25), and the withdrawal, in
April 2001, of the law suit in the South African Supreme Court by 39
pharmaceutical firms against the South African government in order to
enforce drug patents that would have slowed the fight against AIDS. A
WTO dispute settlement panel was set up in January 2001 (cf.
WT/DS199) to examine a US complaint against Brazil's industrial
property law which imposes a "local working" requirement according
to which a patent shall be subject to compulsory licensing if the subject
matter of the patent is not worked in Brazil. Brazil justified its threat of
compulsory licensing for local production of generic drugs at lower
costs by health policy objectives and as a means to put pressure on US
and European pharmaceutical companies to lower their prices for HIV/
AIDS drugs. The US later withdrew its complaint and acknowledged
the right of Brazil to take measures necessary for ensuring supply of
AIDS medicaments at affordable prices to patients in Brazil.

to each WTO member country for dealing with these and other trade and adjustment problems in a manner protecting human rights with due regard to the scarcity of resources. WTO bodies must exercise deference to legitimate balancing decisions by national governments and parliaments which enjoy more democratic legitimacy for the inevitable trade-offs than distant WTO bodies focusing on trade rules.

While the balancing decisions (e.g. on trade rules and non-economic values) should be left to citizens, judges and domestic democratic institutions in accordance with the subsidiarity principle, WTO law should specify more clearly that the balancing principles and balancing procedures must take into account human rights.

Bibliography:

F. Abbott/T. Cottier (2002) (eds.), International Trade and Human Rights, Ann Arbor, MI 2002 (forthcoming).

P. Alston/J. Crawford (2000) (eds.), The Future of UN Human Rights Treaty Monitoring, Cambridge/New York 2000.

P. Alston/M. Bustelo/J. Heenan (1999) (eds.), The EU and Human Rights, Oxford 1999.

G. Amato (1997), Antitrust and the Bounds of Power: the Dilemma of Liberal Democracy in the History of the Market, Oxford 1997.

K. Arambulo (1999), Strengthening the Supervision of the International Covenant on Economic, Social, and Cultural Rights: Theoretical and Procedural Aspects, Antwerpen 1999.

R. E. Barnett (2000), The Structure of Liberty. Justice and the Rule of Law, Oxford/New York 2000.

D. Ben-David/H. Nordström/I Winters (1999), Trade, Income Disparity and Poverty (= WTO Special Study 5), Genève 1999.

L. Betten N. Grief (1998), EU Law and Human Rights Law, New York 1998.

A. Boyle/M. Anderson (1998) (eds.), Human Rights Approaches to Environmental Protection, Oxford/New York 1998.

G. de Búrca/J. Scott (2001) (eds.), The EU and the WTO, Oxford 2001.

E. Cannizzaro (2002) (ed.), The European Union as an Actor in International Relations, Dordrecht 2002.

W. M. Corden (1974), Trade Policy and Economic Welfare, Oxford 1974.

Council of Europe (2000) (ed.), Human Rights in International Law, Strasbourg ²2000.

G. Dutfield (2000), Intellectual property rights, trade, and biodiversity: seeds and plant ..., London 2000.

C. D. Ehlermann/I. Atanasiu (2001) (eds.), European Competition Law Annual 2000: The Modernisation of EC Antitrust Policy, Oxford 2001.

C. D. Ehlermann/L. Gosling (2000) (eds.), European Competition Law Annual 1998: Regulating Communications Markets, Oxford 2000.

R. Elliot (2001), TRIPS and Rights: International Human Rights Law, Access to Medicines, and the Interpretation of the WTO Agreement on Trade Related Aspects of Intellectual Property Rights. Canadian HIV /Aids Legal Network & Aids Law Project, South Africa, Toronto 2001.

J. Elster (2000), Ulysses Unbound: Studies in Rationality, Precommitment, and Constraints, Cambridge/New York 2000.

R. A. Falk (2000), Human Rights Horizons. The Pursuit of Justice in a Globalizing World, New York 2000.

W. Fikentscher (1983), Wirtschaftsrecht, Vol. I, München 1983.

D. P. Forsythe (2000a) (ed.), Human Rights and Comparative Foreign Policy, Tokyo/New York 2000.

D. P. Forsythe (2000b), Human Rights in International Relations, Cambridge 2000.

F. J. Garcia (1999), The Global Market and Human Rights: Trading Away the Human Rights Principle, Brooklyn Journal of International Law 25 (1999) No. 1, 51-98.

J. H. Garvey/T. A. Aleinikoff (1994), Modern Constitutional Theory: A Reader, St. Paul ³1994.

D. Gerber (1998), Law and Competition in Twentieth Century Europe. Protecting Prometheus, Oxford/New York 1998.

F. Gianviti (2001), Economic, Social and Cultural Human Rights and the International Monetary Fund, paper submitted to the UN Committee on Economic, Social and Cultural Rights at its "day of general discussion" on 7 May 2001, available at http://www. unhchr.ch/.

E. Grabitz (1976), Freiheit und Verfassungsrecht, Tübingen 1976.

P. Guyer (2000), Kant on Freedom, Law and Happiness, Cambridge/New York 2000.

A. C. Habbard / M. Guiraud (2001), L'OMC et les droits de l'Homme, International Federation of Human Rights November 2001, Paris 2001.

B. Hawk (1995), System Failure: Vertical Restraints and EC Competition Law, Common Market Law Review 32 (1995) No. 4, 973-989.

M. Hilf/E.-U. Petersmann (1993) (eds.), National Constitutions and International Economic Law, Boston 1993.

International Law Association (2000) (ed.), Report on the 19th Conference, London 2000.

I. Kaul/I. Grunberg/M. A. Stern (1999) (eds.), Global Public Goods. International Cooperation in the 21st Century, New York 1999.

H. H. Koh/R. C. Slye (1999) (eds.), Deliberative Democracy and Human Rights, New Haven 1999.

K. Lenaerts / E. E. De Smijter (2001), A 'Bill of Rights' for the European Union, Common Market Law Review 38 (2001) No. 2, 273-300.

C. B. Macpherson (1977), The Life and Times of Liberal Democracy, Oxford/New York 1977.

P. Marsden (2000), The Divide on Verticals, in *S. J. Evenett/A. Lehmann/B. Steil* (eds.), Antitrust goes global: what future for transatlantic cooperation?, London 2000, 117-136.

M. Mehra (1999) (ed.), Human Rights and Economic Globalisation: Directions for the WTO, Uppsala 1999.

F. L. Morrison/R. E. Hudec (1993), Judicial Protection of Individual Rights under the Foreign Trade Laws of the United States, in *Hilf/Petersmann* (1993), 91-133.

D. C. North (1990), Institutions, Institutional Change and Economic Performance, Cambridge/New York 1990.

OECD (1997) (ed.), The Role of the Competition Agency in Regulatory Reform, Paris 1997.

OECD (2000) (ed.), International Trade and Core Labor Standards, Paris 2000.

M. Olson (2000), Power and Prosperity, 2000.

S. Peers (2001), Fundamental Right or Political Whim? WTO Law and the European Court of Justice, in *de Búrca / Scott* (2001), 111-130.

M. D. Pendleton (1999), A New Human Right – The Right to Globalization, Fordham International Law Journal 22 (1999), 2052-2095.

E.-U. Petersmann (1986), Trade Policy as a Constitutional Problem. On the 'Domestic Policy Functions' of International Trade Rules, Swiss Review of International Economic Relations 41 (1986), 405-439.

E.-U. Petersmann (1991), Constitutional Functions and Constitutional Problems of International Economic Law, Fribourg 1991.

E.-U. Petersmann (1992), Charter of Economic Rights and Duties of States, in *R. Bernhardt* et al. (ed.), Encyclopedia of Public International Law, Vol. 1, Amsterdam / New York 1992, 561-566.

E.-U. Petersmann (1993a), National Constitutions and International Economic Law, in *Hilf/Petersmann* (1993), 3-52.

E.-U. Petersmann (1993b), Constitutional Principles Governing the EEC's Commercial Policy, in *M. Maresceau* (ed.), The European Community's Commercial Policy after 1992: The Legal Dimension, Dordrecht/Boston 1993, 21-62.

E.-U. Petersmann (1998), From the Hobbesian International Law of Coexistence to Modern Integration Law: The WTO Dispute Settlement System, Journal of International Economic Law, 1 (1998) No. 2, 175-198.

E.-U. Petersmann (1999a), How to Constitutionalize International Law and Foreign Policy for the Benefit of Civil Society?, Michigan Journal of International Law 20 (1999) No. 1, 1-30.

E.-U. Petersmann (1999b), Competition-oriented Reforms of the WTO World Trade System, in *R. Zäch* (ed.), Towards WTO Competition Rules, Den Haag/Boston 1999, 43-73.

E.-U. Petersmann (2000a), The WTO Constitution and Human Rights, Journal of International Economic Law 3 (2000) No. 1, 19-25.

E.-U. Petersmann (2000b), From 'Negative' to 'Positive' Integration in the WTO: Time for Mainstreaming Human Rights into WTO Law, Common Market Law Review 37 (2000) No. 6, 1363-1382.

E.-U. Petersmann (2002a), Time for a UN "Global Compact" for Integrating Human Rights into the Law of Worldwide Organizations, European Journal of International Law 2002 (forthcoming).

E.-U. Petersmann (2002b), International Activities of the European Union and Sovereignty of Member States, *Cannizzaro* (2002), 321-345.

E.-U. Petersmann (2002c), Economics and Human Rights, in *Abbott/Cottier* (2002) (forthcoming).

R. Pipes (1999), Property and Freedom, New York 1999.

M. Poiares Maduro (1999), Striking the Elusive Balance between Economic Freedom and Social Rights in the EU, in *Alston et alii* (1999), 449-472.

L. Posner (2001), Unequal Harvest. Farmers' Voices on International Trade and the Rights to Food, International Centre for Human Rights and Democratic Development, Montreal 2001.

P. Prove (1999), Human Rights at the WTO? in *Mehra* (1999), 23-36.

J. Rawls (1999a), A Theory of Justice, revised edition, Cambridge, MA 1999.

J. Rawls (1999b), The Law of Peoples, Cambridge, MA 1999.

M. Robinson (1999), Constructing an International Financial, Trade and Development Architecture: The Human Rights Dimension, in *M. Mehra* (1999), 187-199.

A. D. Rosen (1993), Kant's Theory of Justice, Ithaca 1993.

A. Sen (1999), Development as Freedom, Oxford/New York 1999.

S. Sherry (1987), The Founders' Unwritten Constitution, University of Chicago Law Review 54 (1987), 1127-1177.

H. de Soto (2000), The Mystery of Capital: Why Capitalism Triumphs in the West and Fails Everywhere Else, New York 2000.

E. Stein (2001), International Integration and Democracy: No Love at First Sight, American Journal of International Law 95 (2001) No. 3, 489-534.

A. Sykes (2002), International Trade and Human Rights: An Economic Perspective, in *Abbott/Cottier* (2002) (forthcoming).

B. C. A. Toebes (1999), The Right to Health as a Human Right in International Law, Antwerpen 1999.

United Nations (1995) (ed.), The United Nations and Human Rights 1945-1995, New York 1995.

United Nations Development Program (2000) (ed.), Human Development Report 2000: Human Rights and Human Development, New York/Oxford 2000.

P. L. H. Van den Bossche (1997), The European Community and the Uruguay Round Agreements, in *J. Jackson/A. Sykes* (eds.), Implementing the Uruguay Round, Oxford/New York 1997, 23-102.

W. K. Viscusi/J. M. Vernon/J. E. Harrington (1997), Economics of Regulation and Antitrust, Cambridge, MA ²1997.

A. W. Wood (1999), Kant's Ethical Thought, Cambridge/New York 1999.

World Bank (2000) (ed.), World Development Report 2000/2001: Attacking Poverty, Washington, DC 2000.

WTO Secretariat (ed.) (2001), Guide to the Gats, Genève/Den Haag 2001.

G. A. Zonnekeyn (2001), The Latest on Indirect Effect of WTO Law in the EC Legal Order, Journal of International Economic Law 4 (2001) No. 3, 597-608.

Stefan Griller

International Economic Law as a Means to Further Human Rights? Selective Purchasing Under the WTO Agreement on Government Procurement[*]

I. The Massachusetts Myanmar Law

In September 1998, the EC requested the establishment of a panel pursuant to the Understanding on Dispute Settlement (DSU) of the WTO. Under attack was the so called Massachusetts Law on Myanmar (the former Burma) which allegedly violated several provisions of the Government Procurement Agreement (GPA).

---

[*] I would like to thank *Mag. Katharina Gamharter* for her support in finalizing this contribution.

In June 1996, Massachusetts adopted the Act Regulating State Contracts with Companies Doing Business with or in Burma (Myanmar).[1] Intended as a sanction for the massive violation of human rights by the government, the statute barred state entities from buying goods or services from any person (including business organizations) identified on a "restricted purchase list" of those doing business with Burma.[2] "Doing business with Burma" was defined broadly to cover any person:

"(a) having a principal place of business, place of incorporation or its corporate headquarters in Burma (Myanmar) or having any operations, leases, franchises, majority-owned subsidiaries, distribution agreements, or any other similar agreements in Burma (Myanmar), or being the majority-owned subsidiary, licensee or franchise of such a person;

"(b) providing financial services to the government of Burma (Myanmar), including providing direct loans, underwriting government securities, providing any consulting advice or assistance, providing brokerage services, acting as a trustee or escrow agent, or otherwise acting as an agent pursuant to a contractual agreement;

"(c) promoting the importation or sale of gems, timber, oil, gas or other related products, commerce in which is largely controlled by the government of Burma (Myanmar), from Burma (Myanmar);

"(d) providing any goods or services to the government of Burma (Myanmar)".

There were three exceptions to the ban: (1) if the procurement was essential, and without the restricted bid, there would have been no bids or insufficient competition; (2) if the procurement was of medical supplies; and (3) if the procurement efforts produced no "comparable low bid or offer" by a person not doing business with Burma, meaning an offer no more than 10 percent greater than the restricted bid.

The WTO never decided the case, as the Myanmar Law was declared invalid by US courts, which led first to the suspension and

---

[1]   1996 Mass. Acts 239, ch. 130 [codified at Mass. Gen. Laws §§7:22G-7:22M, 40 F½ (1997)].

[2]   Exempt from boycott were entities present in Burma solely to report the news, or to provide international telecommunication goods or services, or medical supplies.

later to the lapse of the authority of the panel. The US Supreme Court in June 2000[3] held that the law violated the Supremacy Clause of the US Constitution owing to its potential to frustrate federal statutory objectives. According to the far-reaching preemption doctrine, state law is not only naturally pre-empted to the extent that there is a conflict with a federal statute, but must also yield to a congressional Act whenever Congress intends federal law to "occupy the field". As regards the second limb, the supremacy clause is violated if the law "stands as an obstacle to the accomplishment and execution of the full purposes and objectives of Congress".

The Supreme Court found that the Myanmar Law was pre-empted in this sense by a Congressional statute passed in September 1996,[4] three months after the Massachusetts law had been enacted. Congress had imposed a set of mandatory and conditional sanctions on Burma, including a large margin of discretion for the President of the US on how to proceed in order to further human rights standards in Myanmar. The Court saw the law as an obstacle to the accomplishment of Congress' full objectives under the federal Act. According to the Court, the state law undermined the intended purpose and "natural effect" of at least three provisions of the federal Act, namely, its delegation of effective discretion to the President to control economic sanctions against Burma, its limitation of sanctions solely to United States persons and new investment, and its directive to the President to proceed diplomatically in developing a comprehensive, multilateral strategy towards Burma. The introduction of dispute settlement procedures under DSU were relevant in the last mentioned context, but not decisive.

II.   Selective Purchasing Under the GPA

A. The Complaint in the Myanmar Case and General Remarks

The EC had claimed that the Myanmar Law violated several provisions of the GPA, a plurilateral agreement in the framework of the WTO. Its major goals, highlighted in the preamble of the

---

[3]   530 U.S. _ (2000), June 19, 2000, *Crosby v National Foreign Trade Council*.

[4]   Foreign Operations, Export Financing, and Related Programs Appropriations Act, 1997, §570, 110 Stat. 3009-166 to 3009-167 (enacted by the Omnibus Consolidated Appropriations Act, 1997, §101(c), 110 Stat. 3009-121 to 3009-172).

Agreement, are a) liberalization and expansion of world trade, b) non-discrimination and national treatment, c) transparency, d) effective enforcement, and e) respect for the needs of developing countries, in particular the least-developed countries. Currently, some 27 countries are signatories to the GPA, among them Canada, Japan, the USA, the EC and the Member States of the EC respectively. The agreement covers – according to differing commitments of the parties – procurement activities above certain thresholds by central and sub-central government entities, as well as public enterprises and utilities.

In the Myanmar case, the EC invoked Articles III, VIII(b), XIII.4(b), (and XXII.2) of the GPA.[5]

Article III GPA provides for National Treatment and Non-discrimination. Para. 1 requires immediate and unconditional treatment no less favourable than that accorded to domestic products, services and suppliers, and that accorded to products, services and suppliers of any other party. Para. 2 prohibits discrimination between locally established suppliers on the basis of degree of foreign affiliation or ownership or on the basis of the origin of the good or service being supplied, provided that the country of origin is a party to the agreement (which, by the way, Myanmar is not).

Article VIII(b) GPA contains the qualification criteria of the supplier, whereby "any conditions for participation in tendering procedures shall be limited to those which are essential to ensure the firm's capability to fulfil the contract in question. Any conditions for participation required from suppliers, including financial guarantees, technical qualifications and information necessary for establishing the financial, commercial and technical capacity of suppliers, as well as the verification of qualifications, shall be no less favourable to suppliers of other Parties than to domestic suppliers and shall not discriminate among suppliers of other Parties ..."

Article XIII.4(b) GPA regulates the award of contracts and requires that the award has to be made to the "tenderer who has been determined to be fully capable of undertaking the contract and whose tender ... is either the lowest tender or the tender which in terms of the specific evaluation criteria set forth in the notices or tender documentation is determined to be the most advantageous".

Summing up, the EC argued that these provisions of the GPA render illegal a rule which differentiates between tenderers accord-

---

[5]   WT/DS88/3, 9 Sept 1998.

ing to their involvement in transactions with governments that violate human rights. For the purpose of this paper, the issue shall be addressed in this broad sense, and not only with regard to the specific conditions of the Massachusetts law.

The prohibition or justification of Human Rights clauses can, also in the Myanmar case, be scrutinized with regard to various situations, stages of the procurement procedure, and on the grounds of several arguments. I shall address the most important in turn, not claiming to deal with all aspects put forward in the discussion.

B. Assessment of the Legality of Human Rights Clauses Under the GPA

1. Non-discrimination and National Treatment Issues

(1.) In the Myanmar case, a violation of the National Treatment obligation of the GPA is not obvious. Domestic suppliers appear equally affected – as can also be drawn from the fact that it were national suppliers who brought the issue to the Supreme Court. It has been argued that there might still be a *de facto* discrimination for companies which, for historical or geographical reasons, engage more in business with a human rights violating country than others.[6] While certainly such effect cannot be completely excluded, in any event there are further considerations. First, it might still be that on average domestic enterprises are more affected, given that they – for various reasons – are more likely to do business with contracting authorities bound by the Myanmar law. That would result in a *de facto* discrimination of domestic enterprises which would have to be weighed against the *de facto* discrimination of foreign suppliers. Second, it would still be necessary to discuss eventual justifications of such a *de facto* discrimination.[7]

The Non-discrimination clause could be relevant insofar as a local subsidiary of a Myanmar based enterprise would be caught by the provision. However, this seems not to have been pertinent to the facts of either the WTO or the US case. With regard to such situations, however, it is necessary to rely on the safeguard clauses of the agreement.

(2.) A controversial issue is the country based approach which was also chosen in the Myanmar case. It is argued that country

---

[6] *Spennemann* (2001) 54 et seq.

[7] *McCrudden* (1999) 36 et seq.

based restrictions always are *prima facie* violations of the GATT.[8] Regarding the GPA, the situation is less clear. Since Myanmar is not party to the GPA (and also not to the WTO), the contention could be that a company in a third country, say within the EC, doing business with Myanmar, is discriminated against if compared with a company doing business with a country not subject to such restrictions. But it is hard to see how this could be challenged under the equality provisions of the GPA.

Should a GPA party, say Korea, be the target of the restriction, the situation is apparently different. In such a case the Non-discrimination clause quite obviously would apply. Consequently an eventual justification would have to rely on the safeguard clauses of the GPA. The situation might be different if the country specific measure is imposed on the basis of a general provision aiming at equal treatment of all countries violating human rights. However, controversies might still occur, since there is a certain tension emerging from the fact that it is still the contracting parties which are the primary beneficiaries of the rights flowing from the GPA, but that the agreement obviously at the same time (Article XX GPA) includes the right to individual complaints and prohibits discrimination among suppliers of other parties. The result could be that the treatment of the contracting party could be justified as being based on an equality assessment, while the individual company might be affected only because it is situated in the targeted country without being involved in human rights violations.

(3.) The argument that "social conditions" in some cases have been the subject of reservations of GPA parties, which makes them illegal for all the others, is at least partly misleading. The argument is only convincing with regard to discriminatory provisions. The point is that Canada, Korea and the USA made some sort of reservations in their GPA commitments. In the case of Canada, the reservation says that the agreement does not apply to set-asides for small and minority businesses,[9] whereas the USA reserves procurements of sub-central government entities subject to programmes promoting the development of distressed areas and businesses owned by minorities, disabled veterans and women are reserved from coverage.[10] The EC reacted by introducing far-reaching

---

[8]   *Howse/Regan* (2000), *Spennemann* (2001) 71 et seqq.
[9]   Appendix I, General Notes for Canada.
[10] United States, Annex 2.

derogations vis-à-vis Canada (also for other reasons), and by excluding the availability of the Challenge Procedures under the GPA for companies residing in Japan, Korea or the USA in cases of the award of a contract to small or medium sized enterprises to suppliers or service providers located in other countries than those mentioned.[11] The argument is that since the EC has not fought for the inclusion of similar provisions, it has to be concluded that selective purchasing for social reasons is not available to the Communities under the GPA.[12] In itself, the argument is certainly correct insofar as the clauses mentioned are exempting *discriminatory* provisions from the coverage of the GPA. However, the argument is not convincing with regard to non-discriminatory clauses, and especially not with regard to human rights clauses. Thus it is essential to make a difference between protectionist and non protectionist clauses.[13]

(4.) It is a matter of debate whether the National Treatment and the Non-discrimination clause only apply to like products.[14] If this is so, then the finding of an eventual violation of Article III GPA depends to a certain extent on the well known "process – product distinction". On the grounds that non-product related PPMs (processes and production methods) could form part of the scrutiny of likeness, it could be argued that products produced while at the same time violating human rights were unlike, which would exclude them from the clauses under discussion. If such an argument is denied, any differentiation on the grounds of human rights violations would be illegal.

However, mainly for one reason, this point shall not be further developed. Even if non-product related PPMs could not justify differential treatment, the issue appears, contrary to some suggestions in literature, to be of limited importance. It is, at least at first sight, important for suppliers or service providers which are more or less directly involved in the violation of human rights. This could (even) be companies using "affected" raw material for the product subject to the procurement restrictions. However, it might be different with

---

[11] EC, General Notes and Derogations from the Provisions of Article III.

[12] Interpretative Communication of the Commission on the Community law applicable to public procurement and the possibilities for integrating social consideration into public procurement, COM (2001) 566 final, 15.10.2001, at 14.

[13] See also *McCrudden* (1999) at 9.

[14] *McCrudden* (2001) 36 et seqq., *Spennemann* (2001) 55 et seqq.

regard to companies simply doing business by selling products to the targeted country. They would be affected by the measure without their products being the result of human rights violations. In other words: In these cases, the issue is whether the contracting authority may still differentiate between like products according to its preferences.

This point is at the centre of the GPA, and thus has relevance far beyond these specific circumstances. The question is not so much whether products in one or the other way affected by human rights violations are like or unlike products, but whether and to what extent the contracting authority may, in awarding the contract, differentiate between like products. In fact, every decision in a procurement procedure inevitably involves a differentiation between like products. Against this background, it might well be that it is not only by chance or a result of careless drafting that the notion of "like" products does not appear in the text of the GPA.

2. Are the Qualification and Award Criteria Exhaustive?

(1.) The most important question is whether the qualification and/or the award criteria mentioned in the GPA are exhaustive in the sense that they would prohibit every specification of additional criteria, even if such criteria would not be arbitrary or discriminatory on the grounds of nationality or origin. There is no convincing argument which could support such a conclusion. The most relevant provisions included in Article VIII GPA on the qualification of suppliers, and in Article XIII on the award of contracts have already been mentioned. The conditions for participation in tendering procedures are limited to those which are "essential to ensure the firm's capability to fulfil the contract in question".[15] It has rightly been pointed out that it might be essential for the contracting authority that the firm is capable to supply the product while at the same time respecting human rights.[16] Regarding the award of contracts, the GPA is even more vague. The contracting authority has the choice between the lowest tender or "the tender which in terms of the specific evaluation criteria set forth in the notices or tender documentation is determined to be the most advantageous".[17] It is remarkable that the text, contrasting to that of the EC directives,

---

[15] Article VIII(b) GPA.
[16] *Spennemann* (2001) 63 et seqq.
[17] Article XIII 4.(b) GPA.

avoids the expression "most economically advantageous".[18] The tender documentation provided to suppliers has to contain "all information necessary to permit them to submit responsive tenders, including ... the criteria for awarding the contract, including any factors other than price that are to be considered in the evaluation of tenders ...".[19] The wording suggests that it is to a very large extent up to the contracting authority (or the respective legislator) to determine the details of the award criteria. In more general language, one might well say that the GPA is strict as regards transparency and the prohibition of discriminatory practices,[20] but it does not contain a comprehensive "purity" principle[21] rendering non-economic criteria automatically illegal.

However, it should be stressed that this is no authorization to arbitrarily restricting procurement practices. It might well be that the Myanmar law still falls short of this standard by not differentiating according to the degree of involvement in human rights violations, and thus might not be proportionate.[22]

(2.) In this context, it is added that the matter would not be different if selective purchasing criteria would not be applied as qualification and award criteria, but as contract conditions.[23] This seems to be the view, among others and with regard the EC law, of the European Commission. Obviously the position is of considerable importance for those who strictly exclude non-economic qualification or award criteria. The merits of this position under EC law is examined below, however, at this stage it is stressed that the GPA does not support such a differentiation.

3. Safeguard Clauses

Still for those who do not share the view that the GPA at least to a certain extent allows for selective purchasing conditions, and also with regard to certain practices which would not be covered by such a broader interpretation of the agreement either, the safeguard

---

[18] Compare already *Kunzlik* (1998) 206.

[19] Article XII 2(h) GPA.

[20] Compare in this respect also Article XVI GPA on the prohibition of offsets which, among others, are "measures used to encourage local development".

[21] *McCrudden* (1999) 30.

[22] The subject shall not be further developed here. With regard to the proportionality principle, compare also below.

[23] Compare *McCrudden* (1999) 30 et seqq.

clause of the GPA is of crucial importance. Article XXIII GPA, under the heading "Exceptions to the Agreement", in its first paragraph contains a clause referring to "essential security interests" of the parties. More important for the subject of human rights protection is the second paragraph, which – similar to, but not identical with Article XX GATT – reads as follows:

> "Subject to the requirement that such measures are not applied in a manner which would constitute a means of arbitrary or unjustifiable discrimination between countries where the same conditions prevail or a disguised restriction on international trade, nothing in this Agreement shall be construed to prevent any Party from imposing or enforcing measures: necessary to protect public morals, order or safety, human, animal or plant life or health or intellectual property; or relating to the products or services of handicapped persons, of philanthropic institutions or of prison labour".

Arguably,[24] the protection of human rights falls (mainly) under the protection of public morals or order. It is another and more difficult question, which human rights could be invoked under the clause. It is submitted that not only peremptory norms of international law (such as the prohibition of slavery), but also fundamental provisions included in the respective legal order (*ordre public*) could be invoked. Even more controversial might be the requirements of the necessity test which is indispensable under Article XXIII. The measures taken would have to stand not only the efficiency, but also the proportionality, test.[25] To start with the first, it would be required to show that the measures taken are efficient in achieving their goals. But what are legitimate goals? In the Myanmar case, it can be argued that the goal is the promotion of the respect for human rights in Myanmar. In this case it might be questionable that the measure is efficient at all. But if the goal would be to develop and observe a consistent human rights policy of the government which does not allow human rights to be a "non issue" in a specific field of activity, the result could be different. To achieve

---

[24] Compare *McCrudden* (1999) 38-46; *Spennemann* (2001) 77-93.

[25] The premise is that the requirements are comparable to those under Article XX GATT. See in this respect esp the recent Appellate Body Decision in *Korea – Measures Affecting Imports of Fresh, Chilled and Frozen Beef*, AB-2000-8, WT/DS 161 und 169/AB/R (*Korea – Beef*), 11 Dec 2000, paras 161-163.

this goal, selective purchasing might be considered to be effective. Under the proportionality test it would have to be shown that there is no comparably efficient measure which would have less adverse effect on the fulfilment of the GPA. Such a necessity test would be anything but easy to pass, even if it is true that the Appellate Body (AB) in *Korea – Beef* has introduced a more flexible system of scrutiny (under the related provision of Article XX(d) GATT). It might well be that it could not be justified to also target, as the Myanmar law does to a certain extent, companies which are not involved in any practices of violating human rights, but either are residing in the country of the targeted government, or are making business with such companies.

A final point is the so called chapeau of Article XXIII 2 GPA prohibiting "arbitrary or unjustifiable discrimination between countries where the same conditions prevail or a disguised restriction on international trade". It has already been put forward that the banning of products from Myanmar, but not of the PR of China would seem to be an arbitrary discrimination and probably would not pass WTO scrutiny.[26] More generally, it could be argued that country specific restrictions would only satisfy this non-discrimination test if applied equally to all countries with a comparable human rights record. However, contextual interpretation[27] might lead to a modified result. It has to be taken into account that Article XXIII allows for exceptions, *inter alia*, from the GPA specific most favoured nation clause (Article III GPA). Thus, to a certain extent, it inevitably allows for a differentiation between countries which would otherwise be prohibited. Is it really compelling that all countries which may, on the grounds of this safeguard clause, be treated differently, can invoke some sort of a "second order most favoured nation clause" providing for MFN-treatment of all countries "where the same conditions prevail"? If this result was to be achieved, should the treaty not use a similar wording as in Article III 1(b) GPA, stipulating that such differentiation should in itself provide for "treatment no less favourable than that accorded to products,

---

[26] *Spennemann* (2001) 93.

[27] Compare Article 31 1 *Vienna Convention on the Law of Treaties*. As the AB, in *US – Gasoline*, WT/DS2/AB/R, AB-1996-1, 29 April 1996, chapter II, has found, Article 31 as such forms part of the customary rules of interpretation of public international law "which the Appellate Body has been directed, by Article 3(2) of the *DSU*, to apply".

services and suppliers of any other Party" where the same conditions prevail? Instead, the treaty prohibits "arbitrary or unjustifiable discrimination" between such countries, and "a disguised restriction on international trade".

It shall also be noted that the AB has, with regard to the parallel chapeau clause in Article XX GATT, found that it "cannot logically refer to the same standard(s) by which a violation of a substantive rule has been determined to have occurred. To proceed down that path would be both to empty the chapeau of its contents and to deprive the exceptions ... of meaning. Such recourse would also confuse the question of whether inconsistency with a substantive rule existed, with the further and separate question arising under the chapeau of Article XX as to whether that inconsistency was nevertheless justified".[28] Furthermore, the AB decided, in *US – Shrimp*, and again with regard to the parallel provision in Article XX GATT, that it is "but one expression of the principle of good faith", and also corresponding to the doctrine of *abus de droit*.[29] The AB did not at all rule out different treatment between countries where the same conditions prevail. However, it stressed specific *procedural* requirements for the imposition of such restrictions. It called for "serious, across-the-board negotiations with the objective of concluding bilateral or multilateral agreements".[30] The AB could not accept that the US had negotiated "seriously with some, but not with other Members"[31] exporting to the US.

Against this background, it might be contended that country specific restrictions might be justifiable provided that they are based on a reasonable general scheme aiming at the avoidance of "arbitrary or unjustifiable discrimination". On the basis of such a scheme, differentiation between countries where the same conditions prevail could be accepted at least as a transitory measure – allowing for a step-by-step implementation of the general, non-discriminatory scheme[32] – and provided that the restriction is only

---

[28] AB, in *US – Gasoline*, WT/DS2/AB/R, AB-1996-1, 29 April 1996, chapter III near fn 45.

[29] AB-1998-4, *United States – Import Prohibition of Certain Shrimp and Shrimp Products (US – Shrimps)*, WT/DS58/AB/R, 12 Oct 1998, para 158.

[30] *US – Shrimps* (above fn 29), para 166.

[31] *US – Shrimps* (above fn 29), para 172.

[32] For a more generous approach allowing for permanent differentiations between countries where the same conditions prevail compare *Trebil-*

imposed after "serious, good faith efforts"[33] to come to terms on the basis of negotiations, which did not produce sufficient results.

Finally, it should also be said that in *Shrimp*, the AB held "that discrimination results not only when countries in which the same conditions prevail are differently treated, but also when the application of the measure at issue does not allow for any inquiry into the appropriateness of the regulatory program for the conditions prevailing in those exporting countries".[34] It might be in the same vain of thought to call for a differentiation between countries, but even between suppliers or service providers according to their "regulatory environment". Why should a supplier who is "doing business" with a "blacklisted" country but who is at the same time, on the basis of individual scrutiny, avoiding business with companies violating Human rights, categorically be excluded from the award of the contract?

III.   Perspectives for the European Communities

A. Human Rights Clauses Under
the EC Government Procurement Directives?

The substantive law of public procurement within the internal market is mainly governed by four EC directives, the first three on the coordination of procedures for the award of public works, public supply, and public service contracts, and finally the fourth on coordinating the procurement procedures of entities operating in the water, energy, transport and telecommunications sectors (the so

---

cock in this volume, near fn 28. *Trebilcock* argues that differentiation is only prohibited if imposed for protectionist reasons. However, according to the safeguard clauses (of Article XX GATT or Article XXIII GPA) "a balance must be struck between the *right* of a Member to invoke an exception under Article XX and the *duty* of that same Member to respect the treaty rights of the other Members" [AB, *US – Shrimps* (above fn 29), para 156]. Thus, it might be a violation of *the rights of another member* to be treated differently compared to a (third) member where the same conditions prevail. Why should it make a difference *for the targeted member* that the disadvantage with regard to a third member is not founded in protectionist reasons?

[33]   AB-2001-4, *United States – Import Prohibition of Certain Shrimp and Shrimp Products*, Recourse to Article 21.5 of the DSU by Malaysia (*US – Shrimp, Article 21.5.*), WT/DS58/AB/RW, 22 Oct 2001, para 134.

[34]   *US – Shrimps* (above fn 29), para 165.

called *Utilities Directive*).[35] As far as public procurement in goods
is concerned, these directives in principle also regulate the award of
contracts across the EC external borders. However, for services,
external relations are still predominantly a matter for the Member
States (which are, together with the EC, signatories of the GPA).[36]
Consequently, the "human rights question" is a matter to be decided
according to either the EC directives, this is especially so for the
award of contracts within the internal market and for the award of
supply contracts within the scope of the GPA, or national legislation, especially regarding the award of service contracts falling
under the GPA.

The legal status of non-economic criteria in EC public procurement law is controversial. This is the more so regarding human
rights clauses which, to the knowledge of the author, have never
been the centre of litigation. As there has been no judicial clarification, the issue has to be explored on the grounds of the related
topics of the legality of social or environmental criteria.

In its recent Communication on the legality of social considerations in the field of public procurement[37] the European Commission
reconfirmed its rather restrictive position. It is based on the fact that
the relevant EC directives allow the contracting authority to base
the award of contracts either on the lowest price criterion only, or to
choose the "most economically advantageous tender".[38] Regarding
the second option the directives contain a non-exhaustive list of
relevant factors: price, delivery date, running costs, cost-effectiveness, quality, aesthetic and functional characteristics, technical
merit, after-sales service and technical assistance.

---

[35] For a consolidated version of the relevant EC directives see
http://europa.eu.int/eur-lex/en/lif/ind/en_analytical_index_06.html; for
a survey on the actual public procurement system of the EC compare
http://europa.eu.int/comm/internal_market/en/publproc/index.htm.

[36] The complex division of competences between the EC and its Member
States regarding external relations in public procurement shall not be
examined here; compare in this respect *Griller* (2000).

[37] COM (2001) 566 final, 15.10.2001 (above fn 12). Compare *Pache/
Rüger* (2002) 169 et seqq. For a comprehensive analysis of the subject
– but excluding the human rights issue – see *Benedict* (2000).

[38] E.g. Art 26 of the Council Directive 93/36/EEC coordinating procedures for the award of public supply contracts, OJ No 1993/L 199/1, as
amended.

Against this background, the Commission in the mentioned Communication stresses its view that the criteria used should generate an "economic advantage for the contracting authority". Furthermore, according to the Commission, such criteria must "concern the nature of the work which is the subject-matter of the contract or the manner in which it is carried out", and must therefore "be linked to the subject-matter of the contractor or the manner in which it is performed".[39] The Commission observes that social criteria are not among the various examples in the directives, and concludes that contracting authorities might only impose such criteria via contractual clauses. This flows from the position that, according to the Commission, (only) the "execution phase of public procurement contracts is not currently regulated by the public procurement directives". Thus, the Member States might regulate this phase only if they respect general Community law, in particular, not to discriminate against non national tenderers.[40] It is only in this context that the Commission mentions, *inter alia*, the eventual "obligation to comply with the substance of the provisions of ILO core conventions during the execution of the contract". In other words: The Commission tries to interpret the EC procurement directives in a similar manner as the GPA in its complaint filed against the US. However, in the Communication at issue, the Commission does not mention the eventual option to include human rights clauses in contract conditions.

The Commission is certainly right in stressing that the European Court of Justice (ECJ) regards it as "the aim of the directives ... to avoid both the risk of preference being given to national tenderers or applicants" and the possibility that a contracting authority "may choose to be guided by considerations other than economic ones ...".[41] But it has also to be said that the ECJ grants a large margin of discretion to the Member States and the contracting authorities respectively regarding the scope of justifiable economic considerations. This is so since the *Beentjes* case, where the court accepted the criterion of the ability of the tenderer to employ long-time unemployed. The court said that this was an "additional specific condition" which had to be mentioned in the notice, so that contractors

---

[39] COM (2001) 566 final, 15.10.2001, at 13.
[40] COM (2001) 566 final, 15.10.2001, at 16.
[41] From recent jurisprudence, see Case C-380/98, *The Queen/ University of Cambridge*, [2000] ECR, I-8035, para 17.

may become aware of its existence.[42] It should be stressed that the court did so in answering the question whether "the rejection of a tender" on the grounds of this criterion was legal. The court did not treat the criterion as a contract condition, but as a selection criterion. On the basis that the directive at issue did not include "a uniform and exhaustive body of Community rules", the court found that Member States are in principle "free to maintain or adopt substantive and procedural rules".[43] The point was raised in a more recent case when the Commission claimed that a condition relating to employment linked to a local project to combat unemployment constituted an infringement of EC law. The Commission acknowledged that the taking into account of employment-related projects may be regarded as a condition of performance but not, as in the case, as an award criterion in the contract notices. The court, however, said that such criterion was not in itself illegal *as an award criterion*, which had already been the case in *Beentjes*.[44]

As a result, the Commission is simply wrong in claiming that social criteria are, in principle, only allowed as contract conditions. The Commission mentions the ECJ's conflicting jurisprudence, but in a way which does not reveal the divergence of opinions.[45] One may also add that the differentiation drawn by the Commission – and to some extent accepted by legal doctrine – is not very convincing. If a criterion is prohibited as a selection criterion, but nev-

---

[42] Case 31/87, *Beentjes*, [1988] ECR, 4635, para 36.

[43] Case 31/87, *Beentjes*, [1988] ECR, 4635, para 20: "Furthermore, the directive does not lay down a uniform and exhaustive body of Community rules; within the framework of the common rules which it contains, the Member States remain free to maintain or adopt substantive and procedural rules in regard to public works contracts on condition that they comply with all the relevant provisions of Community law, in particular the prohibitions flowing from the principles laid down in the Treaty in regard to the right of establishment and the freedom to provide services ...".

The matter shall not be further developed here. The stance of the ECJ could be challenged by pointing at the original version of the EC directives which partly included *transitional* provisions allowing for the application of "non economic" criteria. The conclusion could have well been that after the lapse of these provisions such criteria should no longer be allowed.

[44] Case C-225/98, *Commission / France (Nord-Pas-de-Calais Region)*, [2000] ECR, I-7445, paras. 50 and 52.

[45] COM (2001) 566 final, 15.10.2001, at 14 et seq.

ertheless accepted as a contract requirement, the result would still be the same: A tenderer not able or willing to fulfil the criterion will never win the contract.

A parallel might exist between social and environmental conditions, at least to some extent. Also with regard to the latter, the Commission has been very restrictive. It has been stressing, among others, that each individual award criterion "has to have an economic advantage which directly benefits the contracting authority".[46] However, in a recent judgment, the ECJ did not follow this view. It held that the contracting authority may "take into consideration ecological criteria ..., provided that they are linked to the subject-matter of the contract, do not confer an unrestricted freedom of choice on the authority, are expressly mentioned in the contract documents or the tender notice, and comply with all the fundamental principles of Community law, in particular the principle of non-discrimination."[47] "Linked criteria" are those "relating to the contract in question".[48]

If transferred to human rights clauses, this requirement might imply that "doing business" with a country violating human rights in the broad sense of the Myanmar law is too unspecific. Rather, it might be necessary to draw on the supplier's or service provider's (direct or indirect) involvement in human rights violating activities; the mere existence of an establishment or a subsidiary in a country violating human rights, or doing business with companies established in such countries, might not be sufficiently "related" to the award of a contract.

It must be noted, however, that the requirement of a sufficient nexus as developed so far by the ECJ is not precise enough to settle the matter, even if it could be transferred to human rights clauses without modification. First, is has to be noted that the criterion of employing long-term unemployed, as already accepted by the ECJ, is quite "remote", if it is understood that it might, in principle, be

---

[46] Commission interpretative Communication on the Community law applicable to public procurement and the possibilities for integrating environmental considerations into public procurement, COM (2001) 274 final, 4.7.2001, at 20.

[47] Case C-513/99, *Concordia Bus Finland Oy Ab (originally Stagecoach Finland)*, 17 Sept 2002, para. 69, nyr. Compare already the Opinion of AG *Mischo* in C-513/99, 13 Dec 2001, nyr.

[48] Case C-513/99, *Concordia Bus Finland Oy Ab (originally Stagecoach Finland)*, 17 Sept 2002, para. 60.

legally applied in *all* procurement procedures, not only in those carried out as a core element of employment policy. Thus, the existing case law seems to accommodate the goal to integrate employment policy into other policies,[49] a goal which is expressly stipulated by the TEC with regard to the promotion of equality between men and women, environmental protection, consumer protection, and animal welfare.[50] Second, it remains to be seen whether, against this background, the integration of a consistent human rights policy into other policies might be considered of minor weight compared to employment policy.[51]

The issue discussed above is also controversial in the ongoing debate on "modernising, simplifying and rendering more flexible"[52] the existing EC legal framework in the field of public procurement. In its recently amended proposal, the European Commission took the concurring view into account, that other than "purely economic" considerations might equally be of relevance and allowed in the course of awarding a contract. The reformulated recital (29) now says in its essential passages, that contract performance conditions "may be aimed at promoting on-the-job training and the employment of people who are facing particular difficulties in finding work, at combating unemployment or at protecting the environment, and may give rise to obligations – applicable to contract performance – to, in particular, recruit the long-term unemployed or implement training schemes for the unemployed and young persons, or to comply with the substance of the provisions of the ILO core conventions, ... to recruit a number of handicapped persons above that required under national legislation". A new Art 26a of the proposed directive reads, under the heading "contract perform-

---

[49] It has to be added that it might be more than difficult to define a concept of employment policy which would be strictly divided from other policies.

[50] Compare Article 3 para. 2, Article 6, Article 153 para. 2 TEC, an the Protocol on Protection and Welfare of Animals.

[51] It must be added that public procurement in the EC takes place against a background of a developed system of human rights protection – compare only *Duschanek/Griller* (2002).

[52] Amended proposal for a European Parliament and Council directive concerning the coordination of procedures for the award of public supply contracts, public service contracts and public works contracts, COM (2002) 236 final, 6.5.2002, at 2.

ance conditions": "Contracting authorities may impose particular conditions concerning performance of the contract, provided that those conditions are compatible with Community law and provided that they are stated in the contract notice or in the contract documents. Contract performance conditions may relate in particular to social and environmental considerations".

The conclusion is that the Member States remain to a very large extent free to determine the relevant criteria for the most economically advantageous tender, including social considerations. If this is correct, there is no compelling reason in sight which would render human rights conditions illegal from the outset. As long as such conditions are "linked to the subject-matter of the contract", do not confer an unrestrictive freedom of choice, are not discriminatory, and are included in the procurement documentation, such criteria would be acceptable. It has to be admitted, though, that the extent to which the respect for human rights is linked to the award of public contracts, is still not a settled issue. What should be demonstrated is that there are good reasons – under EC law – to respect the integration of a Member State's human rights policy into its public procurement policy on a general basis.

B. Consequences of an Eventual EC Prohibition Under the GPA

For those who accept that selective purchasing aiming at the promotion of human rights might be justifiable under the GPA, but not under EC law, things become more complicated. Arguably such a position would inevitably imply that the respect for the National Treatment and the Non-discrimination clause of Article III GPA would bar the application of such criteria also vis-à-vis GPA parties.

IV.   Concluding Remarks

Selective Purchasing under the GPA is a specific example for the tensions between trade liberalization and the protection of Human Rights.[53] It is at the same time an example supporting the view that it would, in principle, be too simplistic to advocate for clear cut solutions according to a strict hierarchy of norms. In international law, such a hierarchy generally does not exist. But even where this is different, which is the case when *ius cogens* is at stake, there are no simple solutions. Is doing business with a country violating the

---

[53]   Compare only recently, *Cottier* (2002), and *Petersmann*, in this volume.

prohibition of torture, or even doing business with a torturer, automatically in itself a violation of the prohibition? Also, many human rights guarantees allow for restrictions on the basis of public interest clauses, which might, *inter alia*, capture trade liberalization rules. Vice versa, trade agreements usually include safeguard clauses allowing for the protection and promotion of "non-economic concerns"[54] including Human Rights.[55] Similar solutions are to be discussed when trade agreements and Human Rights agreements concluded between the same parties are conflicting *prima vista*.

Taken altogether, the relationship between trade liberalization and the protection of Human Rights rather is one of reconciliation and balanced interpretation than one of clear hierarchy.[56] It is contended that this is a rough characterization of the legal situation *de lege lata*, leaving aside the debate on how it should be *de lege ferenda*.[57]

Moreover, when there is a discussion about selective purchasing on the basis of human rights clauses, or, on a broader concept, on the grounds of social clauses, specific characteristic of public procurement provisions should be considered. It is not general import or export restrictions that are at stake, but preferences of the state and state governed entities as customers. It might not be justified to prevent the state in this function to act in consistence with human rights guarantees enshrined in its legal order, as long as this does not happen in a discriminatory manner. As long as these conditions are met, selective purchasing it not *per se* prohibited by the GPA.

---

[54] The expression "non-economic concerns" shall not be further explored although it is readily acknowledged that its use is often, and often and also in this context as well, is too simplistic. Many "economic concerns" are covered by Human Rights, for example the right to property and the freedom to conduct a business protect core features of economic concerns.

[55] This appears to be the prevailing view, even if acknowledging decisions especially of the AB are still missing; compare in this respect *Petersmann* (2002) at 645, and *Howse* (2002) at 655 et seqq.

[56] It can be added that the situation is similar within many national legal systems as well as within EC law.

[57] For the controversy on this subject, see recently *Petersmann* (2002) and *Howse* (2002). Suffice it here to say that a "clear cut hierarchy" might fail to meet the requirements of a balanced application of both Human Rights guarantees and trade liberalization rules.

Bibliography:

C. Benedict (2000), Sekundärzwecke im Vergabeverfahren. Öffentliches Auftragswesen, seine teilweise Harmonisierung im EG/EU-Binnenmarkt und die Instrumentalisierung von Vergaberecht durch vergabefremde Aspekte, Berlin / Heidelberg / New York 2000.

T. Cottier (2002), Trade and Human Rights: A Relationship to discover, Journal of International Economic Law 5 (2002) No. 1, 111-132.

A. Duschanek/S. Griller (2002) (eds.), Grundrechte für Europa. Die Europäische Union nach Nizza (= Publication Series of ECSA Austria, Vol. 3), Wien/New York 2002.

S. Griller (2000), Das Government Procurement Agreement als Bestandteil des Europarechts und des nationalen Rechts, in *H. P. Rill / S. Griller* (eds.) Grundfragen der öffentlichen Auftragsvergabe, Wien 2000, 79-206.

R. Howse/D. Regan (2000), The Product/Process Distinction - An Illusory Basis for Disciplining 'Unilateralism' in Trade Policy, European Journal of International Law 11 (2000) No. 2, 249-289.

R. Howse (2002), Human Rights in the WTO: Whose Rights, What Humanity? Comment on Petersmann, European Journal of International Law 13 (2002) No. 3, 651-659.

P. Kunzlik (1998), Environmental Issues in International Procurement, in *S. Arrowsmith / A. Davies* (eds.), Public Procurement: Global Revolution (= International Economic Development Law, Vol. 8), London/Den Haag/Boston 1998.

C. McCrudden (1999), International Economic Law and the Pursuit of Human Rights: A Framework for Discussion of the Legality of 'Selective Purchasing' Laws under the WTO Government Procurement Agreement, Journal of International Economic Law 2 (1999) No. 1, 3-48.

E. Pache/C. Rüger (2002), Klarheit über soziale Aspekte im Vergaberecht? Zur Auslegungsmitteilung der Kommission vom

15.10.2001, Europäische Zeitschrift für Wirtschaftsrecht 13 (2002), 169-171.

E.-U. Petersmann (2002), Time for a United Nations „Global Compact" for Integrating Human Rights into the Law of Worldwide Organizations: Lessons from European Integration, European Journal of International Law 13 (2002) No. 3, 621-650.

C. Spennemann (2001), The WTO Agreement on Government Procurement – A Means of Furtherance of Human Rights?, Zeitschrift für Europarechtliche Studien 4 (2001), 43-95.

Michael J. Trebilcock[*]

International Trade and International Labour Standards: Choosing Objectives, Instruments, and Institutions

I.   Introduction

The trade / labour linkage has a long history.[1] It has become one of the most contentious contemporary issues in trade and labour policy circles and debates.[2] The idea of using international labour standards to protect workers from economic exploitation was first promoted by individual social reformers in Europe in the first half of the 19th century at the early stages of the Industrial Revolution. The work of these reformers was later taken over by various non-governmental organizations. Calls for international labour legisla-

---

*   I am indebted to *Greg McIlwain* for excellent research assistance, *Jill
     Given-King* for exemplary secretarial assistance, and to *Robert Howse*,
     Brian Langille, *Edward Iacobucci*, *Kevin Davis* and *Debra Steger* for
     helpful discussions.
[1]   See *Charnovitz* (1987) 126; *Leafy* (1996); *Molatlhegi* (2000) Chap. 2.
[2]   For an excellent review of the surrounding debates, see *Langille* (1997)
      27.

tion increased dramatically during the second half of the 19th century and found expression in various international organizations that were formed (often international associations of trade unions).

Intergovernmental action for international labour legislation began to be reflected in international conferences beginning in 1890. Many of these early efforts were motivated by the concern that in the absence of international labour standards, international competition in an environment of increasingly freer trade would precipitate a race to the bottom. The Treaty of Versailles in 1919 established the ILO. The preamble of the ILO Constitution notes that "the failure of any nation to adopt humane conditions of labour is an obstacle in the way of other nations which desire to improve the conditions in their own countries". Under Article 33 of the ILO Constitution, the governing body may recommend that the Conference take such actions as it may deem wise and expedient to secure compliance with recommendations of commissions of inquiry or where the matter has been referred to the International Court of Justice with the recommendation of the Court. Some commentators have suggested that this does not completely rule out the question of trade sanctions, as is apparently contemplated as a possibility in the case of recent adverse ILO determinations against Myanmar (Burma) with respect to forced labour. However, the ILO, a tripartite organization of government, employers and worker representatives, has mostly pursued its mandate by setting minimum international labour standards through Conventions and Recommendations, subject in the former case to ratification by member states and promoted by investigation, public reporting and technical assistance, but not formal sanctions.

The ILO formally entered the trade / labour interface debate in 1994 at the time of discussion of a possible inclusion of a social clause in the GATT / WTO, the establishment of a link between trade and labour in differing forms within NAFTA and the EU, and the conditioning of trade preferences and concessions by some developed countries on respect for labour standards. The ILO set up a Working Party on the social dimensions of the liberalization of international trade but in 1995 the ILO's governing body concluded that the Working Party would not pursue the question of trade sanctions and that further discussion of a link between international trade and social standards or a sanction-based social clause mechanism would be suspended. However, in 1998, the ILO adopted a Declaration of Fundamental Principles and Rights at Work providing that all members have an obligation to respect and promote certain core labour standards (CLS): 1) freedom of association and the right to engage in collective bargaining, 2) the elimination of forced labour, 3) the elimination of child labour, 4) the elimination of discrimination in employment. This Declaration parallels in many respects references to core international labour standards in the UN Universal Declaration of Human Rights (1948) and the UN Covenant on Civil and Political Rights and the UN Covenant on Economic, Social and Cultural Rights that came into force in 1976.[3] The ILO membership, however, rejected a proposal by its Director-General in 1997 that the ILO promote and administer a country-based certification and labelling program for products from countries complying with core labour standards.[4]

The 1948 Havana Charter that was intended to embody the framework for a new world trading system declared that "Members recognize that unfair labour conditions, particularly in production for export, create difficulties in international trade and accordingly each member shall take whatever action may be appropriate and feasible to eliminate such conditions within its territory." However, the Havana Charter was never adopted because of opposition in the US Congress, and the GATT in Article XX refers only to measures relating to products of prison labour (Article XX(e)), measures necessary to protect public morals (Article XX(a)), and measures relating to human life or health (Article XX(b)). The Ministerial Declaration following the first WTO Ministerial Conference in Singapore in 1996 appears to have removed labour issues from the WTO agenda and remitted them to the ILO. The recent Doha Ministerial Declaration re-affirms this position.[5]

A number of international commodity agreements, starting with the first international tin agreement of 1954, contain labour standards provisions but they contain no dispute settlement or enforcement mechanisms, and according to critics the inclusion of such clauses was intended to protect industries in developed countries from competition from developing countries.[6]

Under 1984 US GSP legislation, the US President in determining eligibility for GSP status must take into account, amongst other

---

[3]   See *Molatlhegi* (2000) Chap. 3; *Stirling* 73.
[4]   See *McCrudden/Davies* (2000) 38; *Cullen* (1999) 78.
[5]   Doha Ministerial Declaration, November 14, 2001.
[6]   *Molatlhegi* (2000) Chap. 2.

things, whether the concerned country is taking steps to ensure internationally recognized workers' rights. The Caribbean Basin Economic Recovery Act of 1983 was the first US legislation in recent history to condition trade on foreign labour standards. The Omnibus Trade and Competitiveness Act of 1988 expanded the provisions of the 1974 Trade Act to cover cases involving alleged violation of internationally recognized labour rights: if investigations by the US Trade Representative show that US trade rights have been violated, his or her office may authorize retaliatory measures, including imposition of restrictions on imports from the concerned country. [7]

The EU first mooted the possibility of linking labour standards to trade preferences by proposing the introduction of labour standards into the Lomé Convention in 1978 to ensure that developing countries with labour conditions which met the requirements of international labour conventions should not be penalized in their trade with the EEC by being out-competed by countries that do not comply with such conventions. This proposal was not implemented in the face of intense opposition from developing countries. In 1994, the EU finally established a link between trade and labour standards in the context of its relationship with developing countries through its GSP system where additional GSP preferences were offered to countries committing themselves to respect international labour standards.[8]

With respect to trade and labour standards linkages in regional trading arrangements, within the European Union the social dimension of European integration took concrete form in 1991 when eleven of the twelve member states (excluding the UK) signed the community's Charter of Fundamental Social Rights. Another important step in the development of EU social policy was the adoption by the 11 members (excluding the UK) of the Protocol on Social Policy at Maastricht in 1991. The content of the Social Chapter is fundamentally the same as that of the Charter and contains a number of guarantees of basic labour rights. Under NAFTA, the North American Agreement on Labour Cooperation (NAALC) requires the NAFTA parties to effectively enforce their own labour laws, and they are subject to specialized dispute settlement proc-

---

[7]   For a useful review of the evolution of labour standards in US trade policy legislation, see *Brown/Deardorff/Stein* (1996) Table 1, p. 235.

[8]   *Molatlhegi* (2000) Chap. 2; *Cullen* (1999).

esses and ultimately fines enforceable through trade sanctions in the event of findings of non-enforcement.

President *Clinton*'s statement at the Seattle Ministerial meeting of the WTO in December 1999 that trade sanctions should be available under the WTO multilateral system against countries violating international labour standards provoked an intensely hostile reaction from developing countries and was a significant factor in the failure of members of the WTO to agree on the launch of a new multilateral Round. As noted above, the recent Doha Ministerial Declaration launching a new multilateral Round confirms the 1996 Singapore Ministerial Decision to remit all international labour standards issues to the ILO. However, the issue of a trade / labour linkage seems unlikely to go away. Regionally, the potential expansion of NAFTA into a Free Trade Area of the Americas (FTAA) will raise the scope and status of the NAFTA Labour Side Accord in this broader context. Multilaterally, fast-track negotiating authority from the US Congress to the US Administration in the Doha Round may well be conditioned on the inclusion of a trade / labour linkage. And unilateral trade actions by states on account of labour practices prevailing in other states may well provoke trade disputes that will require adjudication by international trade dispute settlement bodies.

This paper largely focuses on the potential interface between international trade policy and international labour standards in the WTO multilateral trading system. The paper proceeds by reviewing sequentially the choice of policy objectives, the choice of policy instruments, and the choice of institutional regime in structuring a trade policy-labour standards linkage. On choice of objective, the paper will argue for assimilating CLS with universal human rights, but not privileging CLS over other universal human rights. It rejects fair trade and race-to-the-bottom rationales for a trade policy-labour standards linkage. On choice of instrument, it rejects conditioning the linkage of human rights-based trade sanctions on adverse trade effects in the sanctioning country. On choice of institutional arrangement, it favours according a pre-eminent institutional role to the ILO and UN Human Rights Committees in making determinations of systematic and persistent violations of relevant universal human rights, leaving the Dispute Settlement Body of the WTO with the determination of whether trade sanctions with violators have been applied in a non-discriminatory and consistent fashion and meet some basic standard of proportionality.

II.   The Choice of Policy Objective

Reviewing both contemporary and historical debates about the case for a trade policy-labour standards linkage, several normative rationales for a trade policy-labour standards linkage emerge and are often largely elided in debates, which then greatly complicates the task of evaluating the appropriate choice of instrument and choice of institutional arrangement for vindicating the chosen policy objectives.[9]

A. Unfair Competition

It is often argued that countries that sell goods into export markets that are produced by processes that fail to respect or comply with internationally recognized labour standards are engaging in an unfair form of competition that deprives domestic producers in export markets and producers and exporters in third country markets who comply with these standards of legitimate market share. Countries where internationally recognized labour standards are not complied with are often accused of "social dumping" or indirect or implicit and illicit subsidization. These economic activities, entailing either lax labour laws or ineffective enforcement of nominally compliant laws (or both), are analogized to economic dumping and direct subsidization that may attract anti-dumping duties or countervailing duties under Article VI of the GATT and current WTO Agreements on anti-dumping and subsidization and countervailing duties.[10]

Without further and careful specification, this rationale for linking international trade policy and / or sanctions with labour standards is largely incoherent. From the perspective of importing countries, generically lower labour costs in exporting countries enhance consumer welfare in importing countries, and by more than reductions in producer welfare in the latter. From the perspective of exporting countries, particularly developing countries, the latter rightly argue that in the early stages of industrialization, entailing mass production of low technology products e.g. textiles, clothing, footwear, processed agricultural products, low cost and low skilled labour is one of the principal sources of their competitive advantage and to deny them the ability to exploit this is to consign them for-

---

[9]   See *Trebilcock/Howse* (1999) Chap. 16 (Trade and Labour Rights).
[10] See *Rodrik* (1996); *Blackett* (1999).

ever to low value-added commodity production for developed country markets ("hewers of wood and drawers of water").

However, it is crucial not to overstate the significance of this source of comparative advantage. While it is true that the earnings of low skilled workers relative to high skilled workers in the US and other developed countries have declined in recent years (or unemployment levels increased), most empirical studies show that increased trade with low wage developing countries may account for at most twenty per cent of this reduction, and most of the increase in the wage gap between skilled and unskilled workers is attributable to technological change and, in the case of the US, also to rapidly declining rates of unionization.[11] More importantly, there is almost no evidence that the reduction in relative earnings of unskilled workers in developed countries that is reasonably attributable to increased trade with developing countries relates to non-compliance with core labour standards rather than simply lower wages. Even in this latter respect, as *Paul Krugman* and many other economists have pointed out,[12] the growth rate of living standards essentially equals the growth rate of domestic productivity. In the case of the US, exports are only ten per cent of the GNP, which means the US is still almost 90 per cent an economy that produces goods and services for its own use. Data show almost a one-to-one relationship between labour productivity and labour costs in manufacturing in a wide range of developed and developing countries.[13] Labour productivity, or total factor productivity, is a function of many factors, including public investments in education and training, health care, infrastructure and law and order. Thus, it is a fallacy to assume that low wages are the principal driving force behind today's global trade or foreign direct investment flows. This relationship between labour productivity and labour costs explains why internationally most firms are not seeking to relocate to e.g. Bangladesh despite its low wages, and why most international trade and foreign direct investment flows are still dominated by developed countries as countries of origin and countries of destination.

Economic theory strongly suggests that the imposition of common international labour standards across-the-board, based on de-

---

[11] For extensive reviews of the empirical literature, see *Brown* (2000); *Maskus* (1997).
[12] *Krugman* (1997) Chap. 1.
[13] *Rodrik* (1997).

veloped country standards, would substantially reduce total economic welfare as conventionally measured in importing countries, exporting countries, and globally.[14] The welfare implications of insisting only on common adherence to CLS are more complex. Price effects in importing countries are likely to be minor. While some analysts (most prominently the OECD in a 1996 study) have also concluded that such a commitment is likely to have no negative implications for exporting countries in terms of export and growth performance,[15] other analysts are more cautious in their assessments of the welfare implications of particular CLS (for example, the scope of the collective bargaining entitlement, or the peremptory termination of child labour without pre-empting inferior substitution effects through rendering basic education more accessible).[16]

Even stated in fairness rather than welfare terms, if it is unfair for firms and workers in developed countries to have to compete with firms and workers in developing countries with access to low paid, low skilled labour, by the same token it is equally unfair for developing countries to have to compete with firms and workers in developed countries that depend on highly skilled labour forces, highly developed infrastructure, large public investments in education and research and development, extensive health care systems, effective law and order, and superior institutions, in most cases reflecting collective or public investments on a scale that far exceeds the capacity of most developing countries. Thus, this unfair competition argument, in and of itself, is totally indeterminate and carries high risks of the trade policy-labour standards linkage being exploited for protectionist ends. In this respect, it is important to emphasize that the unfair competition argument focuses principally on the welfare implications of non-compliance with international labour standards for citizens or interests in *importing countries*.

B. The Race to the Bottom

As the brief historical exegesis of the trade / labour linkage in the introduction to this paper makes clear, a major motivation for promoting international labour standards in the first place and then subsequently a trade policy-labour standards linkage (as, for example, reflected in the preambles to the ILO Constitution and Havana

---

[14] See *Brown / Deardorff / Stein* (1996); also *Brown* (2000); *Maskus* (1997).
[15] OECD (1996); *Rodrik* (1996).
[16] See *Brown* (2000); *Maskus* (1997).

Charter) is that low labour standards (including low wages) in exporting countries may undermine higher labour standards in importing countries and precipitate a so-called "race to the bottom" – a form of prisoner's dilemma – that can only be pre-empted by international agreement on and enforcement of minimum labour standards.[17]

This argument is a variant on the unfair competition argument reviewed above but instead of assuming that importing countries will maintain the *status quo* with respect to their more stringent labour standards and accept a loss of market share assumes that such countries will in fact progressively dilute them in order to avoid losing market share to imports from countries where these standards are not adhered to, resulting in a low level equilibrium trap where all countries relax their labour standards to what many regard as suboptimal levels, yet all countries simply retain their pre-existing share of trade or investment after the race to the bottom has run its course.

Despite the durability of this concern, for reasons given above, most notably that differences in conditions of employment largely reflect differences in productivity, there is little reason to suppose that liberal trade and investment regimes will precipitate a race to the bottom. Moreover, the empirical evidence provides no support for the claim that liberal international trade and investment regimes are leading developed countries to relax their CLS or labour standards generally or that foreign direct investors are investing in countries with weak CLS. Indeed, the evidence suggests that, with the notable exception of China, countries with weak CLS attract very little FDI either in general or specifically in the sectors where CLS are weak. Even Export Processing Zones (EPZs) typically provide superior employment conditions to surrounding markets.[18] Some commentators, while conceding that weak CLS in some developing countries have not caused a weakening of labour standards generally in developed countries, argue that developing countries with weak CLS that compete against each other in export markets may be stuck in a low-level equilibrium trap with respect to efforts to enhance CLS vis-à-vis each other.[19] If the OECD findings are well-founded – that CLS have no adverse effects on export per-

---

[17] See *Alben* (2001).
[18] See *Brown* (2000); *Maskus* (1997).
[19] See *Maskus* (1997); *Basu* (2001).

formance and economic growth, and may have positive effects – this concern is unfounded. To the extent that this view is excessively optimistic, then trade sanctions designed to enforce common compliance with CLS may have adverse effects on the targeted countries' economic welfare, and may reduce their capacity to eliminate non-compliant practices. However, it is important to emphasize that race-to-the-bottom concerns, like unfair competition concerns, largely emanate from the perceived welfare implications of non-compliance with international labour standards for citizens and interests in *importing countries*.

C. Core Labour Standards as Human Rights

Various core labour standards have been characterized as human rights in the UN Universal Declaration of Human Rights, the subsequent International Covenant on Civil and Political Rights and the International Covenant on Economic, Social and Cultural Rights. The ILO's 1998 Declaration of Fundamental Principles and Rights at Work enumerates a short list of core international labour standards which are defined more fully in eight background Covenants that are incorporated by reference, i.e. freedom of association and collective bargaining, the elimination of forced labour; the elimination of child labour; and the elimination of discrimination in employment, which is also consistent with the characterization of certain core labour standards or rights as human rights, especially those that guarantee basic freedom of choice in employment relations.

As *Amartya Sen* argues in his recent book, "Development as Freedom",[20] the basic goals of development can be conceived of in universalistic terms where individual well-being can plausibly be viewed as entailing certain basic freedoms irrespective of cultural context: freedom to engage in political criticism and association, freedom to engage in market transactions, freedom from the ravages of preventable or curable disease, freedom from the disabling effects of illiteracy and lack of basic education, freedom from extreme material privation. According to *Sen*, these freedoms have both intrinsic and instrumental value. Importantly, in contrast to the unfair competition and race-to-the-bottom rationales for linking international trade policy and international labour standards, the human rights perspective focuses primarily on the welfare of citi-

---

[20]   *Sen* (1999).

zens in *exporting*, not importing countries. The assumption under-lying this concern with basic or universal human rights is that fail-ure to respect them in any country either does not reflect the will of the citizens but rather decisions of unrepresentative or repressive governments, or alternatively majoritarian oppression of minorities, e.g. children, women, racial or religious minorities, or alternatively again paternalistic concerns that citizens in other countries have made uninformed or ill-advised choices to forego these basic rights.

In my view, the linkage of international trade policy, including trade or other economic sanctions, with core labour standards that reflect basic or universal human rights, is a cogent one. When citi-zens in some countries observe gross or systematic abuses of hu-man rights in other countries, the possible range of reactions open to them include diplomatic protests, withdrawal of ambassadors, cancellation of air landing rights, trade sanctions or more compre-hensive economic boycotts, or at the limit military intervention. Arguing that doing nothing is always or often the most appropriate response is inconsistent with the very notion of *universal* human rights. In extreme cases, such as war crimes, apartheid, the threat of chemical warfare in the case of Iraq, genocide in the case of Serbia, or the Holocaust in the case of Nazi Germany, excluding *a priori* economic sanctions from the menu of possible options seems inde-fensible. Whether it is the most appropriate option may, of course, be context-specific and depend both on the seriousness of the abuses and the likely efficacy of the response-choice of instrument issues to which I turn next. But it is sufficient for present purposes to restate the point that to the extent that core labour standards are appropriately characterized as basic or universal human rights, a linkage between trade policy and such labour standards is not only defensible but arguably imperative, in contrast to the other two rationales for such a linkage which, despite their much longer his-torical lineage, seem to me to be largely spurious and inconsistent with the central predicates of a liberal trading system. However, core labour standards viewed as basic or universal human rights, by promoting human freedom of choice, are entirely consistent with a liberal trading regime that seeks to ensure other human freedoms, in particular the right of individuals to engage in market transactions with other individuals without discrimination on the basis of country of location.[21]

Having said this, the scope and definition of the class of human rights viewed as sufficiently universal as to warrant potentially the imposition of trade sanctions for their violation is problematic in various respects. Even CLS are not susceptible to uncontentious understandings of their scope. Should child labour be defined only in terms of a minimum working age or should some subset of exploitative child labour practices be targeted? What practices exactly constitute discrimination in the workplace? What constitutes forced labour beyond slavery? When is freedom of association and the right to engage in collective bargaining fully respected, given that most countries deny or limit the right to strike in various contexts? Beyond CLS, while civil rights, e.g. to be free from genocide, apartheid, torture, detention without trial, etc., may be reasonably well-understood and commonly subscribed to (at least in principle), political rights, e.g. to engage in political association , criticism or dissent or even to vote, are much less widely recognized.[22] Economic, social and cultural rights, are even less universally accepted.[23] These issues have major implications for the choice of instrument and choice of institutional arrangements for structuring the trade policy-labour standards linkage, to which I turn below.

III.   The Choice of Instrument

A. Soft Law Instruments

The ILO's promulgation and promotion of Conventions on minimum international labour standards are the most prominent form of soft law in this context, in that they depend on ratification by individual member states and are subject only to investigation and reporting by ILO organs and the provision of technical assistance to enable countries to build capacity to implement them. Thus, compliance with ILO norms depends on a combination of public identification, embarrassment and shaming (a mild stick), and technical assistance to promote compliance (a mild carrot). The ILO has been widely criticized by proponents of a trade / labour

---

[21]   See *Molatlhegi* (2000) Chap. 3; *McCrudden / Davies* (2000); *Cleveland* (2002).
[22]   *Stirling* (1996).
[23]   Economist magazine, August 18, 2001, "The Politics of Human Rights" 9; "Human Rights" 18 et seq; *Ignatieff* (2001).

linkage for ineffective enforcement of its norms and indeed variable ratification of its Conventions by many countries, including major developed countries such as the US (which has, of course, been a prominent proponent of a trade / labour linkage). Many of the soft law, market-driven mechanisms described below have emerged in part out of frustration by NGOs and other interest groups with the ineffectiveness of the ILO.

One class of soft law instruments entails a range of certification, labelling, and voluntary code of conduct mechanisms that purport to identify firms or products that conform to core international labour standards and hence are responsive to information market failures if consumers in importing countries derive private disutility from consuming goods produced in violation of CLS.[24] The efficacy of these mechanisms turn largely on market reactions to the signals that they entail, principally by consumers and to a lesser extent by investors. These instruments are attractive in some respects in their focus on consumer (not producer) welfare in importing countries in that they depend on consumer preferences and a willingness to pay to vindicate those preferences and hence are consistent with the normative predicate of liberal trade theory, which largely focuses on the potential for free trade to enhance consumer welfare. Typically, such mechanisms are either self-initiated by firms or industry associations or are initiated by non-governmental organizations of various kinds, who negotiate them with firms or trade associations. The most ambitious initiative of this kind to date is the Global Compact, launched by UN Secretary-General *Kofi Annan* in 1999 and entailing voluntary corporate endorsements of nine principles, including CLS.

However, these mechanisms suffer from a number of limitations. Currently, they apparently apply to a small percentage of exports in a number of sectors where non-compliance with core labour standards is thought to be common e.g. about five per cent of exports in the textile and clothing industries, and they vary widely in various dimensions e.g. i) which core labour standards are recognized, ii) how these core labour standards are defined, if at all; iii) and how effectively adherence to these standards is monitored, if at all.[25]

---

[24]   *Freeman* (1994).
[25]   *Diller* (1999) 99; *Blackett* (2001) 401; *Brown* (1999).

In explaining the low, inconsistent, and often ineffective application of these mechanisms, a number of explanations suggest
themselves which in turn raise serious questions about attaching
primacy to consumer preferences in importing countries in this
context, despite the initial appeal of mechanisms that depend on
consumer welfare as their reference point and the compatibility of
this reference point with the predicates of free trade.[26] First, consumers, even if fully informed about conditions under which imports are being produced and violations of core international labour
standards that particular modes of production may entail, in fact do
not care enough about the intrinsic values reflected in these core
labour standards (viewed as basic or universal human rights) to put
their money where their mouth is. However, even if this were to be
the case, the fact that the process of production and exchange may
entail production or consumption externalities for other citizens in
exporting or importing countries, as is largely inherent in the notion
of universal human rights, suggests that consumer preferences cannot be decisive in a human rights context.

A second explanation is that consumers in importing countries
do care about these human rights values but are poorly informed
about the conditions under which the goods they are consuming are
produced in exporting countries. The cost of acquiring this information exceeds the value that they place on this information. In this
respect, the voluntary and decentralized nature of the soft law
mechanisms currently employed in this context almost certainly
exacerbates the information problems faced by consumers in importing countries. As noted above, the proposal by the Director-
General of the ILO in 1997 that the ILO should promote an integrated scheme for increasing the effectiveness of consumer choice
by labelling exports as having been produced in countries that conform to core international labour standards was rejected by the main
decision-making body of the ILO, in large part because of strenuous
opposition from developing countries.

Yet a further explanation for the low, inconsistent and often ineffective application of these mechanisms is that consumers in importing countries do care about these intrinsic human rights values
but confront serious collective action problems in that individual
consumers who may be prepared to pay a premium for goods pro-

---

[26] See Debate "New Democracy Forum: Stepping Up Labour Standards",
      Boston Review, February/March 2001.

duced in conditions that meet core labour standards will be concerned that other consumers who share their concerns may opportunistically purchase lower-priced goods relying on other consumers to bear the financial costs of vindicating their collective preferences. However, if every consumer suspects every other consumer of being likely to behave opportunistically, i.e. to free ride on their sacrifices, an effective voluntary collective response may not emerge.

Beyond these reasons for not according primacy to consumer preferences in this context, a further serious limitation is associated with soft law mechanisms that link consumer responses to imports of offending goods, e.g. goods made with child or forced labour, conflict diamonds, etc. These mechanisms are unresponsive to violations of either core labour standards viewed as universal human rights or universal human rights defined more broadly that are occurring in non-traded goods sectors. For example, it is widely agreed that most child labour is not employed in export sectors (between five and ten per cent) but in domestic agriculture, services, retail and the informal sector generally.[27] Many abuses of civil and political human rights are not related in any direct way to traded goods sectors, e.g. civil rights abuses in Sudan and Burma, to take two current examples.

B. Hard Law Options

The first and most fundamental issue that arises in choosing hard law instruments is the scope of the trade policy-labour standards linkage. If we conceptualize at least core labour standards as universal human rights, how can we justify privileging these particular human rights over at least some subset of universally proclaimed universal human rights (subject to the definitional issues noted above)? Surely genocide, torture, detention without trial, etc. warrant at least as serious concern from the international community, and at least as serious a set of legal sanctions, as violations of core international labour standards. To privilege core labour standards over these other human rights is quite overtly to elide the various normative rationales for intervention reviewed earlier in this paper and to risk a protectionist rationale for trade or other economic sanctions.

---

[27] See *Brown* (2000); *Morici* (2001).

Related to this point, a further issue arises relating to the scope of the linkage between trade policy and core labour standards: Why should trade or other economic sanctions be contingent on imports of offending goods? As in the discussion of market-driven soft law instruments and limitations thereof, why should child labour in non-tradable goods sectors or human rights violations in non-tradable goods sectors warrant any less concern, or any less severe sanctions, than such abuses in tradable goods sectors?

It follows from these two points that in my view trade or other economic sanctions should not be confined to core labour standards, but should extend to at least some subset of universally accepted rights more generally, and that such sanctions should not be limited to imports of goods directly produced by the offending practices. This in fact suggests a very broad domain for linking trade and other economic sanctions with universal human rights. However, it also suggests some significant constraints on their invocation. In particular, both the substantive rules governing their invocation and the procedures by which they may be invoked should be consistent with the human rights rationale for intervention and should exclude the unfair competition and race to the bottom rationales for intervention.

In terms of substantive rules, this requirement assigns considerable significance to rules of non-discrimination and consistency. For example, suppose hypothetically that it is the case that the US has no textile sector but a significant clothing sector and that child labour is employed in producing exports for the US market in India in both sectors but the US seeks to impose trade sanctions only against clothing imports from India and not textile imports. Alternatively, even if the US seeks to apply trade sanctions against both clothing and textile imports from India, it does not seek to do so against similar imports from Pakistan made with child labour for geopolitical or other reasons. The Appellate Body's decisions in *Shrimp / Turtles*, *Beef Hormones*, and *Australian Salmon*[28] in other contexts, in my view, rightly emphasize the importance of non-discriminatory and consistent treatment of imports reflecting the ostensible rationale (in the present context a human rights rationale) for the intervention, and not disguised protectionism. Unless a non-discrimination / consistency requirement is applied rigorously, hard

---

[28] Appellate Body decisions, *Shrimp / Turtles* (1998); *Beef Hormones* (1998); *Australian Salmon* (1998).

law based trade sanctions carry a high risk of constituting a disguised form of protectionism with the human rights rationale a
mere pretext or cover for protectionist measures not motivated by
human rights concerns but in fact the other two illegitimate rationales for intervention discussed earlier in this paper. This is why we
should resist arguments that differences in production and processing methods (PPMs) should render products unlike products for
purposes of Article III of the GATT (National Treatment) and instead adopt an economic definition of like products as the Appellate
Body did in *Asbestos*,[29] focussing on substitutability by consumers,
and remit justifications for inferior treatment of competitive imports
to Article XX (perhaps amended to include a universal human
rights exception but subject to the non-discrimination conditions in
the chapeau).

In defining the elements of a non-discrimination test, we need to
be clear on what purpose it is designed to serve: in my view, it
should be designed to screen out cases of disguised protectionism in
cases where trade sanctions have been unilaterally invoked, osten-
sibly on human rights grounds. But it should not require sanctioning
countries either to apply sanctions to all countries in violation of
CLS (or human rights), or none – an all-or-nothing requirement that
is likely to make "the perfect enemy of the good". In other words,
as a matter of international trade law there should be a negative
duty not to discriminate for protectionist reasons, but there should
be no positive duty to take affirmative action. While a sanctioning
country may choose not to sanction all violations of CLS (or human
rights) everywhere in the world, this form of trade sanction "under-
reach" should surely not be a legitimate concern of an international
trade body, which cannot plausibly be transformed into a global
human rights crusader. In contrast, the problem of sanction "under-
reach" may be a legitimate concern of other international organizations (such as the ILO, or UN Human Rights Committees), but this
calls for action on their part (e.g. by adopting a regime like the
Convention on International Trade in Endangered Species (CITES),
requiring multilateral sanctions by members in particular cases).
For the WTO, the principal concern is sanction "over-reach", where
the sanctioning country's actions in targeting some imports and not
others seems principally explicable on the basis that in the former
case it has a domestic industry to protect and in the latter case it

---

[29] Appellate Body decision, *Asbestos* (2000).

does not. Where it imposes trade sanctions in the latter case they
entail no costs to the domestic producers of competitive products
(who are non-existent), but costs to domestic consumers and thus
can be viewed as an action against material interest that can only be
explained by the sanctioning country's genuine concern with CLS
(or human rights) violations in exporting countries (similarly in the
case of bans on exports or foreign direct investment), where the
government of the sanctioning state, by taking action, is seeking to
solve collective action problems among its own consumers or citizens. On this approach, in the hypothetical example above, the differential treatment of clothing and textile imports from India would
be suspect, but the failure to sanction similar imports from Pakistan,
for non-trade related reasons, would not be. But what if India has
only a clothing industry and Pakistan only a textile industry and the
US acts only against imported clothing from India?

In terms of procedural requirements for the invocation of trade
or other economic sanctions against violations of universal human
rights in other countries, a number of options present themselves.
First, a basic choice has to be made (although often overlooked in
debates over the trade/labour standards linkage) between sticks and
carrots. Rather like the European Community's GSP regime, it is
not difficult to imagine developed countries offering developing
countries significant trade concessions (e.g. accelerated implementation of the phase out of the Multifibre Arrangement) if they commit themselves to an accelerated phase out of offending labour or
other human rights abuses. Unlike the Uruguay Round Agreements,
which entailed for the most part a single undertaking by Member
States, such an arrangement in this context might more appropriately take the form of a plurilateral agreement (like the Uruguay
Round Government Procurement Code) where this is an option
offered to developing countries and for those who choose it developed countries would bind their trade concessions (unlike GSP
treatment). The commitments made by countries to observe core
international labour standards and other universal human rights
would have to be reasonably precisely defined in terms of ILO or
UN Conventions or Covenants, so that violations of these commitments could be rendered reasonably justiciable through an appropriate international dispute settlement process (perhaps vested in
the WTO, but not necessarily or exclusively so as I explore further
below). However, one of the limitations of the carrot option, as

pointed out by *Howard Chang*,[30] is that it creates moral hazard problems in that countries may persist in violations or engage in more egregious violations in order to attract larger concessions (or carrots).

A second option would be to require all countries that are parties to either a regional or multilateral arrangement like the WTO to commit themselves to effectively enforcing their own existing labour laws (as under the NAFTA Labour Side Accord), with enforcement provided through supranational or international dispute settlement processes and penalties. The limitations of this option are obvious enough: first, it addresses only violations of core international labour standards and not other universal human rights; second, it assumes that member countries have already enacted substantive laws that reflect these standards and that the only problem is ineffective enforcement, which in many cases may not be the central problem.

A third option is to allow private party-initiated petitions for trade sanctions under domestic law analogous to anti-dumping duties and countervailing duties. I unequivocally reject this option as espousing in its most naked form the two rationales for a trade / labour standards linkage that I regard as illegitimate and as carrying the highest risk of protectionist abuse of this linkage.

A fourth option would be to allow unilateral *state* action against imports from offending countries (perhaps by amending Article XX of the GATT to include a core international labour standards and universal human rights exception, or by expansive interpretation of the public morals exception already contained within Article XX),[31] subject to such measures satisfying the conditions contained in the chapeau of Article XX prohibiting arbitrary or unjustifiable discrimination between countries where the same conditions prevail or disguised restrictions on trade in the application of such measures, rigorously enforced as argued above. This option is obviously more appealing than expanding the scope of current private contingent protection mechanisms, but risks the capture of states imposing such measures by domestic producer interests. Moreover, this option casts the burden of proof in important respects on the targeted country after such a measure has been imposed to initiate a formal complaint and make out a *prima facie* case that the measure in

---

[30]   *Chang* (1997) 309.
[31]   See *Charnovitz* (1998) 68.

question does not comply with the requirements of Article XX. Similarly, in the absence of an attempt to link a core labour standards / human rights exception under Article XX to relevant background international conventions or covenants, issues of justiciability in international dispute settlement in this context are likely to be acute and place more of a burden on such a dispute settlement process than it can reasonably bear. Moreover, in the absence of a horizontal linkage with other international organizations with central mandates in the labour standards or human rights domains (discussed below), the "necessity" test that attaches to most of the exceptions currently enumerated under Article XX is likely to prove intractable in evaluating the justification for trade sanctions.[32]

A fifth option would be for all member states who are parties to either regional or multilateral trading arrangements to negotiate a comprehensive set of rules setting out commitments to observe core international labour standards and other universal human rights (perhaps incorporating by reference relevant international documents). On this approach, which is analogous in some respects to that entailed in the Uruguay Round TRIPS Agreement (which incorporates by reference the Berne, Paris and Rome Conventions), trade sanctions would come at the end of the dispute settlement process and not at the beginning. In other words, a country complaining that another country was in violation of its core labour standards or other human rights commitment would have to demonstrate a breach of these commitments and would carry the burden of initiating and proving, at least *prima facie*, such violations, and only if the complaint is upheld by the dispute settlement body could retaliatory trade sanctions be authorized in the event that non-compliance continued. This approach has several virtues: first, trade sanctions cannot be imposed until there has been a multilateral judgment that a violation of relevant core international labour standards or other human rights has occurred, and the country seeking to impose such sanctions bears the initial burden of initiating a complaint and proving a *prima facie* case. Second, it has the virtue of any rule-based system of laying out the substantive ground rules with some precision in advance and thus minimizes the potential for protectionist abuse of the regime. Third, and relatedly, it renders problems of justiciability more tractable.

---

[32] See *Brown* (2000); *Maskus* (1997); *Roessler* (2000) Chap. 6, Diverging Domestic Policies and Multilateral Trade Integration.

IV.   The Choice of Institutional Regime

Having discussed the choice of objectives and the choice of instruments in the light of those objectives in shaping a trade / labour standards linkage, the remaining question is the choice of institutions to administer this linkage in the light of choice of objectives and choice of instruments. Two important and related considerations are relevant here: First, institutional specialization, as in many other domains, has many virtues in vindicating desired policy objectives;[33] second, because human rights, not trade effects, motivate the trade / labour linkage that I advocate, vesting exclusive or even primary jurisdiction in an international trade body risks compromising the normative rationale for the linkage, e.g. by giving primacy to adverse trade effects in either importing or exporting countries.

In cases of egregious abuses of universal civil human rights, e.g. apartheid or genocide, it is difficult to imagine as plausible the vesting of this function in a trade organization (like the WTO). Rather, following current international practices, one would imagine that the appropriate international organ for authorizing or perhaps requiring such sanctions is the UN Security Council. In other less egregious cases, there will still obviously be questions of institutional legitimacy and competence in vesting the administration of such a regime in a trade organization. One option here entails a sharp and exclusive institutional division of labour. For example, with respect to core labour standards, the authorization or requirement for the imposition of a trade or other economic sanctions could be vested in the ILO by way of elaboration of its sanctioning power under article 33 of the ILO Constitution. This would follow, by way of analogy, the example of regimes such as the above-mentioned CITES, which requires signatory states to ban imports of endangered species or products there from. However, critics of the ILO are sceptical of the willingness or capacity of the ILO to implement and administer effectively such a regime. Defenders of the ILO, on the other hand, may worry that the attachment of economic sanctions to the powers of the ILO may destabilize the organization, causing states to withdraw from membership or to withhold ratification of its Conventions to an even greater extent than is the case at present.

---

[33]   See *Srinivasan* (1996).

Another option is to imagine some form of horizontal coordination among international agencies, whereby e.g. the ILO would be wholly or largely responsible for determinations of systematic and persistent violations of core labour standards, or UN Committees on Human Rights for systematic and persistent violations of other universal human rights (other than the most egregious abuses), and the WTO would be responsible for overseeing the implementation of sanctions and ensuring that arbitrary and unjustifiable forms of discrimination and disguised protectionism are avoided, as well as proportionality in the scale of the trade sanctions imposed.

A variant on this option would be to have international organizations such as the ILO or UN Human Rights Committees nominate members to dispute settlement panels or the Appellate Body of the WTO in cases involving complaints of violations of core labour standards or other universal human rights, and at the same time take steps to render WTO dispute settlement process both more transparent and more inclusive in terms of admissibility of *amicus curiae* briefs from interested members of civil society.[34]

My preference would be for some form of horizontal co-ordination with specialized international agencies with expertise and legitimacy in the labour standards or human rights fields who would make determinations of systematic and persistent violations of relevant norms despite whatever carrots and sticks (assisting and shaming) that the agency typically first brings to bear on violators. Thus, the "necessity" test would largely fall within these agencies' domains, although such determinations may be precipitated by unilateral state trade action under one of the options reviewed in the previous section, a complaint by the targeted country, and a reference under the DSU (Article 13) by the WTO panel seized with the complaint to a relevant specialized international agency for findings on violations of relevant international norms, which the WTO panel should accept as presumptively dispositive of the referenced issues. Indeed this option becomes much more attractive with this form of horizontal co-ordination. Such determination may also go some distance toward meeting the non-discrimination / disguised discrimination conditions in the chapeau to Article XX of the GATT. With respect to the proportionality of the proposed trade response, the WTO for its part should again be influenced by the nature of the horizontal agency's findings as to the seriousness and persistence of

---

[34]   See *Trebilcock/Howse* (1999) Chap. 3 (Dispute Settlement).

violations. Because adverse trade effects are irrelevant in my pro-posed framework of analysis, trade sanctions cannot be quantified in these terms. Here more imaginative fashioning of trade remedies is called for. As noted above, the NAFTA Labour Side Accord pro-vides for a system of fines, ultimately enforceable by trade sanc-tions, if a member state is found by a specialized panel to have en-gaged in a systematic and persistent practice of not enforcing its own labour laws with the fine payable to the offending country to enhance its labour law enforcement.[35] This form of sanction sug-gests one option. Another option may entail denial of access to the dispute settlement process of the WTO as a complainant for so long as a member state is non-compliant. A yet further option is suspen-sion of voting rights in the WTO while non-compliance persists. Crippling a non-compliant country economically (particularly a poor developing country) with trade sanctions should be reserved as the remedy of last resort.

V.   Conclusions

Much of my thinking on the appropriate linkage between trade policy and labour standards flows out of critical questions that must be answered at the outset of any such analysis relating to the nor-mative rationale for any such linkage at all. As I have attempted to argue in this paper, the unfair competition and race to the bottom rationales for such a linkage are uncompelling, even incoherent, and provide a thinly disguised cover for protectionism, particularly on the part of developed countries vis-à-vis imports from developing countries, and rightly arouse the antagonism and cynicism of devel-oping countries, who already labour under enough disadvantages in trade and other domains without sustaining yet one more encum-brance on their ability to develop. On the other hand, the human rights rationale for a trade / labour standards linkage is much more compelling and has important implications for the scope of the trade / labour standards linkage, as well as the choice of instrument and the choice of institutional regime. While the issues that arise

---

[35]   Under Annex 39 of NAFTA, any monetary enforcement assessment shall be no greater than $1 million (US) for the first year of the Agreement and thereafter no greater than .007 percent of total trade between the Parties during the most recent year for which data are available and must be paid into a fund to improve or enhance labour law enforcement in the Party complained against.

under this rationale with respect to choice of instrument and choice of institutional regime are far from straightforward or uncontentious, resolving these questions is rendered vastly more difficult if we are not clear (as many historical and contemporary debates on the trade / labour linkage have not been) on the foundational normative rationale for a linkage in the first place.

Bibliography:

E. Alben (2001), GATT and the Fair Wage: A Historical Perspective, Columbia Law Review 101 (2001) No. 6, 1410-1447.

K. Basu (2001), The View from the Tropics, in New Democracy Forum: Stepping Up Labour Standards, Boston Review, February / March 2001.

A. Blackett (1999), Whither Social Clause? Human Rights, Trade Theory and Treaty Interpretation, Columbia Human Rights Law Review 31 (1999) No. 1, 1-80.

A. Blackett (2001), Global Governance, Legal Pluralism and the Decentered State: A Labour Law Critique of Codes of Corporate Conduct, Indiana Journal of Global Legal Studies 8 (2001) No. 2, 401-447.

D. Brown (1999), Can Consumer Product Labels Deter Foreign Child Labour Exploitation?, Discussion Paper 99-19, Department of Economics, Tufts University, Medford, MA 1999.

D. Brown (2000), International Trade and Core Labour Standards: A Survey of the Recent Literature, OECD Occasional Papers No. 43, Paris 2000.

D. Brown / A. Deardorff / R. Stein (1996), International Labour Standards and Trade: A Theoretical Analysis, in *J. Bhagwati / R. Hudec* (eds.), Fair Trade and Harmonization, Vol. 1, Cambridge, MA 1996, 236-266.

H. Chang (1997), Carrots, Sticks, and International Externalities, International Review of Law and Economics 17 (1997) No. 3, 309-324.

S. Charnovitz (1987), The Influence of International Labour Standards on the World Trading System: An Historical Overview, International Labour Review 126 (1987), 565-584.

S. Charnovitz (1998), The Morals Exception in Trade Policy, Journal of International Law 38 (1998) No. 4, 689-746.

S. Cleveland (2002), Human Rights Sanctions and International Trade: A Theory of Compatibility, Journal of International Economic Law 5 (2002) No. 1, 133-189.

H. Cullen (1999), The Limits of International Trade Mechanisms in Enforcing Human Rights: The Case of Child Labour, The International Journal of Children's Rights 7 (1999), 1-29.

J. Diller (1999), A Social Conscience in the Global Marketplace? Labour Dimensions of Codes of Conduct, Social Labelling and Investor Initiatives, in International Labour Review 138 (1999) No. 2, 99-129.

R. Freeman (1994), A Hard-Headed Look at Labour Standards, in US Department of Labour, Bureau of International Labour Affairs (ed.), International Labour Standards and Global Economic Integration; Proceedings of a Symposium, Washington, DC 1994.

M. Ignatieff (2001), Human Rights as Politics and Idolatry, Princeton, NJ 2001.

B. Langille (1997), Eight Ways to Think About International Labour Standards, Journal of World Trade 31 (1997), 27.

V. Leafy (1996), Workers' Rights and International Trade: The Social Clause, in *J. Bhagwhati / R. Hudec* (eds.), Fair Trade and Harmonization, Vol. 2, Cambridge, MA 1996, 177-230.

P. Krugman (1997), Competitiveness: A Dangerous Obsession, in Pop Internationalism, Cambridge, MA 1997.

K. E. Maskus (1997), Should Core Labour Standards Be Imposed Through International Trade Policy?, Policy Research Working Paper 1817, World Bank, Washington, DC 1997.

C. McCrudden / A. Davies (2000), A Perspective on Trade and Labour Rights, Journal of International Economic Law 3 (2000) No. 1, 43-62.

B. Molatlhegi (2000), Trade and Labour Interface in the Context of Economic Integration: The Case of the Southern African Development Community, Doctoral Thesis, University of Toronto Faculty of Law 2000.

P. Morici (2001), Labour Standards in the Global Trading System, Economic Strategy Institute, Washington, DC 2001.

OECD (1996) (ed.), Trade, Employment and Labour Standards: A Study of Core Workers' Rights and International Trade, Paris 1996.

D. Rodrik (1996), Labor Standards in International Trade: Do They Matter and What to do About Them, in *R. Lawrence* et al. (eds.), Emerging Agenda for Global Trade: High Stakes for Developing Countries, Policy Essay No. 20, Overseas Development Council, Washington, DC 1996, 35-79.

D. Rodrik (1997), Has Globalization Gone Too Far?, Washington, DC 1997.

F. Roessler (2000), The Legal Structure and Limits of the World Trade Order, London 2000.

A. Sen (1999), Development as Freedom, New York 1999.

T. N. Srinivasan (1996), International Trade and Labour Standards from an Economic Perspective, in *P. van Dijck / G. Faber* (eds.), Challenges to the New World Trade Organization, Den Haag / Boston 1996, 219-244.

P. Stirling (1996), The Use of Trade Sanctions as an Enforcement Mechanism for Basic Human Rights: Proposal for Additions at the World Trade Organization, American University Journal of International Law and Policy 11 (1996), N. 1, 1-46.

M. Trebilcock / R. Howse (1999), The Regulation of International Trade, London / New York [2]1999.

José Manuel Salazar-Xirinachs / Jorge Mario Martínez-Piva

Trade, Labour Standards and Global Governance: A Perspective from the Americas*

---

* Finished in March 2002

I.   Introduction

The idea that the regulatory framework of globalization should have a set of universally agreed human rights regarding working conditions or labour standards is by now widely accepted. This, in and of itself is one of the hallmarks of an increasingly globalized world economy. Although the ILO has since 1919 been charged with the task of international coordination of labour policies and standards, the 1990s saw a growing international consensus on a number of core labour rights which is expressed in the ILO Declaration on Fundamental Principles and Rights at Work, signed in 1998 which binds the 175 ILO members.

However, while there is wide consensus on the need for regulation and international coordination in this area, there are major issues and disagreements about what means should be used to promote higher standards, whether the general concept of "labour rights" could be translated into a precise and operational definition of "labour standards", what allowance should be made for national circumstances and peculiarities, and what should be the role of international institutions like the ILO and the WTO in policing and enforcing labour standards?

In industrialized countries, factors such as: competitive concerns about trade with low-wage developing countries; the perception of the relative inability of the ILO to enforce core labour rights; coupled with the perception of the success of the WTO to enforce trade rules, among others, have led to mounting pressure to include labour provisions in the WTO and in trade agreements in general, as a means of ensuring compliance with universally accepted labour rights. Those that oppose the trade-labour link argue that this is not an effective way of promoting implementation; that there are major difficulties in translating core labour rights into operationally uniform and enforceable labour standards; that it is a mistake to overburden trade institutions with "non-trade" concerns; and that, while there is a lot of scope for a cooperative approach, asymmetries in market size and political economy considerations provide a no win-win scenario for small economies to support a trade sanctions approach in this area.

There is also pressure to include labour provisions in regional trade agreements (RTAs). As one of the most proactive regions in the world in the proliferation of RTAs during the 1990s, the Americas has been a fertile ground for experimentation with new areas of discipline or "deep" integration, and some of the recent agreements in this region have included labour provisions, as well as environmental ones, that go well beyond multilateral disciplines and commitments in these areas.

The purpose of this paper is to analyze and assess the main arguments and related empirical evidence for and against the inclusion of labour provisions in trade agreements. The paper is organized as follows. Section II. contains some general comments on global governance and development issues, Section III. provides an overview of international and regional regulation issues in the labor area. Section IV. deals with the main arguments in favor of including labour provisions in trade agreements, while Section V. analyses the main reasons why most Latin American and Caribbean countries are opposed to this link, particularly if it involves the possibility of restrictions to market access. Section VI. analyzes the three models of labour cooperation agreements that have emerged in the Americas: the NAFTA (1995), the Canada-Chile Agreement (1996), and the Canada-Costa Rica Agreement (2001); as well as the U.S.-Jordan standard or model (2000). It is argued that there are important lessons to be learned from these regional models and that they have contributed to a more sophisticated understanding of the issues involved. The final section draws some conclusions on trade and labour regulation issues.

II.   Global Governance and Development

The debate about globalization, its nature and impacts, has raised a number of fundamental questions relevant to the relationship between trade rules and labour rights and their international governance systems. Substantive policy questions include: Is it correct that global trade and market governance have developed more quickly than global social governance? Is there an imbalance between the economic and social pillars of the global governance system? How to make international trade rules more development friendly? What allowance should be made for national circumstances and peculiarities?

A number of important questions refer to decision making processes: Where and how to negotiate and define rules and institutions for international governance? How participatory and transparent is the process in terms of the engagement of nation-states and in terms of the participation of national or international civil society sectors and NGOs? How representative are NGOs wishes to participate in the policy-making process at the regional and global levels?

The WTO, in particular, has been a victim of its own success in enforcing global trade rules. Impressed by this success many groups have demanded the inclusion of a number of new issues in the WTO agenda. Should the WTO agenda be expanded to include new areas of international and domestic regulation such as labour and the environment? Is this expansion of the agenda in the WTO and centralization of the power to make and enforce rules desirable? Or is decentralization and specialization in the allocation of power for rule making, policing and enforcing a better global architecture? As discussed below, in the WTO Doha Ministerial Meeting some of these questions received specific answers that should reduce anxiety and conflict about these issues, at least for some time.

All of the above and others are legitimate and important questions. In trying to answer them two related traps should be avoided. One is reasoning exclusively from an industrial country perspective about the modern market economy and its institutions. The other is approaching the global trade and social governance issues unarmed with at least some rudimentary elements of that often forgotten subject called "development theory".

As for rules and institutions, the international community has rediscovered their importance for development, the question is what kind of institutions? One of the fundamental insights to emerge from institutional economics is that the state and the market can be combined in many different ways, that there are many different models of the mixed economy that can promote growth.[1] *Dani Rodrik* has put this insight as follows: "There is no single mapping between a well-functioning market and the f o r m of non-market institutions required to sustain it. This finds reflection in the wide variety of regulatory, stabilizing and legitimizing institutions that we observe in today's advanced industrial societies ... We need to maintain a healthy skepticism towards the idea that a specific type of institution – a particular form of corporate governance, social security system, or labour market legislation, for example – is the only type that is compatible with a well functioning market".[2] This point about the institutional diversity found in the international growth and development experience, is a healthy warning against a simplistic importation of international rules and standards that might not fit the specificities of developing countries.

The second trap would be not to give sufficient weight to the role of economic openness, trade and growth in reducing poverty and improving living standards and working conditions. Recent research has shown clearly that growth is important for poverty reduction, and that trade is important for growth. Faster growth is associated with faster poverty reduction, and economic contraction is associated with increased poverty. For poverty to increase with economic growth, there would have to be a drastic worsening of income distribution, and this is not generally the case in most countries. However, it is also equally clear that growth by itself does not necessarily improve income distribution, and that this requires a complex array of accompanying social policies. The point is that increased access to large markets and expanded trade is one of the major contributions that the world trading system can make to growth, poverty reduction and improving working conditions in developing countries. Policies that tend to restrict market access and trade do not contribute to increased standards of living in developing countries.[3]

---

[1] *Chang* (2002), *Easterly* (2001), *Williamson* (1985).

[2] *Rodrik* (2001) 11.

[3] Studies of the relationship between trade and growth, and growth and poverty reduction have followed two main lines. One uses econometric estimates based on cross-country time series data and panel estimation techniques. See *Levine / Renelt* (1992), *Sachs / Warner* (1995), *Sala-i-Martin* (1997), *Frankel / Romer* (1999), *Irwin / Terviö* (2000), *Dollar /*

These "development paradigm" issues are important because, as will become evident in the following sections, where one stands in terms of the trade-labour nexus, depends to a large extent on one's views about the fundamental determinants and links between trade, growth, development and poverty reduction. Let us now briefly review the evolution of international and regional regulation of labour issues.

III.   International and Regional Regulation of Labour Issues

There is a long tradition of international coordination of labour law that dates back to the Industrial Revolution, however, the international labour rights agenda broadened significantly with the creation of the International Labour Organization in 1919. Initially, the ILO's focus was on the eradication of slavery and all forms of forced labour. Later, it expanded its agenda to include the rights to freedom of association and collective bargaining, non-discrimination in employment, and elimination of child labour.[4]

The 1990s saw a growing international consensus on a number of core labour rights, a trend that led to the 1998 ILO Declaration on Fundamental Principles and Rights at Work that binds the 175 ILO members. This Declaration states that:

"... all members, even if they have not ratified the Conventions in question, have an obligation arising from the very fact of membership in the Organization, to respect, to promote and to realize, in good faith and in accordance with the Constitution, the Principles concerning the fundamental rights which are the subject of those conventions, namely:

1. freedom of association and the effective recognition of the right to collective bargaining,

---

Kraay (2001). *Rodriguez / Rodrik* (1999) and *Rodrik* (2001) are skeptical about the robustness of some of these results regarding the relationship between trade openness and growth. *Jones* (2000), however, focusing on trade policy variables, concludes that trade restrictions are almost invariably harmful to long-run growth, although the magnitude of the effect is uncertain. The other line of research has been the development of General Equilibrium Models. World Bank (2002) contains a survey of the latter literature and results and new estimates of the significant gains for developing countries of different trade opening and integration scenarios.

[4]   For history and further analysis of the trade-labour linkage see *Charnovitz* (2001a) Part III; *Leary* (1996).

2. the elimination of all forms of forced or compulsory labour,
3. the effective abolition of child labour, and
4. the elimination of discrimination in respect of employment and occupation".

Over time the ILO has developed a number of Conventions that member countries are free to join and ratify. Table 1 presents the list of Conventions corresponding to the core labour rights.

This broad-based international consensus around a set of general rights or values for the treatment of labour is a remarkable feature of the new realities of the global economy. However, it is one thing to reach consensus based on general rights or values, and quite another, to agree on precise definitions to make common labour standards operational.[5]

Table 1:
Ratification of Core ILO Conventions

	Convention		Ratification	
	Year	Number	Total Members	Western Hemisphere
Minimum Age	1973	138	93	20
Worst Forms of Child Labour	1999	182	43	20
Forced Labour	1930	29	154	31
Abolition of Forced Labour	1957	105	147	34

to be continued

---

[5] *Brown* (2001) analyzes of some of the difficulties of defining common labour standards as well as the complex relationships between labour standards and economic efficiency. The author concludes that "Taking steps to reduce forced labour, child labour, and discriminatory behavior, or to support free association and collective bargaining will often have a mixture of effects ... We cannot make a general statement that universal labour standards derived from commonly held moral values will always produce positive economic outcomes. The effect on economic performance and the lives of workers and their families of legally imposed labour market constraints of the sort contemplated by labour rights activities cannot be presumed to be positive, but instead must be empirically investigated on a country-by-country basis". (97).

Table 1 (continued):
Ratification of Core ILO Conventions

| | Convention | | Ratification | |
	Year	Number	Total Members	Western Hemisphere
Non-Discrimination in Employment and Occupation	1958	111	149	30
Equal Remuneration	1951	100	145	30
Freedom of Association	1948	87	132	30
Right to Organize / Collective Bargaining	1949	98	147	30

Source: ILO

The thirty-four countries in the Western Hemisphere have a fairly good record of ratifying ILO conventions (Table 1, and Table 2 for more detail) and a tradition of cooperation on labour issues. In the Inter-American system there is cooperation at two levels: sub-regional and hemispheric. At the sub-regional level, Central America is a good example, where Ministers of Labour, including those of Panama and the Dominican Republic, meet regularly to undertake joint actions under the auspices of the regional ILO office. The main initiative, however, is Hemispheric. Ministers of Labour of the hemisphere meet every two years. At their meeting in Viña del Mar, Chile, in 1998 the Ministers of Labour agreed on a Plan of Action, and established two working groups: one on Globalization of the Economy and its Social and Labour Dimensions; and another on Modernization of the State and Labour Administration.[6] Minis-

---

[6]   The Working Groups that were established in Viña del Mar, made considerable progress. The Working Group on Globalization of the Economy and its Social and Labor Dimensions promoted a variety of surveys and analysis including: an analysis on "Labour Standards in Integration Agreements in the Americas" conducted by the ILO; and an exhaustive survey of professional training and educational experiences in the region. The group responsible for the Modernization of the

ters identified priority areas and a number of initiatives designed to ensure progress in each area, including: the role of the Ministries of Labour, employment and the labour market, vocational training, labour relations and basic workers' rights, social security, health and safety, enforcement of national labour laws and administration of justice in the labour area, and social dialogue.

Table 2: Western Hemisphere:
Ratification of ILO Core Conventions, 2001

	Freedom of association and collective bargaining		Elimination of Forced and compulsory labour		Elimination of discrimination in respect of employment and occupation		Abolition of child labour	
	Conv. 87	Conv. 98	Conv. 29	Conv. 105	Conv. 00	Conv. 111	Conv. 138	Conv. 182
Americas (34)[7]	30	30	31	34	30	30	20	20
Antigua and Barbuda	x	x	x	x		x	x	
Argentina	x	x	x	x	x	x	x	x
Bahamas	x	x	x	x	x	x		x
Barbados	x	x	x	x	x	x	x	x
Belize	x	x	x	x	x	x	x	x
Bolivia	x	x		x	x	x	x	
Brazil		x	x	x	x	x	x	x
Canada	x			x	x	x		x
Chile	x	x	x	x	x	x	x	x
Colombia	x	x	x	x	x	x	x	
Costa Rica	x	x	x	x	x	x	x	
Dominica	x	x	x	x	x	x	x	x

to be continued

State and Labour Administration developed cooperation projects in the areas of preventive mediation; automatization of trade unions' registration and related services and modernization of labour intermediation systems.

[7]   Includes all countries participating in the Free Trade Area of the Americas (FTAA) process.

Table 2 (continued): Western Hemisphere:
Ratification of ILO Core Conventions, 2001 (continued)

	Freedom of association and collective bargaining		Elimination of Forced and compulsory labour		Elimination of discrimination in respect of employment and occupation		Abolition of child labour	
	Conv. 87	Conv. 98	Conv. 29	Conv. 105	Conv. 00	Conv. 111	Conv. 138	Conv. 182
Dominican Republic	x	x	x	x	x	x	x	x
Ecuador	x	x	x	x	x	x	x	x
El Salvador			x	x	x	x	x	x
Grenada	x	x	x	x	x			
Guatemala	x	x	x	x	x	x	x	
Guyana	x	x	x	x	x	x	x	x
Haiti	x	x	x	x	x	x		
Honduras	x	x	x	x	x	x	x	
Jamaica	x	x	x	x	x	x		
Mexico	x		x	x	x	x		x
Nicaragua	x	x	x	x	x	x	x	x
Panama	x	x	x	x	x	x	x	x
Paraguay	x	x	x	x	x	x		x
Peru	x	x	x	x	x	x		
St. Kitts and Nevis	x	x	x	x	x	x		x
Saint Lucia	x	x	x	x	x	x		x
St. Vincent and the Grenadines		x	x	x				
Suriname	x	x	x	x				
Trinidad and Tobago	x	x	x	x	x	x		
United States				x				x
Uruguay	x	x	x	x	x	x	x	x
Venezuela	x	x	x	x	x	x	x	

Source: ILO web page (http://www.ilo.org/) 2001.

Ministers of Labour of the Americas met again in Washington D.C. in February 2000 and in Ottawa, Canada in October, 2001. Ottawa's Plan of Action established two working groups: one will examine the labour dimensions of the Summit of the Americas process, and has been asked specifically to analyze questions of globalization related to employment and labour, identify areas of agreement and issues where further work needs to be done, and create a process for improved collaboration and cooperation on these labour dimensions with other government ministries. This working group will build upon the results of the Working Group on Globalization of the Economy and its Social and Labor Dimensions created under the Viña del Mar Declaration. It will also examine the implications of the ILO report "Labour Standards and the Integration Process in the Americas". Continuing the work of its predecessor, the second group will focus on capacity building of labour ministries to effectively implement labour laws, and on the promotion of the ILO *Declaration on the Fundamental Principles and Rights at Work,* and its *Follow-Up,* in the Hemisphere.

IV.   Assessment of Rationales for Inclusion of Labour Provisions in Trade Agreements

Many different arguments have been put forward to justify the inclusion of labour provisions in trade agreements. In this section these arguments or rationales are grouped under five categories: common sense arguments; economic justifications; moral, humanitarian and human rights rationales; institutional and political considerations.

A. Common Sense and Trade-Relatedness

The basic common sense argument for linkage says that since trade and labour issues are intimately related, there should be no reason to oppose linkage. Although widely used in political discourse, and perhaps appealing to the intuition, this is not a good basis to make decisions in this area. The fact that trade is related with and affects almost every aspect of human life reduces this position to the absurd. For instance, trade and income distribution issues are also intimately related. Should there be an income distribution clause in trade agreements? Obviously not. A common sense approach does not take us very far.

Departure from common sense can take two directions. One is an analytical direction. *Maskus,* for instance, develops an interesting framework to analyze the degree of trade-relatedness of different areas of regulation such as intellectual property rights, competition policy, labour and environmental issues.[8] Although the impact of these academic ideas should not be underestimated, this issue will not be resolved only on academic grounds. At the other extreme there is the pragmatic view that "trade-related" is ultimately anything that governments decide to define as trade-related. While true, this attitude involves the risk of leaving the issue wide open to the winds of political economy and pressure group politics. Therefore, governments and policy-makers would be well advised to reject common sense and political expediency as rationales for deciding how to respond to the pressures for linkage and how to allocate the powers for policing and enforcing labour rights among international institutions.

B. Economic Arguments

The second category of concerns behind the pressures to include labour provisions in trade agreements is economic. There are four basic sets of economic issues: (1) The race to the bottom argument, (2) the idea that to compete with countries where low-wages prevail is unfair competition, (3) the notion that trade liberalization without harmonization of labour standards is bad for wage dispersion and income distribution in advanced industrial economies, and (4) the concern about job dislocation and displacement produced by competing imports.

1. Race to the bottom

The race to the bottom refers to the fear that in the absence of international coordination, countries will have an incentive to lower their own standards to be more attractive to foreign investment or to gain a competitive advantage. Notwithstanding how appealing this argument may look intuitively, there is simply no evidence to support it. A review of the relevant literature suggest the following:

As regards the link between export performance and labour standards one of the principal findings of the well-known OECD 1996 study was that there is no evidence that countries with low core labour standards enjoy a better global export-performance than high-standards countries. This means that lowering labour standards would do nothing to help a country's export performance. The 2000 update of this study states that this finding has not been challenged

---

[8]   *Maskus* (2000).

by new evidence. On the contrary, a study by *Aggarwal* comparing more export-oriented and less export-oriented sectors indicates that core labour standards are often lower in less export-oriented or non-trade sectors.[9] The evidence is also clear that firms in Export Processing Zones pay higher wages and offer less onerous working conditions than do firms in the rest of the economy.[10] These findings are quite robust across different studies and suggest that export activities actually help to lift people out of poverty and can be seen as contributing to a "race to the top".

As regards the link between investment and labour standards, studies of investment location decisions of multinational companies show that these decisions are influenced by many factors of which critical ones are political and macroeconomic stability, quality of infrastructure, logistics and of labour skills. There is no evidence that low quality of labour standards constitute a significant investment decision variable.[11] On this point, the 2000 OECD study concludes that: "With the notable exception of China, countries where core labour standards are not respected continue to receive a very small share of global investment flows. There is no evidence that low-standards countries provide a haven for foreign firms".[12]

Thus, there is no evidence that export performance or FDI flows are correlated with low labour standards or low wages relative to the rest of the economy. In fact, labour standards and wages are higher in export sectors than in non-traded sectors. Even in cases where there might be an incentive to lower standards, democracy, accountability, strong local institutions and international cooperation are probably the best deterrent for any country to engage in such race.

2.   Low-wage competition is "unfair competition"

The argument that competition from low-wage or low labour-cost countries is "unfair competition" is in direct conflict with the basic principle of comparative advantage and rests on two mistaken ideas: (a) that governments in low-income countries have discretion to define the general level of wages or labour costs, and (b) that a competitive advantage based on low wages is illegitimate and con-

---

[9]   *Aggarwal* (1995)
[10]   OECD (1996); *Maskus* (1997).
[11]   *MacCormack/Newman/Rosenfield* (1994).
[12]   OECD (2000) 13.

sequently unfair. Neither of these propositions is good economics nor supported by evidence.

What determines the general level of wages in an economy and the growth in incomes over time? The key factors include the relative factor endowments; cumulative investments in education, infrastructure and health; the skill profile of the labour force and technological progress. Empirically, there is a close correlation between the growth in the level of wages or labour costs and the growth of productivity over time, in both developed and developing countries. This means that wage levels are closely associated with the country's stage of development. Except on the margin, for instance, to adjust minimum wages, the general wage level is not a variable that governments can establish by decree to gain comparative advantage.

A relatively abundant supply of low cost and low skilled labour has been typical of countries in the early stages of development and industrialization. Differences between countries in factor endowments and their relative prices have always been part of legitimate advantages in trade. In fact, the essence of the gains from trade is that due to differences in underlying fundamentals, countries differ in their abilities to produce different products. The 2001 Communication from the European Commission on Promoting Core Labour Standards recognizes this point by adopting the position that the comparative advantage of countries, particularly low-wage developing countries, must in no way be put into question.[13]

3. Impact of trade with low-wage economies on industrial economies

The third set of economic concerns is linked to the perception that increased trade with low-wage economies (the South), has contributed to wage dispersion and income inequality in rich countries (the North), particularly by hurting employment and income of unskilled workers. In other words, the idea that trade with poor countries hurts the poor in rich countries. It is a fact that since the early 1980s the United States has experienced three trends: (a) a fall in real wages of the lowest skilled workers, measured either in real terms or relative to wages of high-skilled workers; (b) a fall in the relative employment of less-skilled workers; and, as a result, (c) an increase in the share of total labour income going to high-skilled

---

[13]   European Commission (2001).

workers. However, what factors have caused these trends? Many papers and volumes have been written on these issues.[14]

Two main factors are widely cited as possible explanations of these changes: international competition from low-wage countries and skill-biased technological change that has increased the demand for skilled workers. There are two conclusions from this literature that need to be stressed. First, as noted by a recent volume and survey of this literature by the National Bureau of Economic Research: "A large amount of research during the past two decades has sought to evaluate both explanations, with the result that ... skill-biased technological change is often thought to be more important".[15]

Second, there is some degree of consensus around the view that the effect of international competition from low wage countries is small or even negligible.[16] However, *Bhagwati* goes beyond this and develops the plausible theoretical possibility that the effect of trade with the South is favorable, not adverse, to workers in the North.[17] To our knowledge, *Bhagwati*'s interesting economic story of beneficial effects for the North has not yet been tested.

Another strand of this literature analyses not just the differences in the level of wages but the associated question of whether wages are related to labour standards. No robust relationship is found between labour standards and the level of wages. *Robbins* finds that neither theory nor evidence supports the premise that stronger labour standards translate into higher wages.[18] Similarly, *Brown* concludes that in general, the link from low labour standards in low-income countries to the wage of unskilled workers in industrialized countries is not strong.[19]

---

[14] *Wood* (1994) was the first academic study to put forward the view that trade with the South has hurt unskilled workers in the North, reducing their wages and pushing them out of jobs. Since then there has been an extensive analysis of the issue that has overwhelmingly rejected this view. See *Bhagwati / Kosters* (1994); *Krugman* (1994), (1998b); *Krugman / Lawrence* (1994); *Feenstra* (2000).

[15] *Feenstra* (2000) 3.

[16] *Rodrik* (1999).

[17] *Bhagwati* (2000), chapter "Play It Again Sam: A New Look at Trade and Wages".

[18] *Robbins* (1997).

[19] *Brown* (2001)

In conclusion, the notion that trade liberalization without harmonization of labour standards is bad for wage dispersion and income distribution in the North, is not well supported by the available evidence.

4. Job dislocation and displacement

Finally, as regards the job dislocation effect, it is clear that trade and the shifting pattern of comparative advantage can indeed produce job displacement and dislocation. In fact, from a *Schumpeterian* perspective this is essential for the process of "creative destruction" that drives a healthy process of economic transformation and provides vitality to capitalist economies. The right response to this effect is not to resist these changes with protectionist responses but rather to facilitate adjustment via trade adjustment assistance policies, including income support, retraining programs, worker relocation and other safety nets mechanisms. Of course, there are complex political economy dynamics behind any such process and countries must be able to afford these programs. In addition, it must be recognized that the WTO and trade agreements have mechanisms such as transition periods, safeguards against import surges, anti-dumping, and others that can be used to help workers and industries to adapt to the new competitive environment.

In summary, none of the four varieties of economic concerns analyzed provides a solid rationale for inclusion of labour provisions in trade agreements. In fact, as will be discussed in the next section, developing countries are right in suspecting protectionist interest when any one of these different but related types of competitive arguments is expressed. While the economic arguments discussed above focus on the impact of trade on workers and citizens in the importing countries, the next category is concerned with the well being of workers and citizens on exporting countries.

C. Moral, Humanitarian and Human Rights Rationales

The typical moral concerns say that: "We should not do business with countries that violate labour or human rights", or "we should not buy from countries or companies that pay poverty wages". These expressions of moral outrage, common among opponents of globalization, are misguided. First because, as explained above, there is clear evidence that trade is good for growth and productivity and that growth is essential to increase living standards. Export-oriented growth has lifted many workers in developing countries from extreme poverty. In the absence of these export-oriented activities and jobs, even if they are badly paid by developed country standards, workers face the alternative of even lower paid jobs or no jobs at all. Therefore, if the moral or humanitarian concern is about the well being of the majority of the poor in developing countries, limiting trade does not help people in developing countries, it actually punishes them. As *Paul Krugman* has argued, moral indignation about "cheap labour" stems from not thinking the matter through. "And when the hopes of hundreds of millions are at stake, thinking things through is not just good intellectual practice. It is a moral duty".[20]

Think for instance, about the implications of the following fact: according to ILO figures, less than 5% of child labourers in developing countries are employed in export industries, 95% of the problem lies in the non-tradable sectors. This statistic means that even if morally well intended, a trade or sanctions approach to compliance would fail to have any effect on the non-tradable sectors and the general conditions of underdevelopment that are actually at the root of the child labour problem.

A broader humanitarian argument emerges when labour issues are placed in the context of a human rights perspective.[21] While appealing at a philosophical level, this human rights perspective presents a number of problems: First, it is not entirely coherent, because to the extent that it leads to policy prescriptions that restrict trade and curtail growth it goes against the interests of those it purports to defend. Second, being by its very nature universalistic the human rights perspective naturally leads to include many varieties of human rights. Why stop at labour rights? To be coherent, a human rights perspective would have to include also civil, social, economic and cultural rights. Going down this road would end up incorporating the whole international diplomatic agenda into trade institutions. Third, it is important to make a distinction between at least two cases of human rights violations: regimes that systematically violate human rights as a matter of policy (e.g apartheid, genocide, disposition to use weapons of mass destruction). In this case the international system already has a number of mechanisms to act via the United Nations, including interventions from trade sanctions to military operations. But this is not what the trade-labour nexus issue in trade agreements is about. In this latter case the

---

[20]   *Krugman* (1998a) 85.
[21]   *Trebilcock* (2002) analyzes this issue.

issue is whether there is a valid and mutually beneficial justification for using market access restrictions as a lever to deal with labour standards in the context of trade agreements among trading partners with shared economic and political values but in different stages of development. In the view of the authors, the answer to this narrower question is no, at least not under a trade restricting approach. Developing country views on this question are examined in the section V.

D. Institutional Arguments and Issues

The institutional argument for including labour provisions in trade agreements and in the WTO is based on the assumption that the ILO has no "teeth", that is, no enforcement power, while the WTO and trade agreements do. Those that make this argument are not only interested in including labour provisions in trade agreements, but are specifically interested in a sanctions-based approach. These views pose a number of questions: Is the enforcement capacity of the ILO really as weak as sometimes portrayed, and if so, can it be improved? Can the WTO really be a better enforcer than the ILO? How to assess the strengths and weakness of the ILO and WTO to effectively improve compliance with core labour rights?

The idea that the ILO has no teeth is not entirely correct. Traditionally, the ILO has relied on principles of voluntary participation, transparency, dialogue and capacity building to achieve its objectives. In particular, the ILO has traditionally recognized that the feasibility of raising labour standards depends on national circumstances and that a significant time period and capacity building may be required to achieve the recommended improvement. In line with this pragmatic approach the main instruments to promote enforcement at the ILO include:

- The Regular Supervisory System: every two to five years, Members submit a report on the measures taken to give effect to the conventions they have ratified, which is examined by a Committee of Experts. This Committee can identify particular problems and request additional information. This is a "peer pressure" mechanism. Each report is examined by a tripartite Committee on the Application of Conventions and Recommendations, and then submitted to the Annual ILO Conference.

Morici and *Schultz* report a mixed record of enforcement based on this mechanism.[22]

- The complaint procedure: Under the provisions of Article 24 this procedure can lead to the establishment of a Commission of Enquiry. Where a country fails to implement its recommendations, the ILO may apply the provisions of Article 33, under which, in case of grave and persistent violation, the Governing Body can recommend to Member states measures to secure compliance.

- General Surveys on the application of one or more specific conventions. According to a rotational system, one of the four core labour standards is under examination every four years.

Three additional mechanisms were established as follow-up to the 1998 Declaration: (a) a yearly reporting requirement for non-ratifying countries created by the 1998 Declaration, (b) a Global Report that the Director General should present each year, focused on the identification of trends and needs on each one of the four core labour standards, and (c) technical assistance encompassing advising on legislative reform and different aspects of capacity building.

Recently two proposals for further strengthening of the ILOs role in promoting labour standards have been made, one by the Commission of the European Communities[23] and the other by the ILO itself.[24]

The view of the Commission is that "The ILO has in recent years enhanced very substantially its means for promoting respect for core labour standards".[25] The European Commission proposal is quite different from some of the mainstream positions in the US debate on these issues. The proposal has a number of basic tenets: rejection of any sanctions-based approaches; the principle "that the comparative advantage of countries, particularly low-wage developing countries, must in no way be put into question"; the idea that "poverty, poor governance and extensive informal sectors are often the main cause of the weak implementation of core labour standards in developing countries"; and the notion that "sustained economic growth can contribute to the respect and effective application of

---

[22] *Morici / Schultz* (2001).
[23] European Commission (2001).
[24] ILO (2001).
[25] European Commission (2001) 13.

labour standards and of the social regulatory framework and vice versa".

Based on these premises the EU initiative proposes an approach to promote core labour standards and improve social governance that "comprise instruments and actions within different policy fields". A central pillar of this integrated strategy is making the ILO a more effective enforcer by giving more weight to observations in reports; giving greater publicity to the supervisory mechanism; improving the effectiveness of complaint procedures; and consideration of positive incentives in a wider sense.

The European Commission strategy also proposes other specific actions at the EU level as well as at the international level: increasing support for multilateral technical assistance, including the ILO; launching a forum for international dialogue; increasing trade incentives through the generalized system of preferences; addressing the issue in bilateral relations through assistance and capacity strengthening; making better use of the sustainability impact assessment (SIA); supporting private and voluntary schemes for the promotion of core labour standards through social labeling and industry codes of conduct.

In an area where the specificities and particularities of countries make it difficult, if not altogether impossible, to agree on operationally useful and precise definitions of labour standards for countries at very different stages of development, the question emerges as to how to assess the strengths and weakness of the ILO and WTO to effectively improve compliance with core labour rights?

Many consider the fact that the ILO has no teeth, in a trade sanctions sense, as a weakness of the ILO. However, it is persuasive to argue that this is the strength of the organization, not its weakness. The ILO's strength is precisely its pragmatic reliance on principles of voluntary participation, transparency, tripartite social dialogue and cooperation for capacity building rather than on an inflexible and legalistic approach in which little allowance can be made for national peculiarities and where the asymmetries in market size mean that small economies have very limited ability to punish strong countries who break the rules.[26] This pragmatic approach means that weaker and smaller countries do not have reason to regard the ILO as an instrument of more powerful countries or

---

[26]   *Rowthorn* (2000).

sectors within countries, and this induces cooperation rather than confrontation and resentment.

As to the idea that because of its reliance on the trade sanctions tool the WTO is a better enforcer there is a growing body of analysis that puts this conventional wisdom into question. *Charnovitz* reviews this work and makes a strong case that, as he puts it: "The WTO may have the best dispute settlement system of any international organization, but it does not have the best compliance system".[27] Based on the WTO experience so far, *Charnovitz* concludes that the disadvantages of the sanctions tool outweigh its advantages, that the current WTO system is too coercive and state-centric, and that the WTO needs to design better ways to get governments to follow WTO rules. He suggests that pulling out the WTO's teeth and substituting them for a variety of softer, non-trade distorting mechanisms will improve the WTO compliance system. On a first analysis this view might seem extreme, and certainly, as the author recognizes, at present the elimination of sanctions in the WTO system is inconceivable. However, these conclusions are reached after serious and thoughtful analysis. The underlying issues are among the most important challenges facing countries as regards the regulatory framework of globalization, and there is no doubt that they will continue to receive a significant degree of attention in the next few years.

For present purposes, however, the main conclusion from the previous discussion is that the popular institutional rationale to bring labour issues into the WTO, based on the idea that the ILO has no teeth while this is the main strength of the WTO, is highly simplistic. And the same conclusion applies to the institutional justification for incorporating labour issues in regional trade agreements using sanctions as an enforcement tool.

E. Political Economy Arguments and Realities

The fundamental political argument is that intellectual property rights were "given" to Capital, and that it would be fair to "give" labour rights to Labour. For authors like *Maskus*,[28] the labour-trade linkage is a clear matter of political economy as was the issue of intellectual property rights: "To a considerable extent, the answer (to why the TRIPS agreement is in the WTO) relies on considerations of political economy. Three powerful and easily organized

---

[27]   *Charnovitz* (2001) 792.
[28]   *Maskus* (2000) 3.

industries (pharmaceuticals, recorded entertainment, and software) presciently recognized the opportunity afforded by the Uruguay Round to protect their intellectual property in the future and made IPRs a core issue for the United States Trade Representative (USTR)". Some analysts in fact think that the inclusion of IPRs in the WTO family of agreements was a mistake, and that, although it cannot be undone, it should not be repeated. As stated above, there are great risks in leaving the issue wide open to the winds of political economy and pressure group politics. As explained next, developing countries are making an important contribution in balancing these pressures in industrial countries and explaining the nature of their concerns.

V.   Why are Most Latin American Countries Opposed to Inclusion[29]

Most Latin American and Caribbean (LAC) countries are quite willing to cooperate on labour issues globally in the context of the ILO, and hemispherically in the context of the Labour Initiative in the Inter-American system, but are generally opposed to linking trade and labour issues in the WTO and in bilateral or regional Free Trade Agreements, particularly under any approach involving trade restrictions or sanctions.

To provide a better understanding of the motives for this opposition, in this section the main reasons are grouped into six categories: (A) negotiating priorities; (B) political economy perceptions; (C) stage of development issues; (D) questions concerning the logic of trade negotiations, (E) considerations of efficiency in achieving social objectives and (F) arguments related to the architecture of the global trading system.

A. Distraction from Negotiating Priorities

LAC countries' negotiating priorities are closely related to market access issues. These include: elimination of high tariffs and of non-tariff barriers in sectors where they have comparative advantages (textiles, clothing, footwear, leather, food, agriculture); elimination of tariff escalation; tougher disciplines in the application of trade remedies by large industrial countries; further strengthening of dispute resolution mechanisms, and enlarged access for their skilled labour to global markets for services. They are also very

---

[29]   This section draws from *Salazar-Xirinachs* (2000).

interested in more access to international investment flows, but recognize that this is fundamentally a matter for domestic policies to improve the investment climate: from macro-disciplines, to normative frameworks for investment protection, to the core factors of competitiveness.

These priorities are linked to the widely held view that trade and investment are the engines of economic growth and, in conjunction with appropriate social policies, offer the best chance for creating employment and reducing poverty. This focus on growth is the main reason why the priority is expanding trade and obtaining larger and more secure access to the large country markets and to each others' markets. The introduction of other issues that threaten to complicate, delay, or even derail the negotiations is seen as a diversion from the main objectives in terms of growth and development.

B. Political Economy Perceptions

Like many other developing countries, those of LAC understand the pressures in developed countries to include labour issues in trade negotiations emanate from two major constituencies, sometimes acting in alliance: (1) powerful lobbying groups interested in defending protection and privileges, who want to limit international competition from developing countries by raising their production costs and deterring investment flows to them; and (2) morality-driven human rights and other groups that want to see higher standards abroad and have no protectionist agendas. The first group is perceived as not genuinely interested in improving the well-being in developing countries but rather motivated by competitiveness concerns and perceptions that they will be losers from freer trade. Hence, many trade authorities in LAC countries are concerned that the motivations for including labour issues in trade negotiations are at best mixed, and at worst not really humanitarian at all, but rather expressions of protectionist interests. Given these apprehensions, this is a game that these authorities would rather not play.

This attitude is exacerbated by the perception that self-interest or protectionist intent is clear from the selective focus on certain labour issues. Thus, the refusal to include social clauses on issues of importance to some countries – such as the rights of migrant labourers or enhanced access for skilled labour in services contracts – is taken as a signal that even if labour issues were included in negotiations, the playing field would not be level.

C. Stage of Development Issues

These take various forms. One, is the view that since poverty, informality, and labour market conditions in developing countries are quite different from those of an advanced industrial economy, the strict application of uniform labour standards, is at best questionable and at worst technically and politically unfeasible. For example, by including labour issues in trade negotiations, countries might have imposed upon them models of labour / management relations that are inappropriate, be it because of their stage of development, or because changes in labour processes induced by globalization and the technological revolution are rendering such models increasingly obsolete. Questions also emerge as to whether developed countries ought to undertake far greater commitments in the labour rights area than developing countries that are at a much lower stage of development (e.g. union representation on boards and other aspects of the European model of labour relations).

D. Logic of Trade Negotiations

The fundamental asymmetry in market size and relative importance as trading partners between the US on the one hand, and developing countries (LAC in particular), on the other, makes a trade sanctions approach to enforcement of labour rights a no win-win proposition. The argument is that the US is the only country that can threaten with credibility and actually produce damage, in many cases disproportionately so, by closing its market to the other trading partners. Accepting the link between market access or trade sanctions and labour issues, as suggested by US President *Clinton* in Seattle is, in practice, a way of institutionalizing unilateralism in a multilateral context, either in the WTO or in the FTAA. No win-win outcome is perceived in this.

A second line of reasoning, that explains not so much the opposition to linkage as the strong feelings and inflexible positions on this issue by some countries, is the fear that any concession made to establish a Working Group on Trade and Labour, as proposed by the US in Seattle, or a joint ILO / WTO Standing Working Forum on Trade, Globalization, and Labour Issues, as suggested by the EU and several other Members, is a slippery slope. Countries see no end to it. For instance: at which point are trade unions or NGOs in the US going to support fast track? Will this support be delivered upon *establishment* of the Working Group on Trade and Labour in the WTO? Probably not. Countries will have to wait for the recommendations of the Working Group. But what if the recommendations of the group are not acceptable for trade unions and NGOs? Thus, every solution engenders its own problems and some of those seem even worse than the current difficulties.

Third, there is the view that inclusion of labour and environmental issues in trade negotiations entails the risk of overloading negotiations and making them extremely complex, to the point of at best delaying or at worst impeding the achievement of results.

E. Efficiency in Achieving Social Objectives

Are trade sanctions the best way to achieve results in improving labour standards or other social objectives? Are there superior ways of achieving these objectives and agendas? A majority of countries favor a context of cooperation rather than one of negotiation, not only because of the economic and social damage that limitations to market access could inflict on them, but also because they are convinced that, to an important extent, the source of the problem lies in the lack of capacity to implement core labour rights, linked to limitations in institutional infrastructure and human and financial resources. From this perspective, technical assistance and capacity building are seen as first-best instruments to achieve results. In other words, this is not a problem that can be overcome merely by using trade measures as mechanism to bring governments into line. The difficulties that many developing countries are facing in implementing Uruguay Round commitments in areas such as Technical Standards, Intellectual Property, and Customs Valuation illustrate this point. It is not merely a matter of getting provisions and rules into the WTO, but of actual institutional and administrative capacity to implement them.

There is also the view that insisting on linkage creates a confrontational and divisive agenda that undermines the objectives, instead of promoting goodwill and creative solutions and cooperation on labour issues.

F. Global Governance Issues

Finally, there are fundamental global and regional governance questions: What is the appropriate governance at the international level? What is the appropriate architecture for the global trading system?

A rather technical but important point concerns the architecture of the GATT / WTO system. Trade negotiators, in particular – and this is not only a developing country concern – worry about overloading the WTO with issues that the WTO was not designed to deal with and which could ultimately lead to the destruction of the multilateral, rules-based trading system. This can be clearly illustrated with the debate around the proposals to accommodate in the WTO unilateral trade measures based on process and production methods (PPMs) in the country of export. The concern is that discriminating against products on the basis of the method by which they are produced, rather than their intrinsic qualities, amounts to the extra-territorial or extra-jurisdictional application of domestic regulations, perverting the long-established GATT / WTO principle of national treatment of goods in the country of import. The crux of the argument is that the principles of "national treatment" and "most-favoured nation" are intimately linked to the notion of "like product". These are the cornerstones of a multilateral trade regime that works well and has fostered a predictable and stable global trade regime. Allowing discriminatory treatment based on production methods, labour standards, or human rights would destroy the predictability and undermine the fundamentals of the system. So there is a widespread agreement among trade experts that it is not advisable to amend WTO rules to accommodate unilateral discriminatory treatment.

Another issue of concern, particularly for the trade community, is the risk of overloading the dispute settlement procedures of the WTO with disputes that are about environmental or labour issues rather than about trade, even though there might be an overlap. Many believe that the WTO has neither the expertise nor the legitimacy to adjudicate these disputes and that asking it to arbitrate in such matters undermines its credibility and diverts attention from its first priority, enforcing free trade rules.

In the environmental field, arguments like this triggered the proposal to create a World Environment Organization to provide a focal point for Multilateral Environmental Agreements and other environment-related issues and disputes. Originally suggested by *Daniel Esty*, this proposal was adopted by *Renato Ruggiero*, Director-General of the WTO in early 1999.[30] The parallel with labour issues is clear. These discussions further underpin the view that linkage in general is not feasible, and that it should be replaced by appropriate governance at the international level, where each

---

[30]   See *Runge* (2001).

agenda is pursued by a separate responsible agency, with appropriate coordination between them.

In conclusion, for the reasons explained above, the developing countries have been resisting the inclusion of labour provisions in the WTO and in trade agreements generally, particularly under any approach involving trade restrictions. The outcome of Doha represents a success for the developing countries on this issue and a disappointment for certain groups in the United States and the European Union.

In Doha the labour and environmental issues took different roads: while there is now a strengthened mandate to negotiate certain environmental issues,[31] on labour issues in Doha Ministers reaffirmed the Singapore position that the ILO is the competent body to set and deal with labour standards and limited themselves to "take note of work under way in the ILO on the social dimension of globalization" (Doha Declaration, paragraph 8). So it is to be expected that at least for the next few years, and specifically for this round of multilateral trade negotiations, the Doha Declaration put to rest the contentious aspects of the trade-labour nexus issue as a major divider between the developed and developing worlds in multilateral negotiations.

VI.   Regional Innovation on Trade and Labour Issues

Given this outcome in Doha, and building on existing trends, it is probable that the labour issue will be revisited at the regional level, particularly at least in the Americas.

Despite their general opposition to linking, some countries in Latin America have agreed to include labour provisions in reciprocal trade agreements. Three models of incorporation of labour pro-

---

[31]   The Doha Declaration contains a mandate to negotiate three specific issues: (1) the relationship between WTO rules and trade obligations set out in multilateral environmental agreements (MEAs); (2) procedures for information exchange between MEA Secretariats and relevant WTO committees, and the criteria for the granting of observer status; and (3) the reduction or elimination of tariff and non-tariff barriers to environmental goods and services. There is also mandated discussion in the Committee on Trade and Environment on: (1) clarifying WTO rules in relation to the effects of environmental measures on market access; environmental provisions under the TRIPS agreement such as the patenting of life forms and the relationship of TRIPS with the UN Convention on Biodiversity; and eco-labelling.

visions in trade agreements have emerged among countries of the
Americas: the NAFTA (1994), the Canada-Chile Agreement (1996)
and the Canada-Costa Rica Agreement (2001). These three FTAs
incorporate labour provisions in the form of a side Labour Cooperation Agreement (LCA) to the FTA. The first two agreements are
very similar in their characteristics and procedures; the last one is
more unique, simpler and more comprehensive at the same time.
The US-Jordan FTA (2000) contains a fourth, very different model
of incorporation of labour provisions in a FTA. In this case labour
is incorporated as a full discipline in the main text of the agreement.
Among other implications, this means that the dispute settlement
mechanisms of the agreement apply to the labour issue on the same
basis as to all other disciplines, including the possibility of suspension of trade benefits.

This section compares these four models of incorporation of labour issues in trade agreements in the following dimensions: objectives; scope; cooperation activities; institutional mechanisms; procedures for consultation, evaluation and dispute resolution; and
implementation and enforcement. Table 4 contains a summary of
the main features of these agreements under each one of these dimensions.

The Canada-Chile Agreement is very similar to the North
American Agreement on Labor Cooperation (NAALC), in part
because of the explicit desire stated in the agreement to facilitate
the accession of Chile to the NAALC. Consequently, these two
agreements share the same language on objectives, scope, cooperation activities, and, with a few differences, institutional mechanisms
and resolution of conflicts.

A. Objectives

The objective of all four agreements is the promotion of compliance with and effective enforcement by each Party of its own labour
law, they do not establish minimum standards for their domestic
law. Specifically, the general objectives in the three intra-regional
agreements are the following: (a) Improve working conditions and
living standards in each Party's territory; (b) promote, to the maximum extent possible, the labour principles set out in the Annex;[32]

---

[32]   The three agreements have an annex where the following labour principles are listed: (1) Freedom of association and protection of the right
to organize; (2) The right to bargain collectively; (3) The right to
strike; (4) Prohibition of forced labour; (5) Labour protections for chil-

(c) encourage cooperation to promote innovation and rising levels of productivity and quality; (d) encourage publication and exchange of information, data development and coordination, and joint studies to enhance mutually beneficial understanding of the laws and institutions governing labour in each Party's territory; (e) pursue cooperative labour-related activities on the basis of mutual benefit; (f) promote compliance with, and effective enforcement by each Party, of its labour law; and (g) foster transparency in the administration of labour law.[33] The wording of the objectives in the US-Jordan agreement is different, as can be read from Table 4.

B. Scope

Scope of application is one of the most interesting differences between the existing agreements. The three LCAs cover the broad list of labour rights listed in Annex 1 of the Agreements. However, only the political consultations and evaluation process cover this complete list, the independent review panel or "arbitral panel" process for dispute resolution is much more narrow in scope in the NAALC and the Canada-Chile LCA. The NAALC and the Canada-Chile agreement limit the scope of the arbitral panel to the Party's *technical labour standards on occupational safety and health, child labour or minimum wage.*[34] Instead, the "review panel" process of the Canada-Costa Rica LCA has competence to review issues pertaining to all the rights recognized in the *ILO Declaration on Fun-*

---

dren and young persons; (6) Minimum employment standards; (7) Elimination of employment discrimination; (8) Equal pay for women and men; (9) Prevention of occupational injuries and illnesses; (10) Compensation in cases of occupational injuries and illnesses; (11) Protection of migrant workers.

[33] In the Canada-Costa Rica Agreement there is a slight difference in objective (g) which says: foster full and open exchange of information between the Parties in regard to the application of their labour law.

[34] In the NAALC and Canada-Chile LCA, scope is defined in various ways: (a) According to objective 1b to promote, to the maximum extent possible, the labour principles set out in Annex 1; (b) Article 49 in NAALC and article 44 in Canada-Chile LCA define labour law to include laws and regulations, or provisions thereof, that are directly related to all of the above principles; (c) However, the evaluation by the Evaluation Committees of Experts and the resolution of dispute mechanisms cover only the following matters: Party's technical labour standards on occupational safety and health, child labour or minimum wage.

damental Principles and Rights at Work, 1998,[35] which means that it has competence over a much broader set of issues. The US-Jordan agreement covers the basic core labour rights with some exceptions such as elimination of employment discrimination and equal pay for women and men, which are not mentioned in the definition of scope. For the "labour laws" mentioned in paragraph 6 of the labour chapter, the dispute settlement procedures apply.

C. Cooperation Activities

The NAALC and the Canada-Chile agreements commit the parties to promote cooperative activities and list a wide range of specific areas such as: occupational safety and health; child labour; migrant workers; human resource development; labour statistics; social programs; labour-management relations and collective bargaining procedures; employment standards; etc. The Canada-Costa Rica agreement contains instead an "indicative list of areas of possible cooperation" including to: strengthen the institutional capacity of governmental departments responsible for labour affairs; strengthen and modernize labour inspectorates; strengthen the departments and bodies with jurisdiction over social security matters; and modernize systems for alternative dispute resolution as well as for the mediation and conciliation of individual and collective labour conflicts. These three agreements specify in similar fashion that the activities may be done through seminars, training sessions, working groups and conferences; joint research projects, including sectoral studies; technical assistance; and such other means as the Parties may agree.

The US-Jordan Agreement does not mention any specific cooperation activity, it only says that "The Parties recognize that cooperation between them provides enhanced opportunities to improve labour standards. The Joint Committee ... shall, during its regular sessions, consider any such opportunity identified by a Party".

D. Institutional Mechanisms

Institutional mechanisms differ, particularly in the Canada-Costa Rica LCA (see Figure 1). The NAALC establishes the following mechanisms: (a) a Commission on Labor Cooperation comprised

---

[35]   These include: freedom of association and protection of the right to organize; the right to bargain collectively; the right to strike; prohibition of forced labour; labour protections for children and young persons; elimination of discrimination; and equal pay for women and men.

by a Ministerial Council and a Secretariat; (b) a Ministerial Council, comprised of labour ministers or their designees; (c) a Secretariat, headed by an Executive Director and whose task is to assist the Council; (d) a National Administrative Office for each Party as a contact institution and to assist the Commission; (e) a National Advisory Committee may be convened by each Party (including members of labour and business organizations) to advise it on the implementation and further elaboration of the Agreement; (f) a Governmental Committee may be convened by each Party (including members of federal and state or provincial governments), to advice it on the implementation and further elaboration of the Agreement. This institutional complexity of the NAALC is also present in the Canada-Chile agreement, except that this agreement does not set up a Secretariat and instead relies on the National Secretariats.

The Canada-Costa Rica LCA has a much simpler institutional structure. It establishes a ministerial council comprised of the Ministers responsible for labour affairs of the Parties or their designees, and National Points of Contact, within each party's government department responsible for labour affairs.

The US-Jordan agreement does not establish any labour-specific institutional instance. Instead, like all other disciplines in the agreement, labour issues fall under the responsibility of the Joint Committee (see Table 4 for details about this committee).

Fig. 1., Part I:
Labour-Related Institutional Mechanisms in Four Free Trade Agreements

NAFTA – LCA

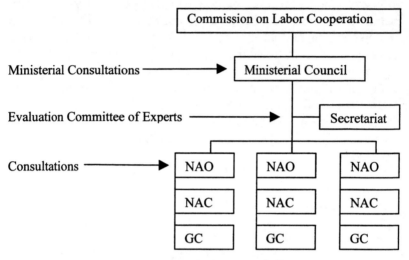

NAO: National Administrative Office

NAC: National Advisory Committee

GC: Governmental Committee

Canada – Costa Rica LCA

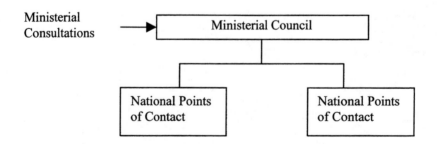

Fig. 1., Part II:
Labour-Related Institutional Mechanisms in Four Free Trade
Agreements

Canada – Chile LCA

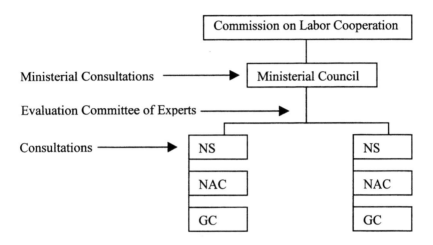

NS: National Secretariat

NAC: National Advisory Committee

GC: Governmental Committee

United States – Jordan FTA

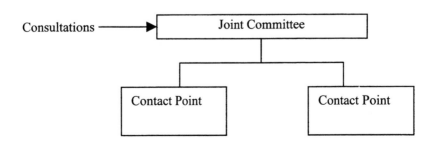

Box 1:
Resolution of Disputes:
North American Agreement on Labor Cooperation (NAALC)
- Phase I: Ministerial Consultations.
- Phase II: Evaluation Committee of Experts (ECE) (300 days).
  - Draft Report (120 days) for consideration by the Council (30 days).
  - The Final Evaluation Report shall be presented to the Council (60 days), should be published (30 days).
  - Parties' written responses to ECE's recommendations (90 days).
  - Final Report and Parties' written responses shall be considered at the next regular session of the Council.
- Phase III: Arbitral Panel (540 days).
  - If there is no resolution in a regular session, Parties may request in writing more consultations (60 days).
  - If Parties fail to resolve the matter, any Party may request a special session of the Council (20 days).
  - If Council cannot resolve the matter within 60 days, the Council may convene an arbitral panel (180 days to present an Initial Report after the last panelist is selected).
  - The Parties may submit within 30 days written comments on the Panel's Initial Report.
- Final Report: 60 days after the presentation of the Initial Report.
  If in its Final Report the panel determines a "persistent pattern of failure to effectively enforce ..." the Parties may agree on an Action Plan consistent with the recommendations of the panel.
- Review of Implementation: If Parties do not agree on an Action Plan or on whether it is being fully implemented, the panel can be reconvened (60-120 days; 180 days).

If the panel determines that the Plan has not been agreed / fully implemented, a "monetary enforcement assessment" can be imposed (90 days after the panel has been reconvened) (simplification).

E. Consultations and Evaluations and Resolution of Disputes

The NAALC as well as the Canada-Chile Agreement LCA have a long and complex procedure for consultations, evaluations, and resolution of disputes. Table 4 contains the details of these procedures and Box 1 a summary of the process for the NAALC and for the Canada-Chile LCA. There are three phases in response to a complaint. The first phase consists of Ministerial Consultations, the second phase involves an evaluation by an Evaluation Committee of Experts (ECE), that could take up to 300 days. If the matter is not resolved, any Party may request that the Ministerial Council convenes an arbitral panel. This third phase of the arbitral panel can last up to 540 days or more, depending on numerous steps and procedures.

The Canada-Costa Rica LCA simplifies these procedures (see Box 2). It defines two phases. Similar to the other agreements, the first phase consists of Ministerial Consultations, but a time limit of 180 days is defined for this stage. If the matter has not been satisfactorily addressed through Ministerial consultations, a party may request that an independent Review Panel be convened, and a time limit of 270 days is defined for the Panel to present an Initial Report containing: (a) findings of fact, (b) determination whether the matter is trade-related and covered by mutually recognized labour law, (c) determination whether there has been a persistent pattern of failure, and (d) recommendations. An interesting innovation is that the Panel is asked that its: "recommendations shall take into account the existing differences in the level of development and size of the economies of the Parties". No such provision is found in the other agreements.

The US-Jordan agreement has a very simple three-stage procedure for consultations: first, between contact points, if not resolved at this stage in 60 days the matter can be referred to the Joint Committee, and if not resolved within 90 days, either Party may refer the matter to a dispute settlement panel.

Box 2:
Review of Effective Enforcement: Canada-Costa Rica Labour Cooperation Agreement
- Phase I: Ministerial Consultations (180 days).
  - Consultations shall be concluded no later than 180 days after the request, unless both Parties agree to other date.
- Phase II: Review Panel (270 days, then two years).
  - If the matter is not resolved, a Party may request that a Review Panel be convened.

---

to be continued

Box 2: (continued)
- Initial Report: 180 days after the last panelist is selected. The recommendations shall take into account the existing differences in the level of development and size of the economies of the Parties.
- Parties may submit written comments within 45 days
- Final Report: Shall be submitted to Ministers 90 days after the Initial Report.
- Final Report shall be available to the public in the three official languages: 120 days after it is transmitted to the Ministers.
- Implementation: If the Final Report determines a "persistent pattern of failure ..." the Party "shall make best efforts to remedy the pattern of failure, including by responding positively to the recommendations of the panel".
- Review of Implementation: Two years after the publication of Final Report, the Panel may be reconvened to review the implementation of recommendations. The Follow-Up Report shall be presented within 90 days to Ministers and published 120 days after it is transmitted to Ministers.

If Panel determines that the Party has not remedied its pattern of failure on issues related to the rights set out in Annex 1, the Party that made the request "may take reasonable and appropriate measures, exclusive of fines or any measure affecting trade, but including the modification of cooperative activities ..."

F. Implementation and Enforcement

In the case of the NAALC and the Canada-Chile LCA, if in its final report, a panel determines a Party's persistent pattern of failure to effectively enforce its occupational, safety and health, child or minimum wage technical labour standards, the disputing Parties may agree on a mutually satisfactory action plan which normally must conform to the determinations and recommendations of the panel. If the disputing Parties have not agreed on an action plan, or cannot agree on whether the Party complained against is fully implementing an action plan, the panel can be reconvened. Where a panel has been reconvened it may establish whether a plan has been proposed or fully implemented and if this is not the case, it may impose a monetary enforcement assessment, no greater than 20 million US dollars (US\$ 10 million in the case of the Canada-Chile LCA). The revenues from these fines "shall be expended at the direction of the Council to enhance the labour law enforcement in the Party complained against".

At this point there is a major difference between the NAALC and the Canada-Chile LCA. In the former, where a Party fails to pay the fine within 80 days after it is imposed by the panel, "any complaining Party or Parties may suspend NAFTA benefits in an amount no greater than that sufficient to collect the monetary enforcement assessment". In the Canada-Chile LCA, in contrast, no suspension of trade benefits – trade sanctions – is contemplated, instead jurisdictional procedures ensure the payment of fines.

The Canada-Costa Rica agreement has neither monetary enforcement – fines – nor suspension of trade benefits:

> "If the panel determines that the Party that was the object of the request has not remedied its persistent pattern of failure to effectively enforce its labour law directly related to principles and rights set out in Annex 1, the Party that made the request may take reasonable and appropriate measures, exclusive of fines or any measure affecting trade, but including the modification of cooperative activities (Art. 12), to encourage the other Party to remedy that persistent pattern, in keeping with the panel's determinations and recommendations." (Art. 23, 5)

That is, the Canada-Costa Rica agreement introduces a totally new approach based exclusively on cooperation and technical assistance to promote compliance and effective enforcement of national labour laws.

In the US-Jordan agreement the dispute settlement panel presents to the Parties a non-binding report. After this "the Joint Committee shall endeavor to resolve the dispute, taking the report into account, as appropriate". And "If the Joint Committee does not resolve the dispute within a period of 30 days after the presentation of the panel report, the affected Party shall be entitled to take any appropriate and commensurate measure".

G. Track Record of Utilization of the Labour Cooperation Agreements

To date, twenty-four submissions have been filed under the NAALC, most of them involve allegations on issues of freedom of association and targeting Mexico enforcement (see details in Table 3). Most important, none of the submissions have ended in trade sanctions and many specific cooperation activities had taken place as result of the ministerial agreements – under the ministerial consultations process.

In the case of the Canada-Chile LCA there are no complaints registered. The parties have emphasized the development of a program of cooperation to promote transparency of labour laws and practices in both countries. This has included exchange of information among experts and civil society actors in a broad range of topics; the organization of numerous forums and seminars in both Canada and Chile involving leaders and representatives of labour, business and academic sectors; as well as exchange and visits of personnel of the Ministries of Labour.[36] The Canada-Costa Rica agreement was signed in April, 2001 and has not yet entered into force.

Table 3:
NAALC Scoreboard

Submissions	Twenty-four submissions have been filed.
Allegations against Canada	Two submissions involved allegations against Canada and were filed with the US NAO
Allegations against Mexico	Fifteen submissions involved allegations against Mexico and were filed fourteen with the US NAO and one with the Canada NAO
Allegations against USA	Seven submissions involved allegations against US and were filed five with the Mexico NAO and two with the Canada NAO
Issues referred in the allegations	Although some submissions involved several issues, there are seventeen out of twenty-four, which involved issues of freedom of association. Safety standards, immigrants rights, gender discrimination, and one case of child labour, were also alleged.

to be continued

---

[36] Information provided by Mr. *Pablo Lazo*, Labour Consultant to the Ministry of Foreign Affaires, Chile.

Table 3:
NAALC Scoreboard (continued)

Status	From the submissions filed with the US NAO, three were withdrawn by the submitters before hearings were held or the review process completed. Hearings were held on nine. Five of the US submissions have gone to ministerial level consultations. The US NAO declined to accept three submissions for review. The US NAO will determine whether to accept US submission 2001-01 for review by August 28, 2001.
	Four Mexican NAO submissions resulted in ministerial consultations. Another Mexican NAO submission has requested ministerial consultations.
	One Canadian NAO submission resulted in a request for ministerial consultations. Canada declined to accept two submissions one is now under appeal.

Source: the US Department of Labor Web Page (http://www.dol.gov/),
August 21, 2001

VII. Conclusions

This paper analyzed and assessed the main arguments for and against inclusion of labour provisions in trade agreements. Of the five rationales identified for inclusion, the following were rejected as incoherent, unfounded either in economic theory or empirical evidence, or otherwise inappropriate: common sense arguments; economic justifications; institutional views that the ILO has no teeth; and purely political considerations. A human rights perspective is the only ground where some defensible arguments for linkage were identified. However, even this perspective presents serious problems, and in the authors' view does not justify a sanctions approach in trade agreements between trade partners with shared economic, political and social values but in different stages of development.

When the perspective, arguments and concerns of developing countries are taken into account, it becomes easier to understand why these countries oppose the trade-labour linkage, particularly under any trade restricting approach. It also becomes apparent why attempts to bring labour issues into global or regional trade agreements, under a sanctions approach, will hardly be feasible and will probably continue to be fiercely resisted. This does not mean developing countries are reluctant to cooperate on labour issues but they strongly prefer compliance systems based on transparency (or sunshine) methods, education, capacity building and stakeholder participation, rather on inflexible and legalistic approaches in which little allowance can be made for national peculiarities and where the asymmetries in market size mean that small economies have very limited ability to punish strong countries who break the rules. From this point of view the ILO's reliance on these "soft" mechanisms can be considered a source of strength not a weakness of the organization. Similarly, such "soft" mechanisms can also be considered a strength of the Labour Cooperation Agreements associated with the Canada-Costa Rica and Canada-Chile FTAs.

The analysis in this paper suggests two general scenarios for the treatment of labour issues in trade agreements and negotiations. If the predominant view on labour issues remains pro-sanctions, the trade-labour issue will continue to be a divisive and confrontational issue in international trade talks. If the predominant view accepts that in this area the best compliance system is one based on transparency, education, capacity building and stakeholder participation, the stage would be set for a truly mutually reinforcing process of improvement in labour rights and conditions driven by more open global and regional trade systems on one hand, and parallel efforts of global and regional international coordination of labour policies and issues on the other.

Table 4:
Treatment of Labour Issues in Four Free Trade Agreements (until page 366)

	NAFTA	Canada-Chile	Canada-Costa Rica	US-Jordan
Modality of Treatment	Side Agreement: labour cooperation agreement	Side Agreement: labour cooperation agreement	Side Agreement: labour cooperation agreement	Incorporates labour as a full discipline in the main text of the agreement (Article 6).
Objectives of the Agreement	(a) Improve working conditions and living standards in each Party's territory; (b) promote, to the maximum extent possible, the labour principles set out in Annex 1; (c) encourage cooperation to promote innovation and rising levels of productivity and quality; (d) encourage publication and exchange of information, data development and coordination, and joint studies to enhance mutually beneficial understanding of the laws and institutions governing labour in each Party's territory;	Same List as NAFTA	Same list from (a) to (f). A different point in (g): foster full and open exchange of information between the Parties in regard to the application of their labour law.	The parties reaffirm their obligation as members of the ILO and their commitments under the ILO Declaration on Fundamental Rights at Work and its Follow-up. The Parties shall strive to ensure that such labour principles and the internationally recognized labour rights set forth in paragraph 6 (see below) are recognized and protected by domestic law. The Parties recognize that it is inappropriate to encourage trade by relaxing domestic labour laws. Accordingly, each Party shall strive to ensure that it does not waive or otherwise derogate

[37] It is an agreement to promote compliance with and effective enforcement by each Party of its labor law; but does not establish minimum standards for their domestic law.

	NAFTA	Canada-Chile	Canada-Costa Rica	US-Jordan
Objectives of the Agreement	(e) pursue cooperative labour-related activities on the basis of mutual benefit; (f) promote compliance with, and effective enforcement by each Party of, its labour law; and (g) foster transparency in the administration of labour law.[37]			from, or offer to waive or otherwise derogate from, such laws as an encouragement for trade with the other Party. Recognizing the right of each Party to establish its own domestic labour standards, and to adopt or modify accordingly its labour laws and regulations, each Party shall strive to ensure that its laws provide for labour standards consistent with the internationally recognized labour rights set forth in paragraph 6 and shall strive to improve those standards in that light.
Scope	Party's technical labour standards on occupational safety and health, child labour or minimum wage.[38]	Party's technical labour standards on occupational safety and health, child labour or minimum wage.[38]	Principles and rights recognized in the ILO Declaration on Fundamental Principles and Rights at Work, 1998 as listed in an-	Paragraph 6: "Labour laws" means statutes and regulations, or provisions thereof, that are directly related to the following

[38] In the NAFTA-LCA and Canada-Chile LCA, scope is defined in various ways:

a. According to objective 1b to promote, to the maximum extent possible, the labor principles set out in Annex 1, which are the following: 1. Freedom of association and protection of the right to organize; 2. The right to bargain collectively; 3. The right to strike; 4. Prohibition of forced labor; 5. Labor protections for children and young persons; 6. Minimum employment standards; 7. Elimination of employment discrimination; 8. Equal pay for women and men; 9. Prevention of

	NAFTA	Canada-Chile	Canada-Costa Rica	US-Jordan
Scope			nexes 1 and 2 of ALC.[39]	labour rights: the right of association; the right to organize and bargain collectively; a prohibition on the use of any form of forced or compulsory labour; a minimum age for the employment of children; and acceptable conditions of work with respect to minimum wages, hours of work, and occupational safety and health.
Cooperation Activities	1. The Council shall promote cooperative activities between the Parties, as appropriate, regarding: (a) occupational safety and	Same as NAFTA except for last sentence: "They (the Parties) shall jointly select, implement and fund all projects falling within the category of coopera-	1. An indicative list of areas of possible cooperation in Annex 3: "(a) strengthen the institutional capacity of the governmental departments responsible for labor	eration between them provides enhanced opportunities to improve labour standards. The Joint Committee ... shall, during its

occupational injuries and illnesses; 10. Compensation in cases of occupational injuries and illnesses; 11. Protection of migrant workers.

b. Article 49 in NAFTA-LCA and article 44 in Canada-Chile LCA define labor law to include laws and regulations, or provisions thereof, that are directly related to all of the above principles.

c. However, the evaluation by the ECE's and the resolution of dispute mechanisms cover only the following matters: Party's technical labor standards on occupational safety and health, child labor or minimum wage.

[39] It includes: freedom of association and protection of the right to organize; the right to bargain collectively; the right to strike; prohibition of forced labor; labor protections for children and young persons; elimination of discrimination; and equal pay for women and men.

	NAFTA	Canada-Chile	Canada-Costa Rica	US–Jordan
Cooperation Activities	health; (b) child labor; (c) migrant workers of the Parties; (d) human resource development; (e) labour statistics; (f) work benefits; (g) social programs for workers and their families; (h) programs, methodologies and experiences regarding productivity improvement; (i) labour-management relations and collective bargaining procedures; (j) employment standards and their implementation; (k) compensation for work-related injury or illness; (l) legislation relating to the formation and operation of unions, collective bargaining and the resolution of labour disputes, and its implementation; (m) the equality of women and men in the workplace; (n) forms of cooperation among workers, management and government; (o) the provision of technical assistance, at the request of a Party, for the development of its labour standards; and (p) such	tive activities ..." Art.11, 3.	affairs particularly in regard to information statistics, studies and research; (b) strengthen and modernize labor inspectorates, by providing them with the appropriate normative frameworks, as well as the structures, functions and means for effective performance; (c) strengthen the departments and bodies with jurisdiction over social security matters, particularly those responsible for the administration of policies and programs for working women, persons with disabilities and the protection of young persons at work; and (d) modernize systems for alternative dispute resolution as well as for the mediation and conciliation of individual and collective labor conflicts, by providing Parties to such conflicts with timely proceedings and trained staff." Annex 3 2. Cooperation activities	regular sessions, consider any such opportunity identified by a Party.

	NAFTA	Canada-Chile	Canada-Costa Rica	US-Jordan
Coope-ration Ac-tivities	other matters as the Parties may agree. 2. Parties may cooperate through: (a) seminars, training sessions, working groups and conferences; (b) joint research projects, including sectoral studies; (c) technical assistance; and (d) such other means as the Parties may agree.		means: same as NAFTA and Canada-Chile ALC	
Institu-tional Mecha-nisms	As institutional instances the Agreement establishes the following: a. Commission on Labour Cooperation comprised by a Ministerial Council and a Secretariat; b. Ministerial Council, comprised of labour ministers or their designees; c. Secretariat, shall be headed by an Executive Director and shall assist the Council; d. National Administrative Office for each Party as a contact institution and to assist the	Same as NAFTA except for the following: a. No (c) Secretariat b. Instead of NAO: National Secretariat	As institutional instances the Agreement establishes the following: a. Ministerial Council comprises Ministers responsible for labour affairs of the Parties or their designees; b. National Points of Contact, within each parties' government department responsible for labour affairs.	No labour-specific institutions are established. Instead, like all other disciplines in the agreement, labour issues fall under the responsibility of the Joint Committee (Art 15), composed by representatives of the Parties and headed by (i) the US Trade Representative and (ii) Jordan's Minister primarily responsible for international trade, or their designees. The Joint Committee may establish ad hoc standing committees or working groups. Each Party shall designate an

	NAFTA	Canada–Chile	Canada–Costa Rica	US–Jordan
Institutional Mechanism	Commission; e. National Advisory Committee may be convened by each Party (including members of labour and business organizations) to advise it on the implementation and further elaboration of the Agreement; f. Governmental Committee may be convened by each Party (including members of federal and state or provincial governments), to advice it on the implementation and further elaboration of the Agreement.			office as contact point.
Consultations and evaluations	1. First stage is ministerial consultations. If not resolved: 2. ECE established by the Council. 3. No ECE may be convened if an independent expert selected by the Council establishes that the matter (a) is not trade-related or; (b) is not covered by mutually recognized labour laws 4. The ECE shall present a draft report within 120 days after it is	Same as NAFTA	1. First stage is ministerial consultations. Consultations shall be concluded no later than 180 days unless both Parties agree to another date.	Either Party may request consultations with the other Party with respect to any matter affecting the operation or interpretation of the Agreement. A party seeking consultations shall submit a request for consultations to the contact point. If the Parties fail to resolve a matter through consultations within 60 days, either Party may refer the matter to the Joint

	NAFTA	Canada–Chile	Canada–Costa Rica	US–Jordan
Consultations and evaluations	established for consideration by the Council. 5. Each Party may submit written views to the ECE on its draft report within 30 days. 6. The ECE shall present a final report to the Council within 60 days after the draft report. 7. The final report shall be published within 30 days after its presentation unless the Council decides otherwise. 8. The Parties shall provide to each other and the Secretariat, responses to the recommendations of the ECE report, within 90 days after its publication. 9. The final report and the Parties' written responses shall be tabled for consideration at the next regular session of the Council.			Committee.
Solution of disputes and enforcement	1. If the matter is not resolved, any Party may request in writing consultations in respect of the general subject of the ECE final report.	1. If the matter is not resolved, any Party may request in writing consultations at special session of the Council in respect of the general subject of the ECE final report.	1. If the matter has not been satisfactorily addressed through Ministerial consultations, a Party may request that a Review Panel be convened (Art. 15).	1. If the matter referred to the Joint Committee is not resolved within 90 days, or within such other period agreed by the Joint Committee, either Party may

	NAFTA	Canada-Chile	Canada-Costa Rica	US-Jordan
Solution of disputes and enforcement	2. If the Parties fail to resolve the matter after 60 days of delivery of request for consultations, a special session may be requested to the Council. 3. The Council shall convene within 20 days of delivery of the request and shall endeavor to resolve the dispute promptly. The Council may: (a) call on such technical advisers or create working groups as it deems necessary; (b) have recourse to good offices, conciliation, mediation or such other dispute resolution procedures, or (c) make recommendations 4. If the matter is not resolved within 60 days after the Council has convened the Council may convene an arbitral panel. 5. Unless the disputing Parties otherwise agree, the panel shall, within 180 days after last panelist is selected, present to the disputing Parties an Initial Report containing: (a) findings of	report. 2. The Council shall convene within 60 days of the request and shall endeavor to resolve the dispute promptly. Following steps, same as NAFTA	2. Unless the Parties otherwise agree, the panel shall, within 180 days after the last panelist is selected, present to the Parties an Initial Report containing (art. 20): (a) findings of fact; (b) determination whether the matter is trade-related and covered by mutually recognized labour law; (c) whether there has been a persistent pattern of failure; (d) recommendations. The recommendations shall take into account the existing differences in the level of development and size of the economies of the Parties. 3. Either Party may submit written comments to the panel on its initial report within 45 days of presentation of the report. 4. Final Report: 90 days after the presentation of the initial report, the Review Panel shall present to Ministers a final report. 5. 120 days after it is transmit-	refer the matter to a dispute settlement panel. 2. The panel shall, within 90 days after the last member is appointed, present to the Parties a report (non binding) containing: findings of fact and its determination as to whether either Party has failed to carry out its obligations or whether a measure taken by either Party severely distorts the balance of trade benefits accorded or substantially undermines the fundamental objectives of the Agreement. At the request of the Parties, the panel may make recommendations for the resolution of the dispute. 3. After a dispute has been referred to a dispute settlement panel and the panel has presented its report, the Joint Committee shall endeavor to resolve the dispute, taking the report into account, as appropriate. 4. If the Joint Committee does

	NAFTA	Canada-Chile	Canada-Costa Rica	US-Jordan
Solution of disputes and enforcement	fact; (b) determination whether there has been a persistent pattern of failure to effectively enforce its occupational safety and health, child or minimum wage technical labour standards in a matter that is trade-related and covered by mutually recognized labour law; (c) recommendations, if any for the resolution of the dispute, which normally shall be that the Party complained against adopt and implement an action plan to remedy the pattern of non-enforcement. 6. Either Party may submit written comments to the panel on its initial report 30 days of its presentation. 7. Final Report: 60 days after the presentation of the initial report, the Panel shall present to the disputing Parties a final report. 8. Disputing Parties shall transmit within 15 days to the Council the final report of the panel and		ted to Ministers the final report shall be available published in the three official languages. 6. Implementation: if in its final report the Review Panel determines a persistent pattern of failure to effectively enforce its labour law, the Party shall make best efforts to remedy the pattern of failure, including by responding positively to the recommendations of the panel. 7. Review of Implementation: Two years after the publication of final report, the Review Panel may be reconvened to review the implementation of recommendations. The panel shall determine whether the persistent pattern of failure to effectively enforce its labour law has been remedied. 8. 90 days after being reconvened the panel shall present to Ministers the Follow-Up Report. 9. The Parties shall make the follow-up report available to the	not resolve the dispute within a period of 30 days after the presentation of the panel report, the affected Party shall be entitled to take any appropriate and commensurate measure.

	NAFTA	Canada-Chile	Canada-Costa Rica	US-Jordan
Solution of disputes and enforcement	their views. 9. Final report shall be published 5 days after transmitted to the Council. 10. Implementation: if in its final report a panel determines a persistent pattern of failure to effectively enforce its occupational safety and health, child or minimum wage technical labour standards, the disputing Parties may agree on a mutually satisfactory action plan which normally shall conform to determinations and recommendations of the panel. 11. Review of Implementation: if the disputing Parties have not agreed on an action plan (Art. 39, 1a), or cannot agree on whether the Party complained against is fully implementing an action plan (Art. 39, 1b), the panel can be reconvened. (Different deadlines to reconvene panel in each case) Where a panel has been recon-		public in the three official languages 120 days after it is transmitted to the Ministers.	

	NAFTA	Canada-Chile	Canada-Costa Rica	US-Jordan
	vened it may establish whether a plan has been proposed / agreed / fully implemented … if not, it may impose, where warranted, a monetary enforcement assessment, within (60 days) after been reconvened.			
Persistent pattern of failure	A monetary enforcement assessment can be established, no greater than 20 Million US Dollars.	A monetary enforcement assessment can be established, no greater than 10 Million US Dollars.	"If the panel determines that the Party that was the object of the request has not remedied its persistent pattern of failure to effectively enforce its labour law directly related to principles and rights set out in Annex 1, the Party that made the request may take reasonable and appropriate measures, exclusive of fines or any measure affecting trade, but including the modification of cooperative activities (Art. 12), to encourage the other Party to remedy that persistent pattern, in keeping with the panel's determinations and recommendations" (Art. 23, 5)	

	NAFTA	Canada-Chile	Canada-Costa Rica	US-Jordan
Revenues	Revenues from fines shall be expended at the direction of the Council to enhance the labour law enforcement in the Party complained against.		Not Applicable	
Suspension of trade benefits –trade sanctions	Where a Party fails to pay a monetary enforcement assessment within 80 days after it is imposed by a panel, any complaining Party or Parties may suspend NAFTA benefits in an amount no greater than that sufficient to collect the monetary enforcement assessment.	No suspension of trade benefits. Jurisdictional procedures ensure the payment of fines.	No suspension of trade benefits.	If the Joint Committee does not resolve the dispute within a period of 30 days after the presentation of the panel report, the affected Party shall be entitled to take any appropriate and commensurate measure (does not rule out suspension of trade benefits).

Prepared by *José Manuel Salazar-Xirinachs and Jorge Mario Martínez-Piva.*

Bibliography:

M. Aggarwal (1995), International trade, labor standards, and labor market conditions: an evaluation of the linkages, U.S. International Trade Commission, Office of Economics, Working Paper No. 95-06-C, June 1995.

J. Bhagwati (2000), The Wind of the Hundred Days, Cambridge, MA 2000.

J. Bhagwati / M. Kosters (1994) (eds.), Trade and Wages: Leveling Wages Down?, Washington, D.C. 1994.

D. Brown (2001), Labor Standards: Where Do They Belong on the International Trade Agenda?, in Journal of Economic Perspectives, 15 (2001) No. 3, Summer 2001, 89-112.

H.-J. Chang (2002), Kicking Away the Ladder: Development Strategy in Historical Perspective, London 2002.

St. Charnovitz (2001a) Essays in Trade Law and Global Governance, London 2001.

St. Charnovitz (2001b), Rethinking WTO Trade Sanctions, American Journal of International Law, 95 (2001) No. 4, October 2001, 792-832.

Commission of the European Communities (2001), Promoting Core Labour Standards and Improving Social Governance in the Context of Globalization, Communication from the Commission to the Council, the European Parliament and the Economic and Social Committee, Brussels 2001, http://europa.eu.int/comm/trade/pdf/comcls_en.pdf.

I. M. Destler / P. J. Balint (1999), The New Politics of American Trade: Trade, Labor, and the Environment, Institute for International Economics, Washington, D.C. 1999.

D. Dollar / A. Kraay (2001), Growth is Good for the Poor, World Bank Policy Department Working Paper No 2587, Washington D.C., April 1999.

W. Easterly (2001), The Elusive Quest for Growth, Cambridge, MA / London 2001.

R. C. Feenstra (2000) (ed.), The Impact of International Trade on Wages, National Bureau of Economic Research, Chicago / London 2000.

J. Frankel / D. Romer (1999), Does Trade Cause Growth?, American Economic Review, 89 (1999) No. 3, 379-399.

Interamerican Conference of Labor Ministers, Declarations and Plans of Action – see www.oas.org/udse/labor.htm.

International Labour Organization (2001), Report of the Director-General: Reducing the decent work deficit - a global challenge, 89th Session, Geneva 2001, http://www.ilo.org/public/ english/standards/relm/ilc/ilc89/rep-i-a.htm.

D. Irwin / M. Terviö (2000), Does Trade Raise Income? Evidence from the Twentieth Century, National Bureau of Economic Research, Working Paper 7745, June 2000, http://www.nber. org/papers/w7745.

C. I. Jones (2001), Comments on F. Rodríguez and D. Rodrik, Trade Policy and Economic Growth: A Sceptic's Guide to the Cross-National Evidence, in *B. S. Bernanke / K. Rogoff* (eds.), NBER Macroeconomics Annual 2000, Cambridge, MA, 2001.

E. Kimberly (2000), Getting Beyond No...! Promoting Worker Rights and Trade, in *J. Schott* (ed.), The WTO After Seattle, Institute for International Economics, Washington, D.C 2000.

P. Krugman (1994), Does Third World Growth Hurt First World Prosperity?, Harvard Business Review, July / August 1994.

P. Krugman (1995), Technology, Trade, and Factor Prices, National Bureau of Economic Research, Working Paper 5355, Cambridge, MA, November 1995, http://papers.nber.org/papers/ w5355.pdf.

P. Krugman (1998a), The Accidental Theorist, New York 1998.

P. Krugman (1998b), Pop Internationalism, Cambridge, MA 1998.

P. Krugman / R. Lawrence (1994), Trade, Jobs and Wages, Scientific American, April 1994.

R. Levine / D. Renelt (1992), A Sensitivity Analysis of Cross-Country Growth Regressions, American Economic Review, 82 (1994) No. 4, 942-963.

A. D. MacCormack / L. J. Newman / D. B. Rosenfield (1994), The New Dynamics of Global Manufacturing Site Location, Sloan Management Review, Summer 1994.

K. Maskus (1997), Should Core Labor Standards Be Imposed through International Trade Policy?, The World Economy 20 (1997) No. 6, September 1997. Also available in: http://www.worldbank.org/research/trade/pdf/wp1817.pdf.

K. E. Maskus (2000), Regulatory Standards in the WTO: Comparing Intellectual Property Rights with Competition Policy, Environmental Protection and Core Labor Standards, University of Colorado, Boulder, http://www2.cid.harvard.edu/cidtrade/Issues/maskus3.pdf.

P. Morici / E. Schulz (2001), Labor Standards in the Global Trading System, Economic Strategy Institute, Washington, D.C. 2001.

OECD (1996), Trade, Employment and Labour Standards: A Study of Core Workers' Rights and International Trade, Paris 1996.

OECD (2000), International Trade and Core Labour Standards, Paris 2000.

A. Panagariya (2000) Trade-Labor Link: A Post-Seattle Analysis, http: //www1.worldbank.org/wbiep/trade/videoconf/panagariya.pdf.

D. Robbins (1997), Facts, Fallacies and Free Trade: A Note on Linking Trade Integration to Labor Standards, Inter-American Development Bank, Working Paper Series 214, May 1997.

F. Rodríguez / D. Rodrik (1999), Trade Policy and Economic Growth: A Skeptic's Guide to the Cross-National Evidence, National Bureau of Economic Research, Working Paper 7081, April 1999, http://www.nber.org/papers/w7081.pdf.

D. Rodrik (1997), Has Globalization Gone Too Far? Institute for International Economics, Washington, D.C. March 1997.

D. Rodrik (2001), Development Strategies for the Next Century, paper Presented at ECLAC-CEPAL Raul Prebisch Anniversary Conference, August 29, 2001, Santiago de Chile, http://www.eclac.org/prensa/noticias/comunicados/6/7616/DaniRodrik 29-08.pdf.

B. Rowthorn (2000), International Labour Standards: Background and Current Issues, University of Cambridge, UK 2000, mimeo.

F. Runge (2001), A Global Environmental Organization (GEO) and the World Trading System, Journal of World Trade, 35 (2001), No 4, 399-426.

J. Sachs /, A. Warner (1995), Economic Reform and the Process of Global Integration, Brookings Papers on Economic Activity, 1, 1-118.

X. X. Sala-i-Martin (1997), I Just Ran Two Million Regressions, American Economic Review 87 (1997) No. 2, 178-183.

J. M. Salazar-Xirinachs (2000), The Trade-Labor Nexus: Developing Countries' Perspectives, Journal of International Economic Law 3 (2000) No. 2, 377-385.

M. Trebilcock (2002), International Trade and International Labour Standards: Choosing Objectives, Instruments, and Institutions, in this volume.

A. Wood (1994), North-South Trade, Employment and Inequality: Changing Fortunes in a Skill-Driven World, Oxford 1994.

World Bank (2002), Global Economic Prospects and the Developing Countries. Making Trade Work for the World's Poor, The World Bank, Washington, D.C. 2002.

Joanne Scott

Integrating Environmental Concerns into International Economic Law[*]

I.   Environmental Concerns and the Dispute Settlement Procedure of the WTO

This paper is concerned with the difficulties associated with integrating environmental concerns into international economic law and in particular, in this first part, into the international trading order constituted by the WTO. The advent of the WTO served to intensify the tension between trade and environment. It did so principally by instituting a profound shift in the premises underpinning international trade relations, taking us beyond a discrimination based approach to one predicated upon a degree of mutual recognition. Thus, put broadly, the scope of the basic prohibition was expanded, thereby subjecting even non-discriminatory trade restrictions resulting from national regulation to the discipline of the WTO. This may be exemplified most clearly by reference to the Agreement on Technical Barriers to Trade (TBT Agreement).[1] Article 2:2 of the TBT Agreement provides that:

---

[*]   This paper is based on a talk given in Vienna in December 2001, and its style and tone reflect its origins as a conference presentation.

[1]   This move beyond discrimination is mirrored in other parts of the WTO Agreement, most infamously perhaps in the Sanitary and Phytosanitary Measures Agreement, the source of so much transatlantic acrimony in the hormones dispute.

"Members shall ensure that technical regulations are not prepared, adopted or applied with a view to or with the effect of creating unnecessary obstacles to international trade. For this purpose,
technical regulations shall not be more trade-restrictive than necessary to fulfil a legitimate objective, taking account of the risks non-
fulfilment would create. Such legitimate objectives are, *inter alia*:
national security requirements, the prevention of deceptive practices; protection of human health or safety, animal or plant life or
health, of the environment. ..."

Thus, as in the EU, it becomes incumbent upon WTO members
to justify technical barriers in the light of a non-exhaustive list of
societal interests. Even where such measures are genuinely even-
handed in their application, they must be demonstrated to be necessary, and not susceptible to realization in a less trade-restrictive
manner.[2] The breadth of this prohibition (on measures which are
not necessary or not the least restrictive of trade) is matched by the
breadth of the concept of a technical regulation as defined in Annex
1 to the TBT Agreement. This encompasses product and process
standards, compliance with which is mandatory, including those
relating to packaging or labelling requirements.

It is thus the case that the TBT Agreement, like other parts of the
WTO Agreement, gives rise to a culture of justification in which
members must defend their regulatory choices in so far as these
impinge upon imported goods. Trade restrictions which rest upon a
failure to comply with domestic standards may be defended only
where those domestic standards are justifiable in the terms laid
down by the WTO Agreement. Such a culture of justification places
a considerable burden upon the dispute settlement bodies of the
WTO, and in particular upon the Appellate Body. It falls to this
body to determine criteria according to which the necessity of
measures is to be assessed, and according to which the adequacy of
a specific justification may be determined. And this then is where
life starts to get difficult for the Appellate Body. Wherever it turns
for inspiration, the resulting criteria emerge as value-laden and
normatively loaded, and thus as strenuously (even violently) contested and resisted. However technocratic the language – reasonableness, rationality, even proportionality – the politics of regulation cannot be convincingly concealed.

---

[2] On this latter requirement see Article 2:3.

Even that last bastion of objective truth – science – is viewed today with some scepticism as a basis for determining regulatory right and wrong. In a climate of uncertainty, where risks are unknown and unknowable, and where attitudes to risk are culturally rather than scientifically constructed, notions of necessity or rationality no longer serve to silence critics who call to their aid past errors, and the language of precaution. In the *hormones* "case" the Appellate Body did not accept that the results of the relevant risk assessment were such as to warrant – or reasonably support – the contested measures. In reaching this conclusion, the Appellate Body was required to establish thresholds according to which the measures could be assessed. In so doing it concluded that it is not open to a state member to take steps to guard against a "merely" theoretical – or hypothetical – risk, where to do so would affect international trade. Thus, while it went out of its way to allow states extensive room for regulatory manoeuvre, it drew the line at the point where there was no evidence of risk, and merely no evidence of no risk. And yet what seems reasonable in the face of such hypothetical risk is a question of judgment, predicated in part upon an assessment of the good associated with the activity which may (or may not) turn out to generate environmental harm, or deleterious effects on public health. Where the negative consequences of human activity are known, parties will disagree about whether their up-side is such that it may be justified. Where they are not known, disagreement will be more intense, and perhaps more intractable. As noted above, any attempt on the part of the WTO dispute settlement bodies to mediate such disputes, will be normatively loaded and strenuously contested.

It is interesting to observe in this respect that recourse to the language of precaution in itself does little to mediate conflicts in this respect. Whereas endorsement of the precautionary principle is increasingly widespread and axiomatic, no single understanding has emerged. This may be illustrated by developments in respect of the regulation of Genetically modified organisms (GMOs). While both the European regime, in the form of a the revised directive,[3] and the international regime in the form of the Cartagena Protocol, speak the language of precaution, uncertainty persists as to what this means. Differences emerge as to the thresholds to be applied, relating for example to the gravity of the threat and the degree of

---

[3]   Directive 2001/18, OJ 2001 L 106 1.

scientific uncertainty, and to the relationship between these two factors. Indeed even within a single regime (e.g. Cartagena) different conceptions of the principle emerge. Thus, whereas Article 1 is parasitic upon the Rio version and hence predicated upon notions of cost-effectiveness and serious and irreparable damage, Cartagena's home-grown version departs from this in a number of important respects.

If, as the above implies, it is accepted that there is no right and wrong in the world of regulation, but only choices which reflect values, preferences, experience, and fears, and moreover that the societal good which flows from that regulation may be assessed and not measured, and hence that its worth is also a question of judgment not truth, it is then apparent that the consequences of entrusting the WTO dispute settlement bodies with the task of pronouncing upon the necessity of a given measure has profound consequences, notably in constitutional terms. It is, in the light of that, not at all surprising that so much attention has come to focus upon legitimacy issues in the context of the WTO, and in particular in the context of the WTO's system of dispute settlement.[4] The Appellate Body – a court in all but name – is experiencing the kind of scrutiny which courts the world over, notably constitutional courts performing a review function, have come to expect.

Two features of the Appellate Body's approach stand out in the light of the comments above. First, as noted above, is the tendency of this body to allow states a wide margin of discretion in the implementation of regulatory choices. Thus, members are allowed considerable room for manoeuvre in justifying their choices as necessary before the Appellate Body. This may be illustrated both by the *hormones* "case" discussed above, and by the more recent *asbestos* report. In the latter the AB continues down the road of softening the application of the proportionality test implied by the concept of necessity, thus increasing the margin of appreciation enjoyed by members in social regulation.[5]

Second, and more interesting perhaps, is the manner in which the Appellate Body has taken tentative steps down a different route, in seeking to walk the fine line between international trade and national regulation. This is most clearly apparent in the *shrimp /*

---

[4] *Howse* (2000) 12.

[5] See *Howse /Türk* (2001) for a fuller discussion of this point, and an overview of the relevant AB jurisprudence.

turtle case.[6] Here the AB in applying GATT Article XX(g) concerning the conservation of exhaustible natural resources, focused attention on the opening sentence of Article XX, or its 'chapeau'. This provides that measures must be applied in a manner which does not constitute a means of arbitrary or unjustified discrimination between countries where the same conditions prevail, or a disguised restriction on trade. In focussing upon this the AB had regard not so much to the substance of the contested US measures, but rather to the circumstances surrounding their application. Notable in this respect was:

- the failure of the United Sates to engage in serious across-the-board negotiations with third countries, with a view to concluding bilateral or multilateral agreements. Thus the measures were applied in a manner which was unilateral or non-consensual;
- the rigidity with which US officials made certification determinations, and the existence of little or no flexibility regardless of how appropriate (or not) the US harvesting model was given conditions prevailing in the state of export;
- the failure of the US to respect standards of basic fairness and due process in the application of the contested measures. Particularly important in this respect were the absence of any opportunity for the applicant to be heard or to respond to the arguments before a certification decision was adopted, the failure to render a formal reasoned decision and to notify the party of it, the absence of any procedure for appeal or review of a decision to deny certification, and overall the 'singularly informal and casual' nature of the procedure, making it impossible for applicants to know whether the measure was being applied in a manner which is fair and just.

II.   'Positive' *vs.* 'Negative' Environmental Integration: The EU as an Example

Thus, while the AB has, over the course of a number of cases, permitted a more open interpretation of Article XX, including the underlying principle of necessity, this is accompanied here by recourse to a kind of proceduralism designed to distinguish the legitimate from the illegitimate in the ostensible pursuit of the relevant social objective. This is a point to which we will return. First

---

[6]   *United States – Import prohibition of certain shrimp and shrimp products* at: http://www.wto.org/english/tratop_e/dispu_e/dispu_e.htm.

though we will turn from "negative" to "positive" integration, and the harmonization of environmental norms.

If the events of recent years have generated a high level of awareness regarding the difficulties associated with defining environmental limits to the free trade imperative, and of the intensely and inherently political nature of this task, they have served also to exemplify the limits of 'positive integration' or harmonisation as a means of promoting sustainable development. While not wishing to disparage the very real achievements of international environmental law, it would nonetheless be naïve to ignore the obstacles which lie in its path. As one leading authority in the field observes:

"Despite impressive achievements, there is reason to doubt the impact of this body of law on actual governmental and human behavior. Limited implementation and enforcement suggests that international environmental law remains in its formative stages. Law making is decentralized, with legislative initiatives being developed in literally dozens of different inter-governmental organizations at the global, regional, and sub-regional level. Coordination between the various initiatives is inadequate, leading to measures which are often duplicative and sometimes even inconsistent. Moreover, the lawmaking process tends to be reactive and somewhat *ad hoc* in nature, often vulnerable to the vagaries of political economic, and scientific events and findings".[7]

The author of this quotation goes on to suggest some positive steps that might be taken to ameliorate the difficulties involved, emphasizing in particular the need for international institutional reform. Such reform is indispensable, he argues, in view of the need to ensure greater coherence and integration of environmental concerns, more effective enforcement and compliance, and also to guarantee the nimbleness of environmental law "in areas where knowledge and needs are fast-moving".[8] To this end he offers us his "wish-list" of reform proposals, all of which seem eminently sensible though, as he would concede, not always realisable. Yet even in an ideal world in which power and short-term politics did not stand in the way of sensible reform, such is the nature of the challenge of environmental protection that norm harmonization at an international level would be hard, if not impossible, to achieve. One need only look to recent initiatives in respect of climate change and

---

[7]   *Sands* (2000) 372.
[8]   *Sands* (2000) 397.

GMOs, as well as to experience in the European Union to appreciate this.

European Union experience in the formulation of transnational environmental law illustrates at least two fundamental difficulties standing in its way. The first is diversity. Even in a European Union characterized by relative homogeneity, at least in political and economic terms, such is the continuing demand for diversity in regulatory outcomes that the system has had to develop structural mechanisms to accommodate it. Thus, for example, recourse to framework directives permit Member States continuing flexibility in implementation even in the wake of the adoption of 'common' standards. This may be exemplified by reference to the important IPPC Directive (Integrated Pollution Prevention and Control) where recourse to benefits based technology standards such as "Best Available Techniques" permit Member States substantial policy discretion in the implementation of the Directive in the sectors concerned.[9] Additional mechanisms designed to accommodate diversity – physical and economic, as well as in terms of political preferences, are reflected both in individual regulatory norms, through for example derogations or exceptions, temporary or permanent, and in the Treaty itself. The legal basis providing for Community level intervention in the environmental sphere, provides for minimum harmonization measures, thereby permitting Member States to enact stricter measures where such measures are inconsistent with the Treaty.[10] Article 95 EC – the internal market legal basis – is more complex in the balance which it strikes between uniformity and diversity. The bottom line, however, is that it too permits departure from uniform norms in specified circumstances, albeit subject to a Commission control procedure.[11] Limited recognition of this move in the direction of flexibility is apparent in the case law of the Court in so far as it acknowledges that the essential aim of environmental measures is to protect the environment, and not to harmonize national laws, and that as such it is not incompatible with a directive (in this case the nitrates directive) that Member States apply in dif-

---

[9] Council Directive 96/61 EC, OJ 1996 L 257 26.

[10] Article 176 EC provides that "The protective measures adopted pursuant to Article 175 shall not prevent any Member State from maintaining or introducing more stringent protective measures. Such measures must be compatible with the Treaty. They shall be notified to the Commission".

[11] See *Vos* (2001).

ferent ways.[12] While the language of subsidiarity and proportionality in Community law has tended to focus attention upon the desirability rather than the feasibility of Community level intervention, the latter in particular has served to legitimate flexible regulation and a less prescriptive approach. Thus, the protocol on the application of the principles of subsidiarity and proportionality establishes a preference for framework directives and for maximum feasible flexibility in implementation, bearing in mind the demands of effective enforcement.

The second difficulty associated with transnational harmonization of environmental norms exemplified by EU experience relates to complexity. Such is the scale, and complexity of the regulatory challenge posed by the environmental dimension (including its role in the protection of public health) that the traditional "Community Method" has been found wanting. Even in view of a significant move in favour of qualified majority voting, the Community legislative process remains cumbersome and slow. In this it stands in contrast to the pace of environmental change according to which new problems are constantly emerging, and old problems constantly demanding re-evaluation and adaptation in policy response. It is, in the light of this, not at all surprising that the EU is tending to turn its back on the Community Method in favour of alternative approaches to governance, such as are better suited to be responsive to rapidly changing circumstances and perceptions. Most crucial perhaps in this respect is the emergence of what is effectively an executive capacity at Community level, permitting the by-passing of the usual legislative institutions, at least in the usual form. Thus, "comitology" as it has come to be known, strikes a subtle balance between different levels and branches of governance, ascribing an important regulatory function to Member State representatives, sometimes political, but most crucially and commonly, expert in orientation. A quick glance at any environmental directive will exemplify the centrality of the role played by such committees, and the significance of these committees in ensuring the adaptability of Community regimes to current circumstances and problems. What is, however, clear is that this executive capacity has been bought at a price; that of political legitimacy. While there are those who have come to the defence of the system,[13] that defence is premised upon

---

[12] Case C-293/97 *Standley and Metson* ECR 1999 I-2605.
[13] See especially *Joerges* (1999).

a fundamental re-thinking of the nature of democratic authority, and a shift away from representation in favour of deliberation as a basis for democracy. While, equally, the European Court has taken important steps to "constitutionalise" comitology,[14] and the European Parliament forced changes which are of crucial importance in this respect,[15] the fundamental dilemma nonetheless remains; adaptability may be bought at a price, when viewed through the lens of traditional conceptions of democracy and accountability.

Such are the difficulties posed by diversity, and the challenge of achieving adaptability without sacrificing (excessively) legitimacy in governance, that the EU has been forced to engage in quite radical experimentation in environmental governance. This experimentation takes a variety of forms, but may broadly be captured by the language of "proceduralization". By this it is meant that environmental governance in the EU tends increasingly to direct the manner in which decisions are adopted at both Member State and Community level, in order to ensure the integration of an environmental dimension, rather than to direct the Member State or Community institution concerned in terms of substantive policy outcome.

Looking first to the level of the Member States this proceduralization is clearly not new. It was as early as 1975 that the Community first enacted the Environmental Impact Assessment Directive, albeit that this has in the meantime been revised and strengthened in certain key respects. More recent years have seen the (eventual) enactment of a "strategic" counterpart to this; requiring the environmental assessment of certain plans and programmes, rather than individual projects.[16] Yet the phenomenon of proceduralization is inherent in other measures, albeit in more subtle ways. Thus, as I have argued previously, the increasing flexibility which tends to accompany Community intervention in the environmental sphere tends also to be accompanied by a degree of procedural prescription. Thus, while Member States are permitted greater substantive autonomy in the implementation of Community environmental law, they are more and more constrained in the manner in which they exercise these all important implementation choices. Such constraints may take a variety of forms, but relate most commonly to

---

[14] See *Scott/Trubek* (2002).
[15] See Decision 1999/468/EC, OJ 1999 L 184 23.
[16] Directive 2001/42/EC, OJ 2001 L 197 30.

public participation, access to information, transboundary consultation, reporting requirements, and obligations to periodically review
and revise decisions adopted. Such requirements may be free
standing, as with the access to environmental information directive,
currently in the course of revision, or they may be integrated into
specific environmental regimes, and again the IPPC Directive is
exemplary in this respect.

Moving on to the EU level, it is apparent that procedural tools
for environmental protection are widely deployed here too. Of crucial importance in this respect is the Article 6 EC "environmental
integration obligation". Though this has not yet formed the subject
matter of adjudication before the European Court, its practical implications are great, notably in the wake of the Cardiff summit and
the adoption of the "Partnership for Integration" report.[17] This
called upon the Council of Ministers and the European Parliament
to assume responsibility for environmental integration, and identified more specific tasks for the councils, including the identification
of best practice regarding environmental integration in the Member
States, and the identification of priority actions for environmental
integration, and the review of current organizational arrangements
to ensure effective integration.[18] More recently, the 6th Environmental Action Programme observes that the environmental integration process needs to be supported by effective environmental assessment of new policy proposals. To this end the Gothenburg
Council conclusions called upon the Commission to present
mechanisms to ensure that all major policy proposals include a
sustainability impact assessment covering their potential economic,
social and environmental consequences. It is anticipated that such
mechanisms will be up and running by the end of 2002. Crucial in
this respect is the development of sustainable development indicators against which progress will be measured. Emphasis upon the
formulation of sustainable development indicators is also central to
the Community's Sustainable Development Strategy.[19] Thus it is on
the basis of "headline indicators" included in this report that the
Commission will evaluate implementation of this strategy in its
annual synthesis report.

---

[17] COM(98) 333 final.
[18] See on this point, and more generally, *Lenschow* (2002).
[19] COM(2001) 264 final, *A Sustainable Europe for a Better World: A
European Union Strategy for Sustainable Development*.

What we see then in the EU is that sustainable development is viewed less as an end-point, than as a process. Decision-making at both Member State and Community level is constrained less by fixed standards to be achieved, than by procedures which seek to promote a high level of environmental awareness, reflexivity as to environmental consequences, and transparency as to outcomes. This is not unique to the EU. Indeed such is the pervasiveness of this procedural turn that even the European Court on Human Rights, in *Hatton*, favoured a procedural reading of Article 8 of the ECHR. Thus, central to its finding of a violation of Article 8 was the Court's conclusion that the UK had not seriously attempted to evaluate the extent or impact of aircraft noise on the applicants' sleep patterns, or concluded a prior, specific and complete study, with the aim of finding the least onerous solution regarding human rights.[20] Also at the international level, procedural instruments such as EIA or information based tools are common. Crucial in this respect are the Arhus and Espoo Conventions, the former concerning Access to Information, Public Participation in Decision-Making and Access to Justice in Environmental Matters, and the latter, Environmental Impact Assessment in Transboundary Matters.[21]

III.   The Role of State-Based Regulation and Private Actors' Initiatives in International Environmental Law

Before concluding this short piece, one final observation may be made. It was argued above that the nature of environmental governance is changing, and that the relevant changes are captured in part by the language of proceduralization. Significantly, it has been argued that this tendency in the direction of a procedural approach to environmental governance is apparent both when it comes to integrating environmental concerns into international trade law, and in respect of the task of the "harmonization" of environmental law at a transnational or even global level. While one aspect of this procedural turn is an emphasis upon public participation in environmental decision-making and, underpinning this, access to environmental information, the argument thus far nonetheless remains focussed upon the role of the state or groups of states in facilitating sustainable development. In this sense it has tended to ignore one

---

[20] See *Hatton* v. *United Kingdom* at: http://www.echr.coe.int/Eng/ Judgments.htm.

[21] See *Birnie/Boyle* (2002) 262 et seq.

additional and important dimension of environmental governance; namely the increasingly central role of non-state actors in the promulgation and application of environmental norms. This is apparent, albeit to a quite limited extent in an EU context, and albeit that in the EU, private sector initiatives tend to be mediated by a normative framework attributable to the "state". This is the case, for example, in respect of the Eco-Management and Audit System (EMAS) initiative, or in relation to voluntary environmental agreements. In this sense what we are witnessing in the EU is an ever closer interaction between public and private in environmental governance, such as is not readily captured by traditional notions of consultation or participation.

At any international level there is some evidence that the role of non-state actors in the promulgation of environmental norms is yet more far-reaching and profound. This is starkly illustrated, and richly discussed, in the work of *Errol Meidinger* who focuses upon forest certification: "a process through which transnational networks of diverse actors set and enforce standards for the management of forests around the world":[22]

"[These] provide frameworks in which firms can be certified as practising good environmental management. Some, such as the chemical industry's 'Responsible Care' program ... and the United States forest product industry's Sustainable Forestry Initiative, are run by industry trade associations. Others, such as the ISO 1400 program, are run by inter-sectoral industry-based groups, some of which are government sanctioned. Still others, such as the Forest Stewardship Council, are established by partially self-organized NGO-industry groups. Depending on the program, firms are entitled to signal their certification status by displaying labels on their literature, facilities or products. ISO-type programs focus on the implementation of sophisticated environmental management systems ("EMS"s) by firms..., while FSC-type programmes also impose performance requirements. The performance requirements almost invariably include traditional pollution and biodiversity concerns, but are now extending to include economic, community, and labour ones as well".[23]

He argues, following a review of the relevant literature, that "... if one takes the criteria discussed above – rule-making and adjudi-

---

[22]   *Meidinger* (2001) 1.
[23]   *Meidinger* (2001) 31.

cation mechanisms, public legitimacy and social usage – there is a good, although not incontrovertible case for treating forest certification as a form of law making, specifically environmental law making",[24] and moves to assess it on the basis of premises often relied upon in the assessment of more traditional forms of environmental law: efficacy, coherence, adaptability and legitimacy. The issues to which this gives rise are interesting and important, but lie outside of the scope of this paper. Nonetheless, the basic fact bears repetition. Environmental values come to be integrated into the global market place, not merely by virtue of state-based, and quasi-state based, regulatory initiatives, but also by virtue of the activities of private actors, including civil society actors. In this way law, or something resembling law, emerges in forms which are increasingly plural and decentered; a phenomenon which forms an important object of study and analysis in legal sociology.[25]

IV.   Conclusion

This paper has examined two dimensions of the task of integrating environmental concerns into international economic law. The first dimension concerned the "greening" of international trade law, and more specifically the articulation of environmentally motivated limits to the free trade imperative. The second dimension concerned the formulation of free standing environmental norms, through the process of transnational law-making or harmonization of norms. In an EU setting these two dimensions would be captured by the language of "negative" and "positive" integration; or market and policy integration.[26] Analysis of these two dimensions revealed a certain coincidence of approach. It became apparent that both dimensions are, to a degree at least, underpinned by, on the one hand, substantial flexibility or regulatory autonomy for states and, on the other, by a certain procedural rigour in terms of the manner in which, or the process whereby, the relevant decision is to be adopted. In this sense Member States are constrained not so much in what they do, but in terms of how they set about doing it.

Having observed this commonality in approach, it is important not to exaggerate it. For one thing, the specific procedural require-

---

[24] *Meidinger* (2001) 24.

[25] See *Teubner* (1997) 16 and *Appelbaum/Felstiner/Gessner* (2001).

[26] "Integration" here is not used in the sense of environmental integration, but the more traditional integration of previously distinct polities.

ments constraining states in the context of departure from WTO
norms, as expressed in *shrimp /turtle*, are different from the procedural constraints imposed by way of EU law, or international law
instruments such as the Arhus Convention. Also, the rationale for
recourse to such procedural techniques might be thought to be different in each case. Whereas, in respect of negative integration,
proceduralization would seem to have its roots in classical due process concerns – broadly speaking, fairness – in respect of positive
integration, the rationale might be thought to be more functional,
with an emphasis upon the contribution which correct procedures
can make to the formulation of effective and appropriate environmental outcomes, such as are capable of responding to the vagaries
of rapidly changing circumstances, and a regulatory backdrop characterized by complexity, diversity, and deep value pluralism.

This trend towards proceduralization in both negative and positive integration raises a multitude of issues and questions, in terms
both of the effectiveness and legitimacy of governance. While these
cannot be addressed here, one observation may be put forward by
way of conclusion.

One issue which continues to puzzle in the world of international law is the relationship between international trade law, and
multilateral agreements for environmental protection (MEAs).
What is at issue here is the hierarchical relationship between the
WTO and MEAs in the event of a conflict. This question is not
merely hypothetical. Take the Cartagena Biosafety Protocol by way
of example. The tension between this and the WTO (in particular
the SPS Agreement) is there for all to see. Whereas the Protocol
permits departure from the free movement of living modified organisms on the basis of a wide range of factors, including conservation and sustainable use of biodiversity, taking into account risks
to human health, the SPS Agreement will assess the legitimacy of
trade restrictions exclusively from the perspective of human, animal
or plant health or life.[27] In addition, the Protocol articulates its own
conception(s) of the precautionary principle, such that is or may be
different from that underpinning, or deemed to underpin, the SPS

---

[27] It is probable that the SPS Agreement would apply in respect of
LMOs, although some doubt persists. For a discussion of this see:
Zedalis (2001). Were the TBT Agreement to apply, there would be
more flexibility in terms of the grounds which could be invoked under
Article 2:2 to justify restrictions.

Agreement. To the extent that conflicts do arise between the Bio-safety Protocol and the WTO, the hierarchical relationship between these two instruments remains contested and confused. The preamble to the Protocol is deeply and inherently contradictory in this respect. Whereas on the one hand it emphasises that the Protocol shall not be interpreted as implying a change in the rights and obligations of parties under existing international law (including the WTO), on the other, it states that the this statement is not intended to subordinate the Protocol to other international agreements.[28] Confusion reigns, and is not susceptible to clear resolution on the basis of the Vienna Convention on the Law of Treaties.[29]

To what extent then might the trend in favour of proceduralization, in respect of both negative and positive integration, serve to ameliorate this tension between the WTO Agreement and MEAs? It is readily apparent that at a general level it might. It marks a step in the direction of coherence in the sense that the procedural premises underpinning both negative and positive integration emerge as shared premises. According to this trend, the legality of departing from the free trade imperative will be assessed, at least in part, on the basis of the procedural circumstances surrounding the adoption and application of the contested decision to restrict free movement. Equally, in so far as MEAs establish process based standards, respect for these will serve to bolster and not to undermine compliance with the WTO. In this scenario, both international environmental law and international trade law exhibit a high level of deference vis-à-vis the regulatory choices of states, but are more intrusive as regards the shape of the governance arrangements according to which these choices emerge.

If, as the above suggests, the procedural turn evident in international and European law, offers one way forward in alleviating tension between trade and environment, it is equally apparent that it begs a wide range of difficult questions. These relate both to the rationale of this approach, and to its capacity to contribute concretely to a high level of environmental protection. Whereas it is likely that this trend will be readily endorsed by the environmental

---

[28] For a more detailed discussion of the problems arising from the Cartagena Protocol, see the contribution of *Gerhard Loibl* in this volume.

[29] See *Sands* (2000) 399-405 for a brief discussion of the implications of this in the environmental sphere.

movement in the context of the WTO, it is certain to be more deeply contested at the level of "positive" international environmental law. Nonetheless, such is the world that we live in – and the complexity and plurality which characterizes it – that alternatives are hard to find.

Bibliography:

P. Appelbaum / W. L. F. Felstiner / V. Gessner (2001), Rules and Networks: The Legal Culture of Global Business Transactions, Oxford 2001.

P. Birnie / A. Boyle (2002), International Law and the Environment, Oxford/New York ^{2}2002.

R. Howse (2000), Adjuticative Legitimacy and Treaty Interpretation in International Trade Law: The Early Years of WTO Jurisprudence, in *J. H. H. Weiler*, The EU, the WTO and the NAFTA. Towards a Common Law of International Trade?, Oxford /New York 2000, 35-69.

R. Howse / E. Tuerk (2001), The WTO Impact on Internal Regulations: A Case Study of the Canada-EC Asbestos Dispute, in *G. de Búrca / J. Scott* (eds.), The EU and the WTO: Legal and Constitutional Issues, Oxford 2001, 283-328.

C. Joerges (1999), "Good Governance" Through Comitology?, in *C. Joerges / E. Vos*, EU Committees: Social Regulation, Law and Politics, Oxford 1999, 311-388.

A. Lenschow (2002), New Regulatory Approaches in "Greening" EU Policies, European Law Journal 8 (2002) No. 1, 19-37.

E. E. Meidinger (2001), Law Making by Global Civil Society: the Forest Certification Prototype, http://law.buffalo.edu/homepage/eemeid/scholarship/GCSEL.pdf.

P. Sands (2000), Environmental protection in the twenty-first century: sustainable development and international law, in *R. Revesz / P. Sands / R. B. Stewart* (eds.), Environmental Law, the Economy and Sustainable Development, Cambridge 2000, 369-409.

J. Scott / D. Trubek (2002), Mind the Gap: Law and New Approaches to Governance in the EU, European Law Journal 8 (2002) No. 1, 1-18.

G. Teubner (1997), Global Law Without a State, Aldershot /Dartmouth 1997.

E. Vos (2001), Differentiation, Harmonisation and Governance, in *B. de Witte /D. Hanf/E. Vos* (eds.), The Many Faces of Differentiation in EU Law, Antwerpen 2001, 145-179.

R. J. Zedalis (2001), Labelling of Genetically Modified Foods: The Limits of GATT Rules, Journal of World Trade 35 (2001) No. 2, 301-347.

Gerhard Loibl

The Cartagena Protocol on Biosafety: A New Model for Environmental Protection on an International Level?

I.   Introduction

On 29 January 2000 the First Extraordinary meeting of the Conference of the Parties to the Convention on Biological Diversity at its resumed session, held in Montreal, Canada, adopted the Cartagena Protocol on Biosafety to the Convention on Biological Diversity.[1] Thus, a long and difficult negotiating process had been brought to a successful end.

Although the issue of living modified organisms (further: LMO) or – as they are sometimes called – genetically modified organisms (GMOs)[2] had not attained the same amount of attention of the pub-

---

[1] International Legal Materials 39 (2000) 1027 et seqq.; UNEP/CBD/ ExCOP/1/L.5. The Cartagena Protocol has not entered into force as 17 January 2002 only twelve States have deposited their instrument of ratification, acceptance or accession. According to Article 37 para. 1 the Protocol will enter into force on the ninetieth day after the date of deposit of the fiftieth instrument of ratification, acceptance, approval or accession by States or regional economic integration organisations. The Cartagena Protocol, which was open for signature from 15 May 2000 to 4 June 2001 (Article 3), was signed by 106 States and the European Community.

It should be noted that according to Article 37 para. 3 any instruments deposited by "a regional economic integration organisation shall not be counted as additional to those deposited by member States of such organisation".

[2] LMOs are defined in Art. 3 of the Cartagena Protocol on Biodiversity as "any living organism that possesses a novel combination of genetic material obtained through the use of modern biotechnology". In this context it should be noted that in European Community Law the term "Genetically Modified Organism (GMO)" is used. Directive 2001/18/ EC on the deliberate release of genetically modified organisms states in Article 2: "'genetically modified organism (GMO)' means an or-

lic as other environmental concerns – such as the ozone layer and climate change –, it proved, however, to be a highly controversial topic.[3] LMOs are used to generate different types of products and applications, such as pharmaceuticals, food or animal feed.[4] The discussions, in particular, in Europe about the health and environmental impacts of genetically modified soya beans and maize as well as about food products containing LMOs led to an increase in international public attention.

A number of States have adopted regulations for the use of LMOs on the national level.[5] During the negotiations it became evident that States had taken different approaches to handle (potential) risks concerning LMOs, which would have effects in a number of areas, such as international trade or human health care.

It is the objective of the Protocol "in accordance with the precautionary approach contained in Principle 15 of the Rio Declaration on Environment and Development" to ensure "an adequate level of protection in the field of safe transfer, handling and use of living modified organisms resulting from modern biotechnology that may have adverse effects on the conservation and sustainable use of biological diversity, taking into account risks to human health, and specifically focusing on transboundary movements".[6] The Protocol is to be regarded as an important step in the elaboration of international regulations dealing with new developments in the area of science as well as addressing the relationship between international trade rules and provisions on the protection of health and the environment.[7]

---

ganism, with the exception of human beings, in which the genetic material has been altered in a way that does not occur naturally by mating and/or natural recombination". The definitions differ to a certain extent, in particular in regard to human beings who do not fall within the scope of the GMO definition, although they may carry GMOs e.g. due to medical treatment.

[3] See on the issue of biotechnology in general *Murphy* (2001).

[4] LMOs are used in various ways: Sometimes LMOs are used directly such as in the case of seeds (e.g. pesticide-resistant seeds of soya or maize). In other instances they are further processed (e.g. tomatoes resulting from pesticide-resistant seeds are processed to tomato ketchup) or are for "contained use" (i.e. no contact with the external environment).

[5] Cf. *Alder/Wilkinson* (1999) 163; *Schulte* (1999) 261 et seqq.

[6] Article 1 of the Cartagena Protocol.

[7] Cf. *Stoll* (1999) 82 et seqq.

This contribution will look at the process leading to the adoption of the Cartagena Protocol and will analyse whether it has elaborated rules that could be regarded as a new model for environmental protection on the international level.

II.   The Elaboration of the Cartagena Protocol

A. The Convention on Biodiversity and the 'Jakarta Mandate'

Already during the negotiations on the Convention on Biodiversity in August 1990 developing countries raised questions concerning biotechnology and biosafety. Some developing countries feared that their territories might be used for "scientific trials" in the use of "modern biotechnology"[8] and that the introduction of LMOs into the environment might have a negative impact. Others wished to gain access to biotechnology and its benefits. No substantive provisions on biotechnology were included in the Convention on Biological Diversity as many developed countries did not regard biotechnology as a major issue that needed internationally agreed rules. Very little was then known about its possible negative effects on biodiversity and the commercial potential of biotechnology.

As a compromise between the different negotiating positions the Convention on Biodiversity states in Article 8 (g) that "each contracting Party shall, as far as possible and as appropriate, [...] establish or maintain means to regulate, manage or control the risks associated with the use and release of living modified organisms resulting from biotechnology which are likely to have adverse environmental impacts that could affect the conservation and sustainable use of biological diversity, taking into account the risks to human health". Thus, the parties are obliged to take measures on the national level to ensure that LMOs do not have an impact on the conversation of biological diversity.

---

[8]   "Modern biotechnology" is defined in Article 3 (i) of the Cartagena Protocol. It reads as follows:

"'Modern biotechnology' means the application of:
  a) In vitro nucleic acid techniques, including recombinant deoxyribonucleic acid (DNA) and direct injection of nucleic acid into cells or organelles,
  b) Fusion of cells beyond the taxonomic family,
that overcome natural physiological reproductive or recombination barriers and that are not techniques used in traditional breeding and selection".

Moreover, Article 19 (3) of the Convention on Biodiversity provides that a protocol dealing with living modified organisms may
be elaborated if the parties would decide that such rules are necessary.[9]
This vague mandate for the elaboration of international rules on
LMOs was specified by the so-called "Jakarta mandate" which was
adopted by the Second Meeting of the Conference of the Parties to
the Convention on Biological Diversity in 1995.[10] The Conference
of the Parties (further: COP) established a negotiating process to
develop "a protocol on biosafety, specifically focusing on transboundary movement, of any living modified organism resulting
from modern biotechnology that may have adverse effect on the
conservation and sustainable use of biological diversity, setting out
for consideration, in particular, appropriate procedure for advanced
informed agreement".[11] The terms of reference for the open-ended
ad hoc working group were set out in more detail in an annex to the
decision.
Thereby, a deadlock in the elaboration of international regulations to deal with LMOs was overcome. A number of reasons led to
this change of attitude of a number of countries, in particular of the
European Community and its member states:

---

[9]   Article 19 para. 3 reads as follows:
"The Parties shall consider the need for and modalities of a protocol
setting out appropriate procedures, including, in particular, advance informed agreement, in the field of the safe transfer, handling and use of
any living modified organism resulting from biotechnology that may
have adverse effect on the conservation and sustainable use of biological diversity".
The possibility to elaborate a protocol to deal with issues of biosafety
was also reaffirmed in the Nairobi Final Act 1992 (Resolution 2, para.
2 subpara. c).

[10]   Decision II/5 entitled "Consideration on the need for and the modalities of a protocol for the safe transfer, handling and use of living modified organisms". This decision was based on the report of a panel of
fifteen experts on biodiversity and the report of an open-ended ad hoc
group of Experts on Biodiversity. It is interesting to note that the question whether there was a "need" for a protocol was not answered, but
guiding principles, possible items to be considered in an international
framework, and options for an international framework on biosafety
were suggested (see Yearbook of International Environmental Law 6
(1995), 317 et seq.).

[11]   Para. 1 of Decision II/5.

- genetically modified field crops had been tested in laboratories and controlled field trials and were about to be released for large-scale commercial use;[12]
- the public within the European Union had become anxious about the impact of LMOs on human health and the environment;[13] and
- developing countries remained sceptical on the economic and social effects of LMOs (e.g. on their agricultural production).

Moreover, during the discussion it became evident that such a protocol would close a gap in international law: to cover environmental and health aspects of transboundary transfers of LMOs.

B. The Different Groupings During the Negotiations

On the basis of the "Jakarta mandate" the international negotiating committee started its work. During the work of the negotiating committee a number of different groupings of states emerged which presented the different interests and positions.

The developing countries formed the so-called "Like Minded Group". It expressed its scepticism about the impact of LMOs for countries that lacked the capacities and resources to deal adequately with modern biotechnology. One of their concerns was that they would not be able to judge risks resulting from the use of LMOs on their territories and to take necessary preventive measures. Moreover, they feared that the increased use of LMOs would increase their dependence from developed countries and they would suffer economic and social disadvantages. The Like Minded Group aimed at a strict regime for transboundary transfer of LMOs which would take into consideration the technological and financial shortcomings of developing countries, as well as socio-economic factors and environmental concerns.

The so-called "Miami-Group" – consisting of the United States, Canada, Australia, Argentina, Chile and Uruguay – did not share in general the concerns of the negative impacts of LMOs. Moreover, the Miami group was strongly opposed to any regulations which could change the existing trade rules. These countries had increased their production of crops based on LMOs in the last years and, therefore, they feared a negative impact on their commodities ex-

---

[12] *Paarlberg* (2000) 25 et seq. In 1996 genetically modified field crops where released for large-scale commercial use by US farmers.

[13] *Paarlberg* (2000) 26 et seqq.

ports and competitive disadvantages. They aimed at protecting their interests in the export of genetically modified products, mainly agricultural products, by avoiding complicated and time-intensive procedures for transboundary movements of LMOs.

The European Union (EU) also favoured a strict control regime for transboundary movements and emphasized the need for a precautionary approach. Its position was strongly influenced by the public opinion in Europe.[14] Moreover, the EU aimed at giving health and environmental concerns a decisive role in international regulations on LMOs, reflecting its own legislation.[15]

The Eastern and Central European Countries were interested in an international regime on LMOs which would take into account their economic situation and lack of resources.

---

[14] In September 1997 in a Eurobarometer Poll, 80% of Europeans considered that biotechnology was useful in detecting hereditary illnesses and for the production of new innovative medicines, but only one in four Europeans would buy genetically altered fruit even if it tasted better and less than one in four Europeans considered that current legislation was adequate against the risks they believed linked to modern biotechnology. The risks seen concerning genetically modified foods/ organisms are mainly the issues of food security, food allergies and antibiotic resistance (*O'Rourke* (1998) 121-125. See also *Paarlberg* (2000), who points to the different view taken by the public in Europe and the United States: in Germany 82% of the respondents to a Canadian survey stated that they would be less likely to buy groceries labelled as genetically modified products, whereas in the United States a low of 57% of the respondents expressed the same concerns (49)).

[15] The European Community has adopted two directives concerning LMOs – or "genetically modified organisms" as they are called in European Community law –:
  • Directive 90/219/EEC on the Contained Use of Genetically Modified Organisms which was amended by Directive 98/81 of the European Parliament and the Council of 26 October 1998, and
  • Directive 90/220/EEC on the Deliberate Release into the environment of genetically modified organisms (to be replaced on 17 October 2002 by Directive 2001/18/EC of the European Parliament and the Council of 12 March 2002).
  See *Epiney* (1997) 256 et seqq.
  Moreover, the European Community has adopted legislation on foodstuffs consisting of GMOs or foodstuffs that are intentionally genetically altered: Regulation 258/97 on novel foods. For a detailed description see *O'Rourke* (1998) 121 et seqq. Cf. also *Krämer* (1998) 26.

The "Compromise Group" – which was formed in the last stages of the negotiations by Switzerland, Norway, Japan, Mexico and the Republic of Korea – shared the concerns on possible effects of LMOs, but tried to bridge the different positions. They aimed to elaborate international regulations which would be compatible with the existing international trade system.

C. The Main Issues

During the negotiations fundamental differences emerged between the five groups on a number of issues:
- the concept and scope of the Advanced Informed Agreed Procedure (further: AIA procedure),
- LMOs intended for direct use as food, feed or processing (i.e. commodities),
- the precautionary principle and its application,
- labelling of LMOs and documentation accompanying LMO,
- liability and redress,
- the relationship between the Cartagena Protocol and international trade rules, and
- financial resources and capacity building.

Although most of these issues have also been raised and discussed intensively during the negotiations of other international environmental agreements, such as the 1989 Basel Convention on the Control of Transboundary Movements of Hazardous Wastes and Their Disposal,[16] the 1998 Rotterdam Convention on the Prior Informed Consent Procedure for Certain Hazardous Chemicals and Pesticides in International Trade[17] or the 2001 Stockholm Convention on Persistent Organic Pollutants,[18] due to the economic implications of international regulations on LMOs they were discussed and analysed more thoroughly during the negotiations. In particular, the precautionary principle, labelling of LMOs and the relationship between the Cartagena Protocol and international trade regulations emerged as central topics. During the negotiations the question was raised whether the Cartagena Protocol was an environmental agreement or an agreement which primarily dealt with trade issues and, therefore, should be subject to supervision of the World Trade Organisation. In the latter case a large number of States feared that

---

[16]   International Legal Materials 28 (1989) 652 et seqq.
[17]   International Legal Materials 38 (1999) 1 et seqq.
[18]   International Legal Materials 40 (2001) 532 et seqq.

the health and environmental aspects of the Cartagena Protocol would recede into the background.

III.   The Main Elements of the Cartagena Protocol

A. *Scope of the Cartagena Protocol*

According to its Article 4 the Protocol "shall apply to the transboundary movement, transit, handling and use of all living modified organisms that may have adverse effects on the conservation and sustainable use of biological diversity, taking into account risks to human health". Article 5 explicitly excludes "LMOs which are pharmaceuticals for humans that are addressed by other international agreements or organisations" from the scope of the Protocol.

Thus, not all LMOs fall as such within the scope of the Cartagena Protocol. It will be seen in the future application whether the limitation of the scope in Article 4 will give rise to disagreements and how they are to be solved between the parties concerned. Although, Article 7 para. 4 provides that the Conference of the Parties serving as the meeting of the Parties (further: COP/mOP) may identify in a decision LMOs to which the Advance Informed Agreement Procedure will not apply as these LMOs are "not likely to have adverse effects on the conservation and sustainable use of biological diversity". But it seems unlikely that such – political – decisions will be adopted by the COP/mOP concerning LMOs unless the current rather cautious – or even negative – attitude of a large number of States towards LMOs changes.[19] As a last resort in

---

[19]   Such a decision in accordance with Article 7 para. 4 of the Cartagena Protocol will have to be adopted according to the "rules of procedure". Article 29 para. 5 determines that the rules of procedure of the Convention on Biodiversity shall apply *mutatis mutandis*.

"Rules of procedure" for the Conference of the Parties of the Convention of Biodiversity have been adopted by Decision I/1 by COP1. But this decision did not include Rule 40 para. 1 which concerns the majority necessary for adopting decisions by the Conference of the Parties. Rule 40 para. 1 provides that if no consensus is to be found on decisions concerning matters of substance, the decision shall be taken by a two-thirds majority of the Parties present and voting. Financial Rules shall be adopted by consensus. Therefore, currently decisions of COPs have to be adopted by consensus.

It is unlikely that an agreement will be reached in the near future on the majority necessary for adopting decisions by COPs under the Convention on Biodiversity. Similar situations exist in regard to other interna-

case of a disagreement between Parties the dispute settlement procedures contained in Article 27 of the Convention on Biodiversity
will have to be applied.[20]

B. AIA Procedure

At the heart of the Protocol is the "Advance Informed Agreement" procedure which "shall apply prior to the first intentional
transboundary movement of LMOs for intentional introduction into
the environment".[21] Thus, the AIA procedure does not apply to
LMOs in transit through the territory of a Party[22] and the transboundary movement of LMOs destined for contained use.[23] Moreover, the AIA procedure does not apply to LMOs which are intended for direct use as food or feed, or for processing as specific
rules have been set up in Article 11 for them.[24]

The AIA procedure is triggered by the notification of the intended transboundary movement to the competent national authority of the Party of import. This notification in writing must contain
minimum information[25] and has either to be done by the exporting
party itself unless it has required the exporter (i.e. a natural or legal
person) to do so.[26] Within 90 days the Party of import has to acknowledge receipt of the notification in writing[27] and inform the

tional environmental agreements, e.g. the United Nations Framework
Convention on Climate Change 1992. Therefore, it is to be presumed
that any decision under the Cartagena Protocol would have to be taken
by consensus, and this seems very unlikely to achieve in regard to Article 7 para. 4.

[20] The Protocol does not contain provisions on dispute settlement itself.
Article 32 of the Protocol entitled "Relationship with the Convention"
states that "except as otherwise provided in this Protocol, the provisions of the Convention relating to its protocols shall apply to this
Protocol". Therefore, as no statement to the negative is contained in
the Protocol concerning the dispute settlement provisions of the Convention, Article 27 of the Convention also applies to disputes under the
Protocol.

[21] Article 7 para. 1.
[22] Article 6 para. 1.
[23] Article 6 para. 2.
[24] Cf. Article 7 paras. 2 and 3.
[25] See Annex I of the Cartagena Protocol.
[26] Article 8 para. 1.
[27] See Article 9 para. 1. According to Article 9 para. 2 this acknow-
ledgement shall state: the date of receipt of the notification; whether
the notification, *prima facie*, contains the necessary information; and

notifier whether the intentional transboundary movement may proceed only after the Party of import has given its written consent, or after no less then ninety days without a subsequent written consent.[28] A decision by the Party of import shall be communicated to the notifier and to the Biosafety Clearing-House[29] within 270 days after the receipt of the notification in writing. Such a decision which is to be taken on the basis of a risk assessment[30] – which is either carried out by the Party of import or the exporter[31] – may be:

- the approval of the import and how the decision will apply to subsequent imports of the same LMO,
- the prohibition of the import,
- requesting additional relevant information, or
- informing the notifier that the period is to be expended by a defined period of time.

A failure of a Party of import to communicate its decision within 270 days does not imply the consent to the intentional transboundary movement.

A decision taken may be reviewed by a Party of import in light of new scientific information.[32]

The above described procedure is similar to the "prior informed consent" procedure, known from other international environmental agreements,[33] but it is more detailed. It does not only set strict time limits and does not allow any intentional transboundary movement without the written consent of the Party of import, it also provides for a detailed decision-making process based on risk assessment. Risk assessment plays the central role in this process as any deci-

---

whether the Party of import will proceed according to its domestic regulatory framework (which is consistent with the Cartagena Protocol) or according to the procedure specified in Article 10.

[28] Article 10 para. 2.

[29] The Biosafety Clearing-House is established by Article 20 of the Cartagena Protocol in order to facilitate the exchange of information and assist Parties in implementing the Protocol.

[30] Article 15 and Annex III specify the risk assessment to be undertaken in detail.

[31] Article 15 para. 2.

[32] Article 12. Under certain circumstances the notifier may request the review of a decision (Article 12 para. 2).

[33] E.g. the 2001 Rotterdam Convention or the 1989 Basel Convention. Cf. *Kummer* (1995) 65 et seqq.

sion will be based on it. Thus, a minimum international standard is to be applied by the Part of import for its decision making process.

Other international environmental agreements do not give such a central role to risk assessment, as they list those products which are prohibited or restricted to be moved across Parties boundaries – e.g. the 1987 Montreal Protocol or the 1998 Rotterdam Convention.

C. Procedure for LMOs Intended for Direct Use as Food or Feed, or for Processing

As has been stated above, one of the most difficult issues during the negotiations was the question whether the AIA procedure should also be applied to LMOs intended for direct use as food or feed, or for processing. The Miami group feared that the application of the AIA procedure to such LMOs would produce competitive disadvantages for their "commodity exports" by way of the time consuming decision making process. As a compromise a special procedure was established to deal with the intentional trans-boundary movement of such LMOs:[34]

A party that makes a decision regarding domestic use of LMOs which may be subject to transboundary movements shall within fifteen days inform the Parties and provide minimum information.[35] Parties then may take decisions on the import of these LMOs under their domestic regulatory framework that is consistent with the objective of the Protocol. Furthermore, Parties shall make available to the Biosafety Clearing-House[36] their national laws, regulations and guidelines for the import of LMOs. In case of developing countries or countries with economies in transition which lack domestic regulatory frameworks Article 11 para. 6 provides that they may take a decision prior to the first import of such an LMO either on the basis of a risk assessment in accordance with Annex III or a decision taken within a period of 270 days.

Thus, the principle of explicit consent of the Party of import has been upheld also in regard to intentional transboundary movement of LMOs intended for direct use as food or feed, or for processing, but a more speedy procedure has been set up. Thereby, a balance has been found between the interests of the importing Party in regard to health and environmental concerns on the one hand and

---

[34] Article 11. See also the specific provisions of the Cartagena Protocol in regard to labelling and accompanying documentation below III.D.

[35] Annex II sets out the information to be provided.

[36] See Article 20.

those of the exporting Party not to unduly hamper transboundary movements of LMOs on the other hand.[37]

D. Labelling and Accompanying Documentation

Closely related to the procedures for the intentional transboundary movement of LMOs are issues of labelling and the accompanying documentation. They are to be seen as an important means for the identification of LMOs, provide information about them and ensure their appropriate handling.

Article 18 para. 1 requires Parties to ensure that LMOs intended for transboundary movement are handled, packaged and transported under conditions of safety, taking into consideration relevant international rules and standards. As has been described above a distinction has been made in regard to the procedures applied to transboundary movements of different types of LMOs depending on their intended use. The provisions concerning labelling and documentation follow this distinction. Thus, Article 18 para. 2 distinguished three different types in regard to labelling and documentation:

- "LMOs that are intended for direct use as food or feed, or for processing" have to be clearly identified as "may contain" living modified organisms and as not being intended for international introduction into the environment. Furthermore, a contact point for further information has to be provided.[38]
- "LMOs that are destined for contained use" have to be clearly identified as LMOs. The accompanying documentation must specify any requirements for the safe handling, storage, transport and use; the contact point for further information, including the name and address of the individual or institution to whom the LMOs are consigned.[39]
- "LMOs that are intended for intentional introduction into the environment" and "any other LMOs within the scope of the Protocol" have to be clearly identified as LMOs. Documentation has to specify the identity and relevant traits and/or characteristics, any requirements for the safe handling, storage, transport and use; the contact point for further information and, as appropriate, the name and address of the importer and exporter. Furthermore, the documentation has to contain a declaration that the

---

[37] Cf. also the provisions on the precautionary principle and labelling.
[38] Article 18 para. 2 (a).
[39] Article 18 para. 2 (b).

movement is in conformity with the requirements of the Protocol applicable to the exporter.

These – minimum – information requirements will not only ensure that individuals handling LMOs will be able to take the necessary precautions. Furthermore, in regard to LMOs intended for direct consumption information will be given to the consumer about the LMO in question and thus, enable her/him to make a deliberate choice. Article 18 para. 2 (a) further provides in regard to such LMOs that the Conference of the Parties serving as the meeting of the Parties to the Protocol shall take a decision on the detailed requirements for these purposes, including specification of their identity and any unique identification, no later than two years after the entry into force of the Protocol".[40]

E. Precautionary Principle

In the discussion on the elaboration of international rules concerning LMOs the precautionary principle/approach – or principle of precautionary approach as it is sometimes called – has played a central role. Due to the novelty of LMOs very little is known about their – short, medium or long-term - impacts on health and environment. Therefore, scientific certainty on the effects of LMOs cannot serve as a basis in the decision-making process, thus making the application of the precautionary principle an essential element.

The exact contents and the application of the precautionary principle have been discussed intensively both in international negotiations[41] and in academic writings,[42] and have been raised in international judicial proceedings.[43] It has given rise to numerous contro-

---

[40] Cf. Fn 19 above on the majority necessary to take decisions by the COP/mOP.

[41] See the discussions within various international bodies such as UNEP, OECD or Commission on Sustainable Development. Furthermore, the precautionary principle has been raised during discussions within the sessions of the Conference of the Parties of the United Nations Framework Convention on Climate Change, the Biodiversity Convention or the Convention on Trade in Endangered Species.

[42] E.g. *O'Riordan/Jordan* (1995); *Freestone/Hey* (1996); *Soljan* (1998) 211 et seqq.; *Boyle/Freestone* (1999); *Epiney/Scheyli* (2000) 85 et seqq; see also *Freytag/Jakl/Loibl/Wittmann* (2002).

[43] See *Nuclear Test* Cases 1995 (*New Zealand* v. *France*), ICJ Reports 1995, 381 et seqq.; *Gabcikovo-Nagymaros* Case (*Hungary* v. *Slovakia*), International Legal Materials 37 (1998) 162 et seqq.; *Southern Blue Fin Tuna* Cases (*Australia and New Zealand* v. *Japan*), Interna-

versies. So far no general understanding has been reached on the legal status and the contents of the precautionary principle.

As in other international environmental negotiations in recent years the application of the precautionary principle in the context of biosafety raised large controversies. Although none of the participants argued that the precautionary principle had no role to play in regard to LMOs, in particular, the Miami group feared that it could be used to the detriment of their commodity exports. Thus, an adequate role for the precautionary principle had to be found.

The Cartagena Protocol refers to the precautionary principle in a number of its provisions:

- Article 1 provides that the objective of the Protocol is to be achieved in accordance with the precautionary approach contained in Principle 15 of the Rio Declaration on Environment and Development,[44]
- the provisions on the AIA procedure specifically provide that "lack of scientific evidence due to insufficient relevant scientific information and knowledge regarding the extent of the potential adverse effects of a LMOs on the conservation and sustainable use of biological diversity in the Party of import, taking into account risks to human health, shall not prevent the Party from taking a decision, as appropriate, with regard to the import of the LMO in question [...] in order to avoid or minimize such potential negative effects".[45]
- A similar reference is also found in the general principles on risk assessment contained in Annex III which is to be undertaken by a Party of import deciding on an intended transboundary movement of an LMO.
- The wording of the provisions concerning the AIA procedure on the precautionary principle is restated in regard to the procedure for LMOs intended for direct use as food or feed, or for processing.[46]

---

tional Legal Materials 38 (1999) 1624 et seqq.; *Mox Plant* Case (*Ireland* v. *United Kingdom*), www.itlos.org.

[44] International Legal Materials 31 (1992) 874 et seqq.

[45] Article 10 para. 6.

[46] Article 11 para. 8.

Although the precautionary principle has been referred to in other international agreements[47] and international instruments before, the Cartagena Protocol is one of the first international multilateral agreements which included the precautionary principle not only in the preamble, the provisions on the objective of the instrument, but also in its substantive provisions.[48] Thus, the precautionary principle is not only a guideline that has to be taken into account in achieving the objective of the Cartagena Protocol, but it is legally binding. Therefore, Parties are permitted to base their decisions on admitting LMOs on their territory on the precautionary principle.

This underlines the fact that the Cartagena Protocol aims at preventing health and environmental impacts as may also be seen by the procedures established concerning intentional transboundary movements of LMOs and, among others, the provision on risk management.[49]

Although the inclusion of the precautionary principle in the Cartagena Protocol has to be seen as an agreement of the international community on the importance of precaution in dealing with LMOs, it did not clarify how the principle is to be applied in a concrete case. It will be seen in the future practice of the Parties which role the precautionary principle will play in the decision-making process concerning LMOs. Unlike Article 6 of the Straddling and Highly Migratory Fishing Stocks Agreement 1995, which sets out measures for the application of the precautionary approach, the Cartagena Protocol does not indicate how the precautionary principle is to be applied.[50]

F. Socio-economic Considerations

In the discussions concerns were expressed – mainly by representatives of developing countries as well by environmental and developmental NGOs – that LMOs would have effects on socio-

---

[47] See e.g. Article 2 of the OSPAR Convention 1992; preambular paragraph 9 of the Convention on Biodiversity 1992; Article 3 para. 3 of the United Nations Framework Convention on Climate Change; and Articles 5 and 6 of the Straddling and Highly Migratory Fish Stocks Agreement 1995.

[48] The Stockholm Convention on Persistent Organic Pollutants 2001 follows a similar pattern as the Cartagena Protocol.

[49] See Article 16.

[50] Cf. *Freestone* (1999).

economic conditions. In particular, they feared that the use of LMOs in agricultural production would have negative impacts on the rural population: economic disadvantages by changing the structure of markets for seeds and agricultural technologies[51] as well as health and environmental impacts could lead to unwanted social effects and changes. Therefore, they argued that socio-economic effects should be taken into account in a Party's decision on the import of LMOs. Others argued that the concept of "socio-economic considerations" was to broad to be applied in a AIA procedure.

The provision of the Cartagena Protocol dealing with socio-economic considerations does not specify them. Article 26 states that the Parties "in reaching a decision on import under this Protocol or under its domestic measures implementing the Protocol, may take into account, consistent with their international obligations, socio-economic considerations arising from the impact of LMOs on the conservation and sustainable use of biological diversity, especially with regard to the value of biological diversity to indigenous and local communities". Furthermore, the Parties are encouraged to cooperate on research and information exchange on any socio-economic impacts of LMOs, especially on indigenous and local communities.[52] The legal implication of Article 26 on the decision-making process on LMOs is unclear as its content is vague and its application is limited by "other international obligations" – e.g. international trade rules.[53] Still, it is to be seen as another factor underlining the cautious approach taken by the Cartagena Protocol towards the risks which may result from LMOs.

---

[51] Concerns were raised that agricultural communities in developing communities will become increasingly dependent on seeds supplied by multilateral corporations, as only such corporations would be able to invest in research and testing. Thus, local economies might face significant changes. It was argued that such a "globalisation" would only have negative impacts.

[52] Article 27 para. 2.

[53] See also below III.I.1 and 2.

G. Unintentional Transboundary Movements as well as Illegal Transboundary Movements

The Cartagena Protocol also addresses unintentional trans-boundary movements[54] and illegal transboundary movements.[55] Such instances occur without the consent of the Parties concerned and, therefore, are outside the direct control of the Party of origin.

In case of an unintentional transboundary movement potentially affected Parties are to be notified as soon as the Party of origin learns about the situation and consultations shall take place to determine appropriate responses and initiate necessary actions, including emergency measures.

Parties are obliged to adopt appropriate domestic measures aimed at preventing and, if appropriate, penalize transboundary movements of LMOs carried out in contravention of their domestic measures to implement the Protocol. Parties affected by such illegal movements may request the Party of origin to dispose, at its own expense, of the LMOs in question by repatriation or destruction, as appropriate.

Similar provisions are found in other international instruments, such as the Basel Convention.[56] They are to be seen as supplementing the provisions on intentional movement of LMOs, thus ensuring that the objective of the Cartagena Protocol is achieved.

H. Provisions which Aim at Ensuring that the Standards Set by the Cartagena Protocol are Implemented and Applied

The Cartagena Protocol – as has been described above – sets an international standard for the transboundary movement of LMOs in order to avoid adverse effects on the conservation and sustainable use of biodiversity. As stated in the Preamble of the Convention on Biodiversity "the conservation of biological diversity is a common concern of humankind".[57] This underlines that it is the interest of the Parties that the rules of the Cartagena Protocol are applied by individual Parties.

The Cartagena Protocol contains a number of provisions that aim at ensuring that its obligations are met:

---

[54] Article 17.
[55] Article 25.
[56] Cf. Article 9 of the Basel Convention.
[57] Preambular paragraph 3.

- Article 14 on bilateral, regional and multilateral agreements and arrangements,
- Article 24 on non-parties,
- Article 33 on monitoring and reporting, and
- Article 34 on compliance.

1. Bilateral, Regional and Multilateral Agreements and Arrangements

According to Article 14 para. 1 parties may enter into bilateral, regional and multilateral agreements and arrangements that are consistent with the objective of the Protocol and do not result in a lower level of protection. Thus, parties may agree to apply different rules on the transboundary movement of LMOs between them, but the international standards set in the Cartagena Protocol are to be upheld. This is also provided in Article 24 in regard of agreements or arrangements concluded between Parties and Non-Parties.[58]

These provisions of the Cartagena Protocol follow Article 11 of the 1989 Basel Convention on Transboundary Movement of Hazardous Wastes and Their Disposal which provides that Parties may enter into bilateral, multilateral or regional agreements or arrangements with Parties or Non-Parties provided that such agreements or arrangements do not derogate from the environmentally sound management of hazardous wastes and other wastes as required by the Convention.

This provision is of particular importance for States that are parties to a free-trade agreement, a custom union or a regional economic integration organisation (further: REIO) as specific rules concerning the transboundary movement of LMOs are admissible within the framework of such organisations.[59]

2. Relationship with Non-Parties

The Cartagena Protocol also intends to ensure that the standards of the Cartagena Protocol are also applied in regard to intentional

---

[58] Cf. below III.I.2.

[59] During the negotiations proposals were made to include a specific provision concerning REIOs. It was argued that without such a clause the Protocol it would not be sufficiently clear whether specific rules may be applied between member states of a REIO. This view was rejected during the negotiations and the conclusion was reached that these concerns in regard to REIOs were covered by Article 14 para. 1. Cf. on Article 11 of the Basel Convention *Kummer* (1995) 137 et seqq.

transboundary movements of LMOs to Non-Parties. Article 24 states that transboundary movements between Parties and Non-Parties shall be consistent with the objective of the Protocol. This provision follows similar provisions contained in other international environmental agreements, such as the 1987 Montreal Protocol on Substances that Deplete the Ozone Layer[60] or the 1989 Basel Convention on the Control of Transboundary Movements of Hazardous Wastes and Their Disposal[61] which deal with transboundary movements between Parties and Non-Parties. But the Cartagena Protocol deals differently with this issue than the Basel Convention. Article 4 para. 5 obliges parties to the Basel Convention not to permit "hazardous wastes or other wastes to be exported to a non-Party or to be imported from a non-Party". Therefore, transboundary movements of hazardous wastes between Parties and Non-Parties may only take place if a legal framework has been set up in accordance with Article 11.[62] In contrast, the Biosafety Protocol does not oblige parties to set up such a legal framework for transboundary movements of LMOs, but obliges parties to ensure that movements shall be consistent with the objective of the Protocol.

The solution found in the Biosafety Protocol differs even further from the provisions of the Montreal Protocol. According to Art. 4 parties are obliged to ban the import or export of any controlled substances under the Montreal Protocol to any non-party. Only if the meeting of the Parties of the Montreal Protocol determines that a Non-Party is in full compliance with the provisions on control measures for ozone depleting substances Parties may import from or export to the States in question.[63] Thus, trade between parties and non-parties is forbidden, whereas under the Biosafety Protocol parties are only obliged to act in accordance with the objective of the Protocol.

Such provisions raise questions in regard to the principle of *pacta sunt servanda* as contained in Article 26 and the provisons of the Vienna Convention on the Law of Treaties 1969 on treaties and

---

[60] Article 4.
[61] Article 7.
[62] Cf. e.g. Yearbook of International Environmental Law 8 (1997) 358 et seq. Austria and the Federal Republic of Germany concluded a bilateral agreement establishing environmentally sound management of hazardous wastes pursuant to Article 11 of the Basel Convention before Germany became a Party to the Basel Convention.
[63] Article 4 para. 8.

third States[64] as according to Article 24 of the Cartagena Protocol States which are not Parties to the treaty are affected by its provisions: Transboundary movements will only take place if the Non-Parties respect standards set in a treaty to which they are not a party. The wording of Article 24 is addressed to the Parties of the Cartagena Protocol which are obliged to ensure that transboundary movements are consistent with the objective of the Protocol. Thus, this provision on Non-Parties is only of legal concern, if this restriction on transboundary movements infringes rights under international law of the States concerned, e.g. resulting from international trade law.[65]

3. Monitoring and Reporting

These provisions also aim to ensure that Parties apply the standards set in the Cartagena Protocol by monitoring the implementation of its obligations and report thereon at intervals determined by the COP/mOP.[66] Such provisions are found in nearly all environmental agreements, but are also included in international agreements dealing with international trade or human rights.

4. Compliance

Like other international environmental agreements[67] the Cartagena Protocol provides for the elaboration of "cooperative procedures and institutional mechanisms to provide compliance with the provisions of this Protocol and to address cases of non-compliance. These procedures and mechanisms shall include provisions to offer advice or assistance, where appropriate".[68] The compliance mechanism is to be adopted by the COP/mOP. Currently, negotiations are undertaken on the establishment of such a compliance system.[69]

---

[64] See Articles 34 to 38 of the 1969 Vienna Convention on the Law of Treaties.

[65] On the relationship between international environmental agreements and GATT/WTO cf. *Cameron/Robinson* (1991); *Lang* (1995); *Tarasofsky* (1996); *Schoenbaum* (1997):

[66] Article 33.

[67] See e.g. the Montreal Protocol (Article 8), the United Nations Framework Convention on Climate Change (Article 13) and the Kyoto Protocol (Articles 16 and 18).

[68] Article 34, 1st sentence.

[69] See on the current status of the negotiations the "Report of the Open-Ended Meeting of Experts on a Compliance Regime under the Cartagena Protocol on Biosafety" (UNEP/CBD/ICCP/2/13/Add.1) and the

It is the aim of such procedures and mechanisms to ensure that States meet their commitments by giving advice and assistance through a "compliance committee" set up by the Parties.[70] By such a compliance process the international community underlines that it is its interest that all Parties honour their obligations.

The compliance procedure as envisaged by Article 34 is also to be seen in the context of Article 10 para. 7 that provides that COP / mOP shall "decide upon appropriate procedures and mechanisms to facilitate decision-making by Parties of import". This could lead to a certain overlap between procedures established under Article 34 and Article 10 para. 7 as well as the dispute settlement procedures of the Cartagena Protocol and may raise question on the relationship between the Cartagena Protocol and the GATT/WTO.[71]

H. Financial Mechanism and Resources; Capacity Building

The issues of the financial mechanism and resources were a central issue in the negotiations. Article 28 builds upon the provisions of the Convention and provides that the financial mechanism of the Convention is also the mechanism of the Protocol.[72]

Thus, the Cartagena Protocol follows the same lines as are known from other international environmental agreements in pro-

---

Report of the Intergovernmental Committee for the Cartagena Protocol on Biosafety on the Work of its Third Meeting" (UNEP/CBD/ICCP/3/10). The proposal of the Expert Group was discussed at the third meeting but no substantial progress has been made. The "draft procedures and mechanisms on compliance" may be found in UNEP/CBD/ICCP/3/10, pp. 34. The main issues to be resolved are the following:

- role of Principle 7 of the Rio Declaration on "common but differentiated responsibilities;
- the size and composition of the Compliance Committee;
- the question who may trigger the procedure;
- the question who may provide information to the Compliance Committee; and
- which measures may be taken if a Party is found in non-compliance.

[70] On compliance procedures under international environmental agreements see *Loibl* (1997); *Werksman* (1998); *Loibl* (1999); *Fitzmaurice/Redgwell* (2000).

[71] On this issue see below III.I.1.

[72] On the discussions about financial issues and capacity building in recent negotiations see the annual reports in the Yearbook of International Environmental Law.

viding financial resources to assist developing countries and countries with economies in transition in the implementation of their obligations.

The same also applies to the provisions of capacity building as contained in Article 22.

I. Relationship between the Protocol and the World Trade Organisation

The relationship between multilateral environmental agreements (further: MEAs) and GATT/WTO has been at the centre of intensive discussions in the last decades. It has been raised both in institutions dealing mainly with international trade issues on the one hand,[73] and institutions dealing mainly with international environmental issues on the other hand.[74] As has been stated above the relationship between the Cartagena Protocol and international trade rules was one key issue in the elaboration of an international agreement on LMOs.

While some States feared that the Protocol might be used by some Parties to restrict the free movement of goods in a discriminatory and arbitrary manner, in particular of commodities, other States feared that health and environmental concerns would only be of secondary importance to the free movement of goods.

These concerns were most evident in the discussions on the following issues:

- the relationship between the Cartagena Protocol and GATT / WTO in case States are Parties two both international agreements; and

---

[73] Cf. the Doha Ministerial Declaration which states that the question of MEAs and GATT/WTO should be a central issue for the future work of the Committee on Trade and Environment (WT/MIN(01)/DEC/W/1). Para. 31 (a) states that "with a view to enhancing the mutual supportiveness of trade and environment, we agree to negotiations without prejudging their outcome, on

(a) the relationship between existing WTO rules and specific trade obligations set out in multilateral environmental agreements (MEAs). The negotiations shall be limited in scope to the applicability of such existing WTO rules as among parties to the MEA in question. The negotiations shall not prejudice the WTO rights of any Member that is not a party to the MEA in question."

[74] Cf. the Malmö Ministerial Declaration adopted by the First Global Ministerial Environment Forum 2000 or decisions of the Governing Council of UNEP, e.g. Decision 21/4 on trade and environment.

- the effect of the Cartagena Protocol on transboundary movements of LMOs between Parties and Non-Parties.

1. Relationship between the Cartagena Protocol and GATT/WTO

As for the potential economic impact of the relationship between
the two treaties on the future transboundary movements of LMOs a
number of countries – in particular the Miami group – wanted to
ensure that the Cartagena Protocol would not affect the rights and
obligations deriving from any existing international agreement.[75]
Wording to this effect in the text of the Protocol would have meant
that the provisions of the GATT/WTO would prevail in case of a
conflict between the two treaties.[76]

Therefore, this proposal was strongly opposed by States arguing
that health and environmental concerns would not be taken adequately into regard as they feared that such conflicts would be settled under the dispute settlement system of GATT/WTO. They argued that the Protocol would become a "second-class" international
instrument.

Similar discussions have taken place in the negotiations of other
instruments. Most recently this issue was discussed during the negotiations of the PIC Convention (Convention on the Prior Informed Consent Procedure for Certain Hazardous Chemicals and
Pesticides in International Trade).[77] Agreement was reached that
environmental and trade policies are to be seen as mutually supportive, that the rights and obligations arising under other international
agreements are not to be affected and that no hierarchy is created

---

[75] Cf. the proposal put forward on "Relationship with other international
agreements" (Article 31 of the Draft Protocol, UNEP/CBD/
ExCOP/1/2) which read as follows:
"The provisions of this Protocol shall not affect the rights and obligations of any Party to the Protocol deriving from any existing international agreement to which it is also a Party, except where the exercise
of those rights and obligations which cause serious damage or threat to
biological diversity."

[76] See Article 30 of the Vienna Convention on the Law of Treaties 1969
which deals with the application of successive treaties relating to the
same subject manner. Para 2 determines that "when a treaty specifies
that it is subject to, or that it is not to be considered as incompatible
with, an earlier or later treaty, the provisions of that treaty prevails".
Cf. also *Sinclair* (1984) 94 et seqq.

[77] International Legal Materials 38 (1999) 1 et seqq.

between the various international instruments dealing with international trade in chemicals.[78]

Thus, the negotiations for the Biosafety Protocol centred on an issue which has been discussed in a number of international forums, such as the OECD and the Committee on Trade and Environment of the WTO. Although these discussions did not lead to an overall conclusion, they showed that the relationship between the various instruments in the environmental field and the WTO has to be judged on a case to case basis. The main multilateral instruments which gave rise to this debate – the 1989 Basel Convention on Control of Transboundary Movement of Hazardous Wastes and their Disposal, the 1987 Montreal Protocol on Substances that Deplete the Ozone Layer and the 1973 Convention on International Trade in Endangered Species – have not been seen as contrary to GATT/WTO as they are seen to fall within the exception of Article XX GATT.[79] Already Principle 12 of the Rio Declaration on Environment and Development laid down the relevant principles of the relationship between trade and environment.[80] The same approach

---

[78] The relevant parts of the preamble read as follows:
"Recognizing that trade and environmental policies should be mutually supportive with a view to achieving sustainable development,
Emphasizing that nothing in this Convention shall be interpreted as implying in any way a change in the rights and obligations of a Party under any existing international agreement applying to chemicals in international trade or to environmental protection,
Understanding that the above recital is not intended to create a hierarchy between this Convention and other international agreements".

[79] During the negotiations of the Montreal Protocol the question of the compatibility with GATT was raised. Upon request a legal expert from the GATT Secretariat stated that trade restrictions were permissible under Art. XX GATT, as they could be considered "necessary to protect human, animal and plant life or health" and "relating to conservation or exhaustion of exhaustible natural resources" (*Benedick* (1991) 91; see also *Tarasofsky* (1996) at 52 et seq.; *Loibl* (1998) at 421 et seqq.).

[80] Principle 12 reads:
"States should cooperate to promote a supportive and open international economic system that would lead to economic growth and sustainable development in all countries, to better address the problems of environmental degradation. Trade policy measures for environmental purposes should not constitute a means of arbitrary or unjustifiable discrimination or a disguised restriction on international trade. Unilateral

was followed in the PIC-Convention's preambular text – as described above – underlining the mutual supportiveness of the two fields of international law.

In the context of the negotiations of the Cartagena Protocol the question of the relationship between environment and trade was – due to the volume of trade in commodities – of essential importance for a number of countries. The Cartagena Protocol follows the patterns of the above mentioned international environmental agreements on this delicate issue. It deals with this relationship in the preamble. Its relevant paragraphs read as follows:

> "Recognizing that trade and environment agreements should be mutually supportive with a view to achieving sustainable development,
>
> Emphasizing that this Protocol shall not be interpreted as implying a change in the rights and obligations of a Party under any existing international agreement,
>
> Understanding that the above recital is not intended to subordinate the Protocol to other international agreements".

These paragraphs underline that the two fields of international law have to be seen as being mutually supportive and none of these provisions is subordinated to other instruments in general.[81] Therefore, the general rules of international law apply to the relationship between the Biosafety Protocol and the WTO.[82]

---

actions to deal with environmental challenges outside the jurisdiction of the importing country should be avoided. Environmental measures addressing transboundary or global environmental problems should, as far as possible, be based on an international consensus" (International Legal Materials 31 (1992) 876 et seqq.).

Similar references to the relationship between trade and environment are found in Chapter 2 of Agenda 21 (A/Conf.151/26 (Vol. I), 17 et seqq.) and the "Non-legally binding authoritative statement of principles for a global consensus on the management, conservation and sustainable development of all types of forests" (para. 13; International Legal Materials 31 (1992) 881 et seqq.).

[81] The wording chosen in the preamble carefully avoids to state that the Protocol is not to be considered as incompatible with other treaties, thus puts the Protocol on the same level with other treaties.

[82] See the 1969 Vienna Convention on the Law of Treaties.

Following the decision in the *Shrimp-Turtle* Case, the trade restrictions are to be regarded as permissible, as they have been agreed and would be applied multilaterally.[83]

A dispute between Parties about the application and interpretation of the Cartagena Protocol might arise, if a Party – relying on the provisions of the Protocol concerning the AIA procedure – prohibits the import of certain goods containing LMOs and the other Party alleges that the provisions of the Cartagena Protocol were not applied adequately or the import was unduly delayed. It is to be hoped that if such a situation arises the concerned parties will be able to find a solution by making use of the dispute settlement provisions of the Convention on Biodiversity which apply for the Biosafety Protocol. As Article 32 states: "except as otherwise provided in this Protocol, the provisions of the Convention relating to its Protocols shall apply to this Protocol". Thus, the provisions on dispute settlement contained in the Convention are also applicable to the Protocol.[84]

But the affected Party might choose to challenge a Party's behaviour under the WTO dispute settlement system. It could argue

---

[83] Cf. *Brack* (1998).

[84] Article 27 under the heading "settlement of disputes" reads:

"1. In the event of a dispute between Contracting Parties concerning the interpretation or application of this Convention, the parties concerned shall seek solution by negotiations.

2. If the parties concerned cannot reach agreement by negotiation, they may jointly seek the good offices of, or request meditation by, a third party.

3. When ratifying, accepting, approving or acceding to this Convention, or at any time thereafter, a State or regional economic integration organization may declare in writing to the Depository that for a dispute not resolved in accordance with paragraph 1 or paragraph 2 above, it accepts one or both of the following means of dispute settlement as compulsory:

a) Arbitration in accordance with the procedure laid down in Part 1 of Annex II;

b) Submission of the dispute to the International Court of Justice.

4. If the parties to the dispute have not, in accordance with paragraph 3 above, accepted the same or any procedure, the dispute shall be submitted to conciliation in accordance with Part 2 of Annex II unless the parties otherwise agree.

5. The provisions of the Article shall apply with respect to any protocol except as otherwise provided in the protocol concerned".

that the trade restrictions taken are not within the scope of the Cartagena Protocol or the provisions of the Cartagena Protocol have been misused. Thus, the WTO dispute settlement system would have to interpret and apply the Cartagena Protocol. Only if it concludes that the situation in question is not covered by the Cartagena Protocol it would only then have to decide whether the Party's behaviour in question is in conformity with GATT/WTO.

This situation is not to be seen as a subordination of the Cartagena Protocol to GATT/WTO, but rather as a question on the forum to settle such a dispute. So far no rules have been established on the choice of fora for such disputes.

2. Effects of the Cartagena Protocol on the Transboundary Movement of LMOs between Parties and Non-Parties

The provision on the effects of transboundary movements of LMOs between Parties and Non-Parties – as has been described above – aims at ensuring that the standards set by the Cartagena Protocol are implemented (and complied with) by its Parties in the interest of health and environmental concerns. But it also raises concerns that it could lead to restrictions of transboundary movements of LMOs between Parties and Non-Parties which would be in conflict with GATT/WTO. Any such restriction which falls within the scope of the general exceptions under Article XX GATT or the relevant provisions of the SPS-Agreement would be justified. But trade restrictions for LMOs outside the scope of these provisions would be a violation of GATT/WTO.

The reports of the Dispute Settlement Panels have been criticised in the past for giving only limited scope to the exception in regard to health and environmental concerns.[85] In the *Tuna-Dolphin* Cases the Panels held that the United States import restrictions on tuna caught with nets that unintentionally also trapped dolphins were not justified under Article XX as the restrictions aimed to protect the extra-territorial environment.[86] But the Appellate Body's Report in *United States – Import Prohibition of Certain Shrimp and Shrimp Products*[87] demonstrates that under specific circumstances

---

[85]   Cf. *Weinstein/Charnovitz* (2001).

[86]   Report of the Panels in *United States – Restrictions on Imports of Tuna* 1991 (International Legal Materials 30 (1991) 1594 et seqq.) and 1994 (International Legal Materials 33 (1994) 839 et seqq.).

[87]   International Legal Materials 38 (1999) 118 et seqq.

Article XX may have a broader scope. The United States had imposed an import ban on shrimp from countries that did not require their fishing fleet to use devices designed to safeguard endangered sea turtles. The Appellate Body stated that the sea turtles covered by US law were "all known to occur in waters over which the United States exercises jurisdiction. Of course it was not claimed that *all* populations of these species migrate to, or transverse, at one time or another, waters subject to United States jurisdiction". The Appellate Body further stated that it does "not pass upon the question of whether there is an implied jurisdictional limitation in Article XX (g), and if so, the nature or extent of that limitation". It noted "only that in specific circumstances of the case before us, there is a sufficient nexus between the migratory and endangered marine populations involved and the United States for purpose of Article XX (g)".[88] Thus, the Appellate Body ruled that the United States were permitted to ban imports to safeguard an endangered species also found outside its jurisdiction.

Following this ruling in the *Shrimp-Turtle* Case trade restrictions on LMOs by Parties to the Cartagena Protocol would be in conformity with GATT / WTO if a sufficient nexus exists between the LMOs and the Party concerned.

Finally, it should be noted that the example of the Montreal Protocol is only of limited relevance for the Cartagena Protocol. In case of import and export bans of substances within the scope of the Montreal Protocol[89] it was affirmed that these trade restrictions were permissible under Article XX GATT/WTO as they could be considered "necessary to protect human, animal, or plant life or health" and "relating to conservation or exhaustion of exhaustible natural resources".[90] This statement does not apply to the Cartagena Protocol as LMOs do not have an effect on all States as does the depletion of the ozone layer. Therefore, trade restrictions between Parties and Non-Parties under the Cartagena Protocol and their compatibility with GATT/WTO have to be judged on a case to case basis following along the lines set out above.

J. Issues to be Further Elaborated

Although the Cartagena Protocol establishes a framework for the handling, use and transboundary movement of LMOs a number of

---

[88] Para. 133.
[89] See Article 4 of the Montreal Protocol.
[90] Cf. *Benedick* (1991) 91; *Loibl* (2001) at 63 et seqq.

issues were not solved during the negotiations and were left to be further elaborated. Some of them have been already mentioned above, such as the question of labelling of LMOs and products which contain or may contain LMOs intended for direct use as food, feed or for processing; procedures and mechanisms to facilitate decision-making by Parties of import, e.g. by assistance rendered by a "roster of experts"; and a compliance system which should give advice and assistance to parties which are in non-compliance or in potential non-compliance. Moreover, another issue "liability and redress", which proved to be a difficult subject during the negotiations, was agreed to be addressed in the future work under the Cartagena Protocol. Agreement was reached that COP / mOP shall "adopt a process with respect to the appropriate elaboration of international rules and procedures in the field of liability and redress for damage resulting from transboundary movements of LMOs, analysing and taking due account of the ongoing processes in international law on these matters, and shall endeavour to complete this process within four years".[91] This Article reflects the view-point that any provisions on liability and redress have to take into account the substantive obligations of the instrument to which they apply. Only when they are known these issues can be addressed adequately. Moreover, the issue of liability and redress has given rise to a number of discussions both on the international and national level, e.g. the work of the International Law Commission on liability.[92] Article 27 refers to these international developments and intends to build on their experience.

IV.   The Cartagena Protocol – a First Evaluation

The history and the main provisions of the Cartagena Protocol demonstrate that in elaborating rules on the transboundary movement of LMOs a delicate balance has to be found between health and environmental concerns on the one hand and international trade rules on the other hand. The result is an international agreement that primarily deals with health and environmental concerns, although it also affects international trade of LMOs.[93]

---

[91]   Article 27.

[92]   *Hafner/Pearson* (2000) at 23 et seqq.

[93]   See Opinion 2/00 of the European Court of Justice which dealt with the question of the legal basis for the conclusion of the Cartagena Protocol by the European Community. The Commission had argued that the

Moreover, the Cartagena Protocol does not only deal specifically with international trade, but with any transboundary movement of LMOs. Thus, it sets general standards to be applied by Parties to ensure that health and environmental concerns are met. In doing so the Cartagena Protocol has addressed new – controversial – issues. By including the precautionary principle/approach as well as socio-economic aspects it has included new aspects in considering whether new technologies and products should be permitted to be used.

Concerning the relationship between environment and trade – which has been one of the central issues of the negotiations – the Cartagena Protocol follows the patterns of other international environmental agreements such as the PIC Convention or the Convention on Persistent Organic Pollutants. But the Cartagena Protocol addresses trade concerns in more detail than other international environmental agreements have done before. It is a delicate balance that has been found. The Protocol addresses the relationship between the two areas of international law as such, but also contains other provisions which affect international trade: it deals with issues such as "non-discrimination" between imported and locally developed LMOs[94] as well as provisions on implementation of the Cartagena Protocol on the national level and establishes a special procedure for commodities.

As has been demonstrated above, if the Parties to the Cartagena Protocol comply with its provisions conflicts with international trade rules are very unlikely to arise. But in case a Party does not comply with the Cartagena Protocol the issue of the relationship between GATT / WTO and the Cartagena Protocol might raise problems.

Cartagena Protocol should be concluded by the European Community on the basis of Article 133 EC (Title on "common commercial policy") and Article 174 (4) EC. It argued that the Protocol deals primarily with external trade and only certain limited issues addressed in the Protocol concern the environment. The ECJ stated that it is clear from Article 1, which refers to Principle 15 of the Rio Declaration on Environment and Development, that the Protocol pursues an environmental objective, highlighted by mention of the precautionary principle, a fundamental principle of environmental protection referred to in Article 174 (2) EC. It concluded that Article 175 (1) EC was therefore the correct legal basis to conclude the Cartagena Protocol.

[94]   Article 16 para. 4.

Furthermore, the Cartagena Protocol includes both provisions on compliance and dispute settlement – as most other international environmental agreements. Like those agreements it does not address the relationship between the two mechanisms in depth, but just follows the idea expressed in other international agreements that the compliance procedure is without prejudice to dispute settlement mechanisms. Although so far no conflict between the two systems has arisen in practice, the likeliness that the question on the relationship between them might arise is bigger in the context of the Cartagena Protocol. An issue of non-compliance concerning the transboundary movement of an LMO is very likely to have a direct effect on an exporting Party, thus allowing the issue to be raised either before the compliance body or put before a means of dispute settlement, or even before both.

As the Cartagena Protocol has not entered into force yet, practical experience in its interpretation and application is lacking. Although the drafters agreed on solutions that take into account most concerns raised, a number of issues have been left open or are only addressed in a general manner. Thus, only the day to day operation will show whether the Cartagena Protocol is an efficient means to deal with transboundary movements of LMOs.

V.   Concluding Remarks

In general the Cartagena Protocol on Biosafety is as an international instrument which follows patterns known from other international environmental agreements. But it is to be seen as a step forward as it deals with an area which is very closely connected to international trade. It has succeeded in building a bridge between environmental and health concerns on the one hand, and trade concerns on the other. Although a number of issues have left to be solved in the future, it has established a framework for the transfer of LMOs without unduly restricting international trade and taking into account environmental and health issues at the same time. By establishing a strict time-frame for the AIA procedure and determining the criteria for decision-making it ruled out arbitrary and discriminatory decisions by States.

The Cartagena Protocol is an international agreement whose main goal is to ensure that health aspects resulting from LMOs are taken into account effectively. Although trade of LMOs was a central topic during the negotiations it has to be underlined that the scope of the Cartagena Protocol is broader: it also covers transboundary movements, transit, handling and use of LMOs for e.g. scientific purposes. Such non-commercial transfers might be less spectacular, but their impact on health and the environment might be more serious. Thus, the Cartagena Protocol aims primarily at the reduction of risks resulting from modern biotechnology and not at the facilitation or restriction of international trade. In this regard the Cartagena Protocol has to be seen as an international instrument which constitutes a careful balance between the different interests.

Bibliography:

J. Alder / D. Wilkinson (1999), Environmental Law and Ethics, London 1999.

R. E. Benedick (1991), Ozone Diplomacy – New Directions in Safeguarding the Planet, Cambridge, MA 1991.

A. Boyle/D. Freestone (1999) (eds.), International Law and Sustainable Development – Past Achievements and Future Challenges, Oxford/New York 1999.

D. Brack (1998), The *Shrimp-Turtle* Case: Implications for the Multilateral Environmental Agreement – World Trade Organisation Debate, Yearbook of International Environmental Law 9 (1998), 13-19.

J. Cameron / J. Robinson (1991), The Use of Trade Provisions in International Environmental Agreements and their Compatibility with the GATT, Yearbook of International Environmental Law 2 (1991), 3-30.

A. Epiney (1997), Umweltrecht in der Europäischen Union – Primärrechtliche Grundlagen, Gemeinschaftliches Sekundärrecht, Köln 1997.

A. Epiney/M. Scheyli (2000), Umweltvölkerrecht. Völkerrechtliche Bezugspunkte des schweizerischen Umweltrechts, Bern 2000.

M. Fitzmaurice / C. Redgwell (2000), Environmental Non-Compliance Procedures and International Law, Netherlands Yearbook of International Law 31 (2000), 35-66.

D. Freestone (1999), International Fisheries Law Since Rio: The Continued Rise of the Precautionary Principle, in *A. Boyle / D. Freestone* (eds.), International Law and Sustainable Development – Past Achievements and Future Challenges, Oxford/New York 1999, 135-164.

D. Freestone/E. Hey (1996) (eds.), The Precautionary Principle and International Law – The Challenge of Implementation, Boston/ Den Haag 1996.

E. Freytag/Th. Jakl/G. Loibl/M. Wittmann (2002) (eds.), The Role of Precaution in Chemicals Policy, Wien 2002.

G. Hafner/H. Pearson (2000), Environmental Issues in the Work of the International Law Commission, Yearbook of International Environmental Law 11 (2000), 3-51.

L. Krämer (1998), E. C. Treaty and Environmental Law, London ³1998.

K. Kummer (1995), International Management of Hazardous Wastes – The Basel Convention and Related Legal Rules, Oxford 1995.

W. Lang (1995), Les mesures commerciales au service de la protection de l'environnement, Revue Générale de Droit International Public (1995), 545-566.

G. Loibl (1997), Dispute Avoidance and Dispute Settlement in International Environmental Law – Some Reflections on Recent Development, in: Comité Jurídico Interamericano, Curso de Derecho Internacional, XXIV (1997), 101-126.

G. Loibl (1998), Trade and Environment – A Difficult Relationship, New Approaches and Trends: The Kyoto Protocol and Beyond, in *G. Hafner et al.* (eds.), Liber Amicorum Seidl-Hohenfeldern, Den Haag 1998, 419-443.

G. Loibl (1999), Compliance with International Environmental Law – The Emerging Regime under the Kyoto Protocol, in *W. Benedek/H. Isak/R. Kicker* (eds.), Development and Developing International and European Law – Essays in Honour of Konrad Ginther on the Occasion of his 65th Birthday, Frankfurt 1999, 263-283.

G. Loibl (2001), The role of international organisations in international law-making: international environmental negotiations – an empirical study, Non-State Actors and International Law 1 (2001), 41-66.

S. Murphy (2001), Biotechnology and International Law, Harvard International Law Journal 42 (2001) No. 1, 47-139.

T. O'Riordan / A. Jordan (1995), The Precautionary Principle in Contemporary Environmental Politics, Environmental Values 4 (1995), 191-212.

R. O'Rourke (1998), European Food Law, Bembridge / Isle of Wright 1998.

R. Paarlberg (2000), The Global Food Fight, Foreign Affairs 79 (May/June 2000), 24-38.

Th. Schoenbaum (1997), International Trade and Protection of the Environment: The Continuing Search for Reconciliation, American Journal of International Law 91 (1997) No. 2, 268-313.

H. Schulte (1999), Umweltrecht, Heidelberg 1999.

I. Sinclair (1984), The Vienna Convention on the Law of Treaties, Manchester ²1984.

L. Soljan (1998), The General Obligations to Prevent Transboundary Harm and its Relation to Four Key Environmental Principles, Austrian Review of International and European Law 3 (1998) No. 2, 209-232.

P.-T. Stoll (1999), Controlling the Risks of Genetically Modified Organisms: The Cartagena Protocol on Biosafety and the SPS Agreement, Yearbook of International Environmental Law 10 (1999), 82-119.

R. G. Tarasofsky (1996), Ensuring Compatibility Between Multilateral Environmental Agreements and the GATT/WTO, Yearbook of International Environmental Law 7 (1996), 52-74.

M. Weinstein / S. Charnovitz (2001), The Greening of the WTO, Foreign Affairs 80 (November/December 2001), 147-156.

J. Werksman (1998), Compliance and the Kyoto Protocol: Building a Backbone into a "Flexible" Regime, Yearbook of International Environmental Law 9 (1998), 48-104.

Deirdre Curtin

Digital Governance in the European Union Anno 2002. Freedom of Information Trumped by 'Internal Security'?

> *"It is usually much easier to reach an agreement if there are no listen-*
> *ers. It is not a question of wishing for secrecy, but of being able to act*
> *more efficiently"*

(EU Commissioner and Vice-President *Neil Kinnock* speaking on the issue
of having open decision-making in the Council of Ministers)[1]

> *"Ensuring that innocent people do not become the victims of counter-*
> *terrorism measures should always be an important component of any anti-*
> *terrorism strategy."*

(UN High Commissioner for Human Rights, *Mary Robinson*)[2]

I.   Introduction

Counter-terrorism strategies pursued after 11 September have at
times undermined efforts to enhance respect for human rights. Not
only have measures been taken in several parts of the world that
suppress or restrict individual rights but as recently highlighted by
the UN High Commissioner on Human Rights, *Mary Robinson*,
there "is increasing evidence that particular groups such as human
rights defenders, migrants, asylum-seekers and refugees, religious
and ethnic minorities, political activists and the media are being
specifically targeted".[3] This is true also in the context of the EU and
the effects may be exacerbated by measures taken by the EU Council of Ministers behind closed doors. The focus of this paper is limited to attacks on freedom of information in the aftermath of September 11 and in particular the effects of the counter-terrorism
strategy followed by the European Union in that regard. This specific issue should however be placed and understood in its broader
context of the effects of the counter-terrorism efforts on human
rights in general and on certain groups in particular.

The US government, followed by certain other governments
around the world, has striven to increase "internal security" by *inter
alia* embarking on a path of secrecy unprecedented in recent years.
In particular freedom of information laws have come under attack
and have been reduced or even suspended in the quest for more

---

[1]   Stated at a press conference in Copenhagen, 19 March 2002, Danish
      newspaper *Jyllands-Posten*.

[2]   See statement by *Mary Robinson*, United Nations High Commissioner
      for Human Rights, Commission on Human Rights, 58th session, 20
      March 2002, http://www.unhchr.ch/huricane/huricane.nsf/view01/
      858EF20492884DD6C1256B82003E2A38?opendocument.

[3]   See, *ibid.*

control over the sources of knowledge. In Canada for example the Anti-Terrorism Act contains a (much-criticised) clause enabling the Minister of Justice to suspend the effect of Access to Information provisions.[4] In the UK, despite 25 years campaigning for a Freedom of Information Act, *Tony Blair* suspended its entry into force in its entirety for a period of four years.[5] In the US, the Attorney General issued a directive to the heads of Agencies to encourage those Agencies to deny access more often to public records if a claim of invasion of privacy or a claim of breach of national security could be alleged.[6] The release of presidential records was moreover halted indefinitely by the assertion of executive privilege.[7] US State legislatures on the whole followed suit attacking open records and meetings laws.[8] Secrecy is in demand: it gives those in government exclusive control over certain areas of knowledge and thereby increases their power, making it more difficult for even a free press to check that power. The culture of secrecy is sometimes referred to as a virus, spreading from one part of government to another, also transnationally, invading concerns where national internal security plays no role at all. The stakes are high: avoiding that freedom of information as a fundamental (constitutional) value of democracy is sacrificed on the altar of internal security, as opportunistically interpreted.

At the level of international organizations the Member State governments of the European Union have *inter alia* used the tragic

---

[4]   See, *A. Roberts*, The department of secrets: The Chretien cabinet is using fears of terrorism to further restrict public access to information, Ottawa Citizen, October 18, 2001, page A 19.

[5]   For details see the UK Campaign for Freedom of Information: http://www.cfoi.org.uk/doubleblow131101pr.html. The FOI Act itself was passed on 30 November 2000 and must be fully implemented by November 2005. An implementation timetable was announced by the Lord Chancellor in the House of Lords on 13 November, and is set out in the Government's First Annual Report on implementation published on 30 November. The timetable confirms that the right of access will not come into force until January 2005. However a provision requiring authorities to produce publication schemes describing information they publish proactively will be phased in earlier, starting with central government departments in November 2002.

[6]   The text of the *Ashcroft* October 12 Memorandum is available at: http://www.usdoj.gov/oip/foiapost/2001foiapost19.htm.

[7]   For details see, *Dalglish / Leslie / Taylor* (2002).

[8]   See, *Dalglish / Leslie / Taylor* (2002).

events of 11 September as a means of adopting legislation in a
highly secretive fashion which gives far-reaching powers to law
enforcement agencies in the various Member States and at the
European Union level to issue a European Arrest Warrant, to freeze
assets and to include demonstrators in data-bases designed for terrorists.[9] At the same time the newly adopted access to information
law in the EU[10] is being implemented in a restrictive fashion with
wide derogations that are used to give priority to internal security
concerns. The point is that the problems that are now emerging in
the context of the European Union and that are the focus of this
paper are not new problems but rather have become more sharply
defined and more urgent given the speed and the content of the
EU's reaction to the terrorist offensive. The problems relate both to
process (the secretive manner in which highly sensitive and far-
reaching decisions are taken) and to substance (in particular the
encroachment on civil liberties such as the freedom of expression,
the freedom of movement, the freedom of assembly and the right to
privacy). And moreover they are digitally embedded in different
ways.

Whereas one might think of digital government as the provision
of services in a more customer-orientated and accessible fashion
(getting citizens "on-line" and not "in-line" as the saying goes) and
the provision of information on-line in an accessible format on both
processes and structures, one can also define digital government as
embracing the use of data-banks and information by a government
or public administration which are digitally embedded and partially

---

[9]   See, in particular, Proposal for a Council Framework Decision on the
      European Arrest Warrant and the Surrender Procedures between Mem-
      ber States, Council 14867/1/01REV1 (Brussels, 10 December 2001)
      approved by the European Parliament on 6 February 2002. See also,
      EP Report on that proposal, A5-0003/2002, 9 January 2002. See also,
      Draft Framework Decision on the execution in the European Union of
      orders freezing assets or evidence, Council 12636/01, 10 October
      2001. See, Council Framework Decision on Combatting Terrorism,
      148445/1/01REV1, of 7 December 2001 which defines "terrorism" in
      such a way that many fear could still embrace protestors: see State-
      watch at www.statewatch.org.

[10] Regulation (EC) No 1049/2001 of the European Parliament and of the
      Council of 30 May 2001 regarding public access to European Parlia-
      ment, Council and Commission documents, OJ L 145/43 (31 May
      2001) that entered into force on 3 December 2001.

available internally to different organs and agencies of government through a closed intra-net facility. It is in this latter wider sense that I will approach the question of digital government in the EU and the manner in which it has taken specific shape and substance. It therefore also includes some discussion of the manner in which the EU system of classified information has been adopted and implemented. Should a sophisticated international organization such as the EU which is replacing by means of supranational law, constitutional and legislative provisions on all kinds of fundamental issues at the national level (from constitutional rights of access to information to the laws on extradition between Member states, the laws on terrorism et cetera) adopt the lowest common denominator or a high standard of protection given the more difficult legitimacy crisis faced by the EU than any Member Nation State? Moreover, given the fact that the Europeanisation of a very wide range of policy areas takes place at much more distance to individual citizens and that the citizens have such difficulty in understanding the incredibly complex decision-making processes and structures at the EU level, does that not make it even more necessary that information is made accessible by digital means in a very timely, very user friendly and very exhaustive fashion? The answers to these questions have of course everything to do with our vision of the nature of the democracy we wish to construct at the European level and how it will interact with the national level.

I do not discuss the nature of the European Union in terms of the classical supra-national/inter-governmental distinction but rather as a (rapidly evolving) institutional entity displaying both in the underlying normative provisions and the practice of the various institutional actors strong evidence of (institutional) unity (paragraph II.A.). In other words this theoretical background will underpin my approach to the question of (democratic) governance in the European Union in a manner which takes account of all the actors acting under the auspices of the European Union as such, recognising at the same time that developments on what used to be the "fringes" of the EU, justice and home affairs for example, now gradually displays supra-national features in terms of the underlying legal system. I then move to the question of governance in the European Union and in particular the manner of exercise of the executive tasks by the public administration at the EU level (paragraph II.B.). These tasks have traditionally been carried out by the European Commission but in recent years and in particular in the field of justice and home affairs a much more variegated and multi-level structure has sprung-up in topsy-like fashion without any appropriate constitutional framework or sufficient checks and balances to capture the complexity of the contemporary phenomenon of public administration as exercised at the level of the EU itself and in partnership with the other levels of governance. Finally, I focus on the digital aspects of governance at the EU level and its evolution in practice (paragraph III.) as well as highlighting by means of a case-study how far-reaching legislation is adopted in secret by one arm of the legislative power in the EU, the Council of Ministers.

II.   Institutional Unity and a Complex EU Public Administration Map

A. The Evolution of Institutional Unity Across the EU?

As recently as a few years ago it could be shown that regarding the existence and nature of a legal system of the European Union there was no clear legal picture at all and certainly no consensus of opinion.[11] In a contribution to the study of evolving European Union law the present author co-authored an article published in 1999 entitled "The EU as a 'Layered' International Organization: Institutional Unity in Disguise" which presented what can perhaps now be regarded as reflecting an Utrecht approach to the nature of an evolving EU legal order.[12] This latter article concentrated on two main questions: whether the European Union could be qualified as an international organization in legal terms, and if so, whether its institutional legal system is developing in practice towards institutional unity, albeit in disguise. In this article the main focus was the European Union itself. We analysed the Union as a legal institution and defended the thesis that the Union is an international organization with a unitary but complex character. This conclusion was not only based on the analysis of the EU-treaties and other basic instruments, but also on the so-called legal practices, i.e. forms of legal action which are – explicitly or implicitly – employed in order to make the legal institution an operational entity. The analysis of the legal practices concerned mainly what the Union had done between 1993 and 1998 in the two new 'pillars', the CFSP (Common Foreign and Security Policy) and the CJHA (Co-operation in Justice

---

[11] For an overview and references, see *Curtin/Dekker* (1999) 83–85, 92-103; *Shaw* (2000) Part I.
[12] *Curtin/Dekker* (1999).

and Home Affairs). Three – interconnected – levels of Union activity were identified, namely, first, the international legal status of the Union, second the functioning of the main organs of the Union, and, third, the application of some fundamental principles and their effects on the legal protection of the citizens of the Member States. The conclusion was that the legal system of the European Union as such was developing as an institutional unity and that this conclusion did not exclude that, at the same time, spaces for developing a variety of sub-legal systems were created. Of course, some of these sub-legal systems already existed, such as the three 'pillars', but also within these 'pillars' legal sub-systems could be traced and be further developed.

One of the remaining problematic aspects of the unity of the legal system of the Union is the relationship with the national legal order of the member states. Already at the level of principle the question is whether the legal system of the Union as such includes the national legal orders of the member states, and if that is the case how should we go about understanding the relationship between them? With regard to the European Communities the relationship with the national legal orders has taken shape to a very considerable extent. Even if both legal systems, under the general overall umbrella of international law, must qua legal validity be considered as relatively independent one from the other they must nevertheless be considered as firmly intertwined through the operation of several general legal principles such as those relating to the applicability of EC law in the national legal orders and the principle of loyalty. However it is not at all clear whether the same understanding can be said to apply to the relationship between the legal system of the *Union* and that of the member states. Some authors even defend the diametrically opposing view that the Union can only be understood in terms of a pure treaty regime and thus that within the Union there can only be horizontal relations between the 'high contracting' parties.[13] But even if one accepts the view that the Union is more correctly to be understood as constituting in its own right a legal person – in particular in the shape of an international organization – it may be clear that the Union is a separate entity in its own right but that as such does not reveal the nature of its relationship with the legal orders of its member states. That latter – vertical – relation-

---

[13] This view is most clearly and consistently expressed in *Koenig / Pechstein* (1995).

ship can be framed either on the basis of the (classical) legal principle of the autonomy of the member states or on the basis of the
(communautarian) legal principle of the unity of the legal systems
of the organizations and its members.

In a further article we analysed the relationship between the
Union legal system and the national legal systems from two perspectives.[14] In the first place, we explored the angle of the structural
principles concerning the validity and application of the Union's
legal system in the national legal orders of the member states. The
second perspective we developed in analysing the relationship between the Union legal order and that of its member states relates
precisely to some of the consequences for those citizens in the
member states. In particular, we explored the question to what
extent the member states can still be regarded as autonomous in the
sense that they are free to go their own way with regard to the
protection of their citizens. This relationship was analysed mainly
from the perspective of the principle of loyalty, as laid down in art.
10 of the EC Treaty and looked at the manner in which that principle is evolving and the important lessons we may draw on the nature of the relationship between the two systems. We have concluded that on the basis of the rules laid down by the EU system
itself (certain) Union law is capable of being directly applicable in
the national legal orders and that moreover national judges and
administrative authorities are under an obligation to give indirect
effect to Union law. In addition we have attempted to explore the
manner in which a principle of loyalty is taking shape at the level of
the EU legal order itself as an illustration of the nature of the relationship between the EU legal order and those of the national legal
orders as well as of assistance in the characterisation process of that
intricate and evolving relationship.

In a sense what may appear at times a rather abstract and theoretical exercise, of interest mainly to international and European
lawyers and legal theorists, is also motivated by a rather concrete
and practical desire to contribute to the ongoing debate about the
future of Europe. After all, given the reality now of the European
Union as such and the manner in which it has penetrated both the
social and legal understanding, why continue to obfuscate a relatively clear institutional reality by drawing elaborate distinctions
between the Community legal order as such and the supposedly

---

[14]   See further, *Curtin/Dekker* (2002).

purely intergovernmental Union order (a social and legal fiction as we hope to have illustrated) and thereby placing outside the range of common understanding the constitutional positioning of various important EU actors? Moreover does the concept of institutional unity (both in a horizontal and vertical sense) not contribute to better understanding of the relationship between the various legal orders involved and potentially have a contribution to make in the coming discussion on the manner in which powers must be shared across the various governance levels and applied in the various legal systems?

If anything has emerged from the debate on the future of the EU in the past months it is the overwhelming inability of the citizens in the various (existing and candidate) member states to understand what the EU as such is, what its tasks are, what the role of its institutions and various other actors and organs are and how this political system relates to their own national political and constitutional systems.[15] It is this exercise of increasing understanding and rationalizing the seemingly irrational and obtusely complicated where the real challenge lies in the coming months and years. And what is essential in all of this is finally that the perspective of the citizen assumes central place and importance in genuinely trying to come to terms with the fact that at the beginning of the twenty-first century there is such widespread distrust in political institutions and politicians at all levels of our increasingly inter-connected societies.[16] That centrality of the individual is in our view enhanced by an approach that recognises and attempts to come to terms with the various levels of the multi-governance structure of the EU and the various intertwined legal systems. The digital medium is ideally suited to the nature of the challenge ahead. But first some mapping out of the uneven terrain of public administration and its undergrowth in the EU context must be attempted.

---

[15] See, in particular, the very useful and revealing study European Commission (2001).

[16] In this regard the long-awaited and much proclaimed *White paper on European Governance*, COM (2001) 428 of 25 July 2001, by the Commission can be regarded as a relatively weak and at times not very profound contribution to this critical and on-going debate. See further EUI Internet Symposium on the White Paper at *Joerges / Meny / Weiler* (2001).

B. The Evolution of EU Public Administration?

In our work on the evolving institutional unity of the EU *Dekker* and I traced the role which the various institutions played or were beginning to play across the spectrum of EU policies, thus weakening the sense of a strict supranational (EC) / intergovernmental (EU) divide. In terms of a developing EU-wide public administration both the role of the Commission as well as that of the Council, in particular its General-Secretariat, was referred to. Since then further developments have taken place, especially in practice which underline the trends already visible in outline back in 1998. One can certainly not refer to "institutional unity" in the sense of one central public administration at the level of the EU. The overall picture is indeed more nuanced and fragmented than that. That said it is possible to trace certain institutional trends which are present across the spectrum of EU policy-making and which are especially pronounced in the newer policy areas.

In the first place it has become especially clear that a secret administrative culture is at the heart of many of the EU's problems and exists right across the spectrum of its institutions and organs. When the *Santer* Commission felt forced to resign in the aftermath of the publication of the First Report of the Committee of Independent Experts in March 1999 (hereafter: CIE) the boils of secrecy and of lack of (collective) responsibility of the Commission were rather publicly lanced.[17] The resulting crisis was, for many Eurosceptics, empirical vindication of the so-called "rottenness in the heart of Europe".[18] The gist of the general problem, according to the Committee, was openness and transparency, as linked with responsibility and accountability. These fundamental principles needed in the CIE's view to urgently permeate the European Union's political and administrative culture *in all areas and at all levels.*

Part of the Commissions' problems carrying out its various tasks, highlighted by the CIE in its reports, lay in the fact that, over the last decade, it had, cumulatively, simply acquired too many, without a concomitant increase in resources.[19] Overload led to con-

---

[17] *Curtin* (2001).
[18] *Craig* (2000).
[19] See, for detail, Committee on Independent Experts, volumes 1 and 2. http://www.europarl.eu.int/experts/default_en.htm. See, in particular,

fused priorities and to inadequate co-ordination.[20] Moreover the Commission felt forced to seek refuge in a rather elaborate system of "contracting out" certain (not so precisely delineated) tasks.[21] The problem was that this did not happen in any agreed constitutional framework subject to the usual checks and balances but took place on an entirely discretionary and *ad hoc* basis. In addition the Commission has shed certain other tasks to an increasing range of functional agencies. On the national (Member State) side of public administration, this, too, has become much more variegated and complex, both as a result of the "hiving-off" of functions to (quasi-) private sector parties and as a result of increasing trends towards decentralisation and regionalization at national levels of administration. The latter trend, in particular, has forced the Commission to recognise that, when it talks both in terms of "indirect administration" at national level and in terms of a more inclusive and participatory approach to policy-making, it needs to take account of the flurry of regional and local actors which de-centralisation processes have spawned in the past decade or more.[22]

The secretive administrative culture condoned by the CIE is fed *inter alia* by the power that "experts" and national civil servants have acquired within the centralised power structure of the Commission via the instigation and exponential growth of the comitology procedures.[23] The growth of committees, both formal and informal, in the field of justice and home affairs is much less well documented but is notoriously extensive[24] and concerns the Council in particular. In these new policy domains the experts that are involved in the system are mainly national civil servants, law enforcement officers etc. In recent years there is a marked growth in the position, tasks and influence of informal committees with no legal basis whatsoever (e.g., Chief of Police tasks, also other examples in CFSP and external relations).[25]

Chapter 7, "Integrity, responsibility and accountability in European political and administrative life", volume 2.

[20] *Metcalfe* (2000) 817.

[21] See, too, *Craig* (2000).

[22] Among the "new actors of Europe" according to the White Paper Governance Team, June 2001
http://europa.eu.int/comm/governance/docs/index_en.htm.

[23] See *Joerges/Vos* (1999).

[24] See, in general, *Peers* (2000).

[25] See further, *Curtin/Dekker* (1999).

Another layer of opaque public administration is contributed by
the increasing number of (sensitive) tasks carried out by a growing
number of independent bodies such as Europol, pro-Eurojust, etc.
often established by the Council and with no very clear role for the
Commission in terms of relationship and or oversight. These bodies
often maintain independent and far-reaching relationships with third
countries and other international organizations.[26] In addition the
Council itself has, via its General Secretariat, acquired tasks similar
to those carried out at the national level in certain policy areas, in
particular justice and home affairs. Such tasks have gradually
grown in importance and significance since the Treaty of Maastricht.[27] To categorise the latter as simply "inter-governmental" in
nature and effect is belied by both the practice and the effects of the
measures in question.[28] Moreover the rise of separate data-bases in
the context of the EU is striking as well as the efforts made to enable the independent bodies operating on the fringes of the EU to
have access to such data-bases alongside the central institutional
actors in this context, the Commission and the Council.[29]

---

[26] See for example, Initiative of the Kingdom of Sweden with a view to
the adoption of a Council Act amending the Council Act of 12 March
1999 adopting the rules governing the transmission of personal data by
Europol to third States and third bodies adopted by JHA Council, 28
Feb. 2002. Council Decision authorising the Director of Europol to
conclude a Cooperation Agreement between Europol and the Republic
of Iceland. Council Decision authorising the Director of Europol to
conclude a Cooperation Agreement between Europol and the Kingdom
of Norway. Council Decision authorising the Director of Europol to
conclude a Cooperation Agreement between Europol and Interpol. Political agreement at 28 / 29 May 2001 JHA Council; formally adopted
by Transport / Telecoms Council, 27/28 June 2001. Draft agreement
between Europol and the Swiss Confederation, not yet adopted.

[27] See *Curtin/Dekker* (1999).

[28] See further, *Curtin/Dekker* (1999).

[29] See further, Council Regulation laying down certain rules to implement Regulation (EC) No 2725/2000 concerning the establishment of
"Eurodac" for the comparison of fingerprints for the effective application of the Dublin Convention. JHA Council on 28 February 2002
adopted the implementing measures for the Eurodac central database
of fingerprints of all asylum-seekers (6328/02, 25.2.02). "Creation of
anti-globalisation units and a database for demonstrators" - "Spanish
Government measures concerning the anti-globalisation movement" -

In conclusion it can be said that the exercise of public administration at the EU level is fragmented both horizontally and vertically. Moreover there is little attempt to date to integrate ideas on holding the public administration accountable and making it more responsive to citizens into an overall (legal or constitutional) framework. Rather the moves that have been made in recent years to impose principles of good governance (rule of law, transparency, access to information, accountability amongst others) often overlook the fact that there is more to rule-making at the level of the EU than simply the Commission and Council (and European Parliament). In fact it has largely been thanks to the efforts of the Ombudsman that even with regard to the fundamental principle in a democracy of the public's right of access is extended, despite the absence of a formal legal obligation, to many of the other actors and organs operating as it were on the fringes of EU activity.[30]

III.   The Digital Dimension of EU Governance

A. The Evolution of a Citizens' Right to Access EU Information?

1. The Legal Background

The first question is whether in the context of EU activity citizens (the public) enjoy in terms of civil and political rights a right of access to information, including the right to receive that information digitally. The background to the question is the way in which access to information has taken shape within the EU over the course of the past eight years or so. First, the aftermath of the

---

"Spain: Creation of anti-globalisation units and a database", 6904/02. Database of visas, 6645/02 of 1 March 2002, not yet available.

[30] See the European Ombudsman's Decision and Recommendation in the own-initiative inquiry into public access to documents held by Community institutions, initiated in June 1996 (616/PUBAC/F/IJH). This Decision is included in the EO Annual Report 1996, 80. Amongst the fifteen bodies and institutions that were subject of his first inquiry are: the EP, the agencies, the ESC, Committee of the Regions and the EIB. In April 1999, the Ombudsman launched another own-initiative inquiry into public access to documents held by four EU bodies, which were not yet operational at the time of the earlier inquiry, namely the European Central Bank (ECB), the European Agency for Safety and Health at Work, the Community Plant Variety Office (PVO) and Europol. See the Annual Report of the European Ombudsman over 1999, 245-259.

Danish "no" to the Maastricht Treaty prompted the first serious
attempts to institutionalize a system of public access to EU
information (documents) which was made operational by the three
main decision-making institutions in a joint Code of Conduct on the
matter. The institutions then made this non-binding Code operational in principle in their own specific institutional context by
adopting decisions respectively based on their own internal Rules of
Procedure. At the time this approach was said to highlight the conviction of the three institutions that this issue of public access to
their documents was something that they had voluntarily assumed
in their internal rules but that they were under no legal obligation to
do so in the absence of any explicit Treaty rules on the subject. In
due course, other institutions and bodies, among which the EP and
the ECB, have adopted similar rules to those of the two political
institutions, mostly pursuant recommendations issued by the Ombudsman in the context of enquiries into the existence of rules on
public access to documents.[31] Despite a number of important limitations, the most critical ones being the exclusion of documents
drawn up by third parties and a number of widely drawn exceptions,[32] the Code of Conduct seemed to work quite well in practice.[33] In the event a request for access had been refused, citizens
could either bring a case to the Court of Justice or complain to the
European Ombudsman.

The role that the European Court of Justice has played teasing
out the implications of the rules adopted by the various institutions
and laying down the broad parameters of their action has been a
significant one. It can very generally be said that whereas the Court
adopted a role of fairly marginal scrutiny of the actions of the institutions in practice it nevertheless, in a whole series of cases testing the exact limits, successfully kept pressure on the institutions to
make incremental steps in changing their culture of secrecy (by
means of requirements such as to balance interests, to scrutinise the
documents on a case by case basis, to grant access to parts of

---

[31] See, *ibid.*

[32] In particular, the exception concerning the protection of the interest in
the confidentiality of the institution's deliberations has been problematic.

[33] In 2001 the Council received 1.234 applications for a total of 7.950
documents. The statistics of the Council over 2001 show further a high
percentage of disclosure, in respect of the Council 88% of the documents have been released for the procedure as a whole.

documents and to interpret the scope of the internal rules broadly, such as for example applying to comitology committees as an effective part of the Commission and as applying to decision making in the two supposedly inter-governmental fields , CFSP and CJHA).[34]

This approach was confirmed by the Court of Justice in a recent judgment on the subject in the case which *Heidi Hautala*, a Green MEP from Finland, brought against the Council for refusing her access to a Report of the Working Group on Conventional Arms Exports.[35] It was drawn up under the COREU special European correspondence system and was therefore not distributed through the normal channels for distributing Council documents. In the Council's practice, the COREU network is reserved for questions falling within Title V of the Treaty (CFSP). Distribution of documents transmitted via the COREU network is restricted to a limited number of authorised recipients in the Member States, the Commission of the European Communities and the General Secretariat of the Council. The General Secretariat of the Council refused access to the report stating that it contained "highly sensitive information, disclosure of which would undermine the public interest as regards public security". In this case the Court implicitly accepted the view that the concept of the right of access to documents must be interpreted as meaning a right of access to the information contained in the documents and applied it to the facts of the case. Actually the truly radical significance of the judgment in this case lies in the fact that the Court does not exclude documents on a restricted digital "intra-net" from the scope of the access to information rules.

It was only the Treaty of Amsterdam in 1999 that gave a constitutional / Treaty basis to access to documents was given and provision made that the three institutions would adopt a legal instrument by co-decision setting out the limits and exceptions to the principle by 1 May 2001. With minor delay but a highly problematic and secretive procedure a draft regulation was indeed adopted. It entered into force recently on 3 December 2001. To some extent it reflects the *status quo* and in certain respects it is more restrictive.[36] This is in particular the case with regard to the issue of inter-

---

[34] See further, *Curtin* (2000).
[35] Case C-353/99, *Heidi Hautala MEP* v. *Council,* judgment of 6 December 2001, nyr.
[36] See, in general on the pre-Regulation *status quo*, *Curtin* (2000).

nal preparatory documents, with regard to sensitive/classified documents and with regard to the fact that it basically overrides more liberal national laws on the subject.[37]

2. The Evolving Digital Practice of the EU Institutions

The reaction of the institutions to the case-law of the Court in particular and to advances in ICT has been to introduce a more structured and pro-active approach to access to their infomation than was their initial inclination or practice. Part of the reaction was to establish a hyper-link (the Europa server) and to make a host of information available through the medium of Internet. As time went on, the approach of various institutions and bodies became more sophisticated in this new digital context. Thus, the Council in 1999 set up a digital register of its documents in a relatively accessible and user-friendly fashion. This has gradually been expanded and refined. Thus, in December 2001 a total of 1,195 documents were listed as having been archived during the month. During December the full-text was available for 735 documents and not available for 460 documents, 62% were available and 38% were not – and some of those were made available were the result of people making applications for their release.[38] A further unjustifiable limitation in the manner in which the Register is operationalized is the fact that even though the Council Register notes the partial release of a document it does not give direct access online to the parts that have been released but rather it must be formally applied for again and again under the new Access regulation.

Moreover it expanded the information it made available on the Internet in terms of its committees, their schedule of meetings and the documents available before the meetings. Also for the first time (in 2000) both the Council and the Commission now include information on the new policy making fields of CFSP and CJHA on their Internet sites and in the Register of Council documents. Article 11 of the new Regulation states that each institution shall provide a public register, that "references to documents shall be recorded without delay" and that the registers must be operational by 3 June 2002. The Commission Rules of Procedure however is very half-hearted in its approach and if followed will almost certainly

---

[37] For critical commentary see Statewatch
http://www.statewatch.org/news.

[38] Source: www.statewatch.org.

breach the obligation imposed by Article 11 of the new Regulation. It states that: "the coverage of the register provided for by Article 11 of Regulation (EC) No 1049/2001 shall be extended gradually". The European Parliament's formally adopted "Register of references" make no such limitations. However, its internal discussions indicate that there are at least four categories of documents which will never be made accessible to the public.[39] By June 2002 it is planned that the European Parliament's public register will only cover legislative documents under what is called a "minimal" stage one of the proposed Register, with stage two and three following at some undefined point in the future.

In complaints brought before the Ombudsman aspects of the (digital) practice of the institutions may also be challenged. Thus it appeared that the Council in its already operational Register does not maintain a list that records all documents circulated in advance or put before the Council in its various compositions and thus constituted part of the decision-making process. Moreover the Public Register of Council Documents that went on-line on 1 January 1999 does not include the category of "confidential, restraint, SN and non-paper documents" in the register and these categories have also been excluded from agendas and the outcomes of proceedings. A real problem is perceived as the fact that the classification category of "RESTRICTED" is not covered by the new Regulation despite having been greatly expanded in practice in recent years. These complaints have been the subject of an inquiry by the Ombudsman and the complaint has been the subject of a rare Special Report by him. The matter is currently pending before the Petitions Committee of the European Parliament.

One of the main ways that the Access to Documents Regulation adopted by the EU is surprising however is precisely the fact that it contains few explicit digital provisions other than to provide that access to the registers which will be set up by the Commission and the European Parliament (the Council already has one) will be provided electronically (Article 11, paragraph 1). In the United States the FOIA originally adopted in 1946 was adapted a few years ago to the new digital reality in an e-FOIA that is quite far-reaching in the scope of obligations placed on the public administration in terms of making their information available digitally and providing

---

[39]   See, in particular, www.statewatch.org.

access in that way.[40] In particular it introduced an "electronic reading room" facility. Moreover when a request for a particular record has been made three times, this record needs to be made available in the Electronic Reading Room. This seems to favourably influence the number of FOIA requests received with potential applicants first checking digitally available material before submitting a request. NASA headquarters in the US system for example receives about 450 FOIA requests per year but the headquarters' electronic reading room averages about 10,000 hits per month.[41] The issue of digital information provision is also at the leading edge in countries such as the Netherlands that has known an Act to Promote Open Government (WOB) since 1978 (amended in 1993). This legislation deals with public access to information about the administration laid down in documents. An E-WOB is currently before the Dutch Parliament with the purpose of providing greater access to information on-line. Of course the concerns are very different and much more basic in a sense in Member States at the other end of the spectrum, such as the UK that has just announced a four year delay on the implementation of its FOI Act, which was the subject of a twenty year campaign in the first place to get it on the statute books, and Germany which still has no federal law on access to information, although a draft is currently being debated.[42]

3. Refining the Digital Practice: the Issue of Access to Classified Information Raises the Stakes

The Council and EP Regulation on Access to Documents in its article 9 makes special provision for a whole category of so-called "sensitive documents" which basically constitute classified documents (Top secret, secret and confidential) originating from the institutions or the agencies established by them, from Member States, third countries or international organizations. The scope of the documents covered by these special rules includes "public security" documents, with the consequence that documents relating to justice and home affairs are covered. It even appears that documents within the scope of the "financial, monetary or economic

---

[40] The e-FOIA amendments were subject to a staged implementation deadline: the last of the provisions were to be phased into US agency operations by the end of 1999.

[41] See *Botterman et al.* (2000).

[42] See the web-site of the Federal Ministry of Home Affairs, http://www.bmi.bund.de.

policy" exception could conceivably be considered "sensitive documents" under the new rules. The effect of a classification as a sensitive document is that only certain persons can process the application for access to those documents and that reference to them can only be recorded in the register or released with the consent of the originator. This not only gives tremendous power to the originator of a document (who also controls downgrading) but it also assumes that even the document number of a document included in a register will somehow threaten public security! Given that originators have full control over classification, registration and release there is no access whatsoever to such documents when authored by the Council or by third parties. This is a real problem in practice with documents originating from the US, from other international organizations such as NATO and even from the Member States themselves being effectively given a veto over access to information in the EU context.[43] However if the recent Court of Justice's judgment in the *Hautala* case is applied to the category of sensitive documents then the originator of a sensitive document could only veto access to the truly sensitive parts of the document and access would under the general EU access rules have to be granted to the non-"sensitive" parts of a document. [44]

According to the new legislative system the three institutions concerned (Council, Commission and European Parliament) had to adopt detailed internal rules on security rules and classifications (in their rules of procedure), which they did before Christmas 2001.[45]

---

[43] See further, Statewatch home page: www.statewatch.org.
[44] See, "Council of the European Union disagrees on giving access to the public of positions taken by EU governments":
www.statewatch.org/news
[45] See, specific provisions regarding access to documents in Annex III to the Council's Rules of Procedure, as amended by Council Decision of 29 November 2001, 2001/840/EC, O.J. L 313/40, 30.11.2001. The detailed rules on access to documents are laid down in an Annex to the Commission's Rules of Procedure, as amended by Commission Decision of 5 December 2001, 2001/973/EC, ECSC, Euratom, O.J. L 345/94, 29.12.2001. See EP Decision adapting its Rules of Procedure to the provisions of European Parliament and Council Regulation (EC) No 1049/2001 on public access to Parliament, Council and Commission documents, 13 November 2001 (Rule 172 and Annex VII) and EP Bureau Decision of 28 November 2001 on public access to European Parliament documents, O.J. C 374/1, 29.12.2001.

The most elaborate is that of the Commission which in effect clearly indicates an agenda of setting up a EU wide network of freely exchangeable "classified information" among the institutions, bodies, offices and agencies of the EU via intra-net or other digital means. Moreover third states, international organizations and other bodies may also be included in this (digital) network and download such information provided that they operate equivalent security rules themselves. The only glint of light from the outside is the fact that references to classified information "may" be included in the (digital) Register of its documents.

To complicate matters even further, the Commission comes up with a definition of EU classified information as "any information and materials, the unauthorised disclosure of which could cause varying degrees of prejudice to EU interests, or to one or more of its Member States" irrespective of its origin. Moreover one of the central purposes of its new rules that entered into force on 3 December is to "safeguard EU *information handled in communications and information systems and networks* against threats to its confidentiality, integrity and availability". This seems to be an important statement of purpose as far as digital governance by the European Commission is concerned. Closer examination reveals that IT information security (IT-INFOSEC) rules apply to "all communications and information systems and networks" handling information classified as EU "confidential" and above.

B. The Adoption of Secret Legislation and Access to Information: a case-study post 11 September

The example of the Framework Decision on the European arrest warrants is a good illustration in terms of substance just how far the Europeanisation process has gone within the context of the EU. It amounts to a rewriting of national laws on extradition and removes some of the safeguards (procedural and substantive) that have traditionally applied in various national contexts. It leaves little to no discretion to Member States once adopted although it will formally have to be implemented into national law. But this can involve virtually no parliamentary input even at that stage. According to the provisions of the Anti-Terrorism, Crime and Security Act[46] adopted by the UK Parliament it can be implemented by Ministerial order and would not even at the stage of national implementation neces-

---

[46]   http://www.statewatch.org.

sarily have to go before national parliament. The situation may of course be different in other Member States. Be that as it may the provisions of the Framework Directive once adopted may well prove in practice directly applicable in the national legal orders and as such be enforced by the administrative and law enforcement arms of the respective Member States.[47]

The only legal quality the provisions of the Framework Decision will in any event not enjoy is direct effect and the only reason is that the framers of the Treaty of Amsterdam specifically stated this in the relevant legal article (Article 34 (2) (b) Treaty on European Union, ex Article K.6). In other words citizens in the various Member States will not be able to rely directly on its provisions and to enforce them in precedence to other national rules before a national court. But the Court of Justice will have jurisdiction to entertain preliminary questions from national courts on questions of interpretation and validity of its provisions (Article 35 (1) Treaty on European Union, ex Article K.7) and in that context to give effect to principles of Union law such as the principle of indirect effect and to a certain extent the principle of supremacy.

My focus is on the process of its adoption and the information available via Internet and other sources at the time of its adoption by the Council (early December 2001). I will trace through the information available via Internet on the Europa server[48] (Council[49] and Commission[50] home pages) on the draft Framework Decision on European Arrest Warrants[51] just prior to its adoption by the Council. I will then compare the information put before the two parliaments I have been in a position to study: the Dutch parliament and the UK parliament. Finally I will explore the documents available on the Internet site of an organization of civil society, Statewatch.[52]

On 19 September 2001 the Commission put forward a draft Commission proposal that can be found on Internet via a link with Eurolex[53] under "legislation in preparation".[54] To find it one needs

---

[47]   See further on this point *Curtin / Dekker* (2002).
[48]   http://europa.eu.int.
[49]   http://ue.eu.int/en/summ.htm.
[50]   http://europa.eu.int/comm/index_en.htm.
[51]   http://europa.eu.int/eur-lex/en/com/pdf/2001/en_501PC0522.pdf.
[52]   http://www.statewatch.org.
[53]   http://europa.eu.int/eur-lex/en/index.html.
[54]   http://europa.eu.int/eur-lex/en/search/search_lip.html.

to know more or less the number one is looking for. A more accessible source is to be found under the link on its home page "justice and home affairs" and then onto the newly established site "Terrorism – the EU on the move"[55] where under the heading "documents" one will find the Commission's draft (COM (2001) 521).[56] In its own words as an introduction to its new section on its web page "the European Commission has put forward proposals aimed at eliminating legal loopholes in the EU that may help *radicals suspected of violence escape justice*" (emphasis added). These proposals were examined by the EU Council of Ministers of Justice and Home Affairs on 20 September 2001[57] and the extraordinary European Council meeting on 21 September 2001.[58] The special Article 36 Committee of senior officials subsequently continued examination of the draft and came up with various reworked drafts during the course of the ensuing months. No reference to Council negotiations or even a link with the web page of the Council is provided under this specially construed terrorism site of the Commission.

If one then went to the Council's web page one found access to certain earlier drafts on the European Arrest Warrant. For example, under the activities headed "justice and home affairs",[59] one could not track anything down as it fell neither under the heading "future proposals for action" nor "lists of decisions adopted under JHA". One in fact had to know that one must go separately to the topic of "transparency" and then to the heading "access to documents / register"[60] in order to try and literally track down possible Council texts. A search in the register with the words "European arrest warrant" produced (at that time) a list of eight entries. This contained the Commission proposal, a Council document transferring the Commission proposal to all delegations and six sets of draft Council texts / amendments (dating in time from 24 September through 10 October to 31 October to 14 November to 19 November to 4 December). Only the text from the Article 36 Committee to CORE-

---

[55] http://europa.eu.int/comm/justice_home/news/terrorism/index_en.htm.

[56] http://europa.eu.int/comm/justice_home/unit/terrorism/
      terrorism_sg_en.pdf.

[57] http://europa.eu.int/comm/justice_home/news/terrorism/
      documents/concl_council_20sep_en.pdf.

[58] http://europa.eu.int/comm/justice_home/news/terrorism/
      documents/concl_council_21sep_en.pdf.

[59] http://ue.eu.int/jai/default.asp?lang=en.

[60] http://register.consilium.eu.int/utfregister/frames/introshfsEN.htm.

PER / Council of 10 October 2001 could be downloaded via the Internet and was a very initial text asking for some political guidance on very specific issues of principle. The four substantive Council texts indicating where the Council's consideration of the Commissions proposal is at are indicated as "not available" on the Internet.

But *Sherlock Holmes* turned to the heading "agendas and timetables to meetings"[61] exploring whether further substantive information could be gleaned as to the content of the Council's work on this particular subject. From the timetables of meetings, it could be learned that a meeting of JHA Council was planned on 6 and 7 December. Under "agendas" of meetings of the Council, on 6 December, the day the scheduled meeting on JHA is to commence, the latest agenda for meetings refers to those that took place a week or more previously! Drawing a blank and being of a rather stubborn disposition, *Sherlock Holmes* turned to the heading "Article 36 Committee" to see if anything could be reconstructed from what is available there, after all this is the preparatory instance of the Council's draft decision. But the latest agendas for this important committee date back to the meeting it held on 12 and 13 November, some several weeks previously (from 9 November). Out of curiosity he looks whether there indeed one might at least find the draft Council decision of 31 October but discovers only that the provisional agenda is that and no more but that a document number is given which on rechecking the Council register turns out to be the draft of 31 October. So on 12 and 13 November the Article 36 committee was discussing the draft of 31 October and since then three further draft texts have been produced and distributed.

Watson on the other hand was active at the same time in two Member States in particular. He discovered that on 12 November the Select Committee on the EU of the House of Lords made a Report *inter alia* on the European Arrest Warrant proposal in order to inform an early debate in the House on some of the proposed EU legislation concerned with terrorism.[62] During the course of drawing up the report they took evidence from the relevant Government Minister and published as is customary that evidence. Both the report itself and the debate in the House of Lords reproduced in Han-

---

[61] http://ue.eu.int/cal/en/index.htm.
[62] http://www.parliament.the-stationery-office.co.uk/pa/ld200102/
ldselect/ldeucom/34/3402.htm.

sard are available on the Internet.[63] The state of the negotiations are those reflected in the Belgian presidency document of 31 October; at the time the evidence was taken and the report made that version was available only in French.

The Dutch Parliament is consulted as a matter of national constitutional law. On 19 November it received from the government what is known as an annotated agenda of the meeting to take place in Brussels on 6 and 7 December. That agenda is published also on the Internet as an official document of the Dutch Parliament (in Dutch).[64] It included the draft arrest warrant but referred also to the version of 31 October, which was supplied in Dutch and to the two later texts, one available in English and the most recent only in French. The explicit rider was added to the annotated agenda to the effect that in any event "it was the subject of on-going negotiations and that the government would provide further information when it became available". On 5 December the Dutch Minister of Justice appeared before the relevant scrutiny committee of the Dutch parliament, only one day before the start of the relevant Council meeting. At that meeting it was given oral information as to the state of play in negotiations but was not given the latest draft of 4 December as that was stated not to be available at that time. The Dutch Parliament was in these circumstances asked to go ahead with agreeing to the substance of a text not made available to it despite the text of the Dutch constitutional provisions to the effect that it would receive such documents fifteen days in advance. In the event the Dutch parliament along with the UK and Sweden imposed parliamentary scrutiny reserves on the text as agreed in Council. Such reserves cannot alter the content of the Decision agreed upon in Council but must be lifted before it can enter into force.

At the same time as *Watson*'s assiduous work in the national context, his young trainee had stumbled across the existence of an organization called Statewatch which maintained a very extensive and very easily accessible web site plus a special Observatory on the anti- terrorism measures under discussion post 11 September.[65] Statewatch describes itself as "a non-profit-making voluntary group founded in 1991 comprised of lawyers, academics, journalists, researchers and community activists. Its European network of con-

---

[63] http://www.parliament.the-stationery-office.co.uk/pa/ld/ldhansrd.htm.

[64] http://www.parlement.nl.

[65] http://www.statewatch.org/observatory2.htm.

tributors is drawn from twelve countries. Statewatch encourages the publication of investigative journalism and critical research in the fields of the state, civil liberties and openness".[66] On that web-site *Watson*'s young assistant printed out with ease and within five minutes of first going on the Web a text of the Proposed Framework Decision on European Arrest Warrant[67] and moreover had access to background material and detailed commentary on the provisions of the draft available.

IV.   Putting Meat on the Bones of EU Digital Government

A. *Reflections on EU Information and Communications Policy*

It is not uncommon to come across statements to the effect that the technology behind ICT has occasioned a very fundamental shift *inter alia* in the role of government and governance.[68] ICT is, at the same time, responsible for a vast increase in the amount of information that is available both in a quantitative sense and in the manner in which it renders information accessible. ICT, in principle, increases the transparency of processes and structures by generating information about the underlying productive and administrative processes through which public administration accomplishes its tasks. The Commission in its White Paper on Governance is however content to adopt a congratulatory and superficial approach to its information policy (including the controversial new regulation on public access to documents) and some meagre thoughts in a separate communication on developing its communications policy.[69] Indeed, further examination of the Report of the (internal) Working Group 2a ("Consultation and Participation of Civil Society") as well as that of Working Group 1a ("Broadening and enriching the public debate on European matters"), reveals that the general attitude displayed within the Commission to the significance of ICT is a highly ambivalent one, confined largely to view-

---

[66]   http://www.statewatch.org/about.htm.

[67]   http://www.statewatch.org/news/2001/sep/euarrest2.pdf

[68]   ICT and Government Committee, *Citizen and Government in the Information Society. The Need for Institutional Innovation.* (Den Haag, September 2001),
http://www.minbzk.nl/international/documents/pub3092.htm.

[69]   Commission: Communication on a New Framework for Co-operation on the Information and Communication Policy of the European Union, COM (2001) 354, 27 June 2001.

ing it in purely *instrumental* terms. In other words, it tends to focus
on the introduction of more *on-line information* (for example, data-
bases providing information on civil society organizations that are
active at European level or listing all consultative bodies involved
in EU policy-making) rather than on reflecting on the *institutio*nal
potential and dynamics of the technology in a broader (citizenship)
framework.[70]

The obligation on institutions to make information available to
the general public on request at the same time entails, in my view,
the obligation to make known the information they have in their
possession. Interested citizens must be able to know what public
information the institutions possess and where and how it can be
found. It is the task of the institutional actors in the formal political
process to pro-actively make this information available and in principle freely available.[71] This includes the establishment of a *public
register* where, as a rule, documents that have been received and
drawn up by a public authority (including all its preparatory instances) must be registered. This would include documents that the
public authority in question estimates initially to be 'secret' or
'classified' (i.e. not falling within the rules on access to documents
but under one of the specific exceptions to the general rule of openness). Only in this way can public activities be opened up to the
citizens (and their representatives) in such a way that they can
choose the information they wish to obtain, without having to rely
on public information services (the information that public authorities choose to give about their work). In June 2002 the Commission,
the Council and the European Parliament must have separately in-
stituted such registers as part of their obligations under the newly
adopted regulation on access to their documents.

Electronic media makes it possible to make such information
widely available.[72] More and more it is considered an obligation on

---

[70] *Bovens* (2002).
[71] The role of commercial publishers in this regard must clearly also be
     considered but here it is a matter more of a supplemental role where
     such publishers charge commercial rates for information to which
     some clear added value in terms of information provision is present.
[72] Of course the assumption cannot be made that individual citizens inter-
     ested in participating in this fashion all necessarily have access to the
     requisite hardware in order to have voice in this fashion. Clearly the
     provision of easy access to the computer hardware in public areas such
     as libraries, community halls and even public kiosks (Portugal and the

the part of all executive and administrative and legislative (and even judicial) authorities within the EU to put on *Internet* extensive information about their tasks, their organization structure, their activities, the agendas for their meetings as well as information on the most important documents under discussion in that context.[73] If the documents are not directly made accessible via Internet then information should be included as to where those documents can be obtained. Initially it could certainly be said that the information placed on the Web pages of the various institutions related to documents already considered within the public domain. In other words the initial function of putting information on the Internet was simply to make such information more speedily available and more readily accessible to a wide range of users (for example, Court judgments, Advocate General opinions, et cetera). Such material was subsequently published elsewhere (generally by the Official Publications Office of the EU and also by commercial publishers) and only available in these sources on payment of quite hefty sums of money. The situation has improved in this regard in the practice of the Council in particular who now includes in its excellent Register documents that certainly previously would not be considered as being in the public domain.

The more radical step of placing on Internet of the entire decision making procedure (including the preparatory instances) as suggested by *Joseph Weiler* and others some years ago in their interesting *Lexcalibur* – the European public square – proposal, has not yet been taken.[74] There are some indications however that in the

---

Netherlands) need to be stimulated at national and local level, possibly with some EC funding.

[73] See the practice of the Europa server in that regard: http://www.europa. eu.int.

[74] What they envisage is that each *Community* decision-making project intended to result in the eventual adoption of a Community norm would have a 'decisional web site' on the Internet within the general *Lexcalibur* 'Home Page' which would identify the scope and purpose of the legislative or regulatory measure(s); the Community and Member States persons or administrative departments or divisions responsible for the process; the proposed and actual timetable of the decisional process so that one would know at any given moment the progress of the process. Moreover the idea is that interested parties could actually access and view all *non-confidential* documents that form part of the process. Finally they could 'under carefully designed procedures' di-

newer thinking on the second generation Europa server and the installation of thematic sites right across the decisional spectrum a step going in that direction may well be taken. By its very nature however the ideal of the 'public square' is of course intrinsically suited to deal with the complex, multi-level and variegated nature of Union decision-making. With regard to the possibility of interested parties actually having input into the decisional process itself I feel that this should be considered within the framework of a more general *interactive* communication *network* for political information and participation, serving as a means of communication between the citizens and the European political system.[75]

An avenue worthy of serious exploration is the granting of digital access *rights* to information also at the level of EU public administration and governance structures. In the Netherlands, the Dutch Commission on Constitutional Rights in the Digital Era drafted proposals to adapt the Dutch Constitution to the information society and included a right of access to information held by the government.[76] Recognition of information rights can help to render the constitutional state an appropriate accommodation for the information society; such embedment is particularly important in the European (constitutional) context. How can our thinking on the role and significance of (broadly based) information rights in the digital era take concrete shape?

How would the ideal, even utopian, digital "reading room" of the Europa server look like? Some ideas to explore further could include the following:

- An effective hyper-link linking the web pages of all EU institutions, organs and independent bodies (Europol, Eurojust etc.) and providing substantive access and links across institutions to particular policy-field developments. In other words an inter-institutional approach such as adopted with regard to the EU Committee on Standards in Public Life and as has been proposed with regard to communication policy (see Commissions recent Communication on the subject).

---

rectly submit input into the specific decisional process. See *Weiler* (1997) 153.

[75] See too, *Nentwich* (1997).

[76] Commission on Constitutional Right in the Digital Era (*Commissie Grondrechten in het Digitale Tijdperk)*: Report, 2000, http://www. minbzk.nl/gdt/index2.htm.

- Subject based Observatories which give the public easy and uptodate access to all developments with regard to grouped policy areas right across the spectrum of Union activity.
- Observatories to include information on all measures of implementation as well as the decisions (legislation) itself.
- Inter-institutional Registers of documents.
- The drafts of Council decisions as they advance through the decision-making process so that interested parties can ensure that they can input views into the formal political process.
- The obligation to refer to sites (via links) which refer to civil society views and views of parliaments (national and European).
- Where the European Parliament enjoys co-decision an invitation to interested parties to make comments before a given date (a kind of adapted "notice and comment").

B. The role of the Non-Governmental Sector

The decision by the Commission not to deal with the key issues of access to information and the linked question of the communication policies of the institutions is a major defect in the White Paper and pre-determined a fairly marginal role for "active" civil society representatives in its development of the governance agenda in the EU. The Commission in its White Paper gravely underestimates the changing relationship between public administration and citizen and the role that ICT is playing in that regard. Any role for the non-governmental sector is inspired by the belief that the non-governmental sector has a crucial role to play in stimulating public deliberation on issues of concern to the general public. It is a rather futile exercise to attempt to pigeonhole as part of an exclusively vertical pyramid of accountability the role of the citizen and their civil society representatives in the manner that the Commission attempts to do in its White Paper on Governance. Rather a re-imagined role for the civil society sector could invigorate considerably not only the institutions of representative democracy but also offset to some extent at least the reality of excessive bureaucratic domination. This perspective does not exclude the profit-making sector that should also be enabled to participate openly in a public debate with its points of view. What is crucial however to this perspective of introducing more spaces for deliberative democracy is that access to the debate is open and transparent and that there is no (or reduced) monopolization of influence behind closed doors. Information is often not sought by interested citizens because they are unaware of its existence.

Providing a greatly improved system of information is only to be considered a first step of a much larger project. It would serve as the basis for a system that allows widespread *participation* in policy-making processes through the mechanisms of interactive dialogue between the Union institutions and interested private actors. Digital networks potentially transform the way we create, exchange and access information. It is this transformation of social (civil) dialogue that can be of such significance to democratic theory. It allows individuals to access the deliberative process as active participators rather than as mere passive receivers of messages. It also enhances the ability of individuals to access relevant information that may be crucial for will formation purposes. Moreover, it may well prove to be a unique opportunity for deliberations of citizens and interest groups beyond the traditional frontiers of the nation state, without the burden of high entry costs for either individual citizens or public interest groups.[77] The danger of resulting information 'overload' is clearly present. Already today citizens, groups and national parliaments all experience difficulty in sifting the information they do receive and evaluating it to know what is important and what not and when precisely action, at what level, is required. This existing situation will only be exacerbated considerably by any active information policy going in the more radical direction of *Lexcalibur*. In this context the role for the more specialized issue-oriented NGOs emerges as a kind of well informed 'early-warning' mechanism helping to stimulate and focus public deliberations on related areas. Such 'active' citizens can also have a pivotal role to play in ensuring the more widespread dissemination and filtering of information with the aim of assuring more concrete possibilities for political participation in the deliberative process itself.[78]

What could still in 1996 be termed the "quiet revolution" of NGO participation in international organizations took a different turn after Seattle in 1999. Ever since then European Council summits have virtually without exception been accompanied by demonstrations and protests. Over time it has also become a clearer focus for anti-globalization protests, the EU being perceived as a "glob-

---

[77] See too, *Weiler et al.* (1996).
[78] See further, *Curtin* (2003).

alizierungsverstarker" and the links between anti-EU protests and anti-globalization protests have strengthened.[79] Such spectacular demonstrations and protests led not only to dismissive comment by a segment of the political elite (such as the statement by *Tony Blair* post Gothenburg, condemning "the travelling circus of anarchists") but also amongst others to greater realization of the need to take on board the sentiments of dissatisfaction being expressed bottom-up (also evidenced in referenda, such as the Irish-Nice one) in the further construction of the EU. Nevertheless the temptation is to react in an overly authoritarian manner to certain post-national threats from "uncivil society" with the risk of unnecessarily radicalizing "civil" society. Thus, the normative response at the EU level to 11 September has been for example to equate protestors at summit meetings etc with terrorists rather than ensuring that "voice " is also given to those who seek change from the political process. What is interesting about this latter example is that it was civil society organizations themselves that successfully made an issue for debate in the (European?) public sphere of the attempt to introduce a new and sweeping definition of terrorism. The combination of immediate digital access to the relevant documents (provided by civil society itself and not by the responsible decision-makers) coupled with sophisticated analysis and an engagement with the formal political actors at the national level (national parliaments in particular) and at the European level (the Council and the European Parliament in particular; the ESC played no role at all) was a formula that resulted in real change to the normative provisions in question.[80]

As a result of engaged, albeit non-traditional, political activity, citizens not only have much greater motivation to seek out information as to the performance of the public administration and formal decision-makers for themselves (or via an association or interest group to which they belong), they are thus better placed than ever to scrutinise the manner in which public administration tasks are carried out . Moreover, it follows that (large groups of) citizens no longer need or wish to have passive relations with the public authorities, but instead wish to play a vigorous part in defining

---

[79] See too, *Wolf* (2001) 113.

[80] See for details the Observatory on Terrorism and the Protection of Civil Liberties on the Statewatch home-page, www.statewatch.org.

these contacts as they see fit.[81] In other words, citizens are themselves developing their role, using the technology offered to them
by ICT both in terms of acquiring information and maintaining
virtual and horizontal relations with no traditional time and space
constraints,[82] and are more willing to engage actively in (specific)
issues now than in times where a more heroic view of politics prevailed.[83]

Bibliography:

M. Botterman et al. (2000), Public Information Provision in the
Digital Age. Implementation and effects of the U.S. Freedom of
Information Act, Leiden 2000.

M. Bovens (2002), Information Rights. Citizenship in the Information Society, Journal of Political Philosophy, forthcoming.

P. Craig (2000), The Fall and Renewal of the Commission: Accountability, Contract and Administrative Organisation, European Law Journal, 6 (2000), No. 2, 98-116.

D. Curtin (2000), Citizens' Fundamental Rights of Access to EU
Information: An Evolving Digital Passepartout?, Common Market Law Review, 37 (2000), 7-41.

D. Curtin (2001) The European Commission in Search of Accountability: From Chamber of Secrets to Good Governance, in *J.
Wouters / J. Stuyck* (eds.), Principles of Proper Conduct for Supranational, State and Private Actors in the European Union:

---

[81] ICT and Government Committee, *Citizen and Government in the Information Society. The Need for Institutional Innovation.* (Den Haag,
September 2001)
http://www.minbzk.nl/international/documents/pub3092.htm.

[82] See further, Scientific Council for Government Policy, Governments
Losing Ground. An Exploration of Administrative Consequences of
ICT (Den Haag 1998).

[83] See, on the role of ICT in strengthening the possibilities for civil society organizations to participate in the process, Internet and Public Administration (*Internet en Openbaar Bestuur*), "De Schaduw Democ-
ratie" (2001), http://www.internetenopenbaarbestuur.nl/.

Towards a *Ius Commune*. Essays in Honour of Walter van Gerven, Antwerpen 2001, 5-20.

D. Curtin (2003), Private Interest Representation or Civil Society Deliberation: A Contemporary Dilemma for European Union Governance, Journal of Law and Society 30 (2003) forthcoming.

D. M. Curtin / I. F. Dekker (1999), The EU as a 'Layered' International Organization: Institutional Unity in Disguise, in *P. Craig / G. de Búrca* (eds.), The Evolution of EU Law, Oxford, 1999, 83-136.

D. M. Curtin / I. F. Dekker (2002), The Constitutional Structure of the European Union: Some Reflections on Vertical Unity-in-Diversity, in *P. Beaumont / C. Lyons / N. Walker* (eds.) Convergence and Divergence in European Public Law, Oxford 2002, 59-78.

L. A. Dalglish / G. P. Leslie / Ph. Taylor (2002) (eds.), Homefront Confidential. How the War on Terrorism Affects Access to Information and the Public's Right to Know, The Reporters Committee for Freedom of the Press White Paper, Arlington / VA 2002 (also available at: http://www.rcfp.org/news/documents/Homefront_Confidential.pdf).

European Commission (2001), Perceptions of the European Union. A Qualitative Study of the Public's Attitudes to and Expectations of the European union in the 15 Member States and the 9 Candidate Countries, Bruxelles 2001.

C. Joerges / Y. Meny / J. Weiler (2001) (eds.), Mountain or Molehill? A Critical Appraisal of the Commission White Paper on Governance, http://www.jeanmonnetprogram.org/papers/01/010601.html.

C. Joerges / E. Vos (1999) (eds.), EU Committees: Social Regulation, Oxford 1999.

Chr. Koenig / M. Pechstein (1995), Die Europäische Union: Der Vertrag von Maastricht, Tübingen 1995.

L. Metcalfe (2000), Reforming the Commission: Will Organizational Efficiency Produce Effective Governance?, Journal of Common Market Studies, 38 (2000), 817-841.

M. Nentwich (1996), Opportunity Structures for Citizens Participation: the Case of the European Union, European Integration Online Papers, 0 (1996), http://eiop.or.at/eiop/texte/1996-001a.htm.

S. Peers (2000), Steve Peers, EU Justice and home affairs law, Harlow 2000.

J. Shaw (2000), Law of the European Union, Basingstoke [3]2000.

J. H. H. Weiler (1997), The European Union belongs to its citizens: three immodest proposals, European Law Review, 22 (1997), 150-156.

J. H. H. Weiler et al. (1996), Certain Rectangular Problems of European Integration, European Parliament. DG Research. Project IV/95/02, http://iue.it/AEI/EP/.

F.-O. Wolf (2001), Zivilgesellschaftliche Netzwerke, Globalisierung, Europäisierung und Demokratisierungschancen. Erwartungen aktiver TrägerInnen und staatliche Handlungsoptionen, unpublished manuscript, 2001, on file with the author.

Sebastian Geiseler-Bonse

Transparency and Democracy in the Internet: ICANN as an Example?

I.   Introduction

The Internet is getting more and more important for the society as a whole and its individual members. For a long time the Internet was seen as an outlaw territory like the "Wild West". Everyone could do whatever he felt like.

This situation has changed appreciably. The "wild" Internet has been domiciled to a certain degree. Not only business activities of the "dotcom" industry but the decisions of ICANN as the governing body of the Internet are closely being observed by the public.

The question will be whether ICANN is in fact a governing body of the Internet and whether this body is suitable of bringing democracy to the new medium. In addition, another question remains in the dark so far. Is ICANN transparent enough to ever become a governing body of the Internet society?

The following article will try to shed some light on the questions posed.

II.   The Internet Corporation of Assigned Names and Numbers

Before getting into the main aspects of the topic it may be useful to first provide a little background on ICANN.

A. What is ICANN?

ICANN stands for *Internet Corporation for Assigned Names and Numbers*. It is a unique entity that may not be familiar to everyone.

ICANN is a non-profit private-sector organisation incorporated in Marina del Rey, California, USA. The organisation was formed in 1998 to undertake certain administrative and technical management aspects of the core resources of the Internet: Internet domain names, protocols, addresses and the root server system.

To maintain the Domain Name System (DNS) is probably the task with the most political effect.

The DNS makes the Internet or more specifically the World Wide Web convenient for human beings. From the technical point every computer connected to the Internet has a unique number, the so called IP-Number, assigned to it in order to be identifiable. This is necessary for the information to be sent only to the targeted computer.

Every server that stores information is accessible by this IP-Number but these are very difficult for human beings to memorise. Here is where the DNS comes into play. Every IP-Number corresponds with a Domain Name. For example the IP-Number 128.176.188.115 corresponds with the domain name www.uni-muenster.de.

This Domain Name System must be managed and administrated by someone and that is ICANN. Other functions like the IP address

System and the setting of standards are also fulfilled by ICANN but the DNS is the most important because most political one.

B. *History of the DNS and ICANN*

The US Government, which financed research for the development of the Internet, contracted the "Internet Assigned Numbers Authority" (IANA) with the DNS management in the late 1980s. The IANA was in fact a one-man institution, represented by one of the creators of the Internet – *Jon Postel*. *Jon Postel* was involved in the developments of the Internet since 1969 where he took part in the APRANet project of the US Department of Defence. The idea was to create a military information system that would survive a nuclear war.

When the Internet evolved to a global and most important commercial medium a more suitable management system was needed.

While *Jon Postel* tried to bring IANA under the influence of the "Internet Society" (ISOC) in the middle of the 1990s, the number of domain names broke the ten-million mark. The increasing importance of the Internet lead national governments and private industry to demand more governmental and business involvement.

After the ITU[1] tried to take the lead to become "governor of the Internet" in 1996, the "International ad hoc Committee" (IAHC) was founded. But the idea of bringing the "global Internet community" (represented by IANA and ISOC), the governments (represented by the ITU and WIPO) and the business world (represented by the International Trademark Association) under this one roof worked only for a short period. The IAHC produced a "Memorandum of Understanding on generic Top Level Domains" (gTLD-MoU) which was signed by about 100 governmental and non-governmental actors in Geneva on 2 May 1997. The ITU got the role of the custodian of the "gTLD-MoU". The project failed in the end because substantial groups, from internet users via national governments to major businesses, were not adequately represented by the IAHC and disagreed with key parts of the MoU.[2]

In the autumn of 1997 the US Government under the presidency of *Bill Clinton* started an alternative initiative and proposed the development of an Internet Governance System under US private sector leadership. The E-Commerce paper from July 1997 expressed the opinion that governments should play, if any, only a

---

[1]   International Telecommunication Union.
[2]   *Kleinwächter* (2001) 268.

limited role in the Internet governance. This US "green paper" was heavily criticised by the European Commission and Internet users around the world.

As a reaction the *Clinton* administration modified the paper and published a "White Paper" in June 1998. This paper paved the way for the incorporation of ICANN.

In October 1998 the US Department of Commerce recognised ICANN as the global Internet governance corporation. The Department of Commerce and ICANN entered into a Memorandum of Understanding which sought to transfer gradually all functions of Internet governance to ICANN within a two years period. This contract was stretched afterwards to 1 October 2001.

C. Principles of ICANN

There are four basic principles laid out in the Memorandum of Understanding founding ICANN. These basic principles could be seen as the four pillars on which ICANN has to stand.

1. Stability

The US Government thought that it was not longer a proper role for it to manage the technical aspects of the Internet and wanted to transfer this task to ICANN but only in a way that did not threaten the stability of the Internet. The principle of maintaining a stable Internet network is the core of the "White Paper".

This is the main and most important principle of ICANN which is sometimes misused as an excuse for certain decisions of ICANN's leadership. Reform ideas are often rejected for being a threat for the stability of the Internet.

2. Competition

ICANN was to increase competition in the DNS as opposed to the existing monopoly of Network Solutions Inc. (NSI) as the sole registry.

The Domain Name System was introduced at a time when the registration of .edu domains outnumbered the .com domains and the registration for free. The .edu domain was mostly used by educational institutions that started the Internet. The Department of Commerce contracted with Network Solutions Inc. Hereby, this Virginian-based, private company received a monopoly for the registration of domain names in the open generic Top Level Domain Name space (gTLDs).

NSI started to charge a registration fee per domain name (US $ 35 per year). With the beginning of the dot-com boom the registration of domain names became a huge business market. Hence, one of the first activities on the agenda of ICANN was to create competition in this monopolistic market. This was done by adopting a policy for the accreditation and licensing of registrars in the gTLD Area.

After trying with only five registrars in the beginning of 1999, ICANN has already recognised around 200 registrars worldwide up to April 2001. By the recognition of the other registrars the still very dominant position of NSI has decreased to nearly 50%.

3. Private Sector, Bottom-up Consensus Development

ICANN is a private entity with a unique structure. It is based on the At-Large Members and several Supporting Organisations. The idea is that within these groups a consensus on issues is developed instead of a deciding board on the top of the organisation. That this is mostly a theoretical idea will be obvious when scrutinising ICANN's structure.

4. Representation

The principle is that a body such as ICANN can only plausibly claim to operate as a consensus development organisation for the Internet community if it is truly representative of that community.

According to the White Paper ICANN should "reflect the functional and geographic diversity of the Internet and its users" and " ensure international participation in decision making". It can be questioned whether this ideal has been fulfilled in the current structure of ICANN. It will be demonstrated that especially individuals are under-represented within ICANN's structure. The only part of ICANN where individuals get the real opportunity to take part in ICANN is the At-Large Membership.

Especially in the Supporting Organisations the interests of individuals are quasi not represented. The representation of commercial interests is prevailing. More detailed aspects will be presented within the discussion of ICANN's level of transparency.

D. The Structure of ICANN

The graphic on the following page serves as an illustration of ICANN's structure:

ICANN consists of a Staff and a Board of Directors. The Board of Directors consists of 19 persons, one chairman and 18 directors.

From these 18 directors five were elected by the At-Large-Membership, four are still from the initial Board of Directors and nine others. These nine are the delegates of the three supporting organisations, the DNSO,[3] PSO[4] and ASO.[5]

These Organisations build constituencies and elected these nine directors into the Board in October 1999.

The ICANN Board is led by a Chair who gets support from a small secretariat, the so-called ICANN Staff. ICANNs first Chair was *Esther Dyson*, America's "First Lady of the Internet" (1998-2000), followed by *Vint Cerf* (2000-20-02), Vice-President of MCI/Worldcom and as the originator of the TCP/IP Protocol one of the "Fathers of the Internet". From 1998-2000 *Mike Roberts*, the first Secretary General of the above-mentioned ISOC, served as CEO. In March 2001 Stuart Lynn became ICANN's new CEO.

In addition, there is the so called GAC, the Governmental Advisory Committee where the more than 180 governments are represented. The GAC is purely advising and not involved in the decision making. The recommendations are not binding for the Board. In addition, governmental representatives are not eligible for a seat in the Board of Directors.

The participation in the GAC is the only involvement the US Government officially still has.

[3] Domain Name Supporting Organisation.
[4] Protocol Supporting Organisation.
[5] Address Supporting Organisation.

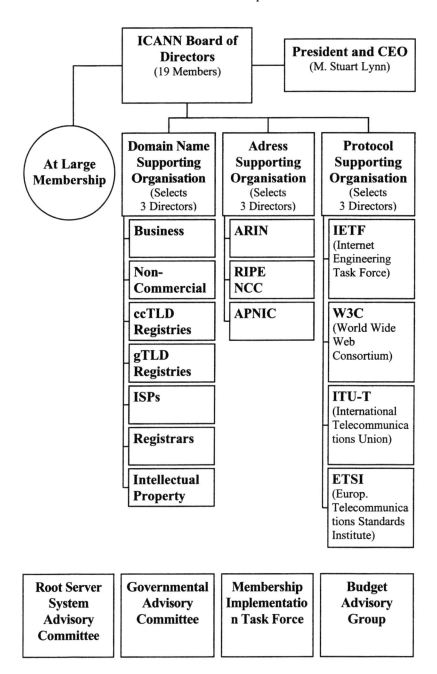

E. The Root Server System

De facto the US Government has a greater influence than it likes to admit. The US Government still has the physical power over the A-Root Server which is the core of the Internet Network.

The root server, which manages the TLDs, can be seen as the material heart of the Internet. The name server finds its way to the desired computer by asking the root server for the relevant Top Level Domain. Each root server mirrors the TLDs of the A-root Server, which is based in Herndon, Virginia and is managed by NSI.

The control over the A-Root Server is the focus of growing controversy. The global Internet community has assumed for a long period that the factual control over the A-Root Server by the US Government would be given up and transferred to ICANN. But this has never been explicitly stated that ICANN would be responsible for it one day. So far the *Bush* Administration has not stated their opinion on the matter.

In March 2001 a Committee of the US Senate asked the General Accounting Office of the US Congress to investigate whether the Department of Commerce has the right to transfer control of the A-Root Server to ICANN.

The control over the A-Root Server is of major importance because of the critical character of this element of the Internet infrastructure. The shut-down of the A-Root Server would in fact result in a total collapse of the Internet. Hence, there are several alternative root server initiatives.

Even the question could be raised whether the US Government could misuse their actual power over the A-Root Server against other countries. If a "country code Top Level Domain" (ccTLD) would be taken out of the A-Root Server, the impact on the respective country would be enormous.

But these aspects seem to be more of a horror-scenario since the US Government has managed the A-Root Server in a very responsible way with respect to the fact that it acts on behalf of the global Internet community.

On the other hand, the legal relationship to the A-Root Server has to be clarified. So far, the other governments simply have to trust the US Government. An international treaty should be considered.

III. Transparency within ICANN

The aspect of transparency within ICANN has to be doubted. There are still too many decisions made behind closed doors without the opportunity for the Internet Society to give comments and suggestions.

Karl Auerbach, the winning candidate for the North American region, once even mentioned that in his opinion ICANN would effectively be led by ICANN's Staff and not the Board of Directors. Making this statement as an elected Member of the Board it shows that the decision-making process lacks transparency and trust.

In addition, ICANN's structure hinders the involvement of a diverse representation of interests. It appears that the commercial interests are over-represented within ICANN's structure. Instead of putting the difficult task of finding a means to create real global representation within the organisation, ICANN has been structured to place commercial entities in a place of privilege within its political community. The favoured position of the Supporting Organisations means that the citizens of ICANN are firms and companies. Firms, which are granted legal personality by states in order for commerce to flow more efficiently, are being granted political personality in cyberspace by virtue of their rights to representation and participation.[6]

One good example for the lack of adequate representation resulting also in a lack of transparency is the structure of the DNSO, one of ICANN's three supporting organisations. The DNSO serves as a forum for debating issues and recommending policies concerning the allocation of domain names. Participants can become members by joining a constituency of the DNSO's General Assembly. The constituencies, in what can be considered a corporatist model of representation, are organised around assumed common interests: Country Code TLD Registries, Commercial and Business Entities, Generic TLD Registries, Internet Service and Connectivity Providers, Non-Commercial Domain Name Holders, Registrars, and Trademark and Other Intellectual Property and Anti-Counterfeiting Interests. Of these seven constituencies only one, the Non-Commercial Domain Name Holders Constituency, articulates the interests of non-profit organisations. But this constituency leaves out the interests of individuals even if they are domain name hold-

---

[6] *Marlin-Bennett* (2001) 303.

ers. To date there is no representation within the DNSO constituencies for individuals.

The rules provide that additional constituencies can be added to the DNSO by a vote of the ICANN Board of Directors.

This rule demonstrates the contradiction to ICANN's third principle of a bottom-up decision-making.

Individuals who want to become members of at least the General Assembly of the DNSO must take a positive step of registering. But the General Assembly is only open to individuals who are knowledgeable about relevant issues and willing to give their time to participate in the work of the DNSO.[7] On the other hand, no explanation is given as to how to evaluate an individual's competence.

Despite all this, the DNSO has the most inclusive membership of ICANN's three supporting organisations. The Address Supporting Organisation and the Protocol Supporting Organisation have stricter limits on who or what is considered a member of the political community.

In general, for-profit organisations have more opportunities to be citizens than non-commercial organisations, and individuals have the least representation. The Board of Directors is not held accountable to those who are not represented.[8]

IV.   Democracy in the Internet

Another question is whether ICANN can provide democratic governance for the Internet. This question could easily be opposed when seeing ICANN as a simply technical coordinating body not governing at all.[9] If ICANN is not governing at all the question of the democratic character of this governance is not plausible.

On the other hand, the fact that ICANN held the "first online election" might be interpreted otherwise. A book remains a book even if called something else. In this sense the different opinion of ICANN's leadership would not hinder the qualification of a democratic body.

But before observing the democratic nature of ICANN, the abstract requirements of democracy should shortly be presented.

---

[7]   ICANN, DNSO, http://www.dnso.icann.org/dnso/aboutdnso.html.
[8]   *Marlin-Bennett* (2001) 304.
[9]   *Dyson* (1999).

A. Preconditions of Democracy

Debate among political theorists over the nature and definition of democracy has generated a rich body of literature. Though there is no universally accepted definition of democracy, and consequently no single agreed-upon meaning of democratic governance, there is general agreement that the procedures of governance must conform to certain standards in order to be labelled "democratic".[10]

The existence of a political community is a precondition of democracy. Political community can be defined in terms of four dimensions.

- Democracy needs a political community to function. A political community is needed. Otherwise there would not be anything to be governed. For bottom-up decision-making to happen, there must be a bottom.[11]

  The political community is defined by membership, communication, interest aggregation and its culture. Each of these requirements posed different difficulties in general and in particular when it comes to an application on a global scale.

  With regard to membership of the political community it is difficult to reason where certain restrictions should be made. Who would be allowed to vote in a potential election? Several national democracies handle this question differently. One criterion in respect to membership is common to all those different system: geographic borders. Normally the right to vote coincide with the link to a certain territory. This condition has to be thought over in a global context.

- The second dimension of a political community is the communication community. Collective decision-making in a democracy requires the ability of the political community to communicate. The first obvious obstacle could be the language. Is one language a necessary requirement or just a hurdle to be overcome?

  But also the ability to spread information to every member of the political community is vital.

- This leads to the third dimension: interest aggregation. This refers primarily to political parties. In a democracy political parties educate voters, formulate collective views, and aggregate the interests of many individuals.[12]

---

[10] *Marlin-Bennett* (2001) 302.
[11] *Marlin-Bennett* (2001).
[12] *Dahl* (1994) 23-34.

- Finally, political community has a cultural dimension. Collective identity between the members of a political community plays an important role. Some degree of mutual trust, solidarity, and respect for the rights of others is necessary for majoritarian decision-making to function effectively.

These are the dimensions of a political community. But a political community is not the only requirement of democratic governance. Democratic governance requires a political community to which the representatives of the governing institution are accountable, equal rights among the members of the political community, and legitimacy for the structure and procedures of the governing institution.

These other requirements will be discussed in their application to ICANN's structure.

B. Feasibility of Global Democracy

Before scrutinising whether ICANN can fulfil the requirements of democratic governance with its structure, a few general remarks on the feasibility of global democracy should be made. This might give some explanations in case ICANN should fall short of certain requirements.

Processes of globalisation raise issues of legitimacy as global governance institutions find themselves making policy decisions that have little grounding in popular consent. Global democracy seems to be the solution but many scholars argue that global democracy is simply not feasible, for the conditions of democracy cannot be realised at a global level.

First of all the global character makes the basic condition of a link to a territory for members of the political community obsolete. By definition territorial boundaries do not apply on a global level.

This leads to two problems often alleged. First, global membership allows too many interests into the decision-making process. A chaos of ungovernability might be the result. Secondly, the relevance of issues varies around the world. Not every issue is of interest to different part of the world.

Another problem within the political community is the result of its globality: Communication within the community. The lack of a global language cannot easily be overcome by a prevailing language. English is the most spread language but results in disadvantages for non-native speakers. Inadequacy of the global media and the impossibility of a global public forum are additional obstacles.

There are too many parts of the world with poor media infrastructure. This makes it difficult if not impossible to participate in something close to a global public forum.

Also the precondition of common values is questionable. At a global level the need for solidarity and common values is problematic. Technology and administration extend globally more easily than human contact. People around the world remain abstract to each other, and so it is unlikely that a global democracy could withstand the strains imposed by decisions that hurt the interests of parts of the community.

Thus the mere feasibility of global democracy remains unclear.

C. ICANN and Global Democracy

With the obstacles to the feasibility of global democracy in mind one has to scrutinise ICANN as a potential example of global democratic governance.

The first question has to be whether ICANN simply by its structure is able to fulfil the mentioned requirements. In the light of this question the passed ICANN elections can be analysed.

Although ICANN's mandate is technical and administrative in nature, its decisions are inextricably linked to global public policy. The control over the domain name allocation and the oversight over the root server system touches on such policy matters as property rights, speech rights and industry structure.

The Uniform Dispute Resolution Policy for domain name disputes defined a new but limited protection of trademarks on a global level without any international treaty. In addition, there is a inherent restriction on the freedom of speech in domain names if conflicting with registered trade marks. The delegation of authority to private entities to operate the domain name servers affects industry structure and competitiveness in the global domain name registration business.[13]

Insofar as it makes public policy, ICANN is similar to other global governance institutions like the World Trade Organisation in sectors like trade and finance.

But the ICANN is different. It embodies mechanisms for democratic governance. In the fall of 2000 ICANN held elections of several members of its Board of Directors. In doing so it implemented a precedent-setting experiment in the practice of global democracy.

---

[13]   *Froomkin* (2000).

Other organisation lack democratic mechanisms, ICANN has such mechanisms in place.

The election was planned even before the foundation of ICANN itself. The US Department of Commerce set out in the Memorandum of Understanding (MoU) with ICANN at its creation that half of the Members of the Board of Directors should be elected by the Internet community. The initial Board of Directors was only set in place on an interim basis with the clear obligation to enable the election of the Board Members.

But this stipulation was by far not as clear as it may sound, at least considering the following turmoil.

The summer of the year 2000 should be the moment that according to the ICANN website when "the first time ... every interested member of the global Internet society would have the opportunity to participate in the online-election of Internet politicians."

To achieve a quasi-democratic legitimacy the elections where foreseen in the White Paper of the US Government.

Being a member in ICANN's voter community was possible for everyone around the world over sixteen years of age with a working E-mail and postal address. One had to register on ICANN's website to become an At-Large Member. The voter identity number was sent by a conventional letter enabling the respective At-Large member to register online for the upcoming elections. The At-Large Membership later on elected the members of the Board of Directors. Hereby ICANN proved that the political community is not necessarily bound by territorial boundaries.

When ICANN planned these elections one might interpret that the Board of Directors at that time was not very happy about it. Therefore, the initial idea was to hold only indirect elections. The At-Large Membership should elect an At-Large-Council consisting of 18 Members with at least two representatives of the five regions in the world.

This plan was uniformly criticised by nearly everyone that showed interest in the online elections. Under this steadily increasing pressure ICANN changed its plans and finally opted for direct elections.

At first two committees were created, a nomination committee (NoCom) and an election committee (ElCom). The nomination committee then accepted proposals for candidates until the 20th July 2000 and presented a list of candidates which it saw as being appropriate. Whoever was not included in the list but nevertheless was interested was given a chance of self-nomination in a second phase lasting from the 20th July until the 20th August.

The NoCom with its members was disputed because it consisted of four residing directors of the Board and three others. Critics regretted that no public *call of interest* was made and ICANN practised a sort of incest. ICANN on the other side argued that the technical qualification of the candidates could only be ensured this way.

After the two phases a list of 35 candidates (seven for each region) was drafted and each candidate was given the platform for a campaign.

The actual elections were held in the first 10 days of October 2000. Until the 31st of August 2000, the end of the registration phase, 158,593 Internet users officially registered as At-Large Members.

This number might not be very impressive compared to approximately 200 million Internet users but it was definitely surprising for ICANN. Its Staff had calculated with a number around 15,000 to 20,000 registrations.

This also explains why the technical circumstances were inadequate towards the end of the registration phase. Many interested users were not able to register due to Server problems.

Another fact puts also more weight on this number of registrations. ICANN itself was very reluctant to advertise the upcoming elections. Only after several press campaigns initiated from independent sources and an ICANN Meeting in Yokohama the rally began. In the end the most registrations came out of Japan, then China, Germany and only on the fourth place the USA where ICANN is situated.

Finally, in the elections only 36,000 At-Large Member took part but many had complained that their election PIN, necessary to vote online, had not be delivered in time.

As the representative for the European region *Andy Müller-Maguhn*, the former speaker of the German Hacker community called "Chaos-Computer-Club", was elected.

These first online-elections showed that global democratic elections are indeed feasible. Obviously various details were generally not satisfying. But then again these first elections have to be seen as experiment providing for many suggestions and experience for future attempts.

The predictions that a global membership would bring an unmanageable range of issues to the election turned out to be false.

The election campaign may have been notable for the small number
of issues raised and the similarity of candidates' positions. Two sets
of issues prevailed. One focused on the need to safeguard the stability of the Internet, to ensure that ICANN's board would be composed of technical experts, and to protect intellectual property
rights. The second set of issues centred on a program of institutional reform. This emphasised ICANN's perceived lack of transparency and accountability, as well as its perceived democratic
deficit. In the election, outspoken advocates of reform were elected
in North America and Europe as opposed to the winning candidate
in the Asian region.

Across the globe, the issues raised in the election were quite
consistent reflecting the sector-specific mandate of ICANN. The
Internet sector's homogeneity counteracted globalism's heteroge-
neity.[14]

In terms of communication community and the ICANN election
the characteristics of the Internet proved to be very valuable. By
definition, every voter in the elections had access to the Internet.
Due to this fact, the first barrier to the creation of a global communication community did not appear. The language problem was
overcome by a self-organising system of communication. The main
language was English but more and more documents were available
in other languages. Because the Internet sector was already very
global and very English language-orientated, it had a comparatively
large population that could communicate. This top-level communication community engaged in a global discussion of issues. On the
other side, more national and non-English forums appeared and
some its members served as liaisons with the global communication
community.

Interest aggregation was not absent in the ICANN elections.
Numerous non-governmental organisations (NGOs) participated
actively in the ICANN elections. NGOs from around the world
joined in a loose Civil Society Internet Forum (CSIF) as a collective
framework for participation in the elections. The CSIF worked to
aggregate interests and define collective positions for voters around
the globe. The CSIF articulated a collective platform in its "Civil

---

[14]   *Klein* (2001) 340.

Society Statement".[15] Some of the leading NGO activists and election candidates composed this document during the summer of 2000, which stated principles for governance and derived from them a series of concrete reforms for ICANN. Although it did not nominate candidates, the CSIF did encourage candidates to voluntarily affiliate themselves with its platform, and such signatories were publicised as "Friends of Civil Society".

In respect of aggregating interests CSIF could be compared to a political party. And CSIF was not alone. The business interests were aggregated in the Global Internet Project (GIP) in which the deregulation of the Internet was advocated. In the weeks before the elections GIP cooperated with the leadership of ISOC to distribute their message.

Analysing the passed ICANN elections one can see all the preconditions for democracy present at least to a certain degree. This contradicts all the sceptics' assertions on the impossibility of global democracy. As we have seen it is not impossible.

The global political community did not result in a chaotic community with an explosion of issues. The Internet served as the first practical global media enabling the global community to communicate. The language barrier was overcome by the interconnection between the global top-level debate and national, smaller debate circles.

But before overestimating the feasibility of global democracy one should realise that certain reasons proved to be of vital importance for the success of the passed elections.

Scholars have underestimated the significance of the sectoral nature of today's globalism. Today's globalism does not raise questions about governance in general but only of governance within specific sectors. The resulting political community is not hopelessly overextended. Scholars have undervalued the distinction between full world government, which no one foresees in the near future, and global sectoral government, which increasingly exists today.[16]

The significance of the Internet should not be underestimated as well. This new technology reduces many barriers to global democ-

---

[15] *Civil Society Internet Forum,* 'Civil Society Statement on the ICANN Elections', July 2000, http://www.civilsocietyinternetforum.org/ statement.html.

[16] *Klein* (2001).

racy. It facilitates the formation of associations which can aggregate interests. An important condition of global democracy. The Internet makes global communication possible and this in a way previously unthinkable. A new degree of citizen involvement is enabled.

V.   The ALSC Report

In March 2000 at the ICANN Meeting in Cairo it was decided that instead of nine only five new Board-Members would be elected by the At-Large Members. Again, this decision was taken behind closed doors.

After the election an At-Large Membership Study Committee (ALSC) was created to evaluate the benefits and problems of the first election. The resulting ALSC report should thereafter be the basis for further elections if there would be any.

This might sound surprising but ICANN actually considered to cancel further elections and hence changed the By Laws accordingly. Without an explicit decision there would be no further elections. This change in the "By Laws" was made behind closed doors at the Cairo Meeting as well.

The Report of the Committee is publicly available[17] and acknowledges the political importance ICANN is having. The report promotes the elections of six Board Members in the future. It also comments on the requirements to register as an At-Large Member.

In the first elections each Internet User older than 16 with a valid e-mail and postal address could register. The report now promotes to change these low requirements. In further elections only domain name holder should be able to vote. This would prevent the misuse by voting-capture groups and would be a better representation of the Internet Society. Only domain name holder were part of the Internet Society since they have proved their interest by registering a domain name.

These proposals were not left uncommented. The main point of criticism is that the requirement of being a domain name holder would influence the At-Large Membership unilaterally. Demographics say that around 80 % of the domain names are held by companies and developing countries are underrepresented.

But even though the report promotes only six Members to be elected instead of nine as foreseen in the White Paper, at least it

---

[17] Available since 5 November 2001 via ICANN's Homepage at http://www.icann.org.

seems to be secured that the first online elections will not be the last.

VI.   Conclusion

ICANN is a particularly unusual international organisation: a private entity deriving authority form the US government, but making rules for the whole world. This leads to questions of legitimacy.

Especially in this context the ICANN elections were of great importance. This might introduce legitimacy to a certain degree, but only if the global Internet Society would be well represented. Representation is unbalanced towards an over-representation of commercial interests. The individuals amongst the Internet Society got their first chance of participation within ICANN when the first online-elections took place in 2000.

These elections have to be seen as a first experiment on the way to a sectoral global governance. Global governance is not at all impossible as was stated by many sceptics. The ICANN elections proved otherwise. But one has to keep in mind that an important part of the success of this experiment was the sectoral character of ICANN. In certain sectors global governance is feasible and the specific characteristics of the Internet facilitated the creation of the necessary political community.

It will be interesting to see whether ICANN's leadership will be able to withstand the public pressure against the cancellation of future elections, especially after the recommendations of the ALSC Report promoting future elections.

Without saying that global democracy can be achieved easily, the ICANN elections have proved that it is at least feasible and that it is vitally important to ensure a balanced representation of interests in a globalising world dominated by commercial interests.

Bibliography:

R. Dahl (1994), A democratic dilemma: system effectiveness versus citizen participation, Political Science Quarterly 109 (1994) No. 1, 23-34.

E. Dyson (1999), Testimony prepared for the US House of Representatives, Committee on Commerce, Subcommittee on Oversight and Investigations, available at http://www.icann.org/dyson_testimony_22july99.htm.

M. Froomkin (2000), Wrong turn in cyberspace: using ICANN to route around the APA and the Constitution, Duke Law Journal 50 (2000) No. 17, 17-184.

H. Klein (2001), The Feasibility of global Democracy: understanding ICANN's at-large election, Camford Info 3 (2001) No. 4, 333-347.

W. Kleinwächter (2001), The silent subversive: ICANN and the new global governance, Camford Info, 3 (2001) No. 4, 259-278.

R. Marlin-Bennett (2001), ICANN and Democracy: contradictions and possibilities, Camford Info 3 (2001) No. 4, 299-310.

John Lewis

How Far Are Governments Interested in International Transparency? The Distribution of Radio Frequencies as a Practical Example

I.   Introduction

This paper commences with a brief description of the International Telecommunication Union (ITU) and its role in the attribution of the radio frequency spectrum/satellite orbit resource at the international level through the application of the ITU Radio Regulations, an international treaty text. This is then extended to cover management of the resource at the national level. The discussion then proceeds to cover trends in privatization and regulation of telecommunications and, in particular, radiocommunications services with particular mention of transparency issues.

II.   The International Telecommunication Union[1]

The ITU was established in 1865 when the First International Telegraph Convention was signed in Paris by 20 participating countries who decided on common rules to standardize equipment in order to guarantee generalized telegraph interconnection and adopted uniform operating instructions. Since that time, telecommunications have continued to develop apace and the history of the ITU fully reflects the advances that have been made.

In 1947, after the Second World War, a major milestone occurred when the ITU held a conference in Atlantic City with the aim of developing and modernizing the organization. Under an agreement with the United Nations, it became the UN specialized agency responsible for international regulation of telecommunica-

---

[1]   This section draws from the official history of the ITU, available at
      http://www.itu.int/itudoc/about/itu/history/history.txt.

tions on 15 October 1947. The headquarters of the organization were transferred in 1948 from Bern, where it had been established in 1868, to Geneva: moreover, the International Frequency Registration Board (IFRB) was set up to manage the frequency spectrum which was becoming increasingly complicated and the Table of Frequency Allocations, introduced in 1912, became mandatory. This Table allocates to each service using radio waves (there are about 40 at the present time) specific frequency bands with a view to avoiding interference between stations – in communications between aircraft and control towers, car telephones, ships at sea and coast stations, radio stations or spacecraft and earth-based stations.

The Radio Regulations, which is the international treaty text controlling access by countries to the radio frequency spectrum / satellite orbit resource, is annexed to ITU Constitution/Convention (CS/CV). These Regulations are continually updated and revised to take account of use of new frequency bands and new radiocommunication services and systems at World Radiocommunication Conferences.

III. Basis of the International Radio Regulations

A. Introduction

Access is gained by Administrations of Member States of the International Telecommunication Union (ITU) to the frequency spectrum / satellite orbit resource for the introduction of their telecommunication systems by application of the International Radio Regulations.

In this context, from the time of the first legislation concerning spectrum usage, international frequency management had always been based on the concept of national sovereignty. National administrations regulated the usage of radio frequencies and access to communication services.

In a large part of the terrestrial radiocommunications domain (microwave links, land mobile, most of broadcasting, radiodetermination, etc.) the administrations are (almost) master of their national frequency management problems. National authorities are effectively able to assign frequencies to users; with, however, some exceptions in particular in the high frequency (HF) bands. Again, except for services using the HF bands, interference and coordination problems and their resolution for terrestrial services normally remain issues limited to the administration concerned and those of its neighbouring countries.

On the other hand, because of the extra-territorial nature of satellite orbits, the usage of frequencies for space radiocommunications should logically be regulated at the international level. The considerable reluctance of Governments to cede sovereignty with respect to resource allocation and the assessment of requirements led to regulations for space services that have been drawn up in such a way that the orbit and spectrum distribution is left to the administrations to be individually managed and negotiated. There is no supranational body to allocate these (common) resources (to "authorise" the use of orbital positions) or to arbitrate in the case of disagreement. The ITU, as the specialised agency of the United Nations responsible for telecommunications, does not have either law enforcement power or any effective control functions. Consequently orbit/spectrum resource exploitation is based on goodwill between administrations and on recognition of the fact that mutual interest will lead to mutual observance of the rules and regulations established by the international community in order that interference is avoided and that equitable access and efficient usage is promoted. In practice, administrations carefully assess the extent to which they follow these rules and regulations based on their national telecommunications policies and priorities as well as their geographical situation.

B. United Nations Texts

Different Declarations and Treaties (most importantly the 1967 Outer Space Treaty) of the United Nations stipulate that outer space (in contrast with air space which is under national sovereignty) is not subject to national appropriation by claim or by occupation but is free for exploitation and use by all states through their governmental or non-governmental entities in conformity with international regulations. Thus nobody owns any orbital position but everybody can use this common resource provided that the international regulations and procedures are applied. Another important element of the UN regulations is that states retain jurisdiction and control over objects that they have launched into outer space and they are responsible for space activities carried out by any of their public or private entities (even if the state does not exercise any direct or indirect control over such activities). States are thus obliged to establish appropriate control and supervision mechanisms (normally in the form of licences).

C. ITU – Major Principles

During the last 30 years, starting with the World Administrative Radio Conference of 1963 (WARC-63) and including the last World Radiocommunication Conference (WRC-2000), many ITU Conferences (WARCs, WRCs) have dealt with the regulation of spectrum/orbit usage by stations of the space radiocommunication services. Member States of the ITU established a legal regime which is codified through the ITU Constitution/Convention and the Radio Regulations. These instruments contain the main principles as well as the specific regulations required to allow, at the international level, access to the spectrum/orbit resource.

The above regulations are based on the main principles of efficient use of and equitable access to the spectrum/orbit resources which are laid down in Nos. 195 and 196 of the ITU Constitution (Article 44), which stipulate that:

"Members shall endeavour to limit the number of frequencies and the spectrum used to the minimum essential to provide in a satisfactory manner the necessary services". (CS195)

"In using frequency bands for radio services, Member States shall bear in mind that radio frequencies and any associated orbits, including the geostationary-satellite orbit, are limited natural resources and that they must be used rationally, efficiently and economically, in conformity with the provisions of the Radio Regulations, so that countries or groups of countries may have equitable access to those orbits and frequencies, taking into account the special needs of the developing countries and the geographical situation of particular countries". (CS196)

As indicated above, further detailed regulations and procedures governing orbit/spectrum use are contained in the Radio Regulations (RR), which is a binding international treaty (No. 31 of the ITU Constitution).

In the process of establishing the ITU's space-related regulations, emphasis was laid from the outset on *efficient and rational utilization*. This concept was implemented through a "first come, first served" procedure. This procedure ("coordination before use") is based on the principle that the right to use a satellite position is acquired through negotiations with the administrations concerned with the actual use of the same portion of the orbital segment. If applied correctly (i.e. to cover genuine requirements), the procedure offers a means of achieving efficient spectrum / orbit management; it serves to fill the gaps in the orbit as needs arise and results, in principle, in a homogeneous orbital distribution of space stations. On the basis of the Radio Regulations, and in the frequency bands where this concept is applied, Member administrations should designate the volume of orbit/spectrum resources that is required to satisfy their actual requirements. It then falls to the national administrations to assign frequencies and orbital positions, to apply the appropriate procedures (international coordination and recording) for the space segment and earth stations of their (governmental, public and private) networks, and to assume continuing responsibility for the networks.

The progressive exploitation of the orbit / frequency resources and the resulting likelihood of congestion of the geostationary-satellite orbit prompted ITU Member countries to consider more and more seriously the question of *equitable access* in respect of the orbit / spectrum resources. This resulted in the establishment (and introduction into the ITU regulatory regime) of frequency / orbital position plans in which a certain amount of frequency spectrum is set aside for future use by all countries, particularly those which are not in a position, at present, to make use of these resources. These plans, in which each country has a predetermined orbital position associated with the free use, at any time, of a certain amount of frequency spectrum, together with the associated procedures, guarantee for each country equitable access to the spectrum/ orbit resources, thereby safeguarding their basic rights. Such plans govern a considerable part of the frequency usage of the most resource-demanding space radiocommunication services; namely, the fixed-satellite and broadcasting-satellite services.[2]

---

2   *Fixed-satellite service:* A *radiocommunication service* between *earth stations* at given positions, when one or more *satellites* are used; the given position may be a specified fixed point or any fixed point within specified areas; in some cases this service includes satellite-to-satellite links, which may also be operated in the *inter-satellite service*; the fixed-satellite service may also include *feeder links* for other *space radiocommunication services.* (RR 1.21) *Broadcasting-satellite service:* A *radiocommunication service* in which signals transmitted or retransmitted by *space stations* are intended for direct reception by the general public. (RR 1.39)

During the last 30 years, this regulatory framework has been constantly adapted to changing circumstances and has achieved the necessary flexibility in satisfying the two major, but not always compatible, requirements of efficiency and equity. With the dramatic development in telecommunication services, increasing demand for spectrum/orbit usage for practically all space communication services has been observed and this has given rise to more complex mechanisms to enable frequency sharing as well as revised (and again often more complex) associated regulatory procedures. New regulatory text and limits for sharing were agreed at WRC-2000 for inclusion in the Radio Regulations and this confirms these ongoing developments.

D. Structure of the Radio Regulations

Since the Atlantic City ITU Conference, held in 1947, international management of the radio frequency spectrum has been based on several main principles, namely:

- A Table of Frequency Allocations which indicates which frequency bands are allocated to the many different radiocommunication services;
- a series of regulatory procedures and technical and operational requirements that are to be applied so that the rights and obligations of Member Administrations are established when obtaining access to the spectrum/orbit resources;
- international recognition of these rights by recording frequency assignments and associated orbital information used or intended to be used in the Master International Frequency Register.

Up until 1963 these principles, as enshrined in the Radio Regulations, dealt only with terrestrial radiocommunication services. After the 1963 Extraordinary Administrative Radio Conference to Allocate Frequency Bands for Space Radiocommunication Purposes and especially after the 1971 World Administrative Radio Conference for Space Telecommunications (both held in Geneva) the Radio Regulations incorporated a large amount of new material in order to take account of the allocations and associated procedures that were agreed concerning space services.

As could be expected, the technological developments at that time were such that the "optimum" bands for space radiocommunications were also used for important terrestrial applications and a system of sharing the use of these bands by the different services had to be developed. The bands of greatest interest at that time were

the 6/4 GHz, 8/7 GHz and 14/11/12 GHz frequency bands. These
were at that time and remain important bands for terrestrial microwave radio relay systems. The sharing mechanisms that were developed had to take account of the different possible radio signal
interference between the space and terrestrial systems and, importantly, the fact that terrestrial systems were already in place. This
latter point meant that a number of technical restrictions on terrestrial systems that were considered in order to facilitate sharing (and
which were incorporated in the Radio Regulations) could not be
made obligatory as many terrestrial systems (which would have not
conformed with these restrictions) were already in operation.

The procedures that were developed had to take account of the
large scale investments that would be necessary to introduce space
systems and a consequential desire of Administrations to have
reasonable security that new space systems could be implemented
and operated with acceptable levels of interference. This was
effected by allowing the different coordination procedures to
commence well in advance of the date of bringing into use of the
systems concerned.

E. Procedures Applying To Non-Planned Services

WRC-95 and WRC-97 consolidated all the coordination
procedures developed at earlier conferences into one single article
of the Radio Regulations, namely Article 9 "Procedure for effecting
coordination with or obtaining agreement of other administrations".
This Article contains all elements of the procedures of former
Articles 11 and 14, those of Resolutions 33 and 46. Associated with
the Article 9 are also Appendix 4, which specifies the various data
that must be furnished in any advance publication or coordination
request (replacing the old Appendices 1-5 in their entirety), and
Appendix 5, which contains criteria for identification of
administrations with which coordination is to be effected or
agreement sought.

The new Radio Regulations have been applied provisionally
since 1 January 1999, with some of the provisions, relating particularly to the outcome on Resolution 18 (Kyoto, 1994), being
applied since 22 November 1997 and for provisions relating to
Resolution 86 (Minneapolis, 1998) since 3 June 2000.

The coordination procedure is based on the principle of "first
come – first served". Successful coordination of space networks or
earth stations paves the way to the international recognition to the

use of frequencies by these networks/stations and the recording of
the frequencies in the Master International Frequency Register
(MIFR). The relevant provisions involve three basic steps:
* advance publication (Section I, Article 9)
* coordination (Section II, Article 9)
* notification/recording (Article 11)

Satisfactory completion of these procedures leads to rights being
acquired through the coordination with other Administrations concerned of the actual usage foreseen for the new system. Coordination is based on establishing acceptable levels of radio frequency
interference for all stations concerned in the coordination process.
This leads to efficient spectrum/orbit management and, in addition,
in the case of satellite systems, leads to homogeneous orbital distribution of space stations in the geostationary-satellite orbit. It should
be noted that this process leads to Administrations and Operators
having a continuing responsibility for the ongoing coordination of
their stations and satellite networks. In more formal terms, they
have obtained what is known as "International Recognition" of their
resource utilisation.

F. Assignment or Allotment Plans

Appendices 30, 30A and 30B to the Radio Regulations contain
plans for the broadcasting-satellite and the fixed-satellite services.
These *a priori* plans were established with a view to guaranteeing
equitable access to the geostationary orbit by all countries. In the
Plans, spectrum and orbit resource is set aside for future use by
all countries. The plans contain orbital positions, a certain
frequency spectrum and a service area which normally covers only
the country's territory. The plan entries are associated with a set of
technical parameters in accordance with which a specific satellite
network may be implemented. The plans also contain implementation procedures for those modified requirements which were not
foreseeable at the time of the establishment of the Plans. In Regions
1 and 3[3] there are also the Lists of additional uses, which are separated from the Appendix 30 and 30A Plans, and which are annexed
to the MIFR. The frequency bands subject to these Plans are listed
in Annex 2.

---

[3] Region 1 is the countries of Europe, the Middle East and Africa,
including all of the ex-Soviet Union; Region 2 is the countries of North
and South America and Region 3 is the countries of Asia and Oceania.

WRC-2000 adopted a revision of the AP30 and AP30A Plans for Regions 1 and 3.

In the case of terrestrial radiocommunication services Plans have been developed for broadcasting services (Sound and Television) on a regional basis and Plans have also been developed for radio-communication safety services for communications with ships and aircraft in the maritime and aeronautical mobile services.

G. Obligations and Rights

Access to the spectrum/orbit resource is obtained by following the *obligatory* procedures and other requirements of the Radio Regulations as indicated above. These *obligations* are with respect to existing or already planned uses of the resource by other admini-strations that have equally had to follow the relevant procedures and other requirements of the Regulations. Once the Radio Regu-latory requirements are being followed, an administration has ob-tained *rights* in terms of the requirements placed on other admini-strations, coming later, seeking to use the resource.

As ITU has no law enforcement or control power, exploitation of the orbit/spectrum resource has been based on goodwill between the administrations of ITU member states. Mutual interest has, in the past, and should continue, in the future, to ensure that interfer-ence is manageable and that use of the resource is efficient and equitable.

H. World Radiocommunication Conferences (WRCs)

At WRCs, which currently meet in a 3-year cycle, decisions are based on proposals presented to the Conference by Administrations and these may be:

- National proposals;
- Regional proposals;
- Proposals by interest groups which can be service or industry based (e.g. IMT-2000 third generation cellular radio, digital broadcasting), government interests (e.g. defence, meteorologi-cal), etc.;
- Proposals for new requirements, usually from developed coun-tries.

The Conference agenda is established by the preceding WRC and it takes account of improvements and modifications to the ex-isting Regulations as well as of new requirements arising from new services and technologies. Industry, operators and users are in-creasingly part of conference delegations and this is a reflection of the increasing importance of non-Government entities in the resource allocation process.

It should be noted that it is only in the case of assignments Plans where ITU denotes an element of the resource which can be considered to pertain to a country, and then only for the lifetime of the Plan.

I. National Authorities

As mentioned above, the specific tasks of the assignment and control of frequency / orbit usage remain with the Governments (administrations). This means that the assignment of frequencies and orbital positions (licences), the application of the appropriate procedures (international coordination and notification) for the space segment and earth stations of their (government and private) networks and the continuing responsibility for the networks are tasks carried out by national administrations.

J. Summary

This overview of the principles and structure will serve as the basis of discussion, in subsequent sections of this paper, of the implications of the application of the Radio Regulations by national administrations in the attribution of radio frequencies to the different service requirements competing for access to the spectrum/orbit resource.

Further details, relating to the above material, can be found in Annex 1.

IV.   National Spectrum Administration

A. Introduction

The nature of radio wave propagation is such that radio frequency interference can occur well beyond national borders, especially in some frequency ranges. Frequencies in ranges below 30 Megahertz (MHz) can propagate over long distances on the Earth's surface and, indeed, this property is used beneficially to offer long range low cost terrestrial services. Furthermore, frequencies in virtually all ranges can propagate over long distances once outside the Earth's atmosphere and, thus, satellite based communications require careful coordination on a global basis so that any radio frequency interference is at acceptable levels.

These fundamental physical phenomena have to be taken into account in radio frequency spectrum management, at the international, regional and national levels. As a result national spectrum management has to be based on decisions taken at the international level and the Radio Regulations are a fundamental tool in the development of national policy in this field.

B. National Regulation

National regulations are based on the ITU Radio Regulations and typically contain a frequency allocation table and technical and operational requirements taken from those texts. The national frequency table may or may not contain all the options existing internationally in terms of allocations of bands to radiocommunication services. Often, at least in some bands, only a subset of those international allocations is included in the national texts; this choice depends on national telecommunications priorities. National users will be expected to respect the requirements of the Radio Regulations with respect to the coordination and notification of frequency assignments, this being carried out via the national spectrum regulatory authority.

National regulations will also include similar texts taken from regional agreements. These can arrive from formal coordination arrangements established by regional bodies (e.g. the European Conference of Postal and Telecommunications Administrations – CEPT) or by specific arrangements between neighbouring countries (e.g. coordination between Australia, New Zealand and Papua New Guinea in particular frequency bands). National regulations will also include specific requirements in terms of licensing processes and fees, technical equipment standards, urban planning and operating methods.

C. Coordination with Neighbours

The amount of national spectrum management activity related to coordination of terrestrial radiocommunications required with neighbouring countries depends both on the size and geographical relationship of the countries concerned as well as on the extent of their telecommunications development. As one extreme, coordination between Australia, New Zealand and Papua New Guinea is necessary only in the lower frequency bands (typically below 25 MHz) and Australia and New Zealand are free to establish services in higher frequency bands without restriction, due to their geographical isolation. Papua New Guinea has to coordinate with Indonesia (a country sharing a common land border) although the state of telecommunications development in the two countries is such that this is not a major issue. The other extreme would be co-ordination between countries in Europe, where countries are of small or medium size and can have several common borders. Tele-communications services are also highly developed and this regional coordination is a major workload in European administrations. Regional coordination is facilitated by agreements and standards established the CEPT, which has an extensive formal structure covering radiocommunication matters. A European Radiocommunications Office (ERO), based in Copenhagen, carries out a number of coordination, standard and research roles for the CEPT in this regard.

Another interesting example is coordination in North America between Canada, the United States and Mexico. All three counties are large and coordination of terrestrial services is largely restricted to services planned to operate close to the long land borders between Canada and the US and between the US and Mexico. Again coordination activity is intensive and bilateral and tri-partite agreements have been established to facilitate the task, for both terrestrial and space radiocommunication services.

A common thread existing in these examples in that the countries concerned established their own local arrangements and did not necessarily seek to involve the ITU in the process. A recent example of this approach in Europe was the planning for Digital Audio Broadcasting (DAB) that was done within the CEPT/ERO, even though earlier planning for television in these frequency bands was established at an ITU Regional conference. Countries use the ITU forum as they feel it is necessary; ITU's role is seen as necessary for coordination of space radiocommunication services as well as for terrestrial services where the countries concerned do not have the necessary technical skills (as in the case of planning television stations in Africa) or where ITU can act as an intermediary in cases where diplomatic contact is difficult or non-existant between the countries concerned.

D. Equipment Standards

Standardisation of equipment is also a strong force leading countries to follow international decisions in their national regulations. This can arise for commercial reasons (lowering the cost of equipment) or from the desire to ensure satisfactory operation of equipment over a wide area encompassing a number of countries. A brilliant example of the latter is the GSM standards for cellular

mobile radio, where users can roam over most of the Earth's surface and use their standard handset.

Equipment standards tend to be set by developed countries as
they reach a particular level of technical sophistication and service
requirement earlier than others. To extend the European example,
bodies such as the European Telecommunications Standards institute (ETSI) play a major role in equipment and system standardisation.

V.   Trends in Privatisation and Regulation

A. The Traditional Approach

Traditionally, the management of spectrum/orbit resources at the
national level was assigned to the government owned PTT. A major
exception was in the USA where the Federal Communications
Commission (FCC) was responsible for commercial uses and the
National Telecommunications and Information Administration
(NTIA) was responsible for Government uses. A perception developed in a number of countries in the 70s and 80s that the PTT was a
first among so-called equals and pressures were brought on Governments to assign the responsibility of national spectrum management to a neutral body. This pressure was increased as competition
was introduced in the provision of telecommunications services and
a neutral regulatory body was seen as essential. Further pressure
sought to remove the spectrum management function from excessive political input by seeking a management body outside traditional ministerial influence and more likely to provide objective and
neutral decision making on resource attribution. This influence has
spread in more recent years as more and more countries took up this
approach.

B. Current Developments

The ITU has been active in providing a forum for the discussion
of regulatory approaches on this subject in recent years. It has published volumes of the ITU's Trends in Telecommunication Reform
each year since 1998 and these reports[4] provide a wealth of infor-

---

4   See *General Trends in Telecommuncation Reform 1998 – World* (published by the ITU in six volumes), *Trends in Telecommunication Reform, Convergence and Regulation 1999* (published by the ITU in one
volume) and *Trends in Telecommunication Reform, Interconnection
Regulation 2000-2001* (published by the ITU in one volume).

mation in this field. In addition ITU has convened each year Global Symposia[5] for Regulators and the trend in the establishment of independent regulatory bodies is striking. Starting with only 30 separate regulatory bodies in 1994, the figure was 77 in 1998 and 110 in 2001.

The Symposia are of increasing importance and they attract a wide range of senior regulators and other interested parties. An interesting aspect is the choice being made by countries as to the nature of the regulatory authority as this process develops with many being collegial bodies and others being led by a Director General or similar high level official.

The regulatory authorities are also faced with need to keep up with the technological changes that are revolutionising the information and technology industry; their task is increasingly complex.

The process of management of the spectrum / orbit resource is becoming much more open with auctions and public hearings more and more prevalent. Auctions are increasingly being used for attribution of the resource for terrestrial services in "popular" frequency bands. In such cases, freedom of use of the bands is usually part of the "package", provided limitations on coverage and interference into adjacent areas are met; this provides considerable scope for creative spectrum usage and the development of new services. Auction schemes have been shown not to be perfect; teething problems have arisen and the process has been considerably refined in recent times. "Beauty contests", where decisions on resource attribution are based on the perception of the ability of the proponents to provide satisfactory services as well as on the license fees they are prepared to pay are also used and this allows regulators more control in decision making.

There is also increasing competition in resource attribution between traditional spectrum users and advocates of new technologies and this is challenging the traditional "first come, first served" approach. Detailed justification of perceived needs is required and decisions to change attributions are increasingly requiring consideration of issues relating to the relocation of existing users and the need for the newcomer to bear the costs of such relocation.

All of this activity is occurring in an environment where the importance of telecommunications facilities in national development

---

[5]   For information on the recent ITU Global Symposium for Regulators –
see http://www.itu.int/ITU-D/treg/Events/Seminar/GSR/index.html.

(one speaks of a country's "nervous system") is increasingly recognised as is the importance of the telecommunications industry in overall economic terms in the post-industrial age.

VI. Transparency Issues

The detailed discussion presented in the above sections of this paper indicate that commercial and industry pressures as well as movements in the political sphere are leading to more open processes in resource attribution in an increasing number of countries. If anything services seen as important public services (safety, defence, etc.) are finding it increasingly difficult to justify their perceived resource needs.

There is an increasing perception that resource allocation processes should be open, accessible and simple and a recognition that transparent processes should eliminate delays and increase the efficiency of resource allocation. Independence of the decision making process from Ministerial involvement is considered especially important. Additionally, it is seen that transparency encourages investment and economic growth.

Another aspect receiving increasing attention is the relationship between the Regulatory Authority and the Competition Authority within a country. This needs to be well specified in order to ensure that the maximum benefit arises to the community at large in the resource attribution process.

Important guidance to national authorities is found in recent decisions of the World Trade Organization (WTO) who have released a number of texts including a Reference Paper on regulatory frameworks for telecommunications ("Definition and Principles on the Regulatory Framework for Basic Telecommunication Services")[6]. Regional telecommunications groups have also released similar texts. As an example both APEC (Asia-Pacific Economic Cooperation)[7] and CITEL (Inter-American Telecommunication Commission)[8] have produced texts on the principle of telecommunications interconnection.

---

[6] See http://www.wto.org/english/news_e/pres97_e/refpap-e.htm.
[7] Information on the "APEC Principles of Interconnection" can be found at http://www.apectelwg.org/apecdata/telwg/interTG/principl.html.
[8] Document PCC.I/doc. 864/99 titled "CITEL Guidelines and Practices for Interconnection Regulation" can be found at http://www.citel.oas.org/RES/p1_res077.asp.

This move towards common approaches to telecommunications regulation is being reinforced with the establishment of regional groupings of regulatory authorities.

All in all, there has been and there continues to be increasing transparency and efficiency in the attribution by countries of the radio frequency spectrum resource as the role of telecommunications and, in particular, radiocommunications in modern economies is becoming more important.

In conclusion, it should be noted that this discussion of the transparency involved in the issue of licenses for spectrum usage should be separated from consideration of the control of message content; this is a separate issue not discussed in this paper and which has its own intriguing aspects.

VII.   Conclusion

In recent times, particularly in the 1990s, privatisation of telecommunications services providers and the establishment of independent regulatory bodies has led to increasing transparent and efficiency in the attribution of the valuable radio frequency spectrum/satellite orbit resource. Commercial and industry interests as well as users of telecommunications services are increasingly involved in the decision making process in a field of increasing complexity and innovation. The importance of telecommunications facilities in national development is being increasingly recognised, as is the importance of the telecommunications industry in overall economic terms in the post-industrial age, and this recognition is driving this trend in the method of resource attribution.

Bibliography:

The list of ITU publications concerning radiocommunication matters or having reference to it is given below. They may be obtained from the ITU Sales Section.

- International Telecommunication Constitution and Convention, Geneva 1992, as amended by the Final Acts of the Plenipotentiary Conference, Kyoto 1994 and the Plenipotentiary Conference, Minneapolis 1998.
- Radio Regulations, 2001 edition.
- Final Acts of the World Radiocommunication Conference (WRC-97) (Geneva, 1997).
- Final Acts of the World Radiocommunication Conference (WRC-95) (Geneva, 1995).
- Manual for use by the maritime mobile-satellite services.

In addition, the Radiocommunication and Telecommunication Standardisation Sectors publish a substantial number of Recommendations in a variety of technical and operational subject areas.[9]

---

[9] Further information can be obtained from the following address: International Telecommunication Union, Place des Nations, 1211 Geneva 20, Switzerland, http://www.itu.int.

Annex 1: The Role of the International Telecommunication Union in the Provision of Radiocommunications Services

A. Brief History of the International Telecommunication Union[10]

1. On 24 May 1844 Samuel Morse sent his first public message over a telegraph line between Washington and Baltimore, thus ushering in the telecommunication age. Barely ten years later, telegraphy had become available to the general public. At this period, however, telegraph lines did not cross national frontiers because each country used a different system and each had its own telegraph code to safeguard the secrecy of its military and political telegraph messages. Messages had to be transcribed, translated and handed over at frontiers before being retransmitted over the telegraph network of the neighbouring country.

2. It is not surprising, therefore, that countries decided to conclude agreements to interconnect their national networks. In view of this expansion of telegraph networks 20 European States decided to meet in order to work out a framework agreement. They also decided on common rules to standardize equipment in order to guarantee generalized interconnection, adopted uniform operating instructions which had hitherto been different from one country to another and laid down common international tariff and accounting rules. On 17 May 1865 after two and a half months of arduous negotiations, the first International Telegraph Convention was signed in Paris by the 20 participating countries and the International Telegraph Union was set up to enable subsequent amendments to this initial agreement to be agreed upon. This marked the birth of the ITU. Today, over 130 years later, the reasons which led to the establishment of the Union still apply and the fundamental objectives of the organisation are basically unchanged.

3. Since that time, telecommunications have continued to develop apace and the history of the ITU fully reflects the advances which have been made. Following the invention of the telephone in 1876 and the subsequent expansion of telephony, the Telegraph Union began, in 1885, to draw up international legislation governing telephony. With the invention in 1896 of wireless te-

---

[10] This section draws from the official history of the ITU, available at http://www.itu.int/aboutitu/overview/history.html.

legraphy – the first type of radiocommunication – and the utilization of this new technique, particularly for maritime purposes, it was decided to convene a preliminary radio conference in 1903 to study the question of international regulations for radiotelegraph communications; at the International Radiotelegraph Conference held in 1906 in Berlin, the first International Radiotelegraph Convention was signed. The annex to this Convention contained the first regulations governing wireless telegraphy; these regulations which have since been amended and revised by numerous radio conferences held throughout the years, are now known as the Radio Regulations.

4. The year 1920 saw the beginning of sound broadcasting at the improvised studios of the Marconi Company. In 1927, at a conference held in Washington D.C., the International Radio Consultative committee (CCIR) was established. The 1927 International Radiotelegraph Conference also allocated frequency bands to the various radio services existing at the time (fixed, maritime and aeronautical mobile, broadcasting, amateur and experimental) to ensure greater efficiency of operation in view of the increase in the number of services using frequencies and the technical peculiarities of each service.

5. At the 1932 Madrid Conference, the Union decided to combine the International Telegraph Convention of 1865 and the International Radiotelegraph Convention of 1906 to form the International Telecommunication Convention. It also decided to change its name and was known as from 1 January 1934 as the International Telecommunication Union in order to reaffirm the full scope if its responsibilities, i.e. all forms of communication, by wire, radio, optical systems or other electromagnetic systems.

6. In 1947, after the Second World War, the ITU held a conference in Atlantic City with the aim of developing and modernizing the organization. Under an agreement with the United Nations, it became a UN specialized agency on 15 October 1947. The headquarters of the organization were transferred in 1948 from Bern, where it had been established in 1868, to Geneva: moreover, the International Frequency Registration Board (IFRB) was set up to manage the frequency spectrum which was becoming increasingly complicated and the Table of Frequency Allocations, introduced in 1912, became mandatory. This Table allocates to each service using radio waves (there are about 40 at the present time) specific frequency bands with a view to avoiding

interference between stations – in communications between aircraft and control towers, car telephones, ships at sea and coast
stations, radio stations or spacecraft and earth-based stations.

7. The year 1957 was marked by the launching of the first artificial
satellite, Sputnik 1, which inaugurated the space age. The first
geostationary satellite was put in orbit in 1963; together with ra-
dio-relay systems and submarine cables, satellites now constitute
the main means of long distance communication. In order to
meet the challenges of the space age, the CCIR set up in 1959 a
Study Group responsible for studying space radiocommunication and an Extraordinary Administrative Conference for space
communications was held in 1963 in Geneva to allocate frequencies to the various space services. ITU has held many Conferences since that time, many of which dealt with space radiocommunication matters.

8. Closer to the present time, in 1989, a Plenipotentiary Conference
held in Nice recognized the importance of placing technical assistance to the developing countries on the same footing within
the ITU as the traditional activities of coordination, standardization and international regulation and set up a Telecommunication Development Bureau (BDT) to step up the efforts being
made for development in the Third World. This Bureau began its
activities at the beginning of 1990.

9. Each major innovation in the field of telecommunications is thus
matched by specification on the part of the Union to integrate
new discoveries into the world network and to provide the necessary resources to respond more effectively to the expectations
of Member States.

B. Mandate of the ITU[11]

10. The basic instruments of the International Telecommunication
Union are the Constitution and Convention, as adopted by the
Plenipotentiary Conference in Nice (1989) and modified by the
Additional Plenipotentiary Conference in Geneva (1992), the
Plenipotentiary Conference in Kyoto (1994) and the Plenipoten-
tiary Conference in Minneapolis in 1998.As of June 1999 there
were 188 Member States and over 500 Sector Members.

11. The purposes of the Union are:

---

[11] The material in this section is drawn from the ITU Constitution and
Convention.

a) to maintain and extend international cooperation among all its Member States for the improvement and rational use of telecommunications of all kinds;

b) to promote and enhance participation of entities and organizations in the activities of the Union and foster fruitful cooperation and partnership between them and Member States for the fulfilment of the overall objectives as embodied in the purposes of the Union;

c) to promote and to offer technical assistance to developing countries in the field of telecommunications, and also to promote the mobilization of the material, human and financial resources needed for its implementation, as well as access to information;

d) to promote the development of technical facilities and their most efficient operation with a view to improving the efficiency of telecommunication services, increasing their usefulness and making them, so far as possible, generally available to the public;

e) to promote the extension of the benefits of the new telecommunication technologies to all the world's inhabitants;

f) to promote the use of telecommunication services with the objective of facilitating peaceful relations;

g) to harmonize the actions of Member States and promote fruitful and constructive cooperation and partnership between Member States and Sector Members in the attainment of those ends;

h) to promote, at the international level, the adoption of a broader approach to the issues of telecommunications in the global information economy and society, by cooperating with other world and regional intergovernmental organizations and those non-governmental organizations concerned with telecommunications.

12. To this end, the Union, in particular:

a) effects allocation of bands of the radio-frequency spectrum, the allotment of radio frequencies and registration of radio-frequency assignments and, for space services, of any associated orbital position in the geostationary-satellite orbit or of any associated characteristics of satellites in other orbits in order to avoid harmful interference between radio stations of different countries;

b) coordinates efforts to eliminate harmful interference between radio stations of different countries and to improve the use made of the radio-frequency spectrum for radiocommunication services and of the geostationary-satellite and other satellite orbits;

c) facilitates the worldwide standardization of telecommunications, with a satisfactory quality of service;

d) fosters international cooperation and solidarity in the delivery of technical assistance to the developing countries and the creation, development and improvement of telecommunication equipment and networks in developing countries by every means at its disposal, including through its participation in the relevant programmes of the United Nations and the use of its own resources, as appropriate;

e) coordinates efforts to harmonize the development of telecommunication facilities, notably those using space techniques, with a view to full advantage being taken of their possibilities;

f) fosters collaboration among Member States and Sector Members with a view to the establishment of rates at levels as low as possible consistent with an efficient service and taking into account the necessity for maintaining independent financial administration of telecommunication on a sound basis;

g) promotes the adoption of measures for ensuring the safety of life through the cooperation of telecommunication services;

h) undertakes studies, makes regulations, adopts resolutions, formulates recommendations and opinions, and collects and publishes information concerning telecommunication matters;

i) promotes, with international financial and development organizations, the establishment of preferential and favourable lines of credit to be used for the development of social projects aimed, inter alia, at extending telecommunication services to the most isolated areas in countries;

j) promotes participation of concerned entities in the activities of the Union and cooperation with regional and other organizations for the fulfilment of the purposes of the Union.

C. *Organization of the ITU*[12]

13. The Union is comprised of the following organs:
    a) the Plenipotentiary Conference, which is the supreme organ of the Union;
    b) the Council, which acts on behalf of the Plenipotentiary Conference;
    c) world conferences on international telecommunications;
    d) the Radiocommunication Sector (ITU-R), including world and regional radiocommunication conferences, radiocommunication assemblies and the Radio Regulations Board;
    e) the Telecommunication Standardization Sector (ITU-T), including world telecommunication standardization assemblies;
    f) the Telecommunication Development Sector (ITU-D), including world and regional telecommunication development conferences;
    g) the General Secretariat.
14. The Plenipotentiary Conference is composed of delegations representing Member States. It is convened every four years.
15. The Council is composed of a number of Member States (not exceeding 25% of the total number of Member States) elected by the Plenipotentiary Conference (in accordance with the provisions of No. 61 of the Constitution) with due regard to the need for equitable distribution of the seats on the Council among all regions of the world.
16. The Conferences on International Telecommunications are convened to consider specific telecommunication matters. The decisions of such conferences must in all circumstances be in conformity with the provisions of the Constitution and the Convention. The Administrative Regulations adopted by the Conferences have treaty force at the international level.
17. The functions of the Radiocommunication Sector are, bearing in mind the particular concerns of developing countries, to fulfil the purposes of the Union relating to radiocommunication:
    - by ensuring the rational, equitable, efficient and economical use of the radio-frequency spectrum by all radiocommunication services, including those using the geostationary-satellite or other satellite orbits, subject to the provisions of Article 44 of the Constitution, and

---

[12] The material in this section is drawn from the ITU Constitution and Convention.

- by carrying out studies without limit of frequency range and adopting recommendations on radiocommunication matters.

The Radiocommunication Sector works through:

a) World and Regional radiocommunication conferences;
b) the Radio Regulations Board;
c) Radiocommunication Assemblies;
d) Radiocommunication Study Groups;
e) the Radiocommunication Advisory Group;
f) the Radiocommunication Bureau, headed by an elected Director.

The Radiocommunication Sector has as members:

a) of right, the administrations of all Member States;
b) any entity or organization which becomes a Sector Member in accordance with the relevant provisions of the Convention.

18. The functions of the Telecommunication Standardization Sector are, bearing in mind the concerns of the developing countries, to fulfil the purposes of the Union relating to telecommunication standardization, by studying technical, operating and tariff questions and adopting recommendations on them with a view to standardizing telecommunications on a worldwide basis.

19. The functions of the Telecommunication Development Sector are to fulfil the purposes of the Union and to discharge, within its specific sphere of competence, the Union's dual responsibility as a United Nations specialized agency and executing agency for implementing projects under the United Nations development system or other funding arrangements so as to facilitate and enhance telecommunications development by offering, organizing and coordinating technical cooperation and assistance activities.

20. The General Secretariat is directed by the Secretary-General who prepares strategic policies and plans for the Union, coordinates its activities and takes all the actions required to ensure economic use of the Union's resources and is responsible to the Administrative Council for all the administrative and financial aspects of the Union's activities. He is assisted by the Deputy Secretary-General.

21. The Radio Regulations Board consists of elected members thoroughly qualified in the field of radiocommunications and possessing practical experience in the assignment and utilization of frequencies. Each member is expected to be familiar with the geographic, economic and demographic conditions within a par-

ticular area of the world. They perform their duties for the Union independently and on a part-time basis.

The duties of the Radio Regulations Board consist of:

a) the approval of Rules of Procedure, which include technical criteria, in accordance with the Radio Regulations and with any decision which may be taken by competent radiocommunication conferences. These Rules of Procedure shall be used by the Director and the Bureau in the application of the Radio Regulations to register frequency assignments made by Member States. These Rules shall be open to comment by administrations and, in case of continuing disagreement, the matter shall be submitted to a forthcoming world radiocommunication conference;

b) the consideration of any other matter that cannot be resolved through the application of the above Rules of Procedure;

c) the performance of any additional duties, concerned with the assignment and utilization of frequencies, in accordance with the procedures provided for in the Radio Regulations, and as prescribed by a competent conference or by the Council with the consent of a majority of the Member States, in preparation for, or in pursuance of the decisions of, such a conference.

22. The structure of the Radiocommunication Sector is shown diagrammatically in Figure 1.

23. The Radiocommunication Bureau (BR) is headed by a Director who organizes and coordinates the work of the Radiocommunication Sector. The Bureau:

a) provides administrative and technical support to Radiocommunication Conferences, Radiocommunication Assemblies and Study Groups, including Working Parties and Task Groups;

b) applies the provisions of the Radio Regulations and various Regional Agreements;

c) records and registers frequency assignments and also orbital characteristics of space services, and maintains the Master International Frequency Register;

d) provides advice to Members on the equitable, effective and economical use of the radio-frequency spectrum and satellite orbits, and investigates and assists in resolving cases of harmful interference;

e) coordinates the preparation, editing and dispatch of circulars, documents and publications developed within the Sector;

f) provides technical information and seminars on national frequency management and radiocommunications, and works closely with the Telecommunication Development Bureau in assisting developing countries.

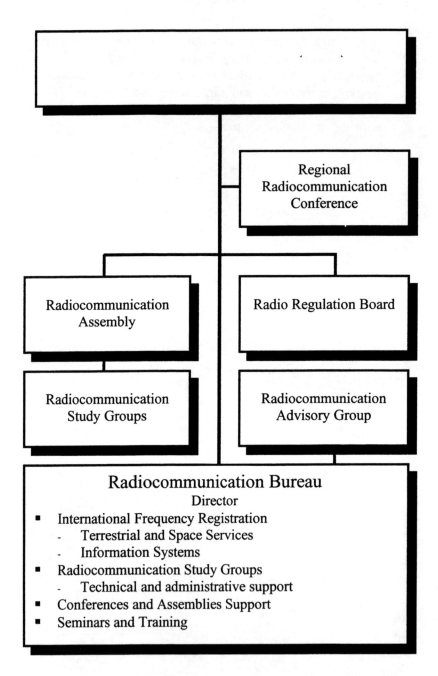

Fig. 1: Structure of the Radiocommunication Sector of the ITU

Annex 2: Frequency Bands Allocated to Space Radiocommunication Services Subject to Planning

The Appendix 30 and 30A Broadcasting Satellite Service (BSS) Plans and Lists cover the following frequency bands:

- Region 1: 11.7 – 12.5 GHz (space-to-Earth);
  14.5 – 14.8 GHz (Earth-to-space);[13]
  17.3 – 18.1 GHz (Earth-to-space).
- Region 2: 12.2 – 12.7 GHz (space-to-Earth);
  17.3 – 17.8 GHz (Earth-to-space);
- Region 3: 11.7 – 12.2 GHz (space-to-Earth);
  14.5 – 14.8 GHz (Earth-to-space);
  17.3 – 18.1 GHz (Earth-to-space).

The AP30B Plan covers the following Fixed Satellite Service (FSS) frequency bands:

- 4 500 – 4 800 MHz (space-to-Earth);
- 6 725 – 7 025 MHz (Earth-to-space);
- 10.70 – 10.95 GHz (space-to-Earth);
- 11.20 – 11.45 GHz (space-to-Earth);
- 12.75 – 13.25 GHz (Earth-to-space);

resulting in a total bandwidth of 800 MHz in each direction.

---

[13] For countries outside Europe.

Abbreviations

AB: Appellate Body
ACP: African, Caribbean and Pacific Group of States
AG: Attorney General
AIA-Procedure: Advanced Informed Agreed Procedure
ALSC: At-Large Membership Study Committee (of ICANN)
APEC: Asia-Pacific Economic Cooperation
Art.:   Article
ASO: Address Supporting Organisation
ATC: Agreement on Textiles and Clothing,

BDT: Telecommunication Development Bureau
BISD: Basic Instruments and Selected Documents (of the
             GATT)
BR: Radiocommunication Bureau
BVerfGE: Bundesverfassungsgerichtserkenntnisse (decisions of
             the German federal court for constitutional law)
B-VG: Bundesverfassungsgesetz (Austrian Constitution)

CAC: Codex Alimentarius Commission
CBD: Convention on Biological Diversity
CCIR: International Radio Consultative committee
ccTLD: Country Code Top Level Domain
CEO: Chief Executive Officer
CEPT: Conference of Postal and Telecommunications
             Administrations
CESCR: Committee on Economic, Social and Cultural Rights
CFSP: Common Foreign and Security Policy
ch: chapter
CHF: Swiss Francs
CIE: Committee of Independent Experts
CIEL: Center for International Environmental Law
CITEL: Inter-American Telecommunication Commission

CITES:	Convention on International Trade in Endangered Species
CJHA:	Co-operation in Justice- and Home Affairs
CLS:	Core labour standards
COP:	Conference of Parties (of the Cartagena Protocol)
CPT:	Consumer Project for Technology
CS:	(ITU) Constitution
CSCE:	Conference for Security and Co-operation in Europe
CSIF:	Civil Society Internet Forum
CV:	(ITU) Convention

DAB:	Digital Audio Broadcasting
DG:	Director General
DNA:	Deoxyribonucleic acid
DNS:	Domain Name System
DNSO:	Domain Name Supporting Organisation
DSB:	Dispute Settlement Body
DSU:	Dispute Settlement Understanding

EC:	European Community
ECB:	European Central Bank
ECHR:	European Convention for the Protection of Human Rights and Fundamental Freedoms
ECJ:	European Court of Justice
ECR:	European Court Reports (Reports of Cases before the Court of Justice and the Court of First Instance)
EEC:	European Economic Community
EIA:	Environmental Impact Assessment
ElCom:	Election Committee (of ICANN)
EMAS:	Eco-Management and Audit System
EO:	European Ombudsman
EP:	European Parliament
EPZ:	Export Processing Zone
ERO:	European Radiocommunications Office
ESC:	Economic and Social Committee
ETSI:	European Telecommunications Standards institute
EU:	European Union
Europol:	European Police Office

FAO:	Food and Agriculture Organization of the UN
FCC:	(US-) Federal Communications Commission

FDI: Foreign Direct Investment
Foe: Friends of the Earth
FOI(A):   Freedom of Information (Act)
FSC: Forest Stewardship Council
FTAA: Free Trade Area of the Americas

G-7:   Group of Seven
G-8:   Group of Eight
GA RES: General Assembly Resolution (of the UN)
GAC: Governmental Advisory Committee
GATS: General Agreement on Trade in Services
GATT: General Agreement on Tariffs and Trade
GHz: Gigahertz
GIP: Global Internet Project
GMO: Genetically modified organism
GNP: Gross National Product
GPA: Government Procurement Agreement
GRAIN: Genetic Resources Action International
GSP: Generalized System of Tariff Preferences
gTLD-MoU: Memorandum of Understanding on generic Top Level
            Domains
gTLDs: generic Top Level Domain Name space

HF: High Frequency
HFCS: High-Fructose Corn Syrup

IAHC: International ad hoc Committee
IANA: Internet Assigned Numbers Authority
IATP: The Institute for Agriculture and Trade Policy
ICANN: The Internet Corporation of Assigned Names and
            Numbers
ICESCR: International Covenant on Economic, Social and
            Cultural Rights
ICJ: International Court of Justice
ICT: Information- and Communication-Technology
ICTSD: International Center for Trade and Sustainable
            Development
IFRB: International Frequency Registration Board
IGO: Intergovernmental Organization
ILA: International Law Association
ILC: International Law Commission

ILEAP: International Lawyers and Economists Against Poverty
ILM: International Legal Materials
ILO: International Labour Organization
ILR: International Law Reporter
IMF: International Monetary Fund
IMT: International Mobile Telecommunications
IOE: International Office of Epizootics
IP: Internet Protocol
IPPC: International Plant Protection Convention
IPPC-Directive: Integrated Pollution Prevention and Control-Directive (Council Directive 96/61 EC, OJ 1996 L 257 26)
IPR: Intellectual property rights
ISO: International Organization for Standardization
ISOC: Internet Society
ITC: International Trade Center
ITU: International Telecommunication Union
ITU-D: ITU Telecommunication Development Sector
ITU-R: ITU Radiocommunication Sector
ITU-T: ITU Telecommunication Standardization Sector

JHA: Justice and Home Affairs

LMO: Living modified organism

MEA: Multilateral Environmental Agreement
MEP: Member of the European Parliament
MFN: Most favourite nation treatment
MHz: Megahertz
MIFR: Master International Frequency Register
mOP: meeting of the Parties (of the Cartagena Protocol)
MoU: Memorandum of Understanding
MSF: Médecins sans Frontières

NAALC: North American Agreement on Labour Cooperation
NAFTA: North American Free Trade Area
NATO: North Atlantic Treaty Organization
NGO: Non-Governmental Organisation
NoCom: Nomination committee (of ICANN)
NSI: Network Solutions Incorporated
NTIA: National Telecommunications and Information Administration (USA)

nyr: not yet reported

ODA: Overseas Development Aid
OECD: Organisation for Economic Co-operation and Development
OJ: Official Journal of the European Communities
OSCE: Organization for Security and Co-operation in Europe
OSPAR: OSlo PARis Convention / Commission for the Protection of the Marine Environment of the North-East Atlantic

Para.: Paragraph
PhRMA: Pharmaceutical Research and Manufacturers of America
PIC Convention: Convention on the Prior Informed Consent Procedure for Certain Hazardous Chemicals and Pesticides in International Trade
PPM: Processes and production methods
PR: People's Republic
PSI: Public Services International
PSO: Protocol Supporting Organisation
PTT: Post-, Telegraph-, and Telephone-Administration
PVO: (European) Plant Variety Office

REIO: Regional Economic Integration Organisation
RR: Radio Regulations

SCM(A): Subsidies and Countervailing Measures (Agreement)
sec.: Section
SPS: Sanitary and Phytosanitary Measures
SUNS: South-North Development Monitor

TBT: Technical barriers to trade
TED: Turtle Excluder Device
TIP: Trade Information Project
TLD: Top Level Domain
TPRM: Trade Policy Review Mechanism
TRIPS: Trade-related aspects of intellectual property rights
UDHR: Universal Declaration of Human Rights
UK: United Kingdom
UN(O): United Nations (Organisation)

UNCCPR: United Nations Covenant on Civil and Political Rights
UNCESCR: United Nations Covenant on Economic, Social and
Cultural Rights
UNCTAD: United Nations Conference on Trade and Development
UNDP: United Nations Development Programme
UNEP: United Nations Environment Programme
UNESCO: United Nations Educational, Scientific and Cultural
Organization
US(A): United States (of America)
USTR: United States Trade Representative

VCLT: Vienna Convention on the Law of Treaties

WARC: World Administrative Radio Conference
WDM: World Development Movement
WHO: World Health Organization
WIPO: World Intellectual Property Organization
WRC: World Radiocommunication Conference
WTO: World Trade Organization
WWF: World Wildlife Fund for Nature

The Authors of this Volume

Armin von Bogdandy was Professor in Frankfurt / Main, Germany, when he finished his manuscript. Since October, 2002 he is Director of the *Max Planck* Institute for Comparative Public Law and International Law in Heidelberg, Germany.

Deirdre Curtin holds a chair for 'Law of International Organizations' at the University of Utrecht, Netherlands, and for Institutional Law of the EU at the College of Europe in Bruges and is Director of the Irish Centre of European Law in Dublin.

Sebastian Geiseler-Bonse is assistant at the Institute for Law of Information, Telecommunication and Media at the University of Münster, Germany.

Goetz J. Goettsche is research and teaching assistant in the field of International Economic Law, University of Hamburg, Faculty of Law.

Stefan Griller is Professor for Public Law with special regard to European Law at the Research Institute for European Affairs – IEF of *Wirtschaftsuniversität*, Vienna. He is also Secretary General of ECSA Austria.

Gerhard Hafner is Professor for public international law and European law at the Institute of International Law and International Relations of the University of Vienna. He was also a member of the UN's International Law Commission.

Meinhard Hilf is Professor for Public, European and Public International Law at Hamburg University.

Robert Howse is Professor of Law at the University of Michigan Law School in Ann Arbor, MI.

John Lewis was head of the Space Publication and Registration Division of the Space Services Department of ITU's Radiocommunication Bureau for years. At present he is consultant in international spectrum management in Geneva, Switzerland.

Gerhard Loibl was Professor at the Institute of International Law and International Relations of the University of Vienna when he finished his manuscript. Since July, 2002 he is working with the Diplomatic Academy in Vienna.

Jorge Mario Martínez-Piva, who is an economist from education, is a consultant in the Trade Unit of the Organization of American States (OAS) in Washington, D.C.

Iulia Motoc is Professor at the University of Bucharest and Director of the Institute for International Law and Politics at the same University. She is UN Commission Special Rapporteur for RDCongo and a member and former President of the UN Sub-Commission on Promotion and Protection of Human Rights.

Ernst-Ulrich Petersmann is Professor of International and European Law at the European University Institute in Florence, Italy. He was legal advisor in the German Ministry of Economic Affairs, GATT and the WTO, and is Chairman of the International Trade Law Committee of the ILA.

José Manuel Salazar-Xirinachs, former Minister of Foreign Trade of Costa Rica, at present is working as Chief Trade Advisor and Director of the Trade Unit at the Organization of American States (OAS) in Washington, D.C.

Michael J. Trebilcock is Professor of Law at the Faculty of Law of the University of Toronto, Ontario, Canada.

Elisabeth Tuerk is working as a staff attorney at the Geneva office of the 'Center for International Environmental Law (CIEL)'.

J. H. H. Weiler is European Union *Jean Monnet* Professor of Law at the New York University School of Law, where he is also the Director of the '*Jean Monnet* Center for International and Regional Economic Law & Justice'.

SpringerLaw

Fritz Breuss, Gerhard Fink, Stefan Griller (eds.)

Institutional, Legal and Economic Aspects of the EMU

2003. VIII, 346 pages.
Softcover **EUR 64,20,** sFr 100,–
(Recommended retail price)
This Euro-price is recommended for Germany and includes 7 % VAT.
ISBN 3-211-83856-2
Schriftenreihe des Forschungsinstituts für Europafragen
der Wirtschaftsuniversität Wien / Research Institute
for European Affairs Publication Series, Volume 23

This books analyses in four parts some of the major aspects of the unique architecture of the Economic and Monetary Union (EMU) of the European Union. The first part deals with the problems of the institutional set-up of the EMU: the legal position of the European Central Bank; the excessive reserves in the Euro system; the "Maastricht conformity" of the public undertakings. The asymmetric architecture of the EMU (centralised monetary policy and decentralised fiscal policy; policy co-ordination; the stability and growth pact) is analysed in part two. The third part covers the monetary aspects of the EMU: the monetary policy of the ECB; the technical aspects of the specific payment system in the ESCB; the role of the Euro as an international currency and the explanations of is weakness. The concluding part looks at the problems connected with EU enlargement: are the candidate countries really ready for the EMU (degree of business cycle conformity); the problems of the banking system in the CEECs.

SpringerWienNewYork

A-1201 Wien, Sachsenplatz 4–6, P.O. Box 89, Fax +43.1.330 24 26, e-mail: books@springer.at, **www.springer.at**
D-69126 Heidelberg, Haberstraße 7, Fax +49.6221.345-229, e-mail: orders@springer.de
USA, Secaucus, NJ 07096-2485, P.O. Box 2485, Fax +1.201.348-4505, e-mail: orders@springer-ny.com
EBS, Japan, Tokyo 113, 3–13, Hongo 3-chome, Bunkyo-ku, Fax +81.3.38 18 08 64, e-mail: orders@svt-ebs.co.jp

SpringerLaw

Fritz Breuss, Stefan Griller, Erich Vranes

The Banana Dispute

An Economic and Legal Analysis

2003. Approx. 300 pages.
Softcover **approx. EUR 64,09,** sFr 99,50
(Recommended retail price)
This Euro-price is recommended for Germany and includes 7 % VAT.
ISBN 3-211-83727-2
Schriftenreihe des Forschungsinstituts für Europafragen
der Wirtschaftsuniversität Wien / Research Institute
for European Affairs Publication Series, Volume 19
Due January 2003

The "Banana dispute" represents one of the central cases in international trade. It has led to several precedents on the international (WTO), EC and national level. It thus constitutes the mandatory starting point for any in-depth study of the WTO system and transatlantic trade relations. Moreover, this dispute casts new light on classic issues of European law, especially the relationship of EC, national law and state liability.

This treatise is the most comprehensive published to date, and also an easily accessible one. The study is supplemented by an economic analysis of the welfare effects of the EC banana import regime for the EC domestic market, and interdisciplinary conclusions for future amendments of the WTO enforcement system.

This book will be of equal interest to practitioners, academics and students of international economic relations.

SpringerWienNewYork

A-1201 Wien, Sachsenplatz 4–6, P.O. Box 89, Fax +43.1.330 24 26, e-mail: books@springer.at, www.springer.at
D-69126 Heidelberg, Haberstraße 7, Fax +49.6221.345-229, e-mail: orders@springer.de
USA, Secaucus, NJ 07096-2485, P.O. Box 2485, Fax +1.201.348-4505, e-mail: orders@springer-ny.com
EBS, Japan, Tokyo 113, 3–13, Hongo 3-chome, Bunkyo-ku, Fax +81.3.38 18 08 64, e-mail: orders@svt-ebs.co.jp

SpringerLaw

Stefan Griller, Birgit Weidel (eds.)

External Economic Relations and Foreign Policy in the European Union

2002. IV, 500 pages.
Softcover **EUR 84,53,** sFr 131,50
(Recommended retail price)
This Euro-price is recommended for Germany and includes 7 % VAT.
ISBN 3-211-83726-4
Schriftenreihe des Forschungsinstituts für Europafragen
der Wirtschaftsuniversität Wien / Research Institute
for European Affairs Publication Series, Volume 20

The challenges of globalisation call for a strong role of the European Union as an international actor. Despite its economic importance, the EU has not been able to assert a corresponding influence on the course of international politics. The artificial distinction between external economic relations, as a subject of the supranational first pillar, and foreign policy, as a subject of the intergovernmental second pillar undermines consistent policy-making and significantly weakens the EU's performance on the international scene.

This book illustrates the inextricable link between political and economic aspects of external relations and the constitutional dimension of this area. Provided with a thorough analysis of competence and representation issues the reader will gain a more profound understanding of the complex area of EU external relations.

SpringerWienNewYork

A-1201 Wien, Sachsenplatz 4–6, P.O. Box 89, Fax +43.1.330 24 26, e-mail: books@springer.at, www.springer.at
D-69126 Heidelberg, Haberstraße 7, Fax +49.6221.345-229, e-mail: orders@springer.de
USA, Secaucus, NJ 07096-2485, P.O. Box 2485, Fax +1.201.348-4505, e-mail: orders@springer-ny.com
EBS, Japan, Tokyo 113, 3–13, Hongo 3-chome, Bunkyo-ku, Fax +81.3.38 18 08 64, e-mail: orders@svt-ebs.co.jp

SpringerLaw

Stefan Griller et al.

The Treaty of Amsterdam

Facts, Analysis, Prospects

2000. XXVII, 643 pages. 3 figures.
Softcover **EUR 117,70,** sFr 178,–
(Recommended retail price)
This Euro-price is recommended for Germany and includes 7 % VAT.
ISBN 3-211-83162-2
Schriftenreihe des Forschungsinstituts für Europafragen
der Wirtschaftsuniversität Wien / Research Institute
for European Affairs Publication Series, Volume 15

The Treaty of Amsterdam has introduced important changes
into the constitution of the European Union, for example, in
the fields of internal and external affairs and employment
policy, which will impact upon the future of the Union. Also
of considerable importance is the new option to establish
closer co-operation between a group of Member States, as
well as certain institutional modifications.
Particular attention is paid to areas of the Treaty of Amsterdam
which are unclear or apparently deficient. All of these topics
are of greatest importance within the course of the ongoing
thematic debate, not the least on future EU-enlargement. The
book is addressed to experts and anyone interested in European affairs.

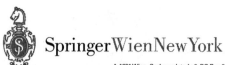

SpringerWienNewYork

A-1201 Wien, Sachsenplatz 4–6, P.O.Box 89, Fax +43.1.330 24 26, e-mail: books@springer.at, **www.springer.at**
D-69126 Heidelberg, Haberstraße 7, Fax +49.6221.345-229, e-mail: orders@springer.de
USA, Secaucus, NJ 07096-2485, P.O. Box 2485, Fax +1.201.348-4505, e-mail: orders@springer-ny.com
EBS, Japan, Tokyo 113, 3–13, Hongo 3-chome, Bunkyo-ku, Fax +81.3.38 18 08 64, e-mail: orders@svt-ebs.co.jp